CASE STUDIES
in
BUSINESS ETHICS

CASE STUDIES
in
BUSINESS ETHICS

SIXTH EDITION

Edited by
Al Gini
Loyola University Chicago

Alexei M. Marcoux
Loyola University Chicago

Upper Saddle River, NJ 07458

Library of Congress Cataloging-in-Publication Data

Case studies in business ethics / edited by Al Gini, Alexei M. Marcoux—6th ed.
p. cm.
ISBN-13: 978-0-13-242432-5 (alk. paper)
ISBN-10: 0-13-242432-0 (alk. paper)
1. Business ethics—Case studies. I. Gini, Al.
HF5387.C36 2008
174'.4—dc22

2007025933

Editor in Chief: Sarah Touborg
Senior Acquisitions Editor: Dave Repetto
Project Manager: Sarah Holle
Editorial Assistant: Carla Worner
Assoc. Marketing Manager: Sasha Anderson Smith
Senior Managing Editor: Mary Rottino
Production Liaison: Fran Russello
Manufacturing Buyer: Cathy Petersen
Cover Design: Bruce Kenselaar
Composition/Full-Service Project Management: Karpagam Jagadeesan/GGS Book Services
Printer/Binder: RR Donnelley & Sons Company

Credits and acknowledgments borrowed from other sources and reproduced, with permission, in this textbook appear on appropriate page within text.

Pearson Education LTD. London
Pearson Education Singapore, Pte. Ltd
Pearson Education, Canada, Ltd
Pearson Education–Japan
Pearson Education Australia PTY, Limited

Pearson Education North Asia Ltd
Pearson Educación de Mexico, S.A. de C.V.
Pearson Education Malaysia, Pte. Ltd
Pearson Education, Upper Saddle River, New Jersey

10 9 8 7 6 5 4
ISBN-13: 978-0-13-242432-5
ISBN-10:   0-13-242432-0

Contents

SEVEN • Women in the Workplace   **241**

Preface

Case Studies in Business Ethics is an attempt to bring together, in a single volume, an overview of the nature of business and ethical reasoning, essays to read, ideas and issues to ponder, and cases to debate. It is our hope that these readings will be both interesting and informative to teachers and students alike.

The first edition of this text (1984) was the brainchild of Thomas Donaldson. Editions two (1990), three (1993), and four (1996) were the joint efforts of Thomas Donaldson and Al Gini. The fifth edition (2005) was produced solely by Al Gini, and the sixth edition has been made possible with the collaboration of Al Gini and Alexei M. Marcoux.

A number of thanks need to be made. To begin with, we owe unending gratitude to Michelle Ambrose, Nicole Hackett, and Jessica L. Searles for their untiring efforts in putting this book together and correcting all of our errors. We want to thank our editor, Mical Moser, for her confidence in us and for making this book possible. And, of course, we also want to thank two very important people in our lives for their unending patience and kindness, Sherry Gini and Arianne Marcoux.

We would like to thank the following reviewers: Karen Gantt, University of Hartford; Jeff Cranford, Bluefield College; Krishna Mallick, Salem State College; Desheng Zong, Utica College; George P. Generas, Jr., University of Hartford; Chalmer Labig, OK State University.

AL GINI
Loyola University Chicago

ALEXEI M. MARCOUX
Loyola University Chicago

Ethics, Business, and Business Ethics

Al Gini and Alexei M. Marcoux

[E]thics distinguishes itself from law and etiquette by going deeper into the essence of our social existence. It distinguishes itself from religion by seeking reasons, rather than authority, to justify its principles. The central purpose of ethics is to secure valid principles of conduct and values that can be instrumental in guiding human actions and producing good character. As such it is the most important activity known to humans, for it has to do with how we are to live.

LOUIS P. POJMAN

We need each other. We are dependent on each other to survive and thrive. Good choices or bad choices, our collective existence requires us to continuously make choices about "what we ought to do" in regard to others. Like it or not, we are by definition moral creatures. Ethics is primarily a communal, collective enterprise, not a solitary one. It is the study of our web-work of relationships with others. As a communal exercise, ethics is the attempt to work out the rights we have and share with others.[1]

Defining ethics is not difficult. Doing it, living it, on the other hand, is. Why? Because ethics requires us to be concerned about the rights and well-being of others. It requires us to stop thinking of ourselves as the sole center of the universe. It requires us to transcend the simplistic equation of "me, myself, and I." It requires us to be just, reasonable, and objective. Perhaps it requires us to do something we either "cannot" or "do not" want to do—be our best rational selves in regard to others.

We believe that the central problem of ethics today is not a lack or moral reasoning or moral imagination, but, rather, a lack of moral engagement.[2] That is, the willingness to take on ethical issues and questions. The willingness to extend ourselves. The willingness to put ourselves in "harm's way" because we are concerned about the well-being of others. We have forgotten a fundamental Socratic lesson: The goal of life is not to escape death, suffering, or inconvenience. The goal is to escape doing wrong, and living well with others.

Publicly, we may live lives that are economically and electronically interconnected and interdependent; but privately, we are both emotionally and ethically withdrawn, unappreciative, and unempathetic to the wants, needs, and desires of others. Too many of us live our lives hopelessly absorbed with self. If we care about anyone else at all, it is only after we have first taken care of our own self-centered wants and needs.

Søren Kierkegaard said that "subjectivity is the starting point of ethics." But subjectivity is neither the end point nor the only point of ethics. Starting from the self, ethics proceeds with the recognition of others. Ethics is always about self in the context of others. Ethics must be open to the "voice of others." For feminist and ethicist Carol Gilligan, caring for others, being responsive to others, being ethical, begins with standing outside of the needs of self and "talking and listening to others."

For Jean-Paul Sartre, we are by definition moral creatures because we are "condemned" by the fact of our collective existence to continuously make choices about "what we ought to do" in regard to others.[3] When Robinson Crusoe found himself marooned and alone on a tiny Pacific atoll, all things were possible. But when Friday came along and they discovered pirates burying treasure and each other on the beach, Crusoe was then involved in a universe of others, an ethical universe.

As a communal exercise, ethics is the attempt to work out the rights and obligations we have and share with others. What is mine? What do I owe you? An act is not wrong (unethical) simply because it advances the well-being of an individual, but an act is wrong if it is unfair and inconsiderate in regard to the rights and just claims of others.

According to the influential political philosopher John Rawls, given the presence of others and that we need others, ethics is elementally the pursuit of justice, fair play, and equity. For Rawls, the study of ethics has to do with developing standards for judging the conduct of one party whose behavior impacts on another.[4] Minimally, "good behavior" intends no harm and respects the rights of all affected, and "bad behavior" is willfully or negligently trampling on the rights and interests of others. Ethics, then, tries to find a way to protect one person's individual rights and needs against and alongside the rights and needs of others. Of course, the paradox and central tension of ethics lies in the fact that while we are by nature communal and in need of others, at the same time we are by disposition more or less egocentric and self-serving.[5]

John Dewey argued that at the pre-critical, pre-rational, pre-autonomous stage of our lives, morality starts as a set of culturally defined rules which are external to the individual and are imposed or inculcated as habits. But real ethical thinking, said Dewey, begins at the evaluative period of our lives, when as independent agents we freely decide to accept, embrace, modify, or deny these rules. Dewey maintained that every serious ethical system rejects the notion that one's standard of conduct should simply and uncritically be an acceptance of the rules of the culture we happen to live in. Even if it is the case that custom, habit, convention, public opinion, or law are correct in their mandates, to embrace them without critical reflection does not constitute a complete and formal ethical act and might be better labeled "ethical happenstance" or "ethics by virtue of circumstantial accident." For Dewey, ethics is essentially "reflective conduct," and he believed that the distinction between custom and reflective morality is clearly marked. The former places the standard and rules of conduct solely on habit; the latter appeals to reason and choice. The distinction is as important as it is definite, for it shifts the center of gravity in morality. For Dewey, ethics is a two-part process. It is never simply enough to do the right thing. We must do the right thing for the right reason, on purpose. In other words, true ethical acts necessitate the unity of theory and action, or, the integration of self in a deliberately chosen act.[6]

Perhaps the two most felicitous definitions of ethics we've ever come across are those of business ethicist Ed Freeman and theologian Frank Griswald. "Ethics is how we treat people face to face, person to person, day in and day out over a prolonged period of time" (Freeman). "Ethics is about the rules we chose to live by once we decide we want to live together" (Griswald). What both of these definitions emphasize is that ethics is an ongoing task, a continuous struggle. Both these definitions emphasize that ethics does exists as *theory* but that it is only truly *alive* when practiced face to face. Ethics is something we *do*. It is an option, a choice. It is something that we make, create, build, maintain, and sustain with our decision making and our actions.

Ethics requires us to take a stance, make a decision. Even when we try to avoid making a decision, we often can't. Most moral dilemmas do not allow us the luxury of neutrality. In the words of Harvey Cox: "Not to decide, is to decide."

Ultimately all of ethics revolves around the resolution of one basic question: "Why should anyone do what is right when doing so is not to their advantage?" Clearly, it is not always personally good, rational, and advantageous to do the right thing. It is as plain as can be, in spite of the many theories to the contrary, that doing right and refraining from doing wrong is not necessarily in accordance with reason; and, conversely, doing wrong and omitting right is not necessarily contrary to reason in the ordinary sense. In fact, people are credited with high moral worth or are called heroes specifically on the grounds of having done what is right even when this is contrary to their own best interest. The point is, if a person wants to be shown that it is always to their advantage, and that their life will invariably be better (or, at least, not made worse) if they adopt the moral way of life, I doubt if this demand can always be met. It must be admitted that anyone who takes the moral road may be called upon to make serious personal sacrifices and, hence, may not have as good a life at the material and practical level as she would otherwise have had. Perhaps the only response to this question is a negative one. It was Aristotle who fathered the notion that at the foundation of morals lies the principle that if morality is to be argued about at all, then the onus of justification lies upon those who propose to deny it.

The term *narcissism* or *narcissistic type* is not often used in philosophical circles, but we think it should be. As a concept, narcissism neatly encapsulates the dark side of why it is so hard "to get free of the shadow of self."

In Greek mythology, the legend of Narcissus is told in a number of slightly different ways, but all versions end with the same moral message. As a child and a young man Narcissus was so beautiful that many lovers, men and women alike, courted him. Even the nymph Echo fell in love with him, but he refused them all.

(The grieving Echo pined away until she was only a voice in the mountains, uttering forever the last syllable of any word that she heard.) One erstwhile lover rejected by Narcissus prayed to Nemesis (the personification of retribution), who condemned Narcissus to the contemplation of his own beauty reflected in a pool of water on Mount Helicon. Maddened by the sight of his own face, Narcissus could not tear himself away from the pool.

Hour after hour, day after day, Narcissus hung over the pool's edge. He had no care for food or drink; he only gazed at the reflection he loved. "Now I know," he wept, "what others have suffered from me, for I burn with love of another self." Crying in vain for the object of his adoration, his heart finally ceased to throb and he lay dead on the shore. The story ends with the gods themselves taking pity on so fair a corpse, and transforming his body into a new and lovely flower they called Narcissus. According to the *Synopsis of Psychiatry*, persons with narcissistic personality disorder are characterized by a heightened sense of self-importance and grandiose feelings that they are unique in some way. They consider themselves special people and expect special treatment. They always want their own way and are frequently ambitious, desiring fame and fortune. Their relationships with others are fragile and limited. They are unable to show empathy, and they feign sympathy for others only to achieve their own selfish ends. Interpersonal exploitation is commonplace.[7]

A narcissistic individual's entire sense of self is devoted to the pursuit of personal pleasure and self-gratification with little or no concern for the wants and needs of others. Narcissists are not necessarily vain in the cosmetic sense of clothing, style, or trends, but, cosmologically speaking, the world begins and revolves around them. Narcissists create for themselves a self-defined, self-contained, self-serving worldview, which rationalizes anything done on their behalf and which does not require justification on any grounds outside of themselves.

In *The Culture of Narcissism*, historian Christopher Lasch argues that to live for the moment, to live for yourself, and not for your contemporaries, predecessors, or posterity is our prevailing ethical *leitmotif.* For Lasch, narcissists feel free to abandon their social roles as parent, neighbor, or citizen for the higher purpose and goal of self-fulfillment and self-gratification. For Lasch the nineteenth-century ideal of "rugged individualism" was outwardly oriented and saw the world as a "wilderness to be shaped and won with and for others." Contemporary individualism, says Lasch, is totally self-absorbed; for them, "the world is a mirror."

The following is a limited list of some of the key methods and behaviors that narcissistic personality types, and those of us locked into our own selfish concerns, implement in order to insulate and isolate themselves from themselves and others and, thereby, "stay within the shadow of self."

INSTANT GRATIFICATION

One of the more fundamental reasons why a lot of us, narcissistic types and otherwise, are unable to be overly concerned with ethical considerations is our tendency to overvalue present gratification and to undervalue future possible benefits and goods. The ability to defer gratification is one of the best measurements of emotional and ethical maturity. The problem is that people who "live in the moment" tend to dismiss the past, because it is no more, and give no thought to the future, because it has not yet arrived. Such a position is impoverished because it lacks perspective. Ethically speaking, reality is the "moment," but only as it comes from the past and leads us into the future. All three dimensions must be considered in order to develop a consistent and ethically attuned character. The problem is that narcissistic types do not merely live in the moment; they are trapped in the moment and captives of its limitations.

THE LACK OF MORAL IMAGINATION

If ethics is an attempt to stir us beyond the "numbness of self," then ethical decision making requires us to look beyond the immediate moment and beyond personal needs, desires, and wants in order to "imagine" the possible consequences of our decisions and behavior on self and others. In its most elemental sense moral imagination is about picturing, foreseeing, imaginatively discerning various outcomes in our interactions with others. In some sense, moral imagination is a "dramatic virtual rehearsal" which allows us to examine and appraise different courses of action in order to determine the morally best thing to do.

According to a number of prominent philosophical thinkers, it is not always a lack of or ignorance of moral principles that causes moral ineptitude; sometimes it is the inability to "imagine," and be sympathetic to the needs, passions, and interests of others. At its core, to sympathize is to place myself in another's situation, "not because of how that situation might affect me, but rather as if I were that person in that situation."[8] Using "moral imagination" allows us to be self-reflective, allows us to step back from our situation and see it from another point of view. In taking such a perspective, a person tries to look at the world or herself from a more dispassionate perspective or from the point of view of another dispassionate reasonable person, who is not solely absorbed with self. This trans-positional perspective has been called *A Disengaged View from Somewhere.*

1. What would a reasonable person judge is the right thing to do?
2. Could one defend this decision publicly?
3. What kind of precedent does this decision set? Would one want it repeated, or made into law?
4. Is this decision or action necessary?
5. Is this the least worse option?[9]

What "moral imagination" suggests, and what narcissistic types rarely try to do, is that in order to make an ethical decision you have to determine: What's at stake? What are the issues? Who else is involved? And, what are the alternatives? Moral imagination allows us the possibility of addressing these questions from a perspective that is both inside and outside the box, a perspective that focuses on self and others.

CALLOUSNESS, CARELESSNESS, AND HABIT

In 1963, Hannah Arendt coined a phrase in her book on the trial of Adolph Eichmann, *Eichmann in Jerusalem,* that remains rife with ethical implications: "the banality of evil." By it she meant the common and unspectacular nature of evil and evil doers. She had expected Eichmann to be powerful, vile, vicious, nonrepentant—in short, the devil incarnate! Instead he was a small, balding man who liked to read, and who complained to his jailers about his nightly insomnia, his bouts of constipation, and how the snobbish politics of the *SS* kept him from being promoted to full colonel! To Arendt's horror, both as a Jew and a philosopher, Eichmann was not writ-large. He was not a monster. He was, rather, a self-involved boring little clerk. A clerk, said Arendt, who carried out every order given to him, including transporting millions of Jews to their deaths in concentration camps.

Arendt pointed out that, for Eichmann, everything beyond his orders, his own well-being, and his own twisted sense of duty and honor, was irrelevant to him. Putting aside the issues of genocide and genuine evil, the same *modus operandi* can be seen in narcissistic personality types. Just as Eichmann is the embodiment of the "banality of evil," the narcissist's lifestyle exemplifies "the irrelevance of others." Narcissistic types are not necessarily cruel or mean or evil, but rather they are serenely unconcerned or indifferent to others. They are hardened, calloused to the plight or needs of others. As a colleague once pointed out: "It's not so much that self-absorbed, narcissistic types are consciously unethical. Rather, they are thoughtless and, in reality, unconscious of others. In fact, they may be genuinely amoral (without moral concern) in regard to others." In time, of course, callousness, carelessness, and self-absorbed indifference progress from simple behavior traits, to habits, and eventually to a way of life that influences if not totally dictates our moral worldview and the choices we make regarding others.

There is unfortunately an even darker side to the habit of callousness and carelessness in regard to others. It is what Nobel laureate Konrad Lorenz called *pseudo-speciation.* From the behavioral point of view, pseudo-speciation is a variation of what sociologists have traditionally referred to as ethnocentrism and its vicious half-brother, racial prejudice. Ethnocentrism—the idea that what is humane and good is defined by the values of one's own group—seems to be a common human experience. As such, ethnocentrism contributes to hostile intergroup images by accentuating the differences between a person's values and habits and those of people who belong to other groups. The beliefs and habits of other people are viewed as discrepant, esoteric, and incomprehensible. Behaviorally, ethnocentrism involves the rejection of members of other groups simply because they are outsiders. In extreme situations—war, for example—nothing is easier than for the human spirit to neglect to recognize the same conditions and characteristics which define and specify one's own humanity in the existence of another. Conflict accentuates the differences between groups. Pseudo-speciation serves the psychological function of image replacement; through its use, human beings become others, objects, or *Untermenschen* (German for subhumans).[10]

At the individual level, pseudo-speciation is nothing more than the narcissistic self-proclamation which in effect states that one's actions, thoughts, standards, and even life are correct and should be emulated by all. At the social/cultural level, Lorenz has stated that pseudo-speciation allows us to consider members of groups other than our own not fully human (a pseudo-species), or at least to regard them as inferior, crude, and contemptuous rivals not worthy of common decency. Pseudo-speciation allows us to denude others of their humanity and individuality so that we do not kill men, but abstract caricatures: Nazis, Commies, Capitalistic Dogs, Redskins, laps, Gooks! Psychoanalyst Erich Fromm adds to this, stating that what happens in pseudo-speciation is that the aggressor cuts the other person off emotionally and freezes him in an unempathetic state. The other ceases to be experienced as human and becomes a thing. Under these circumstances, there are no inhibitions against even the most severe forms of destructiveness. Moreover, said Fromm, there is good clinical evidence for the assumption that most destructive violence occurs in conjunction with momentary or chronic emotional withdrawal and general indifference to the plight of others.[11]

Reportedly, Winston Churchill once said of a political opponent: "Deep down, there's a lot less there than meets the eye." He was referring, of course, to the person's character or lack thereof. And it is just this phenomenon, the absence of character, or, to be more precise, a flawed character, that goes a long way to explain the difficulty that so many people have in figuring out what they "ought to do" in an ethical situation. Aristotle suggested, as did British philosopher G. E. M. Anscombe and many others, that to do ethics properly you must start with what a person needs and must have to flourish and live well with others—character. For Aristotle the ethical life is grounded on the development and expression of character.

The root word of *character* is the Greek word for etching or engraving. *Charaktêr* was originally used to signify the marks impressed upon a coin. As applied to human beings, *charaktêr* refers to the enduring marks or etched-in factors that have been impressed on our mind, our *psyche*, which include our inborn talents as well as the learned and acquired traits imposed upon us by education and experience. These engravings set us apart, define us, and motivate behavior.

Although much of character is imposed on us, engraved on us by the socio-economic environment, the vagaries of time and place, and the biological (genetic) and behavioral influences of our parents, character is also about what a person *chooses* to hold dear, to value, and to believe in. To paraphrase Eleanor Roosevelt, if you want to know what a person values, check their checkbooks. If you want to know about a person's character, check their values. And, if you want to know a person's ethics, check their character.

William James believed that the most interesting and important thing about a person, and that which determines our perspective on the world is our philosophy of life, i.e., our values, ideals, and beliefs. For James, our values, ideas, and beliefs are the things we choose to hold as dear, important, or sacred. They are things we are willing to act for and act on. Our values, ideas, and beliefs are the roadmaps that help us to decipher and explain what James calls the "booming, buzzing confusion" of reality. Our philosophy of life is defined by what we choose to value, and our character in life is defined by actually living out that which we value. James believes that an honest person experiencing hard times will make every effort to sooner or later honor a debt, but that a dishonest person may never repay a debt even if they possess more than sufficient resources to do so.

Like the concept of values, philosopher Robert C. Solomon defines virtues as desirable, lived out behavior traits that contribute to and are essential for achieving happiness, getting along with others, and, in general, living well. For Solomon, like Aristotle, we choose our virtues and make them "second nature" by repetition and habit. Virtuous behavior is not an accident or mere luck or a onetime event. A virtuous act is doing the right thing for the right reason, habitually, and on purpose. Ethics, says Solomon, is a question of one's whole character, not just a question of this particular virtue or that.[12]

The Romans had a perfect Latin word to describe and measure the quality of a person's character, *integritas*. Ethically speaking, integrity means "the state or quality of being entire or complete." It means soundness, being unimpaired, having all the component pieces fit together and be whole. It means an attempt to adhere to a cluster of virtues and values which complement and reinforce each other. Integrity is about self-restraint, self-control, self-mastery, or continence.

Integrity is not just about simple addition. Integrity means "living coherently," what the Greek stoics called *homologoumenôs zên*—presenting a sense of self to the world that is not Janus faced, fractured, or schizophrenic. Integrity is about one's sense of personal identity and honor. It is a matter of integrating the various parts of our personality into a harmonious, intact whole. An integrated character does not do and say one thing when no one else is around and yet another when someone is present. The possession (or lack) of integrity is something that all morally serious people care about and think important. In both personal relationships and public life, to describe someone as exhibiting a lack of integrity is to offer a damning diagnosis.

> It carries the implication that this individual is not to be relied upon, that in some fundamental way they are not someone who we can, or should, view as being wholly unequivocally there. The foundations of self and character are not sound; the ordering of values is not coherent.[13]

In his 1996 bestseller, *Integrity*, Stephen L. Carter suggests that integrity is a kind of über-virtue or a type of "philosophical cement" that contains and coordinates all of one's other virtues and values. Carter understands integrity as having the courage of one's convictions. He suggests that if ethics is living out what we value, then the integrity of a person's character, or lack thereof, is as good a yardstick as any to predict ethical conduct. Carter describes integrity in terms of three characteristics:

1. One must take pains to try to discern what is right from wrong.
2. One must be willing to shape one's actions in accord with that discernment, even when it is difficult or painful to do so. (As Walter Lippman so eloquently phrased it: "He has

honor if he holds himself to an ideal of conduct though it is inconvenient, unprofitable, or dangerous to do so.")

3. One must be willing to acknowledge publicly what one is doing. In short, a person of integrity must be reflective, steadfast, trustworthy, and whole. "A person of integrity," said Carter, "is a whole person, a person somehow undivided."[14]

According to *Chicago Tribune* columnist Eric Zorn, a person of character is someone who has a conscience. Unfortunately, to most modern ears, says Zorn, the word "conscience" is too abstract, ephemeral, and downright old-fashioned to be used in most conventional conversations. What comes to mind, for a lot of people, is the image of a little person sitting on your shoulder who is whispering in your ear and offering advice and judgment on the moral goodness or blameworthiness of your actions. Nevertheless, Zorn argued, even though the word is rarely used, its meaning, function, and purpose is neither obsolete nor irrelevant.[15]

Conscience implies care, concern, or, at the very least, the recognition of others. Our conscience is not just a nagging, faultfinding, superego-cop. Conscience is from the Latin *conscire*—to be conscious; to know. Conscience is the faculty, the power, the instinct, the ability to reflect on, be sensitive to, evaluate, and make judgments about our interactions with others. It is not an infallible instinct. It is not a perfect emotional buzzer that can always distinguish between right and wrong. It is not a perfect truth detector. But if we are lucky, if we are not totally lost in the emotional maze of our own narcissism, conscience at the very least forces us to ponder on our relationships with others, and to make some sort of judgments about what we consider to be acceptable or unacceptable behavior in their regard.

If character is living out what we value, conscience is that computer chip which makes judgments and evaluations about when, how, and with whom that value should or should not be applied. Conscience requires us to consider others.

Being a person of character and consciousness is an ongoing activity, and not a onetime affair or an episodic experience. Ethical character is formed over time and can withstand the test of time. Aristotle reportedly said, "Never judge a person moral until they are dead." What he meant by that is that on any given day or moment we make mistakes, we fail, we act in ways we wish we would not. Who among us is without regret or fault? A person's character must be judged in perspective, over time. Character, like a skill or art form, must be practiced to be perfected and maintained. And yet having said this, some mistakes, some actions, some behavior, intended or not, can change our lives and our reputations forever. Vigilance is required!

John Dewey has argued that we have made a fetish out of the "cult of rugged individualism."[16] We think that all of our rights are personal, private, and proprietary when in fact private rights always and only exist within the context of the collective community. Each generation needs to learn to "forget ourselves on purpose," to let go of our ego needs, to step back from center stage, to, at the very least, be open to the voices and the needs of others. Simple prudence ("to govern and discipline ourselves by the care of reason") should make us aware that we are not the only one at the table, that other issues and needs must to be addressed besides out own. Thomas Merton has pointed out that the paradox of both faith and ethics is the need to lose ourselves (in others) in order to find ourselves.[17]

Self-absorption, self-centeredness, self-involvement are not traits limited to our private lives. Unfortunately, they spill over into our public actions as well. Getting free of the emotional fortress of self—me, myself, and I—may also be the root problem for our failings and ethical indiscretions in the realms of politics, industry, and business.

What is business?[18] It seems a silly question because *we all know* (or at least, think we know) what business is: Business is what *corporations* do. We can easily identify corporations—American Express, Coca-Cola, General Electric, Home Depot, McDonald's, Microsoft, Verizon (to name a handful of the thirty corporations whose stock prices are used to calculate the Dow Jones industrial average)—so, to understand what business is we need only observe what they (corporations) do.[19] And whatever *they* do is business.

This seemingly straightforward understanding of business informs much of what is written in the business ethics literature, but it runs aground on two basic problems. First, not all corporations are *business* corporations. In addition to business corporations, there are, for example, municipal corporations (formed to establish local government entities, like cities) and not-for-profit corporations (formed most frequently to promote charitable endeavors). It would be wrong to say that whatever municipal corporations do (e.g., issue parking citations) or not-for-profit corporations do (e.g., fund or conduct adult literacy programs) is business.

Second, not all doers of business are corporations. In addition to the business corporations with which we are most readily familiar—firms like American Express, Coca-Cola, General Electric, Home Depot, McDonald's, Microsoft, and Verizon, whose ownership shares are traded on public exchanges, like the New York Stock Exchange—business doers include sole proprietorships (business firms wholly owned by an individual person who is liable for all debts of the business venture), general partnerships (business firms owned by two or more persons, called general partners, each of whom is jointly and severably liable for all debts of the business venture), and limited partnerships (business firms owned by one or more general partners and one or more limited partners—partners who share in the profits of the business venture, have no managerial role, and are liable for the debts of the business venture only to the extent of any capital they contribute to it). Business doers include also business corporations whose ownership shares are not traded on public exchanges. These may be vast enterprises whose shares could easily be publicly traded if management and the shareholders wished to go that route (Cargill and Koch Industries being perhaps the best examples), or smaller firms whose ownership shares may be held by only a few family members or managers (so-called close corporations)—availing themselves of the corporate form mainly for the limitation of personal liability and whatever tax advantages accrue to doing business in the corporate, rather than some other, form. Business doers include also cooperatives, whose ownership shares are typically held by those who bear some *other* substantial relationship to the business venture. Thus, there are worker cooperatives (business firms owned by some or all their employees), customer cooperatives (business firms owned by some or all of those who buy the firm's products—like Ace Hardware, which is owned by its franchisees), and supplier cooperatives (business firms owned by some or all of those who sell their products to the firm as inputs to the business venture—like Ocean Spray, which is owned by the farmers who supply it with cranberries and other fruits to make its juices).[20]

So, if not all corporations are business doers and not all business doers are corporations, then whatever *business* is, it is clearly not just whatever corporations do. Amending the initial, failed account of what business is to "business is what business doers do" demonstrates the poverty of this approach: We need an account of what business *is* in order to identify those who are doing it, so saying "business is what business doers do" gets us nowhere closer to saying what business is.

Some would seek to slip this punch by saying that business is what *organizations* do.[21] While this lacks the self-referential difficulties that make "business is what business doers do" a non-starter, it runs aground for the same reasons that "business is what corporations do" ran aground. First, there are organizations that don't do business. The Upper Sandusky Ladies Bridge Club is undoubtedly an organization (presumably of bridge-playing ladies in the greater Upper Sandusky area), but it is such even if it does no business—as it may if, for example, its officers do no more than schedule and publicize to members the next game, and its members do no more than play in the appointed place and at the appointed time, taking tea and sandwiches during the break. Second, there are business-doers who are not organizations. The sole entrepreneur who sells her services, performs them, and accepts the payment for them (like the house cleaner one of the authors regularly hires) is undoubtedly doing business, but she is not an organization and doesn't have recourse to one in order to do business.[22]

The path to progress is to stop focusing on the *entities* ("corporations," "organizations") we associate with business, and focus instead on the *activities* that make those entities *business* entities, rather than entities of another kind.[23] Business firms differ from other kinds of organizations not principally in their organizational features, but in what they are organized to do—business. There is a world of difference between Google Inc. and the Internal Revenue Service, for example, but they are not nearly so different organizationally as they are in the diverging practices each is intended to support.

We have an intuitive grasp of what it is to *do* business and it is that activity, rather than the entities conducting it, that makes it business. Like medicine and like law, business is a *practice.*[24] Characterizing business practice is not easy, but working from clear cases the beginnings of an account emerge.

People do business when they *transact,* or *trade.* One engages in trade by alienating some property rights and acquiring other property rights by means of exchange. Business is, at least in part, a *transaction-executing* practice. But one does not do business only when executing transactions. Transactional opportunities do not always present themselves immediately and transparently. Often, we have to seek them out. It may be as simple as locating a convenient vendor who sells the commodity one seeks or as complex as identifying potential customers for a product yet unmade. Finding transactional opportunities requires alertness to them and imagination about how best to exploit them. Another way to say this is that business is an *entrepreneurial* practice.[25] Because alertness is critical to executing transactions, business is not just a transaction-executing, but also a transaction-*seeking*, practice.

Transactions are sought and executed typically not for their own sake, but in pursuit of some end. Not all ends one seeks through transactions are business ends. The free medical clinic that transacts with medical suppliers, buying their wares with donations from concerned citizens, is transaction-seeking and transaction-executing, but we are rightly reluctant to characterize its transactional activities as business. The clear case is where the transactor seeks to make his transactional activity *self-sustaining*. One engages in business by seeking to identify and implement *profitable* sets of transactions—seeking to yield something of value that was not there before the transactions were initiated.

Nothing in this account depends upon the view that people are motivated exclusively, or even primarily, by profit. It says only that people pursue their aims through *business*, rather than through other means, when they attempt to transact in a profit-generating (self-sustaining) way. Business, on this account, is the pursuit and execution of intentionally self-sustaining transactional activity.

By way of contrast, consider the viewer-supported public television station. Our intuitive understanding is that it, like the free medical clinic, is not engaged in business. Like the free medical clinic, it seems to rely intendedly on monetary gifts to sustain itself and so is not a business doer. Indeed, public television donors are often called *sustaining members*—suggesting that it is not the *transactional* activities of the public television station that are intended to sustain it. But note that these sustaining pledges are not always straightforward gifts. When a donative pledge of $100 nets the viewer a *Best of Peter, Paul & Mary* CD, this seems at first blush like a sale—a transaction—rather than a gift. These pledges are interesting because they seem actually to involve *two* interactions between donor and public television station where at first there appears to be only one. One interaction *is* a transaction—sale of the *Best of Peter, Paul & Mary* CD. But note that the donor likely would not pay *just anyone* $100 for the CD. If the donor's local Virgin Megastore sought $100 for the CD, which commands $20 on Amazon, the donor would likely be uninterested in paying the extra $80. If $20 is indeed the prevailing price for the CD, then the donor and the public television station are more reasonably interpreted as engaging in (1) a $20 transaction for purchase of the *Best of Peter, Paul & Mary* CD and (2) an $80 *gift* to support the public television station. The public television station is not a business doer, on this account, because its *transactions* are not, and are not intended to be, self-sustaining.

By focusing on transactional activity, rather than pre-analytic characterizations of what is or is not a business firm, we see that anybody (not just "corporations," or worse: "organizations") can do business. A proper understanding of business ethics ought to reflect that fact.

If business is a practice, like medicine or law, then business ethics is a form of practice ethics, like medical ethics or legal ethics. Just as medical ethics and legal ethics focus on the moral contours of their defining practices, business ethics focuses on the moral contours of its defining practice. On the account sketched above, business is a practice focused on transactions, seeking self-sustenance from a sum of them. Business ethics, conceived as an account of the moral contours of business practice, is, or should be understood as, a transaction-focused, rather than an organization-focused, intellectual enterprise.

If we understand *ethics* as according proper weight to other-regarding reasons in formulating our plans of action, then *business* ethics seems straightforward: Business ethics is a matter of according proper weight to other-regarding reasons in formulating our plans of action *when doing business*—i.e., pursuing and engaging in intendedly self-sustaining transactions. However, no sooner does one thumb through a business ethics textbook (even a textbook like this one) or business ethics journal than does one encounter readings or articles that seem far removed from explicating the ethics of transaction-seeking and transaction-executing activity.

Robert Solomon seeks to distinguish three levels of business ethics analysis or argument, which he calls the micro, the macro, and the molar.[26] The *micro* level concerns "the rules for fair exchange between two individuals." The *macro* level concerns "the institutional or cultural rules of commerce for an entire society ('the business world'). The *molar* level ("molar" from the Latin *moles*, meaning "mass") concerns "the basic unit of commerce today—the corporation."[27]

Solomon's micro level sounds like what we have characterized above as business ethics. His macro level too, at first blush, sounds like what we have characterized as business ethics. For what, exactly, would "institutional or cultural rules of commerce" be if not "rules of fair exchange"? To ask that question, however, is to raise another: If the micro and macro levels are fundamentally the same, why distinguish them?

The answer, of course, is that for Solomon they are not the same. His characterization of the macro level emphasizes the institutional and the notion that the rules of commerce of which he writes are *for the whole society*. Solomon's macro level business ethics addresses the relationship between political society and economic activity. It "becomes part and parcel of those large questions about justice, legitimacy, and the nature of society that constitute social and political philosophy."[28] He identifies as archetypal inquiries of macro level business ethics such questions as:

> What is the purpose of the 'free market'—or is it in some sense a good of its own, with its own *telos*? Are private property rights primary, in some sense preceding social convention (as John Locke and more recently Robert Nozick have argued), or is the market too to be conceived as a complex social practice in which rights are but one ingredient? Is the free market system 'fair'? Is it the most efficient way to distribute goods and services throughout society? Does it pay enough attention to cases of desperate need (where a 'fair exchange' is not part of the question)? Does it pay enough attention to merit, where it is by no means guaranteed that virtue will be in sufficient demand so as to be rewarded? What are the legitimate (and illegitimate roles of government in business life), and what is the role of government regulation?[29]

These are all important questions—of social and political philosophy. However, it is not clear why one would conceive of them as part of business ethics. Engaging in business practice *presupposes* that most of those questions are answered—and in a particular way. If business ethics is to offer something useful—something that is not subsumed by what are, after all, foundational questions of political philosophy—it should tell us what we ought to do when engaging in business practice. There are gains to be had from an intellectual division of labor between political philosophy and business ethics, and macro level business ethics upsets the division, making business ethics journals and textbooks just another venue for doing political philosophy. Macro level business ethics is more about what many self-described business ethicists really want to talk about—their visions of the just political society—than it is about the ethics of doing business. It is, in other words, more applied political philosophy than applied ethics.

This point is underscored by Solomon's conception of the molar level of business ethics, which sees the corporation as "the basic unit of commerce today." Only if one is moved by the view that questions about the justice of the free market or the proper role of public policy toward business are fundamental to business ethics could one claim that the corporation is the "definitive 'molar' unit of modern business" and that "the central questions of business ethics tend to be unabashedly aimed at the directors and employees of those few thousand or so companies that rule so much of commercial life around the world."[30] One suspects that those companies "rule" commercial life in the same way that a firm whose product enjoys 30 percent market share is said to "command" or to "control" 30 percent of the market. It is a metaphorical usage than depends upon a literal interpretation for its rhetorical bite.

Moreover, as we write, the U.S. economy is in the midst of an entrepreneurial renaissance, begun at the end of the twentieth century, that is transforming the business environment in exciting and unpredictable ways. The great bulk of the workforce is found in firms with 500 employees or fewer. Job growth and surging economic productivity are found mainly in firms with 50 employees or fewer. Unprecedented numbers of Americans are abandoning employment entirely—starting their own firms and living on their profits, rather than on a paycheck. Established members of the economic oligarchy of which so many business ethicists write, like General Motors and Ford, "rule" no marketplace and find themselves on the verge of collapse. They are replaced not by new oligarchs but by no oligarchs—young, nimble, entrepreneurial firms like Google and Skype are at the forefront of business; a forefront easy to miss by focusing on the ossified corporate titans that make up the Fortune 500.

The Prussian military theorist Carl von Clausewitz famously described war as he "continuation of politics by other means." The readings in this text reflect both the ethics-of-business-practice approach to business ethics and the institutional/societal approach that Solomon calls macro-level business ethics. We advise that you approach the readings critically, with an open, but also an active, mind. Does the author try to sell debatable public policy objectives as ethical business practice? Is the reading there to make a point about the ethics of doing business or, following Clausewitz, to continue politics by other means? Sometimes the answer will be yes, sometimes no, and many times it will be unclear. The benefit is found in working through it yourself.

NOTES

1. A more detailed version of the first part of this essay can be found in Al Gini, *Why It's Hard to Be Good* (New York: Routledge, 2006).
2. John Hendry, *Between Enterprise and Ethics* (New York: Oxford University Press, 2004).
3. Al Gini, "Moral Leadership and Business Ethics," *Journal of Leadership Studies* 4(4) (Fall 1997): 67.
4. Ibid., 67.
5. Ibid., 68.
6. Ibid., 66, 67.
7. See, e.g., Donna M. Czuchta Romano, "A Self-Psychology Approach to Narcissistic Personality Disorder: A Nursing Reflection," Perspectives In Psychiatric Care 40(1) (2004): 20–28.
8. Patricia H. Werhane, "Moral Imagination and the Search for Ethical Decision Making and Management," *Business Ethics Quarterly*, Ruffin Series, 1 (n.d.): 81, 82.
9. Ibid., 88–91.
10. A. R. Gini, "Soldiers in Combat: Strategies for Survival," *Thought* 56, 220 (March 1981): 24, 25.
11. Ibid., 25.
12. Robert C. Solomon, *A Handbook for Ethics* (Orlando, Fla.: Harcourt Brace, 1996), 83–88.
13. *Routledge Encyclopedia of Philosophy Online*, "Integrity," http://www.rep.Routledge.com/Article/L134SECT1
14. Stephen L. Carter quoted in Gilbert Meilaender, "Integral or Divided?" in *First Things*, May 1996: 49–71.
15. Eric Zorn, "'Conscience': Old-Fashioned But Not Obsolete," *Chicago Tribune*, Tempo Section, 2, May 23, 2002.
16. John Dewey, *Individualism Old and New* (New York: Capricorn, 1962).
17. A. E. Carr, *A Search for Wisdom and Spirit: Thomas Merton's Theology of Self* (Notre Dame, Ind.: University of Notre Dame Press, 1988), 26.
18. A more detailed and somewhat differently focused version of this discussion can be found in Alexei M. Marcoux, "The Concept of Business in Business Ethics," *Journal of Private Enterprise* 21(2) (2006): 50–67.
19. The idea that "a corporation is what it does" informs the collection of essays in James E. Post, Lee E. Preston, and Sybille Sachs, *Redefining the Corporation: Stakeholder Management and Organizational Wealth* (Stanford, Calif.: Stanford University Press, 2002).
20. On the dazzling and not often commented upon variety of ownership structures that obtain among business ventures, see Henry Hansmann, *The Ownership of Enterprise* (Cambridge, Mass.: Belknap Press of Harvard University Press, 1996).
21. Indeed, the frequency with which business ethics is conflated with organizational ethics in the business ethics literature is something to behold.
22. The sole entrepreneur is the crucial case. If we say that she too is an organization, then that is a *reductio ad absurdum* on the concept of an organization—not because nothing is organizational but because everything is.
23. This is the more sensible approach for another reason: It is likely the case that not all the activities of business doers are *business* activities. Sole proprietors, partners, and corporate managers—business doers all—also sleep, eat, paint their nails, and shoot rubber bands at their workmates. That these activities are engaged in by business doers does not make them business activities.
24. It may be thought that we are hereby arguing that business ethics is, like medical ethics and legal ethics, a species of professional ethics. We are not. Professions are defined by particular expertise and highly technical regularities of practice that are absent in business. Nonetheless, business is a practice, an activity. It is the moral features of that practice that are central to business ethics, properly construed.

25. The alertness-focused account of entrepreneurship is due to Israel Kirzner, *Competition & Entrepreneurship* (Chicago: University of Chicago Press, 1973).

26. Robert Solomon, "Business Ethics," in Peter Singer, ed., *A Companion to Ethics* (Malden, Mass.: Blackwell, 1991), 354–365.

27. Ibid., 359.

28. Ibid.

29. Ibid.

30. Ibid.

Business or Ethics

Albert Carr argues that bluffing in business negotiations is like bluffing in poker: appropriate to the venue and an agreed-on part of business practice. Through his vigorous and entertaining defense of bluffing, Carr by implication asks us to consider to what extent the ethics of a practice (like business) should conform to, and to what extent and for what reason they may deviate legitimately from, our moral judgments about everyday life. Is business analogous to poker, with bluffing justified on the same grounds for both? Or do the disanalogies between business and poker call for us to scrutinize the practice and its effects more deeply?

The word *parable* means "comparison" or "judgment." "The Parable of the Sadhu" asks us to compare, to judge, to make a moral choice. What was an Indian holy man (a *sadhu*) doing unconscious and unclothed at 15,000 feet on a Himalayan mountain slope? Were the people who found him now responsible for him? Should the group or any single individual have taken responsibility for his safety? Does the parable parallel the distinction often made between individual ethical decision making (personal ethics) and collective decision making (professional or business ethics)? Is there an absolute right or wrong to be found here?

As "The Parable of the Sadhu" demonstrates, relatively few issues in life are ever clear cut, especially when they involve a complex series of facts and decisions. However, there are times when the issues, although complex, are clear and demand our attention. Such is the case with two classic examples of what's right and wrong in business ethics: the Beech-Nut apple juice incident and the Tylenol tampering episode.

The Beech-Nut incident raises this question: "Why would one of America's most venerable food companies knowingly produce apple juice that completely omitted apples from its recipe and contained nothing but sugar water and vitamin C?" After all, Beech-Nut is not a mom-and-pop outfit but a firm that annually earned a 17 to 20 percent share of the $760 million U.S. baby food market. This was a firm that was managed at the top by a president and vice president who were pillars of the community. So how did it happen that Beech-Nut broke its sacred trust with the public— "Safe Food for Healthy Kids"?

The Tylenol tampering episode and the position taken by top management at Johnson & Johnson raise this question: "In doing the right thing, can a corporation and business also do well?" Is the lesson of this case that honesty works and the truth can be effective both ethically and economically? Or is the real lesson a cynical, self-serving one à la Mark Twain: "When in doubt tell the truth. It will disarm your friends and befuddle your enemies"?

Essay

Is Business Bluffing Ethical?

Albert Z. Carr

Albert Carr wrote this inflammatory piece in the Harvard Business Review *in 1968. It continues to attract controversy.*

A respected businessman with whom I discussed the theme of this article remarked with some heat, "You mean to say you're going to encourage men to bluff? Why, bluffing is nothing more than a form of lying! You're advising them to lie!"

I agreed that the basis of private morality is a respect for truth and that the closer a businessman comes to the truth, the more he deserves respect. At the same time, I suggested that most bluffing in business might be regarded simply as game strategy—much like bluffing in poker, which does not reflect on the morality of the bluffer.

I quoted Henry Taylor, the British statesman who pointed out that "falsehood ceases to be falsehood when it is understood on all sides that the truth is not expected to be spoken"— an exact description of bluffing in poker, diplomacy, and business. I cited the analogy of the criminal court, where the criminal is not expected to tell the truth when he pleads "not guilty." Everyone from the judge down takes it for granted that the job of the defendant's attorney is to get his client off, not to reveal the truth; and this is considered ethical practice. I mentioned Representative Omar Burleson, the Democrat from Texas, who was quoted as saying, in regard to the ethics of Congress, "Ethics is a barrel of worms"[1]—a pungent summing up of the problem of deciding who is ethical in politics.

I reminded my friend that millions of businessmen feel constrained every day to say *yes* to their bosses when they secretly believe *no* and that this is generally accepted as permissible strategy when the alternative might be the loss of a job. The essential point, I said, is that the ethics of business are game ethics, different from the ethics of religion.

He remained unconvinced. Referring to the company of which he is president, he declared: "Maybe that's good enough for some businessmen, but I can tell you that we pride ourselves on our ethics. In 30 years not one customer has ever questioned my word or asked to check our figures. We're loyal to our customers and fair to our suppliers. I regard my handshake on a deal as a contract. I've never entered into price-fixing schemes with my competitors. I've never allowed my salesmen to spread injurious rumors about other companies. Our union contract is the best in our industry. And, if I do say so myself, our ethical standards are of the highest!"

He really was saying, without realizing it, that he was living up to the ethical standards of the business game—which are a far cry from those of private life. Like a gentlemanly poker player, he did not play in cahoots with others at the table, try to smear their reputations, or hold back chips he owed them.

But this same fine man, at that very time, was allowing one of his products to be advertised in a way that made it sound a great deal better than it actually was. Another item in his product line was notorious among dealers for its "built-in obsolescence." He was holding back from the market a much-improved product because he did not want it to interfere with sales of the inferior item it would have replaced. He had joined with certain of his competitors in hiring a lobbyist to push a state legislature, by methods that he preferred not to know too much about, into amending a bill then being enacted.

In his view these things had nothing to do with ethics; they were merely normal business practice. He himself undoubtedly avoided outright falsehoods—never lied in so many words. But the entire organization that he ruled was deeply involved in numerous strategies of deception.

PRESSURE TO DECEIVE

Most executives from time to time are almost compelled, in the interests of their companies or themselves, to practice some form of deception when negotiating with customers, dealers, labor unions, government officials, or even other departments of their companies. By conscious misstatements, concealment of pertinent facts, or exaggeration—in short, by bluffing—they seek to persuade others to agree with them. I think it is fair to say that if the individual executive refuses to bluff from time to time—if he feels obligated to tell the truth, the whole truth, and nothing but the truth—he is ignoring opportunities permitted under the rules and is at a heavy disadvantage in his business dealings.

But here and there a businessman is unable to reconcile himself to the bluff in which he plays a part. His conscience, perhaps spurred by religious idealism, troubles him. He feels guilty; he may develop an ulcer or a nervous tic. Before any executive can make profitable use of the strategy of the bluff, he needs to make sure that in bluffing he will not lose self-respect or become emotionally disturbed. If he is to reconcile personal integrity and high standards of honesty with the practical requirements of business, he must feel that his bluffs are ethically justified. The justification rests on the fact that business, as practiced by individuals as well as by corporations, has the impersonal character of a game—a game that demands both special strategy and an understanding of its special ethics.

The game is played at all levels of corporate life, from the highest to the lowest. At the very instant that a man decides to enter business, he may be forced into a game situation, as is shown by the recent experience of a Cornell honor graduate who applied for a job with a large company:

- This applicant was given a psychological test which included the statement, "Of the following magazines, check any that you have read either regularly or from time to time, and double-check those which interest you most. *Reader's Digest, Time, Fortune, Saturday Evening Post, The New Republic, Life, Look, Ramparts, Newsweek, Business Week, U.S. News & World Report, The Nation, Playboy, Esquire, Harper's, Sports Illustrated.*"

  His tastes in reading were broad, and at one time or another he had read almost all of these magazines. He was a subscriber to *The New Republic*, an enthusiast for *Ramparts*, and an avid student of the pictures in *Playboy*. He was not sure whether his interest in *Playboy* would be held against him, but he had a shrewd suspicion that if he confessed to an interest in *Ramparts* and *The New Republic*, he would be thought a liberal, a radical, or at least an intellectual, and his chances of getting the job, which he needed, would greatly diminish. He therefore checked five of the more conservative magazines. Apparently it was a sound decision, for he got the job.

  He had made a game player's decision, consistent with business ethics.

A similar case is that of a magazine space sales-man who, owing to a merger, suddenly found himself out of a job:

- This man was 58, and, in spite of a good record, his chance of getting a job elsewhere in a business where youth is favored in hiring practice was not good. He was a vigorous, healthy man, and only a considerable amount of gray in his hair suggested his age. Before beginning his job search he touched up his hair with a black dye to confine the gray to his temples. He knew that the truth about his age might well come out in time, but he calculated that he could deal with that situation when it arose. He and his wife decided that he could easily pass for 45, and he so stated his age on his résumé.

    This was a lie; yet within the accepted rules of the business game, no moral culpability attaches to it.

THE POKER ANALOGY

We can learn a good deal about the nature of business by comparing it with poker. While both have a large element of chance, in the long run the winner is the man who plays with steady skill. In both games ultimate victory requires intimate knowledge of the rules, insight into the psychology of the other players, a bold front, a considerable amount of self-discipline, and the ability to respond swiftly and effectively to opportunities provided by chance.

No one expects poker to be played on the ethical principles preached in churches. In poker it is right and proper to bluff a friend out of the rewards of being dealt a good hand. A player feels no more than a slight twinge of sympathy, if that, when—with nothing better than a single ace in his hand—he strips a heavy loser, who holds a pair, of the rest of his chips. It was up to the other fellow to protect himself. In the words of an excellent poker player, former President Harry Truman, "If you can't stand the heat, stay out of the kitchen." If one shows mercy to a loser in poker, it is a personal gesture, divorced from the rules of the game.

Poker has its special ethics, and here I am not referring to rules against cheating. The man who keeps an ace up his sleeve or who marks the cards is more than unethical; he is a crook, and can be punished as such—kicked out of the game or, in the Old West, shot.

In contrast to the cheat, the unethical poker player is one who, while abiding by the letter of the rules, finds ways to put the other players at an unfair disadvantage. Perhaps he unnerves them with loud talk. Or he tries to get them drunk. Or he plays in cahoots with someone else at the table. Ethical poker players frown on such tactics.

Poker's own brand of ethics is different from the ethical ideals of civilized human relationships. The game calls for distrust of the other fellow. It ignores the claim of friendship. Cunning deception and conceal-ment of one's strength and intentions, not kindness and open-heartedness, are vital in poker. No one thinks any the worse of poker on that account. And no one should think any the worse of the game of business because its standards of right and wrong differ from the prevailing traditions of morality in our society. . . .

'WE DON'T MAKE THE LAWS'

Wherever we turn in business, we can perceive the sharp distinction between its ethical stan-dards and those of the churches. Newspapers abound with sensational stories growing out of this distinction:

- We read one day that Senator Philip A. Hart of Michigan has attacked food processors for deceptive packaging of numerous products.[2]

- The next day there is a Congressional to-do over Ralph Nader's book, *Unsafe At Any Speed*, which demonstrates that automobile companies for years have neglected the safety of car-owning families.[3]

- Then another Senator, Lee Metcalf of Montana, and journalist Vic Reinemer show in their book, *Overcharge*, the methods by which utility companies elude regulating government bodies to extract unduly large payments from users of electricity.[4]

These are merely dramatic instances of a prevailing condition; there is hardly a major industry at which a similar attack could not be aimed. Critics of business regard such behavior as unethical, but the companies concerned know that they are merely playing the business game.

Among the most respected of our business institutions are the insurance companies. A group of insurance executives meeting recently in New England was startled when their guest speaker, social critic Daniel Patrick Moynihan, roundly berated them for "unethical" practices. They had been guilty, Moynihan alleged, of using outdated actuarial tables to obtain unfairly high premiums. They habitually delayed the hearings of lawsuits against them in order to tire out the plaintiffs and win cheap settlements. In their employment policies they used ingenious devices to discriminate against certain minority groups.[5]

It was difficult for the audience to deny the validity of these charges. But these men were business game players. Their reaction to Moynihan's attack was much the same as that of the automobile manufacturers to Nader, of the utilities to Senator Metcalf, and of the food processors to Senator Hart. If the laws governing their businesses change, or if public opinion becomes clamorous, they will make the necessary adjustments. But morally they have in their view done nothing wrong. As long as they comply with the letter of the law, they are within their rights to operate their businesses as they see fit.

The small business is in the same position as the great corporation in this respect. For example:

- In 1967 a key manufacturer was accused of providing master keys for automobiles to mail-order customers, although it was obvious that some of the purchasers might be automobile thieves. His defense was plain and straightforward. If there was nothing in the law to prevent him from selling his keys to anyone who ordered them, it was not up to him to inquire as to his customers' motives. Why was it any worse, he insisted, for him to sell car keys by mail, than for mail-order houses to sell guns that might be used for murder? Until the law was changed, the key manufacturer could regard himself as being just as ethical as any other businessman by the rules of the business game.[6]

Violations of the ethical ideals of society are common in business, but they are not necessarily violations of business principles. Each year the Federal Trade Commission orders hundreds of companies, many of them of the first magnitude, to "cease and desist" from practices which, judged by ordinary standards, are of questionable morality but which are stoutly defended by the companies concerned.

In one case, a firm manufacturing a well-known mouthwash was accused of using a cheap form of alcohol possibly deleterious to health. The company's chief executive, after testifying in Washington, made this comment privately:

"We broke no law. We're in a highly competitive industry. If we're going to stay in business, we have to look for profit wherever the law permits. We don't make the laws. We obey them. Then why do we have to put up with this 'holier than thou' talk about ethics? It's sheer hypocrisy. We're not in business to

promote ethics. Look at the cigarette companies, for God's sake! If the ethics aren't
embodied in the laws by the men who made
them, you can't expect businessmen to fill the
lack. Why, a sudden submission to Christian
ethics by businessmen would bring about the
greatest economic upheaval in history!"

It may be noted that the government failed
to prove its case against him.

CAST ILLUSIONS ASIDE

Talk about ethics by businessmen is often a
thin decorative coating over the hard realities
of the game:

- Once I listened to a speech by a young executive
  who pointed to a new industry code as proof that
  his company and its competitors were deeply
  aware of their responsibilities to society. It was a
  code of ethics, he said. The industry was going to
  police itself, to dissuade constituent companies
  from wrongdoing. His eyes shone with conviction and enthusiasm.

  The same day there was a meeting in a
  hotel room where the industry's top executives
  met with the "czar" who was to administer the
  new code, a man of high repute. No one who
  was present could doubt their common attitude. In their eyes the code was designed
  primarily to forestall a move by the federal government to impose stem restrictions on the
  industry. They felt that the code would hamper
  them a good deal less than new federal laws
  would. It was, in other words, conceived as a
  protection for the industry, not for the public.

  The young executive accepted the surface
  explanation of the code; these leaders, all experienced game players, did not deceive themselves for a moment about its purpose.

The illusion that business can afford to be
guided by ethics as conceived in private life is
often fostered by speeches and articles containing such phrases as, "It pays to be ethical,"
or, "Sound ethics is good business." Actually
this is not an ethical position at all; it is a self-
serving calculation in disguise. The speaker is

really saying that in the long run a company
can make more money if it does not antago-
nize competitors, suppliers, employees, and
customers by squeezing them too hard. He is
saying that oversharp policies reduce ultimate
gains. That is true, but it has nothing to do
with ethics. The underlying attitude is much
like that in the familiar story of the shop-
keeper who finds an extra $20 bill in the cash
register, debates with himself the ethical
problem—should he tell his partner?—and
finally decides to share the money because
the gesture will give him an edge over the
s.o.b. the next time they quarrel.

I think it is fair to sum up the prevailing
attitude of businessmen on ethics as follows:

We live in what is probably the most competitive of the world's civilized societies. Our
customs encourage a high degree of aggres-
sion in the individual's striving for success.
Business is our main area of competition,
and it has been ritualized into a game of
strategy. The basic rules of the game have
been set by the government, which attempts
to detect and punish business frauds. But as
long as a company does not transgress the
rules of the game set by law, it has the legal
right to shape its strategy without reference
to anything but its profits. If it takes a long-
term view of its profits, it will preserve amica-
ble relations, so far as possible, with those
with whom it deals. A wise businessman will
not seek advantage to the point where he
generates dangerous hostility among employees, competitors, customers, government, or
the public at large. But decisions in this area
are, in the final test, decisions of strategy, not
of ethics.

. . . If a man plans to make a seat in the
business game, he owes it to himself to master
the principles by which the game is played,
including its special ethical outlook. He can
then hardly fail to recognize that an occasional bluff may well be justified in terms of
the game's ethics and warranted in terms of

economic necessity. Once he clears his mind on this point, he is in a good position to match his strategy against that of the other players. He can then determine objectively whether a bluff in a given situation has a good chance of succeeding and can decide when and how to bluff, without a feeling of ethical transgression.

To be a winner, a man must play to win. This does not mean that he must be ruthless, cruel, harsh, or treacherous. On the contrary, the better his reputation for integrity, honesty, and decency, the better his chances of victory will be in the long run. But from time to time every businessman, like every poker player, is offered a choice between certain loss or bluffing within the legal rules of the game. If he is not resigned to losing, if he wants to rise in his company and industry, then in such a crisis he will bluff—and bluff hard.

Every now and then one meets a successful businessman who has conveniently forgotten the small or large deceptions that he practiced on his way to fortune. "God gave me my money," old John D. Rockefeller once piously told a Sunday school class. It would be a rare tycoon in our time who would risk the horse laugh with which such a remark would be greeted.

In the last third of the twentieth century even children are aware that if a man has become prosperous in business, he has sometimes departed from the strict truth in order to overcome obstacles or has practiced the more subtle deceptions of the half-truth or the misleading omission. Whatever the form of the bluff, it is an integral part of the game, and the executive who does not master its techniques is not likely to accumulate much money or power.

NOTES

1. *The New York Times*, March 9, 1967.
2. *The New York Times*, November 21, 1966.
3. New York, Grossman Publishers, Inc., 1965.
4. New York, David McKay Company, Inc., 1967.
5. *The New York Times*, January 17, 1967.
6. Cited by Ralph Nader in "Business Crime," *The New Republic*, July 1, 1967, p. 7.

Case Study

The Parable of the Sadhu

Bowen H. McCoy

It was early in the morning before the sun rose, which gave them time to climb the treacherous slope to the pass at 18,000 feet before the ice steps melted. They were also concerned about their stamina and altitude sickness, and felt the need to press on. Into the chance collection of climbers on that Himalayan slope an ethical dilemma arose in the guise of an unconscious, almost naked sadhu, an Indian holy man. Each climber gave the sadhu help but none made sure he would be safe. Should somebody have stopped to help the sadhu to safety? Would it have done any good? Was the group responsible? Since leaving the sadhu on the mountain

---

slope, the author, who was one of the climbers, has pondered these issues. He sees many parallels for business people as they face ethical decisions at work.

Last year, as the first participant in the new six-month sabbatical program that Morgan Stanley has adopted, I enjoyed a rare opportunity to collect my thoughts as well as do some travelling. I spent the first three months in Nepal, walking 600 miles through 200 villages in the Himalayas and climbing some 120,000 vertical feet. On the trip my sole Western companion was an anthropologist who shed light on the cultural patterns of the villages we passed through.

During the Nepal hike, something occurred that has had a powerful impact on my thinking about corporate ethics. Although some might argue that the experience has no relevance to business, it was a situation in which a basic ethical dilemma suddenly intruded into the lives of a group of individuals. How the group responded I think holds a lesson for all organizations no matter how defined.

THE SADHU

The Nepal experience was more rugged and adventuresome than I had anticipated. Most commercial treks last two or three weeks and cover a quarter of the distance we traveled.

My friend Stephen, the anthropologist, and I were halfway through the 60-day Himalayan part of the trip when we reached the high point, an 18,000-foot pass over a crest that we'd have to traverse to reach the village of Muklinath, an ancient holy place for pilgrims.

Six years earlier I had suffered pulmonary edema, an acute form of altitude sickness, at 16,500 feet in the vicinity of Everest base camp, so we were understandably concerned about what would happen at 18,000 feet. Moreover, the Himalayas were having their wettest spring in 20 years, hip-deep powder and ice had already driven us off one ridge.

If we failed to cross the pass, I feared that the last half of our "once in a lifetime" trip would be ruined.

The night before we would try the pass, we camped at a hut at 14,500 feet. In the photos taken at that camp, my face appears wan. The last village we'd passed through was a sturdy two-day walk below us, and I was tired.

During the late afternoon, four backpackers from New Zealand joined us, and we spent most of the night awake, anticipating the climb. Below we could see the fires of two other parties, which turned out to be two Swiss couples and a Japanese hiking club.

To get over the steep part of the climb before the sun melted the steps cut in the ice, we departed at 3:30 A.M. The New Zealanders left first, followed by Stephen and myself, our porters and Sherpas, and then the Swiss. The Japanese lingered in their camp. The sky was clear, and we were confident that no spring storm would erupt that day to close the pass.

At 15,500 feet, it looked to me as if Stephen were shuffling and staggering a bit, which are symptoms of altitude sickness. (The initial stage of altitude sickness brings a headache and nausea. As the condition worsens, a climber may encounter difficult breathing, disorientation, aphasia, and paralysis.) I felt strong, my adrenaline was flowing, but I was very concerned about my ultimate ability to get across. A couple of our porters were also suffering from the height, and Pasang, our Sherpa sirdar (leader), was worried.

Just after daybreak, while we rested at 15,500 feet, one of the New Zealanders, who had gone ahead, came staggering down toward us with a body slung across his shoulders. He dumped the almost naked, barefoot body of an Indian holy man—a sadhu—at my feet. He had found the pilgrim lying on the ice, shivering and suffering from hypothermia.

I cradled the sadhu's head and laid him out on the rocks. The New Zealander was angry. He wanted to get across the pass before the bright sun melted the snow. He said, "Look, I've done what I can. You have porters and Sherpa guides. You care for him. We're going on!" He turned and went back up the mountain to join his friends.

I took a carotid pulse and found that the sadhu was still alive. We figured he had probably visited the holy shrines at Muklinath and was on his way home. It was fruitless to question why he had chosen this desperately high route instead of the safe, heavily traveled caravan route through the Kali Gandaki gorge. Or why he was almost naked and with no shoes, or how long he had been lying in the pass. The answers weren't going to solve our problem.

Stephen and the four Swiss began stripping off outer clothing and opening their packs. The sadhu was soon clothed from head to foot. He was not able to walk, but he was very much alive. I looked down the mountain and spotted below the Japanese climbers marching up with a horse.

Without a great deal of thought, I told Stephen and Pasang that I was concerned about withstanding the heights to come and wanted to get over the pass. I took off after several of our porters who had gone ahead.

On the steep part of the ascent where, if the ice steps had given way, I would have slid down about 3,000 feet, I felt vertigo. I stopped for a breather, allowing the Swiss to catch up with me. I inquired about the sadhu and Stephen. They said that the sadhu was fine and that Stephen was just behind. I set off again for the summit.

Stephen arrived at the summit an hour after I did. Still exhilarated by victory, I ran down the snow slope to congratulate him. He was suffering from altitude sickness, walking 15 steps, then stopping, walking 15 steps, then stopping, Pasang accompanied him all the way up. When I reached them, Stephen glared at me and said: "How do you feel about contributing to the death of a fellow man?"

I did not fully comprehend what he meant.

"Is the sadhu dead?" I inquired.

"No," replied Stephen, "but he surely will be!"

After I had gone, and the Swiss had departed not long after, Stephen had remained with the sadhu. When the Japanese had arrived. Stephen had asked to use their horse to transport the sadhu down to the hut. They had refused. He had then asked Pasang to have a group of our porters carry the sadhu. Pasang had resisted the idea, saying that the porters would have to exert all their energy to get themselves over the pass. He had thought they could not carry a man down 1,000 feet to the hut, reclimb the slope, and get across safely before the snow melted. Pasang had pressed Stephen not to delay any longer.

The Sherpas had carried the sadhu down to a rock in the sun at about 15,000 feet and had pointed out the hut another 500 feet below. The Japanese had given him food and drink. When they had last seen him he was listlessly throwing rocks at the Japanese party's dog, which had frightened him. We do not know if the sadhu lived or died.

For many of the following days and evenings Stephen and I discussed and debated our behavior toward the sadhu. Stephen is a committed Quaker with deep moral vision. He said, "I feel that what happened with the sadhu is a good example of the breakdown between the individual ethic and the corporate ethic. No one person was willing to assume ultimate responsibility for the sadhu. Each was willing to do his bit just so long as it was not too inconvenient. When it got to be a bother, everyone just passed the buck to someone else and took off. Jesus was relevant to a more individualistic stage of society, but how do we interpret his teaching today in a world filled with large, impersonal organizations and groups?"

I defended the larger group, saying, "Look, we all cared. We all stopped and gave aid and comfort. Everyone did his bit. The New Zealander carried him down below the snow line. I took his pulse and suggested we treat him for hypothermia. You and the Swiss gave him clothing and got him warmed up. The Japanese gave him food and water. The Sherpas carried him down to the sun and pointed out the easy trail toward the hut. He was well enough to throw rocks at a dog. What more could we do?"

"You have just described the typical affluent Westerner's response to a problem. Throwing money—in this case food and sweaters—at it, but not solving the fundamentals!" Stephen retorted.

"What would satisfy you?" I said. "Here we are, a group of New Zealanders, Swiss, Americans, and Japanese who have never met before and who are at the apex of one of the most powerful experiences of our lives. Some years the pass is so bad no one gets over it. What right does an almost naked pilgrim who chooses the wrong trail have to disrupt our lives? Even the Sherpas had no interest in risking the trip to help him beyond a certain point."

Stephen calmly rebutted, "I wonder what the Sherpas would have done if the sadhu had been a well-dressed Nepali, or what the Japanese would have done if the sadhu had been a well-dressed Asian, or what you would have done, Buzz, if the sadhu had been a well-dressed Western woman?"

"Where, in your opinion," I asked instead, "is the limit of our responsibility in a situation like this? We had our own well-being to worry about. Our Sherpa guides were unwilling to jeopardize us or the porters for the sadhu. No one else on the mountain was willing to commit himself beyond certain self-imposed limits."

Stephen said, "As individual Christians or people with a Western ethical tradition, we can fulfill our obligations in such a situation only if (1) the sadhu dies in our care, (2) the sadhu demonstrates to us that he could undertake the two-day walk down to the village, or (3) we carry the sadhu for two days down to the village and convince someone there to care for him."

"Leaving the sadhu in the sun with food and clothing, while he demonstrated hand-eye coordination by throwing a rock at a dog, comes close to fulfilling items one and two," I answered. "And it wouldn't have made sense to take him to the village where the people appeared to be far less caring than the Sherpas, so the third condition is impractical. Are you really saying that, no matter what the implications, we should, at the drop of a hat, have changed our entire plan?"

THE INDIVIDUAL VS. THE GROUP ETHIC

Despite my arguments, I felt and continue to feel guilt about the sadhu. I had literally walked through a classic moral dilemma without fully thinking through the consequences. My excuses for my actions include a high adrenaline flow, a superordinate goal, and a once-in-a-lifetime opportunity—factors in the usual corporate situation, especially when one is under stress.

Real moral dilemmas are ambiguous, and many of us hike right through them, unaware that they exist. When, usually after the fact, someone makes an issue of them, we tend to resent his or her bringing it up. Often, when the full import of what we have done (or not done) falls on us, we dig into a defensive position from which it is very difficult to emerge. In rare circumstances we may contemplate what we have done from inside a prison.

Had we mountaineers been free of physical and mental stress caused by the effort and the high altitude, we might have treated the sadhu differently. Yet isn't stress the real test of personal and corporate values? The instant decisions executives make under pressure reveal the most about personal and corporate character.

Among the many questions that occur to me when pondering my experience are: What are the practical limits of moral imagination and vision? Is there a collective or institutional ethic beyond the ethics of the individual? At what level of effort or commitment can one discharge one's ethical responsibilities? Not every ethical dilemma has a right solution. Reasonable people often disagree; otherwise there would be no dilemma. In a business context, however, it is essential that managers agree on a process for dealing with dilemmas.

The sadhu experience offers an interesting parallel to business situations. An immediate response was mandatory. Failure to act was a decision in itself. Up on the mountain we could not resign and submit our résumés to a headhunter. In contrast to philosophy, business involves action and implementation—getting things done. Managers must come up with answers to problems based on what they see and what they allow to influence their decision-making processes. On the mountain, none of us but Stephen realized the true dimensions of the situation we were facing.

One of our problems was that as a group we had no process for developing a consensus. We had no sense of purpose or plan. The difficulties of dealing with the sadhu were so complex that no one person could handle it. Because it did not have a set of preconditions that could guide its action to an acceptable resolution, the group reacted instinctively as individuals. The cross-cultural nature of the group added a further layer of complexity. We had no leader with whom we could all identify and in whose purpose we believed. Only Stephen was willing to take charge, but he could not gain adequate support to care for the sadhu.

Some organizations do have a value system that transcends the personal values of the managers. Such values, which go beyond profitability, are usually revealed when the organization is under stress. People throughout the organization generally accept its values, which, because they are not presented as a rigid list of commandments, may be somewhat ambiguous. The stories people tell, rather than printed materials, transmit these conceptions of what is proper behavior.

For 20 years I have been exposed at senior levels to a variety of corporations and organizations. It is amazing how quickly an outsider can sense the tone and style of an organization and the degree of tolerated openness and freedom to challenge management.

Organizations that do not have a heritage of mutually accepted, shared values tend to become unhinged during stress, with each individual bailing out for himself. In the great takeover battles we have witnessed during past years, companies that had strong cultures drew the wagons around them and fought it out, while other companies saw executives, supported by their golden parachutes, bail out of the struggles.

Because corporations and their members are interdependent, for the corporation to be strong the members need to share a preconceived notion of what is correct behavior, a "business ethic," and think of it as a positive force, not a constraint.

As an investment banker I am continually warned by well-meaning lawyers, clients, and associates to be wary of conflicts of interest. Yet if I were to run away from every difficult situation, I wouldn't be an effective investment banker. I have to feel my way through conflicts. An effective manager can't run from risk either; he or she has to confront and deal with risk. To feel "safe" in doing this, managers need the guidelines of an agreed-on process and set of values within the organization.

After my three months in Nepal, I spent three months as an executive-in-residence at both Stanford Business School and the Center for Ethics and Social Policy at the Graduate Theological Union at Berkeley. These six months away from my job gave me time to assimilate 20 years of business experience. My thoughts turned often to the meaning of the leadership role in any large organization. Students at the seminary thought of themselves as antibusiness. But when I questioned them they agreed that they distrusted all large organizations, including the church. They perceived all large organizations as impersonal and opposed to individual values and needs. Yet we all know of organizations where people's values and beliefs are respected and their expressions encouraged. What makes the difference? Can we identify the difference and, as a result, manage more effectively?

The word "ethics" turns off many and confuses more. Yet the notions of shared values and an agreed-on process for dealing with adversity and change—what many people mean when they talk about corporate culture—seem to be at the heart of the ethical issue. People who are in touch with their own core beliefs and the beliefs of others and are sustained by them can be more comfortable living on the cutting edge. At times, taking a tough line or a decisive stand in a muddle of ambiguity is the only ethical thing to do. If a manager is indecisive and spends time trying to figure out the "good" thing to do, the enterprise may be lost.

Business ethics, then, has to do with the authenticity and integrity of the enterprise. To be ethical is to follow the business as well as the cultural goals of the corporation, its owners, its employees, and its customers. Those who cannot serve the corporate vision are not authentic business people and, therefore, are not ethical in the business sense.

At this stage of my own business experience, I have a strong interest in organizational behavior. Sociologists are keenly studying what they call corporate stories, legends, and heroes as a way organizations have of transmitting the value system. Corporations such as Arco have even hired consultants to perform an audit of their corporate culture. In a company, the leader is the person who understands, interprets, and manages the corporate value system. Effective managers are then action-oriented people who resolve conflict, are tolerant of ambiguity, stress, and change, and have a strong sense of purpose for themselves and their organizations.

If all this is true, I wonder about the role of the professional manager who moves from company to company. How can he or she quickly absorb the values and culture of different organizations? Or is there, indeed, an art of management that is totally transportable? Assuming such fungible managers do exist, is it proper for them to manipulate the values of others?

What would have happened had Stephen and I carried the sadhu for two days back to the village and become involved with the villagers in his care? In four trips to Nepal my most interesting experiences occurred in 1975 when I lived in a Sherpa home in the Khumbu for five days recovering from altitude sickness. The high point of Stephen's trip was an invitation to participate in a family funeral ceremony in Manang. Neither experience had to do with climbing the high passes of the Himalayas. Why were we so reluctant to try the lower path, the ambiguous trail? Perhaps because we did not have a leader who could reveal the greater purpose of the trip to us.

Why didn't Stephen with his moral vision opt to take the sadhu under his personal care? The answer is because, in part, Stephen was hard-stressed physically himself, and because, in part, without some support system that involved our involuntary and episodic community on the mountain, it was beyond his individual capacity to do so.

I see the current interest in corporate culture and corporate value systems as a positive response to Stephen's pessimism about the decline of the role of the individual in large organizations. Individuals who operate from a thoughtful set of personal values provide the foundation for a corporate culture. A corporate tradition that encourages freedom of inquiry, supports personal values, and reinforces a focused sense of direction can fulfill the need for individuality along with the prosperity and success of the group. Without such corporate support, the individual is lost.

That is the lesson of the sadhu. In a complex corporate situation, the individual requires and deserves the support of the group. If people cannot find such support from their organization, they don't know how to act. If such support is forthcoming, a person has a stake in the success of the group, and can add much to the process of establishing and maintaining a corporate culture. It is management's challenge to be sensitive to individual needs, to shape them, and to direct and focus them for the benefit of the group as a whole.

For each of us the sadhu lives. Should we stop what we are doing and comfort him; or should we keep trudging up toward the high pass? Should I pause to help the derelict I pass on the street each night as I walk by the Yale Club en route to Grand Central Station? Am I his brother? What is the nature of our responsibility if we consider ourselves to be ethical persons? Perhaps it is to change the values of the group so that it can, with all its resources, take the other road.

Case Study

Into the Mouth of Babes

James Traub

It is well within the reach of most white-collar criminals to assume an air of irreproachable virtue, especially when they're about to be sentenced. But there was something unusually compelling about the hearing of Niels L. Hoyvald and John F. Lavery as they stood before Judge Thomas C. Platt of the United States District Court in Brooklyn last month— especially in light of what they were being sentenced for. As president and vice president of the Beech-Nut Nutrition Corporation, Hoyvald and Lavery had sold millions of bottles of "apple juice" that they knew to contain little or no apple juice at all— only sugars, water, flavoring and coloring. The consumers of this bogus product were babies.

One prosecutor of the case, Thomas H. Roche, had summed up Beech-Nut's behavior as "a classic picture of corporate greed and irresponsibility." The company itself had pleaded guilty the previous fall to 215 counts of violating Federal food and drug laws, and had agreed to pay a $2 million fine, by far the largest ever imposed in the 50-year history of the Food, Drug and Cosmetic Act. Beech-Nut

---

had confessed in a press release that it had broken a "sacred trust."

Yet there was Niels Hoyvald, 54 years old, tall, silver-haired, immaculately dressed, standing before Judge Platt with head bowed, as his attorney, Brendan V. Sullivan, Jr., described him as "a person we would be proud to have in our family." When it was Hoyvald's turn to address the judge, he spoke firmly, but then his voice cracked as he spoke of his wife and mother: "I can hardly bear to look at them or speak to them," he said. "I ask for them and myself, please don't send me to jail."

Judge Platt was clearly troubled. He spoke in a semiaudible mutter that had the crowd in the courtroom craning forward. Though it was "unusual for a corporate executive to do time for consumer fraud," he said, he had "no alternative" but to sentence Hoyvald to a prison term of a year and a day, plus fines totaling $100,000. He then meted out the same punishment to the 56-year old Lavery, who declined to speak on his own behalf. He received his sentence with no show of emotion.

The combination of babies, apple juice and a well-known name like Beech-Nut makes for a potent symbol. In fact, apple juice is not especially nutritious (bottlers often fortify it with extra Vitamin C), but babies love it and find it easy to digest. Parents are pleased to buy a product that says "no sugar added"—as Beech-Nut advertised—and seem to regard it as almost as pure and natural as mother's milk. That, of course, was the sacred trust Beech-Nut broke, and is now struggling to repair. The company's share of the $760 million United States baby-food market has dropped from a high of 20 percent in 1986, when Beech-Nut and the two executives were indicted, to 17 percent this year. Its losses in the fruit-juice market have been even more dramatic. Richard C. Theuer, the company's president since 1986, still gets a stream of letters from outraged parents "who don't realize that it was a long time ago." Some of them, he says are "almost obscene."

If parents are outraged by Beech-Nut's actions, many people are also baffled. Even after the trial and verdict, the question of motive lingers: why would two men with impeccable records carry out so cynical and reckless a fraud? Except for Theuer, no current Beech-Nut employee who was involved in the events of the trial agreed to be interviewed for this article, nor did Hoyvald or Lavery. But a vivid picture of the economic and psychological concerns that impelled the company along its ruinous course emerges from court documents and a wide range of interviews. The Beech-Nut baby food scandal is a case study in the warping effects of blind corporate loyalty.

For three-quarters of century after its founding in 1891 as a meatpacking company, Beech-Nut expanded steadily into a large, diversified food concern, eventually including Life Savers, Table Talk pies, Tetley tea, Martinson's coffee, chewing gum and, of course, baby food. The company had an image straight from Norman Rockwell—pure, simple, healthful. In 1969, Beech-Nut was taken over by the Squibb Corporation. Only four years later, a remnant of the old company was spun off and taken private by a group led by a lawyer, Frank C. Nicholas. The company that emerged from the Squibb umbrella sold only baby food, and, as in earlier years, regularly divided with Heinz the third or so of the market not controlled by Gerber. It was a completely new world for Beech-Nut's newly independent owners, and an extremely precarious one. Beech-Nut was in a continuous financial bind.

After an expensive and unsuccessful effort in the mid-1970's to market Beech-Nut as the "natural" baby food, the imperative to reduce costs became overwhelming. In 1977, when a Bronx-based supplier, who would later take the name Universal Juice, offered Beech-Nut a less-expensive apple-juice concentrate, the company abandoned its longtime supplier for the new source. The savings would never amount to much more than $250,000 a year, out of a $50 million-plus manufacturing budget, but Beech-Nut was under the gun.

At the time, the decision may have seemed insignificant. Ira Knickerbocker, head of agricultural purchasing at the main Beech-Nut plant in Canajoharie, N.Y., who has since retired, says that in 1977 the new concentrate was only slightly less expensive than the competition's. "There was never a question about the quality or anything else," he insists. Yet no other baby-food company, and no large apple-juice manufacturer, ever bought significant quantities of concentrate from Universal. In early 1981, Heinz would return the product to Universal after samples had failed to pass conventional laboratory tests and the supplier refused to let company officials visit the plant.

Another Federal prosecutor, John R. Fleder, contends that the low price of the Universal concentrate, which eventually reached 25 percent below the market, "should have been enough in itself to tip off anybody" that the concentrate was diluted or adulterated. Jack B. Hartog, a supplier who had sold Beech-Nut much of its apple concentrate until 1977, agrees with Fleder: "There was no question about it in the trade."

John Lavery, Beech-Nut's vice president of operations and manager of the plant in Canajoharie, did not question the authenticity of the concentrate. After spending his entire career at Beech-Nut, Lavery had risen to a position in which he managed almost 1,000 employees. In the small hamlets around Canajoharie, a company town in rural Montgomery County, northwest of Albany, Lavery was known as a figure of propriety and rectitude. "He was as straight and narrow as anything you could come up with," says Ed Gros, an engineer who worked with Lavery at Beech-Nut. Lavery was a fixture in the Methodist church, on the school board and in community organizations.

In 1978, after initial testing indicated the presence of impurities in the new concentrate, Lavery agreed to send two employees to inspect the "blending facility" that Universal's owner, Zeev Kaplansky, claimed to operate in New Jersey. The two reported that all they could find was a warehouse containing a few 55-gallon drums. The bizarre field trip aroused further suspicions among executives at the Canajoharie plant, but only one, Jerome J. LiCari, head of research and development, chose to act on them.

LiCari sent samples of the concentrate to an outside laboratory. The tests, he reported to Lavery, indicated that the juice was adulterated, probably with corn syrup. Rather than return the concentrate, or demand proof of its authenticity, as Heinz would do three years later, Lavery sent down the order that Kaplansky sign a "hold-harmless agreement," indemnifying Beech-Nut against damages arising from consumer and other complaints (Ironically, in May 1987 Beech-Nut settled a class-action suit against it totalling $7.5 million.)

LiCari, however, was scarcely satisfied by Lavery's legalistic approach. Like Lavery, LiCari was also every bit the local boy. Born and raised in neighboring Herkimer County, he had worked in the Beech-Nut plant during summers home from college, and, after 14 years with Beech-Nut, he had achieved his greatest ambitions. Yet it was LiCari who accepted the solitary role of institutional conscience. In April 1979, and again in July, he sent samples of the concentrate to a second laboratory, in California. The April test again found signs of adulteration, but the July test did not. LiCari concluded that Kaplansky had switched from corn syrup to beet sugar, an adulterant that current technology could not detect. Once again he approached Lavery, suggesting that Beech-Nut require Kaplansky to repurchase the concentrate. This time, Lavery instructed that the concentrate be blended into mixed juices, where adulter-ation is far harder to detect. Lavery's attorney, Steven Kimelman, says that his client does not recall his rationale for the decision, but argues that on this matter, as on others, he acted in concert with other executives, includ-ing LiCari.

Lavery and LiCari were locked in a hopeless conflict of roles, values, and personality. Steven Kimelman characterizes Lavery as "more like a general. He's the kind of guy who gives orders, and he has no trouble making up his mind; LiCari was too much of a scientist type to him, and not practical enough." LiCari had become consumed by the issues of the concentrate. By spring of 1981 he was working almost full time on tests to determine its purity. Finally, on Aug. 5, LiCari circulated a memo to executives, including Lavery. "A tremendous amount of circumstantial evidence," he wrote, makes for "a grave case against the current supplier" of apple concentrate. No matter what the cost, LiCari concluded, a new supplier should be found.

Several days later, LiCari was summoned to Lavery's office, where, as he told the jury, "I was threatened that I wasn't a team player, I wasn't working for the company, threatened to be fired." The choice could not have been more stark: capitulate, or leave.

Many of those who know Lavery find this picture of him simply unbelievable. The Canajoharie view is that Lavery was victimized. Ed Gros, Lavery's former colleague, speculates that LiCari "had a personal vendetta" against Lavery. Ira Knickerbocker blames the Govern-ment. Yet even Lavery's friends admit to a kind of moral bafflement. "I've lost a lot of sleep over this," says a former company vice presi-dent, Bill Johnsey.

Steven Kimelman denies that Lavery threatened LiCari, but concedes that his client made a "mistake in judgment." The mistake was in not kicking the matter up to Hoyvald when he received the Aug. 5 memo.

Kimelman insists that Lavery "thought that LiCari tended to overreact," and in any case felt that there was no other concentrate whose purity he could entirely trust In fact, LiCari's tests showed no signs of adulteration in several other, more expensive, concen-trates. A harsher view is that Lavery acted quite consciously. "He just didn't care," says Thomas Roche, one of the prosecutors. "He showed an extraordinary amount of arro-gance. I think his sole objective was to show Beech-Nut and Nestlé's (since 1979, the cor-porate parent) that he could do well."

Or perhaps Lavery had simply blinded him-self to the consequences of his acts. The apple juice had become merely a commodity and the babies merely customers. One exchange between another prosecutor, Kenneth L. Jost, and an executive at the Canajoharie plant, Robert J. Belvin, seemed to sum up Lavery's state of mind:

"Mr. Belvin, what did you do when you found that Beech-Nut had been using a prod-uct in what is called apple juice that was not in fact apple juice?"

"I—I became very upset"

"Why were you very upset?"

"Because we feed babies . . ."

"Did you ever hear Mr. Lavery express a sen-timent similar to that you have just described to the jury?"

"No."

By 1979, Beech-Nut's financial condition had become so parlous that Frank Nicholas admitted failure and sold the company to Nestle S.A., the Swiss food giant. Nestlé arrived with $60 million in working capital and a commitment to restore a hallowed brand name to health. The view in the food industry was that Beech-Nut had been rescued from the brink. Yet evidence presented at the trial gives the exact opposite impression—of a Procrustean bed being prepared for nervous managers. Hoyvald, who chose to testify on his own behalf, admitted that in 1981, his first year as chief executive, he had grandiosely promised Nestlé that Beech-Nut would earn $700,000 the following year, though there would be a negative cash flow of $1.7 million. Hoyvald had arrived at Nestlé only a year before, but he was a seasoned executive in the food business. The answer nevertheless shot back from Switzerland: the cash flow for Beech-Nut, as for all other Nestlé subsidiaries, would have to be zero or better. "The pressure," as he conceded, "was on."

Hoyvald testified that he knew nothing about adulterated concentrate until the summer of 1982. In January 1981, however, LiCari had sent to both Lavery and Hoyvald a copy of an article in a trade magazine discussing signs of adulteration in apple juice, and had written and attached a memo noting, among other things, that "Beech-Nut has been concerned over the authenticity of fruit juice products." LiCari also told the jury that in August of that same year, several weeks after his disastrous confrontation with Lavery, he went to Beech-Nut's corporate headquarters in Fort Washington, Pa., to appeal to Hoyvald—an uncharacteristic suspension of his faith in the chain of command. Hoyvald had been appointed president only four months earlier, and LiCari testified that he liked and trusted his new boss, whom he felt had a mandate from Nestlé to restore Beech-Nut's prestige. The meeting in Fort Washington persuaded LiCari that he had finally found an ally. Hoyvald, LiCari testified, "appeared shocked and surprised" at LiCari's report, and left him feeling "that something was going to be done and they would stop using it."

Then, month after month, nothing happened. Finally, at a late-fall company retreat at a ski resort in Vermont, LiCari raised the issue with Hoyvald one last time. Hoyvald told him, he testified, that he was unwilling to fire Lavery. (In his own testimony, Hoyvald denied that either meeting had taken place.)

LiCari was now convinced that the company was bent on lawbreaking, as he later testified, and rather than acquiesce, he quit, in January 1982. His allies concerned with quality control remained behind, but evidently none was stubborn or reckless enough to press his point.

Hoyvald, like Lavery, was a man with an exemplary background, though one that was a good deal more varied and sophisticated than his subordinate's. Born and raised in a provincial town in Denmark, he had relocated to the United States and received his Master of Business Administration degree from the University of Wisconsin in 1960. An ambitious man, Hoyvald had hopscotched across five companies before joining Beech-Nut as head of marketing in 1980, with the promise that he would be promoted to president within a year. Throughout his career, Hoyvald's watchword had been "aggressively marketing top quality products," as he wrote in a three-page "Career Path" addendum to a 1979 résumé. He had turned around the faltering Plumrose Inc., a large food company, by emphasizing quality, and he viewed the job at Beech-Nut as a chance to do just that.

In June 1982, Hoyvald's principles were abruptly tested when the quality of his own product was decisively challenged. A trade association, the Processed Apples Institute, had initiated an investigation into long-standing charges of adulteration throughout the apple-concentrate business. By April 1982, an investigator working of the institute, a former New York City narcotics detective named Andrew Rosenzweig (who is now chief investigator for the Manhattan District Attorney's office), was prowling around the Woodside, Queens, warehouse of a company called Food Complex, which was Universal's manufacturing arm. By diligent questioning, and searching by flashlight through a dumpster in the middle of many nights, Rosenzweig discovered that Food Complex omitted apples from its recipe altogether, and that its biggest customer was Beech-Nut.

On June 25, Rosenzweig tracked a tanker full of sugar water out of the Food Complex loading dock and up the New York State Thruway to Canajoharie, where he planned to confront management with his findings. He was hoping to persuade the company to join a civil suit being prepared against Universal and Food Complex; but, expecting the worst, he secretly tape-recorded the ensuing conversation.

At the trial, the tape proved to be a damning piece of evidence. In the course of the discussion, Lavery and two other executives, instead of disputing Rosenzweig's claim that Beech-Nut was making juice from suspect concentrate, unleashed a cascade of tortuous rationalizations. When Rosenzweig explained that the trade association had made new strides in lab testing, Lavery, obviously panicking, suddenly announced; "At this point, we've made our last order from Universal." But despite considerable pressure, Lavery refused to give Rosenzweig samples of the concentrate, and declined to join the suit. The one anxiety he expressed was the possibility of bad publicity.

On June 28, Paul E. Hillabush, the head of quality assurance at Canajoharie, called Hoyvald to tell him of Rosenzweig's visit. Hillabush testified that he suggested Beech-Nut recall the product. But Beech-Nut would not only have had to switch to a new and more expensive concentrate, it would have had to admit publicly that the product it had been selling since 1978 was bogus. The cover-up, which Lavery had begun three years earlier with the order to blend the concentrate in mixed juices, was attaining an irresistible momentum.

Hoyvald made the fateful decision to reject Hillabush's advice, and to devote the next eight weeks to moving the tainted products as fast as possible. It would be aggressive marketing, though not of a quality product.

The Apple Institute's suit, as it turned out, was only the first wave to hit the beach. Federal and state authorities had been investigating suppliers of adulterated concentrate since the spring, and the trail led them, too, to Canajoharie. On July 29, an inspector from the United States Food and Drug Administration arrived at the plant, announced that samples taken from supermarket shelves had proved to be adulterated, and took away cases of apple juice ready to be shipped. On Aug. 11, Paul Hillabush received a call from an old friend, Maurice Guerrette, an assistant director with the New York State Department of Agriculture and Markets, who reported much the same conclusion. Guerrette recalls receiving one of the great shocks of his life when Hillabush tried to laugh the whole thing off. It was only then that he realized—as would each investigator in his turn—that Beech-Nut was not the victim of a crime, but its conscious perpetrator.

Guerrette's phone call persuaded Lavery and others—incorrectly, as it turned out—that a seizure action was imminent. After consulting with Hoyvald, executives in Canajoharie decided to move the entire inventory of tainted juice out of the state's jurisdiction. And so, on the night of Aug. 12, nine tractor-trailers from Beech-Nut's trucking company were loaded with 26,000 cases of juice and taken in a ghostly caravan to a warehouse in Secaucus, N.J. One of America's most venerable food companies was fleeing the law like a bootlegger.

By the late summer of 1982, Beech-Nut was racing to unload its stock before regulators initiated a seizure action. On Sept. 1, Hoyvald managed to unload thousands of cases of juice from the Secaucus warehouse to Puerto Rico, despite the fact that the Puerto Rican distributor was already overstocked. Two weeks later, Hoyvald overruled his own lawyers and colleagues, who again suggested a recall, and ordered a feverish "foreign promotion";

under certain circumstances, American law does not prohibit the selling abroad of products banned at home. Within days, 23,000 cases were trucked at great expense from the company's San Jose, Calif., plant to Galveston, Tex., where they were off-loaded for the Dominican Republic, where they were sold at a 50 percent discount.

While Beech-Nut's sales staff shipped the evidence out to sea, its lawyers were holding the Federal and state agencies at bay. On Sept. 24, lawyers scheduled a meeting with F.D.A. officials that was designed to placate their adversaries. It worked. Three more weeks passed before the F.D.A. Administrator, Taylor M. Quinn, threatened to seize the juice, and thus finally wrung from the company a pledge to begin a nationwide recall. New York State authorities, less patient, threatened a seizure before Beech-Nut hurriedly agreed to a state recall. But the delay allowed Niels Hoyvald to virtually complete his master plan.

By the middle of November Hoyvald could boast, in a report to his superior at Nestlé, "The recall has now been completed, and due to our many delays, we were only faced with having to destroy approximately 20,000 cases. We received adverse publicity in only one magazine." As it turned out, of course, Hoyvald's self-congratulation was premature.

Further Federal and state investigations exposed details of the cover-up, as well as the fact that Beech-Nut had continued to sell the juice in its mixed-juice product for six months after the recall. New York State sued Beech-Nut for selling an adulterated and misbranded product, and imposed a $250,000 fine, by far the largest such penalty ever assessed in the state for consumer violations. In November 1986, the United States Attorney obtained indictments of Hoyvald, Lavery, Beech-Nut, Zeev Kaplansky and Kaplansky's colleague Raymond H. Wells, the owner of Food Complex. Beech-Nut eventually settled by agreeing to pay a $2 million fine. Kaplansky and Wells, who had earlier settled the apple institute with a financial agreement and by ceasing production of their concentrate, also pleaded guilty, and await sentencing. The F.D.A. referred the case to the Justice Department for criminal prosecution.

The case against Hoyvald and Lavery seemed overwhelming—so overwhelming that Lavery's first attorney suggested he plead guilty. Why did Lavery and Hoyvald insist on standing trial? Because both men, by most reports, are still convinced that they committed nothing graver than a mistake in judgment.

Hoyvald and Lavery seem to think of themselves as corporate patriots. Asked by one of the prosecutors why the entire inventory of concentrate was not destroyed once it came under suspicion, Hoyvald shot back testily: "And I could have called up Switzerland and told them I had just closed the company down. Because that is what would have been the result of it."

The questions of what Nestlé would have said, or did say, was not resolved by the trial. Jerome LiCari testified that in 1980 and 1981 he had expressed his concerns to six different Nestlé officials, including Richard Theuer, who was then a vice president of Nestlé and would become Beech-Nut's president in 1986. In an extraordinary effort to clear its reputation, Nestlé brought all six officials to court, mostly from Switzerland, and each one either contradicted LiCari's account or stated he had no memory of the alleged conversation. Nestlé is acutely sensitive to its public image, which was tarnished in the 1970's and early 80's when it aggressively promoted infant formula in third-world countries despite public health concerns, sparking international controversy and boycott campaigns.

Nestlé has defended its subsidiary's acts as vigorously as it defended its own in the past.

The company has spent what sources close to the case estimate as several million dollars in defending the two executives, and has agreed to keep both men on the payroll—at annual salaries of $120,000 and $70,000—until their current appeals are exhausted.

In a memo sent to Canajoharie employees after the verdict, James M. Biggar, president of Nestlé's American operations, claimed that LiCari had confused "what he wished he had said" with "what he actually said or did," and faulted management only for failing to keep an "open door."

Richard Theuer, the man Nestlé chose to replace Hoyvald, promises to keep that door open. He hopes to convince the public that at "the new Beech-Nut" decisions will be taken, as he says, "on behalf of the babies."

Case Study

Tylenol's Rebound

Carl Cannon

It's "easier to turn water into wine than to bring back Tylenol. It is dead."

That obituary by the head of a large advertising agency came at the height of the Tylenol crisis, which began a year ago this coming Friday. In the bitter wake of seven deaths in the Chicago area from cyanide-laced Extra-Strength Tylenol capsules, millions of bottles were yanked off the shelves by panicky retailers, unsure of their own liability, and by a confounded manufacturer, Johnson & Johnson. A product that had become almost a household word virtually disappeared in the first weeks after the tragedy.

From 35.4% of the over-the-counter analgesic market before the killings, Tylenol sank to a shaky 18.3% at the end of last year, when the red-and-white capsules began to reappear on the shelves. Johnson & Johnson, an international health-products giant based in New Brunswick, N.J., saw its stock price plunge.

"TEXTBOOK" RECOVERY PLAN

But that ad executive has since profusely apologized. Today, through a recovery plan that some say will be studied in textbooks on marketing, advertising and public relations, the product that only 12 months ago was "buried" by doomsayers has more than a 28.6% share of the $1.2-billion non-prescription pain reliever market, or more than 80% of its total before the crisis.

Johnson & Johnson's management, its agency, Compton Advertising, the unique confidence the public had in the product itself and even the news media share credit for the resurgence of Tylenol. It came against difficult odds, against a backdrop of national fear and a host of copycat crimes that not only threatened Tylenol but for a time cast a pall over the entire non-prescription analgesic industry as well. It was expensive—Johnson & Johnson's massive product recall, media

---

messages and tests of the capsules cost it in the tens of millions of dollars. And it has permanently affected the way non-prescription drugs are packaged as makers of everything from aspirin to eye drops followed Johnson & Johnson's lead in tamper-proofing.

Within the first few hours after the poisonings were traced to Tylenol capsules, Johnson & Johnson set up a task force of its top executives to first assess the damage to the company and then determine how to overcome it.

Over the next two weeks, during which this task force and a Compton Advertising team struggled to come up with a plan for recovery, outside marketing experts were advising that the only course was to change the name and come out with a "new" product. But there was legitimate concern that if such a tactic as merely reissuing Tylenol under a different name were tried, the press would quickly learn of it and the situation for the company would be worse.

There was no feeling within the company or within the agency that the name Tylenol should be dropped, according to Richard Earle, Compton's senior vice president and creative director, and Thomas Lom, senior vice president and managing supervisor for the advertising agency, both of whom worked on the recovery plan.

Tylenol was introduced in the late 1950's to the medical profession and built its reputation in those first years on being medically endorsed as a substitute for aspirin. The company contends its research shows that 70% of the users of the product first tried it on the recommendation of a physician. "With that kind of a profile as a foundation, advertising for the product began in 1976," Earle said. "We did some research and found that it was pretty well known among consumers then as a substitute for aspirin. Over the years our commercials used ordinary people with hidden cameras and showed the relief of actual headaches. The whole

emphasis of our campaigns was how well the product worked."

ADVERTISING CRITICIZED

It was a type of advertising that had been criticized by other Madison Avenue agencies as both boring and insulting to viewers. Critics say consumers were not naive enough to believe that people featured in the commercials were unaware they were on camera. But sales results had proved these critics wrong. Viewers obviously not only believed the advertising, but had faith in the product as well. This was later to stand the company in good stead in the midst of the crisis when competing products saw an opportunity to increase their market share at Tylenol's expense.

The first major decision by Johnson & Johnson, even before the crisis task force was set up, according to a company spokesman who took part, was to pull two lots of Tylenol capsules off the shelves in Chicago. The second was to halt all advertising. In the next few days capsules were taken off shelves across the country.

Johnson & Johnson's next step was to launch consumer research, to judge how the public perceived the company. "Then it was deemed necessary to make sure consumers got rid of Tylenol capsules," a Johnson & Johnson spokesman said. To accomplish this, Compton ran newspaper ads 10 days after the tragedy offering to swap Tylenol tablets for Tylenol capsules. "The press had informed the public so well that the whole country realized the danger was not in tablets, so the response was good," Lorn said.

At the same time, decisions were being made to investigate tamper-resistant packaging, to develop marketing strategies to rebuild the brand—coupons for consumers and discounts for retailers—and to figure out the type of advertising to employ once the crisis was over.

During this period the company also obtained a letter from the Food and Drug Administration stating that the agency was satisfied that there had been no criminal tampering with the product at the plant in which it was manufactured. "We were encountering people in our research who still expressed some lingering doubt, who thought perhaps the damage had been done on our premises," a company spokesman said. Johnson & Johnson widely exhibited the FDA letter to the press to try to erase the doubts.

Then the counterattack—a low-key one—began. "We wrote some ad copy which was essentially a corporate statement," Earle said. "We felt the public should be told that Tylenol would be back. We wrote a commercial early but it was held up and not aired for about four weeks."

The reluctance was born of uncertainty, according to the Compton team. "The company had worries of stirring everything up. So we did some research. Starting a week after the tragedy, we began to conduct man-on-the-street interviews to get a good reading of the general mood of the country. Over the next four weeks, we interviewed more than 800 people in 12 or 15 cities and found little negative feeling against the company itself. Many said they would buy Tylenol again if it were packaged in tamper-proof containers.

"But Mr. Burke (James E. Burke, chairman and chief executive of Johnson & Johnson) wanted to go slowly. He decided not to rush in. There were some concern over the timing. It was very close to Halloween and we were afraid it might spark a 'copycat' crime," Earle said.

AIRED "ROADBLOCK" AD

It was finally concluded that, since the Tylenol killings had been so extensively covered in the press and since Compton's research showed that the public wanted to hear from the company, the commercial should be run. "Our statement was rewritten many times," Lom said.

The first Tylenol commercial after the killings was what ad agencies and networks call a "roadblock": A viewer would see the same commercial no matter which of the three television networks was being watched at, say, 9 P.M. The ad featured Dr. Thomas N. Gates, medical director of McNeil Consumer Products, the Johnson & Johnson subsidiary that produces the analgesic. Gates, obviously used as a symbol of reliability, urged trust in the product and promised tamper-resistant containers.

"We thought about that spot hard and long," acknowledged a Johnson & Johnson spokesman. "There was some risk that it would be interpreted as being too commercial. After all, there were no capsules on the shelves for people to even buy. But, fortunately, it did what the country was expecting from the company and told them Tylenol would be back and it would be safe."

Long thought was given, too, to the press conference by Burke in which he announced—five weeks after McNeil Consumers Products withdrew 22 million bottles from the market—that Tylenol would start to reappear on store shelves in triple-sealed, tamper-resistant packages.

"We had more than 200 inquiries from the media and there simply was no other way" to answer them all, a company spokesman said. Burke appeared in New York and was linked by television to 29 other cities across the country. He said it was a "moral imperative" not to be destroyed by a "terrorist" act. And Johnson & Johnson emerged with the perception of being a responsible company and a champion of consumers.

GRANTED ACCESS TO MEDIA

Both Earle and Lom acknowledge that "a lot that might have been handled by advertising at this time was handled in a public relations sense." They mean that over these weeks Johnson & Johnson executives made themselves extremely available to the press. Burke and aides accepted virtually any and all appearances on talk shows, for instance, in an attempt to get across the company's viewpoint.

Still, according to one of those involved, the Johnson & Johnson task force agonized over a request for an appearance on "60 Minutes" because of the combative and sometimes abrasive style of questioning often used on the show. Among the seven key members of the Burke task force, two voted against the appearance. "We discussed it at length, and decided we had nothing to hide and the rest of the press had done a very complete job, and we thought '60 Minutes' would, too."

Burke not only appeared, but CBS reporter Mike Wallace and a camera crew were also allowed to attend and film a strategy session of the task force. In the telecast, as it had publicly and editorially most other places, the company won empathy from its plight.

It was a plight that would have sunk a smaller and less diverse company than Johnson & Johnson. If Tylenol had been its lone product, the story probably would have been different. As it was, Johnson & Johnson took a $100-million pretax write-off on the Tylenol losses for 1982. Tylenol contributed an estimated 7% of Johnson & Johnson's worldwide sales of $5.4 billion and between 15% and 20% of its profits of $467.6 million in 1981.

Still, despite Tylenol's vulnerability, competitors made surprisingly small headway in grabbing off chunks of its market share. For one thing, some of their products, too, were adulterated in a wave of copycat incidents at the height of the scare. Consumers were frightened by then of most analgesic capsules.

There was apparently an amazing level of brand loyalty. Anacin, the next-biggest seller, picked up only an estimated 1% to give it a 13.5% market share, and Datril's share remained at less than 1%.

A Johnson & Johnson official said the company is currently in litigation with some of its insurance firms over whether or not the company was covered for such product-tampering resulting in deaths.

Finally, the company was confident enough to return to pretty much the same type of advertising it had done before the crisis—non-actors with headaches. On Jan. 3, a San Diego woman appeared in an ad, expressing her trust in the brand. An announcer pointed out the new tamper-resistant packaging, but the crisis was never mentioned.

"We reviewed our advertising campaign just the other day," a company spokeswoman said last week. "We decided to go with the same thing with about the same level of spending."

Truth-Telling and Communication

In Section One, Albert Carr argued that bluffing in business negotiation is morally permissible, an exception to the general rule that one ought not to lie—an exception justified by the venue of business and the understandings that inform those who participate in business practice. But ethical issues in business communication reach well beyond bluffing and, indeed, beyond negotiation.

What should an employee do when confronted by actual or apparent wrongdoing on the job? When, or under what circumstances, is an employee permitted or required to report such wrongdoing to others (e.g., top management, regulatory bodies, or the news media)? Where do the demands of employee loyalty end and the demands of public disclosure begin? These questions are addressed under the rubric of *whistleblowing*. A number of thorny, interrelated moral issues surrounding whistleblowing demand careful attention. We begin our examination of whistleblowing with the articles "Whistleblowing and Employee Loyalty" and "Some Paradoxes of Whistleblowing."

"Purifying an Image: Baxter International and the Dialyzer Crisis" raises the question of when and under what circumstances a firm ought to inform actual or potential customers about the risks attendant to using the product. "Shoe Sales" asks whether deceptive tactics employed in retail shoe sales are harmful to consumers. "The Job Negotiation" reprises one of the issues that Carr raised in "Is Business Bluffing Ethical?"—but with an interesting twist, asking you which of three negotiating tactics you would be willing to employ. "Volvo's Crushing Blow" allows us to consider how advertisements can mislead without directly lying and how the demands of advertising creativity and the ethical requirement of truth-telling ought to be accommodated.

Case Study

Whistleblowing and Employee Loyalty

Ronald Duska

There are proponents on both sides of the issue—those who praise whistleblowers as civic heroes and those who condemn them as "finks." Maxwell Glen and Cody Shearer, who wrote about the whistleblowers at Three Mile Island say, "Without the *courageous* breed of assorted company insiders known as whistleblowers—workers who often risk their livelihoods to disclose information about construction and design flaws—the Nuclear Regulatory Commission itself would be nearly as idle as Three Mile Island. . . . That whistleblowers deserve both gratitude and protection is beyond disagreement."[1]

Still, while Glen and Shearer praise whistleblowers, others vociferously condemn them. For example, in a now infamous quote, James Roche, the former president of General Motors said:

> Some critics are now busy eroding another support of free enterprise—the loyalty of a management team, with its unifying values and cooperative work. Some of the enemies of business now encourage an employee to be *disloyal* to the enterprise. They want to create suspicion and disharmony, and pry into the proprietary interests of the business. However this is labeled—industrial espionage, whistleblowing, or professional responsibility—it is another tactic for spreading disunity and creating conflict.[2]

From Roche's point of view, not only is whistleblowing not "courageous" and not deserving of "gratitude and protection" as Glen and Shearer would have it, it is corrosive and impermissible.

Discussions of whistleblowing generally revolve around three topics: (1) attempts to define whistleblowing more precisely, (2) debates about whether and when whistleblowing is permissible, and (3) debates about whether and when one has an obligation to blow the whistle.

In this paper I want to focus on the second problem, because I find it somewhat disconcerting that there is a problem at all. When I first looked into the ethics of whistleblowing it seemed to me that whistleblowing was a good thing, and yet I found in the literature claim after claim that it was in need of defense, that there was something wrong with it, namely that it was an act of disloyalty.

If whistleblowing is a disloyal act, it deserves disapproval, and ultimately any action of whistleblowing needs justification. This disturbs me. It is as if the act of a good Samaritan is being condemned as an act of interference, as if the prevention of a suicide needs to be justified.

In his book *Business Ethics*, Norman Bowie claims that "whistleblowing . . . violate(s) a *prima facie* duty of loyalty to one's employer." According to Bowie, there is a duty of loyalty that prohibits one from reporting his employer or company. Bowie, of course, recognizes that this is only a *prima facie* duty, that is, one that can be overridden by a higher duty to the public good. Nevertheless, the axiom that whistleblowing is disloyal is Bowie's starting point.[3]

Bowie is not alone. Sissela Bok sees "whistle-blowing" as an instance of disloyalty:

> The whistleblower hopes to stop the game; but since he is neither referee nor coach, and since he blows the whistle on his own team, his act is seen as a *violation of loyalty*. In holding his position, he has assumed certain obligations to his colleagues and clients. He may even have subscribed to a loyalty oath or a promise of confidentiality.... Loyalty to colleagues and to clients comes to be pitted against loyalty to the public interest, to those who may be injured unless the revelation is made.[4]

Bowie and Bok end up defending whistle-blowing in certain contexts, so I don't necessarily disagree with their conclusions. However, I fail to see how one has an obligation of loyalty to one's company, so I disagree with their perception of the problem and their starting point. I want to argue that one does not have an obligation of loyalty to a company, even a *prima facie* one, because companies are not the kind of things that are properly objects of loyalty. To make them objects of loyalty gives them a moral status they do not deserve and in raising their status, one lowers the status of the individuals who work for the companies. Thus, the difference in perception is important because those who think employees have an obligation of loyalty to a company fail to take into account a relevant moral difference between persons and corporations.

But why aren't companies the kind of things that can be objects of loyalty? To answer that we have to ask what are proper objects of loyalty. John Ladd states the problem this way, "Granted that loyalty is the whole-hearted devotion to an object of some kind, what kind of thing is the object? Is it an abstract entity, such as an idea or a collective being? Or is it a person or group of persons?"[5] Philosophers fall into three camps on the question. On one side are the idealists who hold that loyalty is devotion to something more than persons, to some cause or abstract entity. On the other side are what Ladd calls "social atomists," and these include empiricists and utilitarians, who think that at most one can only be loyal to individuals and that loyalty can ultimately be explained away as some other obligation that holds between two people. Finally, there is a moderate position that holds that although idealists go too far in postulating some super-personal entity as an object of loyalty, loyalty is still an important and real relation that holds between people, one that cannot be dismissed by reducing it to some other relation.

There does seem to be a view of loyalty that is not extreme. According to Ladd, "'loyalty' is taken to refer to a relationship between persons—for instance, between a lord and his vassal, between a parent and his children, or between friends. Thus the object of loyalty is ordinarily taken to be a person or a group of persons."[6]

But this raises a problem that Ladd glosses over. There is a difference between a person or a group of persons, and aside from instances of loyalty that relate two people such as lord/vassal, parent/child, or friend/friend, there are instances of loyalty relating a person to a group, such as a person to his family, a person to this team, and a person to his country. Families, countries, and teams are presumably groups of persons. They are certainly ordinarily construed as objects of loyalty.

But to what am I loyal in such a group? In being loyal to the group am I being loyal to the whole group or to its members? It is easy to see the object of loyalty in the case of an individual person. It is simply the individual. But to whom am I loyal in a group? To whom am I loyal in a family? Am I loyal to each and every individual or to something larger, and if to something larger, what is it? We are tempted to think of a group as an entity of its own, an individual in its own right, having an identity of its own.

To avoid the problem of individuals existing for the sake of the group, the atomists insist that a group is nothing more than the individuals who comprise it, nothing other than a mental fiction by which we refer to a group of individuals. It is certainly not a reality or entity over and above the sum of its parts, and consequently is not a proper object of loyalty. Under such a position, of course, no loyalty would be owed to a company because a company is a mere mental fiction, since it is a group. One would have obligations to the individual members of the company, but one could never be justified in overriding those obligations for the sake of the "group" taken collectively. A company has no moral status except in terms of the individual members who comprise it. It is not a proper object of loyalty. But the atomists go too far. Some groups, such as a family, do have a reality of their own, whereas groups of people walking down the street do not. From Ladd's point of view the social atomist is wrong because he fails to recognize the kinds of groups that are held together by "the ties that bind." The atomist tries to reduce these groups to simple sets of individuals bound together by some externally imposed criteria. This seems wrong.

There do seem to be groups in which the relationships and interactions create a new force or entity. A group takes on an identity and a reality of its own that is determined by its purpose, and this purpose defines the various relationships and roles set up within the group. There is a division of labor into roles necessary for the fulfillment of the purposes of the group. The membership, then, is not of individuals who are the same but of individuals who have specific relationships to one another determined by the aim of the group. Thus we get specific relationships like parent/child, coach/player, and so on, that don't occur in other groups. It seems then that an atomist account of loyalty that restricts loyalty merely to individuals and does not include loyalty to groups might be inadequate.

But once I have admitted that we can have loyalty to a group, do I not open myself up to criticism from the proponent of loyalty to the company? Might not the proponent of loyalty to business say: "Very well. I agree with you. The atomists are short-sighted. Groups have some sort of reality and they can be proper objects of loyalty. But companies are groups. Therefore companies are proper objects of loyalty."

The point seems well taken, except for the fact that the kinds of relationships that loyalty requires are just the kind that one does not find in business. As Ladd says, "The ties that bind the persons together provide the basis of loyalty." But all sorts of ties bind people together. I am a member of a group of fans if I go to a ball game. I am a member of a group if I merely walk down the street. What binds people together in a business is not sufficient to require loyalty.

A business or corporation does two things in the free enterprise system: It produces a good or service and it makes a profit. The making of a profit, however, is the primary function of a business as a business, for if the production of the good or service is not profitable, the business would be out of business. Thus nonprofitable goods or services are a means to an end. People bound together in a business are bound together not for mutual fulfillment and support, but to divide labor or make a profit. Thus, while we can jokingly refer to a family as a place where "they have to take you in no matter what," we cannot refer to a company in that way. If a worker does not produce in a company or if cheaper laborers are available, the company—in order to fulfill its purpose—should get rid of the worker. A company feels no obligation of loyalty. The saying "You can't buy loyalty" is true. Loyalty depends on ties that demand self-sacrifice with no expectation of reward. Business functions on the basis of enlightened self-interest. I am devoted to a company not because it is like a parent to me; it is not. Attempts of some companies to create "one big happy family" ought to be looked on with suspicion. I am not devoted to it at all, nor should I be. I work for it because it pays me. I am not in a family to get paid, I am in a company to get paid.

The cold hard truth is that the goal of profit is what gives birth to a company and forms that particular group. Money is what ties the group together. But in such a commercialized venture, with such a goal, there is no loyalty, or at least none need be expected. An employer will release an employee and an employee will walk away from an employer when it is profitable for either one to do so.

Not only is loyalty to a corporation not required, it more than likely is misguided. There is nothing as pathetic as the story of the loyal employee who, having given above and beyond the call of duty, is let go in the restructuring of the company. He feels betrayed because he mistakenly viewed the company as an object of his loyalty. Getting rid of such foolish romanticism and coming to grips with this hard but accurate assessment should ultimately benefit everyone.

To think we owe a company or corporation loyalty requires us to think of that company as a person or as a group with a goal of human fulfillment. If we think of it in this way we can be loyal. But this is the wrong way to think. A company is not a person. A company is an instrument, and an instrument with a specific purpose, the making of profit. To treat an instrument as an end in itself, like a person, may not be as bad as treating an end as an instrument, but it does give the instrument a moral status it does not deserve; and by elevating the instrument we lower the end. All things, instruments and ends, become alike.

Remember that Roche refers to the "management team" and Bok sees the name "whistleblowing" coming from the instance of a referee blowing a whistle in the presence of a foul. What is perceived as bad about whistleblowing in business from this perspective is that one blows the whistle on one's own team, thereby violating team loyalty. If the company can get its employees to view it as a team they belong to, it is easier to demand loyalty. Then the rules governing teamwork and team loyalty will apply. One reason the appeal to a team and team loyalty works so well in business is that businesses are in competition with one another. Effective motivation turns business practices into a game and instills teamwork.

But businesses differ from teams in very important respects, which makes the analogy between business and a team dangerous. Loyalty to a team is loyalty within the context of sport or a competition. Teamwork and team loyalty require that in the circumscribed activity of the game I cooperate with my fellow players, so that pulling all together, we may win. The object of (most) sports is victory. But winning in sports is a social convention, divorced from the usual goings on of society. Such a winning is most times a harmless, morally neutral diversion.

But the fact that this victory in sports, within the rules enforced by a referee (whistleblower), is a socially developed convention taking place within a larger social context makes it quite different from competition in business, which, rather than being defined by a context, permeates the whole of society in its influence. Competition leads not only to victory but to losers. One can lose at sport with precious few consequences. The consequences of losing at business are much larger. Further, the losers in business can be those who are not in the game voluntarily (we are all forced to participate) but who are still affected by business decisions. People cannot choose to participate in business. It permeates everyone's lives.

The team model, then, fits very well with the model of the free market system, because there competition is said to be the name of the game. Rival companies compete and their object is to win. To call a foul on one's own teammate is to jeopardize one's chances of winning and is viewed as disloyalty.

But isn't it time to stop viewing corporate machinations as games? These games are not controlled and are not ended after a specific time. The activities of business affect the lives of everyone, not just the game players. The analogy of the corporation to a team and the consequent appeal to team loyalty, although understandable, is seriously misleading, at least in the moral sphere where competition is not the prevailing virtue.

If my analysis is correct, the issue of the permissibility of whistleblowing is not a real issue since there is no obligation of loyalty to a company. Whistleblowing is not only permissible but expected when a company is harming society. The issue is not one of disloyalty to the company, but of whether the whistleblower has an obligation to society if blowing the whistle will bring him retaliation.

NOTES

1. Maxwell Glen and Cody Shearer, "Going After the Whistle-blowers," *Philadelphia Inquirer,* Tuesday, August 2, 1983, Op-ed page, p. 11A.
2. James M. Roche, "The Competitive System, to Work, to Preserve, and to Protect," *Vital Speeches of the Day* (May 1971): 445.
3. Norman Bowie, *Business Ethics* (Englewood Cliffs, N.J.: Prentice Hall, 1982), pp. 140–143.
4. Sissela Bok, "Whistleblowing and Professional Responsibilities," *New York University Education Quarterly* 2 (1980): 3.
5. John Ladd, "Loyalty," *The Encyclopedia of Philosophy* 5:97.
6. Ibid.

Case Study

Some Paradoxes of Whistleblowing

Michael Davis

By "paradox," I mean an apparent—and, in this case, real—inconsistency between theory (our systematic understanding of whistleblowing) and the facts (what we actually know, or think we know, about whistleblowing). What concerns me is not a few anomalies, the exceptions that test a rule, but a flood of exceptions that seems to swamp the rule.

This paper has four parts. The first states the standard theory of whistleblowing. The second argues that the standard theory is paradoxical, that it is inconsistent with what we know about whistleblowers. The third part sketches what seems to me a less paradoxical theory of whistleblowing. The fourth tests the new theory against one classic case of whistleblowing,

Roger Boisjoly's testimony before the presidential commission investigating the *Challenger* disaster ("the Rogers Commission").

I use that case because the chief facts are both uncontroversial enough and well known enough to make detailed exposition unnecessary. For the same reason, I also use that case to illustrate various claims about whistleblowing throughout the paper.

JUSTIFICATION AND WHISTLEBLOWING

The standard theory is not about whistleblowing as such but about justified whistleblowing—and rightly so. Whether this or that is, or is not, whistleblowing is a question for lexicographers. For the rest of us, mere moral agents, the question is: when, if ever, is whistleblowing justified?

We may distinguish three (related) senses in which an act may be "justified." First, an act may be something morality permits. Many acts, for example, eating fruit at lunch, are morally justified in this weak sense. They are (all things considered) morally all right, though some of the alternatives are morally all right too. Second, acts may be morally justified in a stronger sense. Not only is doing them morally all right, but doing anything else instead is morally wrong. These acts are *morally required.* Third, some acts, though only morally justified in the weaker sense, are still required all things considered. They are mandatory because of some non-moral consideration. They are rationally (but not morally) required.

I shall be concerned here only with moral justification, that is, with what morality permits or requires. I shall have nothing to say about when other considerations, for example, individual prudence or social policy, make (morally permissible) whistleblowing something reason requires.

Generally, we do not *need* to justify an act unless we have reason to think it wrong (whether morally wrong or wrong in some other way). So, for example, I do not need to justify eating fruit for lunch today, though I would if I were allergic to fruit or had been keeping a fast. We also do not need a justification if we believe the act in question wrong. We do not need a justification because, insofar as an act is wrong, justification is impossible. The point of justification is to show to be right an act the rightness of which has been put in (reasonable) doubt.

Insofar as we believe the act wrong, we can only condemn or excuse it. To condemn it is simply to declare it wrong. To excuse it is to show that, while the act was wrong, the doer had good reason to do it, could not help doing it, or for some other reason should not suffer the response otherwise reserved for such a wrongdoer.

Most acts, though what morality permits or requires, need no justification. There is no reason to think them wrong. Their justification is too plain for words. Why then is whistleblowing so problematic that we need *theories* of its justification? What reason do we have to think whistleblowing might be morally wrong?

Whistleblowing always involves revealing information that would not ordinarily be revealed. But there is nothing morally problematic about that: after all, revealing information not ordinarily revealed is one function of science. Whistleblowing always involves, in addition, an actual (or at least declared) intention to prevent something bad that would otherwise occur. Nothing morally problematic in that either. That may well be the chief use of information.

What seems to make whistleblowing morally problematic is its organizational context. A mere individual cannot blow the whistle (in any interesting sense); only a member of an organization, whether a current or a former member, can. Indeed, he can only blow the whistle on his own organization (or some part of it). So, for example, a police officer who makes public information about a burglary ring, though a member of an organization, does not blow the whistle on the burglary ring (in any interesting sense). She simply alerts the public. Even if she came by the information working undercover in the ring, her revelation could not be whistleblowing. While secret agents, spies, and other infiltrators need a moral justification for what they do, the justification they need differs from that whistleblowers need. Infiltrators gain their information under false pretenses. They need a justification for that deception.[1]

Whistleblowers generally do not gain their information under false pretenses.

What if, instead of being a police officer, the revealer of information about the burglary ring were an ordinary member of the ring? Would such an informer be a (justified) whistleblower?

I think not. The burglary ring is a criminal organization. The whistleblower's organization never is, though it may occasionally engage in crime (knowingly or by inadvertence). So, even a burglar who, having a change of heart, volunteers information about his ring to the police or the newspaper, does not need to justify his act in the way the whistleblower does. Helping to destroy a criminal organization by revealing its secrets is morally much less problematic than whistleblowing.

What then is morally problematic about the whistleblower's organizational context? The whistleblower *cannot* blow the whistle using just any information obtained in virtue of membership in the organization. A clerk in Accounts who, happening upon evidence of serious wrongdoing while visiting a friend in Quality Control, is not a whistleblower just because she passes the information to a friend at the *Tribune*. She is more like a self-appointed spy. She seems to differ from the whistleblower, or at least from clear cases of the whistleblower, precisely in her relation to the information in question. To be a whistleblower is to reveal information with which one is *entrusted*.

But it is more than that. The whistleblower does not reveal the information to save his own skin (for example, to avoid perjury under oath).[2] He has no excuse for revealing what his organization does not want revealed. Instead, he claims to be doing what he should. If he cannot honestly make that claim—if, that is, he does not have that intention—his revelation is not whistleblowing (and so, not justified as whistleblowing), but something analogous, much as pulling a child from the water is not a rescue, even if it saves the child's life, when

the "rescuer" merely believes herself to be salvaging old clothes.

What makes whistleblowing morally problematic, if anything does, is this high-minded but unexcused misuse of one's position in a generally law-abiding, morally decent organization, an organization that prima facie deserves the whistleblower's loyalty (as a burglary ring does not).[3]

The whistleblower must reveal information the organization does not want revealed. But, in any actual organization, "what the organization wants" will be contested, with various individuals or groups asking to be taken as speaking for the organization. Who, for example, did what Thiokol wanted the night before the *Challenger* exploded? In retrospect, it is obvious that the three vice presidents, Lund, Kilminster, and Mason, did not do what Thiokol wanted— or, at least, what it would have wanted. At the time, however, they had authority to speak for the company—the conglomerate Morton-Thiokol headquartered in Chicago—while the protesting engineers, including Boisjoly, did not. Yet, even before the explosion, was it obvious that the three were doing what the company wanted? To be a whistleblower, one must, I think, at least temporarily lose an argument about what the organization wants. The whistleblower is disloyal only in a sense, the sense the winners of the internal argument get to dictate. What can justify such disloyalty?

THE STANDARD THEORY

According to the theory now more or less standard,[4] such disloyalty is morally permissible when:

S1. The organization to which the would-be whistleblower belongs will, through its product or policy, do serious and considerable harm to the public (whether to users of its product, to innocent bystanders, or to the public at large);

S2. The would-be whistleblower has identified that threat of harm, reported it to her immediate superior, making clear both the threat itself and the objection to it, and concluded that the superior will do nothing effective; and

S3. The would-be whistleblower has exhausted other internal procedures within the organization (for example, by going up the organizational ladder as far as allowed)—or at least made use of as many internal procedures as the danger to others and her own safety make reasonable.

Whistleblowing is morally required (according to the standard theory) when, in addition:

S4. The would-be whistleblower has (or has accessible) evidence that would convince a reasonable, impartial observer that her view of the threat is correct; and

S5. The would-be whistleblower has good reason to believe that revealing the threat will (probably) prevent the harm at reasonable cost (all things considered).

Why is whistleblowing morally required when these five conditions are met? According to the standard theory, whistleblowing is morally required, when it is, because "people have a moral obligation to prevent serious harm to others if they can do so with little cost to themselves."[5] In other words, whistleblowing meeting all five conditions is a form of "minimally decent samaritanism" (a doing of what morality requires) rather than "good samaritanism" (going well beyond the moral minimum).[6]

A number of writers have pointed out that the relation between the first three conditions and the full five does not seem to be that between the morally permissible and the morally required.[7] If, for example, the whistleblower lacks evidence that would convince a reasonable, impartial observer of the threat in question (S4), her whistleblowing could not prevent harm. Since it could not prevent harm, her whistleblowing would not be even

morally permissible: what could make morally permissible an attempt to help a stranger when the attempt will probably fail and the cost be high both to the would-be Samaritan and to those to whom she owes a competing obligation? The most that can be said for blowing the whistle where only conditions S1–S3 are met seems to be that the whistleblower has an excuse when (without negligence) she acts on inadequate evidence. So, for many writers, the standard view is that S1–S5 state sufficient conditions for morally required whistleblowing even though S1–S3 do not state sufficient conditions for morally permissible whistleblowing but (at best) for morally excusable whistleblowing.

The standard theory is not a definition of whistleblowing or even of justified whistleblowing. The theory purports to state sufficient conditions, not necessary conditions (a "when" but *not* an "only when"). But these sufficient conditions are supposed to identify the central cases of morally justified whistleblowing. Since a theory that did only that would be quite useful, we cannot object to the theory merely because it is incomplete in this way. Incomplete only in this way, the theory would be about as useful as theories of practical ethics ever are.

THREE PARADOXES

That's the standard theory: where are the paradoxes? The first paradox I want to call attention to concerns a commonplace of the whistleblowing literature. Whistleblowers are not minimally decent Samaritans. If they are Samaritans at all, they are good Samaritans. They always act at considerable risk to career and generally at considerable risk to their financial security and personal relations.[8]

In this respect, as in many others, Roger Boisjoly is typical. Boisjoly blew the whistle on his employer, Thiokol: he volunteered information, in public testimony before the Rogers Commission, that Thiokol did not want him to volunteer. As often happens, both his employer and many who relied on it for employment reacted hostilely. Boisjoly had to say goodbye to the company town, to old friends and neighbors, and to building rockets; he had to start a new career at an age when most people are preparing for retirement.

Since whistleblowing is generally costly to the whistleblower in some such large way as this, the standard theory's minimally decent samaritanism provides *no* justification for the central cases of whistleblowing.[9] That is the first paradox, what me might call "the paradox of burden."

The second paradox concerns the prevention of "harm." On the standard theory, the would-be whistleblower must seek to prevent "serious and considerable harm" in order for the whistleblowing to be even morally permissible. There seems to be a good deal of play in the term "harm." The harm in question can be physical (such as death or disease), financial (such as loss of or damage to property), and perhaps even psychological (such as fear or mental illness). But there is a limit to how much the standard theory can stretch "harm." Beyond that limit are "harms" like injustice, deception, and waste. As morally important as injustice, deception, and waste can be, they do not seem to constitute the "serious and considerable harm" that can require someone to become even a minimally decent samaritan.

Yet, many cases of whistleblowing, perhaps most, are not about preventing serious and considerable physical, financial, or psychological harm. For example, when Boisjoly spoke up the evening before the *Challenger* exploded, the lives of seven astronauts sat in the balance. Speaking up then was about preventing serious and considerable physical, financial, and psychological harm—but it was not whistleblowing. Boisjoly was then serving his employer, not

betraying a trust (even on the employer's understanding of that trust); he was calling his superiors' attention to what he thought they should take into account in their decision, not publicly revealing confidential information. The whistleblowing came after the explosion, in testimony before the Rogers Commission. By then, the seven astronauts were beyond help, the shuttle program was suspended, and any further threat of physical, financial, or psychological harm to the "public" was—after discounting for time—negligible.

Boisjoly had little reason to believe his testimony would make a significant difference in the booster's redesign, in safety procedures in the shuttle program, or even in re-awakening concern for safety among NASA employees and contractors. The *Challenger*'s explosion was much more likely to do that than anything Boisjoly could do. What Boisjoly could do in his testimony, what I think he tried to do, was prevent falsification of the record.[10]

Falsification of the record is, of course, harm in a sense, especially a record as historically important as that the Rogers Commission was to produce. But falsification is harm only in a sense that almost empties "harm" of its distinctive meaning, leaving it more or less equivalent to "moral wrong." The proponents of the standard theory mean more by "harm" than that.

De George, for example, explicitly says that a threat justifying whistleblowing must be to "life or health."[11] The standard theory is strikingly narrower in its grounds of justification than many examples of justified whistleblowing suggest it should be. That is the second paradox, the "paradox of missing harm."

The third paradox is related to the second. Insofar as whistleblowers are understood as people out to prevent harm, not just to prevent moral wrong, their chances of success are not good. Whistleblowers generally do not prevent much harm. In this too, Boisjoly is typical. As he has said many times, things at

Thiokol are now much as they were before the disaster. Insofar as we can identify cause and effect, even now we have little reason to believe that—whatever his actual intention—Boisjoly's testimony actually prevented any harm. So, if whistleblowers must have, as the standard theory says (S5), "good reason to believe that revealing the threat will (probably) prevent the harm," then the history of whistleblowing virtually rules out the moral justification of whistleblowing. That is certainly paradoxical in a theory purporting to state sufficient conditions for the central cases of justified whistleblowing. Let us call this "the paradox of failure."

A COMPLICITY THEORY

As I look down the roll of whistleblowers, I do not see anyone who, like the clerk from Accounts, just happened upon key documents in a cover-up.[12] Few, if any, whistleblowers are mere third-parties like the good Samaritan. They are generally deeply involved in the activity they reveal. This involvement suggests that we might better understand what justifies (most) whistleblowing if we understand the whistleblower's obligation to derive from *complicity* in wrongdoing rather than from the ability to prevent harm.

Any complicity theory of justified whistleblowing has two obvious advantages over the standard theory. One is that (moral) complicity itself presupposes (moral) wrongdoing, not harm. So, a complicity justification automatically avoids the paradox of missing harm, fitting the facts of whistleblowing better than a theory which, like the standard one, emphasizes prevention of harm.

That is one obvious advantage of a complicity theory. The other is that complicity invokes a more demanding obligation than the ability to prevent harm does. We are morally obliged to avoid doing moral wrongs. When, despite our best efforts, we nonetheless find ourselves engaged in some wrong, we have an obligation to do what we reasonably can to set things right. If, for example, I cause a traffic accident, I have a moral (and legal) obligation to call help, stay at the scene till help arrives, and render first aid (if I know how), even at substantial cost to myself and those to whom I owe my time, and even with little likelihood that anything I do will help much. Just as a complicity theory avoids the paradox of missing harm, it also avoids the paradox of burden.

What about the third paradox, the paradox of failure? I shall come to that, but only after remedying one disadvantage of the complicity theory. That disadvantage is obvious: we do not yet have such a theory, not even a sketch. Here, then, is the place to offer a sketch:

Complicity Theory

You are morally required to reveal what you know to the public (or to a suitable agent or representative of it)[13] when:

C1. what you will reveal derives from your work for an organization;

C2. you are a voluntary member of that organization;

C3. you believe that the organization, though legitimate, is engaged in serious moral wrongdoing;

C4. you believe that your work for that organization will contribute (more or less directly) to the wrong if (but *not* only if) you do not publicly reveal what you know;

C5. you are justified in beliefs C3 and C4; and

C6. beliefs C3 and C4 are true.

The complicity theory differs from the standard theory in several ways worth pointing out here. The first is that, according to C1, what the whistleblower reveals must derive from his work for the organization. This condition distinguishes the whistleblower from the spy (and the clerk in Accounts). The spy seeks out information in order to reveal it; the whistle-blower learns it as a proper part of doing the job the organization has assigned him. The standard theory, in contrast, has nothing to say about how the whistleblower comes to know of the threat she reveals (S2). For the standard theory, spies are just another kind of whistleblower.

A second way in which the complicity theory differs from the standard theory is that the complicity theory (C2) explicitly requires the whistleblower to be a *voluntary* participant in the organization in question. Whistleblowing is not—according to the complicity theory—an activity in which slaves, prisoners, or other involuntary participants in an organization engage. In this way, the complicity theory makes explicit something implicit in the standard theory. The whistleblowers of the standard theory are generally "employees." Employees are voluntary participants in the organization employing them.

What explains this difference in explicitness? For the samaritanism of the standard theory, the voluntariness of employment is extrinsic. What is crucial is the ability to prevent harm. For the complicity theory, however, the voluntariness is crucial. The obligations deriving from complicity seem to vary with the voluntariness of our participation in the wrongdoing. Consider, for example, a teller who helps a gang rob her bank because they have threatened to kill her if she does not: she does not have the same obligation to break off her association with the gang as someone who has freely joined it. The voluntariness of employment means that the would-be whistleblower's complicity will be more like that of one of the gang than like that of the conscripted teller.[14]

A third way in which the complicity theory differs from the standard theory is that the complicity theory (C3) requires moral wrong, not harm, for justification. The wrong need not be a new event (as a harm must be if it is to be *prevented*). It might, for example, consist

in no more than silence about facts necessary to correct a serious injustice.

The complicity theory (C3) does, however, follow the standard theory in requiring that the predicate of whistleblowing be "serious." Under the complicity theory, minor wrongdoing can no more justify whistleblowing than can minor harm under the standard theory.[15] While organizational loyalty cannot forbid whistleblowing, it does forbid "tattling," that is, revealing minor wrongdoing.

A fourth way in which the complicity theory differs from the standard theory, the most important, is that the complicity theory (C4) requires that the whistleblower believe her work will have contributed to the wrong in question if she does nothing but does *not* require that she believe that her revelation will prevent (or undo) the wrong. The complicity theory does not require any belief about what the whistleblowing can accomplish (beyond ending complicity in the wrong in question). The whistleblower reveals what she knows to prevent complicity in the wrong, not to prevent the wrong as such. She can prevent complicity (if there is any to prevent) simply by publicly revealing what she knows. The revelation itself breaks the bond of complicity, the secret partnership in wrongdoing, that makes her an accomplice in her organization's wrongdoing.[16] The complicity theory thus avoids the third paradox, the paradox of failure, just as it avoided the other two.

The fifth difference between the complicity theory and the standard theory is closely related to the fourth. Because publicly revealing what one knows breaks the bond of complicity, the complicity theory does not require the whistleblower to have enough evidence to convince others of the wrong in question. Convincing others, or just being able to convince them, is not, as such, an element in the justification of whistleblowing.

The complicity theory does, however, require (C5) that the whistleblower be (epistemically) justified in believing both that his organization is engaged in wrongdoing and that he will contribute to that wrong unless he blows the whistle. Such (epistemic) justification may require substantial physical evidence (as the standard theory says) or just a good sense of how things work. The complicity theory does not share the standard theory's substantial evidential demand (S4).

In one respect, however, the complicity theory clearly requires more of the whistleblower than the standard theory does. The complicity theory's C6—combined with C5—requires not only that the whistleblower be *justified* in her beliefs about the organization's wrongdoing and her part in it, but also that she be *right* about them. If she is wrong about either the wrongdoing or her complicity, her revelation will not be justified whistleblowing. This consequence of C6 is, I think, not as surprising as it may seem. If the would-be whistleblower is wrong only about her own complicity, her revelation of actual wrongdoing will, being otherwise justified, merely fail to be justified *as whistleblowing* (much as a failed rescue, though justified an attempt, cannot be justified as a rescue). If, however, she is wrong about the wrongdoing itself, her situation is more serious. Her belief that wrong is being done, though fully justified on the evidence available to her, cannot justify her disloyalty. All her justified belief can do is *excuse* her disloyalty. Insofar as she acted with good intentions and while exercising reasonable care, she is a victim of bad luck. Such bad luck will leave her with an obligation to apologize, to correct the record (for example, by publicly recanting the charges she publicly made), and otherwise to set things right.

The complicity theory says nothing on at least one matter about which the standard theory says much, going through channels before publicly revealing what one knows. But the two theories do not differ as much as this difference in emphasis suggests. If going through channels would suffice to prevent (or undo) the wrong, then it cannot be true (as C4 and C6 together require) that the would-be whistleblower's work will contribute to the wrong if she does not publicly reveal what she knows. Where, however, going through channels would *not* prevent (or undo) the wrong, there is no need to go through channels. Condition C4's if-clause will be satisfied. For the complicity theory, going through channels is a way of finding out what the organization will do, not an independent requirement of justification. That, I think, is also how the standard theory understands it.[17]

A last difference between the two theories worth mention here is that the complicity theory is only a theory of morally required whistleblowing while the standard theory claims as well to define circumstances when whistleblowing is morally permissible but not morally required. This difference is another advantage the complicity theory has over the standard theory. The standard theory, as we saw, has trouble making good on its claim to explain how whistleblowing can be morally permissible without being morally required.

TESTING THE THEORY

Let us now test the theory against Boisjoly's testimony before the Rogers Commission. Recall that under the standard theory any justification of that testimony seemed to fail for at least three reasons: First, Boisjoly could not testify without substantial cost to himself and Thiokol (to whom he owed loyalty). Second, there was no serious and substantial harm his testimony could prevent. And, third, he had little reason to believe that, even if he could identify a serious and considerable harm to prevent, his testimony had much chance of preventing it.

Since few doubt that Boisjoly's testimony before the Rogers Commission constitutes justified whistleblowing, if anything does, we should welcome a theory that—unlike the standard one—justifies that testimony as whistleblowing. The complicity theory sketched above does that:

C1. Boisjoly's testimony consisted almost entirely of information derived from his work on booster rockets at Thiokol.

C2. Boisjoly was a voluntary member of Thiokol.

C3. Boisjoly believed Thiokol, a legitimate organization, was attempting to mislead its client, the government, about the causes of a deadly accident. Attempting to do that certainly seems a serious moral wrong.

C4. On the evening before the *Challenger* exploded. Boisjoly gave up objecting to the launch once his superiors, including the three Thiokol vice presidents, had made it clear that they were no longer willing to listen to him. He also had a part in preparing those superiors to testify intelligently before the Rogers Commission concerning the booster's fatal field joint. Boisjoly believed that Thiokol would use his failure to offer his own interpretation of his retreat into silence the night before the launch, and the knowledge that he had imparted to his superiors, to contribute to the attempt to mislead Thiokol's client.

C5. The evidence justifying beliefs C3 and C4 consisted of comments of various officers of Thiokol, what Boisjoly had seen at Thiokol over the years, and what he learned about the rocket business over a long career. I find this evidence sufficient to justify his belief both that his organization was engaged in wrongdoing and that his work was implicated.

C6. Here we reach a paradox of *knowledge*. Since belief is knowledge if, but only if, it is *both* justified *and* true, we cannot *show* that we know anything. All we can show is that a belief is now justified and that we have no reason to expect anything to turn up later to prove it false. The evidence now available still justifies Boisjoly's belief both about what Thiokol was attempting and about what would have been his part in the attempt. Since new evidence is unlikely, his testimony seems to satisfy C6 just as it satisfied the complicity theory's other five conditions.

Since the complicity theory explains why Boisjoly's testimony before the Rogers Commission was morally required whistleblowing, it has passed its first test, a test the standard theory failed.

NOTES

I should thank Vivian Weil for several discussions provoking this paper, as well as for commenting on several drafts; members of the Program in Ethics, Science, and Environment, Oregon State University, for raising several hard questions after I read an early version of this paper to them, April 24, 1996; those who asked questions (including my co-panelist, Roger Boisjoly) at a session of the annual meeting of the Northwest Section of the American Society of Engineering Educators, Oregon Institute of Technology, Klamath Falls, Oregon, April 26, 1996; the editors of *Business and Professional Ethics Journal,* and, last, attendees at a symposium sponsored by the Centre for Professional Ethics, University of Central Lancashire, Preston, England, November 12, 1996.

1. This is, I think, one (but not the only) reason to reject the forgotten—but perceptive—definition of whistleblowing in Frederick Elliston, John Keenan, Paula Lockhart, and Jane van Schaick, *Whistleblowing Research: Methodological and Moral Issues* (New York: Praeger, 1984), p. 15: "An act of whistleblowing occurs when: 1) an individual performs an action or series of actions intended to make information public; 2) the information is made a matter of public record; 3) the information is about possible or actual, nontrivial wrongdoing in an organization; and 4) the individual who performs the action is a member or former member of the organization." While this definition confounds whistleblowers with spies, informers, and the like, and is designed for research on whistleblowing rather than for developing a justification, its wrong-based approach makes it closer to the complicity theory offered below than to the standard theory. (Though the book has four authors, they credit the whole of the first chapter, including this definition, to someone else, Deborah Johnson.)

2. I do not mean that, for some purpose, for example, a whistleblower protection act, it might not be convenient to include among whistleblowers those who reveal information unwillingly. What I mean is that, for purposes of developing a general theory of justified whistleblowing, such cases are uninteresting. Avoiding contempt of court or Congress generally provides sufficient justification for testifying about serious wrongdoing, and avoiding perjury, a sufficient justification for telling the truth, a stronger justification than can either the standard theory or the alternative I shall offer.

3. There is, of course, a problem about organizational loyalty, especially when the organization is a business

and it understands its employees as instruments rather than members. While justifying whistleblowing is easier the less loyalty one owes the organization in question, we will learn more if we focus on the harder cases, those where we admit significant obligations of loyalty. So, that is what I do here.

4. Throughout this paper, I take the standard theory to be Richard T. De George's version in *Business Ethics*, 3rd ed. (New York: Macmillan, 1990), pp. 200–214 (amended only insofar as necessary to include non-businesses as well as businesses). Why treat De George's theory as standard? There are two reasons first, it seems the most commonly cited; and second, people offering alternatives generally treat it as the one to be replaced. The only obvious competitor, Norman Bowie's, is distinguishable from De George's on no point relevant here. See his *Business Ethics* (Englewood Cliffs, NJ: Prentice-Hall, 1982), p. 143.

5. De George, 200. Later, 214, De George says something more daring: "It is not implausible to claim both that we are morally obliged to prevent harm to others at little expense to ourselves, and that we are morally obliged to prevent great harm to a great many others, even at considerable expense to ourselves." De George (quite rightly) considers the opportunity to prevent great harm (as distinct from serious harm) so rare that he can safely ignore it.

6. There is now a significant literature on the responsibilities of the minimally decent Samaritan. See, for example: Peter Singer, "Famine, Affluence, and Morality," *Philosophy and Public Affairs* 7 (Spring 1972): 229–243; Alan Gewirth, *Reason and Morality* (Chicago: University of Chicago Press, 1978), 217–230; Patricia Smith, "The Duty to Rescue and the Slippery Slope Problem," *Social Theory and Practice* 16 (Spring 1990): 19–41; John M. Whelan, "Charity and the Duty to Rescue," *Social Theory and Practice* 17 (Fall 1991): 441–456; and David Copp, "Responsibility for Collective Inaction," *Journal of Social Philosophy* 22 (Fall 1991): 71–80.

7. See, for example, David Theo Goldberg, "Tuning In to Whistle Blowing," *Business and Professional Ethics Journal* 7 (Summer 1988): 85–94.

8. For an explanation of why whistleblowing is inevitably a high risk undertaking, see my "Avoiding the Tragedy of Whistleblowing," *Business and Professional Ethics Journal* 8 (Winter 1989): 3–19.

9. Indeed, I am tempted to go further and claim that, where an informant takes little or no risk, we are unlikely to describe her as a whistleblower at all. So, for example, I would say that using an internal or external "hot-line" is whistleblowing only when it is risky. We are, in other words, likely to consider using a hot-line as disloyalty (that is, as "going out of channels") only if the organization (or some part of it) is likely to respond with considerable hostility to its use.

10. After I presented this paper in Klamath Falls, Boisjoly told me that, though his motive for testifying as he did

was (as I surmised) to prevent falsification of the record, part of his reason for wanting to prevent that was that he wanted to do what he could to prevent the managers responsible for the disaster from having any part in redesigning the boosters. This *secondary* motive is, of course, consistent with the complicity theory.

11. De George, 210: "The notion of *serious* harm might be expanded to include serious financial harm, and kinds of harm other than death and serious threats to health and body. But as we noted earlier, we shall restrict ourselves here to products and practices that produce or threaten serious harm or danger to life and health."

12. See Myron Peretz Glazer and Penina Migdal Glazer, *The Whistleblowers: Exposing Corruption in Government and Industry* (New York: Basic Books, 1989), for a good list of whistleblowers (with detailed description of each): for an older list (with descriptions), see Alan F. Westin, *Whistle-blowing! Loyalty and Dissent in the Corporation* (New York: McGraw-Hill, 1981).

13. The problems with "public" in any definition of "whistleblowing" are well known (perhaps even notorious). I simply ignore them here. For our purposes, the public to whom the whistleblower reveals information is that individual or group to whom she must reveal it in order to end her complicity. Who is the public will vary with circumstances.

14. Do I claim that slaves, prisoners, inmates in a mental hospital, or students in a school cannot blow the whistle—or, at least, cannot do so justifiably? Well, not exactly. That the usual lists of whistleblowers include no involuntary participants in wrongdoing is, I think, important evidence for the claim that involuntary participants cannot blow the whistle. But, since how we have used a word does not determine how we can use it (especially a word like "whistleblowing" where usage is still evolving), that evidence is hardly decisive. What I think is clear is that involuntary participants will not have the same obligation of loyalty as the typical whistleblower; hence, any theory justifying their "going public" will have a somewhat different structure than the theory developed here. What about *voluntary* participants who are not employees, such as unpaid volunteers in a political campaign? While the complicity theory clearly counts them as capable of justified whistleblowing, the standard theory must make some special provision.

15. If the revelation seems likely to prevent harm as well, or to undo some injustice as well, that will, of course, strengthen the justification, making better a justification already good enough. But, according to the complicity theory, such good consequences are not necessary for justification.

16. We are, of course, assuming the standard case of whistleblowing where complicity involves only information. We can imagine more complicated cases where, in addition to information, there are benefits from the wrongdoing (say, a bonus derived from past wrongdoing). In such complex cases, revealing information (including the bonus) may not be all

that is morally required but, even so, it will, I think, end the complicity relevant to whistleblowing. That, however, is a matter about which I am still thinking.

17. Compare De George, 211: "By reporting one's concern to one's immediate superior or other appropriate persons, one preserves and observes the regular practices of firms, which on the whole promote their order and efficiency; this fulfills one's obligation of minimizing harm, and *it precludes precipitous whistle blowing.*" (Italics mine.)

Case Study

Purifying an Image: Baxter International and the Dialyzer Crisis

Julie A. Davis

This case examines product liability regarding a blood filter produced by Baxter International, a medical supply company. Acting quickly, Baxter used rhetorical strategies of compensation and corrective action to strengthen the company's image. The case poses several challenging issues regarding a company's duty to inform patients of a product's risks and the patients' right to know. In this case, Baxter accepted responsibility without concern for possible litigation over the product, even in the absence of conclusive evidence of fault.

Health and safety are the main products medical supply companies have to sell. However, when these organizations face product liability problems, instead of offering improved health, the products leave death and disability behind them. This is the type of crisis Baxter International, a medical supply company based in Deerfield, Illinois, faced in the summer and fall of 2001.[1] By the time this crisis was resolved, 53 dialysis patients had died, two lines of dialyzers (a type of blood filter) were discontinued, two plants that manufactured the filters implicated in the deaths were closed, and Baxter took a charge to earnings of $189 million. Despite the high number of deaths, the company's quick actions, along with outside circumstances, kept the story from receiving the quantitative and qualitative amounts of press coverage endured by organizations facing crises with much lower death and injury rates.

The patient deaths placed Baxter in an ethical morass, seeking answers to a variety of questions: When should an organization inform customers of potential problems with a product? When should an organization act in the face of incomplete information to accept responsibility for a problem? How much responsibility should an organization take on for a crisis that could have plausibly been the result of several organizations' actions? What are the ethical implications of an organization's action to prevent a tragedy's reoccurrence if those actions cause harm to innocents, including their own employees and customers? Can an organization attempt to be too ethical? To understand Baxter's attempts to answer these ethical questions, an examination of the organization and the dialyzer crisis, Baxter's responses to the deaths, and circumstances that allowed the organization to avoid negative media attention about the crisis and its aftermath is in order.

ORGANIZATIONAL HISTORY OF BAXTER INTERNATIONAL

Before a discussion of the dialyzer crisis can be undertaken, a brief overview of the organization as a whole will be helpful. Baxter International is a $7.7 billion healthcare products organization headquartered in Deerfield, Illinois, outside Chicago. The company began in 1931, founded by Dr. Don Baxter, as a manufacturer and distributor of intravenous solutions (Hammonds, 2002). Its product line is divided into three divisions: Bioscience, which produces vaccines and biopharmaceuticals; Medication Delivery, focusing on dispensing medications to patients; and Renal, where Baxter is the leading supplier of products assisting patients with kidney disease. At this writing, the company employs approximately 50,000 people in over 100 countries worldwide (Baxter International, n.d.).

As best as can be determined, Baxter's problems began on August 15, 2001, when two dialysis patients in Spain died within hours of receiving treatment using dialyzers produced by Althin, one of Baxter's subsidiaries. At first, these deaths, while tragic, did not receive undue attention. The patients had been elderly and ill before beginning treatment. However, within a week, a total of 11 patients died in Spain soon after using the filters. A few weeks later, 21 people died in Croatia. By mid-October, when Baxter issued a worldwide recall of the devices, the deaths of 53 people in seven countries, including 4 in the United States, were linked to the filters ("Baxter's Harry Kraemer: 'I don't golf,'" 2002; Hammonds, 2002; Peterson & Daly, 2001). Criminal investigations into Baxter's role in the deaths were opened in Spain, Sweden, and Croatia. By November, Baxter faced what it called "the worst crisis in its 80-year history" (Firn, 2001, p. 34).

Within days of the first reported deaths in Spain, Baxter began an investigation into the filters and possible causes of death and issued a recall for the lot of filters implicated in the deaths. New products were not shipped to suppliers after these deaths (Greising, 2001). On October 9, Baxter announced the results of internal tests and those of an independent group of analysts, neither of which provided conclusive evidence about why the patients died.

Yet, later that week nearly two dozen deaths in Croatia were being blamed on the devices. Renal Division president Alan Heller feared a problem with the filters. "I knew that there was too much there to be a coincidence" (Hammonds, 2002, n.p.). Immediately, a team of Baxter investigators flew to the scene. The next day, the company issued a worldwide recall for these lines of filters and a distribution hold for filters already produced. Anyone possessing these filters was asked to return them for credit, at a cost to Baxter of about $10 million (Greising, 2001; Hammonds, 2002).

Continued investigation found the presence of a perfluorohydrocarbon-based fluid in some of the dialyzers ("Baxter's A and AF series dialyzers," 2001). This fluid was used to test filters that required leak repairs. Although the fluid was supposed to be removed from filters before shipping, dialyzers from the Romney Plant in Sweden had left the plant containing trace amounts of the fluid. While nontoxic at room temperature, when heated to body temperature in a patient's bloodstream, the liquid turned into a gas, causing fatal pulmonary embolisms. By early November, Baxter's internal tests indicated that the fluid in the filters caused the deaths. Baxter CEO Harry Kraemer decided to permanently discontinue making the filters and close the Romney Plant as well as another Althin plant in Florida, taking a charge of $189 million to cover settlements to the victims' families and close the plants. This charge lowered Baxter's 2001 net income 17% from the previous year ("Baxter's Harry Kraemer: 'I don't golf,'" 2002).

When facing attacks from the Croatian press and the victims' families, coupled with its own sense of ethics, Baxter relied on image restoration strategies to solve the problem and maintain its reputation. The following section will examine Baxter's rhetoric during this time to determine which image restoration strategies the organization chose, or declined, to use.

BAXTER'S RESPONSE TO THE DIALYZER DEATHS

When faced with a public threat to it reputation, as Baxter did in 2001, an organization must use crisis response strategies to defend itself. Much of modern crisis response theory stems from Ware and Linkugel's (1973) discussion of the apologetic genre. These authors argue that *apologia,* or speeches of apology, occur during "the questioning of a person's *moral nature, motives, or reputation*" (p. 274, emphasis in the original). They delineate these types of ethical questions from mere attacks on an individual's policies. Over time, other theorists have added to Ware and Linkugel's typology.

Apologia, Benoit's (1995, 1997) extensions of it, and Coombs's (2000) adjustment of the categories, need not be limited to individuals speaking to clear their reputations of allegations of moral wrongdoing. McMillan (1986) posits that while organizations lack human attributes such as thinking, abstracting, and feeling, "there is a social presence about an organization to which it is possible to assign definite traits and qualities that are readily verifiable" (p. 22). These traits are revealed through symbol use, which "presents an image of the organization that its constituents have come to know and recognize" (p. 22). This image, just like an individual's face or reputation, can be attacked and is vigorously defended. Benoit and Brinson (1994) comment:

> There can be no doubt that government agencies, corporations, and other bodies are as concerned

as individuals with their image or reputation, and for good reason. Since the early 1970s, organizations have become more aware of their responsibility for contributing to society in economic, social, environmental, and political ways. (p. 76)

Benoit (1995) argues that while individuals and organizations may use different image restoration strategies, use different combinations of strategies, or expend different amounts of resources on the strategies, "the basic options are the same for both individual and corporate image repair efforts" (p. 177). The following sections will examine both the crisis response strategies that Baxter chose to use and the strategies it rejected when purifying its image in the aftermath of the dialyzer deaths.

Crisis Response Strategies Baxter Used

Baxter International was forced to choose from a variety of crisis response strategies to explain both the dialyzer crisis itself and its actions during it. In this situation, Baxter selected two strategies from the category of crisis response strategies designed to reduce the perceived offensiveness of the event (Benoit, 1997; Benoit & Czerwinski, 1997). While these strategies accept responsibility for the event, they attempt to convince audience members that the event was not as serious as originally thought. Specifically, Baxter used the strategies of compensation and corrective action to purify an image polluted by patient deaths.

The first of these strategies, *compensation,* offers the victims some form of reparation to repay them for the offensive action (Benoit & Czerwinski, 1997). This strategy hopes that "offering to compensate the injured party may function to reduce the act's offensiveness, and the damage to the accused's image" (Benoit & Brinson, 1994, p. 77). Compensation attempts to right a wrong by providing restitution for the victims' loss.

Baxter immediately pledged to compensate the victims' families for the deaths of their loved ones. Once the problem with the fluid came to light, Baxter immediately took a charge to earnings, in part to pay settlements to the families of patients who died. As early as November, a Baxter spokesperson was quoted as saying, "Baxter will compensate those families affected by this incident" (Japsen, 2001a, n.p.).

By the end of 2001, Baxter had made good on this promise, settling with the families of Spanish victims for approximately $292,000 apiece (Daly, 2001). An attorney representing some of these victims' families also applauded Baxter's actions, saying,

> We feel that the settlement each family reached with Baxter is fair and reasonable. Baxter has treated the families with great respect during this unusually difficult time. The families are comforted in knowing that Baxter continues looking into the science surrounding these tragic events to ensure it will never happen again. (Baxter International Inc., 2001, n.p.)

Baxter refused to release the terms of this settlement, or the settlement it made with the Croatian victims. The only lawsuit involving an American victim had also settled. The plaintiff's attorney in this case said that Baxter "behaved responsibly and appropriately" (Hammonds, 2002, n.p.). Plaintiffs' lawyers in these cases were satisfied with the compensation Baxter offered.

While monetary settlements in product liability suits are nothing new, Baxter's statements surrounding these settlements were. Baxter chairman and CEO, Harry Kraemer, commented in the November 28, 2001, release announcing the Spanish settlement:

> Our goal is to do the right thing. While nothing we do will replace the loss these families have experienced, we understand their need to bring closure to this tragedy. Our hope is that this settlement helps to minimize the distress to

the families involved. (Baxter International, 2001d, n.p.)[2]

This statement recognizes that while compensation is a relatively weak strategy in situations where people are killed, as it cannot return to the situation as it existed before the offensive act, it nonetheless provides some respite to those affected by the offensive act.

Another strategy accused individuals and organizations may use is *corrective action,* which occurs when the "accused promises to correct the problem" when faced with threats to their image (Benoit & Czerwinski, 1997, p. 44). This strategy can take two forms: (1) the accused attempts to return the situation to the state it was in before the offensive action, or (2) the accused takes steps to prevent the offensive action from recurring. Benoit and Czerwinski (1997) differentiate this strategy from compensation, arguing, "Unlike compensation, which seeks to pay for a problem, corrective action seeks to prevent or correct it" (p. 77). Since Baxter could not return the patients who were killed by the defective dialyzers to life, it used the second set of corrective action strategies to convince its audience that no other patients would be injured by the dialyzers.

Throughout the entire crisis, from the first press release issued following the Croatian deaths to the recent retrospective articles on the crisis published by the business press, Baxter officials have emphasized the process aspect of their investigations and their attempts to prevent future deaths, not only for their own customers but also for their competitors. For instance, the October 15, 2001, release about the Croatian deaths stresses how Baxter's concern for safety drives its actions:

> All testing by Baxter, as well as independent testing by TÜV Product Service, has continued to demonstrate the safety of these dialyzers. Nevertheless, in an abundance of caution, Baxter has put a global hold on distribution of this series of dialyzers and is advising customers

worldwide to temporarily discontinue use, pending the evaluation by an expert commission. Baxter will work with customers to find suitable alternative dialyzers to use in the interim. (Baxter International, 2001a, n.p.)

This quotation talks about how Baxter, in the absence of compelling evidence, voluntarily asked its customers to stop using its products, and switch to those of its competitors, until the original dialyzers can be proven safe. This strategy sought to protect Baxter's patients at its own expense. Rarely will organizations voluntarily help their customers shift to competitors' products.

Baxter also aided its competition by informing them of the reason for the deaths. After the dialyzer crisis, Baxter not only explained its investigation and findings to the Food and Drug Administration and regulatory agencies in the affected countries, but also apprised 3M, the manufacturer of the fluid left in the filters, and rival competitors that could use the same manufacturing process that could leave them vulnerable to the same problems (Hammonds, 2002). Not only did Baxter take steps to ensure that a similar crisis never affected them again, they also attempted to keep a related problem from affecting their competitors.

Yet, Baxter went one step further, ceasing production of the entire line of filters implicated in the deaths. Baxter CEO Harry Kraemer commented in a November 5 press release that

> We are greatly saddened by the patient deaths and I would like to extend my personal sympathies to family members of those patients. We have a responsibility to make public our findings immediately and take swift action, even though confirmatory studies remain under way. . . . While a small number of our A and AF dialyzers appear to have played a role in some of these tragic events, we believe there remain substantive gaps in information about the facts associated with many of the patient deaths. Therefore, we have decided that in the interest of patient safety, the most prudent course of

action is to permanently cease manufacturing these dialyzers. (Baxter, 2001b, n.p.)

While some industry analysts considered closing the plants "overkill" (Birchard, 2002, p. 38), Baxter's emphasis on safety and on keeping the problem from recurring required that the filters be discontinued. Kraemer stated, when asked if the filters could have been produced safely, "Were we 100% confident? . . . No. We didn't know" (Hammonds, 2002, n.p.). One of the lead investigators in Spain and Croatia summed up Baxter's investigation this way: "This made us second-guess systems that we'd used for 20 years and that had always worked." Another investigator concluded, "What we know for sure is, this problem will never happen again" (Hammonds, 2002, n.p.). While they may never understand why the problem arose when it did, they took steps to prevent its recurrence, which is a clear example of corrective action. In this case, Baxter jettisoned a product that accounted for 30% of its dialyzer sales, and the $20 million in revenue it brought in, which likely could have been salvaged, to protect its customers.

Another way Baxter used the strategy of corrective action involved the extent of the investigation it pursued into the problems. As one of Baxter's investigators explained in the October 15 release, "Patient safety is our highest priority. . . . That is why we feel it is critical that all aspects of the hemodialysis treatment be thoroughly investigated" (Baxter, 2001a, n.p.). Although earlier tests had exonerated the filters, Baxter continued to investigate its products in an effort to prevent the problem from recurring. In the November 5 letter to customers, Baxter also emphasized the importance of safety, and how it used its investigation to guarantee it:

> Given our utmost concern for patient safety, we continued our intensive investigation, even after exhausting all standard internationally recognized safety and toxicity tests. We diligently

pursued every potential lead based on the facts available to us and even began pursuing other less obvious courses of investigation in search of what could be the cause of the unexplained deaths. (Baxter International, 2001c, n.p.)

The investigative process Baxter used to find the cause of the problem and prevent future instances was so thorough that it continued the investigation past the limits normally imposed on organizations.

When discussing the dialyzer crisis with the media, Baxter decided to use strategies aimed at reducing the offensiveness of the event—compensation and corrective action. However, the strategies Baxter decided to use were not the only interesting decisions it made. Equally important are the strategies the company decided *not* to use.

Crisis Response Strategies Baxter Did Not Use

During its crisis response rhetoric, Baxter chose not to use a variety of tempting and common strategies. At no time did Baxter deny either that the dialyzers were responsible for the patient deaths or claim that other actors could have contributed to the crisis. Both of the strategies fall within a category of strategies that Benoit (1997) labels *denial.* This category is divided into two separate strategies: *simple denial,* where the "firm may deny that the act has occurred, that the firm performed the act, or that the act was harmful to anyone" (p. 179); and *shift the blame,* which argues "that another person or organization is actually responsible for the offensive act" (p. 180).

Despite plausible arguments, Baxter refused to engage in the strategy of shifting blame. They could easily have blamed 3M, who made the fluid used in testing the filters; or Althin, the filters' producer, which Baxter had acquired the March before the crisis began.

They also did not blame Croatian and Spanish officials who opted not to cooperate with the investigation; Baxter never received the Croatian filters for testing (Greising, 2001). Baxter refused to use these strategies, because as Kraemer stated, "If you live in a world of let's find somebody to blame, then you're into a Ford-Firestone thing.... The reality of it is, we're responsible" (Greising, 2001, n.p.). In taking responsibility for the incidents, Baxter limited itself to strategies that would reduce the offensiveness of the original act (compensation) and attempt to prevent future problems (corrective action).

In sum, Baxter used corrective action and compensation to rebuild its image both during and after the dialyzer crisis. Equally as important are the available strategies it decided not to use. In accepting responsibility for this event, Baxter declined to shift the blame to 3M, maker of the fluid found in the dialyzers, or Althin's original management. After evaluating these strategies, this paper will examine how the circumstances surrounding the crisis and Baxter's responses to it helped the company avoid the withering public scrutiny common to many fatal-product liability cases.

HOW BAXTER AVOIDED NEGATIVE MEDIA COVERAGE

Most of the image restoration cases researchers study involve widely publicized events where an organization faces a serious threat to its reputation, if not its continued existence (Benoit & Brinson, 1994; Benoit & Czerwinski, 1997; Boyd, 2001; Sellnow, 1993; Sellnow & Ulmer, 1995; Sellnow, Ulmer, & Snider, 1998). However, the organizations would, in most if not all of the cases, have considered that their crisis responses were more successful had they been able to limit the media coverage of the events in the first place. Baxter reached this goal of avoiding media coverage of the dialyzer crisis through a combination of its situation and its use of crisis response strategies.

Several situational variables prevented the media from paying close attention to this situation. Early in the crisis, the deaths occurred overseas—the first cluster of deaths took place in Spain. By the time the filters were recalled in mid-October, all but four of the deaths had taken place outside the United States. Under the best of circumstances, American media sources subscribe to the "all news is local news" motto and lavish attention on stories occurring in the United States or that affect large numbers of Americans. The four American deaths, two each in Texas and Nebraska, were not enough to catch the press's attention.

Part of the reason the American news media did not spend much time or ink on the Baxter case was due to other news stories. Less than one month after the first death on August 15, 2001, the World Trade Center attacks consumed the media's, and much of the news-consuming public's, attention. Fifty-three deaths caused by medical devices suddenly seemed less important, by comparison. By the time the media returned to business news, Baxter had completed its investigation, accepted responsibility, and begun settlements with victims. There was little left to report.

As well as paling beside the September 11, 2001, tragedies, Baxter also paled beside the size and scope of the domestic corporate scandals making headlines. The Enron, Adelphia, Global Crossing, Anderson, and WorldCom scandals had a greater impact on the pocketbooks and consciousness of the American public. Hence, the media devoted more attention to the larger business stories.

However, Baxter's successful navigation of the crisis cannot be credited entirely to the media's divided attentions. Its investors, and certainly its employees, paid close attention to the crisis. Baxter's strategic choices, in many ways, kept the story from escalating. The speed of Baxter's response and its reliance on

corrective action helped it recover from the crisis. Benoit and Brinson (1994) highlight the importance of a speedy response to crisis situations. In Baxter's case, the speed with which it began the investigation, issued the hold, and ordered the recall may have saved more lives and limited the corporation's potential liability: "They didn't look like they were trying to hide anything. . . . The recall was last month . . . and that is moving fairly quickly for an international company" (Japsen, 2001a, n.p.). Rather than waiting for conclusive evidence of responsibility from an independent agency, which they never received, and risking more deaths in the meantime, Baxter took immediate steps to solve the problem and protect patients.

In moving quickly, Baxter implemented corrective actions designed to prevent future occurrences of the dialyzer contamination. Closing the plant and discontinuing the production of an entire line of products were actions designed to "correct the problem" (Benoit, 1997, p. 181). However, corrective action can also leave an organization vulnerable to lawsuits. Chicago-area attorneys commented that Baxter "has sort of confessed" and this action "makes it [litigation] easier, but also brings in more competing firms" (Klein, 2001, n.p.). Benoit (1997) noticed this contradiction between image restoration and limiting liability when he stated, "image restoration concerns may, admittedly, conflict with a desire to avoid lawsuits, and the firm must decide whether it is more important to restore its image or avoid litigation" (pp. 183–184). Sellnow, Ulmer, and Snider (1998) admit, "we do [not] assume that corrective action should be taken without consideration of the legal consequences" (p. 64). Despite this concern, Baxter seems to have settled the lawsuits related to this case in spite of its early acceptance of responsibility.

Benoit (1997) affirms that accepting responsibility quickly when at fault is "morally the correct thing to do" (p. 184). Without concern for litigation, Baxter used this strategy, even in the absence of conclusive evidence, and won admirers for its crisis management. Lawsuits were settled, stock prices went up soon after the crisis, renal product sales rose, and members of the public familiar with the situation were impressed by Baxter's performance. Hammonds (2002) commented, "The message to CEOs: Investors like honesty, including public apologies. (Kraemer visited New York to apologize in person to the president of Croatia.) So, it turns out, do employees" (n.p.). Owning up to a problem and taking quick action to lessen its impact and prevent its recurrence allowed Baxter International to defuse a potentially devastating crisis and emerge stronger than ever.

AFTERMATH OF DIALYZER CRISIS

Despite facing potential legal liability and damage to its reputation, in the short term Baxter seemed to have weathered the storm of the dialyzer crisis successfully. Both the finances and the prestige of the organization improved after the crisis, and Baxter's response to it, became public. This section will examine Baxter's reputation after the crisis by studying its stock price and its standing in the medical supply community.

In one of the most widely recognized measures of organizational success, stock price, Baxter initially suffered a loss as news of the charge against earnings and potential lawsuits rattled investors. However, as the company began to settle the lawsuits and amid assurances that the initial charge against earnings would cover any potential liability, stock prices began to rebound (Japsen, 2001b). By the end of 2001, Baxter's stock had risen 23% while its companions on the Standard and Poor's health care index dropped 13% ("Baxter's Harry Kraemer: 'I don't golf,'" 2002). The dialyzer crisis did not prevent Baxter from outperforming similar health care stocks operating in the same economic environment.

Stock prices jumped and Baxter's standing in the medical community scored its greatest coup in late November 2001, when the Bush administration awarded the company, in a joint contract with Acambis PLC, the $428 million contract to be the federal government's sole provider of 155 million doses of smallpox vaccine. This contract not only provided a financial boon for the organization, but also a rhetorical shot in the arm, as Baxter was selected over pharmaceutical giants Merck and GlaxoSmithKline. Baxter was moving up in the pharmaceutical market and closer to its goal of becoming a worldwide producer with $1 billion in annual sales by the end of the decade (Japsen, 2001b).

Despite the crisis, and the loss of a $20 million product, Baxter remained number one worldwide in renal care products with sales of $1.94 billion ("Baxter's Harry Kraemer: 'I don't golf,'" 2002). Not only did Baxter rise above other renal care providers, it was also recognized by industry publications for ethical behavior. For instance, *Business Ethics* awarded the company spots on its list of "100 Best Corporate Citizens" in 2001 and 2002. Baxter's environmental policies also earned it head-of-the-class honors in service to the environment.

However, recent years have been more difficult for Baxter. It has repeatedly lowered and often fallen short of its earning projections, eliminated thousands of positions, and faced tumbling stock prices. In mid-March 2003, the Justice Department subpoenaed Baxter's records about the dialyzer crisis, possibly reopening the issue. These problems led Kraemer to resign his position as chairman and CEO in January of 2004 (Japsen & Miller, 2004). While Baxter initially ended the dialyzer crisis with its reputation intact, these later financial problems indicate that organizations cannot rest on past ethical behavior, but must constantly continue to update and revise their practices to remain viable.

NOTES

1. The information for this case came from publicly accessible news accounts, press releases, statements available on Baxter International's Web site, and published statements from its officers.

2. This and other releases from Baxter International were accessed from the organization's Web site, www .baxter.com. While these documents are no longer available online, the author has retained copies and would be happy to share them as requested.

REFERENCES

Baxter International. (2001a, October 15). *Baxter urges comprehensive scientific analysis of hemodialysis treatment safety* [Press Release]. Retrieved November 11, 2002, from www.baxter.com/utilities/news/releases/2001/ 10–15.croatia.html

Baxter International. (2001b, November 5). *Following extensive investigation, Baxter identifies probable cause of recent hemodialysis patient deaths* [Press Release]. Retrieved November 11, 2002, from www.baxter.com/utilities/ news/releases/2001/11–05dialyzer.html

Baxter International. (2001c, November 5). *Stop manufacture letter.* Retrieved November 7, 2001, from www.baxter.com

Baxter International. (2001d, November 28). *Baxter announces agreement with families affected by recent hemodialysis deaths in Spain* [Press Release]. Retrieved November 11, 2002, from www.baxter.com/utilities/ news/releases/2001/11–28spsettlement.html

Baxter International. (n.d.). *Corporate overview.* Retrieved March 29, 2004, from http://www.baxter.com/about_ baxter/company_profile/sub/corporate_overview. html

Baxter International Inc. (2001, November 29). Agreement with families affected by recent hemodialysis deaths—in Spain. *Market News Publishing.* Retrieved July 10, 2005, from General Business File ASAP database.

Baxter's A and AF series dialyzers linked to over 50 deaths. (2001, Fall). *Journal of Clinical Engineering*, pp. 241–242.

Baxter's Harry Kraemer: "I don't golf." (2002, March 28). *Business Week Online.* Retrieved March 29 2002, from www.businessweek. com.

Benoit, W. L. (1995). *Accounts, excuses, and apologies: A theory of image restoration strategies.* Albany: State University of New York Press.

Benoit, W. L. (1997). Image repair discourse and crisis communication. *Public Relations Review, 23*(2), 177–186.

Benoit, W. L., & Brinson, S. L. (1994). AT&T: Apologies are not enough. *Communication Quarterly, 42*(1), 75–89.

Benoit, W. L., & Czerwinski, A. (1997). A critical analysis of USAir's image repair discourse. *Business Communication Quarterly, 60*(3), 38–57.

Birchard, B. (2002, February). Citizen Kraemer. *Chief Executive*, pp. 34–38.

Boyd, J. (2001). The rhetoric of arrogance: The public relations response of the Standard Oil Trust. *Public Relations Review, 27*, 163–178.

Coombs, T. W. (2000). Designing post-crisis messages: Lessons for crisis response strategies. *Review of Business*, pp. 37–41.

Daly, E. (2001, November 29). Baxter settles dialysis deaths in Spain. *New York Times*, p. C4. Retrieved January 14, 2002, from the InfoTrac Custom Newspapers Database.

Firn, D. (2001, November 6). Baxter faces crisis over blood filters. *The Financial Times.* Retrieved November 11, 2002, from the InfoTrac Expanded Academic Index.

Greising, D. (2001, November 7). Baxter gets grip on crisis, responsibility. *Chicago Tribune.* Retrieved November 7, 2001, from http://chicagotribune.com

Hammonds, K. H. (2002, November). Harry Kraemer's moment of truth. *Fast Company.* Retrieved November 6, 2002, from www.fastcompany.com

Japsen, B. (2001a, November 6). Baxter links its filters to deaths. *Chicago Tribune.* Retrieved November 7, 2001, from http://chicagotribune.com

Japsen, B. (2001b, November 30). Smallpox pact may invigorate Baxter. *Chicago Tribune.* Retrieved November 7, 2001, from http://chicagotribune.com

Japsen, B., & Miller, J. P. (2004, January 27). Chief stepping down at Baxter. *Chicago Tribune.* Retrieved March 22, 2004, from http://chicagotribune.com

Klein, S. A. (2001, November 26). Legal eagles eye wounded Baxter; lawyers scouring globe to find more filter victims. *Crain's Chicago Business*, p. 4. Retrieved November 11, 2002, from the InfoTrac Expanded Academic Index.

McMillan, J. J. (1986). In search of the organizational persona: A rationale for studying organizations rhetorically. In L. Thayer (Ed.), *Organization communication: Emerging perspectives I* (pp. 21–45). Norwood, NJ: Ablex.

Peterson, M., & Daly, E. (2001, November 21). Baxter finds possible link in 53 deaths. *New York Times.* Retrieved November 7, 2001, from http://nytimes.com

Sellnow, T. L. (1993). Scientific argument in organizational crisis situations: The case of Exxon. *Argumentation and Advocacy, 30*(1), 28–43. Retrieved November 15, 2002, from the InfoTrac Expanded Academic Index.

Sellnow, T. L., & Ulmer, R. R. (1995). Ambiguous argument as advocacy in organizational crisis communication. *Argumentation and Advocacy, 31*(3), 138–151.

Sellnow, T. L., Ulmer, R. R., & Snider, M. (1998). The compatibility of corrective action in organizational crisis communication. *Communication Quarterly, 46*(1), 60–74.

Ware, B. L., & Linkugel, W. A. (1973). They spoke in defense of themselves: On the generic criticism of the apologia. *The Quarterly Journal of Speech, 59*, 273–283.

Case Study

Shoe Sales

Thomas L. Carson

The following case is taken from a paper that I received from a student. I am using this case with the student's permission. The student did not want me to use his/her name. I have made some minor stylistic and grammatical corrections, but otherwise, the description of this case is taken verbatim from the student's paper.

My introduction to retail sales began at the age of seventeen in a small "stocks-to-suits" men's store. The old-timers I trained under endowed me with several pearls of wisdom that are universal to success in any sales: "don't make friends, make money," and "first you get their confidence, then you get their trust, then you get their money." In order to achieve the objective of making money the tactics employed are often morally questionable. Two examples may help to illustrate the type of tactics I am considering.

1. My present position as a women's shoe salesman often necessitates the use of lying and deception in order to make a sale. For example, it is useful to develop a sense of urgency or *need* on the part of the customer to buy a particular shoe. (It is easier to make the sale if they *need* a shoe rather than simply *want* it.) Once a customer selects a specific shoe the salesman creates the urgency by stating, with much false sincerity and steady eye contact, "Ooh, that may be a tough one, there are only a few left." In fact, there may be several dozen in stock and in all sizes. It is now a simple matter to bring out other comparable shoes, all of a slightly higher price or those which management wants to "blow out," and extol their benefits. If the customer balks, or is visibly upset, a simple, "Let me double check," a short delay in the stock room, and the production of the first shoe, is almost a guarantee of a sale. Telling the truth, that there are several dozen in stock, will eliminate any sense of urgency on the part of the customer; she may decide to come back after her next paycheck as you have plenty. She may never come back, or if she does you may not be there, or she may wind up with another salesman. They waste your time, and on commission time *is* money.

2. Suppose that a customer *wants* a shoe that you do not have in *her* size. In this scenario she needs a size 7, but you only have a 6½ and a 7½. There are two ways to proceed, either of which achieves the same result, a successful sale. Since most women understate their size, I will only explain how to put them into the half size up (7½). While in the stock room lift up the inner sole of the 7½ and insert a foam "tap," apply a small amount of glue to the inner sole and put the inner sole back in place. This gives more cushion under the ball of the foot and takes up the extra space. Bring several shoes out including the 6½ and gimmicked 7½. Put the 6½ on them without telling her what size it is. [Since the customer asked to see a size 7, she will assume that the shoe she is trying on is a size 7.] The customer will of course say it is too tight at which point the salesman replies, "They all cut them a little differently, let's try the 7½." Put the 7½ on her, point out the mirror, and quickly box up the 6½, putting it to the side. Ask how it feels, et cetera, and close the sale. Without this deception it is almost *certain* that she will "walk" which means trouble from management and lost money.

Journal of Business Ethics 17: 725–728, 1998. Copyright © 1998, Kluwer Academic Publishers. Reprinted with permission.

Questions

1. The salesperson in this case suggests that the policies that he/she practiced were economically advantageous to him/her. ("My present position as a women's shoe salesman often *Necessitates* [my emphasis] the use of lying and deception in order to make a sale.") Should we accept this? Will he/she make more money in the long run if he/she engages in such practices? If the answer to this question is "yes," what, if anything, could store owners do to alter these incentives for engaging in lying and/or deception?

2. Is the salesperson lying in the two scenarios described here?
3. Assuming that the answer to question #2 is "yes," is the economic benefit to the salesperson sufficient to justify lying?
4. Is the customer harmed or likely to be harmed in either of the two examples? If so, how? Would you knowingly purchase a pair of shoes that was a half size too large and fitted with a foam rubber tap? [These taps become flattened out rather quickly.]

Case Study

The Job Negotiation

Michael A. Santoro

You are in the final stages of a job negotiation. You would be willing to take the job for $90,000, but of course you would like to make more if you can. Which (any or all) of these tactics would you use to get a higher salary?

1. Say you would be willing to take the job for $110,000
2. Say you wouldn't take the job for less than $110,000
3. Say you have an offer for $110,000 when you really don't have any other offers.

Case Study

Volvo's Crushing Blow

Ronald M. Green

The title card reads "June 12, 1990 Austin, Texas," Visuals move between crowd shots and views of a giant pickup truck with 6-foot-high tires identified as "Bear Foot." The truck drives over a line of cars, leaving only Volvo station wagon intact. "There's one car still standing out there" says an announcer over the public address system. A voice-over adds "Apparently, not everyone appreciates the strength of a Volvo."

In October 1990, executives at Volvo and their advertising agency Scali, McCabe, Sloves were pleased. Their "Bear Foot" spots were adding a sly touch of humor to Volvo's tradition of promoting the safety and reliability of its cars. The ads, first broadcast early in the month on several cable channels, and appearing in print versions in *Forbes* and *Car & Driver*, were also drawing critical praise. In a review of car advertising. *USA Today* described the "Bear Foot" spots as one of the most effective television promotions of the 1991 model year.

But by the end of the month "Bear Foot" had turned into a nightmare for Volvo and Scali. Late in October, James Mattox, attorney general of Texas, announced that he was pressing charges against Volvo North America Corporation, the car maker's American arm. In a lawsuit, Mattox charged that the ads had been shot after production people had reinforced the Volvos and sawed through the pillars on the competing cars. The ads, he told the press, were "a hoax and a sham."

Volvo reacted quickly. Within a week of Mattox's public announcement, the firm withdrew the spots and began running corrective ads explaining its decision in 19 Texas newspapers, *USA Today*, and the *Wall Street Journal*. Volvo also agreed to reimburse the attorney general's office $316,250 for investigative costs and legal fees.

Volvo's corrective ads took the form of a letter "to all interested consumers" from Joseph L. Nicolato, company president-CEO. The letter stated that the advertising "inaccurately characterized the event as a car-crushing exhibition when in fact it was a dramatization of the actual event in Vermont."

The letter continued:

> On Oct. 30 Volvo management learned for the first time that the film production team had apparently made modifications to two of the vehicles. There were two reasons for the modifications, first, to enable the filming to be done without threatening the safety of the production crew, and second, to allow the demonstration Volvo to withstand the number of runs by the "monster truck" required for filming.

As Volvo issued its statement it was still unclear who had authorized the modifications. Perretti Productions, New York, had handled production of the commercial for Scali but Jim Perretti, the spot's director, was unavailable for comment.

In a separate statement to the press, Volvo's manager of public relations, Bob Austin, said that an investigation was under way to determine what caused the mistake. He explained that Milt Gravatt, the importer's marketing services manager, had been in Austin during the shoot but had not been on site at every moment during the 15 to 18 hours over two days it took to film the commercial.

"[Mr. Gravatt] assured us he did not see anything improper," said Austin. "We normally go down to a shoot to be nearby in case we can do anything to facilitate the production, but our basic attitude is to let the professionals do it. At this point, it is unclear what happened when, and who authorized it."

Executives at Scali expressed confusion and dismay. Agency chairman-CEO Marvin Sloves told reporters, "The agency never authorized any alterations of any vehicles at the shoot. We knew of no alterations made to create any misleading impression. I am just overwhelmed and shocked by the whole thing."

Sloves insisted that the agency creative team on site had not seen the alterations being made. "They say, and I believe them, that we had no idea they were doing anything to alter the cars to create a misleading impression." Although the spot itself was a dramatization, Sloves added, "This was a real live thing we had documentation for."

Stephanie Frawley, a development specialist at the Arthritis Foundation of Vermont, supported the claim that the ads were based on fact. The Foundation, she said, had sponsored a "monster truck" event at the fairgrounds in Essex, Vermont, two years earlier and of the four cars that participated, a Volvo was the only one that was not crushed. From other people who were there, and from photos we have it was obvious. She said, "Volvo is telling the truth."

Specialists in advertising law disagreed over the legal norms relevant to the "Bear Foot" spots. Felix Kent, an advertising lawyer with Hall, Dickler, Lawler, Kent & Friednan, said that a U.S. Supreme Court decision in the 1970s clearly established that demonstration ads could not use any form of mock-ups or deception. But Rick Kunit, a partner at Frankfurt, Garbus, Klein & Selz, said that "for the past 10 years or so we've been able to be fairly free about not putting the dramatization and recreation and similar supers basically because a lot of the time you get enough in the context of the commercial that people know it's a dramatization."

As November wore on, Volvo weighed the course of its future advertising. Speaking for the company, Bob Austin insisted that Volvo had no intention of backing off from its emphasis on safety which has been featured in advertising virtually since the company entered the U.S. market in 1956. "Volvo was built around a solid set of basic values safety, reliability, and longevity," Austin said. "We will have to allow the public to decide whether they believe in Volvo."

As for Scali's future on the $40 million account, "We will establish what happened and take appropriate corrective action," said Austin, who acknowledged that some outsiders had suggested Volvo fire the agency.

"Any conversation of that type would be premature," Austin added. "We have resisted the temptation to throw a body out there for the media."

Some advertising industry professionals saw major damage to the industry in the "Bear Foot" incident. DeWitt Helm, president of the Association of National Advertisers, said the episode "feeds the fuel of activists and overly zealous regulators. It's giving all advertising and business a tarnish and black eye we don't deserve."

But not every consumer agreed. Donna Gates, a Chicago public relations executive, said the flap over the ads would not have changed her mind about the car. "As a Volvo owner, I think it's a wonderful car," she said. "It feels like a little tank. I feel very safe in it."

On November 18, 1990, in the wake of a highly publicized scandal involving its "Bear Foot" commercial, Scali, McCabe, Sloves ended a twenty-three-year relationship by resigning the Volvo account. Loss of its oldest, largest flagship account was estimated to cost the agency $40 million in revenues and to require the layoff of thirty-five to fifty staffers.

"I'm devastated by it," said Marvin Sloves, the chairman and chief executive of the agency he had founded twenty-three years earlier with Sam Scali and Ed McCabe. Resigning the account, he said, "was the right thing to do. The executives at Volvo deserve a chance to put this thing behind them."

According to William Hoover, the senior vice-president of marketing for Volvo Cars of North America, an investigation showed that the production company hired by Scali apparently knew the demonstration was a fake. "The agency had to accept responsibility and the only thing to do was to resign," said Hoover.

Despite the resignation, questions remained over who had authorized and who knew of the product rigging that took place at the production shoot June 12 in Austin.

In an interview in October, before Volvo had been contacted by the Texas attorney general's office, Dean Stefanides, Scali executive vice-president and group creative director, explained that the idea for the spot initially came from an account executive at the agency who learned from a friend that a real monster truck exhibition in Vermont had used a Volvo in a lineup of other cars. In that event, the Volvo was the only car uncrushed. Engineering personnel at Volvo confirmed that Volvo's roof supports were theoretically strong enough to sustain the 11,000 pound weight of a monster truck.

"We looked into it and substantiated it. We thought the Volvo audience would find it funny or campy, even though they might not go to those events," Stefanides said. He added that it was simply a fresh and creative way to continue Volvo's long-running safety demonstration spots. Scali subsequently hired Perretti Productions to oversee production of the commercial.

Perretti, in turn, handed the re-creation of the Vermont event to International Productions, a company based in Phoenix, Arizona, that specializes in the promotion and production of motor sport events.

Lesse Spindler, promotion director of International Productions, said that his company did not have any advertising responsibility during the shoot. Our understanding was that we were to recreate that event. The issue of bracing the Volvos came up during the contract negotiation stage with Perretti said Spindler, but "they elected not to because of the cost factor."

According to Spindler, the first of the three Volvos used in the shoot was not reinforced and was crushed early in the day by the monster truck. Once that car was crushed, work to brace the remaining two Volvos immediately got under way. Wooden supports were added to the second Volvo and the third was reinforced with steel. "The decision was also made to weaken the structures of competing cars by cutting their roof supports.

Those at the scene had included Jim Perretti; John Slaven; Scali executive vice-president and management representative; Dean Stefanides; and Larry Hempel, another Scali executive vice-president and group creative director. An initial Volvo inquiry revealed that a Volvo management representative, Milt Gravait, had been at the site from early morning until about 6:30 P.M. At that point, the shooting was declared a wrap and Volvo and top Scali management left the scene. Apparently some filming continued after that using one or more modified Volvos.

Sources reported that before the airing of the spots, Scali submitted to the TV networks a producer's report vouching for the accuracy of the commercial and stating that no special effects or techniques had been used.

Whatever its causes, the episode marked a serious setback for an agency whose creativity had long been the envy of others in the industry. Over the years, Scali had put Perdue and its foul-faced chairman on the map and had held kosher Hebrew National franks accountable to "a higher authority."

Mark Messing, a Scali senior vice-president, noted that the agency could have avoided the fiasco by labeling the ad a "reenactment."

"Rookie error," he said.

The Ad-Cult and Marketing

Advertising and marketing give rise to some of the most complex and interesting issues in business ethics. What ethical boundaries should constrain a sales pitch? A marketing campaign?

When it comes to advertising, the cry of business is often *caveat emptor*—"let the buyer beware." It is often argued that the job of business is to sell its products, and the job of consumers is to spend their money wisely. Short of an outright false-hood or flagrant deception, business should do whatever it can to attract consumers' dollars, especially in a competitive marketplace.

Critics of advertising have suggested that it is nothing more than veiled psychological warfare waged against the buying public. That is, the public are manipulated, cajoled, coerced, and otherwise bamboozled into buying goods and services they would not buy were the portrayal accurate and informative—especially without the emotional and psychological ploys so often used in advertising. A proper ethical evaluation of advertising requires caution, subtlety, and a highly nuanced analysis. This is true with respect not only to what is being presented but also to what is omitted.

In addition, ethics concerns itself with the intended target of advertising—the people to whom these ads are intended to appeal. Ethicists often argue that we need to take into account the intended audience of the advertisement, as well as the nature of the product being advertised. Most would agree that selling designer jeans to an adult audience is ethically different, for example, from selling toys to children. But whether it is also ethically different from selling extrapotent alcoholic beverages to the working poor is a matter of great controversy, pitting respect for consumer autonomy against what some see as justified paternalism.

The cases and essays in this section subject marketing and advertising to close ethical scrutiny. "Is Marketing Ethics an Oxymoron?" asks whether marketers should be ambivalent about what they do when, for example, their efforts persuade an already overweight man to eat another Big Mac. "The Dependence Effect" asks what the costs are of satisfying wants that do not originate in the person but are contrived in her through marketing. "Everquest®: Entertainment or Addiction?" raises the question of whether online game marketers ought to consider the effects of gaming on those who are psychologically or emotionally impaired. "Vioxx" asks the reader to consider how ongoing scientific research and new findings should bear on a pharmaceutical company's efforts to market a drug. Is it morally permissible to spin the science? "Uptown, Dakota, and PowerMaster" considers the ethical implications of marketing specific tobacco and alcoholic beverage products to minority and low-income demographics that are statistically more likely to suffer from the deleterious health effects of tobacco and alcohol consumption. "The Case of the Contested Firearms" raises interesting issues regarding the sale, marketing, and distribution of firearms. Does a firearms manufacturer bear responsibility for marketing guns in a way that enhances their availability to criminals?

Essay

Is Marketing Ethics an Oxymoron?

Philip Kotler

Every profession and business has to wrestle with ethical questions. The recent wave of business scandals over inaccurate reporting of sales and profits and excessive pay and privileges for top executives has brought questions of business ethics to the fore. And lawyers have been continuously accused of "ambulance chasing," jury manipulation, and inflated fees, leaving the plaintiffs with much less than called for in the judgment. Physicians have been known to recommend certain drugs as more effective while receiving support from pharmaceutical companies.

Marketers are not immune from facing a whole set of ethical issues. For evidence, look to Howard Bowen's classic questions from his 1953 book, *Social Responsibilities of the Businessman*:

"Should he conduct selling in ways that intrude on the privacy of people, for example, by door-to-door selling? Should he use methods involving ballyhoo, chances, prizes, hawking, and other tactics which are at least of doubtful good taste? Should he employ 'high pressure' tactics in persuading people to buy?

Should he try to hasten the obsolescence of goods by bringing out an endless succession of new models and new styles? Should he appeal to and attempt to strengthen the motives of materialism, invidious consumption, and keeping up with the Joneses?" (Also see Smith, N. Craig and Elizabeth Cooper-Martin (1997), "Ethics and Target Marketing: The Role of Product Harm and Consumer Vulnerability," *Journal of Marketing*, July, 1–20.)

The issues raised are complicated. Drawing a clear line between normal marketing practice and unethical behavior isn't easy. Yet it's important for marketing scholars and those interested in public policy to raise questions about practices that they may normally endorse but which may not coincide with the public interest.

We will examine the central axiom of marketing: Companies that satisfy their target customers will perform better than those that don't. Companies that satisfy customers can expect repeat business; those that don't will get only one-time sales. Steady profits come from holding on to customers, satisfying

---

Philip Kotler is S.C. Johnson and Son Distinguished Professor of International Marketing, Kellogg School of Management, Northwestern University. He may be reached at pkotler@nwu.edu.

them, and selling them more goods and services.

This axiom is the essence of the well-known marketing concept. It reduces to the formula "Give the customer what he wants." This sounds reasonable on the surface. But notice that it carries an implied corollary: "Don't judge what the customer wants."

Marketers have been, or should be, a little uneasy about this corollary. It raises two public interest concerns: (1) What if the customer wants something that isn't good for him or her? (2) What if the product or service, while good for the customer, isn't good for society or other groups?

When it comes to the first question, what are some products that some customers desire that might not be good for them? These would be products that can potentially harm their health, safety, or well-being. Tobacco and hard drugs such as cocaine, LSD, or ecstasy immediately come to mind.

As for the second question, examples of products or services that some customers desire that may not be in the public's best interest include using asbestos as a building material or using lead paint indiscriminately. Other products and services where debates continue to rage as to whether they are in the public's interest include the right to own guns and other weapons, the right to have an abortion, the right to distribute hate literature, and the right to buy large gas guzzling and polluting automobiles.

We now turn to three questions of interest to marketers, businesses, and the public:

1. Given that expanding consumption is at the core of most businesses, what are the interests and behaviors of companies that make these products?

2. To what extent do these companies care about reducing the negative side effects of these products?

3. What steps can be taken to reduce the consumption of products that have questionable effects and is limited intervention warranted?

EXPANDING CONSUMPTION

Most companies will strive to enlarge their market as much as possible. A tobacco company, if unchecked, will try to get everyone who comes of age to start smoking cigarettes. Given that cigarettes are addictive, this promises the cigarette company "customers for life." Each new customer will create a 50-year profit stream for the cigarette company if the consumer continues to favor the same brand—and live long enough. Suppose a new smoker starts at the age of 13, smokes for 50 years, and dies at 63 from lung cancer. If he spends $500 a year on cigarettes, he will spend $25,000 over his lifetime. If the company's profit rate is 20%, that new customer is worth $5,000 to the company (undiscounted). It is hard to imagine a company that doesn't want to attract a customer who contributes $5,000 to its profits.

The same story describes the hard drug industry, whose products are addictive and even more expensive. The difference is that cigarette companies can operate legally but hard drug companies must operate illegally.

Other products, such as hamburgers, candy, soft drinks, and beer, are less harmful when consumed in moderation, but are addictive for some people. We hear a person saying she has a "sweet tooth." One person drinks three Coca-Colas a day, and another drinks five beers a day. Still another consumer is found who eats most of his meals at McDonald's. These are the "heavy users." Each company treasures the heavy users who account for a high proportion of the company's profits.

All said, every company has a natural drive to expand consumption of its products, leaving any negative consequences to be the result of the "free choice" of consumers. A high-level official working for Coca-Cola in Sweden said that her aim is to get people to start drinking Coca-Cola for breakfast (instead of orange juice). And McDonald's encourages customers to choose a larger hamburger, a larger order of French fries, and a larger cola drink. And these companies have some of the best marketers in the world working for them.

REDUCING SIDE EFFECTS

It would not be a natural act on the part of these companies to try to reduce or restrain consumption of their products. What company wants to reduce its profits? Usually some form of public pressure must bear on these companies before they will act.

The government has passed laws banning tobacco companies from advertising and glamorizing smoking on TV. But Philip Morris' Marlboro brand still will put out posters showing its mythical cowboy. And Marlboro will make sure that its name is mentioned in sports stadiums, art exhibits, and in labels for other products.

Tobacco companies today are treading carefully not to openly try to create smokers out of young people. They have stopped distributing free cigarettes to young people in the United States as they move their operations increasingly into China.

Beer companies have adopted a socially responsible attitude by telling people not to over-drink or drive during or after drinking. They cooperate with efforts to prevent underage people from buying beer. They are trying to behave in a socially responsible manner. They also know that, at the margin, the sales loss resulting from their "co-operation" is very slight.

McDonald's has struggled to find a way to reduce the ill effects (obesity, heart disease) of too much consumption of their products. It tried to offer a reduced-fat hamburger only to find consumers rejecting it. It has offered salads, but they weren't of good quality when originally introduced and they failed. Now it's making a second and better attempt.

LIMITED INTERVENTION

Do public interest groups or the government have the right to intervene in the free choices of individuals? This question has been endlessly debated. On one side are people who resent any intervention in their choices of products and services. In the extreme, they go by such names as libertarians, vigilantes, and "freedom lovers." They have a legitimate concern about government power and its potential abuse. Some of their views include:

- The marketer's job is to "sell more stuff." It isn't the marketer's job to save the world or make society a better place.
- The marketer's job is to produce profits for the shareholders in any legally sanctioned way.
- A high-minded socially conscious person should not be in marketing. A company shouldn't hire such a person.

On the other side are people concerned with the personal and societal costs of "unregulated consumption." They are considered do-gooders and will document that Coca-Cola delivers six teaspoons of sugar in every bottle or can. They will cite statistics on the heavy health costs of obesity, heart disease, and liver damage that are caused by failing to reduce the consumption of some of these products. These costs fall on everyone through higher medical costs and taxes. Thus, those who don't consume questionable products are still harmed through the unenlightened behavior of others.

Ultimately, the problem is one of conflict among different ethical systems. Consider the following five:

Ethical egoism. Your only obligation is to take care of yourself (Protagoras and Ayn Rand).

Government requirements. The law represents the minimal moral standards of a society (Thomas Hobbes and John Locke).

Personal virtues. Be honest, good, and caring (Plato and Aristotle).

Utilitarianism. Create the greatest good for the greatest number (Jeremy Bentham and John Stuart Mill).

Universal rules. "Act only on that maxim through which you can at the same time will that it should become a universal law" (Immanuel Kant's categorical imperative).

Clearly, people embrace different ethical viewpoints, making marketing ethics and other business issues more complex to resolve.

Let's consider the last two ethical systems insofar as they imply that some interventions are warranted. Aside from the weak gestures of companies toward self-regulation and appearing concerned, there are a range of measures that can be taken by those wishing to push their view of the public interest. They include the following six approaches:

1. *Encouraging these companies to make products safer.* Many companies have responded to public concern or social pressure to make their products safer. Tobacco companies developed filters that would reduce the chance of contracting emphysema or lung cancer. If a leaf without nicotine could give smokers the same satisfaction, they would be happy to replace the tobacco leaf. Some tobacco companies have even offered information or aids to help smokers limit their appetite for tobacco or curb it entirely.

Food and soft drink companies have reformulated many of their products to be "light," "nonfat," or "low in calories." Some beer companies have introduced nonalcoholic beer. These companies still offer their standard products but provide concerned consumers with alternatives that present less risk to their weight or health.

Auto companies have reluctantly incorporated devices designed to reduce pollution output into their automobiles. Some are even producing cars with hybrid fuel systems to further reduce harmful emissions to the air. But the auto companies still insist on putting out larger automobiles (such as Hummers) because the "public demands them."

What can we suggest to Coca-Cola and other soft drink competitors that are already offering "light" versions of their drinks? First, they should focus more on developing the bottled water side of their businesses because bottled water is healthier than sugared soft drinks. Further, they should be encouraged to add nutrients and vitamins in standard drinks so these drinks can at least deliver more health benefits, especially to those in undeveloped countries who are deprived of these nutrients and vitamins. (Coca-Cola has some brands doing this now.)

What can we suggest to McDonald's and its fast food competitors? The basic suggestion is to offer more variety in its menu. McDonald's seems to forget that, while parents bring their children to McDonald's, they themselves usually prefer to eat healthier food, not to mention want their children eating healthier foods. How about a first-class salad bar? How about moving more into the healthy sandwich business? Today more Americans are buying their meals at Subway and other sandwich shops where they feel they are getting healthier and tastier food for their dollar.

There seems to be a correlation between the amount of charity given by companies in some categories and the category's degree of "sin." Thus, McDonald's knows that over-consumption of its products can be harmful, but the company is very charitable. A cynic would say that McDonald's wants to build a bank of public goodwill to diffuse potential public criticism.

2. *Banning or restricting the sale or use of the product or service.* A community or nation will ban certain products where there is strong public support. Hard drugs are banned, although there is some debate about whether the ban should include marijuana and lighter hard drugs. There are even advocates who oppose banning hard drugs, believing that the cost of policing and criminality far exceed the cost of a moderate increase that might take place in hard drug usage. Many people today believe that the "war on drugs" can never be won and is creating more serious consequences than simply dropping the ban or helping drug addicts, as Holland and Switzerland have done.

Some products carry restrictions on their purchase or use. This is particularly true of drugs that require a doctor's prescription and certain poisons that can't be purchased without authorization. Persons buying guns must be free of a criminal record and register their gun ownership. And certain types of guns, such as machine guns, are banned or restricted.

3. *Banning or limiting advertising or promotion of the product.* Even when a product isn't banned or its purchase restricted, laws may be passed to prevent

producers from advertising or promoting the product. Gun, alcohol, and tobacco manufacturers can't advertise on TV, although they can advertise in print media such as magazines and newspapers. They can also inform and possibly promote their products online.

Manufacturers get around this by mentioning their brand name in every possible venue: sports stadiums, music concerts, and feature articles. They don't want to be forgotten in the face of a ban on promoting their products overtly.

4. *Increasing "sin" taxes to discourage consumption.* One reasonable alternative to banning a product or its promotion is to place a "sin" tax on its consumption. Thus, smokers pay hefty government taxes for cigarettes. This is supposed to have three effects when done right. First, the higher price should discourage consumption. Second, the tax revenue could be used to finance the social costs to health and safety caused by the consumption of the product. Third, some of the tax revenue could be used to counter-advertise the use of the product or support public education against its use. The last effect was enacted by California when it taxed tobacco companies and used the money to "unsell" tobacco smoking.

5. *Public education campaigns.* In the 1960s, Sweden developed a social policy to use public education to raise a nation of non-smokers and non-drinkers. Children from the first grade up were educated to understand the ill effects of tobacco and alcohol. Other countries are doing this on a less systematic and intensive basis. U.S. public schools devote parts of occasional courses to educate students against certain temptations with mixed success. Girls, not boys, in the United States seem to be more prone to taking up smoking. The reason often given by girls is that smoking curbs their appetite for food and consequently helps them avoid becoming overweight, a problem they consider more serious than lung cancer taking place 40 years later.

Sex education has become a controversial issue, when it comes to public education campaigns. The ultra-conservative camp wants to encourage total abstinence until marriage. The more liberal camp believes that students should be taught the risks of early sex and have the necessary knowledge to protect themselves. The effectiveness of both types of sex education is under debate.

6. *Social marketing campaigns.* These campaigns describe a wide variety of efforts to communicate the ill effects of certain behaviors that can harm the person, other persons, or society as a whole. These campaigns use techniques of public education, advertising and promotion, incentives, and channel development to make it as easy and attractive as possible for people to change their behavior for the better. (See Kotler, Philip, Eduardo Roberto, and Nancy Lee (2002), *Social Marketing: Improving the Quality of Life,* 2nd ed. London: Sage Publications.) Social marketing uses the tools of commercial marketing—segmentation, targeting, and positioning, and the four Ps (product, price, place, and promotion)—to achieve voluntary compliance with publicly endorsed goals. Some social marketing campaigns, such as family planning and anti-littering, have achieved moderate to high success. Other campaigns including anti-smoking, anti-drugs ("say no to drugs"), and seat belt promotion have worked well when supplemented with legal action.

SOCIAL RESPONSIBILITY AND PROFITS

Each year *Business Ethics* magazine publishes the 100 best American companies out of 1,000 evaluated. The publication examines the degree to which the companies serve seven stakeholder groups: shareholders, communities, minorities and women, employees, environment, non-U.S. stakeholders, and customers. Information is gathered on lawsuits, regulatory problems, pollution emissions, charitable contributions, staff diversity counts, union relations, employee benefits, and awards. Companies are removed from the list if there are significant scandals or improprieties. The research is done by Kinder, Lydenberg, Domini (KLD), an independent rating service. (For more details see the Spring 2003 issue of *Business Ethics.*)

The 20 best-rated companies in 2003 were (in order): General Mills, Cummins Engine, Intel, Procter & Gamble, IBM, Hewlett-Packard, Avon Products, Green Mountain Coffee, John Nuveen Co., St. Paul Companies, AT&T, Fannie Mae, Bank of America, Motorola, Herman Miller, Expedia, Autodesk, Cisco Systems, Wild Oats Markets, and Deluxe.

The earmarks of a socially responsible company include:

- Living out a deep set of company values that drive company purpose, goals, strategies, and tactics
- Treating customers with fairness, openness, and quick response to inquiries and complaints
- Treating employees, suppliers, and distributors fairly
- Caring about the environmental impact of its activities and supply chain
- Behaving in a consistently ethical fashion

The intriguing question is whether socially responsible companies are more profitable. Unfortunately, different research studies have come up with different results. The correlations between financial performance (FP) and social performance (SP) are sometimes positive, sometimes negative, and sometimes neutral, depending on the study. Even when FP and SP are positively related, which causes which? The most probable finding is that high FP firms invest slack resources in SP and then discover the SP leads to better FP, in a virtuous circle. (See Waddock, Sandra A. and Samuel B. Graves (1997), "The Corporate Social Performance-Financial Performance Link," *Strategic Management Journal,* 18 (4), 303–319.)

MARKETERS' RESPONSIBILITIES

As professional marketers, we are hired by some of the aforementioned companies to use our marketing toolkit to help them sell more of their products and services. Through our research, we can discover which consumer groups are the most susceptible to increasing their consumption. We can use the research to assemble the best 30-second TV commercials, print ads, and sales incentives to persuade them that these products will deliver great satisfaction. And we can create price discounts to tempt them to consume even more of the product than would normally be healthy or safe to consume.

But, as professional marketers, we should have the same ambivalence as nuclear scientists who help build nuclear bombs or pilots who spray DDT over crops from the airplane. Some of us, in fact, are independent enough to tell these clients that we will not work for them to find ways to sell more of what hurts people. We can tell them that we're willing to use our marketing toolkit to help them build new businesses around substitute products that are much healthier and safer.

But, even if these companies moved toward these healthier and safer products, they'll probably continue to push their current "cash cows." At that point, marketers will have to decide whether to work for these companies, help them reshape their offerings, avoid these companies altogether, or even work to oppose these company offerings.

REMEMBER MARKETING'S CONTRIBUTIONS

Nothing said here should detract from the major contributions that marketing has made to raise the material standards of living around the world. One doesn't want to go back to the kitchen where the housewife cooked five hours a day, washed dishes by hand, put fresh ice in the ice box, and washed and dried clothes in the open air. We value refrigerators, electric stoves, dishwashers, washing machines, and dryers. We value the invention and diffusion of the radio, the television set, the computer, the Internet, the cellular phone, the automobile, the movies, and even frozen food. Marketing has played a major role in their instigation and diffusion. Granted, any of these are capable of abuse (bad movies or TV shows), but they promise and deliver much that is good and valued in modern life.

Marketers have a right to be proud of their field. They search for unmet needs, encourage the development of products and services addressing these needs, manage communications to inform people of these products and services, arrange for easy accessibility and availability, and price the goods in a way that represents superior value delivered vis-à-vis competitors' offerings. This is the true work of marketing.

Author's Note: The author wishes to thank Professor Evert Gummesson of the School of Business, Stockholm University, for earlier discussion of these issues.

Essay

The Dependence Effect

John Kenneth Galbraith

John Kenneth Galbraith was one of the most influential economists of the twentieth century.

The theory of consumer demand, as it is now widely accepted, is based on two broad propositions, neither of them quite explicit but both extremely important for the present value system of economists. The first is that the urgency of wants does not diminish appreciably as more of them are satisfied or, to put the matter more precisely, to the extent that this happens it is not demonstrable and not a matter of any interest to economists or for economic policy. When man has satisfied his physical needs, then psychologically grounded desires take over. These can never be satisfied or, in any case, no progress can be proved. The concept of satiation has very little standing in economics. It is neither useful nor scientific to speculate on the comparative cravings of the stomach and the mind.

The second proposition is that wants originate in the personality of the consumer or, in any case, that they are given data for the economist. The latter's task is merely to seek their satisfaction. He has no need to inquire how these wants are formed. His function is sufficiently fulfilled by maximizing the goods that supply the wants.

The notion that wants do not become less urgent the more amply the individual is supplied is broadly repugnant to common sense. It is something to be believed only by those who wish to believe. Yet the conventional wisdom must be tackled on its own terrain. Intertemporal comparisons of an individual's state of mind do rest on doubtful grounds. Who can say for sure that the deprivation which afflicts him with hunger is more painful than the deprivation which afflicts him with envy of his neighbour's new car? In the time that has passed since he was poor his soul may have become subject to a new and deeper searing. And where a society is concerned, comparisons between marginal satisfactions when it is poor and those when it is affluent will involve not only the same individual at different times but different individuals at different times. The scholar who wishes to believe that with increasing affluence there is no reduction in the urgency of desires and goods is not without points for debate. However plausible the case against him, it cannot be proved. In the defence of the conventional wisdom this amounts almost to invulnerability.

However, there is a flaw in the case. If the individual's wants are to be urgent they must be original with himself. They cannot be urgent if they must be contrived for him. And above all they must not be contrived by the process of production by which they are satisfied. For this means that the whole case for the urgency of production, based on the urgency of wants, falls to the ground. One cannot defend production as satisfying wants if that production creates the wants.

Were it so that man on arising each morning was assailed by demons which instilled in him a passion sometimes for silk shirts, sometimes for kitchen-ware, sometimes for chamber-pots, and sometimes for orange squash, there would be every reason to applaud the effort to find the goods, however odd, that quenched this flame. But should it be that his passion was the result of his first having cultivated the demons, and should it also be that his effort to allay it stirred the demons to ever greater and greater effort, there would be question as to how rational was his solution. Unless restrained by conventional attitudes, he might wonder if the solution lay with more goods or fewer demons.

So it is that if production creates the wants it seeks to satisfy, or if the wants emerge *pari passu* with the production, then the urgency of the wants can no longer be used to defend the urgency of the production. Production only fills a void that it has itself created.

The even more direct link between production and wants is provided by the institutions of modern advertising and salesmanship. These cannot be reconciled with the notion of independently determined desires, for their central function is to create desires—to bring into being wants that previously did not exist.[1] This is accomplished by the producer of the goods or at his behest. A broad empirical relationship exists between what is spent on production of consumers' goods and what is spent in synthesizing the desires for that production. A new consumer product must be introduced with a suitable advertising campaign to arouse an interest in it. The path for an expansion of output must be paved by a suitable expansion in the advertising budget. Outlays for the manufacturing of a product are not more important in the strategy of modern business enterprise than outlays for the manufacturing of demand for the product. None of this is novel. All would be regarded as elementary by the most retarded student in the nation's most primitive school of business administration. The cost of this want formation is formidable. In 1956 total advertising expenditure—though, as noted, not all of it may be assigned to the synthesis of wants—amounted to about ten thousand million dollars. For some years it had been increasing at a rate in excess of a thousand million dollars a year. Obviously, such outlays must be integrated with the theory of consumer demand. They are too big to be ignored.

But such integration means recognizing that wants are dependent on production. It accords to the producer the function both of making the goods and of making the desires for them. It recognizes that production, not only passively through emulation, but actively through advertising and related activities, creates the wants it seeks to satisfy.

The businessman and the lay reader will be puzzled over the emphasis which I give to a seemingly obvious point. The point is indeed obvious. But it is one which, to a singular degree, economists have resisted. They have sensed, as the layman does not, the damage to established ideas which lurks in these relationships. As a result, incredibly, they have closed their eyes (and ears) to the most obtrusive of all economic phenomena, namely modern want creation.

This is not to say that the evidence affirming the dependence of wants on advertising has been entirely ignored. It is one reason why advertising has so long been regarded with such uneasiness by economists. Here is something which cannot be accommodated easily to existing theory. More pervious scholars have speculated on the urgency of desires which are so obviously the fruit of such expensively contrived campaigns for popular attention. Is a new breakfast cereal or detergent so much wanted if so much must be spent to compel in the consumer the sense of want? But there has been little tendency to go on to examine the implications of this for the theory of consumer demand and even less for the importance of production and productive efficiency. These have remained sacrosanct. More often the uneasiness has been manifested in a general disapproval of advertising and advertising men, leading to the occasional suggestion that they shouldn't exist. Such suggestions have usually been ill received.

And so the notion of independently determined wants still survives. In the face of all the forces of modern salesmanship it still rules, almost undefiled, in the textbooks. And it still remains the economist's mission—and on few matters is the pedagogy so firm— to seek unquestioningly the means for filling these wants. This being so, production remains of prime urgency. We have here, perhaps, the ultimate triumph of the conventional wisdom in its resistance to the evidence of the eyes. To equal it one must imagine a humanitarian who was long ago persuaded of the grievous shortage of hospital facilities in the town. He continues to importune the passers-by for money for more beds and refuses to notice that the town doctor is deftly knocking over pedestrians with his car to keep up the occupancy.

And in unravelling the complex we should always be careful not to overlook the obvious. The fact that wants can be synthesized by advertising, catalysed by salesmanship, and shaped by the discreet manipulations of the persuaders shows that they are not very urgent. A man who is hungry need never be told of his need for food. If he is inspired by his appetite, he is immune to the influence of Messrs. Batten, Barton, Durstine and Osborn. The latter are effective only with those who are so far removed from physical want that they do not already know what they want. In this state alone men are open to persuasion.

The general conclusion of these pages is of such importance for this essay that it had perhaps best be put with some formality. As a society becomes increasingly affluent, wants are increasingly created by the process by which they are satisfied. This may operate passively. Increases in consumption, the counterpart of increases in production, act by suggestion or emulation to create wants. Or producers may proceed actively to create wants through advertising and salesmanship. Wants thus come to depend on output. In technical terms it can no longer be assumed that welfare is greater at an all-round higher level of production than at a lower one. It may be the same. The higher level of production has, merely, a higher level of want creation necessitating a higher level of want satisfaction. There will be frequent occasion to refer to the way wants depend on the process by which they are satisfied. It will be convenient to call it the Dependence Effect.

The final problem of the productive society is what it produces. This manifests itself in an implacable tendency to provide an opulent supply of some things and a niggardly yield of others. This disparity carries to the point where it is a cause of social discomfort and social unhealth. The line which divides our area of wealth from our area of poverty is roughly that which divides privately produced and marketed goods and services from publicly rendered services. Our wealth in the first is not only in startling contrast with the meagreness of the latter, but our wealth in privately produced goods is, to a marked degree, the cause of crisis in the supply of public services. For we have failed to see the importance, indeed the urgent need, of maintaining a balance between the two.

This disparity between our flow of private and public goods and services is no matter of subjective judgment. On the contrary, it is the source of the most extensive comment which only stops short of the direct contrast being made here. In the years following World War II, the papers of any major city—those of New York were an excellent example—told daily of the shortages and shortcomings in the elementary municipal and metropolitan services. The schools were old and overcrowded. The police force was under strength and underpaid. The parks and playgrounds were insufficient. Streets and empty lots were filthy, and the sanitation staff was under-equipped and in need of men. Access to the city by those who work there was uncertain and painful and becoming more so. Internal transportation was overcrowded, unhealthful, and dirty. So was the air. Parking on the streets had to be prohibited, and there was no space elsewhere. These deficiencies were not in new and novel services but in old and established ones. Cities have long swept their streets, helped their people move around, educated them, kept order, and provided horse rails for vehicles which sought to pause. That their residents should have a non-toxic supply of air suggests no revolutionary dalliance with socialism.

The contrast was and remains evident not alone to those who read. The family which takes its mauve and cerise, air-conditioned, power-steered, and power-braked car out for a tour passes through cities that are badly paved, made hideous by litter, blighted buildings, billboards, and posts for wires that should long since have been put underground. They pass on into a countryside that has been rendered largely invisible by commercial art. (The goods which the latter advertise have an absolute priority in our value system. Such aesthetic considerations as a view of the countryside accordingly come second. On such matters we are consistent.) They picnic on exquisitely packaged food from a portable icebox by a polluted stream and go on to spend the night at a park which is a menace to public health and morals. Just before dozing off on an air-mattress, beneath a nylon tent, amid the stench of decaying refuse, they may reflect vaguely on the curious unevenness of their blessings. Is this, indeed, the American genius?

The case for social balance has, so far, been put negatively. Failure to keep public services in minimal relation to private production and use of goods is a cause of social disorder or impairs economic performance. The matter may now be put affirmatively. By failing to exploit the opportunity to expand public production we are missing opportunities for enjoyment which otherwise we might have had. Presumably a community can be as well rewarded by buying better schools or better parks as by buying bigger cars. By concentrating on the latter rather than the former it is failing to maximize its satisfactions. As with schools in the community, so with public services over the country at large. It is scarcely sensible that we should satisfy our wants in private goods with reckless abundance, while in the case of public goods, on the evidence of the eye, we practice extreme self-denial. So, far from systematically exploiting the opportunities to derive use and pleasure from these services, we do not supply what would keep us out of trouble.

The conventional wisdom holds that the community, large or small, makes a decision as to how much it will devote to its public services. This decision is arrived at by democratic process. Subject to the imperfections and uncertainties of democracy, people decide how much of their private income and goods they will surrender in order to have public services of which they are in greater need. Thus there is a balance, however rough, in the enjoyments to be had from private goods and services and those rendered by public authority.

It will be obvious, however, that this view depends on the notion of independently determined consumer wants. In such a world one could with some reason defend the doctrine that the consumer, as a voter, makes an independent choice between public and private goods. But given the dependence effect—given that consumer wants are created by the process by which they are satisfied—the consumer makes no such choice. He is subject to the forces of advertising and emulation by which production creates its own demand. Advertising operates exclusively, and emulation mainly, on behalf of privately produced goods and services.[2] Since management and emulative effects operate on behalf of private production, public services will have an inherent tendency to lag behind. Car demand which is expensively synthesized will inevitably have a much larger claim on income than parks or public health or even roads where no such influence operates. The engines of mass communication, in their highest state of development, assail the eyes and ears of the community on behalf of more beer but not of more schools. Even in the conventional wisdom it will scarcely be contended that this leads to an equal choice between the two.

The competition is especially unequal for new products and services. Every corner of the public psyche is canvassed by some of the nation's most talented citizens to see if the desire for some merchantable product can be cultivated. No similar process operates on behalf of the nonmerchantable services of the state. Indeed, while we take the cultivation of new private wants for granted we would be measurably shocked to see it applied to public services. The scientist or engineer or advertising man who devotes himself to developing a new carburetor, cleanser, or depilatory for which the public recognizes no need and will feel none until an advertising campaign arouses it, is one of the valued members of our society. A politician or a public servant who dreams up a new public service is a wastrel. Few public offences are more reprehensible.

So much for the influences which operate on the decision between public and private production. The calm decision between public and private consumption pictured by the conventional wisdom is, in fact, a remarkable example of the error which arises from viewing social behaviour out of context. The inherent tendency will always be for public services to fall behind private production. We have here the first of the causes of social imbalance.

NOTES

1. Advertising is not a simple phenomenon. It is also important in competitive strategy and want creation is, ordinarily, a complementary result of efforts to shift the demand curve of the individual firm at the expense of others or (less importantly, I think) to change its shape by increasing the degree of product differentiation. Some of the failure of economists to identify advertising with want creation may be attributed to the undue attention that its use in purely competitive strategy has attracted. It should be noted, however, that the competitive manipulation of consumer desire is only possible, at least on any appreciable scale, when such need is not strongly felt.

2. Emulation does operate between communities. A new school or a new highway in one community does exert pressure on others to remain abreast. However, as compared with the pervasive effects of emulation in extending the demand for privately produced consumers' goods there will be agreement, I think, that this intercommunity effect is probably small.

Case Study

Everquest®: Entertainment or Addiction?[1]

Judith W. Spain and Gina Vega

"This game was written to keep people online as long as possible," stated Elizabeth Woolley after the suicide of her son, Shawn. "Where are your ethics, Sony?" she wondered.[2] "This isn't just an online game, it's dangerous. I believe if he hadn't been playing that game, he'd be alive today," she said.[3]

THE INCIDENT

At around 6:00 A.M., on Tuesday, November 20, 2001, in Hudson, Wisconsin, Shawn Woolley had logged on to his computer and began playing EverQuest®, his favorite game. A few hours later he committed suicide in his apartment. Two days passed and, when he didn't show up for Thanksgiving dinner, his mother, Liz Woolley, found his body in a rocking chair at his computer desk. He had a .22 caliber rifle at his side and EverQuest® was still running on his computer.[4]

Mrs. Woolley stated to the news media that she believed the cause of Shawn's suicide was his addiction to EverQuest®.[5] But, was this an expected response to the game? The news media picked up on the suicide story and the potential issues of addiction, obsession, or compulsion of today's consumer for online game-playing at the expense of their daily lives. Although the media contacted SOE for comment, the only response from the company was from Mr. McDaniel, Vice President of Marketing for SOE.[6] Denying corporate responsibility, he stated "There's a duty on the consumer to use it responsibly."[7]

EVERQUEST®—THE GAME

Emblazoned across the EverQuest® web-site were the words, "Pause Life. Play Game." EverQuest® was a "real 3D massively multi-player (MMP) fantasy game role playing game (RPG)." A massively multiplayer online game is a video game where a player connects through the Internet to a persistent virtual world, joining with hundreds of thousands of other gamers in a shared experience. Each player chooses a character and develops its "role" in Norrath, by creating its own background and, thus, its future. In a role playing game, there is no "winning" in the traditional sense. After players create their own characters, the characters are then "free" to roam the fantasy world.

The scope of EverQuest® differed from player to player. EverQuest® players entered into an enormous virtual entertainment world named Norrath, with its own species, economic systems, alliances, and politics. The players could wander around seeking allies and knowledge, facing epic challenges, meeting new friends, and more.

Each player defined his/her own character's destiny. The character could be a knight, a misshapen elf, a dwarf, a monster, or a amsel in distress. Characters grew in strength and in power based on the total number of hours they were played. EverQuest® players usually attempted to form "guilds" or teams which worked together to earn points, slay monsters, and capture key positions within the world of Norrath. A monetary value was attached to the characters as they became recognized "rulers" in Norrath. One player who reached the highest EverQuest® levels reported selling three characters on eBay for $4,500.[8]

Pressure for players to continue playing the game and not logging off was tremendous. Logging off could hurt the guild's chances of advancing through the game since strength in numbers was critical for attacking a dragon or another guild, or trying to steal the treasures of another character. In addition, logging off could allow your character be attacked because, even though a player was not online, their character remained in play and actively involved in the land of Norrath.

FINANCIAL IMPLICATIONS

Introduced by Sony Online Entertainment in 1998, EverQuest® retailed for approximately $40. It required either a Sony Playstation game system ($199.00) or could be played on a personal computer. For an additional $12.95 per month, players could sign up to play the game online. Revenues from online subscriptions netted Sony approximately $5 million a month in 2002.[9] The game and its expansions were widely popular. One expansion of the EverQuest® game, "The Shadow of Luclin," sold 120,000 copies on the day it was released.

Since Norrath existed online, the players were from all around the world, increasing the likelihood that play would be intense even when most of America was sleeping. Indeed, demand in Europe for this game became so great that in November 2001, Sony had to construct and bring online a new server dedicated to EverQuest®.[10]

More than 1,000 computers kept the game running, with forty-seven Sony staffers continually adding items and quests to the game and approximately 128 "game masters"

functioning online, wandering around in Norrath answering questions.[11] Because the game became so popular, Norrath was likely to become overpopulated. To combat this, Sony launched 42 versions of the game so that players could relocate their character to a different "world" for a $50 fee.[12] The revenue stream was so good that Sony planned to introduce EverQuest® II, a project costing $20 million.[13]

Sony was committed to increasing its market. "SOE's goal has always been to bring gamers new content and dynamic communities," said Scott McDaniel, vice president of marketing, Sony Online Entertainment. "By continuing to expand the types of games offered, we are driving the growth of the massively multiplayer market."[14] "*EverQuest* currently has more than 430,000 active subscribers with new fans logging on daily. With recent free additions to the game, including a new user-friendly interface, and more areas to explore, we are confident that *EverQuest* will continue to dominate the online role-playing game segment."[15]

THE TYPICAL PLAYER

As of May 2003, there were approximately 430,000 registered players of EverQuest®, with approximately 12,000 more signing up each month.[16] On any given night, approximately 100,000 players roamed the world of Norrath.[17] The average age of an EverQuest® player was 25.6 years old with 31.7% of the players being students.[18] Average household income for a player ranged from below $30,000 (27.6%), $30,000 to $49,999 (21.4%), $50,000 to $74,999 (20.4%), to over $75,000 (27.8%).[19]

In one survey, 45.2% of the 1,989 respondents considered themselves addicted to EverQuest®. The typical player logged more than 20 hours per week playing the game,[20] with one survey estimating that 15% of the users played between 40–50 hours per week.[21] Another survey of 3,166 players indicated that for the 18–22 year old age group, 50.7% of the males and 44.7% of the females have lost sleep over their playing habits.[22] In many ways, Shawn Woolley fit this model, but there were some differences.

AN ATYPICAL PLAYER?

Shawn Woolley, a 21 year old shy, overweight young man, had been diagnosed with depression in conjunction with schizoid personality behavior. He also had a history of seizures. Shawn lived in a group home for a short time, but had checked himself out after several months and rented his own apartment. He had held a variety of different jobs over the preceding year, but he quit his last job about a week before the suicide.[23]

Shawn began playing EverQuest® approximately one year before his death. When he committed suicide, he left no note. The only clues for what he had been doing prior to his suicide were notes about names and terms related to EverQuest®. His family claimed that the lure of the game for Shawn was the camaraderie with other players. Mrs. Woolley related one incident in which Shawn cried because another player had stolen some of the treasures he had collected playing the game.[24] She feared that Shawn's suicide was the result of something happening to one of his treasured characters, called "I Love You."

ONLINE ADDICTION: ANOTHER ILLNESS?

Numerous mental health organizations are dedicated to dealing with online addiction.[25] Experts such as Jay Parker, a chemical dependency counselor and co-founder of Internet/Computer Addiction Services in Redmond, Washington, believed that online gaming was a significant addiction problem, causing a growing number of people spending huge chunks of time at the computer.[26] David Walsh, president of the National Institute on Media and the Family in Minneapolis, stated, "This game is so addictive in nature that many EverQuest® players refer to it as "EverCrack."[27] The peer pressure to stay online and help your guild, the lure of playing anonymously, and the thrill of the hunt made EverQuest® very appealing to consumers. A three-year long study of 4,100 massively multiplayer role-playing game users indicated that 40% of these players considered themselves addicted to the game and 15% of them "reported symptoms of withdrawal, such as anger and anxiety, when prevented from playing."[28]

However, some psychologists believed that the online gaming was not addictive. Sara Kiesler, PhD, a researcher at Carnegie Mellon University, stated, "No research has yet established that there is a disorder of Internet addiction that is separable from problems such as loneliness or problem gambling, or that a passion for using the Internet is long-lasting."[29] Instead, most psychologists say that the personality of the particular player is what puts him or her at risk. Shawn Woolley's diagnosed personality disorders made it easy for him to reinvent himself online, which is what he appeared to do. This "escape from reality" feature of the game could be very alluring to individuals with low self-esteem. The thrill of anonymity may have lured Shawn and other players to continue playing and playing and playing. . . .

A PARENT'S RESPONSE

Mrs. Woolley developed her own web-site, Online Gamers Anonymous (Olganon), in her quest to educate people about the dangers of playing Everquest®.[30] Two additional web-sites appeared for EverQuest® "widows," dedicated to providing a support group for those individuals dealing with a husband, wife, girlfriend, son, etc. addicted to playing the game. An active web-site with links to numerous online addiction services, "EQ Widows" listed 3,654 members.[31] A similar web-site provided opportunities for aggrieved family members to vent their anger about the game and receive moral support.[32] One member stated that her fiancé "picked the game over me on Mother's Day. He picks the game over when I have my family from out of town."[33] Other members responded with advice and encouragement, including one member who opined that she should "move on . . . There is no reason for you to suffer when there are other men out there in the real world that you can date."[34]

"This is an underground epidemic," said Woolley. "Just like alcohol was in the 1920s. People then were told to hide their family members who had problems with alcohol away. Families today want to hide the problem. They think online addiction is shameful, and they don't want to talk about it."[35]

FUTURE OF SOE AND ONLINE GAMING

SOE introduced EverQuest II® in late 2004. Destined to be as popular as EverQuest®, the new version would be set in a new age—the Age of Destiny. Players' quests would directly affect the structure of the game, thus changing the plot line on a monthly basis. SOE was anticipating high profits and favorable customer response with this new product.

But, SOE had some possible legal issues looming. Mrs. Woolley was contemplating filing a lawsuit against SOE for its alleged role in her son's suicide. In Tampa, Florida, the EverQuest® game was implicated in the death of a young child when the father threw the

child into a closet after the child's crying had interrupted his game playing.[36] Some time after January 2003, a warning label appeared on EverQuest®'s website: "Photosensitive. Seizure Warning."

"EverQuest" is a game," McDaniel said in an e-mail interview. "The vast majority of our 430,000 subscribers play the game in moderation, enjoying the game-play as well as the community interaction the game provides. As with any form of entertainment, it is the responsibility of each individual player to monitor his or her own playing habits and prioritize his or her time as necessary. It is not our place to monitor or limit how individuals spend their free time."[37]

As big a money-maker as it promised to be, was SOE justified in releasing it? Was the game really responsible, even in part, for death, abuse, or other personal emotional damage to players? Was there something Scott McDaniel should be doing besides preparing the ad campaign?

NOTES

1. An earlier version of this case was used as the centerpiece for the 10th Annual Vincentians International Conference Promoting Business Ethics (October 2004, Garden City, New York). That version, along with the related exercises and Oxford debate transcript, will be published in a special issue of *The Journal of Business Ethics,* forthcoming.
2. Spain, J. (2003, August 27). Telephone Interview with Mrs. Woolley.
3. Harter, K. (2002, April 28). Mother: Game sucked son in. *Pioneer Press.* Retrieved May 25, 2004 from http://www.twincities.com/mld/pioneerpress.news/local/3146855.htm?lc
4. Irvine, M. (2002, May 26). Online game blamed for son's suicide. *Lexington Herald Leader,* p. A5.
5. Miller, S., (2002, March 30) Death of a game addict. *Milwaukee Journal Sentinel.* Retrieved May 1, 2003 from http://www.jsoline.com/news/State/mar02/31536.asp
6. Scott McDaniel Biography. Retrieved May 1, 2003 from http://www.sonyonline.com/corp/company.info/bios.jsp
7. Irvine, M. (2002, May 26). Online game blamed for son's suicide. *Lexington Herald Leader,* p. A5.

8. Scheeres, Julia. (2001, December 5). The Quest to End Game Addiction. *Wired News.* Retrieved May 1, 2003 from http://www.wired.com/news/holidays/0,1882,48479,00.html

9. Keighley, Geoff. (2002, August). The Sorcerer of Sony. *Business 2.0,* 49–53.

10. Press Release. www.sonyonline.com/corp/press.jsp. October 29, 2001.

11. Keighley, Geoff. (2002, August). The Sorcerer of Sony. *Business 2.0,* 49–53.

12. Keighley, Geoff. (2002, August). The Sorcerer of Sony. *Business 2.0,* 49–53.

13. Keighley, Geoff. (2002, August). The Sorcerer of Sony. *Business 2.0,* 49–53.

14. Sony online entertainment continues to lead the online gaming industry with its new roster of massively multiplayer games. (May 13, 2000). http://eqlive.station.sony.com/news_section/newsview.jsp?story=43027 Retrieved January 6, 2005.

15. Everquest experiences a record number of simultaneous players. (July 29, 200). http://eqlive.station.sony.com/news_section/newsview.jsp?story=50196. Retrieved January 6, 2005.

16. Keighley, Geoff. (2002, August). The Sorcerer of Sony. *Business 2.0,* 49–53.

17. EverQuest Or EverCrack. (2002, May 28). *CBS News.com.* Retrieved May 1, 2003 from http://cbsnews.com

18. Yee, N. (2001). The Norrathian Scrolls: A Study of EverQuest. Retrieved May 1, 2003 from http://www.nickyee.com/eqt/demographics.html

19. Yee, N. (2001). The Norrathian Scrolls: A Study of EverQuest. Retrieved May 1, 2003 from http://www.nickyee.com/eqt/demographics.html

20. Everquest or Evercrack. (2002, May 28). *CBS News.com.* Retrieved May 1, 2003 from http://cbsnews.com

21. Yee, N. (2001). The Norrathian Scrolls: A Study of EverQuest. Retrieved May 1, 2003 from http://www.nickyee.com/eqt/report.html

22. Yee, N. (2002). Ariadne—Understanding MMORPG Addiction. Retrieved May 1, 2003 from http://www.shinyspinning.com/weblog/archieves/00000036.html

23. Patrizio, A. (2002, April 3). Did Game Play Role in Suicide?. *Wired News.* Retrieved May 1, 2003 from http://www.wired.com/news/games/0,2101,51490,00.html

24. Irvine, M. (2002, May 26). Online game blamed for son's suicide. *Lexington Herald Leader,* p. A5.

25. Media Family.org—Media Influence on children: Making Media Manageable for Families and Children (Home page for Media and Family), (n.d.). Retrieved May 1, 2003 from http://www.mediafamily.org and see Internet/Computer Addiction Services (Home page for Computer Addiction Services), (n.d.). Retrieved May 1, 2003 from http://www.icaservices.com

26. Miller, S., (2002, March 30) Death of a game addict. *Milwaukee Journal Sentinel.* Retrieved May 1, 2003 from http://www.jsoline.com/news/State/mar02/31536.asp

27. Miller, S., (2002, March 30) Death of a game addict. *Milwaukee Journal Sentinel.* Retrieved May 1, 2003 from http://www.jsonline.com/news/State/mar02/31536.asp

28. Jacobs, Timothy. Video gamers play on as their lives fall apart. www.jrn.columbia.edu/studentwork/cns/2003–06–22/282.asp. Retrieved January 6, 2005.

29. Review of journal article by DeAngelis, T. *Is Internet Addiction Real.* Retrieved May 16, 2004 from http://www.apa.org/monitor/apr00/addiction.html. Published in Monitor on Psychology, Volume 31, No. 4, April 2000.

30. Online Gamers Anonymous. (Home page for Online Gamers Anonymous), (n.d.). Retrieved May 1, 2003 from http://www.olganon.org

31. Yahoo! Groups: EverQuest Widows (Home page for EverQuest Widows), (n.d.). Retrieved May 1, 2003 from http://groups.yahoo.com/group/EverQuest-Widows/

32. Yahoo! Groups: Spouses against EverQuest. (Home page for Spouses against EverQuest). (n.d.). Retrieved May 1, 2003 from http://groups.yahoo.com/group/spousesagainsteverquest

33. Yahoo! Groups: Spouses Against EverQuest. (2003, May 30). Message Board—Message 407. Retrieved June 21, 2003 from http://groups.yahoo.com/group/spousesagainsteverquest

34. Yahoo! Groups: Spouses Against EverQuest. (2003, May 30) Message Board—Message 407. Retrieved June 21, 2003 from http://groups.yahoo.com/group/spousesagainsteverquest

35. Jacobs, Timothy. Video gamers play on as their lives fall apart. www.jrn.columbia.edu/studentwork/cns/2003–06–22/282.asp. Retrieved January 6, 2005.

36. Becker, D. (2002, April 12). When games stop being fun. *CNET News.com.* Retrieved May 1, 2003 from http://news.com/2102–1040–881673.html
    John Smedley Biography. Retrieved May 1, 2003 from http://www.sonyonline.com/corp/company_info/bios.jsp

37. Jacobs, Timothy. Video gamers play on as their lives fall apart. www.jrn.columbia.edu/studentwork/cns/2003–06–22/282.asp. Retrieved January 6, 2005.

Case Study

Vioxx

Ronald M. Green

As the millennial year 2000 progressed, senior executives at Merck had many reasons to be pleased. Sales of Vioxx, Merck's recently approved osteoarthritis drug, were strong and were pulling ahead of those of competitor Pfizer's Celebrex. Such success was welcome since the patents on some of Merck's other major drugs, including its very successful anti-cholesterol drug Mevacor, were nearing expiration. With sales of Vioxx already passing the billion-dollar mark, Merck knew it had a winner.

Vioxx (chemical name rofecoxib) had been seven years in development before its FDA approval in May 1999. Classified as a COX-2 inhibitor, Vioxx works by impeding production of the enzyme cyclooxygenase-2 that is responsible for producing pain and inflammation, while not inhibiting COX-1, the enzyme involved in the protection of the stomach lining. Inhibition of COX-1 can result in potential serious consequences such as stomach ulcers and perforation, a recognized side effect of non-steroidal anti-inflammatory drugs (NSAIDS).

By early 2000, several studies had shown that Vioxx was an effective pain reliever for patients with osteoarthritis of the hip or knee. Further studies were done or in progress to determine the value of Vioxx for the treatment of rheumatoid arthritis. If all those studies panned out, Vioxx could go on to become the largest selling drug in Merck's history.

Four doses of Vioxx (5, 12.5, 25, and 50 mg.) were available, and patients at all of the doses studied reported significant improvement in nearly all categories of physical functioning when compared to patients taking placebo. Treatment with Vioxx was generally well tolerated among all studied doses. Diarrhea, headache, insomnia, and upper respiratory infection were among the most commonly reported side effects, but the same effects were observed in patients treated with placebo.

There were some clouds on Merck's horizon. Several pre-approval studies had shown cardiovascular side effects of Vioxx and other COX-2 inhibitors. The mechanisms of these effects were not really well understood. Some researchers speculated that the COX-1 enzyme, which Vioxx and the other drugs did not inhibit, might cause platelet coagulation. These concerns had led a handful of clinicians to speak out against the new class of drugs.

For every study showing worrisome CV effects, there were others showing no adverse effects, and even protective benefits of Vioxx. Merck's marketing managers had tried to handle these issues by preparing a series of targeted instructional materials for the over 3,000 company sales representatives across the country that were assigned to engage in face-to-face discussions with physicians about Vioxx.

One of the items already available for use by sales reps was the "Cardiovascular Card," a convenient tri-fold. It featured data from several pre-approval studies that supported the safety of Vioxx. One panel depicting "Overall Mortality Rates" indicated that patients on Vioxx were 11 times less likely to die than patients on standard anti-inflammatory drugs, and 8 times less likely to die from heart attacks and strokes. Another panel indicated that the rate of heart attack among patients on Vioxx was less than half of the rate of patients receiving placebo and virtually identical to that of patients receiving other anti-inflammatory drugs. Merck executives knew that these pre-approval studies, based on very limited populations and not always targeted at cardiovascular effects, were of limited scientific value, but they supported their gut-level confidence in the new drug.

There was one looming cloud on the horizon—no one was quite sure how large it was—in the form of one incidental finding in a just completed study whose results had been known to Merck executives at least since February.

The study had actually been sponsored by Merck in the hopes of demonstrating Vioxx's minimal gastrointestinal effects and possibly doing away with usual NSAID gastrointestinal warnings on the drug's label. Aimed specifically at determining the benefits of Vioxx for the treatment of rheumatoid arthritis, it was a double blind, randomized trial comparing the occurrence of gastrointestinal toxicity of Vioxx and naproxen (Aleve, a nonsteroidal anti-inflammatory). It had enrolled over 8,000 patients and involved a team of Merck-supported and independent researchers known as the Vigor Study Group (for Vioxx Gastrointestinal Outcomes Research).

Overall, the Vigor Study seemed very good news for Merck. It showed that while Vioxx and naproxen had similar treatment efficacy, Vioxx caused roughly half as many serious gastrointestinal events (perforation, obstruction and severe upper gastrointestinal bleeding) as the older drug.

The cloud in this sunny picture was the finding that the incidence of myocardial infarction (irreversible heart damage usually resulting from blockage of a coronary artery) was approximately five times higher among patients in the Vioxx group than among those in the naproxen group. But this effect was found only among the 4 percent of the study population with the highest risk of a myocardial infarction and for whom low-dose aspirin was an indicated therapy. (Aspirin had been withheld during the study to prevent its confounding of gastrointestinal effects.) No increase in MI was found for healthier patients. Furthermore, the study showed that despite these instances of MI, the overall mortality rate and death rates from cardiovascular causes were similar in the two groups.

A number of scientists, both inside and outside Merck, believed that the higher incidence of MI in the Vigor study resulted, not from any risks of Vioxx, but from possible heart protective effects of naproxen. These effects, which were well established for aspirin but relatively unstudied for naproxen, could easily account for different MI rates in the study population. In a series of conferences and prepared press releases, Merck was stressing naproxen's cardioprotective effects as a way of explaining the findings of the Vigor Study.

At mid-year, Merck executives had much to celebrate—and some decisions to make. What should they do about the findings of the Vigor Study? Would further studies be appropriate? And if so, what kinds of studies would be needed to clarify the benefits and risks of Vioxx? Above all, how should they now continue to market their new blockbuster drug?

Case Study

Uptown, Dakota, and PowerMaster

N. Craig Smith

UPTOWN

In December 1989, the R.J. Reynolds Tobacco Co. (RJR) announced plans to introduce Uptown, a menthol cigarette designed to appeal strongly to black smokers. Cigarette sales had declined 6% in 1989 alone and tobacco companies were aggressively seeking new customers. While 29% of the adult U.S. population smoked at that time, the figure was 34% for blacks. Market research showed 69% of black smokers preferred menthol as against 27% for all smokers. RJR's Salem already was the top-selling menthol cigarette with a 6.8% market share (a 1% share was around $250 million in sales), but research suggested many blacks would favor the lighter menthol planned for Uptown. The company's marketing plan for the Philadelphia test market included advertising suggesting glamour, high fashion and nightlife, with the slogan "Uptown. The place. The taste." It would run in black newspapers and in black-oriented magazines such as *Jet* and *Ebony*. Research on the Uptown name suggested it was "classy sounding" and, accordingly, the product packaging was black and gold, in contrast to the usual green for menthol cigarettes. Moreover, the cigarettes were to be packed with the filters down, a response to a research finding showing that many blacks opened cigarette packs from the bottom. In short, RJR had studied carefully the market and customer needs and responded with a sharply focused marketing program targeting black smokers.

For a number of years, public health officials had attacked cigarette advertising directed at specific groups, especially minorities. Statistics showed that during the 1980s the gap between the number of black and white smokers was widening, as whites were more likely to quit. However, the attack on RJR's marketing plans for Uptown by the black Health and Human Services Secretary, Louis W. Sullivan, was unprecedented. In a January 18, 1990, speech to medical students at the University of Pennsylvania (in the city where RJR planned to test market Uptown) he said: "This brand is cynically and deliberately targeted toward black Americans. At a time when our people desperately need the message of health promotion. Uptown's message is more disease, more suffering and more death for a group already bearing more than its share of smoking-related illness and mortality. At a time when we must cultivate greater personal responsibility among our citizens, Uptown's slick and sinister advertising proposes instead a greater degree of personal irresponsibility." In a letter to RJR's CEO, Sullivan wrote, "I strongly urge you to cancel your plans to market a brand of cigarettes that is specifically targeted to black smokers."

Sullivan's speech received extensive media coverage. Among those commenting on his remarks, Reed Tuckson, the D.C. health commissioner, noted: "The prevalence of smoking is by far the single most important issue that accounts for the poor quality of health for people of color in this country. The predatory behavior and the degree of intensity to which these companies market their products of death and disease for the sake of profit is just immoral." An RJR spokeswoman initially commented: "We believe that black smokers have the right to buy products that fit their preference. The introduction of a new brand will not affect the decision to smoke." However, on January 19, RJR announced that it had cancelled plans for Uptown. Peter Hoult, executive vice president for marketing commented: "We regret that a small coalition of antismoking zealots apparently believes that black smokers are somehow different from others who choose to smoke. This represents a loss of choice for black smokers and a further erosion of the free enterprise system."

RJR's conflict with Sullivan did not end with Uptown. Confidential RJR documents leaked to the Advocacy Institute were released to the press to coincide with a Senate hearing on cigarette advertising targeting specific groups. This time, the marketing plans were for a new brand that targeted women.

DAKOTA

RJR had planned to test market Dakota in April, 1990. It was positioned against Philip Morris Co.'s Marlboro, the leading cigarette brand with a 26% overall market share and the leading brand among women. Marlboro was the most popular entry-level brand for teenage women and was smoked by almost half of young female smokers aged 18 to 24. RJR saw an opportunity in addressing a weakness in Marlboro's appeal to women: the difficulty for a woman to completely identify with the "Marlboro man" image. Women were "one of the few bright spots" in the shrinking cigarette market, with a rate of smoking

declining, but not as fast as for males. Moreover, while there were still more adult male smokers (32%) than females (27%), among teens, girls smoked at higher rates than boys. Philip Morris had pioneered female cigarettes in the late 1960s with Virginia Slims, the dominant brand with a 3% share. While around a dozen other brands only held in total a 3% market share, there had been much activity in the late 1980s; for example, BAT Industries' Capri, a much thinner cigarette, had gained a 0.5% market share in 16 months, prompting Philip Morris to launch Superslims and other innovations. As a marketing VP for Liggett commented, "if the female segment keeps growing, more companies will come into it." RJR was no exception.

Dakota was not positioned as a conventional female cigarette with a "soft, feminine sell." Its image was rugged. The target customer was a white, 18–24 year-old, "virile" female, with only a high school degree and for whom work was a job, not a career. Her free time was spent with her boyfriend, doing whatever he was doing, including tractor pulls and hot rod shows. Proposed promotions included "hunk-oriented" premiums, such as calendars, that would tie in with Dakota-sponsored male strip shows. The Dakota cigarette would be similar in taste and number of puffs to a Marlboro. Again, RJR had developed a marketing program clearly aimed at a well-defined target market.

Women's groups already had been strongly critical of the increased efforts by tobacco companies to target women. Twisting the Virginia Slims ad slogan, they were telling women smokers: "You've come the *wrong* way, baby." The Women's Tennis Association had been pressured to end its ties with Philip Morris, the sponsor of the Virginia Slims tennis tour. The marketing VP of Philip Morris commented that it was "reprehensible at best and sexist at worst to assume that adult women are not capable of making their own decisions about whether or not to smoke." Another industry spokesperson noted that it's "prudent marketing to go after your market." The demise of Uptown prompted increased attention to the targeting of women and the suggestion that they too could "resist exploitation by the tobacco industry." Having noted that slim cigarettes appealed to women with a "freedom from fat" message, one commentator suggested Sullivan should "blast cigarette companies for targeting women." With the announcement of RJR's plans for Dakota, Sullivan was able to oblige. He was also critical of the Virginia Slims tennis tour for fostering "a misleading impression that smoking is compatible with good health."

Primed by the Uptown story, commentators offered more insightful analysis on the controversy over target marketing, going beyond charges of "exploitation" and "manipulation." Consumer vulnerability was suggested in explanation: "Dakota is an unscrupulous attempt to exploit a vulnerable group" (Kornheiser 1990); "the company is under heavy fire for a plan to market the new brand to one of the industry's most vulnerable segments: young, poorly-educated, blue-collar women" (Freedman and McCarthy 1990). Target marketing was acknowledged as a standard marketing tool and a tactic of choice among tobacco companies because in a declining market the best opportunities were with specific groups the poor, the young, blacks and Hispanics. These perceived vulnerable groups were left because "The well-to-do and well-educated . . . have quit smoking. Those who remain are the disadvantaged. It's logical to target them, except you are sending a message society can't accept." Targeting had become hazardous for tobacco companies because "targeting specific consumer groups suggests they're creating victims" (Freedman and McCarthy 1990).

However, the hazards of targeting were not restricted to tobacco. The alcohol industry soon realized that it too faced the prospect of similar pressures and going "down Tobacco Road" (Abramson 1991). With driving after drinking the leading cause of death among teenagers, the industry had already faced criticism over targeting youth from groups and public health officials, such as Surgeon General Koop.

POWERMASTER

Like the tobacco industry, alcohol producers, also faced with declining consumption, were increasingly targeting their marketing programs, especially at heavy users. These targets included "the most vulnerable elements of society," according to Michael Jacobson of the Center for Science in the Public Interest (CSPI), a consumer advocacy group coordinating a coalition of 22 public interest groups critical of the emphasis on black and Hispanic consumers in advertisements for malt liquor. A CSPI video, "Marketing Booze to Blacks," suggested alcohol was connected to many social problems, from spousal and child abuse to homicide. The Beer Institute charged the Center with elitism: "The elitists at CSPI believe that only middle- to upper-class white males have the capacity to view ads without endangering themselves" (Folt 1991). In San Francisco, the city's health commissioner commented: "It is the height of irresponsibility for the beer industry to target poor ethnic communities with these genocidal beer promotions." Community leaders charged that heavy promotion of "high octane" malt liquor in black and Latino neighborhoods resulted in social problems similar to those created by crack cocaine. The following year, another new product introduction was to go the way of Uptown and Dakota.

In 1990, G. Heileman Brewing Co., the fifth largest brewer in the U.S., had seen its volumes decline for the seventh year in a row. Market share was also down. It was in bankruptcy proceedings and desperately in need of successful new product introductions. It had developed 40% of the 87 new beer products introduced in the 1980s. While beer consumption was on the decline (along with most other alcoholic beverages), the $500m. malt liquor market was growing. It experienced a 7% volume increase to 79.7 m. 2.5-gallon cases in 1990, about 3% of the total beer market. Some malts had even seen annual increases of 25–30%. Malt liquor, brewed from a base that contains a higher degree of fermentable sugars than regular beer, has a higher alcohol content, is paler in color and has a more aromatic and malty taste. It was disproportionately consumed in low income neighborhoods, where its appeal was attributed to its "quicker high." Heileman dominated the malt liquor market with a volume market share of around one-third. In July, 1991, it planned to introduce PowerMaster, which at 5.9% alcohol was 31% stronger than Heileman's Colt 45, the market leader, and had 65% more alcohol than regular beer. Heileman had spent more than $2m on research and marketing for the brand.

The announcement of PowerMaster had anti-alcohol groups and black leaders up in arms. CSPI and other groups asked the brewer to stop distribution of the product because "higher octane alcoholic beverages have no place on the market, especially in communities where residents already suffer disproportionately from alcohol and other drug problems." Boycotts were planned. Surgeon General Antonia Novello described the promotion of PowerMaster as "socially irresponsible." PowerMaster's target marketing to minorities also was criticized by Congressional representatives. On June 20, 1991, the Bureau of Alcohol, Tobacco and Firearms (BATF) announced that its approval of the PowerMaster label was a mistake and required Heileman to drop the word *power* because it was a veiled reference to alcohol strength. (The Federal Alcohol Administration Act banned the mention of alcohol content on beer labels to discourage competition on that basis.) On July 3, Heileman announced that it would discontinue PowerMaster following BATF's withdrawal of approval for its label, because "the brand name was the product," commented the Heileman director of marketing. BATF gave the brewer four months to sell existing stocks.

Anti-alcohol groups criticized the agency because it made its move only after public outrage over PowerMaster's potency and the targeting of low-income blacks, who suffer disproportionately from alcohol-related diseases (CSPI found that black men had a 40% higher death rate from cirrhosis of the liver than whites). Industry commentators, anticipating further action by BATF against power claims widely used by malt liquor brands, suggested this would "strip away the whole basis for business" in the category. Also under scrutiny was advertising that associated malt liquors with aphrodisiacs, drug use, and street gangs. The director of the National Coalition to Prevent Impaired Driving commented: "Alcohol producers will think twice before targeting vulnerable, inner-city groups again." While a *New York Times* editorial had lambasted Heileman for "deliberately zeroing in on a section of society that already has problems enough," the president of the Beer Institute accused critics of PowerMaster of "patronizing" blacks and Hispanics. The trade journal *Beverage World* in its obituary to PowerMaster said it became "a magnet of controversy from the moment it reared its alcohol-enhanced head. Federal officials, industry leaders, black activists, and media types weighed in with protests that PowerMaster . . . was an example of bad product, bad marketing, and, essentially, a bad idea."

Later in 1991, BATF cracked down on other malt liquors, such as Black Sunday, Crazy Horse, and St. Ides, while cans of PowerMaster fast became collectors' items. Some observers noted the failure of some black organizations and media to criticize alcohol and tobacco and educate on health effects, suggesting they were "bought off" by these industries. *Fortune* described Power-Master as one of the biggest business goofs of 1991, noting that "targeting black consumers with anything less wholesome than farina has become politically risky." A line extension of Colt 45, Colt 45 Premium, was introduced by Heileman in May 1992 and described by BATF as being identical in content to PowerMaster.

SOURCES

Abramson, Jill (1991). "Selling Moderation, Alcohol Industry Is at Forefront of Efforts to Curb Drunkenness," *Wall Street Journal*, May 21, p. A1.

Alters, Diane (1989). "As Youths Are Urged to Stay Sober, Beer Ad Blitz Tries to Lure Them," *Boston Sunday Globe*, June 25, p. 1.

Bureau of National Affairs (1991). "Brewer Decides to Withdraw New High Alcohol Malt Liquor," *Antitrust and Trade Regulation Report*, Vol. 61, No. 1524 (July 11), p. 41.

Chicago Tribune (1991). "U.S. Seeking to Dilute New Malt Liquor's Name," *Chicago Tribune*, June 21, p. 10.

Cohen, Richard (1990). "More Work for Dr. Sullivan," *Washington Post*, January 30, p. A19.

Cornwell, Rupert (1991). "Out of the West: Trouble Brews for a Powerful Beer," *The Independent*, July 3, p. 10.

Farnham, Alan (1992). "Biggest Business Goofs of 1991," *Fortune*, January 13, p. 81.

Foltz, Kim (1991). "Alcohol Ads Aimed at Blacks Criticized," *New York Times*, January 16, p. D6.

Freedman, Alix M. (1991). "Potent New Heileman Malt Is Brewing Fierce Industry and Social Criticism," *Wall Street Journal*, June 17, p. B1.

Freedman, Alix M. (1991). "Malt Advertising That Touts Firepower Comes Under Attack by U.S. Officials," *Wall Street Journal*, July 1, p. B1.

Freedman, Alix M. (1991). "Heileman, Under Pressure, Scuttles PowerMaster Malt," *Wall Street Journal*, July 5, p. B1.

Freedman, Alix M. and Michael J. McCarthy (1990). "New Smoke from RJR Under Fire," *Wall Street Journal*, February 20, p. B1.

Gardner, Marilyn (1990). "Women and Cigarettes: Smoking out the Truth," *Christian Science Monitor*, January 30, p. 14.

Gladwell, Malcolm (1990). "HHS Chief Assails Tie Between Tobacco Firms, Sporting Events," *St. Petersburg Times*, February 24, p. 6A.

Glater, Jonathan (1992). "Federal Crackdown Alcohol, Regulators Target Ads Over Claims of Potency," *San Francisco Chronicle*, July 24, p. B1.

Hardie, Chris (1994). "Heileman Shipments Cut in Half Since '83," *La Crosse Tribune*, January 13.

Hilts, Philip J. (1990). "Health Chief Assails a Tobacco Producer for Aiming at Blacks," *New York Times*, January 19, p. A1.

Inman, David (1990). "Black Strike Back at Ad Campaigns: Amidst Uproar, Will Marketing Change?" *Sunday Tennessean*, April 8, p. ID.

Jackson, Derrick Z. (1991). "Miller's Mockery," *Boston Globe*, December 29, p. 63.

Kornheiser, Tony (1990). "Cigarettes and Virile Chicks," *Washington Post*, February 23, p. B1.

Lacey, Marc (1992). "Marketing of Malt Liquor Fuels Debate," *Los Angeles Times*, December 15, p. A32.

Lang, Perry (1990). "Hard Sell to Blacks of Potent Malt Brew Called 'Irresponsible,'" *San Francisco Chronicle*, November 3, p. A2.

Rothenberg, Rondall (1989). "Groups Plan to Protest Malt Liquor Campaigns," *New York Times*, August 23, p. D17.

Specter, Michael (1990). "Sullivan Denounces Reynolds Tobacco; New Brand Said Aimed at Blacks," *Washington Post*, January 19, p. A1.

Specter, Michael (1990). "Reynolds Cancels Plans to Market New Cigarette; Uptown Brand Attacked as Aimed at Blacks," *Washington Post*, January 20, p. A3.

Waldman, Peter (1989). "Tobacco Firms Try Soft, Feminine Sell: But in Targeting Women, They Spark Backlash," *Wall Street Journal*, December 19, p. B1.

Case Study

The Case of the Contested Firearms

George Brenkert

"Our lawyers are handling the current case," said Bob Graham, CEO of Magnum Industries, a major gun manufacturer doing business across the United States. "I want you to come up with some overall plan as to where we should be going. Start with a clean slate. What should we be doing with regard to manufacturing and marketing in our handgun division? Should we try to defend our current practices? What about altering them? In what ways? What are our responsibilities and to whom?" Those were the marching orders given to John Diller, Senior VP for Marketing. Diller had been recently been hired by Graham in the hope that he could help the beleaguered firm find a way out of its current difficulties. These difficulties had been brought upon them by increasing numbers of lawsuits filed against them and public charges which accused them of everything from crass indifference to moral culpability in the deaths and injuries of those caused by handguns.

Magnum had been very successful in recent years in the development and marketing of new firearms. Though Magnum offered a full range of firearms, including hunting rifles and target pistols, this market had leveled off. In response, several years ago, it had introduced two other models that had attracted special attention. One was a small, semi-automatic pistol, the Defender, which had a barrel length of only 2.75 inches and an overall length of 5 inches. It was easily concealable, lightweight, and powerful. The other was a special model, the Wildfire, which they advertised as "the gritty answer to tough problems." With a 40 round detachable magazine, a combat-style trigger guard, and surfaces specially treated to resist fingerprints, it had captured the imagination of movie makers, gun magazines and chat rooms on the Internet. There was no doubt that these two models had helped shore up their sales in recent years. But it was these two models that were under attack by the anti-gun lobby and their lawyers. These attacks had not been numerous and had been dismissed by most gun makers as unlikely to succeed until lately. Now the situation seemed to be changing.

THE LEGAL AND MORAL COMPLAINTS

What had particularly caught the attention of Magnum (and that of all other gun manufacturers) was the verdict of a federal jury in New York City that had found nine gun makers collectively liable for several shootings, even though plaintiff lawyers could not prove what brand of gun had been used in any of the cases. The jury had determined that the manufacturers were liable because of their negligent marketing and distribution of handguns. Even though the manufacturers were ordered to pay only 13% of the full amount, one of the plaintiffs was awarded an eye-popping $3.95 million.[1]

The jury found that manufacturers had oversupplied their products in states with weak gun laws, leading to illegal sales in those with strict regulations, like New York.[2] Elisa Barnes, the plaintiff's chief lawyer in this case, claimed that "the gun makers made no attempts to keep their products from falling into criminal hands, like requiring wholesalers not to supply dealers suspected of selling the weapons to questionable buyers." "They don't care" asserted Michael Feldberg, attorney for one of the plaintiffs.[3] In describing the overall situation, Ms. Barnes said: "This huge pool (of handguns) is like toxic waste. It's been sent down the river by different companies."[4]

Now Chicago, New Orleans, Miami, Atlanta, Newark (N.J.), Cleveland (Ohio), and Bridgeport (Connecticut) had filed similar suits; Philadelphia, Baltimore, and Los Angeles also had lawsuits under consideration. Chicago's action sought $433 million in damages, claiming that gun manufacturers have created a public nuisance and burdened the city with extra costs for public hospitals as well as extra police and fire protection.[5]

No one was denying that most large cities continue to be faced with high levels of violent crime. Many of these crimes are committed with firearms that are possessed and used illegally. Firearms were used to commit 69% of all homicides in 1995 and 68% in 1996. In 1995, there were 35,957 deaths attributable to firearms.[6] The high level of gun violence has had a particularly drastic impact on young persons; homicide is the second leading cause of death for youths aged 15–19.

In 1997, in Chicago alone, there were 8,866 robberies, 4,390 aggravated batteries and 3,963 aggravated assaults in which handguns were used. That same year, only 147 robberies were committed in the city with a firearm other than a handgun. Overall, approximately 87% of firearms used in all crimes in Chicago are handguns. A recent survey showed that 45% of persons arrested in the city obtained their guns in the illegal

firearms market. Although most major cities faced the same general set of problems, they approached the legal issues in different ways.

The New Orleans suit, for example, raised a number of relatively straightforward but disturbing issues. It claimed that gun manufacturers, by failing to incorporate appropriate safety devices to prevent use by children and other unauthorized persons, had failed to "personalize" handguns. The suit claimed that at least 30 patents for personalized guns have been granted since 1976. Designs such as combination locks, magnetic locks, radio frequency locks, and encoded chip locks are among the devices patented in attempts to limit the unauthorized use of handguns. Under the Louisiana product liability statute, a manufacturer can be held liable for damage caused by a product that is unreasonably dangerous in design. Under this doctrine, just as car manufacturers have been held liable for failing to install seat belts and air bags, gun makers should be liable for failing to install feasible safety systems.[7] The New Orleans suit alleges that guns that fail to incorporate safety systems to prevent their use by children and other unauthorized users are unreasonably dangerous in design. As a result, the United States leads the world in the number of children who are killed or injured by handguns, with "an average of more than four accidental shootings of children under 15 occur[ring] each day, one of whom dies every other day."[8]

Other cities, such as Chicago (and New York), have taken a more aggressive and less traditional approach to litigation, arguing that gun manufacturers oversupply guns in nearby suburban communities. These guns then end up in Chicago, a city with one of the strictest gun control laws in the nation. This is a result, the City of Chicago contends, of the sales practices of dealers in surrounding communities as well as the manufacturing and marketing practices of the gun manufacturers.

Many of the firearms illegally possessed in Chicago were purchased in a way that should have put the defendant dealers on reasonable notice that the buyer was not obtaining firearms for his own lawful use. For example, Stanley Malone, a resident of Bellwood, Illinois, purchased fourteen pistols from Bell's Gun & Sport Shop and from Suburban Sporting Goods between August, 1994 and June, 1996. He purchased the majority of these firearms to resell to gang members, making a profit of about $60 per firearm ("a straw purchase").[9] Other individuals made similar multiple purchases of handguns over similar periods of time. Sales clerks often made recommendations to undercover police officers regarding means of purchasing the guns to avoid investigation by the Bureau of Alcohol, Tobacco, and Firearms and other authorities. Clerks frequently disregarded comments about how these "buyers" wanted to settle scores with someone. In short, the City of Chicago claims that the practices of dealers in the surrounding communities have caused a large underground market for illegal firearms to flourish within its city limits, making it easy for Chicago residents to obtain firearms in clear violation of the "spirit" of the law.

The role of manufacturers and distributors in this process, the City of Chicago claims, is to knowingly oversupply or "saturate" the market with handguns in areas where gun control laws are less restrictive, knowing that they will be resold in jurisdictions where they cannot be sold legally. By shipping large numbers of firearms to these jurisdictions, the gun manufacturers enhance their profits while disclaiming any knowledge of or responsibility for where their products end up or how they are used. They also distribute substantial quantities of firearms through low-end retailers such as pawn shops and gun stores known to be frequented by criminals and gang members.

They choose not to supervise, regulate, or standardize their network of distributors and dealers because such practices would limit sales in one of their most lucrative markets.

In addition, gun manufacturers are alleged to design and advertise their products to appeal to illicit buyers (both directly and indirectly), including those who wish to use them for criminal purposes. Among the design features of these handguns are: 1) surfaces that offer "resistance to fingerprints"; 2) short barrel lengths and overall lengths; 3) lightweight, detachable magazines; and 4) semi-automatics that can be easily modified to fully automatic. Some models tout the fact that they do not have a hammer, meaning that they are easier to withdraw from a pocket (for quick firing) without snagging on clothing. Advertisements include descriptions of guns as "assault-type pistols" that "deliver more gutsy performance and reliability than any other gun on the market." Another is advertised as being "[c]onsidered the ultimate hideaway, undercover, backup gun available anywhere." The manufacturer, the S. W. Daniels Corporation, marketed this 9-millimeter semiautomatic pistol as the "weapon of choice of the drug lords of the 80s."[10] Another manufacturer called one of its products the "Streetsweeper."[11]

THE GUN INDUSTRY AND THE NATIONAL RIFLE ASSOCIATION

Although they rarely dispute the magnitude of crime problems in major cities, the "pro-gun" sector takes issue with the legal and moral claims made against gun makers. To most gun manufacturers the legal reasoning and arguments above have seemed sophistical and dangerous. The National Rifle Association has held that "this is the beginning [of an attempt] to accomplish . . . through the back door . . . what could not be accomplished through the legislative front door—the elimination of private gun owner-ship in America."[12]

The attempt to control the misuse of guns in this manner is fraught with other problems as well, according to the pro-gun group. "What's next," Wayne Lapierre, spokesman and CEO of the NRA asked, "blaming car manufacturers instead of drunk drivers. . . . Under this theory of law you could eliminate virtually every manufactured product in America."[13] Ralph Boyd, a lawyer who advises gun industries, agreed. "The auto industry makes vehicles that exceed . . . the lawful speed limit in any jurisdiction. What would stop someone from using this type of legal theory from saying, 'Hey, you know those commercials that show cars speeding across the countryside, making tight turns on mountains, zipping around pylons on race courses? Why isn't that negligent marketing? Why isn't the auto industry responsible for all the accidents resulting from excessive speed?' "[14]

Of course the gun industry has sought innovation in style, weight, size, capacity, and speed so as to boost its sales.[15] It is merely responding to the increased competition it faces and the softening of its markets. In general, it feels that its responsibility ends once its product are sold to licensed distributors. "The job of policing gun runners should be left to the Bureau of Alcohol, Tobacco and Firearms, which has never required manufacturers to track their products to the street."[16] Since it considers these lawsuits to pose significant dangers to legitimate rights, the NRA has introduced legislation in at least 20 states that would preclude local governments from suing gun manufacturers and distributors. The latest bill, proposed in Florida, is the toughest, making it a felony for any local official to file a lawsuit of this type.[17]

Besides, gun makers argue, someone ought to raise some questions about the ethics of the lawyers and cities who have brought legal suits against them. Outside of the case in New York, they have little reason, based on the present and past record, to believe that these suits will succeed. Indeed, they have with remarkable consistency been rejected. Instead, they are using these suits to apply financial pressure, or coercion, against the gun makers to pay the cities what amounts to extortion. And yet there have been few complaints raised against such moral tactics. Defenders of the gun makers see this as simply another example of individuals failing to take responsibility for their own behavior and seeking Big Brother, or rather some big law firm, to do for them what people will not do for themselves. It is the morals and lawful behavior of individuals which needs to be addressed in our society, not that of the gun makers.

DILLER'S DILEMMA

In light of all these charges and counter-charges and with significant legal threats in clear view, Magnum needed a coherent plan regarding both its response to the suits and the operation of its business in this new environment. John wondered what he should recommend. The theories of public nuisance, of product liability, and of collective liability advanced in the lawsuits seemed to extend well beyond their past applications. Besides, this was not simply a legal challenge to gun makers. Strong moral charges against the gun manufacturers were also part of the situation they faced. Magnum had to be prepared for all these charges. John wondered whether society and the gun manufacturers had responsibilities for the actions of other adults. How far back up the commercial path should responsibility be pushed and under what conditions? Should Magnum alter its design or marketing of the Defender or the Wildfire? John worried that he would have to have some idea how to answer these questions when he made his recommendation to Graham regarding both their immediate response to this legal situation and their long run approach to producing and marketing firearms.[18]

NOTES

1. Chris Hawke, "Jury Finds Gun Maker Negligence Responsible for Shooting," *Agence France Press,* Feb. 12, 1999. The case was that of Hamilton v. Accu-Tek. No. 95–0049.

2. Joseph P. Fried, "9 Gun Makers Called Liable for Shootings," *New York Times,* Feb. 12, 1999.

3. Ibid.

4. Tom Hays, "AP-Gens-on-Trail," *AP Online,* Feb. 12, 1999.

5. Resa King, "Firepower for the Antigun Lobby," *Business Week,* Feb. 1, 1999.

6. David Kairys, "Legal Claims of Cities Against the Manufacturers of Handguns," *Temple Law Review* 71 (Spring 1998), 2.

7. "Background Information on New Orleans Lawsuit Against Gun Industry," http://www.handguncontrol.org/legalaction/noqa.htm, Hand Gun Control, Feb. 19, 1999.

8. Kairys, 2.

9. Cf. City of Chicago and Country of Cook v. Beretta et al.

10. Daniel Wise, *New York Law Journal,* Jan. 7, 1999.

11. Kairys, 4.

12. Chris Hawke, "NRA Concerned About Gun Suit Verdict," United Press International, Feb. 12, 1999.

13. Ibid.

14. Laura Mansnerus, "Cities' Suits Against Gun Makers Raise Complicated Legal Issues," *Star Tribune* (Minneapolis, Minn.), Feb. 14, 1999.

15. Cf. King.

16. Cf. Hays.

17. Sharon Walsh, "NRA Pushing to Block Gun Suits," *Washington Post,* Feb. 26, 1999.

18. Thomas M. Jones gave me insightful help in preparing this case.

Everything Old to New Again

Conventional wisdom paradoxically tells us that even though change is constant, certain things never really change, and even when things appear to change, they wind up coming back again. This insight is clearly true in regard to certain aspects of men's fashion. For example, the width and pattern of ties are in constant flux, but sooner or later they all come around again. All the men we know over the age of forty-five possess at least three different widths of their very favorite paisley or striped tie. Boot-cut jeans, left for dead in the late 1970s, are back with a vengeance in the first decade of the twenty-first century.

This general principle seems also to apply to literature and fiction. What's that old rule of thumb about there being only twelve possible story lines? But even if this figure is wrong and should be doubled or even tripled, the fact is there are only so many plots, so many story lines, and so many possible dramatic narrative structures out there. When you think about it, isn't *West Side Story* just a mid-twentieth-century *Romeo and Juliet?* Isn't *Star Wars* a futuristic rendering of American westerns like *How the West Was Won?* And aren't the various adventures of Indiana Jones kitsch portrayals of the constant age-old struggle between good and evil?

On a more serious note, the poet and philosopher George Santayana suggested that conventional wisdom, far from being just a casual cliché, is often true. He warned us that things can and will repeat themselves, again and again: "Those who cannot remember the past are condemned to repeat it." Neither encyclopedic knowledge nor huge leaps of imagination are required to generate examples that support Santayana's thesis. Charles Ponzi's "postal coupon scam," the scourge of the 1920s, reemerged as Robert Vesco's "mutual funds scam" in the 1970s and as Charles Keating's savings-and-loan industry "multiple-book accounting scam" in the 1980s.

Ivan Boesky and Michael Milken were brought down in the 1980s on charges of insider trading—similar to the charges that led ultimately to America's favorite doyenne of domesticity, Martha Stewart, serving her recent prison sentence. "The Fall of Michael Milken" tells an important part of that story. "Enron: The Good, The Bad, and The Really Ugly" provides an insightful take on the firm whose name has become synonymous with fraud and whose fall led to the largest corporate bankruptcy in American history. "Kozlowski's Tyco—'I Am The Company!'" supplies perhaps the most egregious example of the self-serving CEO running a company he doesn't own for his own benefit. "The Parmalat Affair," recounting the spectacular unraveling of the Italian food conglomerate, demonstrates that large-scale corporate fraud is not a uniquely American phenomenon. "The Good Old Boys at WorldCom" and "The Ford Pinto" provide valuable insight into the sometimes shocking ways top managers think about and manage their firms and their products.

Case Study

The Fall of Michael Milken

O.C. Ferrell and John Fraedrich

Drexel Burnham Lambert, Inc. was an investment banking firm that rose to prominence during the 1980s, only to be toppled by one of the biggest scandals ever to hit Wall Street. Michael Milken, senior vice-president and head of Drexel's high-yield and convertible bond department, based in Beverly Hills, California, also succumbed to the scandal. Milken's and Drexel's rapid rise to the top came about as a result of their virtual creation and subsequent domination of the billion-dollar "junk bond" market that helped finance the 1980s takeover boom and change the face of corporate America. Their downfall was the result of a Securities and Exchange Commission (SEC) investigation that eventually led to Milken's incarceration and Drexel's bankruptcy.

THE "JUNK BOND KING"

Before Milken's ascent to the top of financial circles, junk bonds were a relatively obscure financial investment shunned by most investors. Junk bonds are debt securities that offer high rates of return at high risk. Often, they are securities that previously had been graded as "investment quality" but later were downgraded to low-grade, high-risk, high-yield status because of doubts about the issuer's financial strength. Drexel preferred to call these securities "high-yield bonds."

Michael Milken was the driving force behind Drexel's domination of the high-yield bond market. People familiar with the firm say Milken's office was responsible for 80 to 90% of Drexel's profits. In addition to bringing in huge profits for the company, Milken also amassed for himself a huge fortune. In the four-year period ending in 1987, he is believed to have made over $1.1 billion. In 1987 alone he earned $550 million in salary and bonuses—more than the firm he worked for—making him easily the highest-paid employee in history.

During the early 1980s, Milken recognized a tremendous opportunity in borrowing needs of relatively small companies. At that time, only about eight hundred companies issued bonds labeled investment grade, but there were thousands of firms with annual revenues of $25 million or more. Drexel's success was built on meeting those financing needs. The company's ability to raise capital through the high-yield bond market allowed many firms to borrow much-needed funds although they had not previously been considered creditworthy. In this sense, Drexel's activities supported growth. Nevertheless, Milken and Drexel have been sharply criticized, particularly in recent years, because their financial activities helped fuel the bitter takeover battles of the 1980s. Investment analysts generally view junk bonds and the companies that issue them as risky and unsafe. Milken continues to defend the use of

---

high-yield bonds; he argues that at the time, "We were matching capital to entrepreneurs who could use it effectively. We were creating investments that money managers needed in volatile markets."

THE CASE AGAINST MILKEN

In addition to criticism by some Wall Streeters, Drexel Burnham Lambert and Michael Milken also attracted the attention of the Securities and Exchange Commission, which between 1980 and 1985 launched four separate investigations into Drexel's activities. None of the investigations turned up enough evidence of wrongdoing to justify action. Only in 1986, when Ivan Boesky agreed to cooperate with prosecutors, was the government able to put together a case strong enough to warrant bringing charges against Drexel Burnham Lambert. During government investigations into a Wall Street insider-trader ring, Dennis Levine, a former Drexel investment banker, blew the whistle on Boesky. As a part of his deal with prosecutors, Boesky agreed to name people who had participated in insider trading and other illegal activities. Boesky's testimony led prosecutors to Drexel and to Milken, their number-one target.

In September 1988, after an investigation spanning two and a half years, the SEC filed a 194-page civil lawsuit against Drexel Burnham Lambert, Inc. The SEC also named Michael Milken, his brother Lowell, and other Milken aides in the suit. In its most sweeping enforcement action since the securities laws were written, the SEC charged Drexel with insider trading, stock manipulation, "parking" of securities to conceal their true ownership, false disclosures in SEC filings, maintaining false books and records, aiding and abetting capital rules violations, fraud in securities offerings materials, and various other charges. (Parking involves hiding ownership of securities by selling them to another with the understanding that they will

be sold back to the original owner, usually at a prearranged time and price.)

The SEC suit also raised questions about Drexel's supervision of Milken's Beverly Hills' operations. Milken reported to Edwin Kantor, head of trading in New York. The two reportedly spoke several times a day over the phone, but otherwise Milken ran the office with little intervention. In an interview held after the investigation and ensuing criminal case were completed, Drexel Burnham Lambert's chief executive officer Fred Joseph stated that he was "appalled and surprised by the organized nature of the crime wave." In retrospect, he admitted to "surprising naiveté." With leadership so loose, it is not clear who, if anyone, was overseeing Milken's activities.

While the SEC was putting together its case, the U.S. Department of Justice was building a criminal case against Drexel and its employees. This effort was led by Rudolph Giuliani, the U.S. attorney for the Manhattan district. At the same time the SEC filed its civil suit against Drexel, Giuliani's office notified Michael Milken, his brother Lowell (who managed many of Michael's accounts), and two other key traders that they would probably soon be indicted on securities laws violations. Drexel Burnham Lambert was notified of its impending indictment a few weeks later. Notification of an impending indictment usually means the prosecution has completed its investigation and is prepared to go to court.

The SEC and the U.S. attorney's office had worked together, sharing resources, information, and investigators, and both had good cases. Their adversary was also well prepared. Drexel had 115 lawyers to the SEC's 15, and the firm made it clear it could outspend the SEC. In fact, Drexel's legal defense budget was bigger than the entire SEC budget. Drexel had $2.3 billion in capital, and for two years it had been setting aside huge reserves to cover any litigation. Despite the bad publicity Drexel experienced, it continued to gain market share and became more profitable throughout the investigation. Even competitors were impressed by the loyalty of Drexel's clients, many of whom at the time of the SEC announcement vowed to remain loyal to Drexel and especially to Milken, who had helped many of them make millions of dollars.

Drexel Burnham Lambert faced charges from the U.S. attorney's office on securities, wire, and mail fraud as well as charges of racketeering under the Racketeering Influenced and Corrupt Organizations Act (RICO). RICO was enacted in 1970 to give the government a powerful weapon to go after organized crime; under the act, a person or business that commits two or more felonies as part of a pattern can be charged with racketeering. RICO allows prosecutors to charge entire organizations with crimes and to seize assets before trial to ensure payment of any subsequent penalties. In addition, RICO requires firms to forfeit any profits made or any property used during the period of wrongdoing. RICO laws carry heavy fines and long prison sentences, and they award triple damages to successful plaintiffs in civil suits.

RICO was first used against a securities firm in August 1988, when Giuliani's office indicated the five general partners of Princeton/Newport Partners, a small New Jersey-based investment firm, on racketeering charges. A former Drexel trader was involved in the transactions on which the partners were indicted. The firm folded within five months of the indictment. Princeton/Newport officials blamed the firm's demise on the fact that clients were scared off from doing business with a racketeer. At the time of the charges against Drexel, some observers expressed surprise that Drexel itself was named rather than the senior executives as individual persons, as in the Princeton/Newport Partners case.

Giuliani's office set out to prove that Drexel used Boesky as a front for secretly trading some stocks. By so doing, Drexel could increase the price of takeover stocks so that it could get higher fees and trigger unwanted takeovers.

The profits were then funneled back into the firm using dubious payments, with false paperwork covering the trail. In many cases Drexel's goal appeared to be power as much as profit—the ability to control the outcome of the deals it financed. Giuliani's case against the firm centered around a $5.3 million payment Boesky made in March 1987 to Drexel for "consulting services." The prosecution alleged this amount was actually part of the profits on stock that Drexel had parked with Boesky's firm. There were also allegations that Drexel and Boesky deliberately destroyed documents to cover up their activities. Of the six charges initially brought against Drexel, all involved transactions allegedly initiated by Michael Milken, and five of the six transactions allegedly involved Boesky. Drexel set out to discredit Boesky as Giuliani's office supported his claims against Drexel with written documentation and other informants—Charles Thurnher, James Dahl, Cary Maultesch, and Terrence Peizer—all of whom had worked for Michael Milken.

As the possibility of a court trial increased, defense lawyers began negotiations with prosecutors to drop the racketeering charges. They argued that RICO was intended to be used against the Mafia and that such charges would be unfair to business, disruptive to the equity and debt markets, and harmful to the economy. Giuliani initially wanted Drexel and its employees to waive their client-attorney privileges so that he could get access to Drexel's records on its own internal investigation of employees in the matter. After several rounds of negotiations, it was clear that Giuliani wanted a settlement. It was also clear that he would not hesitate to invoke the full force of the RICO statutes if he did not get one.

In December 1988, after spending more than $100 million on its legal defense and denying any misconduct or wrongdoing for more than two years, Drexel pleaded guilty to a six-count felony indictment on charges of securities, wire, and mail fraud and agreed to pay a record $650 million in fines and restitution. Drexel also gave in to the government demand that it had most vehemently opposed: It agreed to cooperate in all continuing investigations, including investigations of some of its own clients and employees—including Michael Milken. In return, the prosecutor dropped the racketeering charges against the company. CEO Fred Joseph said Drexel's decision was the only alternative that gave the company a chance to survive.

The settlement with the Justice Department was contingent on Drexel's settling with the SEC, which it did in the spring of 1989. Under that agreement, Drexel submitted to unprecedented federal supervision, agreed to a three-year probation, and had to appoint board members approved by the SEC. In addition, Drexel was required to move its Beverly Hills operation back to New York and to sever ties with Michael Milken. In the agreement, Drexel neither admitted nor denied guilt. By agreeing to plead guilty to the felony charges in which Michael Milken was also implicated and by cooperating with the prosecution in all continuing investigations, Drexel in effect withdrew all support from its most productive employee. The firm was also asked to withhold Milken's 1988 salary and bonus. Some saw the guilty plea as a bargaining chip that Drexel used to gain other concessions from the prosecutor and said Drexel was passing sentence on Milken before he got a trial. Milken's attorney later protested that this denied his client due process.

MILKEN IS INDICTED

Michael Milken was handed his own ninety-eight count felony indictment, including charges of racketeering, in March 1989. In June he resigned from Drexel to form his own company—just before the federal court approved the terms of the SEC settlement that would have forced his termination anyway.

This, along with the fact that Milken continued to proclaim his innocence, widened a rift that had existed in the firm since 1978, when Milken had set up the junk bond operations on the West Coast. Milken's office had become a company within a company, employing about 600 of the elite among Drexel's 9,100 people. Those in "Drexel East," as they came to be called by those in the Beverly Hills office, were often jealous of the high commissions and big bonuses paid to the employees in the junk-bond department. Those in the West saw the men on the board as nonproducers who got rich off Milken and then sold him out to preserve their positions and capital.

Drexel Burnham Lambert CEO Joseph had been a principal negotiator in working out the settlement. He was caught between trying to wring as many concessions from Giuliani as he could and trying to keep an increasingly bitter work force of traders, analysts, and brokers from quitting. However, Joseph made matters worse for himself when, at the board meeting held to accept or reject the settlement, he and five of the other twenty-two members of the board voted against the agreement Joseph had just negotiated.

This token support fooled no one and, in the view of some, made him appear hypocritical, Joseph later admitted privately that what he had done had been a mistake. In talking with a client who happened to be a Milken supporter, Joseph mentioned that he viewed Giuliani as a worthy adversary and that the prosecutor could have come down harder on the firm if he had chosen to do so. The client saw the prosecutor as having "taken Joseph, turned him, and made him his own." Many Milken loyalists within the firm regarded Joseph as a "traitorous wimp."

Some observers say that RICO is a tool that allows prosecutors to scare defendants into submission before getting close to court. Certainly, Joseph initially had no intention of settling, for he believed that firms that had recently settled with the government in other types of cases had not fared well. Other observers, however, are less sympathetic. The $650 million fine, they point out, is not due all at once and is partially (20%) tax deductible. Moreover, $650 million may not be a very significant penalty for a firm that made as much as $200 million on a single deal. In fact, for a while the most popular joke on Wall Street was that the "latest buyout" referred to the way Drexel handled the U.S. attorney's office.

Drexel Burnham Lambert did manage to avoid a lengthy court trial and its accompanying expense and publicity. It avoided the severe penalties of RICO, including jail sentences for top management and the stigma of a racketeering-conviction label. In addition, Drexel was not prohibited from doing business in the junk-bond market. It was, however, a convicted felon and without the services of Michael Milken and other key employees. And, although many clients remained loyal to the firm, others followed Milken or broke ties altogether. Drexel lost its dominance in the junk-bond market.

THINGS GET WORSE

To maintain some degree of profitability, Drexel sold its retail brokerage and mutual fund businesses and trimmed about 40% of its work force from the payroll. Despite Drexel Burnham Lambert's efforts to remain a player in financial markets, the collapse of the junk-bond market in late 1989 was the final blow to the company. Unable to maintain the liquidity needed to buy and sell huge quantities of securities, the company declared bankruptcy in February 1990.

In a plea-bargain arrangement, Michael Milken pleaded guilty on April 24, 1990, to six felony charges, ranging from mail and wire fraud to conspiracy and net-capital violations. He was sentenced to ten years in prison and

three years of community service on his release. He must pay $200 million in fines and penalties as well as $400 million in restitution to victims of his crimes. Additionally, he was barred forever from the securities industry. In return, prosecutors dropped all charges against Lowell Milken (although he, too, was forever barred from the securities industry) and the remaining charges filed against Michael Milken in 1989.

Michael Milken was released to a halfway house in Los Angeles on January 3, 1993. After Milken served twenty-two months in federal prison, his original ten-year sentence was reduced to two years. He spent two months in the halfway house work-release program, but he is still barred by the Securities and Exchange Commission from the investment brokerage industry. His halfway house employment was through his lawyer's firm, Victor and Sandler, researching civil legal cases. In early 1993, it was estimated that Michael Milken had paid $1.1 billion in fines and settlements connected with his work in the securities business at Drexel Burnham Lambert.

After spending 22 months in a federal prison, Michael Milken at the age of 46 indicated that he had inoperable prostate cancer. Milken said he was the victim of a Wall Street witch hunt that had him as a prize trophy. Milken pointed out thousands of emerging businesses he helped to grow, including MCI, Turner Broadcasting, and the largest black-owned business, TLC Beatrice. In June of 1993, he was worth $500 million after paying $1 billion in fines and settlements. He continues to work on 1,800 hours of court-ordered community service with a drug prevention program in inner-city Los Angeles. In a June 5, 1993 interview with Barbara Walters, on the television program *20/20*, he presented himself as a humanitarian, philanthropist, and builder of business. He told Walters in the interview that, "I was involved with over 3 million transactions in my career. Did we have an oversight in bookkeeping in one or two transactions? Yes.

No one thought it was criminal. I am not perfect, and I've never met a person who was."

NOTE

These facts are from Stephen J. Adler and Laurie P. Cohen, "Using Tough Tactics. Drexel's Lawyers May Advance While Appearing to Lose," *The Wall Street Journal*, October 12, 1988, p. 138; Laurie P. Cohen, "Drexel Lawyers. Justice Agency to Meet, Discuss RICO Status in Possible Charges," *The Wall Street Journal*, October 20, 1988, p. A3; Laurie P. Cohen, "Drexel Learns U.S. May Soon Ask an Indictment from Grand Jurors," *The Wall Street Journal*, October 19, 1988, p. A3; Laurie P. Cohen, "Drexel Pact Contains Concessions by U.S.," *The Wall Street Journal*, December 27, 1988, p. A3; Laurie P. Cohen, "Milken's Stiff 10-Year Sentence Is Filled with Incentives to Cooperate with the U.S.," *The Wall Street Journal*, November 23, 1990, p. A3; Laurie P. Cohen, "SEC, Drexel Expected to Request Approval of Proposed Settlement." *The Wall Street Journal*, June 15, 1989, p. B4; Laurie P. Cohen and Stephen J. Adler, "Indicting Milken, U.S. Demands $1.2 Billion of Financier's Assets," *The Wall Street Journal*, March 30. 1989, p. A1; John R. Ernshwiller, "Milken's Pursuit of Business Opportunity Built a Personal Fortune, Brought Drexel to the Fore," *The Wall Street Journal*, September 8, 1988, p. 7A; Michael Calen, with Dean Foust and Eric Schine, "'Guilty, Your Honor'"; Now, Will Milken Help the Feds Nab Other Wall Street Criminals?" *Business Week*, May 7, 1990, pp. 33–34; Colin Lernster and Alicia Hills Moore, "I Woke Up with My Stomach Churning," *Fortune*, July 3, 1989, p. 120; Michael Milken, interviewed by Barbara Walters, *20/20*, June 5, 1995; Michael Milken, as told to James W. Michaels and Phyllis Berman, "My Story—Michael Milken," *Forbes*, March 16, 1992, pp. 78–100; "Milken Move," *USA Today*, December 28, 1992, p. B1; "Mixed Feelings About Drexel's Decision; Some Call It Wise; Others, a Lack of Will," *The Wall Street Journal*, December 23, 1988, p. B1; Thomas E. Ricks, "SEC's Failed Probes of Milken in Past Show Difficulty of Its Mission," *The Wall Street Journal*, January 30, 1989, p. A1; Michael Siconolfi, William Power, Laurie P. Cohen, and Robert Guenther, "Rise and Fall: Wall Street Era Ends as Drexel Burnham Decides to Liquidate; Junk Bonds' Creator Becomes Their Victim as Securities It Holds Plunge in Value," *The Wall Street Journal*, February 14, 1990, pp. A1, A12; Randall Smith, "How Drexel Wields Its Power in Market for High Yield Bonds," *The Wall Street Journal*, May 26, 1988, pp. 1, 12; James B. Stewart, Steven J. Adler, and Laurie P. Cohen, "Out on a Limb, Drexel's Milken Finds Himself More Isolated as Indictment Nears," *The Wall Street Journal*, December 23, 1988, p. A1; James B. Stewart and Daniel Hartzberg, "SEC Accuses Drexel of a Sweeping Array of Securities Violations," *The Wall Street Journal*, September 8, 1988, pp. 1B, 7B: James B. Stewart and Daniel Hartzberg, "U.S. Reportedly to Seek Charges Tied to Transactions of Princeton/Newport," *The Wall Street Journal*, August 4, 1988, pp. 2, 4; James B. Stewart, Daniel Hartzberg, and Laurie P. Cohen, "Biting the Bullet, Drexel Agrees to Plead Guilty and Pay Out a Record $650 Million," *The Wall Street Journal*, December 22, 1988, p. A1; "Still Drawing a Crowd," *USA Today*, January 6, 1993, p. B3; Steve Swartz, "Why Mike Milken Stands to Qualify for Guinness Book," *The Wall Street Journal*, March 31, 1989, p. A1; Steve Swartz and Bryan Burrough, "Tough Choice, Drexel Faces Difficulty Whether It Settles Case or Gambles on a Trial," *The Wall Street Journal*, September 9, 1988, pp. 1, 7; Blair S. Walker, "Milken Rewrites His Life Story," *USA Today*, June 7, 1993, p. 3B; Monci Jo Williams, "Can Fred Joseph Save Drexel?" *Fortune*, May 8, 1989, p. 89; and Monci Jo Williams, "Drexel's Profit and Potential Loss," *Fortune*, February 27, 1989, p. 8.

Case Study

Enron: The Good, The Bad, and The Really Ugly

Denis Collins

Enron. The name conjures up images of everything wrong with corporate America. And for good reason. The poster child of the "New Economy" and a darling of Wall Street, Enron's stock price soared through the 1990s, enriching millions of investors. If you bought the stock in

---

August 1999 and sold it one year later, you more than doubled your money. For five consecutive years, Enron won *Fortune* magazine's award for being the nation's most innovative company. In 2000, with revenue climbing to $100 billion, *Fortune* named Enron America's best-managed company; it was ranked #7 on the Fortune 500 list. One year later Enron imploded into bankruptcy. Twenty thousand people lost their jobs and pensions, and hundreds of thousands lost their investment.

Enron's demise can be attributed to a wide range of diverse factors, including the personalities of key decision-makers, the organizational culture, economic and political trends, and the nature of capitalism. The same deadly ingredients can destroy any organization, if owners and managers are not careful.

THE BEGINNING

Exposed in late 2001, Enron's fraudulent accounting techniques can be traced back to the early 1990s when Enron adopted aggressive accounting measures for calculating revenue. At the time, the company was trying to financially grow out of the heavy debt incurred following the 1985 merger of the two natural gas pipeline companies that became Enron. Minneapolis investor Irwin "The Liquidator" Jacobs had set his sights on raiding Omaha's financially troubled InterNorth natural gas company. The hostile takeover was averted when Ken Lay, the CEO of the much smaller Houston Natural Gas (HNG), agreed to sell his company to InterNorth for $2.4 billion. Lay and other HNG shareholders were paid $70 a share for stock selling at $47. The combined InterNorth/HNG entity had a daunting $4.3 billion debt to manage, leading Jacobs to withdraw his initial offer.

Lay soon impressed a majority of InterNorth/HNG's board of directors with his astute responsiveness to the Reagan Administration's deregulation policies. Just six months later, the board promoted Lay to CEO, making him the fifth-highest-paid chief executive in the United States. The combined corporate entity was renamed Enron, and Lay moved its headquarters from Omaha to his adopted city, Houston.

KEN LAY'S RAGS TO RICHES

Becoming Enron's CEO was a dream come true for Ken Lay, the ambitious forty-two-year-old son of an ordained Southern Baptist preacher. Born in 1942, Lay grew up in rural poverty as a Missouri farm boy, living without indoor plumbing until the age of eleven. He received a scholarship to attend the University of Missouri, where he earned a master's degree in economics, and later became a senior economist for a Houston oil company. Being of draft age during the Vietnam War, Lay enlisted in the Navy and was assigned to conduct economic analyses at the Pentagon, work that he leveraged into a doctoral degree in economics in 1970 from the University of Houston.

After completing his military career, Lay served as a chief aide to the Federal Power Commission and Deputy Undersecretary of Energy in the Department of the Interior, where he specialized in deregulation policies. His work led to a job as vice-president of governmental affairs at Florida Gas, where he was promoted to president within two years. Through hard work and the right connections, Lay advanced from childhood poverty, when he felt lucky to have lunch meat to eat on Thanksgiving, to becoming president of a regulated monopoly before the age of forty, with an annual salary of $268,000, equivalent to more than $700,000 in 2006 dollars. A few years later he became CEO of Enron.

SKILLING'S GAS BANK TO THE RESCUE

Enron, which had dug a deep financial hole to avoid Jacobs's hostile takeover attempt, reported losses of $14 million in 1986, and almost defaulted on its debt payments. Lay relied heavily on McKinsey and Company, the world's most prestigious consulting firm, to help him manage Enron's operational problems. He was very impressed with one particular McKinsey consultant—Jeffrey Skilling.

Whereas Lay's "rags-to-riches" story appropriately earned him the Horatio Alger Award, Skilling had always been a master of the universe. While still in high school, Skilling had saved an amazing $15,000—equivalent to $81,000 in today's money—working as a production manager for a cable television station. He invested all of it in the stock market, and lost it when a bull market turned bear. Despite losing a small fortune, Skilling was hooked on the intellectual excitement of trying to outsmart other stock market investors in predicting a company's future performance. He went on to earn a finance degree from Southern Methodist University and an MBA from Harvard.

With the collapse of communism in 1989, Lay and Skilling understood that the world would eventually become one transparent global market. The first companies to take advantage of the new political and economic landscapes would jump to the head of the Fortune 500 list. They predicted that natural gas would play a more prominent role in the nation's future energy portfolio, and Enron owned the largest natural gas pipeline in the United States.

But the natural gas industry was a mess. Public utilities purchased natural gas every thirty days on the highly unpredictable spot market, making accurate long-term budgeting for suppliers and customers nearly impossible.

Skilling's genius was to create a Gas Bank, where natural gas producers could sell their reserves to Enron, which would then sell them to customers under long-term contracts. Enron would take on the price fluctuation risk for both producers and consumers. Lay hired Skilling in August 1990 to be the CEO of Enron's new Gas Bank Division. In addition to a $275,000 salary and a $950,000 loan, Skilling negotiated for a $10 million cash bonus when the division grew to a valuation of $200 million, and $17 million more when the Gas Bank reached a valuation of $400 million.

Skilling focused on reaching those financial goals. A mere four months after taking the job, he struck gold with his first long-term deal, a $1.3 billion contract to sell natural gas to the New York Power Authority for the next twenty-three years. By the end of 1990, Enron had become the nation's largest natural gas company with $13.2 billion in revenue, a 40% increase from the previous year. The thirty-six-year-old Skilling became an instant corporate hero.

Lay, who didn't like personal conflict, particularly with someone as headstrong and successful as Skilling, gave Skilling plenty of latitude to run his division as he saw fit. Skilling changed Enron's corporate culture from a southern, conservative, good-old-boy system in a highly regulated industry to a very competitive "survival-of-the-fittest" system by attracting the brightest students graduating from the nation's elite MBA programs, tasking them to exploit new market opportunities. The "Skillingites" he employed tended to be extremely intelligent, creative, competitive, single-minded MBAs willing to work eighty-hour weeks. Dangling lucrative stock options and pay for performance bonuses, Skilling offered them an opportunity to become multi-millionaires by the age of forty, just as he did.

MARK-TO-MARKET ACCOUNTING

By mid-1991, the Gas Bank division had long-term contracts with more than 35 natural gas producers and 50 users, generating tremendous financial value for Enron. But it didn't look that way to the outsiders Skilling wanted to impress because Enron's traditional pipeline accounting system only recognized revenue when received. Skilling wanted this changed so that his division's financial statements would reflect the almost guaranteed long-term future revenue streams from public utilities, entities that state governments would not allow to fail.

He looked to the financial industry for an alternative accounting method because his Gas Bank division traded energy in much the same way that brokerage firms traded capital. He found what he was looking for in mark-to-market accounting. Financial institutions calculated the value of their stock portfolios by marking the stock against the current market price, not the original purchase price. By applying the same accounting logic to his Gas Bank division, Enron could claim the current economic value of its almost guaranteed long-term contracts with public utilities.

The Securities and Exchange Commission (SEC) rejected Skilling's initial request to do so, in part because trading companies rely on the market system, an external independent source, to determine the value of their assets, whereas Enron employees would be determining the long-term value of Gas Bank assets, making the valuation more prone to abuse. Skilling insisted such manipulation could be prevented through rigorous auditor oversight, and Enron employed one of the most prestigious auditing firms in the world, Arthur Andersen. With strong support from Arthur Andersen and Enron's board of directors, the SEC approved Enron's use of mark-to-market accounting for the first quarter of 1992. Skilling retroactively applied mark-to-market accounting for the recently completed 1991 fiscal year, which favorably impacted executive bonuses.

ANDY FASTOW AND SPECIAL PURPOSE ENTITIES

Enron still had a lot of debt. Skilling hired Andy Fastow, an expert on cutting-edge finance activities and husband to the heir of a Houston fortune, to do something about the company's debt problems. Fastow, who had majored in economics and Chinese at Tufts University and earned an MBA from Northwestern, quickly became Skilling's confidant. He even named his first son "Jeff" in honor of his new mentor. Fastow, who was loud, vulgar, obnoxious, and prone to temper tantrums, fit in well with the boys-will-be-boys culture being developed by Skilling. Fastow also shared an important attribute with both Lay and Skilling—a propensity for financial risk-taking.

Fastow quickly became an expert on Special Purpose Entities (SPEs), "off-balance-sheet" arrangements that protect company assets from risky business projects. A wide variety of companies, including airlines and large manufacturers, use SPEs to finance the purchase of assets, such as an airplane or new technology. Accounting-wise, an SPE is treated as a separate business entity rather than a subsidiary. If an SPE fails, the sponsoring company's assets are legally protected from the SPE's creditors. According to accounting standards, SPE status can be declared if the business entity meets two important criteria: (1) an independent owner maintains at least a 3% equity investment that remains at risk at all times, and (2) the independent owner exercises managerial control of the SPE.

With some creativity, Fastow constructed SPEs that generated large financial benefits for both Enron and the SPE. He funded SPEs with as much as 97% Enron stock, the highest amount legally allowed, thus requiring no cash from Enron. As Enron's stock increased, so did the economic value of the SPE, making the SPE more attractive to outside investors. Fastow then used the SPEs to add revenue to, and decrease liabilities from, Enron's financial statement. By purchasing an asset *for* Enron's use, the debt associated with the purchase would appear on the SPE's, not Enron's, balance sheet. By purchasing an asset *from* Enron, the SPE would help inflate Enron's revenue and remove the purchased asset's debt from Enron's balance sheet.

Why would an SPE's outside investors agree to this arrangement? These transactions significantly improved Enron's financial statements, which attracted the attention of Wall Street investors, who then drove Enron's stock price to higher levels. Because an SPE's financial foundation was primarily based on Enron stock, SPE outside investors earned very favorable return-on-investments whenever Enron's stock price increased. The win-win relationship between Enron and the SPE would continue for as long as Enron's stock price continued to increase in value. Fastow quickly became one of Skilling's favorite employees.

INTERNATIONAL EXPANSION AND REBECCA MARK

Enron's International Operations Division, under Rebecca Mark's leadership, rivaled the Gas Bank's growth potential. During Mark's ascendancy, Enron negotiated a contract to construct the world's largest cogeneration plant, one that would supply 3 to 4% of Great Britain's electricity needs. Mark, an attractive woman who frequently exploited her good looks in the macho work of international development, possessed a missionary's zeal to provide developing nations in South America and Asia with the energy required for industrialization. She hired well-known high level dignitaries, such as former Secretaries of State James Baker and Henry Kissinger, to open international doors.

Entering new markets requires substantial start-up costs. To attract high quality managers, executive bonuses were based on the economic value of a deal, not profits. For instance, Mark and her executive team skillfully negotiated a $2.9 billion contract to build a power plant in Dabhol, India that would meet the region's increasing energy needs. The deal was justified based on future revenue projections from the sale of energy. The executives were not expected to return their bonuses when, several years later, the agreement collapsed due to local political problems.

Unfortunately for Enron, Mark was typically out-negotiated. When Argentina privatized its water system, Mark's winning bid of $438.6 million exceeded the next highest bid by $288 million. Even worse, the agreement did not include the water company's main office building, a major oversight by Enron's negotiating team. Yet what turned out to be a terrible financial deal for Enron benefited Marx and her management team, whose bonuses were linked to the price of the winning bid.

MANAGING CASH FLOW PROBLEMS

Enron faced several major financial hurdles as its debt kept growing. Skilling's use of mark-to-market accounting techniques made it more difficult to achieve new annual revenue targets. Wall Street analysts continually increased revenue expectations based on the amount of reported revenue. Each year Skilling's division had to exceed its inflated revenue calculations by 15%. This created a cash flow problem because a substantial amount of the Gas Bank's reported revenue was projected, not actual. Skilling considered the cash crunch to be a short-term problem and turned to his protégé, Andy Fastow, to pull him out of the cash hole. Fastow found a complex way to obtain loans from an investment banker that could be recorded as cash on Enron's financial statements through an intricate web of SPEs.

Lay, impressed with the Gas Bank's annual 20% growth rate, promoted Skilling to Chief Operating Officer (COO) for the entire company, a step away from succeeding Lay as Enron's CEO. With his power extended to other divisions, Skilling inserted loyalists in key executive positions throughout the company. He promoted Fastow to vice-president of Treasury and Business Funding, with a goal of raising $20 billion a year in capital. Everyone at Enron who needed capital would have to cooperate with Fastow's growing staff.

Skilling challenged his executive team to apply the successful Gas Bank business model to other operational areas. The plan was simple: find an untapped area of business, buy some assets, don't worry about initial costs, get the revenue numbers up, and control 20% of the market. Soon, sales volume would more than make up for the initial sunk costs. Skilling went on a buying spree, purchasing assets in other industries, such as electricity, paper and coal. Enron then created ways to trade key commodities between potential buyers and sellers within these industries, with Enron getting a small percentage of each transaction.

VIOLATING ACCOUNTING REGULATIONS

Skilling began with the electricity industry due to its similarities to the natural gas industry. Enron focused on California because the state was on the verge of deregulating electricity. The first major problem Fastow had to deal with was what to do with an asset Enron already owned in the state, which would lose its tax advantage if Enron became a major player in the California electricity market. Fastow created an SPE called RADR to purchase the asset from Enron in a way that protected the tax advantage.

Outside investors had profited quite nicely from Fastow-structured SPEs. Fastow now wanted to have some of the economic rewards that RADR would likely generate. However, Enron's Code of Ethics prohibited senior executives from having a financial stake in any organization doing business with Enron. The potential conflict of interest seemed obvious: would Fastow represent Enron's interest by selling an asset to RADR for the highest possible price, or represent RADR's interest by buying an asset from Enron at the lowest possible price?

Enron's Code of Ethics prohibited only senior executives, not their assistants. Looking to exploit the loophole, Fastow initially considered making his assistant and protégé, Michael Kopper, serve as the RADR's outside investor. Fearing that the link would be too obvious, Fastow created "Friends of Enron" to serve as RADR's outside investor. The investment group was led by Bill Dodson, Kopper's domestic partner, who borrowed $419,000 from Fastow's wife to create the group. Kopper funneled RADR's profits back to Fastow by writing "gift" checks to the Fastow family in amounts just under the IRS minimum required for tax reporting and other schemes.

This network of relationships, hidden from Arthur Andersen auditors, violated company policy and Generally Accepted Accounting Principles (GAAP). Next, Fastow created an even more problematic SPE called Chewco that was ultimately 99% funded by Enron, a clear violation of accounting rules and regulations. Fastow named Kopper as Chewco's managing director, and gave his wife Lea an administrative position with an annual salary of $54,000.

CONQUERING THE CHECKS AND BALANCES

Fastow, as well as Skilling, managed his way around every check and balance established by Enron and federal authorities.

Internally, Enron's risk assessment and control (RAC) department was responsible for calculating the economic impact of Fastow's deals, ensuring their fairness from Enron's perspective. However, Fastow and Skilling controlled Enron's semiannual 360 degree performance evaluation process. One negative performance evaluation submitted by a Skillingite could undo a host of favorable comments submitted on behalf of an RAC employee. Not cooperating with Fastow could end one's career at Enron.

Externally, outside auditors and lawyers have professional obligations to protect shareholder interests. However, Arthur Andersen and Vinson & Elkins, Enron's law firm, earned substantial consulting fees from Enron. Disagreeing with Fastow could threaten future consulting assignments. The relationships among the SPEs and Enron had become so complex, and Fastow's presentations about them so misleading, that only someone dedicated to finding a known fraud in the web of relationships would be able to unravel the illegality.

In addition, many Enron accountants were former Arthur Andersen employees. Richard Causey, Enron's Chief Accounting Officer, was a former Andersen auditor. In early 1997, David Duncan, a relatively young partner at thirty-eight years old, had worked with Causey on one of Fastow's first SPEs, and became Andersen's lead auditor on the $40 million Enron account. Duncan would be reviewing his former trusted colleague's work. Furthermore, Duncan's annual bonus and advancement within Arthur Andersen depended on his increasing client fees by 20%. Critically questioning Enron's accounting transactions and financial arrangements could mean career suicide, something Fastow and Skilling pointed out to Duncan and his subordinates.

Lastly, members of the board of directors, who owned significant amounts of stock in Enron, have a fiduciary duty to represent shareholder interests. However, several board members earned consulting fees from Enron, which made it difficult for them to confront Lay or Skilling about potential improprieties. In addition, they considered Lay and Skilling to be their friends and respected them as colleagues.

At each level of checks and balances, an assumption was made that questionable or illegal SPE arrangements would be detected by the next level. Those holding authority at each successive level assumed that Fastow's deals were legitimate because the previous level had not objected to them. The board of directors, which has ultimate responsibility, signed off on the questionable transactions under the assumption that they had the approval of Enron's RAC department, Andersen auditors, and Vinson & Elkins lawyers.

THE BOOM YEARS

Throughout 1998, Enron's stock price steadily climbed 48%, to $57.10 a share. Lay promised to double employees' annual salary in Enron shares of stock if the company continued to hit its performance targets. With everyone's attention fixated on Enron's stock price momentum, Skilling went on a buying spree funded by Enron stock, acquiring 41 companies. He also invested $1 billion to jump-start broadband activities, sending a strong message to employees: Enron's future success would be grounded in trading commodities and Internet expansion, not brick-and-mortar pipelines. Skilling promoted Fastow to Chief Financial Officer (CFO) and removed Mark as CEO of Enron's financially overextended International Division. Fastow hid her many financial failures with a web of SPEs; again, these SPEs were funded primarily with Enron stock.

On April 7, 1999, Enron hit the Initial Public Offering (IPO) jackpot with its investment in Rhythms NetConnections, an Internet service provider. Enron's 5.4 million pre-IPO shares, worth $10 million at the beginning of the day, skyrocketed in value to $372 million by the end of the day. When the investment value declined to $300 million a month later, Skilling wanted to claim the $290 million profit before the stock price declined further. But pre-IPO investors had a legal obligation to hold the stock for six months after the public offering before selling it.

Fastow found a way around this rule by creating an SPE called "LJM1" (named after his wife Lea and sons Jeff and Matthew) to purchase a "put option" from Enron that would lock in the profit. Among LJM1's outside investors were some of the largest investment banks doing business with Enron. When investors questioned how LJM1 would profit from such transactions, Fastow noted that they should trust him; not only would he be directing the fund, he would also be one of the investors, with Enron's permission.

Fastow and Skilling convinced Enron's Board of Directors to waive the company's Code of Ethics so that Fastow could invest $1 million in LJM1 and serve as its director. This was a clear violation of GAAP because LJM1 was being managed by Enron's CFO rather than an independent manager. Fastow was now negotiating on both sides of the table. He favored LJM1 and scolded Enron employees if they negotiated too hard. After all, Fastow argued, LJM1 was helping Enron get debt off its financial statements. When Enron's treasurer complained to Skilling about Fastow's strong-armed negotiating tactics, Skilling reassigned the treasurer.

Even though Fastow favored LJM1 in the negotiations, the results were still so beneficial for Enron that Skilling granted Fastow permission to create LJM2 to serve a similar purpose. The professional staff of LJM2 included Fastow's protégé's Michael Kopper and Ben Glisan, both of whom were on the Enron payroll. During the last eleven days of 1999,

Fastow orchestrated seven deals between Enron and the LJMs that provided Enron with badly needed cash and helped different business units meet quarterly projection targets.

Fastow's schemes included an illegal arrangement, wherein Merrill Lynch investment bankers created a company called Ebarge to temporarily purchase three electricity-generating power barges off the coast of Nigeria that Enron owned. Enron claimed a $12 million profit from the sale, with the understanding that it would purchase the barges back within six months at a price favorable to Ebarge. The parking of an asset with a guaranteed buy-back was a clear violation of GAAP rules. Another complicated set of maneuvers involved an SPE called Southampton Place. In less than two months, the Fastow Family Foundation and Kopper's domestic partner each received $4.5 million for their $25,000 investment, and an Enron lawyer and Ben Glisan, Enron's new treasurer, each received $1 million for their $5,800 investment.

Fastow had become everyone's savior. His creative financing of Enron's mergers and acquisitions were widely acclaimed in the media and earned him *CFO Magazine's* 1999 CFO Excellence Award. That year, Enron succeeded General Electric as the winner of *Fortune* magazine's best-managed company in America.

TROUBLES IN PARADISE

The year 2000 was a wild roller coaster ride for Enron. The dot.com bubble burst in April 2000 and the Internet bull market soon came to a screeching halt. As a result, by mid-year, Enron's new broadband division surpassed its projected $100 million in annual losses and raised its projected loss expectation to $500 million.

Enron's financial statements were saved by a California heat wave and traders who manipulated the electricity market to the detriment of rate-payers. Enron relied on creative accounting techniques to prevent disgruntled electricity consumers and California politicians from determining how much the company profited from the state's turmoil. Skilling and Causey created "Schedule C," an account that did not appear on Enron's balance sheet, to hide $1 billion in profits from its California business that they could use to offset any future losses and to help other business units meet their quarterly targets.

The announcement of a twenty-year partnership with Dallas-based Blockbuster to provide videos on demand through the Internet helped boost Enron's stock price to $90.56 a share by late August. Consumers would be able to choose from a library of the most recently released movie videos from the comfort of their homes. However, the companies were not even close to developing the necessary cost-effective technology. Given a stock split, Enron stock purchased for $40 when Skilling became COO in March 1997 was now worth $181. Rebecca Mark was finally pushed out of Enron for her many failures, and cashed out $82.5 million in stock options. Causey sold a more modest $10 million in stock and Skilling sold more than $7 million in stock options.

Skilling, a hero in the financial press, was now poised to take on Lay's CEO duties and steer the course of Enron's future in 2001. As 2000 came to a close, Enron rose to #7 on the Fortune 500 list with $100 billion in revenue, a 150% increase from the previous year, and $1.3 billion in reported profits.

SKILLING'S REIGN AS ENRON CEO

On February 12, 2001, Ken Lay stepped aside and named Skilling, at age forty-eight, CEO of Enron. Lay wanted to gradually retire and, if all went well, Skilling would replace Lay as chairman of the board at the end of the year.

Skilling predicted that Enron's stock would climb to $126 during his first year as CEO.

Things started to unravel; Enron's stock went down, not up. With Enron trading assets in so many markets, a handful of stock market analysts had compared Enron's financial performance to investment banks, rather than energy companies, and concluded that either the investment banks were significantly undervalued or Enron was significantly overvalued. During an analyst conference call, Skilling cursed at a short-seller who questioned Enron's lack of financial transparency. Soon the broadband market collapsed, as did Enron's partnership with Blockbuster. Enron's international businesses were failing and the company was being blamed for California's electricity problems. Meanwhile, Lay was purchasing a $41 million state-of-the-art corporate jet for Enron, and construction continued on Enron's new $300 million office building in downtown Houston.

Skilling's dream job was turning into a nightmare. His biggest headache was Fastow's network of more than one thousand SPEs. As the financial value of Enron's stock continued to decline, so did the financial value of the SPEs funded mostly with Enron stock. After references to LJM appeared in the media, Skilling told Fastow that his dual role as CFO of Enron and managing director of SPEs doing business with Enron had to end. Fastow chose to stay with Enron and sold his financial interests in the LJMs to his protégé Kopper, who quit Enron to manage them.

Despite these financial problems, Enron announced $50 billion in revenue for the second quarter of 2001. Yet, the very next day, Skilling, struggling with depression, told an astonished Ken Lay he wanted to resign. Ken Rice, Skilling's good friend and former broadband CEO, prepared for Skilling's resignation by selling 772,000 shares for a $28 million profit.

On Monday, August 13, Skilling notified Enron's board of directors that he was resigning due to "family matters." As a sign of good faith to the company, Skilling repaid a $2 million loan and forfeited $20 million in severance pay. Lay informed stunned reporters that he would temporarily return as CEO. The board of directors rewarded Lay with what he needed most, a $10 million bonus and more stock options to help pay margin calls on Enron's declining stock price. While recommending that employees buy Enron stock, Lay sold 78,500 shares for a $2.1 million profit and Skilling sold $37 million of stock options over the next month.

$7 BILLION IN HIDDEN LOSSES

Following Skilling's resignation, a suspicious Sherron Watkins, an Enron vice-president and former Arthur Andersen accountant, submitted an anonymous one-page letter to Lay highlighting some of Fastow's accounting manipulations. When Lay avoided addressing her concerns at an all-employee meeting, she admitted authorship of the letter and met with him directly. Lay hired Vinson & Elkins to investigate Watkins' claims. Fastow demanded that the disloyal Watkins be fired immediately and confiscated her laptop. Enron's lawyers recommended against firing Watkins because the resultant legal fight would be played out in the media, to the detriment of Enron's already ailing stock price.

Lay learned more about the inner workings of Enron during the last two weeks of August than he had his previous fifteen years as CEO. The most urgent problem was financial—what to do about $7 billion in losses hidden by overvalued assets and SPE balance sheets. Officially, Enron had a debt of $12.8 billion, but the actual total was nearly three times that amount, around $35 billion.

Then another unexpected catastrophe occurred. On September 11, 2001, a terrorist attack on the World Trade Center and the Pentagon killed more than three thousand civilians. The stock market halted trading, and analysts predicted a negative effect on all stocks. The credit market tightened at the worst time possible, just when people were beginning to question Enron's creditworthiness.

Arthur Andersen was already under a cease and desist order from the SEC for its role in a $1.7 billion accounting fraud uncovered at Waste Management. In June 2001, prior to Skilling's resignation, the SEC threatened to disbar Andersen from practicing public accounting if the company knowingly approved fraudulent accounting again. Just a few months later, Andersen realized that it had been fraudulently certifying the books of another client—Enron.

Duncan, the Arthur Andersen engagement team's lead auditor, informed Fastow and Causey that some of Enron's SPEs violated GAAP and, as a result, Enron would have to restate earnings going back several years by $1 billion. In addition, Enron would have to restate its third quarter earnings by another $1.2 billion, to reflect an accounting mistake in calculating shareholder equity that had been made the previous year. Fastow, fearing an SEC investigation, ordered Kopper to destroy his laptop and any office or home computer files that contained damaging information about the LJMs.

Lay and Causey continued to keep Andersen auditors in the dark about billions of dollars in hidden losses. Although Duncan was demanding at least $1 billion in write-offs, Lay knew that there was another $6 billion in hidden losses that Andersen had not yet uncovered. Lay now faced a decision that would directly impact Enron's 20,000 employees—how honest should he be with stockholders? With the collapse of the dot.com market compounded by a recession and the World Trade Center tragedy, Wall Street analysts predicted Enron would announce $2 billion in loses for the third quarter of 2001. Lay sought counsel from his executive team, which felt confident that Enron could reasonably explain losses totaling $1.2 billion. Enron's stock price would decline further, but the company wouldn't be destroyed, which would probably happen if $7 billion in losses were unexpectedly announced. This would give Enron another three months to improve operating revenues before acknowledging the additional hidden loses.

THE FALL OUT

Early Tuesday morning, October 16, 2001, Lay announced third quarter operating losses of $618 billion and a total of $1.01 billion in non-recurring write-offs. The next day, a disgruntled group of shareholders filed a class-action lawsuit against Enron for insider trading. Worse yet, the *Wall Street Journal* published the first of a series of articles about Fastow's SPE arrangements. Anticipating a formal investigation by the SEC, Duncan activated Arthur Andersen's documentation retention and destruction policy. On October 23, Andersen employees in the Houston office were directed to start destroying all extraneous documents, emails, and computer files related to the Enron audit. The policy was also invoked in Andersen's Chicago, Portland, and London offices.

When questioned by Enron board members upset with the *Wall Street Journal* exposés, Fastow admitted that he had earned $45 million from the two LJM SPEs. This was in addition to the $33.6 million of Enron stock he previously had sold and $3 million in bonuses. Enron's leading banks refused to lend any more money as long as Fastow remained CFO. As Enron's stock further declined, the board instructed Lay to fire Fastow in order to restore investor confidence. Unfortunately, Enron employees who had overloaded their pension plans with Enron stock were unable to sell their holdings because their accounts had been temporarily frozen until a long planned changeover in pension plan administrators was completed.

Warren Buffet, General Electric, Royal Dutch Shell, GE Capital, the Carlyle Group, and a Saudi prince all refused overtures from Lay to bail out Enron. Pressured by Arthur Andersen, Enron announced in early November that, between 1997 and 2001, income had been overstated by $586 million due to accounting errors related to recording SPE transactions. Profits in 1997, Skilling's first year as COO, had been $9 million rather than the reported $105 million.

Enron was now losing $2 billion a week and lawsuits from employees and creditors were beginning to pile up. Its stock price, which had been $90 a year ago, was down to $8.40. Then Dynegy, a much smaller energy competitor located in Houston that had copied some of Enron's best strategies, announced its intentions to acquire the company for $9 billion. Enron had been saved!

But when Enron's credit rating was downgraded to just one level above junk bond status, an SPE collapsed and Enron had two weeks to pay back the $690 million the SPE had borrowed on behalf of Enron. The extent of Enron's new financial problems caught Dynegy executives and stockholders by surprise.

On November 28, credit agencies admitted the obvious—Enron was unable to pay its debts. Dynegy immediately pulled out of merger negotiations. The value of Enron's stock dropped to 61 cents, as trading volume soared to 345 million shares, compared to the 4 million shares traded on a normal day. The stock of a company that, a mere six weeks earlier, had reported annual sales of $130 billion and assets worth $62 billion, was now worthless.

Lay, who had risen from rural poverty to the top of the corporate ladder, was now relegated to meeting with bankruptcy lawyers. On December 2, having no cash left to pay bills, Enron temporarily closed its doors to reorganize. The following day, 4,000 Enron employees received termination notices. Most of them were given thirty minutes to pack their personal possessions and leave the building.

A month later, Enron was delisted from the New York Stock Exchange, and Lay submitted his resignation. All that remained of Enron were the lawyers there to settle legal claims.

More than four years later, at a joint jury trial, Lay was convicted on six counts of fraud and conspiracy and Skilling on nineteen counts of fraud, conspiracy, and insider trading. Six weeks after the verdict, Lay died of a heart attack while awaiting sentencing. Skilling was sentenced on October 24, 2006 to a twenty-four year term in prison. Causey pled guilty to fraud and Kopper pled guilty to two counts of conspiracy. As of October 2006, thirteen other Enron employees have pled guilty, and three have been convicted. After being indicted on 98 counts of fraud, conspiracy, insider trading, money laundering, and other criminal conduct, the wheeling and dealing Fastow pled guilty to two counts of conspiracy. He received a reduced sentence of six years in jail for providing evidence against Lay, Skilling, and other defendants.

Case Study

Kozlowski's Tyco—"I Am the Company!"

Denis Collins

He who knows he has enough is rich.

LAO TZU

If you are fully immersed in working long hours every day over the course of many years, the line between your work life and your personal life may start to blur. You also might begin to feel entitled to special "perks," particularly if the organization you work for has prospered because of your efforts and personal sacrifices. To counter this very human tendency, company policies and accounting regulations seek to clearly differentiate between corporate use of assets and personal use of assets; employees, of course, are financially responsible for the latter.

Dennis "Deal-A-Month" Kozlowski, one of the highest paid CEOs in the world, ignored this distinction. He considered his entire life to be work-related, treating Tyco's executive loan programs as a personal line of credit, despite an income of $170 million in 1999. He schemed to not pay sales tax on artwork purchased for his company-funded, luxury apartment. After Kozlowski was indicted for tax fraud, an investigation revealed that he and other Tyco executives had defrauded shareholders of more than $600 million. As a result, Kozlowski, at 60 years of age, entered a federal prison to serve a sentence of up to 25 years, and unable to benefit from the lucrative pension plan he had set up for his retirement.

MOVING UP THE SOCIAL AND CORPORATE LADDER

Kozlowski was born in 1946 to middle class parents in Newark, New Jersey. Ironically, his father was a false claims investigator with the

New Jersey bus system; his mother was a school crossing guard. Kozlowski's jobs as a youth included being a paperboy and car wash attendant. In college, he worked 30 hours a week, mostly playing guitar for a wedding band, while obtaining a business degree in finance and accounting at nearby Seton Hall University. He also earned a pilot's license. When dreams of becoming a commercial pilot collapsed, Kozlowski became an auditor in the Mergers & Acquisitions department of SCM in New York City.[1]

Talented, ambitious, and restless, Kozlowski changed jobs several times early in his career. In 1975, at age 28, a headhunter recruited him to help Tyco CEO Joseph Gaziano fulfill a plan to grow the $15 million Exeter, New Hampshire firm into a $1 billion corporation through mergers and acquisitions. Tyco was a public company, founded in 1960 as a research laboratory for energy conversion. Kozlowski served as the internal auditor for Tyco's latest acquisition, a fire protection company whose corporate staff would be reduced from 200 to 30 employees.

In 1982, with new acquisitions pushing Tyco's annual revenue over $500 million, Gaziano died unexpectedly of cancer. John F. Fort III, the new CEO, added healthcare to complement the company's three other business segments: fire protection, electronics, and packaging. Kozlowski's continued climb up the corporate ladder enabled him to purchase a $900,000 estate in North Hampton, New Hampshire for his family, which consisted of his wife and two daughters. Fort gave him a seat on Tyco's Board of Directors in 1987. Two years later, Kozlowski was promoted to President and Chief Operating Officer. In July 1992, as Tyco struggled with a nationwide recession, the Board replaced Fort with Kozlowski. At the age of 46, Kozlowski had reached the top of the corporate ladder, CEO and Chairman of the Board of a $3 billion corporation, with a $1 million salary and $2.6 million in stock grants.

CROSSING THE LINE

Unfortunately, Kozlowski's corporate success took a toll on his marriage. He spent most of his time flying from one acquisition meeting to another. Kozlowski had an affair with a Tyco employee in the late 1980s and then fell in love with a married waitress, Karen Lee Mayo. He separated from his wife, let her and his two children keep the estate, and purchased a second New Hampshire mansion for his own residence. Kozlowski muddied the line between his corporate and personal expenditures, charging Tyco $269,000 in furnishings for his new home and its yearly maintenance costs.[2]

CEOs have a fiduciary duty to act in the best interest of the company's shareholders. Charging the company to furnish a corporate office is acceptable. Charging such large amounts to the company to furnish a home, even if the CEO works conducts business and entertains clients there, is suspicious. Kozlowski, a professionally trained auditor, was manipulating accounting rules and regulations for his own benefit. He got away with it, and would get away with a lot more before being exposed.

MISUSING THE RELOCATION LOAN PROGRAM

By 1995, Tyco had outgrown its modest, two-story, New Hampshire headquarters. Yet, Kozlowski wanted to maintain shareholders' assumption that Tyco had very low corporate overhead. With minimal publicity, Kozlowski quietly purchased a new corporate office overlooking Central Park in New York City, a mere 12 miles from his middle class childhood neighborhood. Economically, Kozlowski had evolved from a tadpole in the New Jersey swamps, to a big fish in a small New Hampshire pond, to a moderate size fish in the world's largest and most exciting lake.

The move to New York City meant finding new housing for his management team. Kozlowski proposed a very generous 15-year interest-free relocation loan program for six executives, himself included. Corporate lawyers and the Board's Compensation Committee approved a more modest plan, available to all salaried employees relocating to New York. Without informing the Board, Kozlowski implemented his initial proposal.[3] Among the recipients of his largesse was his former mistress, Tyco's events planner, who kept her New Hampshire apartment and purchased a $500,000 Fifth Avenue apartment that she only used 35 days a year.[4] Given the Manhattan real estate market, it was an excellent long-term personal investment.

Also in 1995, Kozlowski promoted Mark Swartz, the Director of Mergers & Acquisitions, to Chief Financial Officer and Executive Vice President, and gave him a seat on the Board of Directors. Similar to Kozlowski, the 35 year old Swartz had an auditing background, having worked for Deloitte & Touche before joining Tyco in 1991. CFOs, like CEOs, have a fiduciary duty to serve the best interests of stockholders. As part of his New York City relocation, Swartz, who would be indicted along with Kozlowski in 2002, sold his New Hampshire home to a Tyco subsidiary far above market housing rates, earning a windfall profit for himself at the expense of shareholders.

MISUSING THE KEY EMPLOYEE LOAN PROGRAM

As did most corporations, Tyco provided executives with company stock as part of their compensation package, to further align management interests with shareholder interests. After a pre-determined length of time, the executive can purchase company stock at the price when the option to buy was first granted. If the stock price went up, which benefited all shareholders, the executives earned a corresponding profit. But immediate tax liabilities on the stock profit provided a disincentive to cashing in. In 1983, Tyco established an employee benefit called the Key Employee Loan Program (KELP) that allowed executives to borrow money at a low-interest rate in order to pay these taxes.

Beginning in 1996, Kozlowski and Swartz began misusing KELP loans to pay for personal expenditures. In addition, they did not disclose these loans on executive financial indebtedness forms that would have been accessible to shareholders. By August 1999, Kozlowski owed Tyco $55.9 million in low-interest KELP loans, and $28.5 million in interest-free relocation loans.[5] He used KELP loans to buy a $15 million yacht, an $8.3 million investment in a professional basketball team, a $700,000 investment in a Hollywood movie, $72,042 for jewelry, $155,067 for clothing, $96,943 for flowers, $60,427 for club memberships, and $52,334 for wine. He also purchased a $90,000 Porsche Carrera and a $5 million diamond ring for Karen, his long-term mistress.[6] Tyco's executive loan programs had become his personal piggy bank, though he promised to repay the money. Other times, Kozlowski simply charged personal expenditures to the company.

Tyco's loan programs sparked Kozlowski's interest in real estate. Shortly after relocating corporate offices to New York City, Kozlowski secured a Fifth Avenue apartment with an annual rent of $264,000, and charged it to Tyco. He also bought an $875,000 New Hampshire estate from board member John Fort, Tyco's former CEO, through a Tyco subsidiary, and a summer estate in Nantucket, Massachusetts for $5 million. Kozlowski eventually repaid Tyco for the latter two houses, although he expensed their maintenance to the firm.[7]

MINIMIZING CORPORATE TAXES AND A FLORIDA RELOCATION

Multinational firms incorporated in the United States are taxed for income earned by businesses they own in other countries. Many other countries, such as Bermuda, do not tax income earned in other countries.[8] In 1997, Tyco acquired ADT, a home security system company incorporated in Bermuda, for $6.2 billion, the company's largest acquisition at that time. Kozlowski worked out a "reverse merger" deal with Sir Michael Ashcroft, CEO of ADT, in which ADT would acquire Tyco and then change its name to Tyco. The company, now incorporated in Bermuda, no long had to pay U.S. taxes on overseas businesses.[9]

Kozlowski and Swartz also established a subsidiary in Luxembourg to finance Tyco's debt. Tyco could now, legally, obtain loans from the Luxembourg subsidiary and deduct the interest payments from its taxable income. The new Bermuda incorporation and the Luxembourg subsidiary enabled Tyco to reduce its tax rate from 36% to 25%, a $500 million tax savings. Tyco's U.S. tax rate soon dropped below 20%, approximately half that of other corporations.[10]

In addition, ADT's U.S. headquarters was located in luxurious Boca Raton, Florida, which meant more housing relocations for Tyco executives. Without the Board's permission, Kozlowski added Boca Raton to Tyco's housing relocation program. In 1998, more than forty Tyco employees were given 15-year relocation loans, with little or no interest, to purchase homes in Florida. Kozlowski was the primary beneficiary, purchasing $29.7 million of real estate with interest free loans. Ashcroft, who joined Tyco's board, sold his Boca Raton home to his wife, who then immediately sold it to a Tyco Vice President as a guest house for visiting executives. Kozlowski lived in that home at company expense while his new waterfront mansion was under construction.[11]

Kozlowski's continued misuse of Tyco's executive loan programs required the cooperation of Tyco's new Chief Corporate Counsel, Mark Belnick. Kozlowski met Belnick through former New Hampshire Senator Warren Rudman, who served as a $35,000 per year Tyco consultant. While new acquisitions were being forced to cut labor costs, Kozlowski granted Belnick a $5.9 million three-year contract, more than doubling his previous salary, and 200,000 shares of Tyco stock. Belnick, whose previous office was a few blocks from Tyco's Central Park headquarters, already owned a suburban New York City home. Nonetheless, he was granted a $4 million relocation loan to purchase a Central Park apartment.[12]

SECRETLY FORGIVING EXECUTIVE LOANS

Under Kozlowski's acquisition leadership, Tyco became a "hot" stock in the second half of the 1990s, increasing at an annual rate of 67%. During his first seven years as CEO, Tyco acquired 400 companies, most of them small and medium-sized. His six person Mergers & Acquisition team screened one thousand potential acquisitions annually and finalized deals within two weeks, while competitors took ten times longer.[13] For his efforts, Kozlowski's official salary was a modest $1.25 million a year. However, the stock portion value of his annual compensation package escalated. Over a three year period, Kozlowski's total annual income rose from $8.9 million in 1997, to $70 million in 1998, to $170 million in 1999, making him the second highest paid CEO in the world.[14]

But Kozlowski also owed Tyco $84.4 million for his relocation and KELP loans. In August 1999, Swartz fraudulently credited Kozlowski's KELP account $25 million and his own KELP account $12.5 million in August 1999. Neither Tyco's Vice President of Human Resources, PricewaterhouseCooper's auditors, Board members, nor stockholders were informed of this action. As a result, company shareholders lost $37.5 million in loan obligations. According to tax laws, an employee must declare the amount of a loan forgiveness as income on tax returns. Neither executive disclosed this new compensation in annual reports, proxy statements, or SEC forms. Kozlowski and Swartz also forgave a $1 million loan to a Tyco employee who had been Kozlowski's mistress in the 1980s, and a $300,000 loan to another mistress who had since left the company.[15]

Kozlowski and Swartz repeated this process twice in 2000, and included more executives in their scheme to defraud shareholders. In September, they falsely informed Patricia Prue, Tyco's Vice President of Human Resources, that the Board approved a $100 million loan forgiveness plan for the more than 40 Tyco employees who moved to Florida in 1998. This included Prue, who had received a $748,309 Florida relocation loan.[16] Prue was told that Tyco would pay all income taxes associated with the loan forgiveness plan. Under the guise of preventing Tyco's 215,000 other employees from becoming jealous, Prue obtained signed confidential agreements from each loan forgiveness recipient that, if breached, would cancel the new perk. Everyone signed. The largest Florida relocation loan forgiveness amounts were received by Kozlowski ($32.9 million) and Swartz ($16.6 million). Three months later, Kozlowski gave himself another $16 million in loan forgiveness, and gave Swartz half that amount.[17]

Kozlowski was also using Tyco's philanthropic contributions for personal gain. He no longer differentiated himself from Tyco. What was good for him was good for Tyco, and vice versa. Between 1997 and 2002, Tyco donated more than $100 million to nonprofit organizations. Many of these donations directly benefited Kozlowski, such as $1.3 million to the Nantucket Conservation Foundation to preserve undeveloped land adjacent to his estate, and $5 million to Seton Hall University, his alma mater, to have its Business School building named after him.[18]

MORE REAL ESTATE AND INCOME

In 2000, Kozlowski finalized his divorce so he could marry Karen Mayo, his long-term mistress. After the divorce, a Tyco subsidiary purchased from Kozlowski the New Hampshire estate occupied by his ex-wife for $4.5 million, three times its fair market value; she continued to live there at company expense. Kozlowski then purchased the Tyco-owned $7 million Fifth Avenue apartment, at no profit for Tyco despite soaring New York City real estate prices, and gave it to his ex-wife. He borrowed the full purchase price from Tyco, repaid $5.1 million, and forgave the remaining $1.9 million he still owed Tyco on the transaction.[19]

In honor of Karen's 40th birthday, Kozlowski instructed Tyco's events planner to organize a $2 million party on the exotic Italian island of Sardinia. Plans for the Romanesque themed event included gladiators welcoming the seventy guests to the island, an ice sculpture of Michelangelo's David where Soli vodka was poured into the upper back area and came out the statue's genitals, and a concert performance by pop-singer Jimmy Buffet that cost $250,000. Kozlowski charged half the birthday celebration expenses to Tyco, on the grounds that the event coincided with a subsidiary's board meeting at the same resort and half the attendees were company employees.[20]

Needing a new place to live in New York City, Kozlowski purchased another Fifth Avenue apartment for $16.8 million, charged it to Tyco, and lived in it rent-free. Kozlowski charged his KELP account $3 million in improvements and $11 million in furnishings, such as a $6,000 shower curtain in the maid's bathroom and a $15,000 umbrella stand.[21] Following in the footsteps of his mentor, Swartz bought an Upper East Side apartment in Tyco's name and lived there for an annual savings of $216,000.[22] These financial dealings were done without board permission, nor were they reported as executive income on financial statements.

Meanwhile, Kozlowski's reported W-2 income for 2000 was $137.5 million. His end of the year bonuses included 148,000 more shares of common stock and a $700,000 cash bonus. Swartz received half these totals. Belnick, the Chief Legal Counsel, was rewarded with a $4 million cash bonus and 300,000 shares of Tyco stock. During the year, Belnick cashed in $11 million in stock options.[23]

Kozlowski and Swartz continued to scheme ways, both legal and illegal, to charge their personal expenses to Tyco and to take as much compensation from the company as they could get away with. Kozlowski developed very generous retention agreements for his management team. To ensure Kozlowski's continued leadership the next seven years, until his anticipated retirement on his 62nd birthday in 2008, Kozlowski and Swartz proposed to the Board, and the Board agreed, that Kozlowski be granted a retention plan consisting of 800,000 shares of stock with a current value of $38 billion, a continuation of benefits after age 62, ongoing compensation and proxy bonuses until age 65, a $135 million severance payment, and a lifetime consulting contract worth $3.4 annually.[24]

Swartz and Belnick also signed retention agreements. Swartz was entitled to a $63 million severance payment, $8.5 million in stock, and 500,000 shares of Tyco stock worth $24 million that would start vesting five years

later.[25] Belnick signed a retention agreement that entitled him to $10.6 million if still employed by Tyco on October 1, 2003.[26]

ACQUIRING A FINANCIAL SERVICES COMPANY

Kozlowski long admired Jack Welch's management accomplishments at General Electric, including an acquisition that resulted in GE Capital Services, which financed customer purchases of GE products. Kozlowski sought a similar benefit for Tyco and focused on The CIT Group, the nation's largest independent commercial finance company, which could provide $4–6 billion in customer financing.[27] This would be particularly ironic: early in his professional career, the New Jersey company had rejected Kozlowski for a low-level auditing position.

Frank Walsh, who joined the board when Kozlowski became CEO in 1992, initiated acquisition discussions between Kozlowski and Al Gamper, CIT's Chairman and CEO. Tyco bought CIT Group for $9.5 billion, a 54% premium. After terms of the agreement were finalized in June 2001, Kozlowski paid Walsh a $20 million acquisition finder's fee, with $10 million in cash and $10 million donated to a charitable fund for which Walsh served as trustee. Kozlowski, already with a long list of compensation secrets, told Walsh not to inform the Board about the $20 million payment.[28] Walsh, who as a board member had a fiduciary duty to act in the best interest of stockholders, remained quiet.

With Tyco's stock price robust and his personal expenses mounting, Kozlowski, without Board approval, accelerated the vesting of some employee stock options owned by a few key executives. This resulted in an $8 million profit for himself, $4 million for Swartz, and $3 million for other senior managers, all at the expense of shareholders.[29]

SALES TAX AVOIDANCE SCAMS

Kozlowski's managerial skills were lauded by the media. *Business Week* ranked Tyco #1 on the magazine's best performing company list and Kozlowski among the top 25 corporate managers. Kozlowski's picture adorned the cover of *Business Week*'s May 28, 2001 issue. While the rest of the corporate world struggled through a deepening national recession, Tyco earned $4.7 billion in profits on sales of $30.3 billion for 2000, and 26% sales growth and 30% earnings growth for the first quarter of 2001.[30]

Yet Tyco had its critics. A research analyst accused Tyco of questionable accounting and tax practices. For instance, three weeks prior to finalizing the acquisition of Raychem, Tyco instructed Raychem to pay $60 million in outstanding bills, even if not immediately due. The extra pre-Tyco acquisition supplier payments made it easier for Kozlowski to claim that Raychem immediately improved financially under Tyco's new ownership.[31] Although the SEC, following a six month informal investigation of 120 acquisitions, dismissed these concerns in 2000, the SEC investigation and Kozlowski's huge personal write-offs caught the attention of fraud investigators in Manhattan District Attorney Robert Morgenthau's office and New York State banking authorities.[32]

Kozlowski's personal legal problems began when he and his wife went on an art buying spree to decorate their new Fifth Avenue Apartment, and fraudulently charged the purchases to Tyco. In August 2001, Kozlowski instructed a New York art dealer to purchase three paintings for $1,975,000 from a London art gallery. The paintings were unloaded from a plane at Newark International Airport and then transported to Tyco headquarters in New Hampshire. Without ever removing the paintings from the truck, Kozlowski's assistant signed documents verifying that the artwork had been received. The next day the Tyco-owned art was trucked back to New York for display in his apartment.

His illegal art purchasing activities multiplied when Kozlowski conspired to commit tax fraud on locally purchased artwork. According to New York sales tax laws, art purchased in New York for display in New York is subject to an 8.25% sales tax. The sales tax is not charged if the art is purchased for out-of-state use. In late November and early December, the Kozlowskis purchased more than $4.5 million in artwork from Manhattan art galleries for delivery to their Fifth Avenue apartment. Kozlowski avoided paying more than $375,000 in New York sales tax by claiming these were out-of-state sales. When one of the art dealers became uncomfortable with this fraud, the painting was removed from Kozlowski's apartment, trucked to Tyco's New Hampshire headquarters for the appropriate invoice signature, and then returned to his Fifth Avenue apartment. Kozlowski avoided paying an additional $1 million in New York sales tax when he purchased $12.8 million of art from New York galleries and then had five empty art boxes transported to New Hampshire for appropriate corporate signatures, while the actual paintings were delivered directly to his Manhattan apartment.[33]

Kozlowski, well-known for cost-cutting, continued to shower generous benefits among those aware of his misuse of corporate assets. Belnick earned more than $34 million from stock sales between 1999 and 2001 and was illegally granted $10 million in relocation loans by Kozlowski to purchase a ski chalet in Park City, Utah, a state where Tyco had no corporate presence.[34]

BOARD SCRUTINY

The first leak in Kozlowski's wall of secrecy occurred on January 9, 2002. Tyco's Board consisted of ten directors. Six of the eight external directors had been on the Board for at least a decade, some as long as two decades. It was a close network of friends and business acquaintances who earned annual salaries of $75,000 and 10,000 shares of Tyco stock in return for protecting shareholder interests.[35]

Several Board members reviewing Tyco's annual proxy statements were taken aback when they read that, without their knowledge or approval, Walsh had been paid a $20 million finders fee for the CIT Group acquisition. During the formal Board meeting the following week, they demanded that Walsh return the money to Tyco.[36] Walsh refused, stormed out of the meeting, and resigned his Board seat. The Board, dissatisfied with explanations provided by Kozlowski and Swartz, initiated an investigation of all financial transactions involving senior management, including executive compensation.

STOCK PRICE COLLAPSE

At the beginning of 2002, Tyco's stock stood at a healthy $59 a share. Following the sudden implosion of Enron in late 2001, investigative journalists and short-sellers (investors who profit when a company's stock declines) were looking for the next Enron.[37] Tyco was a prime target due to its aggressive accounting techniques, incomprehensible financial statements, massive debt, and rumors about insider trading; its stock declined steadily the first two weeks of January. In mid-January, Tyco unexpectedly announced an anticipated 20% revenue reduction for its electronics products business unit.[38] By the third week of 2002, Tyco's stock had dropped 25% since January 1, a loss of $30 billion in market value.

Kozlowski disagreed with the public's negative assessment, and maintained that the company was simply too big for any research analyst or investor to understand. He announced

a major change in corporate strategy that would untangle Tyco's complex financial statements and improve the company's sagging stock price. Rather than growing through acquisitions, as the firm had been doing for more than thirty years, he planned to break up the $38 billion corporation over the next year. First, Kozlowski would sell the plastics businesses for a quick $3 billion cash infusion. Second, the rest of the corporation would be reorganized into four separate businesses: health care, fire protection, financial services, and home/office securities and electronics. Kozlowski estimated the total share price value of these four business units at $73.50, far higher than Tyco's current $47 selling price.[39] Third, Kozlowski planned to sell the financial services business (CIT Group) to the public as an IPO, followed by the health care and fire protection businesses. The anticipated IPO income would reduce Tyco's $11 million debt to $4 billion. Fourth, Kozlowski would remain in charge of Tyco's largest business unit, securities and electronics.

But one week after this grand plan was announced, the *Wall Street Journal* published an article exposing Walsh's $20 million finders' fee; Tyco's stock dropped 20% by the end of the trading day.[40] Two days later, Tyco's "the next Enron" aura gained additional substance when the *Wall Street Journal* reported that Kozlowski had sold 748,000 shares of stock worth $40 million back to the company, rather than on the open market.[41] Then, on February 4, a *Wall Street Journal* headline blared that "Tyco Made $8 Billion of Acquisitions Over 3 Years But Didn't Disclose Them." The article noted that Tyco wasn't required to do so by law, as many of these were small acquisitions, but the secrecy sounded a lot like another Enron. Tyco's stock closed that day at $29.20, a one day decline of 20%. Tyco's stock had declined by 50% in slightly more than one month.[42] Over the following week, the *Wall Street Journal* reported that Tyco would layoff

2,250 employees in its Telecom unit, and that it would have to rely on a back-up line of credit to pay nearly $10 billion in debt payment due within a year.[43] Kozlowski had to do something to stop the mass sell-off of Tyco stock, the primary basis of his fortune.

UNSUCCESSFULLY BACKTRACKING

Kozlowski changed his mind about restructuring Tyco. In mid-February, he announced that Tyco would not sell either the health care or the fire protection business units as IPOs, due to the depressed stock market.[44] Investors wondered how the Board of Directors could unanimously agree to break-up Tyco in mid-January and one month later unanimously agree that this was not a good idea.

Making matters worse, Kozlowski had trouble finding buyers for Tyco's plastic business and CIT Group. He initially projected that the CIT Group IPO would generate $6.5 billion in cash to help pay down Tyco's ballooning debt. Kozlowski now admitted that the CIT Group acquisition, which led to his Board problems, was a colossal mistake. He announced that a CIT Group IPO would raise just $4.6 billion, less than half the $9.5 billion Tyco originally paid for it the previous year.[45] After the company declared a $1.9 million quarterly net loss, Tyco's first quarterly loss in a decade, the stock price declined to $17, its lowest since 1997.[46] Five years of stock market gains had been wiped out. In just four months, Tyco's stock had declined 71%, which felt a lot like Enron.

The Board lost confidence in Kozlowski and initiated new internal investigations. In May, the Board requested all company records on charitable contributions over $10,000, apartments and company assets used by employees, company plane use, executive loans, and stock transactions involving Kozlowski, Swartz, and Belnick.[47] The Board hired independent legal counsel to represent Tyco in its investigation of the Walsh affair.

CRIMES AND PUNISHMENTS

In early May, Kozlowski was subpoenaed by the New York County District Attorney's office for information related to his state sales tax avoidance scheme. Neither Kozlowski nor Belnick informed the Board about the criminal investigation. Then, on Friday, May 31, Kozlowski and Belnick told the Board that Kozlowski would be indicted the following week for tax fraud. The Board immediately went into crisis management mode and, late Sunday evening, demanded Kozlowski's resignation. John Fort, who preceded Kozlowski as Tyco's CEO, was named interim CEO.

On Tuesday, June 4, Kozlowski was indicted on eleven felony counts for evading more than $1 million in New York sales tax, each count punishable by up to four years in prison. A week later, Fort fired Belnick for removing confidential Tyco documents from the company's New York office.[48] Three months later, Swartz was also forced to resign.

In September 2002, the SEC filed a civil complaint documenting the following wrongdoings by Kozlowski, Swartz and Belnick:[49]

- *Relocation Loans:* Between 1996 to 2002, Kozlowski inappropriately borrowed $28 million, Swartz $9 million, and Belnick $14 million from Tyco's relocation loan programs.
- *KELP loans for stock option taxes:* Between 1997 to 2002, Kozlowski inappropriately borrowed $241 million and Swartz $72 million in KELP loans.
- *Loan Forgiveness:* Between 1999 and 2001, Kozlowski inappropriately forgave approximately $74 million in company loans to himself and $37 million in company loans to Swartz; neither claimed this as income.

In December 2002, Walsh pled guilty to felony charges of receiving $20 million and was fined $2.25 million. Kozlowski and Swartz' criminal trail began in late 2003. Six months later, with the jury in deliberations, a mistrial was declared because the media released the name of one of the jurors. At the time, eleven of the twelve jurors had already agreed on a guilty verdict.[50]

In July 2004, Belnick was found not guilty by a jury after the government had failed to prove beyond a reasonable doubt that he was guilty of grand larceny, securities fraud, and falsifying business records. The defense lawyers successfully argued that Belnick believed that Tyco's board had approved his compensation and loans. Then the SEC filed suit for fraud, which Belnick settled by agreeing to a $100,000 fine and a five-year ban from serving as a corporate officer.[51]

The retrial of Kozlowski and Swartz began in January, 2005. Six months later, both former executives were found guilty on 22 of 23 charges for stealing $150 million from Tyco.[52] In September 2005, they were each sentenced to 8 1/3 to 25 years in jail, and taken away from the courthouse in handcuffs.[53] The court ordered Kozlowski to pay $167 million, and Swartz $72 million, in fines and restitution. Ten months later, Karen Kozlowski filed for divorce, requesting half of Kozlowski's remaining fortune.[54]

NOTES

1. Anthony Bianco, William Symonds, Nanette Byrnes & David Polek, "The Rise and Fall of Dennis Kozlowski," *Business Week*, December 23, 2002; William C. Symonds & Pamela L. Moore, "The Most Aggressive CEO," *Business Week*, May 5, 2001.

2. *Tyco International Ltd. v. L. Dennis Kozlowski*, United States Southern District of New York, September 12, 2002, p. 32. [Hereafter *Tyco v. Kozlowski*]

3. *Tyco v. Kozlowski*, pp. 9–10.

4. Mark Maremont, "Tyco Ex-Manager Tells of Her Perks, *Wall Street Journal*, October 24, 2003.

5. *Tyco v. Kozlowski*, pp. 12–13.

6. Chad Bray, "Tyco Ex-Officer Tells of Fund Transfers," *Wall Street Journal*, December 3, 2002; Chad Bray, "Tyco Aide Testifies About Incidents, *Wall Street Journal*, January 6, 2004; *Tyco v. Kozlowski*, pp. 32–33; Tyco, pp. 32–33; *WSJ*, 12/3/03, 1/6/04.

7. David Armstrong, James Bandler, John Hechinger & Jerry Guidera, "Tyco Directors Involved in Deals," *Wall Street Journal*, June 14, 2002; Mark Maremont & Laurie P. Cohen, "How Tyco's CEO Enriched Himself," *Wall Street Journal*, August 7, 2002; *Securities and Exchange Commission v. L. Dennis Kozlowski, Mark H. Swartz, and Mark A. Belnick*, United States Southern District of New York, September 9, 2002 [Hereafter *SEC v. Kozlowski, et al.*]; *Tyco v. Kozlowski*, pp. 10 & 32.

8. Editorial, "The Bermuda Inversion," *Wall Street Journal*, May 21, 2002.

9. Symonds & Moore, May 28, 2001.

10. Mark Maremont, John Hechinger, Jerry Markon & Gregory Zuckerman, "Kozlowski Quits Under a Cloud," *Wall Street Journal*, June 4, 2002.

11. Laurie P. Cohen & Mark Maremont, "Tyco Relocations to Florida Are Probed," *Wall Street Journal*, June 10, 2002; Maremont & Cohen, August 7, 2002; *Tyco v. Kozlowski*, p. 15.

12. Laurie P. Cohen, "Tyco's Top Lawyer Joins CEO on Hot Seat," *Wall Street Journal*, September 13, 2002; Laurie P. Cohen, "How a Tyco Lawyer Channeled Windfall Into Unlikely Cause," *Wall Street Journal*, June 4, 2003; *Tyco v. Kozlowski*, p. 17.

13. Symonds & Moore, May 28, 2001.

14. Bianco, et al., December 23, 2002; Mark Maremont & Joseph Weber, "Tyco's Deal-A-Month Man," *Business Week*, January 27, 1997; *Tyco v. Kozlowski*, p. 12.

15. Chad Bray, "Former Official at Tyco Testifies He Was Directed to Forgive Loans," *Wall Street Journal*, February 17, 2005; Colleen DeBaise, "Kozlowski Aide Details Lucrative Salary, Benefits," *Wall Street Journal*, November 14, 2003.

16. Laurie P. Cohen & Mark Maremont, "Tyco Ex-Director May Face Charges," *Wall Street Journal*, September 19, 2002.

17. *SEC v. Kozlowski, et al.*, pp. 9–10.

18. *Tyco v. Kozlowski*, pp. 33–34.

19. *Tyco v. Kozlowski*, pp. 11 & 32.

20. James Bandler & Jerry Guidera, "Tyco Ex-CEO's Party for Wife Cost $2.1 Million, But Had Elvis," *Wall Street Journal*, September 17, 2002.

21. Colleen DeBaise, "Newest 'Tyco Gone Wild' Video Is Out, and Jurors See $6,000 Shower Curtain," *Wall Street Journal*, November 26, 2003.

22. *SEC v. Kozlowski, et al.*, p. 13.

23. *SEC v. Kozlowski, et al.*, p. 10; *Tyco v. Kozlowski*, pp. 17 & 21.

24. Robert Barker, "The High Cost of Kozlowski's Keep," *Business Week*, February 25, 2002.

25. John Hechinger & Gregory Zuckerman, "Is Clock Ticking for Tyco's Swartz," *Wall Street Journal*, June 6, 2002.

26. Laurie P. Cohen & John Hechinger, "Tyco Dismisses General Counsel After a Dispute," *Wall Street Journal*, June 11, 2002.

27. William C. Symonds, Pamela L. Moore & Heather Timmons, "Tyco Breaks Out of Its Mold," *Business Week*, March 26, 2001.

28. Symonds & Moore, May 28, 2001; *Tyco v. Kozlowski*, pp. 25–28.

29. *Tyco v. Kozlowski*, p. 24.

30. Anonymous, "Dennis Kozlowski: Tyco International," *Business Week*, January 8, 2001; Symonds & Moore, May 28, 2001.

31. Mark Maremont, "Tyco Inflated Cash Flow of Acquisition," *Wall Street Journal*, March 19, 2002.

32. Nanette Byrnes, "Kozlowski's Comedown," *Business Week*, June 5, 2002; Mark Maremont & Jerry Markon, "Ex-Tyco Chief Evaded $1 Million in Taxes on Art, Indictment Says," *Wall Street Journal*, June 5, 2002.

33. *The People of the State of New York v. L. Dennis Kozlowski*, Supreme Court of the State of New York, June 4, 2002.

34. Cohen, September 13, 2002; *SEC v. Kozlowski, et al.*, pp. 14–15.

35. Joann S. Lublin, "Two Board Criticized on Kozlowski," *Wall Street Journal*, June 7, 2002.

36. Mark Maremont, "Tyco Discloses It Paid Director on Merger Deal," *Wall Street Journal*, January 29, 2002.

37. Denis Collins, 2006, *Behaving Badly: Ethical Lessons from Enron*, Indianapolis, Ind.: Dog Ear Publishers.

38. David Armstrong, "Tyco International Says Soft Demand Will Depress Fiscal Second-Quarter Results," *Wall Street Journal*, January 16, 2002.

39. Laura Johannes, "Tyco Aims to Boost Shareholder Value With Breakup," *Wall Street Journal*, January 23, 2002.

40. Maremont, January 29, 2002; Mark Maremont, "Tyco Stock Stumbles 20% in Latest Reaction to Corporate Behavior," *Wall Street Journal*, January 30, 2002.

41. Ruth Simon & Kale Kelly, "Executives Use Delaying Tactic in Insider Sales," *Wall Street Journal*, January 31, 2002.

42. Mark Maremont, "Tyco Made $8 Billion of Acquisitions Over 3 Years But Didn't Disclose Them," *Wall Street Journal*, February 4, 2002.

43. John Hechinger, "Tyco to Lay Off 44% of Its Workers at Telecom Unit," *Wall Street Journal*, February 8, 2002; John Hechinger, "Tyco Offers Proof It Is Healthy; Yet It Faces a Huge Debt in 2003," *Wall Street Journal*, February 11, 2002.

44. Mark Maremont, "Tyco Seems to Back Off From Breakup," *Wall Street Journal*, February 14, 2002.

45. William C. Symonds, Heather Timmons & Diane Brady, "Behind Tyco's Accounting Alchemy," *Business Week*, February 25, 2002.

46. Mark Maremont, "Tyco Abandons Plan for Breakup," *Wall Street Journal*, April 26, 2002; Mark Maremont & Robert Frank, "Tyco Shares Fall 15% on Worries About Company's Strategy, Debt," *Wall Street Journal*, April 30, 2002.

47. *Tyco v. Kozlowski*, p. 28.

48. Byrnes, June 5, 2002.

49. *SEC v. Kozlowski, et al.*, pp. 5–11.

50. Mark Maremont, Kara Scannell & Charles Forelle, "Mistrial Scuttles Possible Guilty Verdicts in Tyco Case," *Wall Street Journal*, April 5, 2004.

51. Chad Bray & Colleen DeBaise, "Tyco Ex-Lawyer Is Acquitted in Bonuses Trial," *Wall Street Journal*, July 16, 2004; Jennifer Levitz, "Former Tyco Lawyer Will Pay Fine to Settle SEC Charges Over Loans," *Wall Street Journal*, May 3, 2006.

52. Mark Maremont & Chad Bray, "Tyco Trial Jurors Say Defendants Weren't Credible," *Wall Street Journal*, June 20, 2005.

53. Mark Maremont, "Tyco Figures Will Be Jailed at Least 7 Years," *Wall Street Journal*, September 20, 2005.

54. Anonymous, "Tyco Ex-CEO Is Sued for Divorce," *Wall Street Journal*, August 17, 2006.

Case Study

The Parmalat Affair: Europe's Largest Bankruptcy Scandal

Peter Madsen and Antonino Vaccaro

"It is all too clear to me now that to be a good businessman you need to have a handle on the financial side."

—CALISTO TANZI (FOUNDER OF PARMALAT; STATEMENT MADE WHILE
ON TRIAL FOR MARKET RIGGING, PROVIDING FALSE ACCOUNTING
INFORMATION, AND MISLEADING ITALY'S STOCK MARKET REGULATOR)

A BRIEF HISTORY OF PARMALAT

The Italian food conglomerate Parmalat was founded by Calisto Tanzi in 1961, after he inherited a Parma prosciutto business while still in college. Over the next 25 years, Tanzi parlayed his business into a successful global brand with product lines in milk, dairy, beverages, and baked goods. Parmalat S.p.A. went public on the Milan stock exchange in 1988, with the Tanzi family retaining a majority holding. During the 1990s, Parmalat expanded globally through a series of franchising arrangements and takeovers; however, it eventually emerged that the company was never on a sound financial footing from the time it went public until it declared bankruptcy on December 27, 2003. Over nearly 15 years, the company had falsified its accounts to cover growing and finally enormous edebt.

In 2003, Parmalat was one of the world's largest companies, with 36,000 employees in 30 countries, €10 billion ($13 billion) in assets, and €7.6 billion ($9.88 billion) in annual sales. With estimated liquidity of €3.7 billion ($4.81 billion), eyebrows were raised in the financial sector when the company defaulted on a November 2003 bond payment of €150 million ($195 million). This surprising default triggered a government-led audit which revealed that the company had incurred more than €14 billion ($18.2 billion) in previously unreported debt, primarily through illegal, off-balance sheet transactions. The audit revealed that 38% of Parmalat assets, which were thought to be in a Bank of America account held by the Bonlat Financial Corporation, a Cayman Islands-based Parmalat subsidiary, did not exist at all. The company had created fictitious assets to balance the unreported debt, thus hiding Parmalat's worsening financial picture from the investing public's view. Calisto Tanzi had also directed the transfer of €500 million ($636.2 million) in company assets to other family-led firms to balance losses that were incurred by those holdings. An additional €8 billion ($10.4

Peter Madsen is Distinguished Service Professor for Ethics and Social Responsibility at Carnegie Mellon University (CMU). He is executive director of the Center for the Advancement of Applied Ethics and Political Philosophy at CMU. He teaches courses in business, professional, environmental and computer ethics at CMU and at the Graduate School of Public and International Affairs, University of Pittsburgh.

Antonino Vaccaro is a researcher in the Department of Engineering and Public Policy at Carnegie Mellon University and of the Nucleo de ética empresarial of the Universidade Católica Portuguesa—Faculdade de Ciências Económicas e Empresariais.

billion) or more in company assets has not been accounted for, although it is suspected that much of this money was diverted to Tanzi family private bank accounts. On December 27, 2003, Parmalat was forced into bankruptcy. Today, government-appointed administrator Enrico Bondi struggles to restore Parmalat to solvency and financial transparency.

To maintain the appearance of a successful and flourishing firm in spite of its debt, Parmalat falsified its books on a breathtaking scale. One of the means by which it did so was purposefully overstating its assets, including the value of its brands and of its industrial plants and other infrastructures. More egregiously, Parmalat invented wholly fictitious company assets—most notoriously, a Bank of America account that supposedly held €3.9 billion (nearly $4.8 billion) in company assets. According to high-ranking Parmalat executives, Calisto Tanzi himself ordered the falsification of the account. Later, in order to convince Parmalat's accountants that the funds existed, Parmalat CFO Luciano Del Soldato ordered the forgery of an account verification letter from Bank of America. One of the CFO's top assistants has testified that he used scanners and faxes to cut and paste the letter together (see Figure 1), and then faxed it to the accounting firm.

In addition to inventing company assets, Parmalat also created several fictitious companies that existed only to further camouflage the extent of the company's debt. A common practice was for a genuine Parmalat subsidiary to transfer its uncollectible receivables to one of its shell companies, and then fictitious trade dealings and financial transactions were contrived at the shell company so as to offset the Parmalat subsidiary's losses. Derivative instruments, fictitious loan participation agreements, and other complex financial transactions were all used to offset debt on paper.

Another widespread practice was the declaration of false income on the books. To provide one example, another Parmalat CFO, Fausto Tonna, recorded the sale of 300,000 tons of dry milk powder to Empresa Cubana Importadora de Alimentos, a food importer based in Havana. This improbably large sale would have made nearly 2.8 billion liters of milk, enough to distribute hundreds of liters to every person in Cuba. In subsequent legal proceedings, Tonna and other top Parmalat executives have testified to falsifying many such transactions. Parmalat also declared on its books that payables had been met when they had not, and otherwise misstated or eliminated debts from its balance sheet.

Parmalat also failed to safeguard its genuine company assets. Parmalat funds were misappropriated on a vast scale. Court-appointed consultants first estimated that €25 million ($30 million) of Parmalat's funds had been misappropriated, but this estimate was later increased. Some sources claim that more than €800 million were siphoned into the Tanzi family's personal bank accounts or diverted to unprofitable, family-run subsidiaries. For example, it is estimated that Tanzi ordered the diversion of €500 million ($638 million) from Parmalat to Parmatour.

Finally, Parmalat misrepresented its true financial picture to current and potential investors. Despite its severe financial problems, Parmalat continued to issue corporate bonds and make efforts to attract public investment.

PARMALAT GOVERNANCE

An important enabling factor in the Parmalat scandal was the company's unusual governance structure. In a typical public corporation, shareholders are recognized as the owners of the company while top managers serve to control the company by their decision-making. In this governance model managers exercise day-to-day control over the company, but through a shareholder-elected Board of Directors

DEC 17 2003 16:01 FR Bank of America　　　　2019743539 To 516437334972

Bank of America
New York Branch

Grant Thornton SpA　　　　　　　　　　　　　　　　　　March 6, 2003
Largo Augusto. 7
20122 MILANO, ITALY

Re: Bonlat Financing Corporation
BANK Account No: 6550-2-52252
BANK Securities Deposits No: 6550-2-85419

Dear Sir/Madam

We have received your request for audit purposes dated December 20, 2002. We confirm our response to furnish information concerning account balances and securities deposits from our records at this office.

1. As of the close of business on December 31, 2002, our records indicate the following deposit balance(s):

Account Type	Account Name	Account Number	Account Balance
Demand Deposit	Bonlat Financing Corporation	6550-2-52252	USD $336,812,328.64 CR
Autoinvest Account	Bonlat Financing Corporation	N/A	N/A

2. As of the close of business on December 31, 2002, our records indicate the following securities deposit balance(s):

Account Type	Account Name	Account Number	Account Balance
Securities Deposit	Bonlat Financing Corporation	6550-2-85419	EUR €2,811,000,000.00
Securities Deposit	Bonlat Financing Corporation	6550-2-85419	USD $849,000,000.00

3. As of the close of business on December 31, 2002, our records indicate the following letter of credit balance.

Trade Finance	Customer Name	Reference Number	Outstanding
	N/A	N/A	N/A

This information is for your CONFIDENTIAL use and is furnished in reply to your inquiry. No responsibility is assumed by Bank of America or its officers to the accuracy or completeness of this information. Its representation is made as to any other relationship the subject may have with other Bank of America offices.

Sincerely,

Agnes Balgrave

Bank of America
100 West 33rd Street, New York, NY 10001

Figure 1:　The Bonlat Bank of America forgery

shareholders have an oversight mechanism for scrutinizing managerial decisions. A strong Board of Directors—one that is able to exercise independent oversight over management—is desirable from the shareholders' point of view.

Parmalat's governance structure was in some ways more typical of a small family business than of a large public corporation (see Figure 2).

Calisto Tanzi and members of his family were effectively majority shareholders by way of their family holding company, Coloniale S.p.A., but they were also in control of its day-to-day operations. Tanzi was the CEO, and he installed his daughter, son, brother, and many close friends to top management positions in Parmalat or Parmalat-owned companies. This structure

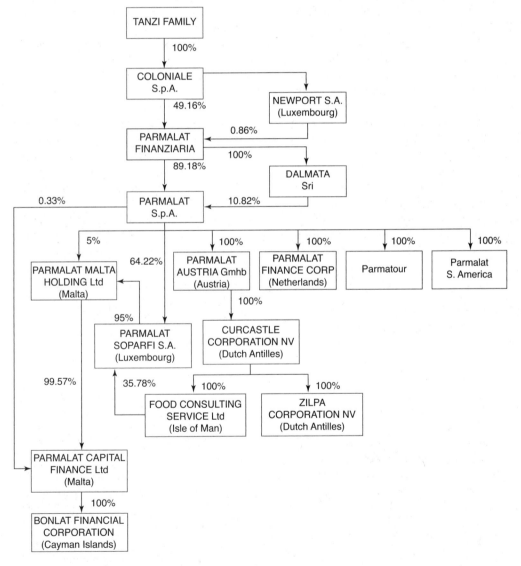

Figure 2:   A simplified framework of the Parmalat group

effectively allowed the interests of the Tanzi family to be served at the expense of minority shareholders in Parmalat Finanziaria unimpeded.

Among the actions beneficial to the Tanzi family but not necessarily to Parmalat Finanziaria's other shareholders were the acquisition of several high-status but hugely unprofitable subsidiaries in such industries as sports, tourism, and media. Tanzi initiated Parmalat's purchase of a 45% stake in Parma AC (now Parma FC), a soccer team in the glamorous Serie A league, installing his son, Stefano Tanzi, as its president. The soccer team won a number of Italian and European championships, but was a continual money loser. Similarly, Tanzi initiated the purchase of Parmatour, a major Italian tourism company, and installed his daughter, Francesca Tanzi, as its head. However, Parmatour proved to be an enormous balance sheet liability. The 1989 Tanzi-led purchase of Odeon TV, a television network intended to form the basis of a media conglomerate to compete with then-future prime minister Silvio Berlusconi's Berlusconi Group, was another miscalculation that further added to the debt burden at Parmalat, later being sold at a €45 million loss.

THE FALLOUT: PARMALAT IN COURT

In 2004, Calisto Tanzi was indicted for market-rigging, falsifying accounts, and obstructing Consob, the Italian equivalent of the US Securities and Exchange Commission (SEC). Numerous lawsuits are pending in the case, and thousands of irate shareholders have sought legal remedies for their losses. As of this writing, sixty-four individuals, including Calisto Tanzi himself, are still facing charges. Under a plea bargain, eleven people have already been sentenced by a Milan court. These eleven people include Calisto Tanzi's son, his younger brother, and two former Parmalat CFOs. Although they have been given prison sentences, it is uncertain whether they will be required to actually serve jail time.

Calisto's son, Stefano Tanzi, received a sentence of one year and eleven months. In addition to serving as the soccer team president, Stefano Tanzi also had a seat on the Parmalat S.p.A. board and had ties to Parmatour. Stefano Tanzi claims that he was duped by his father and had never known about Parmalat's fraudulent bookkeeping. He and his father are said to be estranged.

Calisto's younger brother. Giovanni Tanzi, also received a sentence of one year and eleven months. Giovanni Tanzi held seats on the boards of both the Parmalat group and Coloniale. He and Calisto Tanzi are also said to be estranged.

Former Parmalat CFO Fausto Tonna received a sentence of two and a half years. Tonna had been a director of the Bonlat Financial Corporation, the Cayman Islands-based Parmalat subsidiary in which the fictitious Bank of America account was supposedly held. Another former CFO, Luciano Del Soldato, was the person who ordered the Bank of America letter forgery and the destruction of any evidence that could be used to make a case against Parmalat. He was sentenced to one year and ten months.

In its 2004 lawsuit against Parmalat, the US Securities and Exchange Commission summarized Parmalat's financial irregularities as follows:

As of September 30, 2003, Parmalat Finanziaria had understated its reported debt of €6.4 billion by at least €7.9 billion. Parmalat Finanziaria used various tactics to understate its debt, including: (a) eliminating approximately €3.3 billion of debt held by one of its nominee entities; (b) recording approximately €1 billion of debt as equity through fictitious loan participation agreements; (c) removing approximately €500 million of liabilities by falsely describing the sale of certain receivables as non-recourse, when in fact the company retained an obligation to ensure that the receivables were ultimately paid; (d) improperly eliminating approximately €300 million of debt associated with a Brazilian subsidiary during the sale of the subsidiary; (e) mischaracterizing approximately €300 million of bank debt as intercompany debt, thereby inappropriately eliminating it in consolidation; (f) eliminating approximately €200 million of Parmalat S.p.A. payables as though they had been paid when, in fact, they had not; and (g) not recording a liability of approximately €400 million associated with a put option.

THE FALLOUT: WATCHDOGS ON TRIAL

In addition to the misconduct of Parmalat executives and employees, concerns have also been raised about the conduct of the accountants and banks responsible for the oversight of Parmalat. The government-appointed administrator overseeing Parmalat's restructuring, Enrico Bondi, has claimed that Parmalat's auditors and numerous banks were complicit in Parmalat's misdealings and has sued several of them for damages.

The Italian affiliates of two multinational accounting firms, "Big Four" member Deloitte & Touche and the second-tier Grant Thornton, were Parmalat's auditors, responsible for ensuring the accuracy and transparency of Parmalat's books. Grant Thornton was Parmalat's original and primary accounting firm, but in 1998, owing to a change in Italian law, Parmalat appointed Deloitte & Touche as primary auditors, retaining Grant Thornton as auditors for Parmalat's offshore entities. Prosecutors in Milan found enough evidence to seek indictments against four auditors, two from each firm, to stand trial for assisting Parmalat in hiding its massive debts.

Banks have also come under scrutiny for their role in the Parmalat scandal. Hoping to recover some of the €14 billion ($18.2 billion) that Parmalat had been unable to account for, Bondi has brought lawsuits against numerous big international banks, including Citicorp, UBS, Deutsche Bank, J.P. Morgan Chase & Co., and UniCredito Italiano, S.p.A., since they

had arranged structured financing for 80% of Parmalat's bank debt. It is claimed that American bankers at Citicorp assisted Tanzi in looting funds. It is further alleged that Swiss and German bankers at UBS and Deutsche Bank made last minute loans to Parmalat that violated Italian law, but highly favorable to the lending banks. Bondi sued J.P. Morgan Chase & Co. and UniCredito Italiano, S.p.A. for €4.4 billion ($5.4 billion) for their alleged role in issuing Parmalat bonds from 1997 to 2001, when many of the fraudulent transactions were initiated. In their defense, the banks aver that their transactions were valid, that Bondi's tactics are "cynical," and that they will defend themselves successfully.

Numerous consumer associations are proceeding against banks involved with Parmalat on behalf of bank clients who invested in Parmalat bonds. Bolstered by the slow pace of Italian legal proceedings, banks have been firm in their refusal to settle with those who lost money on Parmalat bonds. For example, Banca Intesa, an important Italian bank, refuses to provide reimbursement to those investors "holding any kind of managerial position in any kind of firm." Banca Intesa maintains that anyone who holds a managerial position is capable of making sound investment choices and, consequently, there is no reason to reimburse them. By the same token, Banca Unicredit, the largest Italian bank, has undertaken to provide partial restitution to only 400 of its 3009 customers who had purchased Parmalat bonds following the recommendations of Unicredit brokers.

PUTTING PARMALAT BACK TOGETHER AGAIN

As Parmalat was one of Italy's largest companies, its bankruptcy was widely thought to threaten Italy's economy. To forestall economic collapse, Italy quickly passed laws making it easier for Parmalat and other large firms to restructure through bankruptcy. Turnaround expert Enrico Bondi was appointed by the Italian government as an "extraordinary administrator" with the role of overseeing Parmalat's bankruptcy restructuring and return to solvency. This task is ongoing.

Early in his assignment, Bondi discovered that the group had no financial liquidity at all and that it was necessary to develop a new and more reliable accounting system. At the end of 2003, Parmalat was unable to pay any debt owed to suppliers, investors, or creditors. Due to extensive falsification of the company's books, it was impossible to quantify the exact amount of Parmalat's losses.

Following Italian law, Bondi worked first to pay Parmalat's suppliers, and recently he has had some success in developing a reconstituted and more solid firm. He developed a new accounting system and has begun to eliminate unprofitable lines of business for the firm.

Under the new direction led by Bondi, Parmalat has partially outpaced its performance after its crisis of 2003. The March 2006 financial report of the Parmalat board stated that during the first trimester of the year 2006, Parmalat's Earnings Before Interest and Taxes, Depreciation and Amortization (EBITDA) had increased 18.4% compared with the first quarter of 2005. Analogously, sales had reached €953.2 million ($1,239.13 million), an increase of 9.8% in relation to the same period in 2005. Although these results are encouraging, at the end of 2006, the amount of total debt of the group still reached €367.4 million ($477.2 million). This fact foretells that Parmalat needs yet to pass through significant structural changes before coming back to normalcy.

Although initially jailed in Milan, Calisto Tanzi was placed under house arrest in his luxurious villa in the proximity of Parma, pending the verdict of the Italian court there. Likewise, his daughter, son and brother were out of prison in late 2006 as they await verdicts.

Initially, Parmalat was taken as a case where a couple of rogue managers simply invented assets to offset huge liabilities as they falsified their accounts over a period of almost 15 years, finally forcing the company into bankruptcy on December 27, 2003. As it seems now, though, Parmalat and its investors were victims not only of the Tanzi family's criminality and executives blindly following orders, but also of the catastrophe that occurred when banks and auditors did not bring responsible oversight and transparency to Parmalat's financial operations.

Case Study

"The Good Old Boys at WorldCom"

Dennis Moberg and Edward Romar

2002 saw an unprecedented number of corporate scandals: Enron, Tyco, Global Crossing. In many ways, WorldCom is just another case of failed corporate governance, accounting abuses, and outright greed. But none of these other companies had senior executives as

---

colorful and likable as Bernie Ebbers. A Canadian by birth, the six foot three inch former basketball coach and Sunday School teacher emerged from the collapse of WorldCom not only broke but with a personal net worth as a negative nine-digit number.[1] No palace in a gated community, no stable of racehorses, or multi-million dollar yacht to show for the telecommunications giant he created. Only debts and red ink—results some consider inevitable given his unflagging enthusiasm and entrepreneurial flair. There is no question that he did some pretty bad stuff, but he really wasn't like the corporate villains of his day: Andy Fastow of Enron, Dennis Koslowski of Tyco, or Gary Winnick of Global Crossing.[2]

Personally, Bernie is a hard guy not to like. In 1998 when Bernie was in the midst of acquiring the telecommunications firm MCI, Reverend Jesse Jackson, speaking at an all-black college near WorldCom's Mississippi headquarters, asked how Ebbers could afford $35 billion for MCI but hadn't donated funds to local black students. Businessman LeRoy Walker, Jr., was in the audience at Jackson's speech, and afterwards set him straight. Ebbers had given over $1 million plus loads of information technology to that black college. "Bernie Ebbers," Walker reportedly told Jackson, "is my mentor."[3] Rev. Jackson was won over, but who wouldn't be by this erstwhile milkman and bar bouncer who serves meals to the homeless at Frank's Famous Biscuits in downtown Jackson, Mississippi, and wears jeans, cowboy boots, and a funky turquoise watch to work.

It was 1983 in a coffee shop in Hattiesburg, Mississippi that Mr. Ebbers first help create the business concept that would become WorldCom. "Who could have thought that a small business in itty bitty Mississippi would one day rival AT&T?" asked an editorial in Jackson, Mississippi's *Clarion-Ledger* newspaper.[4] Bernie's fall and the company's was abrupt. In June, 1999 with WorldCom's shares trading at $64, he was a billionaire,[5] and

WorldCom was the darling of The New Economy. By early May of 2002, Ebbers resigned his post as CEO, declaring that he was "1,000 percent convinced in my heart that this is a temporary thing."[6] Two months later, in spite of Bernie's unflagging optimism, WorldCom declared itself the largest bankruptcy in American history.[7]

This case describes three major issues in the fall of WorldCom, the corporate strategy of growth through acquisition, the use of loans to senior executives, and threats to corporate governance created by chumminess and lack of arm's length dealing. The case concludes with a brief description of the hero of the case—whistle blower Cynthia Cooper.

THE GROWTH THROUGH ACQUISITION MERRY-GO-ROUND

From its humble beginnings as an obscure long distance telephone company WorldCom, through the execution of an aggressive acquisition strategy, evolved into the second largest long distance telephone company in the United States and one of the largest companies handling worldwide Internet data traffic.[8] According to the WorldCom website, at its high point the company:

- Provided mission-critical communications services for tens of thousands of businesses around the world
- Carried more international voice traffic than any other company
- Carried a significant amount of the world's Internet traffic
- Owned and operated a global IP (Internet Protocol) backbone that provided connectivity in more than 2,600 cities, and in more than 100 countries
- Owned and operated 75 data centers on five continents. [Data centers provide hosting and allocation services to businesses for their mission critical business computer applications.[9]]

WorldCom achieved its position as a significant player in the telecommunications industry through the successful completion of 65 acquisitions.[10] Between 1991 and 1997, WorldCom spent almost $60 billion in the acquisition of many of these companies and accumulated $41 billion in debt.[11] Two of these acquisitions were particularly significant. The MFS Communications acquisition enabled WorldCom to obtain UUNet, a major supplier of Internet services to business, and MCI Communications gave WorldCom one of the largest providers of business and consumer telephone service. By 1997, WorldCom's stock had risen from pennies per share to over $60 a share.[12] Through what appeared to be a prescient and successful business strategy at the height of the Internet boom, WorldCom became a darling of Wall Street. In the heady days of the technology bubble Wall Street took notice of WorldCom and its then visionary CEO, Bernie Ebbers. This was a company "on the make," and Wall Street investment banks, analysts and brokers began to discover WorldCom's value and make "strong buy recommendations" to investors. As this process began to unfold, the analysts recommendations, coupled with the continued rise of the stock of the stock market, made WorldCom stock desirable and the market's view of the stock was that it could only go up. As the stock value went up, it was easier for WorldCom to use stock as the vehicle to continue to purchase additional companies. The acquisition of MFS Communications and MCI Communications were, perhaps, the most significant in the long list of WorldCom acquisitions. With the acquisition of MFS Communications and its UUNet unit, "WorldCom (s)uddenly had an investment story to offer about the value of combining long distance, local service and data communications."[13] In late 1997, British Telecommunications Corporation made a $19 billion bid for MCI. Very quickly, Ebbers made a counter offer of $30 billion in

WorldCom stock. In addition, Ebbers agreed to assume $5 billion in MCI debt, making the deal $35 billion or 1.8 times the value of the British Telecom offer. MCI took WorldCom's offer making WorldCom a truly significant global telecommunications company.[14]

All this would be just another story of a successful growth strategy if it wasn't for one significant business reality—mergers and acquisitions, especially large ones, present significant managerial challenges in at least two areas. First, management must deal with the challenge of integrating new and old organizations into a single smooth functioning business. This is a time-consuming process that involves thoughtful planning and a considerable amount of senior managerial attention if the acquisition process is to increase the value of the firm to both shareholders and stakeholders. With 65 acquisitions in six years and several of them large ones, WorldCom management had a great deal on their plate. The second challenge is the requirement to account for the financial aspects of the acquisition. The complete financial integration of the acquired company must be accomplished, including and accounting of asset, debts, good will and a host of other financially important factors. This must be accomplished through the application of generally accepted accounting practices (GAAP).

WorldCom's efforts to integrate MCI illustrate several areas senior management did not address well. In the first place, Ebbers appeared to be an indifferent executive who "paid scant attention to the details of operations."[15] For example, customer service deteriorated. One business customer's service was discontinued incorrectly, and when the customer contacted customer service, he was told he was not a customer. Ultimately, the WorldCom representative told him that if he was a customer, he had called the wrong office because the office he called only handled MCI accounts.[16] This poor customer stumbled "across a problem stemming from

WorldCom's acquisition binge: For all its talent in buying competitors, the company was not up to the task of merging them. Dozens of conflicting computer systems remained, local systems were repetitive and failed to work together properly, and billing systems were not coordinated."[17]

Poor integration of acquired companies also resulted in numerous organizational problems. Among them were:

1. Senior management made little effort to develop a cooperative mindset among the various units of WorldCom.
2. Inter-unit struggles were allowed to undermine the development of a unified service delivery network.
3. WorldCom closed three important MCI technical service centers that contributed to network maintenance only to open twelve different centers that, in the words of one engineer, were duplicate and inefficient.
4. Competitive local exchange carriers (Clercs) were another managerial nightmare. WorldCom purchased a large number of these to provide load service. According to one executive, "(t)he WorldCom model was a vast wasteland of Clercs, and all capacity was expensive and very underutilized. . . . There was far too much redundancy, and we paid far too much to get it."[18]

Regarding financial reporting, WorldCom used a liberal interpretation of accounting rules when preparing financial statements. In an effort to make it appear that profits were increasing, WorldCom would write down in one quarter millions of dollars in assets it acquired while, at the same time, it "included in this charge against earnings the cost of company expenses expected in the future. The result was bigger losses in the current quarter but smaller ones in future quarters, so that its profit picture would seem to be improving."[19] The acquisition of MCI gave WorldCom another accounting opportunity. While reducing the book value of some MCI assets by several billion dollars, the company increased the value of "good will," that is, intangible assets, a brand name, for example, by the same amount. This enabled WorldCom each year to charge a smaller amount against earnings by spreading these large expenses over decades rather than years. The net result was WorldCom's ability to cut annual expenses, acknowledge all MCI revenue and boost profits from the acquisition.

WorldCom managers also tweaked their assumptions about accounts receivables, the amount of money customers owe the company. For a considerable time period, management chose to ignore credit department lists of customers who had not paid their bills and were unlikely to do so. In this area, managerial assumptions play two important roles in receivables accounting. In the first place, they contribute to the amount of funds reserved to cover bad debts. The lower the assumption of non-collectable bills, the smaller the reserve fund required. The result is higher earnings. Secondly, if a company sells receivables to a third party, which WorldCom did, then the assumptions contribute to the amount or receivables available for sale.[20]

So long as there were acquisition targets available, the merry-go-round kept turning, and WorldCom could continue these practices. The stock price was high and accounting practices allowed the company to maximize the financial advantages of the acquisitions while minimizing the negative aspects. WorldCom and Wall Street could ignore the consolidation issues because the new acquisitions allowed management to focus on the behavior so welcome by everyone, the continued rise in the share price. All this was put in jeopardy when, in 2000, the government refused to allow WorldCom's acquisition of Sprint. The denial stopped the carousel and put an end to their acquisition-without-consolidation strategy and left management a stark choice between focusing on creating value from the previous acquisitions with the possible loss of share value or trying to find other creative ways to sustain and increase the share price.

In July 2002, WorldCom filed for bankruptcy protection after several disclosures regarding accounting irregularities. Among then was the admission of improperly accounting for operating expenses as capital expenses in violation of generally accepted accounting practices (GAAP). WorldCom has admitted to a $9 billion adjustment for the period from 1999 thorough the first quarter of 2002.

SWEETHEART LOANS TO SENIOR EXECUTIVES

Bernie Ebbers' passion for his corporate creation loaded him up on common stock. Through generous stock options and purchases Ebbers' WorldCom holdings grew and grew, and he typically financed these purchases with his existing holdings as collateral. That was not a problem until the value of WorldCom stock declined, and Bernie faced margin calls (a demand to put up more collateral for outstanding loans) on some of his purchase. At that point he faced a difficult dilemma. Because his personal assets were insufficient to meet the substantial amount required to meet the call, he could either sell some of his common shares to finance the margin call or request a loan from the company to cover the calls. Yet, when the board learned of his problem, it refused to let him sell his shares on the grounds that it would depress the stock price and signal a lack of confidence about WorldCom's future.[21] Had he pressed the matter and sold his stock, he would have escaped the bankruptcy financially whole, but Ebbers honestly thought WorldCom would recover. Thus, it was enthusiasm and not greed that trapped Mr. Ebbers. The executives associated with other corporate scandals sold at the top. In fact, other WorldCom executives did much, much better than Ebbers.[22] Bernie borrowed against his stock. That course of action makes sense if you believe the stock will go up, but it's the road to ruin if the stock goes down. Unlike the others, he intended to make himself rich taking the rest of the shareholders with him. In his entire career, Mr. Ebbers sold company shares only half a dozen times. Detractors may find him irascible and arrogant, but defenders describe him as a principled man.[23]

The policy of boards of directors authorizing loans for senior executives raises eyebrows. The sheer magnitude of the loans to Ebbers was breathtaking. The $341 million loan the board granted Mr. Ebbers is the largest amount any publicly traded company has lent to one of its officers in recent memory.[24] Beyond that, some question whether such loans are ethical. "A large loan to a senior executive epitomizes concerns about conflict of interest and breach of fiduciary duty," said former SEC enforcement official Seth Taube.[25] Nevertheless, 27% of major publicly traded companies had loans outstanding for executive officers in 2000 up from 17% in 1998 (most commonly for stock purchase but also home buying and relocation). Moreover, there is the claim that executive loans are commonly sweetheart deals involving interest rates that constitute a poor rate of return on company assets. WorldCom charged Ebbers slightly more than 2% interest, a rate considerably below that available to "average" borrowers and also below the company's marginal rate of return. Considering such factors, one compensation analyst claims that such lending "should not be part of the general pay scheme of perks for executives. . . . I just think it's the wrong thing to do."[26]

WHAT'S A NOD OR WINK AMONG FRIENDS?

In the autumn of 1998, Securities and Exchange Commissioner Arthur Levitt, Jr. uttered the prescient criticism, "Auditors and analysts are participants in a game of nods and winks.[27] It should come as no surprise that it was Arthur

Andersen that endorsed many of the accounting irregularities that contributed to WorldCom's demise.[28] Beyond that, however, were a host of incredibly chummy relationships between WorldCom's management and Wall Street analysts.

Since the Glass-Steagall Act was repealed in 1999, financial institutions have been free to offer an almost limitless range of financial services to its commercial and investment clients. Citigroup, the result of the merger of Citibank and Travelers Insurance Company, who owned the investment bank and brokerage firm Salomon Smith Barney, was an early beneficiary of investment deregulation. Citibank regularly dispensed cheap loans and lines of credit as a means of attracting and rewarding corporate clients for highly lucrative work in mergers and acquisitions. Since WorldCom was so active in that mode, their senior managers were the target of a great deal of influence peddling by their banker, Citibank. For example, Travelers Insurance, a Citigroup unit, lent $134 million to a timber company Bernie Ebbers was heavily invested in. Eight months later, WorldCom chose Salomon Smith Barney, Citigroup's brokerage unit, to be the lead underwriter of $5 billion of its bond issue.[29] But the entanglements went both ways. Since the loan to Ebbers was collateralized by his equity holdings, Citigroup had reason to prop up WorldCom stock. And no one was better at that than Jack Grubman, Salomon Smith Barney's telecommunication analyst. Grubman first met Bernie Ebbers in the early 1990's when he was heading up the precursor to WorldCom, LDDS Communications. The two hit it off socially, and Grubman started hyping the company. Investors were handsomely rewarded for following Grubman's buy recommendations until stock reached its high, and Grubman rose financially and by reputation. In fact, *Institutional Investing* magazine gave Jack a Number 1 ranking in 1999,[30] and *Business Week* labeled him "one of the most powerful players on Wall Street."[31]

The investor community has always been ambivalent about the relationship between analysts and the companies they analyze. As long as analyst recommendations are correct, close relations have a positive insider quality, but when their recommendations turn south, corruption is suspected. Certainly Grubman did everything he could to tout his personal relationship with Bernie Ebbers. He bragged about attending Bernie's wedding in 1999. He attended board meeting at WorldCom's headquarters. Analysts at competing firms were annoyed with this chumminess. While the other analysts strained to glimpse any tidbit of information from the company's conference call, Grubman would monopolize the conversation with comments about "dinner last night."[32]

It is not known who picked up the tab for such dinners, but Grubman certainly rewarded executives for their close relationship with him.[33] Both Ebbers and WorldCom CFO Scott Sullivan were granted privileged allocations in IPO (Initial Public Offering) auctions. While the Securities and Exchange Commission allows underwriters like Salomon Smith Barney to distribute its allotment of new securities as it sees fit among its customers, this sort of favoritism has angered many small investors. Banks defend this practice by contending that providing high net worth individuals with favored access to hot IPOs is just good business.[34] Alternatively, they allege that greasing the palms of distinguished investors creates a marketing "buzz" around an IPO, helping deserving small companies trying to go public get the market attention they deserve.[35] For the record, Mr. Ebbers personally made $11 million in trading profits over a four-year period on shares from initial public offerings he received from Salomon Smith Barney.[36] In contrast, Mr. Sullivan lost $13,000 from IPOs, indicating that they were apparently not "sure things."[37]

There is little question but that friendly relations between Grubman and WorldCom helped investors from 1995 to 1999. Many trusted Grubman's insider status and followed his rosy recommendations to financial success. In a 2000 profile in *Business Week*, he seemed to mock the ethical norm against conflict of interest: "what used to be a conflict is now a synergy," he said at the time. "Someone like me . . . would have been looked at disdainfully by the buy side 15 years ago. Now they know that I'm in the flow of what's going on."[38] Yet, when the stock started cratering later that year, Grubman's enthusiasm for WorldCom persisted. Indeed, he maintained the highest rating on WorldCom until March 18, 2002 when he finally raised its risk rating. At that time, the stock had fallen almost 90% from its high two years before. Grubman's mea culpa was to clients on April 22 read, "In retrospect the depth and length of the decline in enterprise spending has been stronger and more damaging to WorldCom than we even anticipated."[39] An official statement from Salomon Smith Barney two week later seemed to contradict the notion that Grubman's analysis was conflicted, "Mr. Grubman was not alone in his enthusiasm for the future prospects of the company. His coverage was based purely on information yielded during his analysis and was not based on personal relationships."[40] Right.

On August 15, 2002, Jack Grubman resigned from Salomon where he had made as much as $20 million per year. His resignation letter read in part, "I understand the disappointment and anger felt by investors as a result of [the company's] collapse, I am nevertheless proud of the work I and the analysts who work with me did."[41] On December 19, 2002, Jack Grubman was fined $15 million and was banned for securities transactions for life by the Securities and Exchange Commission for such conflicts of interest.

The media vilification that accompanies one's fall from power unearthed one interesting detail about Grubman's character—he repeatedly lied about his personal background. A graduate of Boston University, Mr. Grubman claimed a degree from MIT. Moreover, he claimed to have grown up in colorful South Boston, while his roots were actually in Boston's comparatively bland Oxford Circle neighborhood.[42] What makes a person fib about his personal history is an open question. As it turns out, this is probably the least of Jack Grubman's present worries. New York State Controller H. Carl McCall sued Citicorp, Arthur Andersen, Jack Grubman, and others for conflict of interest. According to Mr. McCall, "this is another case of corporate coziness costing investors billions of dollars and raising troubling questions about the integrity of the information investors receive."[43]

THE HERO OF THE CASE

No integrity questions can be raised about Cynthia Cooper whose careful detective work as an internal auditor at WorldCom exposed some of the accounting irregularities apparently intended to deceive investors. Originally charged with responsibilities in operational audit, Cynthia and her colleagues grew suspicious of a number of peculiar financial transactions and went outside their assigned responsibilities to investigate. What they found was a series of clever manipulations intended to bury almost $4 billion in misallocated expenses and phony accounting entries.[44]

A native of Clinton, Mississippi where WorldCom's headquarters was located, Ms. Cooper's detective work was conducted in secret, often late at night to avoid suspicion. The thing that first aroused her curiosity came in March, 2002 when a senior line manager complained to her that her boss, CFO Scott Sullivan, had usurped a $400 million reserve account he had set aside as a hedge against anticipated revenue losses. That didn't seem kosher, so Cooper inquired of the firm's accounting firm, Arthur Andersen. They brushed her off, and Ms. Cooper decided to press the matter with the board's audit committee. That put her in direct conflict with her boss, Sullivan, who ultimately backed down. The next day, however, he warned her to stay out of such matters.

Undeterred and emboldened by the knowledge that Andersen had been discredited by the Enron case and that the SEC was investigating WorldCom, Cynthia decided to continue her investigation. Along the way, she learned of a WorldCom financial analyst who was fired a year earlier for failing to go along with accounting chicanery.[45] Ultimately, she and her team uncovered a $2 billion accounting entry for capital expenditures that had never been authorized. It appeared that the company was attempting to represent operating costs as capital expenditures in order to make the company look more profitable. To gather further evidence, Cynthia's team began an unauthorized search through WorldCom's computerized accounting information system. What they found was evidence that fraud was being committed. When Sullivan heard of the ongoing audit, he asked Cooper to delay her work until the third quarter. She bravely declined. She went to the board's audit committee and in June, Scott Sullivan and two others were terminated. What Ms. Cooper had discovered was the largest accounting fraud in U.S. history.[46]

As single-minded as Cynthia Cooper appeared during this entire affair, it was an incredibly trying ordeal. Her parents and friends noticed that she was under considerable stress and was losing weight. According to the *Wall Street Journal*, she and her colleagues worried "that their findings would be devastating to the company [and] whether their revelations would result in layoffs and obsessed about whether they were jumping to unwarranted conclusions that their colleagues at WorldCom were committing fraud. Plus, they feared that they would somehow end up being blamed for the mess."[47]

It is unclear at this writing whether Bernie Ebbers will be brought to bear for the accounting irregularities that brought down his second in command. Jack Grubman's final legal fate is also unclear. While the ethical quality of enthusiasm and sociability are debatable, the virtue of courage is universally acclaimed, and Cynthia Cooper apparently has it. Thus, it was not surprising that on December 21, 2002, Cynthia Cooper was recognized as one of three "Persons of the Year" by *Time* magazine.

NOTES

1. This is only true if he is liable for the loans he was given by WorldCom. If he avoids those somehow, his net worth may be plus $8.4 million according to the *Wall Street Journal* (see S. Pulliam & J. Sandberg [2002]. Worldcom Seeks SEC Accord As Report Claims Wider Fraud [November 5], A-1).

2. Colvin, C. (2002). Bernie Ebbers' Foolish Faith. *Fortune, 146,* (11 [November 25]), 52.

3. Padgett, T., & Baughn, A. J. (2002). The Rise and Fall of Bernie Ebbers. *Time, 159,* (19 [May 12]), 56+.

4. Morse, D., & Harris, N. (2002). In Mississippi, Ebbers Is a Man to Be Proud Of. *Wall Street Journal,* May 2, 2002, B-1.

5. Young, S., & Solomon, D. (2002). WorldCom Backs Chief Executive for $340 Million. *Wall Street Journal* (February 8), B-1.

6. Ibid.

7. Romero, Simon, & Atlas, Rava D. (2002). WorldCom's Collapse: The Overview. *New York Times* (July 22), A-1.

8. Ibid.

9. WorldCom website (www.worldcom.com/global/about/facts/).

10. Eichenwald, Kurt, (2002). For WorldCom, Acquisition Were Behind Its Rise and Fall. *New York Times* (August 8), A-1.

11. Romero & Atlas, op. cit.

12. Browning, E. S. (1997). Is the Praise for WorldCom Too Much? *Wall Street Journal* (October 8), p. C-24. All acquisition amounts are taken from this article.

13. Eichenwald, op. cit., p. A-3.

14. Ibid.

15. Ibid.

16. Ibid., p. A-2.

17. Ibid., p. A-4.

18. Ibid., p. A-5.

19. Ibid., p. A-4.

20. Ibid., p. A-5; Sender, Henry (2002). Inside the WorldCom Numbers Factory. *Wall Street Journal* (August 21), C-1.

21. Solomon, D., & Blumenstein, R. (2002). Telecom: Mississippi Blues: Loans Proved to Be Ebber's Downfall. *Wall Street Journal* (May 1), A-8.

22. According to David Leonhardt of the *New York Times* (8/25/02, p. 10), Director Francesco Galesi made $31 million, John Sidgmore, the senior manager who replaced Ebbers as CEO, made $25 million, and CFO Scott Sullivan, who many think was responsible for the accounting abuses at WorldCom, pocketed $23 million.

23. Sandberg, J. (2002). Bernie Ebbers Bet the Ranch—Really—on WorldCom Stock. *Wall Street Journal* (April 14), A-13.

24. Salomon, D., & Sandberg, J. (2002). Leading the News. *Wall Street Journal* (November 6), A-3, report that Bernie used 8% of this load for personal use, an uncharacteristically self-serving move for Mr. Ebbers.

25. Young, S. (2002). Big WorldCom Loan May Have Spurred Inquiry. *Wall Street Journal* (March 14), A-3.

26. Lublin, J. S., & Young, S. (2002). WorldCom Loan to CEO of $341 Million Is the Most Generous in Recent Memory. *Wall Street Journal* (March 15), A-4.

27. Byrne, J. A. (2002). Fall from Grace: Joe Berardin Presided over the Biggest Accounting Scandals Ever and the Demise of a Legendary Firm. *Business Wall* (August 12), 50+.

28. These amounted to over $9 million in overstated income. For an explanation as to how some of this was done, see Elstrom, P. (2002). How to Hide $3.8 Billion in Expenses. *Business Week* (July 8), 41+.

29. Morgenson, G. (2002). More Clouds over Citigroup in Its Dealings with Ebbers. *New York Times* (November 3), 1.

30. Smith, R., & Salomon, D. (2002). Heard on the Street: Ebbers' Exit Hurts WorldCom's Biggest Fan. *Wall Street Journal* (May 3), C-1.

31. Rosenbush, S. (2002). Inside the Telecom Game. *Business Week* (August 5), p. 34+.

32. Ibid.

33. On December 20, 2002, Jack Grubman was fined $15 million and was banned for securities transactions for life by the Securities and Exchange Commission for such conflicts of interest.

34. Editors. (2002). Citi Defends IPO Allocations to Shamed Worldcom Execs. *Euroweek* (August 30), 18.

35. Murray, A. (2002). Political Capital: Let Capital Markets, Not Financial Firms, Govern Fate of IPOs. *Wall Street Journal* (September 10), A-4.

36. Craig, S. (2002). Offerings Were Easy Money for Ebbers. *Wall Street Journal* (September 3), C-1.

37. Ibid.

38. Rosenbush, op. cit., 34.

39. Smith, op. cit., C-1.

40. Ibid.

41. Editors. (2002). Salomon's Jack Grubman Resigns. *United Press International* (August 15), 10082777w0186.

42. Rosenbush, op. cit., 34.

43. Weil, J. (2002). Leading the News: An Ebbers Firm Got Citigroup Loans. *Wall Street Journal* (October 14), A-3.

44. Pelliam, S. (2002). Questioning the Books: WorldCom Memos Suggest Plan to Bury Financial Misstatements. *Wall Street Journal* (July 9), A-8.

45. Orey, M. (2002). Career Journal: WorldCom-Inspired "Whistle-Blower" Law Has Weaknesses. *Wall Street Journal* (October 1), B-1.

46. Colvin, G. (2002). Wonder Women of Whistleblowing. *Fortune* (August 12), 56+.

47. Pelliam, S., & Solomon, D. (2002). Uncooking the Books: How Three Unlikely Sleuths Discovered Fraud at WorldCom. *Wall Street Journal* (October 30), A-1.

Case Study

The Ford Pinto

W. Michael Hoffman

I

On August 10, 1978 a tragic automobile accident occurred on U.S. Highway 33 near Goshen, Indiana. Sisters Judy and Lynn Ulrich (ages 18 and 16, respectively) and their cousin Donna Ulrich (age 18) were struck from the rear in their 1973 Ford Pinto by a van. The gas tank of the Pinto ruptured, the car burst into flames and the three teenagers were burned to death.

Subsequently an Elkhart County grand jury returned a criminal homicide charge against Ford, the first ever against an American corporation. During the following 20-week trial, Judge Harold R. Staffeldt advised the jury that Ford should be convicted of reckless homicide if it were shown that the company had engaged in "plain, conscious and unjustifiable disregard of harm that might result (from its actions) and the disregard involves a substantial deviation from acceptable standards of conduct."[1] The key phrase around which the trial hinged, of course, is "acceptable standards." Did Ford knowingly and recklessly choose profit over safety in the design and placement of the Pinto's gas tank? Elkhart County prosecutor Michael A. Cosentino and chief Ford attorney James F. Neal battled dramatically over this issue in a rural Indiana courthouse. Meanwhile, American business anxiously awaited the verdict which could send warning ripples through board rooms across the nation concerning corporate responsibility and product liability.

II

As a background to this trial some discusses of the Pinto controversy is necessary. In 1977 the magazine *Mother Jones* broke a story by Mark Dowie, general manager of *Mother Jones* business operations, accusing Ford of knowingly putting on the road an unsafe car—the Pinto—in which hundreds of people have needlessly suffered burn deaths and even more have been scarred and disfigured due to burns. In his article "Pinto Madness" Dow charges that:

> Fighting strong competition from Volkswagen for the lucrative small-car market, the Ford Motor Company rushed the Pinto into production in much less than the usual time. Ford engineers discovered in pre-production crash tests that rear-end collisions would rupture the Pinto's fuel system extremely easily. Because assembly-line machinery was already tooled when engineers found this defect, top Ford officials decided to manufacture the car anyway—exploding gas tank and all—even though Ford owned the patent on a much safer gas tank. For more than eight years afterwards, Ford successfully lobbied, with extraordinary vigor at some blatant lies, against a key government safety standard that would have forced the company to change the Pinto's fire-prone gas tank. By conservative estimates Pinto crashes had caused 500 burn deaths to people who would not have been seriously injured if the car had not burst into flames. The figure could be high as 900. Burning Pintos have become such an embarrassment to Ford that its advertising agency, J. Walter Thompson, dropped a line from the ending of a radio spot that read "Pinto leaves you with that warm feeling."

Ford knows that the Pinto is a firetrap, yet it has paid out millions to settle damage suits out of court, and it is prepared to spend millions more lobbying against safety standards. With a half million cars rolling off the assembly lines each year, Pinto is the biggest-selling subcompact in America, and the company's operating profit on the car is fantastic. Finally, in 1977, new Pinto models have incorporated a few minor alterations necessary to meet that federal standard Ford managed to hold off for eight years. Why did the company delay so long in making these minimal, inexpensive improvements?

Ford waited eight years because its internal "cost-benefit analysis," which places a dollar value on human life, said it wasn't profitable to make the change sooner.[2]

Several weeks after Dowie's press conference on the article, which had the support of Ralph Nader and auto safety expert Byron Bloch, Ford issued a news release attributed to Herbert T. Misch, vice president of Environmental and Safety Engineering at Ford, countering points made in the *Mother Jones* article. Their statistical studies significantly conflicted with each other.

For example, Dowie states that more than 3,000 people were burning to death yearly in auto fires; he claims that, according to a National Highway Traffic Safety Administration (NHTSA) consultant, although Ford makes 24% of the cars on American roads, these cars account for 42% of the collision-ruptured fuel tanks.[3] Ford, on the other hand, uses statistics from the Fatality Analysis Reporting System (FARS) maintained by the government's NHTSA to defend itself, claiming that in 1975 there were 848 deaths related to fire-associated passenger-car accidents and only 13 of these involved Pintos; in 1976, Pintos accounted for only 22 out of 943. These statistics imply that Pintos were involved in only 1.9% of such accidents, and Pintos constitute about 1.9% of the total registered passenger cars. Furthermore, fewer than half of those Pintos cited in the FARS study were struck in the rear.[4] Ford concludes from this and other studies that the Pinto was never an unsafe car and has not been involved in some 70 burn deaths annually as *Mother Jones* claims.

Ford admits that early model Pintos did not meet rear-impact tests at 20 mph but denies that this implies that they were unsafe compared to other cars of that type and era. In fact, its tests were conducted, according to Ford, some with experimental rubber "bladders" to protect the gas tank, in order to determine how best to have their future cars meet a 20 mph rear-collision standard which Ford itself set as an internal performance goal. The government at that time had no such standard. Ford also points out that in every model year the Pinto met or surpassed the government's own standards, and

> it simply is unreasonable and unfair to contend that a car is somehow unsafe if it does not meet standards proposed for future years or embody the technological improvements that are introduced in later model years.[5]

Mother Jones, on the other hand, presents a different view of the situation. If Ford was so concerned about rear-impact safety, why did it delay the federal government's attempts to impose standards? Dowie gives the following answer:

> The particular regulation involved here was Federal Motor Vehicle Safety Standard 301. Ford picked portions of Standard 201 for strong opposition way back in 1968 when the Pinto was still in the blueprint stage. The intent of 301, and the 300 series that followed it, was to protect drivers and passengers after a crash occurs. Without question the worst post-crash hazard is fire. Standard 301 originally proposed that all cars should be able to withstand a fixed barrier impact of 20 mph (that is, running into a wall at that speed) without losing fuel.
>
> When the standard was proposed, Ford engineers pulled their crash-test results out of their files. The front ends of most cars were no problem—with minor alterations they could stand the impact without losing fuel. "We were already working on the front end," Ford engineer Dick Kimble admitted. "We knew we could meet the test on the front end." But with the Pinto particularly, a 20 mph rear-end standard meant redesigning the entire rear end of the car. With the Pinto scheduled for production in August of 1970, and with $200 million worth of tools in place, adoption of this standard would have created a minor financial disaster. So Standard 301 was targeted for delay, and with some assistance from its industry associates, Ford succeeded beyond its wildest expectations: the standard was not adopted until the 1977 model year.[6]

Ford's tactics were successful, according to Dowie, not only due to their extremely clever lobbying, which became the envy of lobbyists all over Washington, but also because of the pro-industry stance of NHTSA itself.

Furthermore, it is not at all clear that the Pinto was as safe as other comparable cars with regard to the positioning of its gas tank. Unlike the gas tank in the Capri which rode over the rear axle, a "saddle-type" fuel tank on which Ford owned the patent, the Pinto tank was placed just behind the rear bumper. According to Dowie,

Dr. Leslie Ball, the retired safety chief for the NASA manned space program and a founder of the International Society of Reliability Engineers, recently made a careful study of the Pinto. "The release to production of the Pinto was the most reprehensible decision in the history of American engineering," he said. Ball can name more than 40 European and Japanese models in the Pinto price and weight range with safer gas-tank positioning.

Los Angeles auto safety expert Byron Bloch has made an in-depth study of the Pinto fuel system. "It's a catastrophic blunder," he says. "Ford made an extremely irresponsible decision when they placed such a weak tank in such a ridiculous location in such a soft rear end. It's almost designed to blow up—premeditated."[7]

Although other points could be brought out in the debate between *Mother Jones* and Ford, perhaps the most intriguing and controversial is the cost-benefit analysis study that Ford did entitled "Fatalities Associated with Crash-Induced Fuel Leakage and Fires" released by J.C. Echold, Director of Automotive Safety for Ford. This study apparently convinced Ford and was intended to convince the federal government that a technical improvement costing $11 per car which would have prevented gas tanks from rupturing so easily was not cost-effective for society. The costs and benefits are broken down in the following way:

Benefits

Savings:	180 burn deaths, 180 serious burn injuries, 2,100 burned vehicles
Unit Cost:	$200,000 per death, $67,000 per injury, $700 per vehicle
Total Benefit:	$180 \times (\$200,000) + 180 \times (\$67,000) + 2,100 \times (\$700) = \$49.5$ million.

Costs

Sales:	11 million cars, 1.5 million light trucks
Unit Cost:	$11 per car, $11 per truck
Total Cost:	$11,000,000 \times (\$11) + 1,500,000 \times (\$11) = \$137$ million

Component	1971 Costs
Future Productivity Losses	
Direct	$132,000
Indirect	41,300
Medical Costs	
Hospital	700
Other	425
Property Damage	1,500
Insurance Administration	4,700
Legal and Court	3,000
Employer Losses	1,000
Victim's Pain and Suffering	10,000
Funeral	900
Assets (Lost Consumption)	5,000
Miscellaneous	200
TOTAL PER FATALITY	$200,725

(Although this analysis was on all Ford vehicles, a breakout of just the Pinto could be done.) *Mother Jones* reports it could not find anybody who could explain how the $10,000 figure for "pain and suffering" had been arrived at.[8]

Although Ford does not mention this point in its News Release defense, it might have replied that it was the federal government, not Ford, that set the figure for a burn death. Ford simply carried out a cost-benefit analysis based on that figure. *Mother Jones*, however, in addition to insinuating that there was industry-agency (NHTSA) collusion, argues that the $200,000 figure was arrived at under intense pressure from the auto industry to use cost-benefit analysis in determining regulations. *Mother Jones* also questions Ford's estimate of burn injuries: "All independent experts estimate that for each person who dies by an auto fire, many more are left with charred hands, faces and limbs." Referring to the Northern California Burn Center which estimates the ratio of burn injuries to deaths at ten to one instead of one to one, Dowie states that "the true ratio obviously throws the company's calculations way off."[9] Finally, *Mother Jones* claims to have obtained "confidential" Ford documents which Ford did not send to Washington, showing that crash fires could be largely prevented by installing a rubber bladder inside the gas tank for only $5.08 per car, considerably less than the $11 per car Ford originally claimed was required to improve crash-worthiness.[10]

Instead of making the $11 improvement, installing the $5.08 bladder, or even giving the consumer the right to choose the additional cost for added safety, Ford continued, according to *Mother Jones*, to delay the federal government for eight years in establishing mandatory rear-impact standards. In the meantime, Dowie argues, thousands of people were burning to death and tens of thousands more were being badly burned and disfigured for life, tragedies many of which could have been prevented for only a slight cost per vehicle. Furthermore, the delay also meant that millions of new unsafe vehicles went on the road, "vehicles that will be crashing, leaking fuel and incinerating people well into the 1980s."[11]

In concluding this article Dowie broadens his attack beyond just Ford and the Pinto.

> Unfortunately, the Pinto is not an isolated case of corporate malpractice in the auto industry. Neither is Ford a lone sinner. There probably isn't a car on the road without a safety hazard known to its manufacturer . . .
>
> Furthermore, cost-valuing human life is not used by Ford alone. Ford was just the only company careless enough to let such an embarrassing calculation slip into public records. The process of willfully trading lives for profits is built into corporate capitalism. Commodore Vanderbilt publicly scorned George Washington and his "foolish" air brakes while people died by the hundreds in accidents on Vanderbilt's railroads.[12]

Ford has paid millions of dollars in Pinto jury trials and out-of-court settlements, especially the latter. *Mother Jones* quotes Al Slechter in Ford's Washington office as saying: "We'll never go to a jury again. Not in a fire case. Juries are just too sentimental. They *see* those charred remains and forget the evidence. No sir, we'll settle."[13] But apparently Ford thought such settlements would be less costly than the safety improvements. Dowie wonders if Ford would continue to make the same decisions "were Henry Ford II and Lee Iacocca serving 20-year terms in Leavenworth for consumer homicide."[14]

III

On March 13, 1980, the Elkhart County jury found Ford not guilty of criminal homicide in the Ulrich case. Ford attorney Neal summarized several points in his closing argument before the jury. Ford could have stayed out of the small car market which would have been the "easiest way," since Ford would have made more profit by sticking to bigger cars. Instead Ford built the Pinto "to take on the imports, to save jobs for Americans and to make a profit for its stockholders."[15] The Pinto met every fuel-system standard of any federal, state or local government, and was comparable to other 1973 subcompacts. The engineers who designed the car thought it was a good, safe car and bought it for themselves and their families. Ford did everything possible quickly to recall the Pinto after NHTSA ordered it to do so. Finally, and more specifically to the case at hand, Highway 33 was a badly designed highway, and the girls were fully stopped when a 4,000-pound van rammed into the rear of their Pinto at at least 50 miles an hour. Given the same circumstances, Neal stated, any car would have suffered the same consequences as the Ulrichs' Pinto.[16] As reported in the *New York Times* and *Time*, the verdict brought a "loud cheer" from Ford's Board of Directors and undoubtedly at least a sigh of relief from other corporations around the nation.

Many thought this case was a David against a Goliath because of the small amount of money and volunteer legal help Prosecutor Cosentino had in contrast to the huge resources Ford poured into the trial. In addition, it should be pointed out that Cosentino's case suffered from a ruling by Judge Staffeldt that Ford's own test results on pre-1973 Pinto's were inadmissible. These documents confirmed that Ford knew as early as 1971 that the gas tank of the Pinto ruptured at impacts of 20 mph and that the company was aware, because of tests with the Capri, that the over-the-axle position of the gas tank was much safer than mounting it behind the axle. Ford decided to mount it behind the axle in the Pinto to provide more trunk space and to save money. The restrictions of Cosentino's evidence to testimony relating specifically to the 1973 Pinto severely undercut the strength of the prosecutor's case.[17]

Whether this evidence would have changed the minds of the jury will never be known. Some, however, such as business ethicist Richard De George, feel that this evidence shows grounds for charges of recklessness against Ford. Although it is true that there were no federal safety standards in 1973 to which Ford legally had to conform and although Neal seems to have proved that all subcompacts were unsafe when hit at 50 mph by a 4,000-pound van, the fact that the NHTSA ordered a recall of the Pinto and not other subcompacts is, according to De George, "*prima facie* evidence that Ford's Pinto gas tank mounting was substandard."[18] De George argues that these grounds for recklessness are made even stronger by the fact that Ford did not give the consumer a choice to make the Pinto gas tank safer by installing a rubber bladder for a rather modest fee.[19] Giving the consumer such a choice, of course, would have made the Pinto gas tank problem known and therefore probably would have been bad for sales.

Richard A. Epstein, professor of law at the University of Chicago Law School, questions whether Ford should have been brought up on criminal charges of reckless homicide at all. He also points out an interesting historical fact. Before 1966 an injured party in Indiana could not even bring civil charges against an automobile manufacturer solely because of the alleged "uncrashworthiness" of a car; one would have to seek legal relief from the other party involved in the accident, not from the manufacturer. But after *Larson v. General Motors Corp.* in 1968, a new era of crashworthiness suits against automobile manufacturers began. "Reasonable" precautions must now be taken by manufacturers to minimize personal harm in crashes.[20] How to apply criteria of reasonableness in such cases marks the whole nebulous ethical and legal arena of product liability.

If such a civil suit had been brought against Ford, Epstein believes, the corporation might have argued, as they did to a large extent in the criminal suit, that the Pinto conformed to all current applicable safety standards and with common industry practice. (Epstein cites that well over 90% of U.S. standard production cars had their gas tanks in the same position as the

Pinto.) But in a civil trial the adequacy of industry standards is ultimately up to the jury, and had civil charges been brought against Ford in this case the plaintiffs might have had a better chance of winning.[21] Epstein feels that a criminal suit, on the other hand, had no chance from the very outset, because the prosecutor would have had to establish criminal intent on the part of Ford. To use an analogy, if a hunter shoots at a deer and wounds an unseen person, he may be held civilly responsible but not criminally responsible because he did not intend to harm. And even though it may be more difficult to determine the mental state of a corporation (or its principal agents), it seems clear to Epstein that the facts of this case do not prove any such criminal intent even though Ford may have known that some burn deaths/injuries could have been avoided by a different placement of its Pinto gas tank and that Ford consciously decided not to spend more money to save lives.[22] Everyone recognizes that there are trade-offs between safety and costs. Ford could have built a "tank" instead of a Pinto, thereby considerably reducing risks, but it would have been relatively unaffordable for most and probably unattractive to all potential consumers.

To have established Ford's reckless homicide it would have been necessary to establish the same of Ford's agents since a corporation can only act through its agents. Undoubtedly, continues Epstein, the reason why the prosecutor did not try to subject Ford's officers and engineers to fines and imprisonment for their design choices is because of "the good faith character of their judgment, which was necessarily decisive in Ford's behalf as well."[23] For example, Harold C. MacDonald, Ford's chief engineer on the Pinto, testified that he felt it was important to keep the gas tank as far from the passenger compartment as possible, as it was in the Pinto. And other Ford engineers testified that they used the car for their own families. This is relevant information in a criminal case which must be concerned about the intent of the agents.

Furthermore, even if civil charges had been made in this case, it seems unfair and irrelevant to Epstein to accuse Ford of trading cost for safety. Ford's use of cost-benefit formulas, which must assign monetary values to human life and suffering, is precisely what the law demands in assessing civil liability suits.

The court may disagree with the decision, but to blame industry for using such a method would violate the very rules of civil liability. Federal automobile officials (NHTSA) had to make the same calculations in order to discharge their statutory duties. In allowing the Pinto design, are not they too (and in turn their employer, the United States) just as guilty as Ford's agents?[24]

IV

The case of the Ford Pinto raises many questions of ethical importance. Some people conclude that Ford was definitely wrong in designing and marketing the Pinto. The specific accident involving the Ulrich girls, because of the circumstances, was simply not the right one to have attacked Ford on. Other people believe that Ford was neither criminally nor civilly guilty of anything and acted completely responsibly in producing the Pinto. Many others find the case morally perplexing, too complex to make sweeping claims of guilt or innocence.

Was Ford irresponsible in rushing the production of the Pinto? Even though Ford violated no federal safety standards or laws, should it have made the Pinto safer in terms of rear-end collisions, especially regarding the placement of the gas tank? Should Ford have used cost-benefit analysis to make decisions relating to safety, specifically placing dollar values on human life and suffering? Knowing that the Pinto's gas tank could have been made safer by installing a protective bladder for a relatively small cost per consumer, perhaps Ford should have made that option available to the public. If Ford did use heavy lobbying efforts to delay and/or influence federal safety standards, was this ethically proper for a corporation to do? One might ask, if Ford was guilty, whether the engineers, the managers, or both are to blame. If Ford had been found guilty of criminal homicide, was the proposed penalty stiff enough ($10,000 maximum fine for each of the three counts = $30,000 maximum), or should agents of the corporations such as MacDonald, Iacocca, and Henry Ford II be fined and possibly jailed?

A number of questions concerning safety standards are also relevant to the ethical issues at stake in the Ford trial. Is it just to blame a corporation for not abiding by "acceptable standards" when such standards are not yet determined by society? Should corporations like Ford play a role in setting such standards? Should individual juries be determining such standards state by state, incident by incident? If Ford should be setting safety standards, how does it decide how safe to make its product and still make it affordable and desirable to the public without using cost-benefit analysis? For that matter, how does anyone decide? Perhaps it is putting Ford, or any corporation, in a catch-22 position to ask it both to set safety standards and to competitively make a profit for its stockholders.

Regardless of how the reader answers these and other questions it is clear that the Pinto case raises fundamental issues concerning the responsibilities of corporations, how corporations should structure themselves in order to make ethical decisions, and how industry, government, and society in general ought to interrelate to form a framework within which such decisions can properly be made in the future.

NOTES

1. *Indianapolis Star,* March 9, 1980, sec. 3, p. 2.
2. Mark Dowie, "Pinto Madness," *Mother Jones,* Sept./Oct., 1977, pp. 18 and 20. Subsequently Mike Wallace for *60 Minutes* and Sylvia Chase for *20/20* came out with similar exposés.
3. Ibid., p. 30.
4. Ford News Release (Sept. 9, 1977), pp. 1–3.
5. Ibid., p. 5.
6. Dowie, "Pinto Madness," p. 29.
7. Ibid., pp. 22–23.
8. Ibid., pp. 24 and 28. Although this analysis was on all Ford vehicles a breakout of just the Pinto could be done.
9. Ibid., p. 28.
10. Ibid., pp. 28–29.
11. Ibid., p. 30.
12. Ibid., p. 32. Dowie might have cited another example which emerged in the private correspondence which transpired almost a half century ago between Lammot du Pont and Alfred P. Sloan, Jr., then president of GM. Du Pont was trying to convince Sloan to equip GM's lowest-priced cars, Chevrolets, with safety glass. Sloan replied by saying: "It is not my responsibility to sell safety glass.⪙You can say, perhaps, that I am selfish, but business is selfish. We are not a charitable institution—we are trying to make a profit for our stockholders." Quoted in Morton Mintz and Jerry S. Cohen, *Power, Inc.* (New York: The Viking Press, 1976), p. 110.
13. Ibid., p. 31.
14. Ibid., p. 32.
15. Transcript of report of proceedings in *State of Indiana v. Ford Motor Company,* Case No. 11–431, Monday, March 10, 1980, pp. 6202–3. How Neal reconciled his "easiest way" point with his "making more profit for stockholders" point is not clear to this writer.
16. Ibid., pp. 6207–9.
17. *Chicago Tribune,* October 13, 1979, p. 1, sec. 2, p. 12; *New York Times,* October 14, 1979, p. 26; *Atlanta Constitution,* February 7, 1980.
18. Richard De George, "Ethical Responsibilities of Engineers in Large Organizations: The Pinto Case," *Business and Professional Ethics Journal,* vol. I, no. 1 (Fall 1981), p. 4. *New York Times,* October 26, 1978, p. 103, also points out that during 1976 and 1977 there were 13 fiery fatal rear-end collisions involving Pintos, more than double that of other U.S. comparable cars, with VW Rabbits and Toyota Corollas having none.
19. Ibid., p. 5.
20. Richard A. Epstein, "Is Pinto a Criminal?" *Regulation,* March/April, 1980, pp. 16–17.
21. A California jury awarded damages of $127.8 million (reduced later to $6.3 million on appeal) in a Pinto crash where a youth was burned over 95% of his body. See *New York Times,* February 8, 1978, p. 8.
22. Epstein, p. 19.
23. Ibid., pp. 20–21.
24. Ibid., pp. 19–21.

Corporations and Businesses, Large and Small

Legally, corporations are *persons* (although their personhood is often described as a legal fiction), having many of the rights, duties, and powers that attend personhood. Corporations, like persons, can enter into contracts, conducting business in their own name. Corporations have assets that are separate from those of their shareholders and managers, just as persons have assets that are separate from those of other persons. Corporate income, like personal income, is subject to taxation (and taxed again when it is distributed to shareholders in the form of dividends, just as income you might earn is taxed again if you give it to another as a gift).

In the literature of business ethics, perhaps the single most discussed topic has been the *moral* status of the corporation. Are corporations (as distinct from their shareholders, managers, and employees) moral agents? If so, are they moral agents in the same way that individual persons are moral agents? Beyond the requirements of law, what moral duties have corporations to their shareholders, employees, customers, suppliers, and communities—a collection sometimes referred to as their *stakeholders*? Are fiduciary duties that a business corporation's management owe to its shareholders, and to its shareholders alone, morally defensible?

Even good corporations (to the extent that locution makes sense) sometimes do (or are the locus of) bad things. Included in this section is an example of a corporation with a solid track record that temporarily lost its way and almost lost its good name, for good. A.H. Robins ("A.H. Robins: The Dalkon Shield") naively and perhaps unintentionally produced a product that caused injury and harm to many women. But when Robins discovered the problem, it didn't come forward and tell the truth. Rather, it conspired to misinform its customers about the health factors involved with the Dalkon Shield. Why?

Case Study

Sears Auto Shock

Ronald M. Green

"There's a saying, 'You Can Count on Sears.' I'm here to tell you in auto repair you cannot."

—JIM CONRAN, DIRECTOR, CALIFORNIA DEPARTMENT OF
CONSUMER AFFAIRS, PRESS CONFERENCE, JUNE 13, 1992.[1]

A

For most of his life, Michael J. Stumpf considered himself a walking advertisement for Sears, Roebuck & Co. "We had an all-American relationship with Sears," said Stumpf, a 32-year-old industrial video producer who lives in San Francisco. But when his fiancée brought their 1987 Ford to a local Sears Automotive Center for an advertised $89.99 strut job, she ended with a $650 repair bill instead.[2]

Ruth Hernandez had a similar experience. In October 1991, she went to a Sears Automotive Center in Stockton, California, to buy new tires for her 1986 Honda Accord. The mechanic who worked on the car told her that she also needed new struts, at a cost of $419.95. Hernandez, 53, sought a second opinion. Another auto-repair store told her the struts were fine. Furious, Hernandez returned to Sears, where the mechanic admitted his diagnosis was wrong. "I kept thinking," she adds, "how many other people has this happened to?"[3]

Apparently it happened to many others. On June 10, 1992, California's Bureau of Automotive Repairs (BAR) moved to revoke the operating permits of 72 Sears auto service centers in the state. Announcing the results of an 18-month-long undercover investigation into repair practices at 33 Sears auto centers throughout the state, BAR accused Sears automotive operations in California of fraud and willful departures from accepted trade standards.

BAR launched its unprecedented sting operation in December of 1990 after receiving 250 consumer complaints about Sears—enough to suggest a pattern of abuse. During this period Sears advertised brake service specials ranging from $48–$58 that had attracted many customers. Between December 1990 and December 1991, state workers posing as motorists took unmarked state cars for brake inspections 48 times at 27 Sears outlets. Before taking the cars in, state mechanics took apart the brakes and suspension, inspected and marked the parts, and had them photographed and catalogued. Worn brake pads were purposely placed on most of the cars.

The cars were then trailered to a few blocks from the targeted Sears outlet and driven there by the undercover employee. According to BAR investigators, in 42 out of 48 runs Sears employees recommended and performed unnecessary service or repairs. The highest overcharge occurred at the San Bernadino store, where the bill came to $550. On average, according to the state, consumers were bilked $250 each. Many of the replaced parts were nearly new.

On several occasions, BAR officials said, the cars emerged from Sears in worse or unsafe condition, with loose brakes or improperly installed parts. According to state investigators, Sears service personnel were not above using scare tactics to up the bill. According to Jim Schoning, BAR's chief, one of the undercover operators was told that the front calipers on his car were so badly frozen that the car would fishtail if the brakes were applied quickly. "The calipers were in fine working order," Schoning said.[4]

The investigation was a serious blow to Sears, whose auto service business was the largest in California. Nationwide, Sears $3 billion service and parts business was also threatened by similar investigations being launched in New Jersey, New York, and Florida. Overall, auto repair and service accounted for $2.8 billion or 9% of the retail giant's $31.4 billion in revenues in 1991.

What led a company that was once regarded as one of the nation's most enlightened retailers into such difficulties? One factor, in the minds of some observers, was a change of compensation policies in Sears auto service and some of its other retail businesses. In 1990 mechanics, who had previously been paid at an hourly rate, were told that commissions would replace a part of their compensation. A manager formerly earning, say, $15 an hour would now receive $12 an hour and was told to make up the difference through increased sales of services and parts.

Investigators at BAR found that Sears also instructed employees to sell a certain number of repair or services during every eight-hour work shift, including a specified number of alignments, springs, and brake jobs. Employees were pressured to sell a specified number of shock absorbers or struts for every hour worked. If they failed to meet their goals, Sears employees told investigators, they often received a cutback in hours or were transferred to other Sears departments.[5] One Sears mechanic described his experience under this system as "pressure, pressure, pressure to get the dollars."[6]

Changes in compensation policies were part of Sears overall effort to improve its sagging profit posture. During the late 1980s Sears had been hurt by a national recession and new competition from discount outlets and an emerging industry of specialized mail order businesses. In 1990, Sears announced a 40% drop in earnings and a $155 million write-off. Its Merchandise group, which includes auto centers and appliance sales, dropped 60%. During this period Sears Roebuck's new Chairman Edward A. Brennan scrambled to shake up the retail giant, slashing costs by $600 million in 1991. Brennan began renovating the company's 868 lackluster stores, and pushed new low prices. His overall thrust was to make every employee, from the sales floor to the chairman's suite, focus on profits.[7]

Caught off guard by news of the California investigation, the company's response was angry and defensive. Saying it would fight the allegations in court, Sears blasted the investigation as "incompetent, very seriously flawed." In a press statement the company said the investigation "simply does not support the allegations." Pointing out that Sears has offered automotive repair for more than 60 years, the statement went on to say that "we have a hard-earned and outstanding reputation for trust with our customers."[8] The company suggested there may have been political motives behind the charges, a case of a state agency trying to gain support at a time when it was threatened by severe budget cuts.

Perry Chlan, a company spokesman, denied that a quota system existed in Sears 850 auto service centers nationwide. "We have sales goals, but that in no way affects what we recommend in service to a customer's car."[9] Other Sears spokesmen said that the company routinely audits the performance of its sales advisors and mechanics and surveys customers to see that service is satisfactory. Because the company believes in preventive maintenance, they pointed out, some of the problems may have resulted from overzealous efforts on the part of individual mechanics or sales personnel to serve customers. But Roy Liebman, a deputy Attorney General in California, disagreed. Sears's behavior, he charged, shows that "there was a deliberate decision by Sears management to set up a structure that made it totally inevitable that the consumer would be oversold."[10]

Whoever is right, the controversy was clearly something Sears did not need at this difficult moment in its history. With each day's headlines reporting new investigations into its auto business, Sears executives and employees struggled to manage an escalating corporate crisis.

B

On June 15, Sears chairman Edward F. Brennan called a press conference in Chicago as his company struggled to contain a widening crisis. Less than a week before, the state of California had charged Sears with improper sales practices in its California auto service centers. Since then, New Jersey, Florida, and Alabama had announced similar investigations and hundreds of new complaints had been lodged against the company in California.

The day before, the company began a national campaign featuring full-page advertisements in *USA Today, The Wall Street Journal,* and 25 large metropolitan newspapers. An "Open Letter to Sears Customers" signed by Brennan claimed the company would never violate customers' trust, and that in repairing more than 2 million vehicles annually in the state, "mistakes may have occurred." (See Exhibit 1 for a copy of this ad.)

By addressing customer concerns, the Sears campaign represented a change in course from the company's initial response to the crisis, which insisted on the company's legal innocence and denied that Sears had done anything wrong. According to Charles Ruder, Sears vice president for public affairs, chairman Brennan had played an integral role in developing the ad campaign. The weekend before, after canceling a business trip, he had worked on the advertisements with members of management, the company's advertising agency, Ogilvy & Mather, and several unnamed public relations advisors.

Ruder explained that a decision had been made not to hold a news conference with Mr. Brennan or to ask the chairman to appear on television programs to address the charges being leveled at the company. "We thought it was appropriate for Ed to be part of the process of putting the ad together, but we did not think it was necessary to take it to a higher level of escalation," Mr. Ruder said.[11]

C

By late 1992 Sears chairman Edward Brennan and other senior managers could start to believe that they had put behind them the serious embarrassment and legal threat posed by a California investigation of practices at Sears auto centers in that state.

Sears's handling of the crisis had been marked by several changes in course. Following an initial response based on legal issues, the company had shifted attention to its customers, launching an advertising campaign that conceded mistakes, but denied that the

EXHIBIT 1
An Open Letter to Sears Customers

On June 10th, the California Bureau of Automotive Repair made charges concerning the practices of Sears Auto Centers in California.

With over 2 million automotive customers services last year in California alone, mistakes may have occurred. However, Sears wants you to know that we would never intentionally violate the trust customers have shown us for 105 years.

You rely on us to recommend preventive maintenance measures to help insure your safety, and to avoid more costly future repairs. This includes replacement of worn parts, when appropriate, before they fail. This accepted industry practice is being challenged by the Bureau.

Our report policy is to:

1. Consult with you before the repair.
2. Prepare a written estimate.
3. Perform only repairs you authorize.
4. Guarantee all work performed.

Sears has been providing Customer Satisfaction in auto repairs for over 60 years. In addition to our own extensive training program, our technicians have over 14,000 Automotive Service Excellence (ASE) certifications.

Sears's hallmark has always been Satisfaction Guaranteed or Your Money Back. If you have any doubt or question about service performed on your car, we urge you to call or stop by your local Sears Auto Center.

I pledge we will do our utmost to resolve any concern you may have,

ED BRENNAN
Chairman and Chief Executive Office
Sears, Roebuck and Co.

company had intentionally sought to violate its customers' trust. This ad was apparently met with a measure of skepticism by many of its readers. (See Exhibit 2 for one such response.)

Less than a week later, with sales in its auto centers down 15% nationally and 20% in California, Sears chairman Edward F. Brennan held a news conference in Chicago. While continuing to deny that Sears had intentionally wronged its customers, Brennan conceded that the company's incentive compensation program and sales goals had created an environment where mistakes occurred.

Stating that the mistakes "may have been the result of rigid attention to goals, or . . . the result of aggressive selling," Brennan said that the company now realized that the incentive systems were an error. He announced that they would be replaced by a noncommission program intended to reward service personnel for high customer-satisfaction levels. "We want to eliminate anything that could even lead to the perception that our associates could be motivated to sell our customers unneeded repairs."[12] Brennan added that Sears would eliminate sales goals for specific products and would hire an independent organization to perform shopping audits of Sears auto centers. The aim was to insure that company policies and standards were being met.

Over the next few months, Sears sought to put its legal difficulties behind by arriving at out-of-court settlements with state officials

---

EXHIBIT 2
"A Little Searing Commentary" (Excerpts)
by Tony Kornheiser

By now you've undoubtedly seen the full-page ad Sears has placed in newspapers around the country. It begins. "You may have heard recent allegations that some Sears Auto Centers in California and New Jersey have sold customers parts and services they didn't need."

They say, "You may have heard . . ." as though it is some sort of wild rumor that is circulating, like a sighting of bigfoot by some toothless man in a trailer park.

In fact, the reason you may have heard about this is that California consumer affairs officials, after an extensive investigation, have charged Sears with "organized planned fraud." Between December 1990 and August 1991, investigators made 38 visits to 27 Sears Auto Centers with cars that needed minor brake repair, but had no other mechanical problems, and in 34 cases—34 out of 38, mind you, a higher percentage than might be attributable to, say, "wind shear"—Sears mechanics performed work that was unnecessary. That's like going to a doctor's office for a cholesterol test and coming out without a gall bladder . . .

How many Sears mechanics does it take to change your oil?

Fourteen. One to change the oil, and 13 to rebuild your engine as "preventive maintenance."

I knew I was in trouble when I went to a Sears Auto Center for a routine change of fluids, a $29 job, and they looked under the hood and said I needed a new washer.

"No big deal," I said.

When I came back, they handed me a bill for $795.

"What's this for?" I asked.

"Your new washer," they said. And they pointed to the open trunk where they had installed a deluxe Kenmore with three rinse cycles. . . .

There are a number of priceless lines in this ad. One of my favorites is: "As always, no work will ever be performed without your approval."

Oh sure, they get your approval beforehand. They get it by saying, "I don't want to alarm you, but I just thank God you came in when you did. Because if you don't have your froindoid adjusted, and that's this small set of rings underneath your engine block—it's an essential component of the reverse tramiclater—if you don't do this, and again, believe me, I don't want to do anything that isn't absolutely necessary, I want you to keep coming back, but if you don't do this, well, you won't get five blocks from here without your car exploding like a can of Right Guard in a microwave, and you and your beautiful children dying in a fiery wreck, and I don't want to be responsible for that. So, like I said, it's up to you."[13]

---

and the many individual customers who had joined together in class action suits against it. In July, Sears settled an investigation in New Jersey by paying $3,000 in penalties and $200,000 to set up an Auto Repair Industry Reform Fund. Late in October, the company announced a settlement in California by agreeing to pay $8 million to end a consolidated class-action against it, and by providing $3.5 million to finance auto repair training programs at the state's community colleges.

In November Sears announced a final aspect of its settlement effort: a year-long nationwide offer of $50 coupons, redeemable for any Sears product or service, to any customer who bought one or more of the five commonly sold Sears auto parts between August 1, 1990 and January 31, 1992. Given the nearly 1 million eligible for the coupon, Sears could pay out as much as $46.7 million, although it expected to pay out far less.[14]

As the year ended and Sears top managers turned their attention back to the company's long-term struggle back to profitability, it was not clear what impact the auto center flap would have. In that struggle against new competitors, Sears had one major asset: its century-old reputation for quality and integrity. Ian Mitroff, co-director of the University of Southern California Center for Crisis Management, put the problem facing the company succinctly: "If I put my trust in you and you betray me, that creates a very deep response."

NOTES

1. Judy Quinn, "Repair Job," *Incentive* (October 1992), 40.
2. Julia Flynn, Christina Del Valle, and Russell Mitchell, "Did Sears Take Other Customers for a Ride?" *Business Week*, August 3, 1992, 24.
3. Kevin Kelly and Eric Schine, "How Did Sears Blow This Gasket?" *Business Week*, June 29, 1992, 38.
4. UPI, June 11, 1992.
5. Lawrence M. Fisher, "Sears's Auto Centers to Halt Commissions," *The New York Times*, June 23, 1992, D5.
6. Flynn et al., "Did Sears Take Other Customers for a Ride?" 25.
7. Kelly and Schine, "How Did Sears Blow This Gasket?" 38.
8. John Schmeltzer and Jim Mateja, "Sears Auto Centers Charged with Fraud; California Probe 'Flawed,' Retailer Says," *Chicago Tribune*, June 12, 1992, 1.
9. Ibid.
10. Flynn et al., "Did Sears Take Other Customers for a Ride?" 24.
11. Richard W. Stevenson, "Sears Crisis: How Did It Do?" *The New York Times*, June 17, 1992, D4.
12. Fisher, "Sears Auto Centers to Halt Commissions," D1.
13. *Washington Post*, July 28, 1992, Style, 1.
14. Quinn, "Repair Job," *Incentive* (October 1992), 41.

Case Study

The New Year's Eve Crisis[1]

William Naumes and Margaret J. Naumes

It was Monday morning, New Year's Eve Day, 2001. On a day that many people were enjoying at home, Mike Valenti was in his office at Michael's Homestyle Pasta. Since he had acquired the Southern Pasta Company on December 10th, he had been learning the business, trying to get his arms around it, as he described it. Distance was a factor: Michael's headquarters and plant were in Connecticut, while Southern was located in Florida. Mike would have liked to be in Tampa, working directly with his new employees and trying to integrate the two companies' cultures, but his wife was expecting their third child in early January and he needed to stay near home. In the due diligence period leading up to the purchase, it had seemed as though a new problem developed every week.

Finally, three weeks after closing, things seemed to be under control.

The telephone rang. When Mike answered, he was not surprised to hear Ted Brewer on the other end of the line. Ted, Michael's Vice President for Administration and Operations, spent part of every week at the Florida plant. Ted began, "I hope you're sitting down." He went on to tell Mike that Southern's Quality Assurance manager, Fred Jones, was in his office, and "You need to hear what he has to say!" He put Fred on the phone.

Mike listened as Fred told him that the seafood-stuffed pasta shells that Southern had just shipped to its biggest customer were tainted with salmonella.

"That can't be true," Mike responded. "We have the lab results that show it's fine!"

"I know," replied Fred, "but those results were falsified." In tears, the quality assurance manager explained that he had taken the samples of stuffed pasta that were to be sent to an independent lab for testing and baked them to make sure that any bacteria were killed, then had frozen them and repackaged them to look like packages just off the production line. Southern's president, Hans Schmidt, had threatened his job if the stuffed shells didn't test clean.

Mike was stunned. New Year's Eve was one of the biggest nights in the year for restaurants. The shells stuffed with chunks of lobster, crab and shrimp were custom made for a chain of over 200 restaurants, and were one of its featured menu items. The chain accounted for almost half of the revenues of Southern Pasta, and was one of the most important reasons why Michael's had acquired Southern. Salmonella contamination was a serious problem. Salmonella was a bacterium that thrived in undercooked food containing eggs, poultry or meat, responsible for about 600 deaths a year. Small children, the elderly, and people with weakened immune systems were particularly at risk.[2]

"Ted, we need to talk about this," Mike said. "I'm going to set up a conference call and call you back."

MICHAEL'S HOMESTYLE PASTA

Mike Valenti had written a business plan for a homemade-style pasta company in 1991, while he was a college undergraduate. His goal, in the plan, was to reach $3 million in sales. After graduation, he started the company, making stuffed pasta by hand upstairs from his father's bakery. By 2001, the company had moved twice as it expanded, first to the corner of an old textile mill building, then to its own new plant. It had over 100 employees, and sales had reached $17 million.

Michael's Homestyle Pasta produced a range of specialty products including fettuccine and linguini, but its signature product was gourmet stuffed pasta shells. Mike had studied competitors' mass produced products and compared them with home-made. He had identified an important difference— machine-made stuffed pasta, no matter how tasty, had fillings made with chopped up ingredients, while hand-made shells had large, identifiable chunks of vegetables or meat or cheese. So Mike designed machines that could handle the irregular chunks. His focus on research and development and on customer service led him to develop new pasta products for specific clients. By 2001, nearly half of his sales were to national or regional restaurant chains, with independent distributor selling most of the rest.

SOUTHERN PASTA COMPANY

While there were small "Mom and Pop" companies making specialty pasta in many local markets, there was only one other company that was able to produce stuffed shells similar to Michael's on a large scale. Southern Pasta Company, located in Florida, was smaller, but had a wider range of products, including a number of non-pasta items. Like Michael's, its customers included restaurant chains, several of which ordered custom products. Southern was the only company, other than Michael's, that made pasta shells stuffed with identifiable chunks of seafood. At Southern, however, employees made and stuffed some of the pasta products by hand.

Mike had first approached Friedrich Walz, the founder and owner of Southern, in 1999 when the companies were roughly equal in size. The two companies were competing for the same pool of customers, and Mike wanted to know whether Walz would be willing to sell. Walz would only consider a merger, and talks didn't progress far. Shortly afterwards, Michael's succeeded in signing Southern's largest customer.

Two years later, Walz was willing to sell. Despite signing some new customers, sales at Southern had been steadily decreasing and his company had lost $1 million in each of the last two years. In May, 2001, Southern had to recall its seafood-stuffed shells due to salmonella contamination. The plant had to be thoroughly cleaned and then inspected by the FDA. For the first time, the company put in a system to track individual production lots and made other changes in the production process. The customer for whom Southern made the shells stuffed with seafood sent people to inspect, help retool, and develop approved cooking procedures. The recall cost Southern more than half a million dollars.

While Walz had been willing to shoulder the losses out of personal funds from selling a previous business in Europe, the emotional drain of the recall process had taken its toll. He wanted to return home to Europe. The deal was important to Mike because of his concern that a major food company might become interested in buying Southern,

enabling it to become an effective competitor. By the end of June, 2001, Mike and Walz had signed a letter of intent for Michael's purchase of Southern. However, Walz provided as little information as possible during the next few months, while Mike and his management team were attempting to do due diligence analysis. Mike recalled, "There was a point in time during the due diligence where we really didn't feel we had the information to close the deal." Dan Rivers, Michael's VP of Sales and Marketing, was more optimistic. "We knew a lot about the company from competing against them," Dan said. "We felt comfortable that we could make it work."

They did learn the name of some, but not all, of Southern's customers. The May salmonella recall was an issue, but not a major one. As Mike said, "We had done as much due diligence as we could possibly do without going into the plant. To make sure, they provided documentation, consulting documentation saying they'd cured the problem and they'd cured it well into the summer." Mike and his management team were concerned about the limited information they were able to secure from the company. They realized that Walz was not going to provide any further information. They felt that they could build in insurance clauses to cover any expected contingencies. One concern was Southern's large volume of accounts receivable, half of which were more than 90 days old. Mike negotiated an escrow account to cover any receivables that turned out to be uncollectible. Other problems surfaced in the weeks prior to closing, but on December 10, 2001, control of the company passed from Friedrich Walz to Mike Valenti.

MANAGING SOUTHERN PASTA

Mike decided to leave the management team and operations at Southern intact, at least for the time being. He ran Michael's with a lean staff, and he did not have people that he could spare to send to Southern on a full-time basis. Mike also realized, "When you acquire a company, the biggest challenge you have is to overcome their culture and weld it into yours." While he understood Southern's production and markets, his difficulties in getting company information before the takeover left him concerned about what else might not have been disclosed.

Two days after the acquisition, Walz and the president went home to Europe for the holidays. They stated that they would be back after New Year's. For the first few weeks, Mike commuted to Florida as often as possible. While he would have liked to move to Florida temporarily, he knew this was impossible because of the late term pregnancy of his wife. His two top people, Dan, VP of Sales and Marketing, and Ted, VP of Administration and Operations, split their time between Connecticut and Florida, each spending half the week in their new plant to learn the business and begin the process of integrating the company into Michael's. Mike joked that everybody at Bradley International (Hartford CT's airport) knew his name, because "I racked up so many frequent flyer miles." Shortly after December 10th, Michael's director of Quality Assurance moved to Florida temporarily. "He was whipping them into shape," particularly in the area of cleanliness, according to Ted.

It became obvious quickly that the cultures of the two companies were very different. As Mike and his team began digging into the company's operations, they discovered that many of the employees intensely disliked the former owner. The Southern employees indicated that Walz and Schmidt ran the company with a top down management style. The employees stated that when the two top managers gave an order, they expected it to be followed by their subordinates. Otherwise, they had little interaction with lower level employees.

Mike, on the other hand, explained his own approach as "very interactive, very hands-on. I wanted to go out there and see what people were doing. They took it as a breath of fresh air." One of Mike's staff compared Walz's management style with Mike's: "Mike, your people would throw themselves in front of a bus for you. His people would throw him in front of the bus."

Once his wife's due date approached, Mike felt that he couldn't travel until after the baby was born, since "I would never want to miss that!" It wasn't easy for him, however. He described himself as: "I'm the kind of guy that says, 'Look, we're going to solve the problem, so you'd better believe I'm going to be there. I want to know what you're doing, I want to know how you're doing it, I want to know what my impact is going to be, I want to know what my exposure is, I want to see it all.'"

THE CALL FROM FLORIDA

Mike sat back and considered what he had just heard from Fred Jones: "The long and short of what he's telling me is, 'You have a major regulatory problem which could shut you down completely, number one, and number two, you can pretty much kiss goodbye fifty percent of the revenue stream you just bought three weeks ago!'"

One of the changes made after Southern's salmonella problem in May had been the installation of a lot tracking system, so that every batch of each product could be traced and its location identified. The stuffed shells produced during November and early December had been stockpiled and shipments had only recently been made to the customer from these potentially contaminated batches. Fred reported that he had managed to stop two shipments on Southern's loading docks. Ted was checking with the distributors, trying to locate the rest of the contaminated lots. Mike realized the magnitude of the problem:

Once we traced the product, we realized that the product had left distribution already. It was in the restaurants.

There are recalls that go on that you never hear about. And the reason you never hear about them is that the lots never hit flow, they never hit consumer marketplaces. So what happens is the companies will simply pull them back out of distribution and destroy them. And the FDA is fine with that, as long as it can be proved that the product is contained.

If the product had reached consumers, however, the FDA would take action. And what the FDA does, is they put out a press release, and depending on how many states you're in, depends on what sort of media they use to issue the press release. So, fifty states would generally mean US News and World Reports and CNN. . . . We were extremely close to that very harmful situation.

The problem was the cooking system in the plant. The filling mixture of the shells was cooked, but then allowed to cool. The final processing step didn't get the temperature high enough to kill the salmonella.

Mike had learned from Fred that "everybody knows that, down there. It said right in the specs that the product needed to go up to 158 [degrees Fahrenheit], and all of the documentation behind it states that it never hit more than 140." The seafood filling was more vulnerable to contamination than other fillings. In the month before Southern Pasta was acquired, virtually every lot of the seafood-stuffed shells had been contaminated. Hans Schmidt, Southern's President, who was the only person in the company other than Walz who knew about the impending sale, had coerced Fred to make sure that the pasta got clean test results. What Schmidt didn't know was that Fred had also kept his own records of all of the failing test results. Now, after three weeks

under new management, he had finally worked up the nerve to come forward.

THE DECISION

Mike's conference call with his management team had lasted more than four hours, and no definite decision had been reached. Soon, the restaurants would be starting to serve their patrons who were happily celebrating New Year's Eve.

Dan, Ted and Mark had been as shocked as Mike was. Dan's word for it was "dumfounded." "Nobody could finish a sentence: 'How could they . . . ? What did they . . . ?'" Mike remembered.

Southern's sales manager who handled the restaurant account and Michael's lawyer were also brought in on the call. The lawyer noted that the restaurant chain had some responsibility here due to its stated policy of certifying production by its suppliers. There were also the FDA and health department requirements to cook the product at a sufficient level to kill contaminants such as salmonella. The lawyer argued that even if there were a problem at the restaurants, Southern had produced the product prior to the acquisition, and any liability could be placed on Southern's previous owner. He felt that Michael's liability could be limited if anyone were to get sick from the tainted food. They went back and forth on what to do, whether to tell the customer. "Effectively, all my inventory was bad, and all of their inventory was bad except for a very small residual of the older stuff that they had," Mike told his team. Would it matter that the inventory had been produced before Michael's had bought the company? Who would be sued if any customers got sick?

The restaurant chain had cooking standards that required the stuffed shells to be cooked to at least 160 degrees Fahrenheit.

After the May recall, the chain had sent representatives to Southern's plant and assisted in the retooling process. Mike's team discussed the probability that the product would be cooked correctly:

We went through a scenario where, from a legal standpoint, they have documentation saying they need to come up above 160 which means that they should have been cooking the product, so from FDA and health departments standpoints, would they have been at fault? Probably (the restaurant company) would have been co-fault because it meant they didn't have checks and balances in place on their end, to make sure that they were cooking the product properly.

One option would be to trust the chain's cooking standards. Another option would be to contact the chain and have them notify all restaurants, to make sure that the cooking temperature was high enough. Either option could have ramifications, however.

Dan felt,

I think we were scared of a couple of things. One, we were scared that [the customer] would go to another vender. And they were a big reason why we bought the company, $3.5 million out of $8m or so that they were doing. And two, we were scared that they would take it off the menu altogether … just say, 'This was the second time, we can't do this any more. It's too big of a risk to our customers.'

Mike thought back about the call:

It went up, it went down, it got heated, it calmed down: Well, what do we do? What if we called? We could lose the business! Well we could lose the business anyway. I played out every scenario that I could possibly play out. Don't call. Well, what if they call you and say, 'Did you know about this?' What if a pregnant lady comes in there, eats the product, and has a stillborn?

I said, 'My God, I can't believe this. I just spent three and a half million dollars—I just spent three and a half million dollars on nothing!' I thought for sure we were done. Damned if you do, damned if you don't. If somebody gets sick, not only are we done here, but the resulting impact through the industry would have been devastating for us.

By now, it was late afternoon. After the conference call ended, Mike had called back and talked to each person separately, probing to find out what they thought and how comfortable they were with the different options. Ultimately, however, it was his company. Soon, the restaurants would be starting to serve their patrons, happily celebrating New Year's Eve. Mike had to decide what to do.

NOTES

1. The names in this case have been disguised.
2. For information on Salmonellosis, see www.about-salmonella.com

---

Case Study

The Wal-Mart Way

Edward C. Brewer

This case examines criticisms of Wal-Mart and the assertion that its economic impact "limits the ability of local businesses to survive." The case study also examines how the company has responded to charges that it negatively affects local businesses. It raises questions regarding the effect of large businesses on other stakeholders, including whether company goals are aligned with community goals and whether the company communicates responsibly with its publics.

---

*It also addresses the utility, or consequences, of economic development and its impact on rela-
tionships with others, among other ethical perspectives.*

Wal-Mart has had a tremendous impact upon our society. Its pervasive presence has affected communities all over the United States. The first Wal-Mart store opened in 1962 in Rogers, Arkansas. By 1970, there were 38 stores with 1,500 "associates" (employees) and sales of $44.2 million. In 1990, Wal-Mart became the nation's number one retailer. In 2002, Wal-Mart had the biggest single-day sales in history: $1.43 billion on the day after Thanksgiving. Today, Wal-Mart is the world's largest retailer with 13 million "associates" in more than 3200 facilities and sales of $244.5 billion in the fiscal year ending January 31, 2003.[1] Because of this impact, Wal-Mart has been confronted with many ethical challenges.

One of the challenges the huge retailer has faced is to have a positive impact upon the communities it enters. Whether Wal-Mart has acted ethically may be a matter of perspective. Certainly, Wal-Mart does much for the communities in which it operates, but it has also faced criticism that its economic impact limits the ability of local businesses to survive.[2] This case study will examine some of the issues and explain how Wal-Mart has responded to them. It is up to the reader, then, to determine the ethical qualities of Wal-Mart's communication and actions. Does Wal-Mart show ethical consideration to the communities it enters? Do the communities have an ethical obligation to embrace Wal-Mart or fight Wal-Mart? Is Wal-Mart destroying jobs and communities or helping to revitalize them? Does the big-box retail model, which Wal-Mart has perfected, cause an ethical dilemma for local communities?
According to their Web site (www.walmart stores.com), Wal-Mart stores are committed to our communities:

> Wal-Mart Stores, Inc. believes each Wal-Mart store, SAM'S CLUB, and distribution center has

THE WAL-MART PHILOSOPHY

Wal-Mart claims the following impact for the United States (accessed 4/1/04 from http://www.walmartstores.com):

Wal-Mart—Economic Impact*

WAL-MART STORES INC.	
WAL-MART STORES	1,636
SUPERCENTERS	1,093
NEIGHBORHOOD MARKETS	31
SAM'S CLUBS	502
DISTRIBUTION CENTERS	106
ASSOCIATES EMPLOYED IN UNITED STATES	1,043,970
COMMUNITY INVOLVEMENT	$196 million
TOTAL AMOUNT SPENT WITH U.S. SUPPLIERS	$107 billion
TOTAL FEDERAL, STATE AND LOCAL TAXES PAID	$1.2 billion
SALES TAXES COLLECTED AND REMITTED	$8.5 billion

* Total state and local taxes paid include real estate, personal property, other taxes and licenses, unemployment, use, and state income taxes. Sales taxes collected and remitted are state and local sales tax collected by Wal-Mart and remitted to government authorities.

a responsibility to contribute to the well being of the local community. Our more than 3,400 locations contributed more than $150 million to support communities and local non-profit organizations. Customers raised an additional $75 million with the help of our stores and clubs.[3]

Wal-Mart also claims that their philosophy is to do good works:

> Wal-Mart's Good Works community involvement program is based on the philosophy of operating globally and giving back locally. In our

experience, we can make the greatest impact on communities by supporting issues and causes that are important to our customers and associates in their own neighborhoods. We rely on our associates to know which organizations are the most important to their hometowns, and we empower them to determine how Wal-Mart Foundation dollars will be spent. Consequently, our funding initiatives are channeled directly into local communities by associates who live there.

Wal-Mart's approach to implementing this community involvement (again according to their Web site, noted above) is

unique, combining both financial and volunteer support. We encourage our associates to be involved in their local communities and to support the programs that are making a positive difference. In addition, associates conceive and carry out creative fundraising efforts on behalf of local charitable causes, particularly Children's Miracle Network (CMN) and the 170-plus children's hospitals nationwide that receive support from CMN.

Wal-Mart does fund a number of programs to support communities and local nonprofit organizations. They claim to have given the following (http://www.walmartfoundation.org/wmstore/goodworks/scripts/index.jsp)[4]:

- More than $88 million in community grants
- More than $265 million in 15 years for Children's Miracle Network (CMN)
- More than $184 million in 19 years to United Way chapters
- $80 million in scholarships since 1979
- $1.7 million in Environmental Grants
- $3.1 million in Volunteerism Always Pays grants
- $20 million raised and contributed during the 2002 holidays

COMMUNITY COMPLAINTS

Clearly Wal-Mart has participated in helping to make communities better, but there is another side to the story as well. In his book, *In Sam We Trust,* Bob Ortega (1998) suggests that Wal-Mart is devouring America. Among other issues, Representative George Miller's (D-CA) 25-page Report by the Democratic Staff of the Committee on Education and the Workforce, U.S. House of Representatives (Miller, 2004), suggests that Wal-Mart's low wages and unaffordable or unavailable health care cost taxpayers money. In recent years, the downtown areas of many towns have been suffering as communities have become increasingly suburban. According to critics, Wal-Mart often contributes to the decline of the downtown of small towns because they build stores at the outskirts of towns, drawing traffic away from the downtown areas.

Downtown Deterioration

For example, Wilmington, Ohio (a community of about 10,000 when Wal-Mart moved in) saw the decline of their downtown as the traffic flow headed west of town, toward the shopping center that housed Wal-Mart. The K-Mart on the eastern edge of town eventually shut down because of the competition. A small craft store in downtown Wilmington (Clinton Art Craft) soon discovered that Wal-Mart was selling craft supplies to customers at a lower price than Clinton Art Craft could purchase them from their suppliers. Wal-Mart's return policy was also problematic for Clinton Art Craft. Their suppliers would not take back returned items like suppliers did for Wal-Mart. Customers would often get agitated when Clinton Art Craft wouldn't (because they couldn't afford to) have the same return policy as Wal-Mart. Other downtown establishments experienced similar problems and, as a result, they shut down. Business moved to the western edge of town, away from the downtown area, to be closer to the Wal-Mart traffic. Clinton Art Craft was able to stay in business in part because their service, with special attention to the customer, maintained a loyal customer base. However, some of those customers began going to Clinton Art Craft for advice and then heading to Wal-Mart to buy the materials they needed. Clinton Art Craft was forced to add an additional focus to their business (framing and matting) in order to survive. They did survive and thrive, but only because they were able to adapt to the environment Wal-Mart created. It was difficult for a Mom and Pop store run by a husband and wife with an occasional part-time employee to make such adaptations. Resources were limited. Clinton Art Craft survived for over 30 years (until the couple's retirement). For a small business, that is quite a feat, especially in the wake of Wal-Mart's impact on a small town.

The Nevada Small Business Association has claimed that Wal-Mart practices "predatory pricing" to destroy smaller competitors (Reed, 2000). According to Ronna Bolante (2003), "Hawaii [small business] retailers have learned how to co-exist with big boxers: Don't compete with 'em" (p. 16). The plan is to find a niche of different products and services that will not be in competition with Wal-Mart. However, "that's easier said than done, considering Wal-Mart and Sam's Club sell almost everything under the sun" (Bolante, 2003, p. 16). In a town in Colorado, the local government gives Wal-Mart credit for turning the economy around:

> In Sterling, officials point to the local Wal-Mart, which opened a decade ago and expanded to Supercenter in 1995, as a key to turning around a once moribund economy. "They draw from a large geographic area," said City Manager Jim Thomas. "I see license plates from Kansas, Nebraska, and Wyoming" (Peterson, 2002, p. 20).

But while public officials feel the town has benefited from Wal-Mart's presence, local business owners are not of the same opinion:

> To be sure, some of the benefits reaped from Sterling's Wal-Mart have come at the expense of local businesses. "When they come to town, if you're in competition with them, you're going to feel it," said Larry Hilty, proprietor of the Sterling Grocery Mart. "They just tear you up."
>
> When the Supercenter opened, Hilty's business suffered an immediate 50% drop in sales. "I'm surviving," he said, "but it'll never be back to what it was." (Peterson, 2002, p. 20)

Small towns all over the country have felt the impact of Wal-Mart. This is not a new phenomenon. Wal-Mart began having tremendous impact on communities in the 1980s. For example, by the late 1980s, Iowa had felt the effects of the growing retail giant. According to an article by Edward O. Welles (1993), "Iowa towns within a 20-mile radius felt Wal-Marts [sic] pull. Their retail sales declined by 17.6% after five years" (para. 13).

But it wasn't just the retail stores that suffered. The specialty stores also felt the impact. The only hope for small merchants was to find a niche. Because of Wal-Mart's size and strength with suppliers (which has grown tremendously since the late 1980s), the burden has been on the small business owner to change and adapt. Even if they had successful businesses, providing the same goods and products for as long as 50 years, small merchants have been forced to adapt to survive as Wal-Mart enters their territory.

As Wal-Mart prepared to enter Maine in the early 1990s, Ken Stone, a professor of economics at Iowa State University, traveled to the state to give them some advice:

> His advice was simple and direct: don't compete directly with Wal-Mart; specialize and carry harder-to-get and better-quality products; emphasize customer service; extend your hours; advertise more. (Welles, 1993, para. 25)

Merchants in small-town Maine had similar concerns to the Ohio and Iowa merchants—"that Wal-Mart would accelerate the drift of business out of downtown" (Welles, 1993, para. 48). In the minds of merchants, however, the impact goes beyond simply business. One Maine merchant put it this way:

> There's no argument that you can get a damn light bulb for 10 cents cheaper at Wal-Mart than you can at John Hichborns [sic] hardware store. But do people know that John Hichborn is a major contributor to Elmhurst [a local trade school for the handicapped]? He works at finding jobs for people from Elmhurst. If Hichborn goes out of business because people want a cheaper light bulb, then you lose more than just the tax revenues that business generated. (Welles, 1993, para. 69)

Wal-Mart has been the topic of discussion at many Main Street associations across the nation. "'Wal-Mart has gone a long way to reduce opportunity for downtowns to be successful as far as traditional retailers,' said Bob Wilson, director of program services for the Mississippi Main Street Association" (Gillette, 2002, p. 16). Wilson goes on to explain:

> It is a phenomenon a lot of downtowns are going through. A lot of areas have seen the short-term retail tax increases that happen when Wal-Mart comes to town, but it is not a long-term solution. Full-time jobs are replaced by part-time jobs with no benefits. And more employees come from surrounding areas so they don't really have that economic boost to the community. (Gillette, 2002, p. 16)

According to Wilson, Wal-Mart does not have loyalty to the communities it enters and has no problem abandoning its original building in town to move to a larger facility with better traffic flow at the outskirts of town, with no concern as to whether or not it remains in the same taxing district (Gillette, 2002).

Beyond the Small-Town Communities

But it is not just small towns and businesses that are affected. Wal-Mart is preparing to enter the grocery market with its Supercenters around the Chicago area:

> The Jewel and Piggly Wiggly stores serving Antioch will be the first local grocers to feel the Wal-Mart effect. Eventually, the impact will spread to all Chicago-area grocery stores, including two other major combination discount/grocery chains, Meijer Inc., and Target Corp. (Murphy, 2004, para. 6)

The impact can be brutal for business owners. "In exurban Sycamore, Brown County Market lost 40% of its sales after a Wal-Mart Supercenter opened in nearby DeKalb in the late 1990s" (Murphy, 2004, para. 8). The store's owner laments one of the issues: "'I pay my grocery clerks $13 an hour plus benefits. Wal-Mart pays $7 an hour with no benefits,' says owner Daniel Brown. 'It's hard for me to compete against that'" (Murphy, 2004, para. 9).

Recently, an article in *Fast Company* discussed the impact of Wal-Mart's low prices on its suppliers. A gallon-sized jar of Vlasic pickles sold for $2.97. What a deal! As Fishman (2003) puts it:

> Therein lies the basic conundrum of doing business with the world's largest retailer. By selling a gallon of kosher dills for less than most grocers sell a quart, Wal-Mart may have provided a service for its customers. But what did it do for Vlasic? The pickle maker had spent decades convincing customers that they should pay a premium for its brand. Now Wal-Mart was practically giving them away. And the fevered buying spree that resulted distorted every aspect of Vlasic's operations, from farm field to factory to financial statement. (p. 70)

Because Wal-Mart has grown so big, it has developed the power to determine suppliers' prices. They put the pressure on suppliers to lower their prices, and because Wal-Mart has such a big market share of retail sales, the suppliers concede to the Wal-Mart way of doing things. Wal-Mart offers to deliver low prices to consumers. The enticement to small towns is to make them feel as if they have some of the same amenities as a big city. After Wal-Mart has descended on a town and local businesses (hardware stores, dime stores, clothing stores, etc.) have disappeared, Wal-Mart offers to make things even better. As Leslie "Buzz" Davis puts it,

> Later the Wal-Mart front man swoops into your little town, slaps you on your back and says, "Boys, have I got something you are going to love: a Supercenter! This baby will be the size of four football fields and have everything you need to live except a birthing room and a funeral parlor. You won't ever have to shop anywhere else again. Aren't you lucky we chose your little city for all those great jobs the Supercenter will bring? And all that tax base we're just giving you free? Because you are such nice guys, I am going to throw in a large, late model used car lot at this Supercenter. This is a new business we are going into and you'll love it. Why, you'll be living just like those folks in the big city! Gee, aren't you lucky I came to town?" (Davis, 2003, para. 6)

Perhaps Davis's tone is a bit cynical, but there is an element that rings true. It all depends upon your perspective. Community members in Bristol, Tennessee, lost a battle to the retail giant on a rezoning issue. According to an online editorial entitled "Bristol Wal-Mart Controversy" (see www.sullivan-county.com/id2/wal-mart/),

> As accusations of "back room deals" and community anger fly in Bristol, city officials decide to sue citizens for opposing their despotic rule. All of this boils down to locating a Wal-Mart "super center" adjacent to two subdivisions and rezoning the property for business to accommodate them. Bristol goes even beyond "good old boy" politics to new lows. Citizens never had a chance.

Economic Spin-Off

Yet, Wal-Mart has grown to be such a behemoth exactly because it has given customers what they wanted (or at least thought they wanted)—low prices and convenience. One can head to the local Wal-Mart and do virtually all of one's shopping in one huge building. It is often possible to find a reasonable substitution for those specialty items that can't be found at Wal-Mart. But if low prices are causing other local merchants to go out of business, are the conveniences that Wal-Mart provides worthwhile in the long run? There is a whole other side to this community economic impact in terms of the economic spin-off of a dollar spent at Wal-Mart versus a dollar spent at other local merchants. There have been myriad stories about low wages and minimal benefits provided to Wal-Mart "associates," not to mention the hiring of illegal aliens or the fact that China has become a major supplier for the retail giant that used to boast that it only carried products that were made in America.

Wal-Mart's average employee works a 30-hour week and earns about $11,700 a year, which is nearly $2,000 below the poverty line for a family of three (Miller, 2004; Wal-Mart Watch, 2004). Only 38% of "associates" have company-provided health coverage—as compared to the national average of over 60% (Miller, 2004; United Food and Commercial Workers Union [UFCW] Local 227, 2004; UFCW Local 770, 2004; Wal-Mart Watch, 2004). According to the United Food and Commercial Workers International Union Local 227, "Wal-Mart has increased the premium cost for workers by over 200% since 1993—medical care inflation only went up 50% in the same period" (UFCW Local 227, 2004). Furthermore, the UFCW indicates that "[t]he Walton family [owner of Wal-Mart] is worth about $102 billion—less than 1% of that could provide affordable health care for associates" (UFCW Local 227, 2004).

There have also been a number of class action law suits against Wal-Mart for underpaying associates by not paying them for overtime and making them work through daily scheduled 15-minute breaks. In addition, there is a suit alleging that Wal-Mart "systematically deprived illegal workers of labor-law protections during at least the last three years" (Rasansky, 2003, p. 34). There is evidence that Wal-Mart actually destroys more jobs than it creates and lowers community standards. "Research shows that for every two jobs created by a Wal-Mart store, the community loses three" (Flagstaff Activist Network, 2004; UFCW Local 227, 2004; UFCW Local 770, 2004; Wal-Mart Watch, 2004).

Wal-Mart touts their "buy America" program, yet over 80% of the clothing sold in their stores is produced overseas (Flagstaff Activist Network, 2004; UFCW Local 227, 2004; UFCW Local 770, 2004; Wal-Mart Watch, 2004). In order to keep costs low enough to keep them in Wal-Mart stores, suppliers are often forced to move their production overseas. This outsourcing has become more widespread in part because Wal-Mart is big enough to demand the price it desires from its suppliers. A Salt Lake City paper addresses this issue:

> The millions of people flocking to the Wal-Marts, etc., in order to save $0.11 per roll of toilet paper have exactly the same motivation as Corporate America has in seeking a lower price for what it wants to buy. This is not to say that outsourcing American jobs to China or India is OK. In fact, this newspaper has for many years been on record as not supporting that notion. It is, however, to say that if outsourcing is not OK because of the devastating impact on parts of our population, then the local government cooperation with the spread of the Wal-Mart virus is not OK either. ("Outsourcing American jobs," 2004)

COMMUNITY SATISFACTION

However one wants to criticize Wal-Mart, though, one would be hard pressed to find someone who has not purchased from a Wal-Mart store. The other side of the argument is that Wal-Mart does indeed help communities and give them exactly what they desire—low prices and convenience. It saves the customer time because he or she can consolidate shopping needs. Why go to four or five different stores when you can get everything you need at Wal-Mart? Often, you will be able to purchase the same brand for less money as well. Some suggest that Wal-Mart is good for consumers, business, and the economy. An article in Advertising Age ("Wal-Mart Creates Winners All 'Round,'" 2003) claims, "Wal-Mart functions as the consumer's advocate and purchasing agent, badgering suppliers to get the best deal." The article further argues, "Economists say low Wal-Mart prices help keep inflation in check, and its efficiencies have been pushed down the supply chain, further improving productivity." Sheila Danzey (2002) opined that the St. Thomas (New Orleans) housing development would greatly benefit from a proposed Wal-Mart in a "formerly troubled high crime-devalued neighborhood" through a proposed Tax Increment Financing (TIF) plan that would help in the rebuilding of St. Thomas.

Customer Choice

Karen De Coster and Brad Edmonds (2003) dispel some of the rumors often heard about Wal-Mart, such as coming to town and selling below cost until the competition is gone and then jacking up the prices. De Coster and Edmonds argue that if community members want to discourage the acceptance of Wal-Mart in their town, "they have scores of non-bullying options to pick from in order to try and persuade their fellow townsfolk that a new Wal-Mart is not the best option" (para. 16). The authors suggest that it is not easy to convince people to trade convenience for "the sake of undefined moral purposes" (para. 17). Certainly the growth of Wal-Mart is evidence of what the American public as a whole value:

> To be sure, if Americans didn't love Wal-Mart so much it wouldn't be sitting at the top of the 2002 Fortune 500 with $219 billion in revenues. And we do love Wal-Mart. We love it because it gives us variety and abundance. We love it because it saves us time and wrangling. And we love it because no matter where we are, it's always there when we need it. (De Coster & Edmonds, 2003, para. 22)

Business Success

Wal-Mart is big. Davis (2003) suggests that retailers of such size tend to monopolize markets:

> Wal-Mart is on its way to monopolizing the retail discount store and grocery trades. Over 1.4 million people now work for Wal-Mart. It's three times larger than General Motors. It's the largest private employer in the United States and the largest employer in over 20 states. It already has nearly 50% of the discount retail market. It already is the largest grocery store business in America. The company grosses over $250 billion a year, with profits over $8 billion per year. It is the largest corporation in the world. Wal-Mart is mean and hungry for more. Why stop at $500 billion in sales? Why not try for $1 trillion in sales and have 6 million employees? (para. 8)

But isn't that the American way—to want more? In fact, accumulating more wealth is one of the things De Coster and Edmonds (2003) suggest Wal-Mart helps enable its customers to do:

> Families who shop carefully at Wal-Mart can actually budget more for investing, children's college funds, or entertainment. And unlike other giant corporations, Wal-Mart stores around the country make an attempt to provide a friendly atmosphere by spending money to hire greeters, who are often people who would have difficulty finding any other job. This is a friendly, partial solution to shoplifting problems; the solution K-mart applied ("Hey, what's in that bag?") didn't work as well. (para. 19)

Edwin A. Locke (2004), dean's professor emeritus of leadership and motivation at the University of Maryland at College Park and a senior writer for the Ayn Rand Institute in Irvine, California, suggests, "Wal-Mart is one of the most impressive success stories in the history of business" (p. 32). He bemoans the fact that Wal-Mart is so often criticized for running its business effectively and attracting "hoards of customers." Locke admits that Wal-Mart has been successful in competing against other stores, but suggests it does this by "discovering new ways of using computer systems and other technology to manage its inventory and costs better and to reap the benefits of economy of scale" (p. 32). Wal-Mart, according to Locke, has earned its success:

> Wal-Mart is especially popular among low-income shoppers who cannot afford the prices of the more upscale stores. It has put other stores out of business, but that is the way capitalism works. The automobile replaced the horse and buggy. Sound motion picture replaced the silents. No one has a "right" to business success or a "right" to be protected from competitors through government intervention. One only has a right to try to compete through voluntary trade. In a free economy, companies that offer the best value for the dollar win and the losers invest their money elsewhere. (p. 32)

Locke believes Wal-Mart should be admired, rather than feared, and that communities should thank Wal-Mart for being so good at giving customers what they want.

Helping Hand

Wal-Mart claims to contribute to the well-being of communities. Since June 10, 1996, when Wal-Mart began posting pictures of missing children in the lobbies of Wal-Mart facilities, 5,710 children have been featured. More than 4,365 have been recovered. Wal-Mart's customers and associates have assisted in the recovery of 107 of those children.[5] It is clear that Wal-Mart does much in the way of scholarships and philanthropy in addition to offering convenience and low prices. Wal-Mart's rhetoric centers on the three basic beliefs that Sam Walton established in 1962 (see www.walmartstores.com):

1. Respect for the Individual
2. Service to Our Customers
3. Strive for Excellence

If you are in a Wal-Mart store at the right time, you can hear raucous sounds from the back of the store as the "associates" perform the Wal-Mart cheer:

Give me a W!

Give me an A!

Give me an L!

Give me a Squiggly!

Give me an M!

Give me an A!

Give me an R!

Give me a T!

What's that spell?

Wal-Mart!

Whose Wal-Mart is it?

My Wal-Mart!

Who's number one?

The Customer! Always!

A MATTER OF PERSPECTIVE

From the perspective of the Wal-Mart executives, and many patrons, it's all about the customer and the community. But often the community leaders have a different perspective. As the *Economist* ("My Wal-Mart 'tis of Thee," 1996) put it:

Like America itself, Sam Walton's monument excites strong reactions. People are wary of this superpower. They mistrust its motives, fear its cultural clout, deride its brashness and scoff at its contradictions. Yet they also marvel at its convenience and admire its success. And, as with America, the people keep coming. (para. 15)

Does Wal-Mart communicate and act in an ethical manner? You make the call.

NOTES

1. See a complete timeline at http://www.walmart stores.com. Click "news" and then "fact sheets—history, people, commitment."
2. See economic impact statements for all 50 states as well as the national numbers by going to http://www.walmartstores.com and searching their entire site for "economic impact" at the top of their home page.
3. You can find Wal-Mart's philosophy concerning their commitment to communities by going to their Web site at http://www.walmartstores.com and then clicking the "About Wal-Mart" button, then "Research Information," and then "Our Commitment to Communities."
4. From this site, click "What We Fund" button.
5. See Wal-Mart Good Works at http://www.walmart foundation.org/wmstore/goodworks.html.

REFERENCES

Bolante, R. (2003, September). Friend or foe? How Wal-Mart will change urban Honolulu. *Hawaii Business,* 16–20.

Bristol Wal-Mart controversy. (n.d.). Retrieved February 6, 2004, from http://www.sullivan-county.co/id2/wal-mart/

Danzey, S. (2002, January 21). Why we win with Wal-Mart. *New Orleans CityBusiness,* p. 29.

Davis, L. (2003, September 1). Leslie "Buzz" Davis: *Wal-Mart threatens our way of life, must be unionized.* Retrieved February 6, 2004, from www.madison.com/captimes/opinion/column/guest/55885.php

De Coster, K., & Edmonds, B. (2003, January 31). *The case for Wal-Mart.* Retrieved February 3, 2004, from http://www.mises.org/fullarticle.asp?control=1151

Fishman, C. (2003, December). The Wal-Mart you don't know: Why low prices have a high cost. *Fast Company,* 67–80.

Flagstaff Activist Network. *Wal-Mart myths and reality.* Retrieved April 1, 2004, from http://www.flagstaff activist.org/campaigns/walmyths.html

Gillette, B. (2002, June 10–16). Small town retailers finding ways to compete with big chains. *Mississippi Business Journal*, p. 16.

Locke, E. A. (2004, February 20). Thwarting Wal-Mart is simply un-American. *The Central New York Business Journal, 18*(8), 32.

Miller, G. (D-CA), Senior Democrat. (2004, February 16). *Everyday low wages: The hidden price we all pay for Wal-Mart.* A report by the democratic staff of the Committee on Education and the Workforce, U.S. House of Representatives.

Murphy, H. L. (2004, March 15). Wal-Mart set to launch grocery invasion here. *Crain's Chicago Business 27*(11), 9. Retrieved April 1, 2004, from EBSCOhost database.

My Wal-Mart 'tis of thee. (1996, November 23). *The Economist, 341*(7993). Retrieved April 1, 2004, from EBSCOhost database.

Ortega, B. (1998). *In Sam we trust.* New York: Times Business/Random House.

Outsourcing American jobs: Wal-Marts and the quality of life. (2004, March 8–14). *The Enterprise*, 24.

Peterson, E. (2002, November). Wal-Mart's fans and foes. *ColoradoBiz*, p. 18.

Rasansky, J. (2003, December 5–11). Always lower prices? Wal-Mart could face epic battle over unpaid overtime claims. *Fort Worth Business Press*, 34.

Reed, V. (2000, January 10). Small business group decries chamber position on Wal-Mart. *Las Vegas Business Press*, 3.

United Food and Commercial Workers (UFCW) International Union Local 227. (n.d.). [Web site home page] Retrieved April 1, 2004, from http://www.ufcw227.org/organizing/walmart.htm

United Food and Commercial Workers (UFCW) International Union Local 770. (n.d.). [Web site home page] Retrieved April 1, 2004, from http://www.ufcw770.org/index.html

Wal-Mart creates winners all 'round. (2003, October 6). *Advertising Age, 74*(40), 20.

Wal-Mart Watch. *Bad neighbor fact sheet.* Retrieved April 1, 2004, from http://www.walmartwatch.com/bad/page.cfm?subid=108

Welles, E. O. (1993, July). When Wal-Mart comes to town. *Inc., 15*(7), 76–83. Retrieved February 4, 2004, from Business Source Premier database: http://www.walmartstores.com/wmstore/wmstores/HomePage.jsp

---

Case Study

Who Should Pay?[1]

Manuel G. Velasquez

The stakes were high for Gene Elliot, whose on-the-job injuries were estimated to be serious enough to merit at least a $2.4 million settlement. But who should pay for his injuries: Turner Construction or B&C Steel? Or should he be forced to pay for at least part of his injuries because of his own carelessness?

Gene Elliot worked for Mabey Bridge and Shore, a small business that rented temporary steel pedestrian foot bridges to other companies. The temporary bridges had to be put together by the renter, and Gene Elliot's job

was to go to the site where the steel bridge was going to be installed, show the renter how to bolt the bridge sections together and how to install the bridge over a river or waterway, and inspect the bridge to make sure it was done properly and according to Mabey Bridge's high standards. Elliot was a devoted hard worker who strove to do everything possible to ensure that a bridge installation was successful and according to Mabey's standards.

Turner Construction was a general contractor hired to build Invesco Field at the

---

Mile High Stadium in Denver, Colorado. Part of the job involved installing a temporary pedestrian bridge over the Platte River near the stadium. Turner Construction subcontracted (hired) B&C Steel to build and install the bridge, which Turner Construction would pay for. B&C Steel was a small company that specialized in putting together and installing steel structures like those Mabey Bridge rented out. B&C Steel would pick up the bridge, put it together, and install it for Turner.

Turner Construction rented the long steel bridge from Mabey Bridge. Mabey Bridge agreed that the rental included the services of Gene Elliot, who would be loaned to Turner to instruct and inspect the bridge assembly and installation. B&C Steel's workers picked up the bridge sections from Mabey Bridge's warehouse and drove them to the river but didn't unload the bridge sections where they had to be assembled. B&C then had to move the sections to the correct site but didn't plan for the fence, guardrails, and trolley tracks that were in the way and later had to work around these obstructions. B&C Steel began bolting the bridge sections together. When Elliot inspected the job, he found the bridge had been bolted together upside down. Elliot made B&C do the job over, while he climbed up and down and over the bridge, continuously checking and making sure that all the bolts were tight and all the pieces were in the right place so that the installation would be a success. When the bridge was finished, B&C workers used a truck to move the long steel structure to the edge of the river. Unfortunately, B&C had not adequately checked the route and their truck hit a low-hanging power line, which sparked and started a fire. The fire department arrived and put out the fire. Afterwards, the installation job continued.

B&C workers set up a crane on the other side of the river near a retaining wall, and a strong nylon strap was strung from the crane, over the water, and tied to one end of the bridge, which was set on rollers. The B&C crane would lift and pull the bridge over the river to its side, while workers on the other side of the river pushed on their end of the bridge. The work began, and as the pulling crane held the bridge suspended in the air about a quarter of the way over the river, Elliot noticed that the retaining wall which was supporting the crane on the other side of the river was beginning to collapse, causing the crane to begin to tip sideways. The B&C crane operator on the other side began to untie the strap holding the bridge. Concerned that once the strap was cut the bridge would fall into the river and the installation would end in failure, Elliot ran up on the bridge and gave the standard emergency OSHA all-stop signal that all construction workers know means not to move anything. But the bridge, still attached to the crane, somehow moved, and Elliot fell, sustaining numerous pelvic injuries and a severed urethra (the tube that carries urine). The cause of the movement was never established.

Elliot sued Turner Construction and B&C Steel for negligence resulting in economic losses of $28,000, noneconomic injuries of $1,200,000, and permanent impairment of $1,200,000. These figures were established by a qualified expert in the field of worker injuries and were not seriously contested.

Turner Construction, however, denied its responsibility. It claimed that Turner was Elliot's temporary employer and workers' compensation law required employers to pay only the economic losses, here only $28,000, suffered by their employees. Turner Construction pointed to the law, which stated: "Any company leasing or contracting out any part of the work to any lessee or subcontractor, shall be construed to be an employer and shall be liable to pay [only] compensation for injury resulting therefore to said lessees and subcontractors and their employees." Turner Construction claimed that Mabey was a subcontractor to Turner to the extent that it provided the services of Elliot to Turner, so Turner should be construed to be Elliot's temporary employer. Moreover, Colorado's workers' compensation law, which was designed to ensure that employers always paid for worker injuries "grants an injured employee compensation from the employer without regard to negligence and, in return, the responsible employer is granted immunity from common law negligence liability."

B&C claimed that it, too, was not responsible, because according to the law a company is not responsible for negligence when an injury is not "reasonably foreseeable" to the company. B&C contended that a reasonable person could not have anticipated that placing the crane near to the retaining wall and subsequently attempting to remove the nylon strap holding up the bridge might end by prompting someone to get on the bridge in an attempt to save it from falling into the river. On the other hand, B&C claimed, since "Elliot chose to remove himself from a secure and safe position and placed himself in one that he understood was potentially unsafe," Elliot was himself responsible for his injuries.

Elliot claimed that he was not really Turner's employee, since he was working for Mabey. He also argued that B&C had shown a pattern of negligence from the time that the bridge was received until the time that it was installed. B&C and its employees, he said, were unprepared for the project and negligently failed to adequately plan for it, as shown by the sequence of events leading up to his injury. B&C therefore did not exercise the degree of care that a reasonably careful person should have exercised in similar circumstances and so was liable to him for his injuries. He himself was not responsible, he said, because a good, devoted employee would try his best to ensure that the bridge installation did not end in failure, and he would have been perfectly safe if the standard OSHA all-stop signal had been followed by B&C employees, as he had a right to expect it to be.

NOTE

1. This case is based entirely on *Eugene Elliot v. Turner Construction Company and B&C Steel*, United States Court of Appeals, Tenth Circuit, August 24, 2004, case no. 03–1209.

Case Study

Selling Your Sole at Birkenstock

Michael Lewis

One day this spring, two students from the Haas Business School, imbued with the values of public corporate life, traveled to a small private company to explain why it should reconsider its ways. The company was Birkenstock Footprint Sandals, or, as the employees like to call it, Birkenstock USA. Just to say the name, of course, is to hear the sound of granola crunching and the rustle of female underarm hair in the wind. The shoe company of choice for hippies is slightly more complicated than its reputation. It was founded in 1966 by a woman named Margot Fraser to sell orthopedic shoes manufactured by the German shoemaker Birkenstock. In the beginning the only retail outlets that would stock the sandals Fraser imported were health-food stores (then novel), and so the company's first customers had a counter-cultural flavor. The American distributor now sells many different kinds of shoes, including a line for the striving office worker. It has a strain of hippie in it, but other strains too.

At any rate, Birkenstock USA is still a private company, subject to ordinary market forces but immune to pressures from outside investors. When the Haas Business School students went into the company's headquarters in Novato, Calif., they found something of a mess, at least by public corporate standards. Birkenstock had been doing good works, willy-nilly, for 30 years. It paid employees to volunteer and gave away sacks of cash to worthy causes without telling a soul about it. The company was reluctant to disclose the recipients of its philanthropy; after all, wouldn't it violate the spirit of good works to publicize them? But the business-school students were able to uncover a few specifics. For instance, they discovered that Birkenstock gave money to the Elizabeth Glaser Pediatric AIDS Foundation. And that, from the investor-driven corporate point of view, was a problem: sick kids are nice and all, but what do they have to do with selling shoes, especially if you don't spend a lot of time explaining to them why they should be grateful to you?

The students recommended that Birkenstock ditch most of their good works and put all of their energy into a single very public act that connected up naturally to footwear. They shrewdly recommended that Birkenstock

sponsor walks for causes. The cause did not matter so much as the fact that potential customers would be walking many miles on its behalf, and, somewhere along the line, encounter a giant sign that said BIRKENSTOCK.

The C.E.O. of Birkenstock, Matt Endriss, listened politely to what the business-school students had to say. "I wrestle with the words and phrases they throw around," he said afterward. " 'Formalize' . . . 'standardize' . . . 'best practices' . . . 'bang for your buck.' Those words don't live in this organization on a daily basis. A lot of them are words we try to abolish." He tells me, "There's a lot of discussion inside Birkenstock about 'authenticity.' " While that concept is notoriously hard to define, its opposite is not. It is inauthentic to seem not to care too much about making money in the interest of making even more of it. It is inauthentic to go bragging about corporate goodness, in hopes of selling more shoes. When you are honest only because honesty pays, says Birkenstock's C.E.O., you risk forgetting the meaning of honesty. When you are socially responsible only because social responsibility pays, you lose any real sense of what responsibility means.

Put another way: the instinct to give quietly to a pediatric AIDS foundation is second cousin to the instinct not to use slave labor to make your shoes, or not to manipulate your earnings. It is part of a struggle against the market's relentless pressure on the business executive to behave a bit too selfishly—to become one of those corporate villains whom investors can one day profitably sue. "The whole concept of marketing corporate social responsibility seems odd," Endriss says. "Hit folks over the head and tell them how good we are and, in exchange, there's a monetary return for us."

But the matter is clearly not so simple: the people on the receiving end of Birkenstock's social conscience may be grateful, and there's no law to prevent them from telling others what the company has done. Word spreads. And it's possible that the brand Birkenstock is actually strengthened by a less conventionally corporate approach—that is, that the company, in the long run, makes more money by doing its good works on the sly. "People subconsciously think that the company is doing the right thing," Endriss says. "But you ask them, 'Why do you think it's a good company?" And they can't tell you." If it somehow pays for Birkenstock not to publicize its good works—if stealth charity is just a clever strategy for marketing to hippies—then the company is simply strolling down a different path to the biggest pot of gold. But if so, the path is long and poorly marked. "We're not as profitable as we could be," Endriss says, and then goes on to say that if he wanted to maximize the company's earnings he would fire 60% of the workers (the ones who build long-term relationships with customers and vendors) and jack up the price of the shoes.

"Maximizing our profits is not our chief goal," Endriss says. "The exchange of goods and services for money—Birkenstock feels it's here for different reasons." Those reasons can be summarized in a sappy sentence: the happiness of employees and customers and a feeling that it is contributing to the general well-being of the world around it. Make money, yes, but don't make a fetish of it. "If the company were compelled to answer to shareholders," the C.E.O. says, "it would destroy us."

This kind of talk is daft to most investors. Birkenstock USA has existed for nearly 40 years, but it still has only about $120 million in annual sales. It has grown slowly, generating steady but modest profits and exhibiting no great ambition to grow a lot faster. Who'd want to invest in that? To the financial market these guys are a bunch of mediocrities. But that's the idea: when you make a point of behaving extremely well you are unlikely to make as much money as when you don't. A few highly desirable companies (Google?) might be able to dictate morality to investors, but most cannot. The highest moral standards have a price, and most investors do not wish to pay it. But businesspeople who don't have distant, amoral shareholders to answer to are able to pay whatever price they can afford, for the sake of some other goal. And these goals can include behavior so admirable as to make an investor weep.

Three years ago, the founder of Birkenstock, Margot Fraser, by then a septuagenarian, realized that for her company to survive her it would require another owner. She controlled 60% of the outstanding shares, and the question was what to do with them. Rather than take them into the public market and find the highest bidder—who would, of course, demand the fastest-rising share price—Fraser decided that she wanted to sell them all to the company's employees in a way that turned just about every employee into an owner. To calculate the price of her shares, the board, aware of the founder's desires, took the current fair-market value, then reduced it as much as they could without making the price so ridiculously low that it could be construed as a gift. But when they presented her with a price for her shares, Fraser's only question was, "Why can't you make it lower?"

Case Study

A.H. Robins: The Dalkon Shield

Al Gini and T. Sullivan

On August 21, 1985, A.H. Robins of Richmond, Virginia—the seventeenth largest pharmaceutical house in America and corporately rated as number 392 in the Fortune 500—filed for reorganization under chapter 11 of the 1978 Federal Bankruptcy Code. On the surface, Robins seemed to be a thriving company. Its popular products, including Robitussin cough syrup, Chap Stick lip balm, and Sergeant's flea and tick collars for cats and dogs, generated record sales in 1985 of $706 million with a net income in excess of $75 million. Robins's petition for protection under Chapter 11 stems directly from the "blitz of litigation" over a product it has not produced since 1974, the Dalkon Shield intrauterine birth control device. At the time it filed for bankruptcy Robins had been deluged with more than 12,000 personal injury lawsuits charging that the Dalkon Shield was responsible for countless serious illnesses and at least 20 deaths among the women who used it.

In many ways this bankruptcy petition mimes and mirrors (Johns-) Manville's unprecedented request for reorganization in 1982. Manville, the nation's, if not the world's, largest producer of asbestos, claimed that it was succumbing to a "blitz of toxic torts" and therefore could not carry on with business as usual. In August 1982 Manville was facing 16,500 suits on behalf of people who claimed to have contracted cancer and other diseases caused by asbestos and the asbestos-related products that the company produced.

Like Manville, A.H. Robins is defending and explaining its actions by claiming that it simply cannot go on and fulfill its immediate and potential obligations to its stockholders, customers, employees, and litigants (claimants) unless it takes dramatic financial action. In filing for Chapter 11 Robins has won at least temporary respite from its legal woes. Although the company will continue operating during the reorganization, all suits now pending are frozen and no new suits can be filed. While the company develops a plan to handle its liabilities, it is up to the bankruptcy courts to deal with all present claims as well as to establish guidelines for the handling of any future claims.[1] Whatever the final results, the Dalkon Shield case may well turn out to be the worst product liability nightmare that a U.S. drugmaker or major corporation has ever suffered.[2] The A.H. Robins company is essentially a family owned and operated organization. The original company was founded by Albert Hartley Robins, a registered pharmacist, in 1866 in Richmond, Virginia. His grandson, E. Claiborne Robins, built and directed the company into a multinational conglomerate which was able to obtain Fortune 500 status by the middle of the twentieth century. While E. Claiborne Robins remains Chairman of the Board, E. Claiborne Junior is now the firm's president and CEO. Both the family and the company are much liked and respected in their home state. Generations of employees have repeatedly claimed that E. Claiborne Senior was at his worst a "benevolent despot" and at his best a kind and gentle man sincerely interested in quality control as well as his employees' well being. By all reports E. Claiborne Junior seems to be following in his father's footsteps. Moreover, the family's kindness has not been limited to its employees. In 1969 E. Claiborne Senior personally donated over $50 million to the University of Richmond. Since then the Robins family has given at least $50 million more to the university, and additional millions to other universities and to diverse other causes. In December 1983 *Town and Country* magazine listed Claiborne Senior among the top five of "The Most Generous Americans."

Both the family and the company take pride in having "always gone by the book" and always giving their customers a good product at a fair price. In its 120 years of operation the company had done business without having a single product-liability lawsuit filed against it. Critics now claim that Robins has been involved in a directly ordered, prolonged institutional cover-up of the short- and long-term effects of the use of the Dalkon Shield. Moreover, many critics, claim that, more than just stonewalling the possible side effects of the Shield, Robins is guilty of marketing a product they knew to be relatively untested, undependable, and therefore potentially dangerous. Robins is accused of having deceived doctors, lied to women, perjured itself to federal judges, and falsified documentation to the FDA. According to Morton Mintz, Robins's most outspoken critic, thousands, probably tens of thousands, of women who trusted the doctors who trusted A.H. Robins paid a ghastly price for the use of the Dalkon Shield: chronic pelvic infections, impairment or loss of childbearing capacity, children with multiple birth defects, unwanted abortions, recurring health problems, and chronic pain.

IUDs are among the most ancient forms of contraception, known for more than two thousand years. Exactly how an IUD prevents conception is not known. It may interfere with the fertilization of the eggs, but most experts believe that when inserted into the uterus it prevents pregnancy by making it difficult for a fertilized egg to attach itself to the wall of the uterus. Over the centuries the materials used in the fabrication of IUDs include ebony, glass, gold, ivory, pewter, wood, wool, diamond-studded platinum, copper, and plastic.[3] The Dalkon Shield was developed by Dr. Hugh J. Davis, a former professor of obstetrics and gynecology at the Johns Hopkins University, and Irwin Lerner, an electrical engineer. In 1970 they sold their rights to the Shield to Robins, who agreed to pay royalties on future sales and $750,000 in cash. Between 1971 and 1974 Robins sold 4.5 million Dalkon Shields around the world, including 2.85 million in the United States.

By the late 1960s large numbers of women had become concerned about the safety of the Pill. These women formed an ever-growing potential market for an alternative means of birth control. Many of these women switched to "barrier" methods of birth control, particularly the diaphragm, which, when used with spermicidal creams or jellies, can be highly effective, though inconvenient. Others turned to IUDs, which, although convenient, previously had been considered unsafe—causing pelvic infections, irregular bleeding, uterine cramps, and accidental expulsion. Robins leapt at an opportunity to develop a new market with their product. The company's task was to convince physicians that the Shield was as effective as oral contraceptives in preventing pregnancies and that it was safer, better designed, and afforded greater resistance to inadvertent expulsion from the uterus than other IUDs.[4]

In January 1971 Robins began to sell the Dalkon Shield, promoting it as the "modern, superior," "second generation" and—most importantly—"safe" intrauterine device for birth control. The Shield itself is a nickel-sized plastic device that literally looks like a badge or a shield with spikes around the edges and a thread-sized "nylon tail string," which allowed both the wearer and the physician a means to guarantee that the device had not been expelled. The Shield was relatively inexpensive. The device itself sold for between $3.00 and $4.50 (its production costs were an incredibly low figure of $.25 a Shield). The only other cost associated with the Shield was the doctor's office fee for insertion and a recommended yearly pelvic examination. Dr. Hugh Davis claimed that the Dalkon Shield was the safest and most effective IUD because it is "the only IUD which is truly anatomically engineered for optimum uterine placement, fit, tolerance, and retention."[5] Davis was able to persuade a large number of physicians of the effectiveness of the Shield in an article he published in the "Current Investigation" section of the *American Journal of Obstetrics and Gynecology* in February 1970. The article described a study conducted at the Johns Hopkins Family Planning Clinic involving 640 women who had worn the Shield for one year. His analysis was based on 3,549 women-months of experience. Davis cited five pregnancies, ten expulsions, nine removals for medical reasons, and three removals for personal reasons. His startling results: tolerance rate (non-expulsion), 96%; pregnancy rate, 1.1%. The A.H. Robins Company reprinted no fewer than 199,000 copies of the Davis article for distribution to physicians.[6]

While various executives strongly recommended that other studies be commissioned to validate Davis's results, in January 1971 Robins began to market and sell the Shield on the basis of Davis's limited analysis. Robins's decision to produce and sell the Shield based on Davis's statistics may not coincide with the highest standards of scientific research, but it did not violate any FDA statutes and was therefore perfectly legal. At the time Robins produced the Shield, FDA had no regulatory policies in force regarding IUDs of any kind. While FDA had the authority to regulate the production, testing, and sales of all new prescriptions, it could only *recommend* testing on new medical devices. It could not monitor, investigate, or police a device unless charges of lack of effectiveness, injury, or abuse were formally leveled against the device or the producer.

In December 1970 Robins commissioned a major long-term study to reinforce Davis's results. The study concentrated on ten clinics, seven in the United States and one each inCanada, Nova Scotia, and British Columbia. Between December 1970 and December 1974 (six months after Robins suspended domestic sales) 2,391 women were fitted with the Shield. The first results came out in November 1972, and only about half of the women enrolled in the study. The statistics showed a sixteen-month pregnancy rate of 1.6%. The Robins home office was more than pleased and immediately communicated this information to its sales staff. Thirteen months later, with all the women now participating in the program, less happy figures began to show up. The pregnancy rate after six months was 2.1%; after twelve months, 3.2%; after eighteen months, 3.5%; and after twenty-three months, 4.1%. In a final report published as a confidential internal document in August 1975 the final figures and results were even more devastating. The pregnancy rate after six months was 2.6%; after twelve months, 4.2%; after eighteen months, 4.9%; and after twenty-four months 5.7%. Two of the scientists involved in this project submitted a minority report claiming that the Shield was even less effective than these already damaging figures indicated. They claimed that the pregnancy rate during the first year was much higher; after six months, 3.3%; and after twelve months, 5.5%. This twelve-month pregnancy rate is exactly five times *higher than* the rate Robins advertised and promoted—1.1%—to catapult the Shield to leadership in the IUD business.[7] This minority report was never disclosed to the medical community by Robins. Nor did Robins communicate these results to its own sales force. It did report some of these findings to FDA in July 1974, but only after the company had suspended domestic sales earlier that June.

Soon after the Shield entered the marketplace, independent research results began to appear in both national and foreign journals of medicine. In 1970 and 1971 Dr. Mary O. Gabrielson, working out of clinics in San Francisco and Oakland, did an eighteen-month study on 937 women with results that Robins would not want to advertise. The rate of medical removals was 26.4%; the pregnancy rate, 5.1%. In 1973 the *British Medical Journal* published a study showing a 4.7% pregnancy rate in Shield users.[8] Again because there was no law requiring disclosure of this new research information, Robins did not rush to inform the general public, the medical community, or the FDA.

At the same time that the Robins Company was receiving research results pointing to poor statistical effectiveness of the Shield, they also began to receive more and more "single physician experience" reports warning and complaining about some of the medical consequences from using the Shield. These physician's reports plus the statistics generated from controlled clinical reports began to portray the Shield as neither effective nor safe.

The primary cause of concern for Shield users proved to be a much higher incidence of uterine/pelvic bacterial infections. PID (pelvic inflammatory disease) is a highly virulent and very painful, difficult to cure, life threatening infection, which more often than not impairs or destroys a woman's ability to bear children. Of those women who conceived with the Shield in place (approximately 110,000 in the United States), an estimated 60% of them miscarried after suffering severe bacterial infections (PID). In 1974 FDA reported that over 245 women in their fourth to sixth month of pregnancy suffered the relatively rare bacterially induced miscarriage called septic spontaneous abortions. For fifteen women, these septic abortions were fatal.[9] Moreover, hundreds of women throughout the world who had conceived while wearing the Shield gave birth prematurely to children with grave congenital defects, including blindness, cerebral palsy, and mental retardation.[10]

Scientists now believe that the systemic cause for these virulent forms of bacterial infection is the nylon tail of the Shield itself. The Dalkon Shield tail string runs between the vagina, where bacteria are always present, and the uterus, which is germ free. It then passes through the cervix, where cervical mucus is the body's natural defense against bacterial invasion of the uterus. Robins claimed that cervical mucus would stop all germs from entering and infecting the uterus. To the naked eye, the Dalkon Shield tail string is an impervious monofilament, meaning that bacteria on it could not get into it. Actually, however, it is a cylindrical sheath encasing 200 to 450 round monofilaments separated by spaces. While the string was knotted at both ends, neither end was actually sealed. Therefore, any bacteria that got into the spaces between the filaments would be insulated from the body's natural antibacterial action while being drawn into the uterus by "wicking," a phenomenon similar to that by which a string draws the melting wax of a candle to the flame. Scientists believe that the longer the Shield and its string/tail is in place, the greater the chances for its deterioration and infiltration, thereby inducing infection in the uterus. Scientists now also contend that the "syndrome of spontaneous septic abortions" that occurred to women who had the Shield in place in the early second trimester of their pregnancy was caused by the tail string. That is, radical and sudden infection occurred with the uterus expanded to the point where it tended to pull the tail string into itself thereby bringing on instant, often lethal, contamination.[11]

In the summer of 1983 the Centers for Disease Control in Atlanta and the FDA recommended that all women still using the Shield should contact their physicians and have it immediately removed. The Agencies found that women using the Shield had a five-fold increase in risk for contracting PID as compared to women using other types of IUDs. No change in contraceptive practice was recommended for women using any other type of IUD.[12] In April 1985 two studies funded by the National Institute of Health announced yet another dire warning. These studies showed that childless IUD wearers who have had PID run a higher risk of infertility if their devices were Shields than if they were other makes.[13]

Throughout all of this, A.H. Robins officials appeared to be unaware of, or at best indifferent to, the issues, facts, and effects of their product. The company assumed the position of complete denial of any intentional wrongdoing or any malicious intent to evade full public disclosure of pertinent medical information about the safety and effectiveness of the Shield. On numerous separate occasions both in public forums and under oath, E. Claiborne Robins, Senior, has claimed near ignorance of Robins's sixteen-year involvement with the Dalkon Shield. At a series of depositions taken in 1984 Robins Senior swore that he was unable to recall ever having discussed the Shield with his son, the company's chief executive officer and president. When asked, "You certainly knew, when you started marketing this device, that PID was a life-threatening disease, did you not?" Robins testified: "I don't know that, I never thought of it as life-threatening." Did he know it could destroy fertility? "Maybe I should, but I

don't know that. I have heard that, but I am not sure where." Carl Lunsford, senior vice-president for research and development, swore he could recall no "expression of concern" by any company official about PID, and he didn't remember having "personally wondered" about the toll it was taking. He had not tried to find out how many users had died. He had not "personally reviewed" *any* studies on the Shield's safety or effectiveness. When asked if he had "any curiosity" regarding the millions of dollars the company had been paying out in punitive damages to settle lawsuits, his answer was, "No."[14] The case of William Forrest, vice-president and general counsel of A.H. Robins, further strains belief. He has been described by E. Claiborne Junior as one of the company's "two most instrumental" persons in the Dalkon Shield situation. He was in effect in charge of all Shield matters and related legal issues for over a decade. In a trial proceeding, Forrest testified that his wife had worn a Shield until it was surgically removed. She had also had a hysterectomy. Although IUD removals and hysterectomies were frequently connected and simultaneous events for many infected Shield wearers, Forrest steadfastly denied any connection in his wife's case and gave vague and widely differing dates for the two events. He and his wife, he explained, did not discuss such matters in detail. Indeed, Forrest gave a series of confusing accounts of his wife's hysterectomy and its possible relationship to the Shield she had worn.

Q: Did her doctor advise her that her hysterectomy was in any way related to the Dalkon Shield?

A: Not that I know of, no, sir.

Q: Did you ever ask her that?

A: I don't recall. I may have asked her that, I don't recall the doctor telling her that. . . .

Q: . . . Are you telling the ladies and gentlemen of the jury that you and your wife have never had a discussion concerning whether or not the Dalkon Shield played a part in her hysterectomy?

A: Well, certainly, as I indicated to you, we have very general discussions. Now, if I asked her whether that played a part, I don't recall specifically if I did. If I did, to my knowledge, there was no indication that it did.[15]

The company's response to all claims of faulty product design and limited testing procedures has been counter assertions or counter claims regarding the faulty or improper use of the product by the user or the physician. The company has steadfastly maintained that there were no special dangers inherent in the device. In a report to FDA they stated: "Robins believes that serious scientific questions exist about whether the Dalkon Shield poses a significantly different risk of infection than other IUDs." Their continuous theme has been that doctors, not the device, have caused any infections associated with the Shield. The company was committed to the notion that pregnancy and removal rates could be kept extremely low by proper placement of the Shield. They also contended that user abuse played a part in the Shield's supposed malfunctioning. They defined user abuse as poor personal hygiene habits, sexual promiscuity or excessive sexual activity, or physical tampering with the device itself.

According to three different independent investigative reports,[16] the company's public face of calm denial and counterargument masked an internal conspiring to conceal information from the public, the court system, and the FDA. These reports (books) claim documented evidence of the multilevel cover-up. They claim that Robins quashed all documentation debating and contesting Dr. Hugh Davis's celebrated pregnancy rate of only 1.1%, and that Robins knew of the real significance and traumatic effect of the

wicking process of the tail string but did nothing about it. Not only did the company know that the nylon cord used on the tail could degenerate and cause infection, but as early as the summer of 1972 the company was warned in writing by one of its chief consultants, Dr. Thad Earl, that pregnant women should have the Shield immediately removed to avoid "abortion and septic infection." These reports also contend that on at least three separate occasions, executives and officials of Robins lost or destroyed company files and records specifically requested by the Federal Appellate Courts and the FDA.

By May 1974 Robins could no longer avoid the evidence presented to it by FDA implicating the Shield in numerous cases of spontaneous septic abortions and in the death of at least four women as a result. These findings were disclosed in a letter sent by the company to 120,000 doctors. In June 1974 Robins suspended the U.S. distribution and sale of the Shield. In January 1975 Robins called back and completely removed the Shield from the market. The company termed the action a "market withdrawal," not a recall, because it was undertaken voluntarily and not at the direct order of FDA. In September 1980 Robins again wrote the medical community suggesting as a purely precautionary measure that doctors remove the Shield from their patients. In October 1984 Robins initiated a $4 million television, newspaper, and magazine advertising campaign warning and recommending that all women still wearing the device have it removed at Robins's expense. In April 1985 Robins publicly set aside $615 million to settle legal claims from women who had used the Shield. This reserve is the largest provision of its kind to date in a product liability case. In May 1985 a jury in Wichita, Kansas, awarded nearly $9 million to a woman who had charged that the use of the Shield caused her to undergo a hysterectomy. The award was the largest ever made in the history of litigation involving the Shield. Officials of the Robins Company felt that adverse decisions of this magnitude could mean that their $615 million fund would prove to be inadequate. On August 21, 1985, Robins filed for Chapter 11 protection, citing litigation relating to the Shield as the main cause for its actions. Company spokesmen said that it hoped that the Federal Bankruptcy Court in Richmond would set up a payment schedule that would enable it to survive while insuring that victims "would be treated fairly." E. Claiborne Robins, Junior, called it "essential that we move to protect the company's economic viability against those who would destroy it for the benefit of a few."[17] The intriguing financial irony in all of this is that when Robins filed for Chapter 11 it had already spent, at a conservative estimate, $500 million in settlements, litigation losses, and legal fees for a product it had only manufactured for three years and from which it had only realized $500,000 in real profits![18]

In all candor it must be remembered that Robins's actions are not without danger. To the extent that Robins is using Chapter 11 as a shelter against the rush of product-liability litigation, the company is nevertheless taking a gamble. Robins must now operate under the eye of a federal bankruptcy judge, and as Lawrence King, Professor of Law at NYU, has said in regard to the Manville case, "Once you file, there is always a risk of liquidation."[19] For example, as part of their reorganization arrangement with the court, Robins agreed to a class action procedure in which they would begin a 91-nation advertisement campaign to announce to all former users their right to file a claim for compensation for any health problems that may have been caused by the Shield. All potential claimants are given a case number and sent a questionnaire to determine if they qualify for a financial settlement. As of June 1986 more than 300,000 claims have been filed against Robins![20] Numbers such as these

may completely overwhelm the bankruptcy court's ability to reorganize and reestablish the company on a sound financial basis.

Given all of this data, perhaps there is only one thing we can say with certainty in regard to Robins's production of the Dalkon Shield: "In the pharmaceutical world, products that fail can cripple companies as well as people."[21]

AN UPDATE

Since filing for Chapter 11 in 1985 A.H. Robins has received at least three serious takeover bids. Two of these bids were made by the Rorer Group of Philadelphia and Sanoli, the Paris-based pharmaceutical and cosmetics house. Both were rejected primarily because of their inability or unwillingness to guarantee the $2.475 billion escrow fund that the court has mandated be established for the payment of all possible liability and injury claims now pending against Robins.[22] On July 26, 1988, however, Judge Robert R. Merhige approved a plan for the acquisition of Robins by American Home Products of New York. Under this plan, American Home would pay Robins's shareholders about $700 million in American Home stock and provide for most of the Dalkon Shield trust fund with Aetna Life and Casualty Co. contributing $425 million. The judge decreed that since 94% of the Shield claimants and 99% of the Robins's stockholders approved of the plan, the reorganization, pending appeal, would become final on August 25, 1988.[23]

Yet even in an era of corporate raiders and mergers, why would so many major organizations want to take over a company bogged down in bankruptcy proceedings?

The answer lies in such mundane but popular items as Robitussin and Dimetapp cold medicines, Chap Stick lip balm, and Sergeant's flea-and-tick collars. These are among the products that make Robins one of the most profitable bankrupt companies in history. In the first three quarters of 1987, Robins earned $60 million on sales of $621 million, compared with profits of $55 million on revenues of $579 million during the same period of 1986.[24]

Nevertheless, as Guerry Thorton Jr., a lawyer for the Dalkon Shield Victims Association, has pointed out, "the plans confirmation was a phenomenal success story. It has set a precedent by not allowing Robins to escape liability by filling for bankruptcy."[25]

NOTES

1. Al Gini, "Manville: The Ethics of Economic Efficiency?" *Journal of Business Ethics,* 3 (1984), p. 66.
2. *Time,* September 2, 1985, p. 32.
3. Morton Mintz, *At Any Cost* (New York: Pantheon Books, 1985), p. 25.
4. Ibid., p. 29.
5. Ibid., p. 82.
6. Ibid., pp. 29–31.
7. Ibid., pp. 86–88.
8. Ibid., pp. 81, 82.
9. *FDA Consumer,* May 1981, p. 32.
10. Morton Mintz. "At Any Cost." *The Progressive,* November 1985, p. 21.
11. *At Any Cost,* pp. 131–48 and 149–72.
12. *FDA Consumer,* July–August 1983, p. 2.
13. *Wall Street Journal,* April 11, 1985, p. 1.
14. Mintz, "At Any Cost," *The Progressive,* p. 24.
15. Mintz, *At Any Cost,* p. 111.
16. Mintz, *At Any Cost* (New York: Pantheon Books, 1985). Sheldon Engelmayer and Robert Wagman, *Lord's Justice* (New York: Anchor Press/Doubleday, 1985). Susan Perry and Jim Dawson, *Nightmare: Women and the Dalkon Shield* (New York: Macmillan Publishing, 1985).
17. *New York Times,* August 22, 1985, pp. 1, 6.
18. *Time,* November 26, 1984, p. 86.
19. Gini, "Manville: The Ethics of Economic Efficiency?" p. 68.
20. *Wall Street Journal,* June 26, 1986, p. 10.
21. *U.S. News and World Report,* September 2, 1985, p. 12.
22. *Time,* January 11, 1988, p. 59.
23. *New York Times—National Edition,* July 27, 1988, p. 32.
24. *Time,* January 11, 1988, p. 59.
25. *New York Times—National Edition,* July 27, 1988, p. 32.

The Global Marketplace

We live in amazing times. We can go to our local market and buy products from all over the world. Widespread international and transnational commerce is helping transform our global village into a global marketplace. "Sales territories" are now more important commercially than national boundaries. It is becoming increasingly difficult to discern the "nationality" of the products we buy. A car may be designed in the United States and assembled in Mexico, from parts fabricated in Japan, Korea, the United States, and Singapore. Through the power of the Internet, electronic commerce allows us to buy directly from some of the remotest parts of the world, without leaving the comfort of our own homes. We've come a long way from an all too recent era in human history in which we purchased mainly locally produced goods with only a smattering of merchandise traded between neighboring villages.

As we ponder the increasingly international nature of our buying habits, as well as our investments, we pay perhaps too little attention to what it is like to live, to work, and to do business in other parts of the world. Television and the Internet allow us to see that the world is populated by a variety of cultures; that "things are different over there." These differences add a layer of complexity to ethical analysis of how business ought to be transacted. How should a business firm conduct its transactions on foreign soil, in light of these differences? Are these differences simply differences, or do they determine right and wrong? The business practices of different cultures can either mesh or clash. If they clash, how are we to settle on the ethical course of action? Can competing views about ethical standards be equally valid? How can and should cultural differences bear on business ethics?

Not all national economies are vigorous and thriving. Besides differing cultural mores, how ought the economic disparities between nations figure into ethical business practice? For example, consumers in more affluent societies enjoy lower prices because the goods they buy are produced abroad by workers who toil for wages and under conditions—often characterized as *sweatshop* conditions—that consumers would not accept at home. How, if at all, does this fact bear on business ethics?

"Sweatshops and Respect for Persons" makes the case against the strategic use of sweatshop labor. "The Great Non-Debate over International Sweatshops" counters, pointing out some of the not often reflected on benefits of sweatshop labor—*to* sweatshop laborers and the countries in which they work. "Big Blue in Argentina" recounts IBM's efforts to secure business in Argentina by exploiting that nation's rampant official corruption. "Ellen Moore: Living and Working in Bahrain" pits the ambitions and conception of fairness that inform a talented Western business-woman against the needs of her firm and the realities of doing business in the Middle East. "Nike's Suppliers in Vietnam" indicates the good and the bad that comes from the world's leading athletic shoe manufacturer subcontracting shoe assembly in Southeast Asia. "Chrysler and Gao Feng: Corporate Responsibility for Religious and Political Freedom in China" considers the behavior of American automakers operating in China and asks us to ponder how differing standards can be accommodated in an ethically sensitive manner. "H. B. Fuller in Honduras" asks what a company that sets up shop with the best of intentions ought to do when their product gains notoriety for a use they never intended—with tragic consequences for the local community.

Essay

Sweatshops and Respect for Persons

Denis G. Arnold and Norman E. Bowie

In recent years labor and human rights activists have been successful at raising public awareness regarding labor practices in both American and off-shore manufacturing facilities. Organizations such as Human Rights Watch, United Students Against Sweatshops, the National Labor Coalition, Sweatshop Watch, and the Interfaith Center on Corporate responsibility have accused multinational enterprises (MNEs), such as Nike, Wal-Mart, and Disney, of the pernicious exploitation of workers. Recent violations of American and European labor laws have received considerable attention.[1] However, it is the off-shore labor practices of North American and European based MNEs and their contractors that have been most controversial. This is partly due to the fact that many of the labor practices in question are legal outside North America and Europe, or are tolerated by corrupt or repressive political regimes. Unlike the recent immigrants who

toil in the illegal sweatshops of North America and Europe, workers in developing nations typically have no recourse to the law or social service agencies. Activists have sought to enhance the welfare of these workers by pressuring MNEs to comply with labor laws, prohibit coercion, improve health and safety standards, and pay a living wage in their global sourcing operations. Meanwhile, prominent economists wage a campaign of their own in the opinion pages of leading newspapers, arguing that because workers for MNEs are often paid better when compared with local wages, they are fortunate to have such work. Furthermore, they argue that higher wages and improved working conditions will raise unemployment levels.

One test of a robust ethical theory is its ability to shed light on ethical problems. One of the standard criticisms of Immanuel Kant's ethical philosophy is that it is too abstract and

---

formal to be of any use in practical decision making. We contend that this criticism is mistaken and that Kantian theory has much to say about the ethics of sweatshops.[2] We argue that Kant's conception of human dignity provides a clear basis for grounding the obligations of employers to employees. In particular, we argue that respecting the dignity of workers requires that MNEs and their contractors adhere to local labor laws, refrain from coercion, meet minimum safety standards, and provide a living wage for employees. We also respond to the objection that improving health and safety conditions and providing a living wage would cause greater harm than good.

I. RESPECT FOR PERSONS

Critics of sweatshops frequently ground their protests in appeals to human dignity and human rights. Arguably, Kantian ethics provides a philosophical basis for such moral pronouncements. The key principle here is Kant's second formulation of the categorical imperative: "Act so that you treat humanity, whether in your own person or in that of another, always as an end and never as a means only."[3] The popular expression of this principle is that morality requires that we respect people. One significant feature of the idea of respect for persons is that its derivation and application can be assessed independently of other elements of Kantian moral philosophy. Sympathetic readers need not embrace all aspects of Kant's system of ethics in order to grant the merit of Kant's arguments for the second formulation of the categorical imperative.[4] This is because Kant's defense of respect for persons is grounded in the uncontroversial claim that humans are capable of rational, self-governing activity. We believe that individuals with a wide range of theoretical commitments can and should recognize the force of Kant's arguments concerning respect for persons.

Kant did not simply assert that persons are entitled to respect, he provided an elaborate argument for that conclusion. Persons ought to be respected because persons have dignity. For Kant, an object that has dignity is beyond price. Employees have a dignity that machines and capital do not have. They have dignity because they are capable of moral activity. As free beings capable of self-governance they are responsible beings, since freedom and self-governance are the conditions for responsibility. Autonomous responsible beings are capable of making and following their own laws; they are not simply subject to the causal laws of nature. Anyone who recognizes that he or she is free should recognize that he or she is responsible (that he or she is a moral being). As Kant argues, the fact that one is a moral being entails that one possesses dignity.

> Morality is the condition under which alone a rational being can be an end in himself because only through it is it possible to be a lawgiving member in the realm of ends. Thus morality, and humanity insofar as it is capable of morality, alone have dignity.[5]

As a matter of consistency, a person who recognizes that he or she is a moral being should ascribe dignity to anyone who, like him or herself, is a moral being.

Although it is the capacity to behave morally that gives persons their dignity, freedom is required if a person is to act morally. For Kant, being free is more than freedom from causal necessity. This is negative freedom. Freedom in its fullest realization is the ability to guide one's actions from laws that are of one's own making. Freedom is not simply a spontaneous event. Free actions are caused, but they are caused by persons acting from laws they themselves have made. This is positive freedom. Onora O'Neill puts the point this way.

Positive freedom is more than independence from alien causes. It would be absent in lawless or random changes, although these are negatively free, since they depend on no alien causes. Since will is a mode of causality it cannot, if free at all, be merely negatively free, so it must work by nonalien causality . . . it [free will] must be a capacity for self-determination or autonomy.[6]

When we act autonomously we have the capacity to act with dignity. We do so when we act on principles that are grounded in morality rather than in mere inclination. Reason requires that any moral principle that is freely derived must be rational in the sense that it is universal. To be universal in this sense means that the principle can be willed to be universally binding on all subjects in relevantly similar circumstances without contradiction. The fact that persons have this capability means that they possess dignity. And it is as a consequence of this dignity that a person "exacts respect for himself from all other rational beings in the world."[7] As such, one can and should "measure himself with every other being of this Kind and value himself on a footing of equality with them."[8]

Respecting people requires honoring their humanity; which is to say it requires treating them as ends in themselves. In Kant's words,

Humanity itself is a dignity; for a man cannot be used merely as a means by any man . . . but must always be used at the same time as an end. It is just in this that his dignity . . . consists, by which he raises himself above all other beings in the world that are not men and yet can be used, and so over all *things*.[9]

Thomas Hill Jr. has discussed the implication of Kant's arguments concerning human dignity at length.[10] Hill argues treat treating persons as ends in themselves requires supporting and developing certain human capacities, including the capacity to act on reason; the capacity to act on the basis of prudence or efficiency; the capacity to set goals; the capacity to accept categorical imperatives; and the capacity to understand the world and reason abstractly.[11] Based on Kant's writings in the *Metaphysics of Morals*, we would make several additions to the list. There Kant argues that respecting people means that we cannot be indifferent to them. Indifference is a denial of respect.[12] He also argues that we have an obligation to be concerned with the physical welfare of people and their moral well-being. Adversity, pain, and want are temptations to vice and inhibit the ability of individuals to develop their rational and moral capacities.[13] It is these rational and moral capacities that distinguish people from mere animals. People who are not free to develop these capacities may end up leading lives that are closer to animals than to moral beings. Freedom from externally imposed adversity, pain, and want facilitate the cultivation of one's rational capacities and virtuous character. Thus, treating people as ends in themselves means ensuring their physical well-being and supporting and developing their rational and moral capacities.

With respect to the task at hand, what does treating the humanity of persons as ends in themselves require in a business context—specifically in the context of global manufacturing facilities? In an earlier work Bowle has spelled out the implications of the Kantian view for businesses operating in developed countries.[14] Here we apply the same strategy in order to derive basic duties for MNEs operating in developing countries. Specifically, we derive duties that apply to MNEs that are utilizing the vast supplies of inexpensive labor currently available in developing economies. To fully respect a person one must actively treat his or her humanity as an end. This is an obligation that holds on every person *qua* person, whether in the personal realm or in the marketplace. As Kant writes, "Every man has a legitimate claim to respect from his fellow men and is *in turn* bound to respect every other."[15] There are, of course, limits to what managers of MNEs can accomplish. Nonetheless, we believe that the analysis we have provided entails that MNEs operating in developing nations have an obligation to respect the humanity of their employees. We discuss the implications of this conclusion below.

It is noteworthy that an application of the doctrine of respect for persons to the issue of the obligations of employers to employees in developing economies results in conclusions similar to the capabilities approach developed by Amartya Sen.[16] Over the last twenty years Sen has argued that development involves more than an increase in people's incomes and the GNP of the country. He argues that we should be concerned with certain basic human capabilities, the most important of which is freedom. Sen's perspective is similar in important respects to our own because both are concerned with providing work that enhances the positive freedom of the worker. The United Nations utilizes both the Kantian view and the capabilities view as a dual theoretical foundation for its defense of human rights. Among the rights identified by the UN are freedom from injustice and violations of the rule of law; freedom to decent work without exploitation; and the freedom to develop and realize one's human potential. It argues that all global actors, including MNEs, have a moral obligation to respect basic human rights.[17] This general approach to poverty and development has recently been embraced by the World Bank.[18] James Wolfensohn, President of The World Bank, writes:

> A better quality of life for the poor calls for higher Incomes. This requires sound economic policies and institutions conducive to sustained growth. Achieving higher incomes and a better quality of life also calls for much more—improved and more equitable opportunities for education and jobs, better health and nutrition, a cleaner and more sustainable natural environment, on impartial judicial and legal system, greater civilian and political liberties, trustworthy and transparent institutions, and freedom of access to a rich and diverse cultural life. . . . Poor women and men from around the world [note] emphatically the importance of dignity, respect, security, gender issues, a clean environment, health, and inclusion in addition to material well-being.[19]

Significantly, The World Bank has recognized "crucial gaps" in its efforts to encourage development and eliminate poverty through market liberalization. What has been missing is "adequate attention to the quality and sustainability of growth." The World Bank now explicitly acknowledges chat all major stakeholders have important roles to play in this process. "Functioning markets and liberalization are crucial" to poverty reduction. "But so is acknowledging the limits of the market and an essential role for governments *and other stakeholders* in the reform process."[20] MNEs have a significant interest in developing nations as sources of natural resources and inexpensive labor, and as emerging markets. As such, The World Bank properly recognizes MNEs as stakeholders with important moral obligations in the global reform process.

II. OUTSOURCING AND THE DUTIES OF MNEs

One significant feature of globalization that is of particular relevance to our analysis is the increase in outsourcing by MNEs. Prior to the 1970s most foreign production by MNEs was intended for local markets, In the 1970s new financial incentives led MNEs to begin outsourcing the production of goods for North American, European, and Japanese markets to manufacturing facilities in developing countries. Encouraged by international organizations such as The World Bank and the

International Monetary Fund, developing nations established "free trade zones" to encourage foreign investment via tax incentives and a minimal regulatory environment. In the 1980s the availability of international financing allowed entrepreneurs to set up production facilities in developing economies in order to meet the growing demand by MNEs for offshore production.[21] Outsourcing production has many distinct advantages from the perspective of MNEs. These include the following:

Capacity. Companies can expand their business more rapidly by focusing on marketing their products rather than investing in plant capacity, employees, and upgrading capital equipment. Companies can also accept special orders they would not be able to offer to large volume customers if their production capacity were fixed.

Specialization. Companies can market products requiring specialized skills or equipment that the firm does not have in-house.

Reduced Production Costs. In competitive industries where firms compete largely on the basis of price, outsourcing permits companies to reduce the size of their payroll and profit sharing obligations and shop around for lower and lower cost producers all across the globe.

Cycle Time. Outsourcing gives companies the flexibility to turn products around quickly in order to meet consumer demand and also avoid inventory build-ups.

Flexibility. The outsourcing model of production offers unique flexibility to firms that seek to cut costs in production or increase their capacity in that it offers opportunities to experiment with product lines and supplier relationships with minimal financial risk. The expense of developing new samples, for example, is borne by the factory that hopes to receive the order.[22]

Outsourcing has been especially popular in consumer products industries, and in particular in the apparel industry. Nike, for example, outsources all of its production.

Are MNEs responsible for the practices of their subcontractors and suppliers? We believe that they are. Michael Santoro has defended the view that MNEs have a moral duty to ensure that their business partners respect employees by ensuring that human rights are not violated in the workplace. Santoro argues as follows:

> [M]ultinational corporations are morally responsible for the way their suppliers and subcontractors treat their workers. The applicable moral standard is similar to the legal doctrine of *respondeat superior*, according to which a principal is "vicariously liable" or responsible for the acts of its agent conducted in the course of the agency relationship. The classic example of this is the responsibility of employers for the acts of employees. Moreover, ignorance is no excuse. Firms must do whatever is required to become aware of what conditions are like in the factories of their suppliers and subcontractors, and thereby be able to assure themselves and others that their business partners don't mistreat those workers to provide a cheaper source of supply.[23]

We concur with Santoro's judgment and offer the following two-fold justification for the view that MNEs have a duty to ensure that the dignity of workers is respected in the factories of subcontractors. First, an MNE, like any other organization, is composed of individual persons and, since persons are moral creatures, the actions of employees in an MNE are constrained by the categorical imperative. This means MNE managers have a duty to ensure that those with whom they conduct business are properly respected.[24] Second, as Kant acknowledges, individuals have unique duties as a result of their unique circumstances. One key feature in determining an individual's duties is the power they have to render assistance. For example, Kant famously argues that a wealthy person has a duty of charity that an impoverished person lacks. Corollary duties apply to organizations. Researchers have noted that the relationship of power between

MNEs and their subcontractors and suppliers is significantly imbalanced in favor of MNEs:

> [A]s more and mere developing countries have sought to establish export sectors, local manufacturers are locked in fierce competitive battles with one another. The resulting oversupply of export factories allows U.S. companies to move from one supplier to another in search of the lowest prices, quickest turnaround, highest quality and best delivery terms, weighted according to the priorities of the company. In this context, large U.S. manufacturer-merchandisers and retailers wield enormous power to dictate the price at which they will purchase goods.[25]

MNEs are well positioned to help ensure that the employees of its business partners are respected because of this imbalance of power. In addition, MNEs can draw upon substantial economic resources, management expertise, and technical knowledge to assist their business partners in creating a respectful work environment.

III. THE RULE OF LAW

Lawlessness contributes to poverty[26] and is deeply interconnected with human and labor rights violations. One important role that MNEs can play to help ensure that the dignity of workers is properly respected is encouraging respect for the rule of law. The United Nations has emphasized the importance of ensuring that citizens in all nations axe not subject to violations of the rule of law.

> The rule of law means that a country's formal rules are made publicly known and enforced in a predictable way through transparent mechanisms. Two conditions are essential: the rules apply equally to all citizens, and the state is subject to the rules. How state institutions comply with the rule of law greatly affects the daily lives of poor people, who are very vulnerable to abuses of their rights.[27]

It is commonplace for employers in developing nations to violate worker rights in the interest of economic efficiency and with the support of state institutions. Violations of laws relating to wages and benefits, forced overtime, health and safety, child labor, sexual harassment, discrimination, and environmental protection are legion. Examples include the following:

1. Human Rights Watch reports that in Mexican maquiladoras, or export processing zones, U.S. companies such a Johnson Controls and Carlisle Plastics require female job applicants to submit to pregnancy screening; women are refused employment if they test positive. Employment discrimination based on pregnancy is a violation of Mexican law.[28]

2. A Guatemalan Ministry of the Economy study found that less than 30 percent of maquiladora factories that supply MNEs make the legally required payments for workers into the national social security system which gives workers access to health care. The report was not made public by the Ministry of the Economy due to its "startling" nature.[29]

3. An El Salvadoran Ministry of Labor study funded by the United States Agency for International Development found widespread violation of labor laws, including flagrant violation of the freedom to organize and unionize, in maquiladora factories that supply MNEs. The report was suppressed by the Ministry of Labor after factory owners complained.[30]

4. In North and Central Mexico widespread violation of Mexican environmental laws by MNEs and their contractors has been documented by both U.S. and Mexican nongovernmental organizations, and local Mexican governmental officials.[31]

5. In Haiti apparel manufacturers such as L V. Myles Corporation, producing clothing under license with the Walt Disney Company in several contract factories, paid workers substantially less than the Haitian minimum wage. These clothes were sold in the U.S. at Wal-Mart, Sears, J.C. Penney, and other retailers. This practice continued until the National Labor Committee documented and publicized this violation of Haitian law.[32]

Furthermore, in many nations in which MNEs operate those responsible for administering justice are violators of the law. Factory workers frequently have no legal recourse when their legal rights are violated.

The intentional violation of the legal rights of workers in the interest of economic efficiency is fundamentally incompatible with the duty of MNEs to respect workers. Indifference to the plight of workers whose legal rights are systematically violated is a denial of respect. At a minimum, MNEs have a duty to ensure that their offshore factories, and those of their suppliers and subcontractors, arc in full compliance with local laws. Failure to honor the dignity of workers by violating their legal rights—or tolerating the violation of those rights—is also hypocritical. In Kantian terms, it constitutes a pragmatic contradiction. A pragmatic contradiction occurs when one acts on a principle that promotes an action that would be inconsistent with one's purpose if everyone were to act upon that principle. In this case, the principle would be something like the following: "It is permissible to violate the legal rights of others when doing so is economically efficient." MNEs rely on the rule of law to ensure, among other things, that their contracts are fulfilled, their properly is secure, and their copyrights are protected. When violations of the legal rights of MNEs take place, MNEs and business organizations protest vociferously. Thus, MNEs rely on the rule of law to ensure the protection of their own interests. Without the rule of law, MNEs would cease to exist. Therefore, it is inconsistent for an MNE to permit the violation of the legal rights of workers while at the same time it demands that its own rights be protected.

IV. COERCION

We have shown why it is reasonable to believe that all persons possess dignity and that this dignity must be respected. The obligation that we respect others requires that we not use people as a means only, but instead that we treat other people as capable of autonomous law guided action. The requirement not to use people can be met passively, by not treating them in certain ways. However, the requirement to treat them as ends-in-themselves entails positive obligations. We will explore these positive obligations as they relate to sweatshops in Section VI. In this section and the next we explore the requirement that we not use people as a means only. One common way of doing so recognized by Kant is coercion. Coercion violates a person's negative freedom. Coercion is prima facie wrong because it treats the subjects of coercion as mere tools, as objects lacking the rational capacity to choose for themselves how they shall act.

Are sweatshops in violation of the no coercion requirement? An answer to this question depends both on the definition of the concepts in question and on the facts of the particular case. Elsewhere Arnold has provided accounts of physical and psychological coercion.[33] Physical coercion occurs when one's bodily movements are physically forced. In cases where one person (P) physically coerces another person (Q), Q's body is used as an object or instrument for the purpose of fulfilling P's desires. We assume that readers of this essay will agree that using physical coercion to keep people working in sweatshops against their will is disrespectful and morally wrong. While comparatively rare, physical coercion, or the threat of physical coercion, does take place. For example, at a shoe factory in Guangdong, China, it is reported that 2,700 workers were prevented from leaving the factory by 100 live-in security guards that patrolled the walled factory grounds.[34]

For psychological coercion to take place, three conditions most hold. First, the coercer must have a desire about the will of his or her victim. However, this is a desire of a particular kind because it can only be fulfilled through the will of another person. Second, the coercer must have an effective desire to compel his or her victim to act in a manner that makes efficacious the coercer's other regarding desire. The distinction between an other regarding desire and a coercive will is important because it provides a basis for delineating between cases of coercion and, for example, cases of rational persuasion. In both instances a person may have an other regarding desire, but in the case of coercion that desire will be supplemented by an effective first-order desire that seeks to enforce that desire on the person, and in cases of rational persuasion it will not. What is of most importance in such cases is that P intentionally attempts to compel Q to comply with another regarding desire of P's own. These are necessary, but not sufficient conditions of coercion. In order for coercion to take place, the coercer must be successful in getting his or her victim to conform to his or her other regarding desire. In all cases of coercion P attempts to violate the autonomy of Q. When Q successfully resists P's attempted coercion, Q retains his or her autonomy. In such cases P retains a coercive will.

In typical cases, people work in sweatshops because they believe they can earn more money working there than they can in alternative employment, or they work in sweatshops because it is better than being unemployed. In many developing countries, people are moving to large cities from rural areas because agriculture in those areas can no longer support the population base. When people make a choice that seems highly undesirable because there are no better alternatives available, are those people coerced? On the definition of coercion employed here, having to make a choice among undesirable options is not sufficient for coercion. We therefore assume that such persons are not coerced even though they have no better alternative than working in a sweatshop.

Nonetheless, the use of psychological coercion in sweatshops appears widespread. For example, coercion is frequently used by supervisors to improve worker productivity. Workers throughout the world report that they are forced to work long overtime hours or lose their jobs. In Bangladesh factory workers report that they are expected to work virtually every day of the year. Overtime pay, a legal requirement, is often not paid. Employees who refuse to comply are fired.[35] In El Salvador a government study of maquiladora factories found that

> In the majority of companies, it is an obligation of the personnel to work overtime under the threat of firing or some other kind of reprisal. This situation, in addition to threatening the health of the workers, causes family problems in that [the workers] are unable to properly fulfill obligations to their immediate family.
>
> On some occasions, because the work time is extended into the late hours of the night, the workers find themselves obligated to sleep in the factory facilities, which do not have conditions necessary for lodging of personnel.[36]

Bangladesh, El Salvador, and other developing economies lack the social welfare programs that workers in North America and Europe take for granted. If workers lose their jobs, they may end up without any source of income. Thus, workers are understandably fearful of being fired for noncompliance with demands to work long overtime hours. When a worker is threatened with being fired by a supervisor unless she agrees to work overtime, and when the supervisor's intention in making the threat is to ensure compliance, then the supervisor's actions are properly understood as coercive. Similar threats are used to ensure that workers meet production quotas, even in the face of personal injury. For example, a 26-year-old worker who sews steering wheel covers at a Mexican maquila owned by Autotrim reports the following:

> We have to work quickly with our hands, and I am responsible for sewing 20 steering wheel covers per shift After having worked for nine years at the plant, I now suffer from an injury in my right hand. I start out the shift okay, but after about three hours of work, I feel a lot of sharp pains in my fingers. It gets so bad that I can't hold the steering wheel correctly. But still the supervisors keep pressuring me to reach 100 percent of my production. I can only reach about 70 percent of what they ask for. These pains began a year ago and I am not the only one who has suffered from them. There are over 200 of us who have hand injuries and some have lost movement in their hands and arms. The company has fired over 150 people in the last year for lack of production. Others have been pressured to quit. . . .[37]

We do not claim that production quotas are inherently coercive. Given a reasonable quota, employees can choose whether or not to work diligently to fill that quota. Employees who choose idleness over industriousness and are terminated as a result are not coerced. However, when a supervisor threatens workers who are ill or injured with termination unless they meet a production quota that either cannot physically be achieved by the employee, or can only be achieved at the cost of further injury to the employee, the threat is properly understood as coercive. In such cases the employee will inevitably feel compelled to meet the quota. Still other factory workers report being threatened with termination if they seek medical attention. For example, when a worker in El Salvador who was three months pregnant began hemorrhaging she was not allowed to leave the factory to receive medical attention. She subsequently miscarried while in the factory, completed her long work day, and took her fetus home for burial.[38] Other workers have died because they were not allowed to leave the factory to receive medical attention.[39] In

cases where workers suffer miscarriages or death, rather than risk termination, we believe that it reasonable to conclude that the workers are coerced into remaining at work.

According to the analysis provided here, workers choose to work in sweatshops because the alternatives available to them are worse. However, once they are employed, coercion is often used to ensure that they will work long overtime hours and meet production quotas. Respecting workers requires that they be free to decline overtime work without fear of being fired. It also requires that if they are injured or ill—especially as a result of work related activities—they should be allowed to consult healthcare workers and be given work that does not exacerbate their illnesses or injuries. Using coercion as a means of compelling employees to work overtime, to meet production quotas despite injury, or to remain at work while in need of medical attention, is incompatible with respect for persons because the coercers treat their victims as mere tools. It is important to note that even if the victim of coercion successfully resisted in some way, the attempted coercion would remain morally objectionable. This is because the coercer acts as if it is permissible to use the employees as mere tools.

V. WORKING CONDITIONS

Critics of MNEs argue that many workers are vulnerable to workplace hazards such as repetitive motion injuries, exposure to toxic chemicals, exposure to airborne pollutants such as fabric particles, and malfunctioning machinery. One of the most common workplace hazards concerns fire safety. In factories throughout the world workers are locked in to keep them from leaving the factory. When fires break out workers are trapped. This is what happened in 1993 when a fire broke out at the Kader Industrial Toy Company in

Thailand. More than 200 workers were killed and 469 injured. The factory had been producing toys for U.S. companies such as Hasbro, Toys "R" Us, J.C. Penney, and Fisher-Price.[40] In Bangladesh alone, there have been seventeen fires that have resulted in fatalities since 1995. A recent fire at Chowdhury Knitwears claimed 52 lives.[41]

Workers are also exposed to dangerous toxic chemicals and airborne pollutants. For example, a Nike commissioned Ernst & Young Environmental and Labor Practices Audit of the Tae Kwang Vina factory outside Ho Chi Minh City, Vietnam, was leaked to the press. Among the many unsafe conditions reported by Ernst & Young at this 10,000 person facility was exposure to toluene (a toxic chemical used as a solvent in paints, coatings, adhesives, and cleaning agents) at amounts 6 to 177 times that allowed by Vietnamese law.[42] The U.S. Environmental Protection Agency identifies the following acute effects of toluene exposure:

> The central nervous system is the primary target organ for toluene toxicity in both humans and animals for acute (short-term) and chronic (long-term) exposures, CNS dysfunction (which is often reversible) and narcosis have been frequently observed in humans acutely exposed to low or moderate levels of toluene by inhalation; symptoms include fatigue, sleepiness, headaches, and nausea. CNS depression and death have occurred at higher levels of exposure. Cardiac arrhythmia has also been reported in humans acutely exposed to toluene.[43]

In addition to toluene, workers at the Tae Kwang Vina factory were exposed to airborne fabric particles and chemical powders at dangerous levels. It is implausible to think that the (mainly) young women who work in the Tae Kwang Vina factory were informed about these health risks before they were hired. Ernst & Young reports that the employees received no training concerning the proper handling of chemicals after they were hired.

Since that time Nike has overseen substantial health and safety improvements at the Tae Kwang Vina factory, and at the other Southeast Asian factories with which it contracts. Nonetheless, available evidence indicates that unsafe workplace conditions remain common among MNE factories.[44] Consider, for example, the report of Mexican maquila worker Omar Gil:

> Back in 1993 I got my first job in a maquiladora, at Delphi Auto Parts. They paid 360 pesos a week (about $40). There was a lot of pressure from the foreman on the assembly lines to work hard and produce, and a lot of accidents because of the bad design of the lines. The company didn't give us adequate protective equipment to deal with the chemicals—we didn't really have any idea of the dangers, or how we should protect ourselves. The Union did nothing to protect us.
>
> Prom Delphi I went to another company, National Auto parts. In that plant we made car radiators for Cadillacs and Camaros, and there was a lot of sickness and accidents there too. I worked in the area with the metal presses. There were not ventilators to take the fumes out of the plant, and they didn't give us any gloves. We had to handle the parts with our bare hands, and people got cut up a lot. I worked in an area with a lot of lead. If you worked with lead, you're supposed to have special clothing and your clothes should be washed separately. But the company didn't give us any of that. We had to work in our street clothes.
>
> For all of that they paid 400 pesos a week (about $43). We had no union, and there was the same pressure for production from the foreman and the group leaders as I saw at Delphi.
>
> Now I work at TRW, where I've been for about a month and a half. There's really no difference in the conditions in any of these plants—if anything, my situation now is even worse.[45]

If our analysis is correct, then those MNEs that tolerate such health and safety risks have a duty to improve those conditions. Lax health and safety standards violate the moral requirement that employers be concerned with the physical safety of their employees. A failure to implement appropriate safeguards means that employers are treating their employees as disposable tools rather than as beings with unique dignity.

We cannot provide industry specific health and safety guidelines in the space of this essay. However, we believe that the International Labour Organization's carefully worked out Conventions and Recommendations on safely and health provide an excellent template for minimum safety standards.[46] For example, the ILO provides specific recommendations regarding airborne pollutants in "Occupational Exposure to Airborne Substances Harmful to Health" (1980) and exposure to chemicals in "Safety in the Use of Chemicals at Work" (1993). Ethicists, business people, and labor leaders with widely divergent views on a number of issues can agree on a minimum set of health and safety standards that should be in place in factories in the developing world. We return to this issue in Section VII.

VI. WAGES

One of the most controversial issues concerning sweatshops is the demand that employers raise the wages of employees in order to provide a "living wage." Workers from all over the world complain about low wages. For example,

[E]mployees of a maquiladora in Ciudad Acuna, Mexico, owned by the Aluminum Company of America (Alcoa), calculated that to buy the most basic food items needed by a factory worker—items such a beans, tortilla, rice, potatoes, unions and cooking oil, and excluding such "luxuries" as milk, meat, vegetables and cereal—cost U.S. $26.87 per week. At the time, weekly wages at the plant ranged only from $21.44 to $24.60.[47]

While a living wage is difficult to define with precision, one useful approach is to use a method similar to that used by the U.S. government to define poverty. This method involves calculating the cost of a market basket of food needed to meet minimum dietary requirements and then adding the cost of other basic needs. The Council on Economic Priorities uses this approach to define a wage that meets basic needs in different countries. Their formula is as follows:

1. Establish the local cost of a basic food basket needed to provide 2,100 calories per person.
2. Determine the share of the local household income spent on food. Divide into 1 to get total budget multiplier.
3. Multiply that by food spending to get the total per person budget for living expenses.
4. Multiply by half the average number of household members in the area. (Use a higher share if there are many single-parent households.)
5. Add at least 10% for discretionary income.[48]

The United Nations Development Programme employs a similar method to distinguish between three different levels of poverty (see Table 6.1).[49]

It is our contention that, it a minimum, respect for employees entails that MNEs and their suppliers have a moral obligation to ensure that employees do not live under conditions of overall poverty by providing adequate wages for a 48 hour work week to satisfy both basic food needs and basic non-food needs. Doing so helps to ensure the physical well-being and independence of employees, contributes to the development of their rational capacities, and provides them with opportunities for moral development. This in turn allows for the cultivation of self-esteem.[50] It is difficult to specify with precision the minimum number of hours per week that employees should work in order to receive a living wage. However, we believe that a 48 hour work week is a reasonable compromise that allows employees sufficient time for the cultivation of their rational capacities while providing employers with sufficient productivity.

TABLE 6.1

Types of Poverty	Deficiencies	Measures
Extreme Poverty (also known as Absolute Poverty)	Lack of income necessary to satisfy basic food needs	Minimum caloric intake and a food basket that meets that requirement
Overall Poverty (also known as Relative Poverty)	Lack of income necessary to satisfy basic non-food needs	Ability to secure shelter, energy, transportation, and basic health care, e.g.
Human Poverty	Lack of basic human capabilities	Access to goods, services, and infrastructure, e.g.

In addition, MNEs and their suppliers have an obligation to pay appropriate host nation taxes and meet appropriate codes and regulations to ensure that they contribute in appropriate ways to the creation and maintenance of the goods, services, and infrastructure necessary for the fulfillment of human capabilities. Anything less than this means that MNEs, or their suppliers, are not respecting employees as ends in themselves.

VII. ECONOMIC CONSIDERATIONS

The failure of many MNEs to meet the standards required by the application of the doctrine of respect for persons has not gone unnoticed. Through consumer boycotts, letter writing campaigns, opinion columns, and shareholder resolutions, activists have been successful in persuading some MNEs to implement changes. For example, Nike recently created the position of Vice President for Corporate Social Responsibility, hired a public affairs specialist to fill the position, and began to aggressively respond to activist complaints. In a recent open letter to its critics Nike concedes that "Several years ago, in our earlier expansion into certain countries, we had lots to learn about manufacturing practices and how to improve them."[51] However, Nike reports that it has fully embraced the goals of higher wages, the elimination of child labor, and the creation of better working condition. In short, Nike's response to its critics is ". . . guess what? You've already succeeded!"[52] Asked whether or not Nike would have made improvements without public pressure, a Nike official responded "Probably not as quickly, probably not to the degree."[53] Thus, ethical theory and a significant number of citizens of good will stand as one on this issue.

In a recent paper, Ian Maitland criticizes both the labor and human rights activists who have accused MNEs of unjust labor practices, as well as MNEs, such as Nike, that have responded by acquiescing to some of the activists demands.

> In this confrontation between the companies and their critics, neither side seems to have judged it to be in this interest to seriously engage the issue at the heart of the controversy, namely: What are the appropriate wages and labor standards in international sweatshops? . . . the companies have treated the charges about sweatshops as a public relations problem to be managed so as to minimize harm to their public images. The critics have apparently judged that the best way to keep public indignation at boiling point is to oversimplify the issue and treat it as a morality play featuring heartless exploiters and victimized third world workers. The result has been the great non-debate over international sweatshops.[54]

Maitland hopes to do better. In addition to assessing the veracity of claims regarding worker exploitation, he sets out to determine "the ethically appropriate levels of wages and labor standards in international sweatshops."[55] He argues that philosophers, such as Thomas Donaldson and Richard DeGeorge, who object to letting market determinations alone set wage standards, are misguided on the grounds that "attempts to improve on market outcomes may have unforeseen tragic consequences."[56] Maitland's arguments regarding ethically appropriate levels of wages and labor standards may be summarized as follows:

1. Workers in the urban, formal sector of developing nations earn better wages than do workers in the rural, informal sector.
2. The imposition of wages or labor standards greater than that demanded by the market increases costs.
3. Increased costs result in layoffs and slow investment in the formal sector.
4. Formal sector layoffs result in a surplus supply of labor in the informal sector.
5. A surplus of informal sector workers depresses income in the informal sector.

Conclusion: Higher wages or labor standards increase poverty and limit economic growth in developing nations.

Appealing as it does to textbook economic theory, Maitland's conclusion retains an authoritative quality. Naive critics of MNEs fail to lake into consideration rudimentary economic theory, and cynical corporate managers ignore these economic realities in order to preserve their brand images and corporate reputations. Maitland has done a valuable service by raising issues of central importance to the welfare of millions of powerless and impoverished people. However, is his conclusion correct? In the remaining portion of essay we argue that it is not.

First, despite Maitland's faith in the ability of international markets alone to generate ethically acceptable wage and labor standards for MNEs and their contractors, and despite

his criticisms of Donaldson and DeGeorge's recommendations for improving market outcomes, Maitland does not himself defend an unrestricted market approach. It is not clear, however, that Maitland recognizes this fact. The most obvious evidence in support of this conclusion is his criticism of corporate managers who, he believes, merely seek to appease their critics. "Not a single company has tried to mount serious defense of its contracting practices. They have judged that they cannot win a war of soundbites with the critics. Instead of making a fight of it, the companies have sued for peace in order to protect their principal asset—their image."[57] Thus, according to Maitland, corporate managers have made the strategic decision to respond to market forces—in this case consumers' preferences and other marketing considerations—in the manner they deem most consistent with profitability. Given Maitland's faith in the free market, one might expect him to criticize this strategy because it is inefficient.[58] However, Maitland does not pursue this approach. Instead, he argues that managers should not appease their critics—even if managers regard this as the strategy most consistent with profitability—because doing so will have undesirable economic and moral outcomes, namely, higher unemployment and slower economic growth. There is, then, a contradiction at the heart of Maitland's analysis. He argues in favor of improvements to current market outcomes, while at the same time he argues against attempts to improve on market outcomes on the grounds that doing so will result in undesirable moral consequences.[59]

Second, some of the most compelling evidence in support of the proposition that MNEs can improve workplace health and safety conditions while avoiding "tragic outcomes" comes from MNEs themselves. Companies such as Levis Strauss, Motorola, and Mattel have expended considerable resources to ensure that employees in their global sourcing operations work in healthy and safe environments. For example, Levis Strauss & Company stipulates that "We will only utilize business partners who provide workers with a safe and healthy environment."[60] Levis is known for acting in a manner consistent with this policy. Motorola explicitly endorses the idea of respect for persons in their Code of Business Conduct. The Code is built on two foundations:

> *Uncompromising integrity* means staying true to what we believe. We adhere to honesty, fairness and "doing the right thing" without compromise, even when circumstances make it difficult.
>
> *Constant respect for people* means we treat others with dignity, as we would like to be treated ourselves. Constant respect applies to every individual we interact with around the world.[61]

The physical instantiation of these principles can be seen at Motorola's factory in Tianjin, China:

> In the company cafeteria, workers queue up politely for a variety of free and nutritious meals. One area is set aside for a pregnancy well-care program. A booth is open at which appointments can be made with the company medical staff. There is a bank branch dedicated to employee needs. It is a scene that one might expect in a Fortune 500 corporate campus in the United States. The overwhelming sense is of a pleasant, orderly place in which people are fulfilled in their work.[62]

Recently Mattel announced the creation of a global code of conduct for its production facilities and contract manufacturers. It has spent millions of dollars to upgrade its manufacturing facilities in order to improve worker safety and comfort. Furthermore, it has invited a team of academics lead by S. Prakash Sethi to monitor its progress in complying with its self-imposed standards and to make their findings public.[63] This is believed to be the first time that a major MNE has voluntarily submitted to external monitoring. The examples set by Levis, Motorola, and Mattel provide evidence that MNEs are capable of improving worker health and safety without causing further hardship in the communities in which they operate.

Finally, it is not clear that improving employee wages will inevitably lead to the "tragic consequences" that Maitland and others predict. The economic issues under consideration are complex and we cannot address them here in the detail they deserve. Nonetheless, several reasons are provided for thinking that Maitland's conclusion is incorrect. With regard to the lowest paid formal sector wage earners in developing countries, the assumption that productivity is independent of wage levels is dubious.

> As exceptionally low wages are raised, there may be increases in productivity either because of induced management improvements or because of greater labour efficiency due to a decrease in wasteful labour turnover and industrial disputes and to improvements in workers morale and nutrition resulting, in turn, in an increase in the workers' willingness and capacity to work and a reduction in the incidence of debilitating diseases, time off due to illness and accidents caused by fatigue. If higher wages, at least over a certain range, are accompanied by certain improvements in labour productivity, it is conceivable that labour costs could decrease rather than increase and to such an extent that employment would not fall.[64]

Put simply, workers whose minimum daily caloric intakes are met, and who have basic non-food needs met, will have more energy and better altitudes at work; will be less likely to come to work ill; and will be absent with less frequency. Workers are thus likely to be more productive and loyal. Economists refer to a wage that if reduced would make the firm worse off because of a decrease in worker productivity as the efficiency wage. Empirical evidence supports the view that increased productivity resulting from better nutrition offsets the cost of higher wages.[65] Thus, if workers are being paid less than the efficiency wage in a particular market there are good economic reasons, in addition to moral reasons, for raising wages. Higher productivity per hour could also help alleviate the need for overtime work and facilitate a 48 hour work week.

One might object that our analysis implies that MNE managers are unaware of the correlation between wages and productivity, and that such ignorance on the part of MNE managers is implausible. Our reply is two-fold. First, workers in developing nations *are* frequently paid less than the efficiency wage in those labor markets. Second, findings from an El Salvadoran Ministry of Labor study of maquiladora factories are instructive. Researchers found that "According to the production managers interviewed, some companies use North American and Asian efficiency and productivity levels as a parameter for establishing production goals, without considering the different nutritional conditions and technical capacity of our workers."[66] We believe that such erroneous assumptions may be widespread among MNE managers.

Part of Maitland's analysis rests on the assumption that increased labor costs will inevitably result in higher unemployment in competitive markets. Maitland is correct to identify this view as a common belief among many economists, especially as it relates to minimum wage legislation.[67] However, this view has been challenged in recent years. In their recent influential book-length study of the impact of minimum wage increases on employment, David Card and Alan Krueger argue that their reanalysis of the evidence from the Unites States, Canada, the United Kingdom, and Puerto Rico indicates that the existing data does not provide compelling evidence for the textbook view.[68] In addition, Card and Krueger analyzed new data for recent increases in the minimum wage in the U.S. Their analysis is complex, but the results of their analysis are straightforward. "In every

case . . . the estimated effect of the minimum wage was either zero or positive."[69] Increased labor costs appear to have been passed on to consumers in the form of higher prices without increasing unemployment. Again, this data undermines the textbook view regarding the impact of increases in the minimum wage. Economist Richard Freeman summarizes the impact of Card and Krueger's work as follows:

> [T]he Card-Krueger work is essentially correct: the minimum wage at levels observed in the United States has had little or no effect on employment. At the minimum, the book has changed the burden of proof in debates over the minimum, from those who stressed the potential distributional benefits of the minimum to those who stress the potential employment losses.[70]

After evaluating recent work on the impact of minimum wages, economists William Spriggs and John Schmitt reached a more determinate conclusion: "The overwhelming weight of recent evidence supports the view that low-wage workers will benefit overwhelmingly from a higher federal minimum."[71]

Two points concerning wages should be distinguished. First, conclusions concerning the impact of U.S. minimum wage legislation on unemployment cannot automatically be assumed to apply to developing nations. Careful study of the unique conditions of those labor markets is necessary before corollary claims can be assessed. Nonetheless, the textbook view rests significantly on studies concerning the U.S. labor market. As such, we believe that the burden of proof remains with those who maintain that increased labor costs must inevitably result in higher unemployment. Second, we wish to emphasize that we are not taking a position in this essay on increasing federally mandated minimum wages in developing nations. Rather, our contention is that it is economically feasible for MNEs to voluntarily raise wages in factories in developing economies without causing increases in unemployment. MNEs may choose to raise wages while maintaining existing employment levels. Increased labor costs that are not offset by greater productivity may be passed on to consumers, or, if necessary, absorbed through internal cost-cutting measures such as reductions in executive compensation.

VIII. CONCLUSION

As Kant argues, it is by acting in a manner consistent with human dignity that persons raise themselves above all things. Insofar as we recognize the dignity of humanity, we have an obligation to respect both ourselves and others.[72] We have argued that MNE managers who encourage or tolerate violations of the rule of law; use coercion; allow unsafe working conditions; and provide below subsistence wages, disavow their own dignity and that of their workers. In so doing, they disrespect themselves and their workers. Further, we have argued that this moral analysis is not undermined by economic considerations. Significantly. MNEs are in many ways more readily able to honor the humanity of workers. This is because MNEs typically have well defined internal decision structures that, unlike individual moral agents, are not susceptible to weakness of the will.[73] For this reason, MNE managers who recognize a duty to respect their employees, and those of their subcontractors, are well positioned to play a constructive role in ensuring that the dignity of humanity is respected.

NOTES

Earlier versions of this essay were presented to the Annual Meeting of the Society for Business Ethics, Washington D.C., August, 2001; and the American Philosophical Association 100th Anniversary Conference, "Morality in the 21st Century," Newark. Del., October, 2001. We are grateful to audience members for their comments on those occasions. Thanks also to George Brenkert, Heather Douglas, Laura Hartman, John McCall, Sara Arnold, and an anonymous reviewer for helpful comments on earlier drafts of this essay. Special thanks to Ian Maitland and Norris Peterson for detailed written comments; although we continue to disagree with them on some matters, their comments lead to several improvements in this essay.

1. See, for example, Susan Chandler, "Look Who's Sweating Now," *Business Week*, October 16, 1995; Steven Greenhouse, "Sweatshop Raids Cast Doubt on an Effort By Garment Makers to Police the Factories," *New York Times*, July 18, 1997; and Gall Edmondson et al., "Workers in Bondage," *Business Week*, November 27, 2000.

2. For the purposes of this paper we define the term as any workplace in which workers are typically subject to two or more of the following conditions: income for a 48 hour work week less than the overall poverty rate for that country (see Table 1 below); systematic forced overtime; systematic health and safety risks that stem from negligence or the willful disregard of employee welfare; coercion; systematic deception that places workers at risk; and underpayment of earnings.

3. Immanuel Kant, *Foundations of the Metaphysics of Morals*, Lewis White Beck, trans. (New York: Macmillan, 1990), 46.

4. In making this claim we explicitly reject the conclusion reached by Andrew Wicks that one must either "fully embrace Kant's metaphysics" or "break from the abstract universalism of Kant." See Andrew Wicks, "How Kantian A Theory of Capitalism," *Business Ethics Quarterly*, The Ruffin Series: Special Issue 1 (1998): 65.

5. Kant, *Foundations of the Metaphysics of Morals*, 52.

6. Onora O'Neill, *Constructions of Reason* (Cambridge: Cambridge University Press, 1989), 53.

7. Immanuel Kant, *The Metaphysics of Morals*, Mary Gregor, trans. (Cambridge: Cambridge University Press, 1991), 230.

8. Ibid.

9. Ibid., 255.

10. Thomas Hill Jr., *Dignity and Practical Reason in Kant's Moral Theory* (Ithaca: Cornell University Press. 1992).

11. Ibid., 40–41.

12. Kant, *Metaphysics of Morals*, 245.

13. Ibid., 192–193 and 196–197.

14. Norman E. Bowle, *Business Ethics: A Kantian Perspective* (Maiden, Mass.: Blackwell, 1999). See 41–81 for further discussion of the second categorical imperative.

15. Kant, *Metaphysics of Morals*, 255.

16. His latest book is *Development as Freedom* (New York: Anchor Books, 1999). Martha Nussbaum has developed her own version of the capabilities approach, one that pays particular attention to the unique circumstances of women's lives. *Women and Human Development: The Capabilities Approach* (Cambridge: Cambridge University Press, 2000).

17. United Nations Development Programme, *Human Development Report 2000* (New York: Oxford University Press, 2000).

18. See, for example, Vinod Thomas et al., *The Quality of Growth* (Washington D.C.: The World Bank, 2000); Deepa Narayan et al., *Voices of the Poor: Crying Out for Change* (Washington D.C.: The World Bank, 2000); and Deepa Narayan et al., *Voices of the Poor: Can Anyone Hear Us?* (Washington D.C.: The World Bank, 2000).

19. Thomas et al., *The Quality of Growth*, xiv.

20. Ibid., xvii–xviii (Italics added by authors).

21. Pamela-Varley, ed., *The Sweatshop Quandary: Corporate Responsibility on the Global Frontier* (Washington D.C.: Investor Responsibility Research Center, 1998), 185–186.

22. Ibid., 85.

23. Michael A. Santoro, *Profits and Principles: Global Capitalism and Human Rights in China* (Ithaca: Cornell University Press, 2000), 161.

24. For a fuller discussion of this matter see Bowle, *Business Ethics: A Kantian Perspective*, esp. chap. 2.

25. Varley, ed., *The Sweatshop Quandary*, 95.

26. Better rule of law is associated with higher per capita income. See *World Development Report 2000/2001: Attacking Poverty* (New York: Oxford University Press. 2000), 103.

27. Ibid., 102. See also the United National Development Programme's *Human Development Report 2000* (New York: Oxford University Press, 2000), esp. 37–38.

28. Human Rights Watch, "A Job or Your Rights: Continued Sex Discrimination in Mexico's Maquiladora Sector," volume 10, no. 1(B) December 1998. Available at http://www.hrw.org/reports98/women2/.

29. Varley, ed., *The Sweetshop Quandary*, 131.

30. Republic of El Salvador, Ministry of Labor, Monitoring and Labor Relations Analysis Unit, "Monitoring Report on Maquilas and Bonded Areas" (July 2000). Available at http://www.nlcnet.org/elsalvador/0401/translation.htm.

31. Edward J. Williams, "The Maquiladora Industry and Environmental Degradation in the United States-Mexican Borderlands," paper presented at the annual meeting of the Latin American Studies Association, Washington, D.C., September, 1995. Available at http://www.natlaw.com/pubs/williams.htm. See also Joan Salvat, Stef Soetewey, and Peter Breuls, *Free Trade Slaver*, 58 min. (Princeton, N.J.: Films for the Humanities and Sciences, 1999), videocassette.

32. National Labor Committee, "The U.S. in Haiti: How to Get Rich on 11 Cents an Hour," 1995. Available at http://www.nlcnet.org/Halti/0196/index.htm.

33. Denis G. Arnold, "Coercion and Moral Responsibility," *American Philosophical Quarterly* 38 (2001): 53–67. The view of psychological coercion employed here is a slightly revised version of the view defended in that essay. In particular, the condition that cases of psychological coercion always involve psychological compulsion has been replaced with the condition that cases of psychological coercion always involve the victim's compliance with the threat.

34. Varley, ed., *The Sweatshop Quandary*, 72.

35. Barry Bearak, "Lives Held Cheap In Bangladesh Sweatshops," *New York Times*, April 15, 2001.

36. Republic of El Salvador, Ministry of Labor, Monitoring and Labor Relations Analysis Unit, "Monitoring Report on Maquilas and Bonded Areas."

37. Varley, ed., *Sweatshop Quandary*, 68.

38. Salvat et al., *Free Trade Slaves*, 58 min. (Princeton. N.J.: Films for the Humanities and Sciences, 1999), videocassette.

39. Ibid.

40. Varley, ed., *The Sweatshop Quandary*, 67.

41. Bearak, "Lives Held Cheap in Bangladesh Sweatshops."

42. "Ernst & Young Environmental and Labor Practice Audit of the Tae Kwang Vina Industrial Ltd. Co., Vietnam." Available at http://www.corpwatch.org/trac/nike/ernst/audit.html.

43. United States Environmental Protection Agency, Office of Air Quality, Planning, and Standards, "Toluene." Available at http://www.epa.gov/ttnuatw1/hlthef/toluenc.html.

44. See, for example, Varley, ed., *The Sweatshop Quandary*, esp. 59–398.

45. Campaign for Labor Rights, "The Story of a Maquiladora Worker: Interview with Omar Gil by David Bacon," September 6, 2000. Available at www.summersault.com/-agj/clt/alerts/thestoryofamaqulladoraeworker. html.

46. International Labour Organization, "SafeWork: ILO Standards on Safety and Health." Available at http://www.ilo.org/public/english/protection/safework/standard.htm.

47. After the complaint was raised in a shareholder meeting Alcoa raised the wages of the workers by 25%. Pamela Varley, ed., *The Sweatshop Quandary*, 63.

48. Aaron Bernstein, "Sweatshop Reform: How to Solve the Standoff," *Business Week*, May 3, 1999.

49. *Poverty Report 2000: Overcoming Human Poverty* (New York: United Nations Development Programme, 2000).

50. Self-esteem is grounded in the conscious recognition of one's dignity as a rational being.

51. Nike, "An Open Letter Response to USAS Regarding Their National Protest of Nike Through August 16, 2000." Available at http://nikeblz.com/labor/usas_let.shtml.

52. Ibid.

53. Frank Denton, "Close Look at Factory for Nikes," *Wisconsin State Journal*, July 30, 2000.

54. Ian Maitland, "The Great Non-Debate Over International Sweatshops," reprinted in Tom L. Beauchamp and Norman E. Bowle, *Ethical Theory and Business*, 6th ed. (Englewood Cliffs: Prentice Hall, 2001), 595. First published in *British Academy of Management Conference Proceedings*, September 1997, 240–265.

55. Ibid.

56. Ibid., 603.

57. Ibid., 594.

58. Such an argument would likely maintain that corporate managers fail to recognize that a public relations strategy that includes higher wages and improved workplace standards is more costly than an alternative strategy that does not. The details of such a strategy would then need to be worked out.

59. Maitland, "The Great Non-Debate Over International Sweatshops," 602.

60. Ibid., 539.

61. Motorola, "Code of Business Conduct." Available at http://www.motorola.com/code/code.html.

62. Santoro, *Profits and Principles*, 6.

63. S. Prakash Sethi, "Codes of Conduct for Multinational Corporations: An Idea Whose Time Has Come," *Business and Society Review* 104 (1999): 225–241.

64. Gerald Start, *Minimum Wage Filing* (Geneva: International Labour Organization, 1981), 157.

65. C. J. Bliss and N. H. Stern, "Productivity, Wages, and Nutrition, 2: Some Observations," *Journal of Development Economics* 5 (1978): 363–398. For theoretical discussion see C. J. Bliss and N. H. Stern, "Productivity, Wages, and Nutrition, 1: The Theory," *Journal of Development Economics* 5 (1978): 331–362.

66. Republic of El Salvador, Ministry of Labor, Monitoring and Labor Relations Analysis Unit, "Monitoring Report on Maqullas and Bonded Areas."

Available at http://www.nlenet.org/elsalvador/0401/translation.htm.

67. See, for example, the essays collected in *The Economics of Legal Minimum Wages*, Simon Rottenberg, ed. (Washington D.C.: The American Enterprise Institute, 1981).

68. See David Card and Alan B. Kruger, *Myth and Measurement; The New Economics of the Minimum Wage* (Princeton: Princeton University Press, 1995). See also the special symposium on *Myth and Measurement* in *Industrial & Labor Relations Review* (July 1995) with contributions by Charles Brown, Richard Freeman, Daniel Hamermesh, Paul Osterman, and Finis Weleh; David Neumark and William Wascher, "Minimum Wages and Employment: A Case Study of the Fast-Food Industry in New Jersey and Pennsylvania: Comment," *The American Economic Review* (December 2000); 1362–1396; and David Card and Alan B. Krueger, "Minimum Wages and Employment: A Case Study of the Fast-Food Industry in New Jersey and Pennsylvania: Reply," *The American Economic Review* (December 2000): 1397–1420. For a discussion of the living wage issue in the context of the U.S. economy see Robert Pollin and Stephanie Luce, *The Living Wage: Building a Fair Economy* (New York: The New Press, 1998).

69. Card and Krueger, *Myth and Measurement*, 389.

70. Richard B. Freeman, "In Honor of David Card: Winner of the John Bates Clark Medal," *Journal of Economic Perspectives* (Spring 1997): 173.

71. William Spriggs and John Schmitt, "The Minimum Wage: Blocking the Low-Wage Path," in *Reclaiming Prosperity: A Blueprint for Progressive Economic Reform*, Todd Schafer and Jeff Faux (Armonk, N.Y.: MB Sharpe, 1996), 170.

72. Kant, *Foundations of the Metaphysics of Morals*, 255.

73. For a fuller defense of this position see Peter A. French, *Corporate Ethics* (Fort Worth, Tex.: Harcourt Brace, 1995), 79–87.

Essay

The Great Non-Debate over International Sweatshops

Ian Maitland

In recent years, there has been a dramatic growth in the contracting out of production by companies in the industrialized countries to suppliers in developing countries. This globalization of production has led to an emerging international division of labor in footwear and

From Ian Maitland, "The great non-debate over international sweatshops," *British Academy of Management Annual Conference Proceedings*, September, pp. 240–265, 1997. Reprinted with permission.

apparel in which companies like Nike and Reebok concentrate on product design and marketing but rely on a network of contractors in Indonesia, China, Central America, etc., to build shoes or sew shirts according to exact specifications and deliver a high quality good according to precise delivery schedules. As Nike's vice president for Asia has put it, "We don't know the first thing about manufacturing. We are marketers and designers."

The contracting arrangements have drawn intense fire from critics—usually labor and human rights activists. These "critics" (as I will refer to them) have charged that the companies are (by proxy) exploiting workers in the plants (which I will call "international sweatshops") of their suppliers. Specifically the companies stand accused of chasing cheap labor around the globe, failing to pay their workers living wages, using child labor, turning a blind eye to abuses of human rights, being complicit with repressive regimes in denying workers the right to join unions and failing to enforce minimum labor standards in the workplace, and so on.

The campaign against international sweatshops has largely unfolded on television and, to a lesser extent, in the print media. What seems like no more than a handful of critics has mounted an aggressive, media-savvy campaign which has put the publicity-shy retail giants on the defensive. The critics have orchestrated a series of sensational "disclosures" on prime time television exposing the terrible pay and working conditions in factories making jeans for Levi's or sneakers for Nike or Pocahontas shirts for Disney. One of the principal scourges of the companies has been Charles Kernaghan who runs the National Labor Coalition (NLC), a labor human rights group involving 25 unions. It was Kernaghan who, in 1996, broke the news before a Congressional committee that Kathie Lee Gifford's clothing line was being made by 13- and 14-year-olds working 20-hour days in factories in Honduras. Kernaghan also arranged for teenage workers from sweatshops in Central America to testify before Congressional committees about abusive labor practices. At one of these hearings, one of the workers held up a Liz Claiborne cotton sweater identical to ones she had sewn since she was a 13-year-old working 12-hour days. According to a news report, "[t]his image, accusations of oppressive conditions at the factory and the Claiborne logo played well on that evening's network news." The result has been a circus-like atmosphere—as in Roman circus where Christians were thrown to lions.

Kernaghan has shrewdly targeted the companies' carefully cultivated public images. He has explained: "Their image is everything. They live and die by their image. That gives you a certain power over them." As a result, he says, "these companies are sitting ducks. They have no leg to stand on. That's why it's possible for a tiny group like us to take on a giant like Wal-Mart. You can't defend paying someone 31 cents an hour in Honduras. . . ."[1] Apparently most of the companies agree with Kernaghan. Not a single company has tried to mount a serious defense of its contracting practices. They have judged that they cannot win a war of soundbites with the critics. Instead of making a fight of it, the companies have sued for peace in order to protect their principal asset—their image.

Major U.S. retailers have responded by adopting codes of conduct on human and labor rights in their international operations. Levi-Strauss, Nike, Sears, JCPenney, Wal-Mart, Home Depot, and Philips Van-Heusen now have such codes. As Lance Compa notes, such codes are the result of a blend of humanitarian and pragmatic impulses: "Often the altruistic motive coincides with "bottom line" considerations related to brand name, company image, and other intangibles that make for core value to the firm."[2] Peter Jacobi, President of Global Sourcing for Levi-Strauss, has advised: "If your company owns a popular brand, protect this priceless asset at all costs. Highly visible companies have any number of reasons to conduct their business not just responsibly but also in ways that cannot be portrayed as unfair, illegal, or unethical. This sets an extremely high standard since it must be applied to both company-owned businesses and contractors. . . ."[3] And according to another Levi-Strauss spokesman. "In many respects, we're protecting our single largest asset: our brand image and corporate reputation."[4] Nike recently published the results of a generally favorable review of its international operations conducted by former American U.N. Ambassador Andrew Young.

Recently a truce of sorts between the critics and the companies was announced on the White House lawn with President Clinton and Kathie Lee Gifford in attendance. A presidential task force, including representatives of labor unions, human rights groups and apparel companies like L.L. Bean and Nike, has come up with a set of voluntary standards which, it hopes, will be embraced by the entire industry. Companies that comply with the code will be entitled to use a "No Sweat" label.

OBJECTIVE OF THIS PAPER

In this confrontation between the companies and their critics, neither side seems to have judged it to be in its interest to seriously engage the issue at the heart of this controversy, namely: What are appropriate wages and labor standards in international sweatshops? As we have seen, the companies have treated the charges about sweatshops as a public relations problem to be managed so as to minimize harm to their public images. The critics have apparently judged that the best

way to keep public indignation at boiling point is to oversimplify the issue and treat it as a morality play featuring heartless exploiters and victimized third world workers. The result has been a great non-debate over international sweatshops. Paradoxically, if peace breaks out between the two sides, the chances that the debate will be seriously joined may recede still further. Indeed, there exists a real risk (I will argue) that any such truce may be a collusive one that will come at the expense of the very third world workers it is supposed to help.

This paper takes up the issue of what are appropriate wages and labor standards in international sweatshops. Critics charge that the present arrangements are exploitative. I proceed by examining the specific charges of exploitation from the standpoints of both (a) their factual and (b) their ethical sufficiency. However, in the absence of any well-established consensus among business ethicists (or other thoughtful observers), I simultaneously use the investigation of sweatshops as a setting for trying to adjudicate between competing views about what those standards should be. My examination will pay particular attention to (but will not be limited to) labor conditions at the plants of Nike's suppliers in Indonesia. I have not personally visited any international sweatshops, and so my conclusions are based entirely on secondary analysis of the voluminous published record on the topic.

WHAT ARE ETHICALLY APPROPRIATE LABOR STANDARDS IN INTERNATIONAL SWEATSHOPS?

What are ethically acceptable or appropriate levels of wages and labor standards in international sweatshops? The following three possibilities just about run the gamut of standards or principles that have been seriously proposed to regulate such policies.

1. *Home-country standards:* It might be argued (and in rare cases has been) that international corporations have an ethical duty to pay the same wages and provide the same labor standards regardless of where they operate. However, the view that home-country standards should apply in host-countries is rejected by most business ethicists and (officially at least) by the critics of international sweatshops. Thus Thomas Donaldson argues that "[b]y arbitrarily establishing U.S. wage levels as the benchmark for fairness one eliminates the role of the international market in establishing salary levels, and this in turn eliminates the incentive U.S. corporations have to hire foreign workers."[5] Richard DeGeorge makes much the same argument. If there were a rule that said that "that American MNCs [multinational corporations] that wish to be ethical must pay the same wages abroad as they do at home, . . . [then] MNCs would have little incentive to move their manufacturing abroad; and if they did move abroad they would disrupt the local labor market with artificially high wages that bore no relation to the local standard or cost of living."[6]

2. *"Living wage" standard:* It has been proposed that an international corporation should, at a minimum, pay a "living wage." Thus DeGeorge says that corporations should pay a living wage "even when this is not paid by local firms."[7] However, it is hard to pin down what this means operationally. According to DeGeorge, a living wage should "allow the worker to live in dignity as a human being." In order to respect the human rights of its workers, he says, a corporation must pay "at least subsistence wages and as much above that as workers and their dependents need to live with reasonable dignity, given the general state of development of the society."[8] As we shall see, the living wage standard has become a rallying cry of the critics of international sweatshops. Apparently, DeGeorge believes that it is preferable for a corporation to provide no job at all than to offer one that pays less than a living wage. . . .

3. *Classical liberal standard:* Finally, there is what I will call the classical liberal standard. According to this standard a practice (wage or labor practice) is ethically acceptable if it is freely chosen by informed workers. For example, in a recent report the World Bank invoked this standard in connection with workplace safety. It said: "The appropriate level is therefore that at which the costs are commensurate with the value that informed workers place on improved working conditions and reduced risk."[9] Most business ethicists

reject this standard on the grounds that there is some sort of market failure or the "background conditions" are lacking for markets to work effectively. Thus for Donaldson full (or near-full) employment is a prerequisite if workers are to make sound choices regarding workplace safety: "The average level of unemployment in the developing countries today exceeds 40 percent, a figure that has frustrated the application of neoclassical economic principles to the international economy on a score of issues. With full employment, and all other things being equal, market forces will encourage workers to make trade-offs between job opportunities using safety as a variable. But with massive unemployment, market forces in developing countries drive the unemployed to the jobs they are lucky enough to land, regardless of the safety."[10] Apparently there are other forces, like Islamic fundamentalism and the global debt "bomb," that rule out reliance on market solutions, but Donaldson does not explain their relevance.[11] DeGeorge, too, believes that the necessary conditions are lacking for market forces to operate benignly. Without what he calls "background institutions" to protect the workers and the resources of the developing country (e.g., enforceable minimum wages) and/or greater equality of bargaining power exploitation is the most likely result.[12] "If American MNCs pay workers very low wages . . . they clearly have the opportunity to make significant profits."[13] DeGeorge goes on to make the interesting observation that "competition has developed among multinationals themselves, so that the profit margin has been driven down" and developing countries "can play one company against another."[14] But apparently that is not enough to rehabilitate market forces in his eyes.

THE CASE AGAINST INTERNATIONAL SWEATSHOPS

To many of their critics, international sweatshops exemplify the way in which the greater openness of the world economy is hurting workers. . . . Globalization means a transition from (more or less) regulated domestic economies to an unregulated world economy. The superior mobility of capital, and the essentially fixed, immobile nature of world labor, means a fundamental shift in bargaining power in favor of large international corporations. Their global reach permits them to shift production almost costlessly from one location to another. As a consequence, instead of being able to exercise some degree of control over companies operating within their borders, governments are now locked in a bidding war with one another to attract and retain the business of large multinational companies.

The critics allege that international companies are using the direct of withdrawal or withholding of investment to pressure governments and workers to grant concessions. "Today [multinational companies] choose between workers in developing countries that compete against each other to depress wages to attract foreign investment." The result is a race for the bottom—a "destructive downward bidding spiral of the labor conditions and wages of workers throughout the world. . . ."[15] . . . Thus, critics charge that in Indonesia wages are deliberately held below the poverty level or subsistence in order to make the country a desirable location. The results of this competitive dismantling of worker protections, living standards and worker rights are predictable: deteriorating work conditions, declining real incomes for workers, and a widening gap between rich and poor in developing countries. I turn next to the specific charges made by the critics of international sweatshops.

Unconscionable Wages

Critics charge that the companies, by their proxies, are paying "starvation wages" and "slave wages." They are far from clear about what wage level they consider to be appropriate. But they generally demand that companies pay a "living wage." Kernaghan has said that workers should be paid enough to support their families and they should get a

"living wage" and "be treated like human beings."[16] . . . According to Tim Smith, wage levels should be "fair, decent or a living wage for an employee and his or her family." He has said that wages in the maquiladoras of Mexico averaged $35 to $55 a week (in or near 1993) which he calls a "shockingly substandard wage," apparently on the grounds that it "clearly does not allow an employee to feed and care for a family adequately."[17] In 1992, Nike came in for harsh criticism when a magazine published the pay stub of a worker at one of its Indonesian suppliers. It showed that the worker was paid at the rate of $1.03 per day which was reportedly less than the Indonesian government's figure for "minimum physical need."[18]

Immiserization Thesis

Former Labor Secretary Robert Reich has proposed as a test of the fairness of development policies that "Low-wage workers should become better off, not worse off, as trade and investment boost national income." He has written that "[i]f a country pursues policies that . . . limit to a narrow elite the benefits of trade, the promise of open commerce is perverted and drained of its rationale."[19] A key claim of the activists is that companies actually impoverish or immiserize developing country workers. They experience an absolute decline in living standards. This thesis follows from the claim that the bidding war among developing countries is depressing wages. . . .

Widening Gap Between Rich and Poor

A related charge is that international sweatshops are contributing to the increasing gap between rich and poor. Not only are the poor being absolutely impoverished, but trade is generating greater inequality within developing countries. Another test that Reich has proposed to establish the fairness of international trade is that "the gap between rich and poor should tend to narrow with development, not widen."[20] Critics charge that international sweatshops flunk that test. They say that the increasing GNPs of some developing countries simply mask a widening gap between rich and poor. "Across the world, both local and foreign elites are getting richer from the exploitation of the most vulnerable."[21] And, "The major adverse consequence of quickening global economic integration has been widening income disparity within almost all nations. . . ."[22] There appears to be a tacit alliance between the elites of both first and third worlds to exploit the most vulnerable, to regiment and control and conscript them so that they can create the material conditions for the elites' extravagant lifestyles.

Collusion with Repressive Regimes

Critics charge that, in their zeal to make their countries safe for foreign investment, Third World regimes, notably China and Indonesia, have stepped up their repression. Not only have these countries failed to enforce even the minimal labor rules on the books, but they have also used their military and police to break strikes and repress independent unions. They have stifled political dissent, both to retain their hold on political power and to avoid any instability that might scare off foreign investors. Consequently, critics charge, companies like Nike are profiting from political repression. "As unions spread in [Korea and Taiwan], Nike shifted its suppliers primarily to Indonesia, China and Thailand, where they could depend on governments to suppress independent union-organizing efforts."[23]

EVALUATION OF THE CHARGES AGAINST INTERNATIONAL SWEATSHOPS

The critics' charges are undoubtedly accurate on a number of points: (1) There is no doubt that international companies are chasing cheap labor. (2) The wages paid by the international sweatshops are—by American standards—shockingly low. (3) Some developing country governments have tightly controlled or repressed organized labor in order to prevent it from disturbing the flow of foreign investment. Thus, in Indonesia, independent unions have been suppressed. (4) It is not unusual in developing countries for minimum wage levels to be lower than the official poverty level. (5) Developing country governments have winked at violations of minimum wage laws and labor rules. However, most jobs are in the informal sector and so largely outside the scope of government supervision. (6) Some suppliers have employed children or have subcontracted work to other producers who have done so. (7) Some developing country governments deny their people basic political rights. China is the obvious example; Indonesia's record is pretty horrible but had shown steady improvement until the last two years. But on many of the other counts, the critics' charges appear to be seriously inaccurate. And, even where the charges are accurate, it is not self-evident that the practices in question are improper or unethical, as we see next.

Wages and Conditions

Even the critics of international sweatshops do not dispute that the wages they pay are generally higher than—or at least equal to—comparable wages in the labor markets where they operate. According to the International Labor Organization (ILO), multinational companies often apply standards relating to wages, benefits, conditions of work, and occupational safety and health, which both exceed statutory requirements and those practiced by local firms."[24] The ILO also says that wages and working conditions in so-called Export Processing Zones (EPZs) are often equal to or higher than jobs outside. The World Bank says that the poorest workers in developing countries work in the informal sector where they often earn less than half what a formal sector employee earns. Moreover, "informal and rural workers often must work under more hazardous and insecure conditions than their formal sector counterparts.[25]

The same appears to hold true for the international sweatshops. In 1996, young women working in the plant of a Nike supplier in Serang, Indonesia, were earning the Indonesian legal minimum wage of 5,200 rupiahs or about $2.28 each day. As a report in the *Washington Post* pointed out, just earning the minimum wage put these workers among higher-paid Indonesians: "In Indonesia, less than half the working population earns the minimum wage, since about half of all adults here are in farming, and the typical farmer would make only about 2,000 rupiahs each day."[26] The workers in the Serang plant reported that they save about three-quarters of their pay. A 17-year-old woman said: "I came here one year ago from central Java. I'm making more money than my father makes." This woman also said that she sent about 75 percent of her earnings back to her family on the farm.[27] Also in 1996, a Nike spokeswoman estimated that an entry-level factory worker in the plant of a Nike supplier made five times what a farmer makes.[28] Nike's chairman. Phil Knight, likes to teasingly remind critics that the average worker in one of Nike's Chinese factories is paid more than a professor at Beijing University.[29] There is also plentiful anecdotal evidence from non-Nike sources. A worker at the Taiwanese-owned King Star Garment Assembly plant in Honduras told a reporter that he was earning seven times what he earned in the country-side.[30] In Bangladesh, the country's fledgling garment industry was paying women who had never worked before between $40 and $55 a month in 1991. That compared with a national per capita income of about $200 and the approximately $1 a day earned by many of these women's husbands as day laborers or rickshaw drivers.[31]

The same news reports also shed some light on the working conditions in sweatshops. According to the *Washington Post*, in 1994 the Indonesian office of the international accounting firm Ernst and Young surveyed Nike workers concerning worker pay, safety conditions and attitudes toward the job. The auditors pulled workers off the assembly line at random and asked them questions that the workers answered anonymously. The survey of 25 workers at Nike's Serang plant found that 23 thought the hours and over-time worked were fair, and two thought the overtime hours too high. None of the workers reported that they had been discriminated against. Thirteen said the working environment was the key reason they worked at the Serang plant while eight cited salary and benefits.[32] The *Post* report also noted that the Serang plant closes for about ten days each year for Muslim holidays. It quoted Nike officials and the plant's Taiwanese owners as saying that 94 percent of the workers had returned to the plant following the most recent break. . . .

There is also the mute testimony of the lines of job applicants outside the sweatshops in Guatemala and Honduras. According to Lucy Martinez-Mont, in Guatemala the sweatshops are conspicuous for the long lines of young people waiting to be interviewed for a job.[33] Outside the gates of the industrial park in Honduras that Rohter visited "anxious onlookers are always waiting, hoping for a chance at least to fill out a job application [for employment at one of the apparel plants]."[34]

The critics of sweatshops acknowledge that workers have voluntarily taken their jobs, consider themselves lucky to have them, and want to keep them. . . . But they go on to discount the workers' views as the product of confusion or ignorance, and/or they just argue that the workers' views are beside the point. Thus, while "it is undoubtedly true" that Nike has given jobs to thousands of people who wouldn't be working otherwise, they say that "neatly skirts the fundamental human-rights issue raised by these production arrangements that are now spreading all across the world."[35] Similarly the NLC's Kernaghan says that "[w]hether workers think they are better off in the assembly plants than elsewhere is not the real issue."[36] Kernaghan, and Jeff Ballinger of the AFL-CIO, concede that the workers desperately need these jobs. But "[t]hey say they're not asking that U.S. companies stop operating in these countries. They're asking that workers be paid a living wage and treated like human beings."[37] Apparently these workers are victims of what Marx called false consciousness, or else they would grasp that they are being exploited. According to Barnet and Cavanagh, "For many workers . . . exploitation is not a concept easily comprehended because the alternative prospects for earning a living are so bleak.[38]

Immiserization and Inequality

The critics' claim that the countries that host international sweatshops are marked by growing poverty and inequality is flatly contradicted by the record. In fact, many of those countries have experienced sharp increases in living standards—for all strata of society. In trying to attract investment in simple manufacturing, Malaysia and Indonesia and, now, Vietnam and China, are retracing the industrialization path already successfully taken by East Asian countries like Taiwan, Korea, Singapore, and Hong Kong. These four countries got their start by producing labor-intensive manufactured goods (often electrical and electronic components, shoes, and garments) for export markets. Over time they graduated to the export of higher value-added items that are skill-intensive and require a relatively developed industrial base.[39]

As is well known, these East Asian countries achieved growth rates exceeding eight percent for a quarter century. . . . The workers in these economies were not impoverished by growth. The benefits of growth were widely diffused: These economies achieved essentially full employment in the 1960s. Real wages rose by as much as a factor of four. Absolute poverty fell. And income inequality remained at low to moderate levels. It is true that in the initial stages the rapid growth generated only moderate increases in wages. But once essentially full employment was reached, and what economists call the Fei-Ranis turning point was reached, the increased demand for labor resulted in the bidding up of wages as firms competed for a scarce labor supply.

Interestingly, given its historic mission as a watchdog for international labor standards, the ILO has embraced this development model. It recently noted that the most successful developing economies, in terms of output and employment growth, have been "those who best exploited emerging opportunities in the global economy."[40] An "export-oriented policy is vital in countries that are starting on the industrialization path and have large surpluses of cheap labour." Countries which have succeeded in attracting foreign direct investment (FDI) have experienced rapid growth in manufacturing output and exports. The successful attraction of foreign investment in plant and equipment "can be a powerful spur to rapid industrialization and employment creation." "At low levels of industrialization, FDI in garments and shoes and some types of consumer electronics can be very useful for creating employment and opening the economy to international markets; there may be some entrepreneurial skills created in simple activities like garments (as has happened in Bangladesh). Moreover, in some cases, such as Malaysia, the investors may strike deeper roots and invest in more capital-intensive technologies as wages rise."

According to the World Bank, the rapidly growing Asian economies (including Indonesia) "have also been unusually successful at sharing the fruits of their growth."[41] In fact, while inequality in the West has been growing, it has been shrinking in the Asian economies. They are the only economies in the world to have experienced high growth *and* declining inequality, and they also show shrinking gender gaps in education. . . .

Profiting from Repression?

What about the charge that international sweatshops are profiting from repression? It is undeniable that there is repression in many of the countries where sweatshops are located. But economic development appears to be relaxing that repression rather than strengthening its grip. The companies are supposed to benefit from government policies (e.g., repression of unions) that hold down labor costs. However, as we have seen, the wages paid by the international sweatshops already match or exceed the prevailing local wages. Not only that, but incomes in the East Asian economies, and in Indonesia, have risen rapidly. . . .

The critics, however, are right in saying that the Indonesian government has opposed independent unions in the sweatshops out of fear they would lead to higher wages and labor unrest. But the government's fear clearly is that unions might drive wages in the modern industrial sector *above* market-clearing levels—or, more exactly, further above market. It is ironic that critics like Barnet and Cavanagh would use the Marxian term "reserve army of the unemployed." According to Marx, capitalists deliberately maintain high levels of unemployment in order to control the working class. But the Indonesian government's policies (e.g., suppression of unions, resistance to a higher minimum wage and lax enforcement of labor rules) have been directed at achieving exactly the opposite result. The government appears to have calculated that high unemployment is a greater threat to its hold on power. I think we can safely take at face value its claims that its policies are genuinely intended to help the economy create jobs to absorb the massive numbers of unemployed and underemployed.[42]

LABOR STANDARDS IN INTERNATIONAL SWEATSHOPS: PAINFUL TRADEOFFS

Who but the Grinch could grudge paying a few additional pennies to some of the world's poorest workers? There is no doubt that the rhetorical force of the critics' case against international sweatshops rests on this apparently self-evident proposition. However, higher wages and improved labor standards are not free. After all, the critics themselves attack companies for chasing cheap labor. It follows that, if labor in developing countries is made more expensive (say, as the result of pressure by the critics), then those countries will receive less foreign investment, and fewer jobs will be created there. Imposing higher wages may deprive these countries of the one comparative advantage they enjoy, namely low-cost labor.

We have seen that workers in most "international sweatshops" are already relatively well paid. Workers in the urban, formal sectors of developing countries commonly earn more than twice what informal and rural workers get. Simply earning the minimum wage put the young women making Nike shoes in Serang in the top half of the income distribution in Indonesia. Accordingly, the critics are in effect calling for a *widening* of the economic disparity that already greatly favors sweatshop workers.

By itself that may or may not be ethically objectionable. But these higher wages come at the expense of the incomes and the job opportunities of much poorer workers. As economists explain, higher wages in the formal sector reduce employment there and (by increasing the supply of labor) depress incomes in the informal sector. The case against requiring above-market wages for international sweatshop workers is essentially the same as the case against other measures that artificially raise labor costs, like the minimum wage. In Jagdish Bhagwati's words: "Requiring a minimum wage in an overpopulated, developing country, as is done in a developed country, may actually be morally wicked. A minimum wage might help the unionized, industrial proletariat, while limiting the ability to save and invest rapidly which is necessary to draw more of the unemployed and nonunionized rural poor into gainful employment and income."[43] The World Bank makes the same point: "Minimum wages may help the most poverty-stricken-workers in industrial countries, but they clearly do not in developing nations. The workers whom minimum wage legislation tries to protect—urban formal workers—already earn much more than the less favored majority. . . . And inasmuch as minimum wage and other regulations discourage formal employment by increasing wage and nonwage costs, they hurt the poor who aspire to formal employment."[44]

The story is no different when it comes to labor standards other than wages. If standards are set too high they will hurt investment and employment. The World Bank report points out that "[r]educing hazards in the workplace is costly, and typically the greater the reduction the more it costs. Moreover, the costs of compliance often fall largely on employees through lower wages or reduced employment. As a result, setting standards too high can actually lower workers' welfare. . . ."[45] Perversely, if the higher standards advocated by critics retard the growth of formal sector jobs, then that will trap more informal and rural workers in jobs which are far more hazardous and insecure than those of their formal sector counterparts.

The critics consistently advocate policies that will benefit better-off workers at the expense of worse-off ones. If it were within their power, it appears that they would reinvent the labor markets of much of Latin America. Alejandro Portes' description seems to be on the mark: "In Mexico, Brazil, Peru, and other Third World countries, [unlike East Asia], there are powerful independent unions representing the protected sector of the working class. Although there rhetoric is populist and even radical, the fact is that they tend to represent the better-paid and more stable fraction of the working class. Alongside, there toils a vast, unprotected proletariat, employed by informal enterprises and linked, in ways hidden from public view, with modern sector firms." . . .

Of course, it might be objected that trading of workers' rights for more jobs is unethical. But, so far as I can determine, the critics have not made this argument. Although they sometimes implicitly accept the existence of the trade-off (we saw that they attack Nike for chasing cheap labor), their public statements are silent on the lost or forgone jobs from higher wages and better labor standards. At other times, they imply or claim that improvements in workers' wages and conditions are essentially free. . . .

In summary, the result of the ostensibly humanitarian changes urged by critics are likely to be (1) reduced employment in the formal or modern sector of the economy, (2) lower incomes in the informal sector, (3) less investment and so slower economic growth. (4) reduced exports, (5) greater inequality and poverty.

CONCLUSION: THE CASE FOR NOT EXCEEDING MARKET STANDARDS

It is part of the job description of business ethicists to exhort companies to treat their workers better (otherwise what purpose do they serve?). So it will have come as no surprise that both the business ethicists whose views I summarized at the beginning of this paper—Thomas Donaldson and Richard DeGeorge—objected to letting the market alone determine wages and labor standards in multinational companies. Both of them proposed criteria for setting wages that might occasionally "improve" on the outcomes of the market.

Their reasons for rejecting market determination of wages were similar. They both cited conditions that allegedly prevent international markets from generating ethically acceptable results. Donaldson argued that neoclassical economic principles are not applicable to international business because of high unemployment rates in developing countries. And DeGeorge argued that, in an unregulated international market, the gross inequality of bargaining power between workers and companies would lead to exploitation.

But this paper has shown that attempts to improve on market outcomes may have unforeseen tragic consequences. We saw how raising the wages of workers in international sweatshops might wind up penalizing the most vulnerable workers (those in the informal sectors of developing countries) by depressing their wages and reducing their job opportunities in the formal sector. Donaldson

and DeGeorge cited high unemployment and unequal bargaining power as conditions that made it necessary to bypass or override the market determination of wages. However, in both cases, bypassing the market in order to prevent exploitation may aggravate these conditions. As we have seen, above-market wages paid to sweatshop workers may discourage further investment and so perpetuate high unemployment. In turn, the higher unemployment may weaken the bargaining power of workers vis-à-vis employers. Thus such market imperfections seem to call for more reliance on market forces rather than less. Likewise, the experience of the newly industrialized East Asian economies suggests that the best cure for the ills of sweatshops is more sweatshops. But most of the well-intentioned policies that improve on market outcomes are likely to have the opposite effect.

Where does this leave the international manager? If the preceding analysis is correct, then it follows that it is ethically acceptable to pay market wage rates in developing countries (and to provide employment conditions appropriate for the level of development). That holds true even if the wages pay less than so-called living wages or subsistence or even (conceivably) the local minimum wage. The appropriate test is not whether the wage reaches some predetermined standard but whether it is freely accepted by (reasonably) informed workers. The workers themselves are in the best position to judge whether the wages offered are superior to their next-best alternatives. (The same logic applies *mutatis mutandis* to workplace labor standards).

Indeed, not only is it ethically acceptable for a company to pay market wages, but it may be ethically unacceptable for it to pay wages that exceed market levels. That will be the case if the company's above-market wages set precedents for other international companies which raise labor costs to the point of discouraging foreign investment. Furthermore, companies may have a social responsibility to transcend their own narrow preoccupation with protecting their brand image and to publicly defend a system which has greatly improved the lot of millions of workers in developing countries.

NOTES

1. Steven Greenhouse, "A Crusader Makes Celebrities Tremble," *New York Times* (June 18, 1996), p. B4.

2. Lance A. Compa and Tashia Hinchliffe Darricarrere, "Enforcement Through Corporate Codes of Conduct," in Compa and Stephen F. Diamond, *Human Rights, Labor Rights, and International Trade* (Philadelphia: University of Pennsylvania Press. 1996), p. 193.

3. Peter Jacobi in Martha Nichols, "Third-World Families at Work: Child Labor or Child Care," *Harvard Business Review* (Jan-Feb., 1993).

4. David Sampson in Robin G. Civhan, "A Stain on Fashion: The Garment Industry Profits from Cheap Labor," *Washington Post* (September 12, 1995), p. Bl.

5. Thomas Donaldson, *Ethics of International Business* (New York: Oxford University Press, 1989), p. 98.

6. Richard DeGeorge, *Competing with Integrity in International Business* (New York: Oxford University Press, 1993), p. 79.

7. Ibid., pp. 356–7.

8. Ibid., p. 78.

9. World Bank, *World Development Report 1995, "Workers in an Integrating World Economy"* (Oxford University Press, 1995), p. 77.

10. Donaldson, *Ethics of International Business,* p. 115.

11. Ibid., p. 150.

12. DeGeorge, *Competing with Integrity,* p. 48.

13. Ibid., p. 358.

14. Ibid.

15. Terry Collingsworth, J. William Goold, and Pharis J. Harvey, "Time for a Global New Deal," *Foreign Affairs* (Jan-Feb., 1994), p. 8.

16. William B. Falk, "Dirty Little Secrets," *Newsday* (June 16, 1996).

17. Tim Smith, "The Power of Business for Human Rights," *Business & Society Review* (January 1994), p. 36.

18. Jeffrey Ballinger, The New Free Trade Heel." *Harper's Magazine* (August, 1992), pp. 46–7. "As in many developing countries, Indonesia's minimum wage . . . is less than poverty level." Nina Baker, "The Hidden Hands of Nike," *Ortgonian* (August 9. 1992).

19. Robert B. Reich, "Escape from the Global Sweatshop; Capitalism's Stake in Uniting the Workers of the World," *Washington Post* (May 22.1994). Reich's test is intended to apply in developing countries "where democratic institutions are weak or absent."

20. Ibid.

21. Kenneth P. Hutchinson, "Third World Growth," *Harvard Business Review* (Nov.–Dec., 1994).

22. Robin Broad and John Cavanaugh, "Don't Neglect the Impoverished South," *Foreign Affairs* (December 22, 1995).

23. John Cavanagh and Robin Broad, "Global Reach; Workers Fight the Multinationals," *The Nation* (March 18, 1996), p. 21. See also Bob Herbert, "Nike's Bad Neighborhood," *New York Times* (June 14, 1996).

24. International Labor Organization, *World Employment 1995* (Geneva: ILO. 1995), p. 73.

25. World Bank, *Workers in an Integrating World Economy,* p. 5.

26. Keith B. Richburg, and Anne Swardson, "U.S. Industry Overseas: Sweatshop or Job Source?: Indonesians Praise Work at Nike Factory," *Washington Post* (July 28, 1996).

27. Richburg and Swardson, "Sweatshop or Job Source?" The 17-year-old was interviewed in the presence of managers. For other reports that workers remit home large parts of their earnings see Seth Mydans, "Tangerang Journal; For Indonesian Workers at Nike Plant: Just Do It," *New York Times* (August 9, 1996), and Nina Baker, "The Hidden Hands of Nike."

28. Donna Gibbs, Nike spokeswoman on ABC's *World News Tonight,* June 6, 1996.

29. Mark Clifford, "Trading in Social Issues: Labor Policy and International Trade Regulation," *World Press Review* (June 1994), p. 36.

30. Larry Rohter, "To U.S. Critics, a Sweatshop; for Hondurans, a Better Life," *New York Times* (July 18, 1996).

31. Marcus Brauchli, "Garment Industry Booms in Bangladesh," *Wall Street Journal* (August 6, 1991).

32. Richburg and Swardson, "Sweatshop or Job Source?"

33. Lucy Martinez-Mont, "Sweatshops Are Better Than No Shops," *Wall Street Journal* (June 25, 1996).

34. Rohter, "To U.S. Critics a Sweatshop."

35. Barnet and Cavanagh, *Global Dreams,* p. 326.

36. Rohter, "To U.S. Critics a Sweatshop."

37. William B. Falk, "Dirty Little Secrets," *Newsday* (June 16, 1996).

38. Barnet and Cavanagh, "Just Undo It: Nike's Exploited Workers," *New York Times* (February 13, 1994).

39. Sarosh Kuruvilla, "Linkages Between Industrialization Strategies and Industrial Relations/Human Resources Policies: Singapore, Malaysia, The Philippines, and India," *Industrial & Labor Relations Review* (July 1996), p. 637.

40. The ILO's Constitution (of 1919) mentions that: ". . . the failure of any nation to adopt humane conditions of labour is an obstacle in the way of other nations which desire to improve the conditions in their own countries." ILO, *World Employment 1995*, p. 74.

41. World Bank, *The East Asian Miracle* (New York: Oxford University Press. 1993), p. 2.

42. Gideon Rachman, "Wealth in Its Grasp, a Survey of Indonesia," *Economist* (April 17, 1993), pp. 14–15.

43. Jagdish Bhagwati and Robert F. Hudec, eds. *Fair Trade and Harmonization* (Cambridge: MIT Press, 1996), vol. 1, p. 2.

44. World Bank, *Working in an Integrating World Economy*, p. 75.

45. Ibid., p. 77. As I have noted, the report proposes that the "appropriate level is therefore that at which the costs are commensurate with the value that informed workers place on improved working conditions and reduced risk. . . ." (p. 77).

Case Study

Big Blue in Argentina

The High Technology of Corruption

Miguel Alzola (Rutgers University)

"Este tipo (Cattáneo) me dijo: mirá, el proyecto que va a salir es éste y hay dos millones y medio de dólares para vos. No necesitamos nada, simplemente que dejes de joder con el otro proyecto. Y ahí me quebré. Por primera vez en mi vida hice algo de lo que me arrepentiría al otro día. Pero ya era tarde."[1]

ALFREDO ALDACO (FORMER BANCO NACIÓN DIRECTOR),
BUENOS AIRES NEWSPAPER, PÁGINA 12, MAY 7, 1998.

ARGENTINA AND IBM: AN ENDURING RELATIONSHIP

Argentina is the world's eighth largest country, occupying an area more extensive than Mexico and Texas combined. Achieving its independence from Spain in 1816, Argentina was governed for much of the 20th century by alternating military and civilian administrations. In 1989, Carlos Menem, a candidate from the populist Peronist Party, was elected president. President Menem adopted comprehensive market-based policies, dismantling protectionist barriers and business regulations, and implementing a privatization program conforming to International Monetary Fund (IMF) and World Bank (WB) advice.

These reforms contributed to significant increases in investment and growth through most of the 1990s. But some years after the end of Menem's term, the combination of fixed-rate convertibility and high fiscal deficits proved unsustainable. Despite massive loan support from the IMF, these policies were abandoned in 2002, with disastrous effects on the Argentine economy.

During his tenure as President, Menem repeatedly claimed that, through the privatization of large numbers of state enterprises, corruption was being reduced by his administration. Economists and corruption specialists supported that diagnosis.[2] Nonetheless, the media, several NGOs and business executives said strong pressure remained to pay bribes to

---

land government contracts. As of the mid-1990s, 71 Menem government officials, including ministers, governors, and cabinet secretaries, were accused in the courts of acts of corruption. None was convicted by the partisan, Menem-appointed judiciary, but they were convicted after Menem left power.

International Business Machines Corporation (IBM) is a multinational computer technology corporation headquartered in Armonk, New York. Known colloquially as Big Blue, the company was founded in 1888, incorporated in 1911, and listed on the New York Stock Exchange in 1916. Latin America has been an important market for IBM, accounting for $6 billion of the company's $72 billion revenues in the middle 1990s.[3] Argentina, Brazil, and Mexico represented the bulk of IBM's Latin America business. Big Blue has been in Argentina for 75 years. Though Unisys, Hewlett-Packard and Sun Microsystems had a growing presence, IBM was the main supplier of the mainframe and midrange computers that Argentine businesses both large and small relied on to meet their computing needs.

BIG BLUE, BIG CONTRACTS, BIG BRIBES

Since its founding in 1891, the state-owned Banco Nación (assets: $11 billion) has been the leading lender in Argentina. By the middle 1990s, however, Banco Nación was technologically antiquated, with relatively few computers and a poor communications system. Of its 525 branches, only 30 were wired to the head office.

In 1994, Banco Nación's board of directors awarded IBM Argentina a $250 million contract to build a modern technological infrastructure for the bank—from revamping its telephone systems to training its 12,000 employees to use computers. IBM hired Dallas-based Hogan Systems Inc. to develop an all-encompassing software program for Banco Nación. In addition, IBM sub-contracted some of the work to *Consultores Argentines para el Desarrollo SA* (CONSAD), an Argentine information-services consulting company.

Oddly, IBM signed the subcontract with CONSAD's president in 1994—even though the president had died in 1991. CONSAD, through related company "Capacitación y Computación Rural S.A" (CCR), charged IBM $37 million for a computer back-up system that was never required by Banco Nación.

Suspicions of corruption were raised in 1994 by the Argentine tax authority, the Dirección General Impositiva (DGI), which identified a pizza-parlor waitress, a rugby coach and the dead man among the supposed payees of very large checks issued by CCR. The waitress denied ever having received any money from CCR. The dead man was predictably unable to cash the $760,000 check that the company said it had written him. A simple case of suspected tax evasion became more newsworthy when it was discovered that the $37 million were paid to CCR by IBM Argentina. IBM said it had paid $21 million to CCR but declared that it had received nothing in return for those payments. Prosecutors alleged that some of this money was used to pay bribes to government officials. Subsequent investigations found that some $8 million ended up in a numbered account at the Geneva branch of Bank Brussels Lambert, while the remainder was spread among various accounts in Argentina, Uruguay and the USA.

Why did IBM subcontract CONSAD and CCR? CONSAD and CCR offered such a mix of competent software engineers and top political connections that they became valued partners to Big Blue in Argentina. They were subcontractors on virtually every major government contract won by IBM after President Menem was elected in 1989. By contrast, CONSAD was less valuable to IBM in the private sector: IBM used CONSAD for only one major private-sector job during that same period.

Ricardo Martorana, President of IBM Argentina, acknowledged that IBM formed a strong business alliance with CONSAD during the Menem era, but argued that it was due to CONSAD's technical skill in developing software programs, not because of the political skills of Juan Carlos Cattàneo in opening doors to government contracts. Mr. Cattàneo was a 46 year-old political operative, fund-raiser, and later deputy chief of staff for President Menem. His brother, Marcelo Cattàneo, was director of CONSAD and had strong ties to CCR. The Cattàneos had close relationships with Gustavo Soriani, IBM Argentina's vice president in charge of sales. Information industry executives said the IBM-CONSAD alliance became so powerful that competitors often refused to bid on government contracts. "There was a point, maybe two or three years ago, where companies decided it was a waste of time to go against them," said Hugo Strachan, president of Hewlett-Packard Argentina in 1995.[4]

JUDICIAL INVESTIGATIONS, PUBLIC DISCLOSURE AND VENDETTA

Eventually, the United States Federal Bureau of Investigation and the Securities and Exchange Commission began an inquiry into IBM's possible involvement in a bribery scandal that could violate the Foreign Corrupt Practices Act.[5] In Argentina, Federal Judge Adolfo Bagnasco charged a total of thirty people, including IBM officials, employees of the international accounting and consulting firm Deloitte & Touche, and the former president and entire board of Banco Nación with defrauding the state. The judge found that the deal was riddled with irregularities related to the amount of the contract and the

$37 million bribe that IBM Argentina agreed to pay to CCR. Judge Bagnasco commissioned a study by University of Buenos Aires engineers, who found the cost of the Banco Nación contract should have been $129 million (as opposed to the contracted-for $250 million). That amount corresponded with independent estimates offered by executives at two multinational computer companies in Argentina. A report by the Buenos Aires newspaper *Clarin* claimed the deal's price was 53 times higher than a similar contract IBM signed with Banco Rio, a private Argentine bank, when prices were compared on a per-branch basis. "We don't know if IBM added the extra $120 million as a profit margin or a contingency cost," the judge said.[6]

Some of the alleged bribe money crossed the Atlantic several times on its way to the recipients. Judge Bagnasco won the cooperation of Switzerland, Luxembourg and Uruguay banking authorities, allowing him to uncover Swiss bank accounts in the names of two former Banco Nación directors.[7] Both men admitted receiving money from IBM and named Marcelo Cattaneo as the man who had paid them. One of them admitted receiving $1.5 million from IBM but declined to call that payment a bribe. Rather, he said, it was "an acknowledgment I understood it was a way of participating in IBM's happiness."[8]

Public disclosure of the irregular payments in July 1995 resulted, first, in a scramble of denials, and then in a wave of resignations which reached the highest levels of the Menem administration and IBM Argentina. Corporate parent IBM denied any link to the alleged bribes. The president of Banco Nación reportedly denied that the bank had accepted bribes from IBM. However, one month later he resigned, along with three directors. The contract was canceled in 1995, after allegations about it surfaced in the press. The scandal led also to the resignation of Juan Carlos Cattàneo, Menem's deputy chief of staff. In September

1995—i.e., fifteen months after local tax authorities first raised questions on the Banco Nación contract—the US headquarters told IBM Argentina President Ricardo Martorana and deputy Javier Orcoyen to resign or be fired, and COO Gustavo Soriani was fired outright.

Santiago Pinetta, the Argentine journalist who uncovered the IBM bribery case, told reporters that an unknown individual had warned him in two phone calls to his home to stop investigating the bank's activities. The next day, in September 1995, he was hit by a taxi while crossing the street. Police said it was an accident. Nevertheless, in 1996, the attackers were more explicit: Pinetta was beaten by two men and two women outside his home. "They beat me and robbed me and marked me with a knife—I want people to see it,[9] the journalist told reporters. His face was bruised and bloody and his chest slashed 20 times and marked with the letters I-B-M.

In October 1998, CONSAD director Marcelo Cattáneo was found dead, hanging by the neck from a radio antenna in a lonely spot alongside the River Plate. The 41-year-old businessman was wearing sunglasses, a cheap blue jogging suit and trainers—none of which his family had ever seen before. Although there were no marks of violence on the body, neatly folded into eight and placed under the dead man's tongue was a newspaper cutting reporting his own disappearance a few days before[10]—all earmarks of a Mafia message. In testimony before the investigating federal judge investigating, two former Banco Nación directors had acknowledged that Cattáneo had funneled $21 million in cash to Swiss bank accounts bearing their names.

BIG BLUE RESPONDS

To deal with the rising tide of legal challenges, IBM organized a team of accountants, lawyers and public relations executives. Big Blue's strategy was threefold. First, the company denied all charges of corruption, claimed that there was no evidence of illegal payments, and argued that IBM had legitimately won the Banco Nación contract because it offered the best deal. Second, the US headquarters conducted an internal investigation, which turned up a failure to abide by internal controls. On the basis of this finding, the parent company fired the IBM Argentina executives who were indicted by Judge Bagnasco. Third, the company attempted to settle the cases for corruption out of court and did not cooperate with the judicial investigations regarding the links between IBM Argentina and the US and Latin America headquarters.

The IBM investigation, conducted by a team sent from the US, found evidence of a breakdown in management controls, but ruled out any illegal activity. "If you're asking me were bribes paid by IBM officials to win the Nación contract, the answer is No," said Fred McNeese, director of international public relations, in an initial statement. "It is our position that IBM won the contract because it was the most qualified company."[11] However, officials admitted that the contracts involving CONSAD and CCR, were "highly unusual" because $21 million was paid in advance for a back-up service that, in the event, was never required. And the contracts were described as the product of "a grave and unacceptable management decision" by Wilmer Guecaimburu, the then-newly appointed head of IBM Argentina. The company suspended its contracts with CCR and CONSAD. Eventually, IBM attempted to renegotiate the Banco Nación contract with a view to lowering the price, but the Argentine bank decided to terminate the contract and asked for compensation.

IBM said that US headquarters had been misled by its Argentine unit. McNeese insisted that IBM's US executives knew nothing of the subcontract with CCR The company fired or forced the resignation of the top three executives of IBM Argentina, but only after confirmation that IBM Argentina President Ricardo Martorana and chief of operations Gustavo Soriani had been indicted. IBM's Argentine spokesman was confident that its swift action in sacking three executives, including the president of IBM Argentina, would help ensure that the company escaped the insinuations of bribery. "In the long run, this will not damage the image of IBM in Argentina, gained through 72 years of impeccable ethics."[12]

THE BLAME GAME: CORPORATE EVIL AND INDIVIDUAL SCAPEGOATS

But Martorana and Soriani told a different story about the involvement of the US headquarters in the transaction. Soriani, who was one of the most respected executives in Argentina, said he was a scapegoat, set up by top IBM managers, who initially approved the subcontractor payments but later, when the judicial investigations started, said they knew nothing of them. "IBM totally distorted my role. They unfairly singled me out as the villain in this case and ruined my name."[13] He declared that the firm had made him a sacrificial lamb because it could be found in violation of the Foreign Corrupt Practices Act. Regarding the backup system, he said that it should not have come as a surprise to IBM because it was clearly noted in the original contract, which was approved by Steve Lew, the manager for systems integration at IBM Latin America, who reviews the technical details of all contracts. Yet IBM spokesman McNeese said that no one in IBM Latin America headquarters was informed orally or by written document that any money would be paid to CCR. Soriani argued that IBM was not telling the truth and trying to blame a few individuals to avoid prosecution.

Weeks before the scandal, Martorana had been praised publicly by IBM Chairman Louis Gerstner Jr. Nevertheless, after he was indicted by Judge Bagnasco he was fired. Martorana declared that "Steve Lew had more power than me to decide the implementation of the contract because he was sent by the US headquarters to supervise the transaction. Hence, IBM US had complete knowledge of the deal, not just about the technical details."[14] None of the senior executives of IBM's Latin American division was held responsible by the company. Peter Rowley, the executive to whom Martorana reported, was promoted to a new position in Europe, only days after the sackings in Buenos Aires.

In June 1996, Banco Nación cancelled the contract and demanded that IBM refund $85 million that was paid on the contract and asked for penalties. Big Blue fired back, suing the bank in July for more than $86 million and alleging "wrongful revocation" of the contract. In August 1996, Banco Nación countersued for $174 million. Although it admitted errors, IBM denied any malicious intent. In an out-of-court settlement, IBM returned half of the $85 million that so far had been paid. In addition, in 2000, IBM agreed to pay a $300,000 fine when the US Securities and Exchange Commission alleged that the company had failed to report the bribes to its own investors.

In spite of the IBM claim that its US headquarters were unaware of the dirty dealings, Judge Bagnasco was determined to find out whether IBM's head office and other IBM officials were involved. He sought extradition from the US for two former IBM officials in an effort to prove that the company's US headquarters knew about the bribes: Steve Lew, who allegedly oversaw some of the technical aspects of the contract, and Peter Rowley, chief marketing executive for Latin America. Bagnasco also sought extradition from Brazil for Robeli Libero, retired IBM

Latin America general manager, and Marcio Kaiser, formerly in charge of outsourcing.

IBM insisted that headquarters knew nothing of the subcontract's fraudulent details. The company declared that Judge Bagnasco's investigation did not produce evidence that the US and Latin America headquarters had been aware of any misuse of funds stemming from the contract or any other wrongdoing. Although Bagnasco won the cooperation of the Swiss, Luxembourg and Uruguay banking authorities, he obtained similar cooperation from neither the US headquarters nor the US government to extradite the IBM officials. The White House sent mixed messages to Buenos Aires, vacillating between condemning corruption in Latin America and defending US trade interests in the region.

CORRUPT CORPORATE CULTURE: MORE EVIDENCE

Martorana and Soriani were not the only rotten apples in the barrel. Nor was Argentina the only venue for dirty IBM deals. Besides the Banco Nación's contract, Argentine prosecutors began judicial investigations into data-processing contracts worth $513 million between IBM and Argentina's tax authority, DGI, after allegations that the two contracts, signed in 1994, were overpriced and were awarded in disregard of standard government procedures. The investigators also looked into a $28 million software deal that IBM had made with a state social services office, a $30 million contract with the western province of Mendoza, a $28.7 million deal for the computerization of a bank in the northeastern province of Santa Fe, and IBM contracts for $2.5 million with the municipalities of Lomas de Zamora and Avellaneda in the province of Buenos Aires. Argentine Defense Minister Jorge Dominguez was convicted of fraud for acts committed as Mayor of Buenos Aires in

January 1995, when he illegally negotiated and signed a $40 million deal with IBM to integrate its computer systems with a program that was ill-suited to the municipality's needs.

But tainted contracts were awarded to IBM not only by Argentine officials. Although IBM officially maintained that its US and Latin American headquarters did not know the details about the bribes, in June 1998 the authorities in Mexico issued arrest warrants against three senior IBM executives and 19 Mexico City officials charged with conspiracy in an unlawful bidding process in the award of a contract to supply a computer system for the city's prosecutors. The Mexican unit of IBM sought to have the charges thrown out, but when a judge ordered the three executives to face trial, IBM's general manager in Mexico signed a legal agreement and paid Mexico City $37.5 million in cash and new computer products to resolve the dispute. The agreement appeared to be an admission by IBM Mexico that its executives had acted inappropriately. John Reilly, an IBM spokesman for Latin America, said that the agreement reached with city officials resolved the civil dispute and underlined the company's "commitment to customer satisfaction." As in the Argentine case, he insisted that the executives had not been guilty of any wrongdoing. However, Rogelio Ramirez de la O, a prominent consultant to foreign businesses in Mexico, said that "IBM could never have been forced to give up so much unless the government had proved its accusations. This agreement makes clear that IBM's dealings here were a flop if not completely fraudulent."[15]

IBM said it would no longer bid for government contracts in Latin American countries in which it would be the sole bidder. But IBM bribery scandals were not limited to Latin America. In 2004, some 48 South Korean government officials and corporate executives, mainly from IBM ventures, were charged with bribery in a case involving state contracts for computer parts and servers. Fourteen government officials and IBM Korea executives received bribes. As in the Argentine case, IBM Korea said it did not condone the activities. IBM spokesman John Bukovinsky said that three employees were involved and subsequently fired. Executives of IBM's wholly owned IBM Korea and LG & IBM PC Corp—a joint venture 51 percent owned by IBM and 49 percent owned by LG Electronics Inc.—bribed government officials to get deals. The Seoul District Prosecutor's Office said that through illegal actions IBM Korea had won orders for servers and PC parts worth $42.7 million and LG & IBM PC Corp. had won orders worth $900,000. "IBM Korea and LG & IBM PC Corp had bribed computer-related department officials in state-run corporations and colluded with them in auctions to supply servers and PC parts," the prosecutor's office said.[16] In return for bribes, the National Tax Office and the Information Ministry officials gave these companies' technology high marks when they bid for government contracts. Fourteen government officials provided auction information in advance, including a 49-year-old tax official, who is alleged to have received 80 million won ($80,000) in bribes from IBM Korea.

SOME OPEN QUESTIONS

In most countries, the name IBM connotes high technology, but in Argentina, IBM makes people think of scandal, corruption and even assassination. During the late 1990s, on Argentine radio and television talk shows, callers and guests routinely bashed IBM and expressed support for the Government's aggressive prosecution of the company.

Why do people complain about the IBM bribes? Public opinion polls showed that Argentine citizens consistently ranked corruption as one of the country's top problems during the Menem Administration. In addition,

business executives admitted that paying bribes was the usual way to land government contracts while Menem was in office—not just for IBM, but for everyone. Should we blame IBM for doing what many others were doing?

Big Blue never publicly admitted that it paid bribes. It just claimed that the company was misled by the Argentine unit of the company. IBM parted company with Martorana and Soriani for "failing to manage the contract negotiations correctly." Yet, after months of front-page headlines about the scandal, there were few people in Argentina who believed IBM when it said that the US headquarters did nothing wrong, especially after the executives declared under oath that the US and Latin-American headquarters did know and authorized the illegal payments.

Should Big Blue be held criminally liable for the bribes ultimately paid by IBM Argentina, IBM de Mexico and IBM Korea? Is IBM morally responsible for those payments even if the US and Latin American headquarters were misled by the Argentine subsidiary?

Should the company avoid doing business and selling its products in countries where corruption is rampant? Many companies have refused to participate in those countries in which corruption flourishes. For instance, Bell South declined to bid in the privatization of the main Argentine telecommunication company in the early 1990s, given the rumors of bribes surrounding the transaction. Was paying bribes the price that IBM should have taken as a way to expand business in Latin America? It might have been justified from a cost-benefit perspective. But is it permissible for a company like IBM to behave inconsistently with ethical attitudes at home when the ethical standards at the host country are lower?

Decent behavior may be expected from a world-class company such as IBM. Latin Americans expected Big Blue not only to obey the law but also to conduct its business in accordance with ethical standards, which entails abstaining from paying bribes and making contributions to solve one of the main problems of the continent. That may be required not only to behave as a good citizen but also to strengthen its corporate culture. Victor Savanti, former president of IBM Argentina and the executive who made IBM a dominant force in the Argentine market, thought that the IBM-Banco Nación scandal was more than a mere public relations issue. Following his well-thumbed copy of "A Business and Its Beliefs," the 1963 guide to moral corporate behavior written by Thomas Watson Jr. (the son of IBM's founder), Mr. Savanti says, "Our honesty was always a tremendous plus . . . being aware that IBM reputation for honesty in Argentina was destroyed.

This case was prepared by Miguel Alzola[17] and is based on the following sources:

Silvana Bosch, "IBM-Nación: el Estado pagó 53 veces más caro," *Clarin,* April 27, 1998.

Lucinda Low, Report on US FCPA Prosecutions, May 5, 2006.

S.E.C. v. International Business Machines Corporation (00-Civ.-3040) (D.D.C. 2000)

S.E.C. Litigation Release No. 16839 (Dec. 21, 2000)

Sandra Sugawara, "IBM Settles to End Bribery Case," *Washington Post,* December 22, 2002.

Calvin Sims, "Argentine Cloud over IBM Grows Darker," *The New York Times,* June 29, 1996.

David Pilling, Argentina to Probe More IBM Deals," *Financial Times,* June 14, 1996.

Robert S. Leiken, "An End to Corruption," *The Washington Post,* April 16, 1996.

Michael S. Serrill, "A Black Eye for Big Blue IBM's Argentine Subsidiary Is Twisting in a Fraud Scandal," *Time International,* April 15, 1996.

David Haskel, "US Wants Top Argentine Officials to Testify on IBM," *Reuters New,* February 7, 1996.

Stephen Brown, "Another Head Rolls in IBM Argentina Bribe Scandal," *Reuters News,* March 13, 1996.

Jonathan Friedland, "Sour Deal: Did IBM Unit Bribe Officials in Argentina to Land a Contract?—Scandal Claims Top Members of Menem Government, 3 Big Blue Executives—Millions for a Rugby Coach," *The Wall Street Journal,* December 11, 1995.

"Dead Man's Cheque Bounces into IBM Probe," *Financial Times,* October 19, 1995.

David Pilling, "IBM Continues Probe Of Argentine Subsidiary," *Financial Times,* September 18, 1995.

"Gang Attacks Figure In Argentine Case Involving IBM," *The Washington Post,* August 1, 1996.

Calvin Sims, "In Argentine Bribery Scandal, an Ex-Executive of IBM Says He Is a Scapegoat," *The New York Times,* November 5, 1996.

Stephen Fidler and Ken Warn, "Corporate Culture—Corruption Still Saps Economic Potential," *Financial Times,* July 1, 1997.

Silvana Bosch, "Un ex director del Banco Nación admitió que cobró por la firma del contrato," *Clarin,* April 24, 1998.

"IBM's Tale of Woe," *Financial Times,* July 22, 1997.

Sam Dillon, "IBM to Pay Mexico City Millions for Failed System," *The New York Times,* July 24, 1998.

"IBM's Last Tangle in Argentina," *The Economist,* August 1, 1998.

Glenn R. Simpson, "Senate Unanimously Ratifies Pact Against Bribes to Foreign Officials to Fight Corruption Abroad," *The Wall Street Journal,* August 3, 1998.

Ken Warn, "Witness in IBM Scandal Found Dead in Buenos Aires," *Financial Times,* October 6, 1998.

"Argentine Judge Beards Big Blue in Its US Den as Corruption Allegations Spread," *Financial Times,* October 21, 1998.

"Argentina Receives Money from Swiss in IBM Bribe Case," *The Wall Street Journal,* June 9, 1999.

Clifford Krauss, "Money-Laundering Report Gives Argentine Leader a New Woe," *The New York Times,* March 1, 2001.

Kim Kyoung-wha and Caroline Humer, "2 IBM Execs, S. Korea Officials Charged over Bribery," *Reuters News,* January 5, 2004.

Rafael Di Tella, "Corrupción, Compelencia y Eficiencia Burocrática," in Beliz, G. (Ed.), No robarás: ¿Es posible ganarle a la corrupción? Buenos Aires: Editorial de Belgrano, 1997.

NOTES

1. English translation: "This guy (Cattáneo) told me: look, the project that will be favored is this one and there are $2.5 millions for you. We do not need anything, just that you stop bothering with the other project. And there I fell. For the first time in my life, I did something I would regret for ever. But it was too late."

2. Harvard Business School professor and Argentine scholar Rafael Di Tella, one the most important Latin American specialists in economics of corruption, stated in 1997: "It would not be difficult to argue that both Menem and Cavallo—*his minister of Economy*—have made some of the most effective reforms to control corruption." See Di Tella, R. 1997. "Corrupción, Competencia y Eficiencia Burocratica." In Beliz, G. (Ed.), *No robarás: ¿Es posible ganarle a la corrupción?* Buenos Aires: Editorial de Belgrano, p. 322.

3. United States accounted for $27 billion revenues while Europe, Middle East and Africa represented S 25 billion revenues and Asia Pacific accounted for $14 billion revenues. Available at ftp://ftp.software.ibm.com/annualreport/1995/ibm_1995.pdf.

4. Jonathan Friedland, "Sour Deal: Did IBM Unit Bribe Officials in Argentina to Land a Contract?—Scandal Claims Top Members Of Menem Government, 3 Big Blue Executives—Millions for a Rugby Coach," *The Wall Street Journal*, December 11, 1995.

5. The Foreign Corrupt Practices Act of 1977 (15 USC. §§ 78dd-1, et seq.) is a United States federal law which made it unlawful for American persons and firms to make payments to a foreign official for the purpose of obtaining or retaining business.

6. Silvana Bosch, "IBM-Nación: el Estado pagó 53 veces más caro," *Clarin,* April 27, 1998.

7. Eventually, in 1999, Switzerland handed over to Argentina $4.5 million of suspected bribe money frozen in Geneva bank accounts.

8. "Argentine Judge Beards Big Blue in Its US den as Corruption Allegations Spread," *Financial Times,* October 21, 1998.

9. "Gang Attacks Figure In Argentine Case Involving IBM," *The Washington Post,* August 1, 1996.

10. "Encontraron ahorcado al acusado de repartir la coima del caso IBM-Nacion," *Clarin,* October 5, 1998.

11. David Pilling, "IBM Continues Probe of Argentine Subsidiary," *Financial Times,* September 18, 1995.

12. Financial Times, "Dead Man's Cheque Bounces into IBM Probe," October 19, 1995.

13. Calvin Sims, "In Argentine Bribery Scandal, an Ex-Executive of IBM Says He Is a Scapegoat," *The New York Times,* November 5, 1996.

14. Hugo Morales, "Ex presidente de IBM comprometió más a casa matriz," *Ambito Financiero,* April 30, 1998.

15. Sam Dillon, "IBM to Pay Mexico City Millions for Failed System," *The New York Times,* July 24, 1998.

16. Kim Kyoung-wha and Caroline Humer, "2 IBM Execs, S.Korea Officials Charged over Bribery," *Reuters News,* January 5, 2004.

17. The development of this case greatly benefited from the comments of Michael Santoro, Edwin Hartman, and Anne-Laure Winkler.

Case Study

Ellen Moore (A):

Living and Working in Bahrain

Gail Ellement and Martha Maznevski

The General Manager had offered me a choice of two positions in the Operations area. I had considered the matter carefully, and was about to meet with him to tell him I would accept the Accounts Control position. The job was much more challenging than the Customer Services post, but I knew I could learn the systems and procedures quickly and I would have a great opportunity to contribute to the success of the Operations area.

This case was prepared by Gail Ellement and Martha Maznevski of the Richard Ivey School of Business. Copyright © 1990 by Ivey Management Services. Reprinted with permission, Ivey Management Services.

It was November 1989, and Ellen Moore was just completing her second year as an expatriate manager at the offices of a large American financial institution in Manama, Bahrain. After graduating with an MBA from a leading business school, Ellen had joined her husband, who was working as an expatriate manager at an offshore bank in Bahrain. Being highly qualified and capable, she had easily found a demanding position and had worked on increasingly complex projects since she had begun at the company. She was looking forward to the challenges of the Accounts Control position.

ELLEN MOORE

Ellen graduated as the top female from her high school when she was 16, and immediately began working full time for the main branch of one of the largest banks in the country. By the end of four years, she had become a corporate accounts officer and managed over twenty large accounts.

> I remember I was always making everything into a game, a challenge. One of my first jobs was filing checks. I started having a competition with the woman at the adjacent desk who had been filing for years, except she didn't know I was competing with her. When she realized it, we both started competing in earnest. Before long, people used to come over just to watch us fly through these stacks of checks. When I moved to the next job, I used to see how fast I could add up columns of numbers while handling phone conversations. I always had to do something to keep myself challenged.

While working full time at the bank, Ellen achieved a Fellowship in the Institute of Bankers after completing demanding courses and exams. She went on to work in banking and insurance with one of her former corporate clients from the bank. When she was subsequently promoted to manage their financial reporting department, she was both the first female and the youngest person the company had ever had in that position.

Since she had begun working full time, Ellen had been taking courses towards a bachelor's degree at night in one of the city's universities. In 1983 she decided to stop working for two years to complete her Bachelor's Degree. After she graduated with a major in accounting and minors in marketing and management, she entered the MBA program.

> I decided to go straight into the MBA program for several reasons. First, I wanted to update myself. I had taken my undergraduate courses over ten years and wanted to obtain knowledge on contemporary views. Second. I wanted to tie some pieces together—my night school degree left my ideas somewhat fragmented. Third, I wasn't impressed with the interviews I had after I finished the Bachelor's degree, and fourth I was out of work anyway. Finally, my father had already told everyone that I had my MBA, and I decided I really couldn't disappoint him.

Just after Ellen had begun the two year MBA program, her husband was offered a position with an affiliate of his bank, posted in Bahrain beginning the next spring. They sat down and examined potential opportunities that would be available for Ellen once she completed her MBA. They discovered that women could work and assume positions of responsibility in Bahrain, and decided they could both benefit from the move. Her husband moved to Bahrain in March, while Ellen remained to complete her masters. Ellen followed, with MBA in hand, 18 months later.

BAHRAIN

Bahrain is an archipelago of 33 islands located in the Persian Gulf. The main island, Bahrain, comprises 85% of the almost 700 square kilometers of the country, and is the location of the capital city, Manama. Several of the islands are joined by causeways, and in 1987 the 25 kilometer King Fahad Causeway linked the principal island to the mainland of Saudi Arabia, marking the end of island isolation for the country. In 1971, Bahrain gained full independence from Britain, ending a relationship that had lasted for almost a century. Of the population of over 400,000 people, about one third were foreigners.

Bahrain has had a prosperous history. Historically, it has been sought after by many countries for its lush vegetation, fresh water, and pearls. Many traditional crafts and industries were still practiced, including pottery, basket-making, fabric-weaving, pearl-diving, dhow (fishing boat) building, and fishing. Bahrain was the pearl capital of the world for many centuries. Fortunately, just as the pearl industry collapsed with the advent of cultured pearls from Japan, Bahrain struck its first oil.

Since the 1930s, the oil industry had been the largest contributor to Bahrain's Gross National Product. The country was the first in the Persian Gulf to have an oil industry, established with a discovery in 1932. Production at that time was 9600 barrels a day. Eventually, crude output had reached over 40,000 barrels a day. Bahrain's oil products included crude oil, natural gas, methanol and ammonia, and refined products like gasoline, jet fuels, kerosene, and asphalts.

The Bahraini government had been aware for several years that the oil reserves were being seriously depleted. It was determined to diversity the country's economy away from a dependence on one resource. Industries established since 1971 included aluminum processing, shipbuilding, iron and steel processing, and furniture and door manufacturing. Offshore banking began in 1975. Since Bahraini nationals did not have the expertise to develop these industries alone, expatriates

from around the world, particularly from Western Europe and North America, were invited to conduct business in Bahrain. By the late 1980s, the country was a major business and financial center, housing many Middle East branch offices of international firms.

Expatriates in Bahrain

Since Bahrain was an attractive base from which to conduct business, it was a temporary home to many expatriates. Housing compounds, schools, services, shopping and leisure activities all catered to many international cultures. Expatriates lived under residence permits, gained only on the basis of recruitment for a specialist position which could not be filled by a qualified and available Bahraini citizen.

To Ellen, one of the most interesting roles of expatriate managers was that of teacher. The Arab nations had been industrialized for little more than two decades, and had suddenly found themselves needing to compete in a global market. Ellen believed that one of her main reasons for working in Bahrain was to train its nationals eventually to take over her job.

Usually the teaching part was very interesting. When I first arrived in the office, I was amazed to see many staff members with micro computers on their desks, yet they did not know the first thing about operating the equipment. When I inquired about the availability of computer courses, I was informed by a British expatriate manager that 'as these were personal computers, any person should be able to use them, and as such, courses aren't necessary.' It was clear to me that courses were very necessary when the computer knowledge of most employees consisted of little more than knowing where the on/off switch was located on a microcomputer.

Although it was outside of office policy, I held "Ellen's Introduction to Computers" after office hours, just to get people comfortable with the machines and to teach them a few basics.

Sometimes the amount of energy you had to put into the teaching was frustrating in that results were not immediately evident. I often worked jointly with one of the Bahraini managers who really didn't know how to develop projects and prepare reports. Although I wasn't responsible for him, I spent a great deal of time with him, helping him improve his work. Initially there was resistance on his part, because he was not prepared to subordinate himself to an expatriate, let alone a woman. But eventually he came around and we achieved some great results working together.

The range of cultures represented in Bahrain was vast. Expatriate managers interacted not only with Arabic nationals, but also with managers from other parts of the world, and with workers from developing countries who provided a large part of the unskilled labor force.

The inequality among nationalities was one issue I found very difficult to deal with during my stay in Bahrain. The third world immigrants were considered to be the lowest level possible in the pecking order, just slightly lower than nationals from countries outside the Gulf. Gulf Arabs, being of Bedouin origin, maintained a suspicious attitude towards "citified" Arabs. Europeans and North Americans were regarded much more highly. These inequalities had a major impact on daily life, including the availability of jobs and what relations would develop or not develop between supervisors and subordinates. Although I was well acquainted with the racial problems in North America, I haven't seen anything compared to the situation in Bahrain. It wasn't unusual for someone to be exploited and discarded, as any expendable and easily replaceable resource would be, because of their nationality.

Although many expatriates and their families spent their time in Bahrain immersed in their own cultural compounds, social groups, and activities, Ellen believed that her interaction with the various cultures was one of the most valuable elements of her international experience.

MANAGING IN BAHRAIN

Several aspects of the Middle Eastern culture had tremendous impact on the way business was managed, even in Western firms located in Bahrain. It seemed to Ellen, for example, that "truth" to a Bahraini employee was subject to an Arab interpretation, which was formed over hundreds of years of cultural evolution. What Western managers considered to be "proof" of an argument or "factual" evidence could be flatly denied by a Bahraini: if something was not believed it did not exist. As well, it seemed that the concept of "time" differed between Middle Eastern and Western cultures. Schedules and deadlines, while sacred to Western managers, commanded little respect from Bahraini employees. The two areas that had the most impact on Ellen's managing in a company in Bahrain were the Islamic religion and the traditional attitude towards women.

Islam

Most Bahrainis are practicing Muslims. According to the Muslim faith, the universe was created by Allah who prescribed a code of life called Islam and the Qur'an is the literal, unchanged World of Allah preserved exactly as transcribed by Muhammad. Muhammad's own acts as a prophet form the basis for Islamic law, and are second in authority only to the Qur'an. The five Pillars of Islam are belief, prayer, fasting, almsgiving and pilgrimage. Muslims pray five times a day. During Ramadan, the ninth month of the Islamic calendar, Muslims must fast from food, drink, smoking and sexual activity from dawn until dusk, in order to master the urges which sustain and procreate life. All Muslims are obliged to give a certain proportion of their wealth in alms for charitable purposes; the Qur'an stresses that the poor have a just claim on the wealth of the prosperous. Finally, if possible, all Muslims should make a pilgrimage to Mecca during their lives, in a spirit of total sacrifice of personal comforts, acquisition of wealth, and other matters of worldly significance.

> Certainly the Muslim religion had a tremendous impact on my daily working life. The first time I walked into the women's washroom at work I noticed a tap about three inches off the floor over a drain. I found this rather puzzling; I wondered if it was for the cleaning crew. When a woman came in, I asked her about the tap, and she explained that before going to the prayer room, everyone had to wash all uncovered parts of their bodies. The tap was for washing their feet and legs.
>
> One time I was looking for one of my employees, Mohammed, who had a report due to me that afternoon. I searched for him at his desk and other likely spots throughout the office, but to no avail, he just wasn't around. I had had difficulties with Mohammed's work before, when he would submit documents long after deadlines, and I was certain he was attempting to slack off once again. I bumped into one of Mohammed's friends, and asked if he knew Mohammed's whereabouts. When he informed me that Mohammed was in the prayer room, I wasn't sure how to respond. I didn't know if this prayer room activity was very personal and if I could ask questions, such as the length of time one generally spends in prayer. But I needed to know how long Mohammed would be away from his desk. Throwing caution to the wind, I asked the employee how long Mohammed was likely to be in prayers and he told me it usually takes about ten minutes. It wasn't that I felt I didn't have the right to know where my employee was or how long he would be away, I just wasn't certain my authority as a manager allowed me the right to ask questions about such a personal activity as praying.
>
> During Ramadan, the hours of business are shortened by law. It is absolutely illegal for any Muslim to work past two o'clock in the afternoon, unless special permits are obtained from the Ministry of Labor. Unfortunately, business coming in to an American firm does not stop at two, and a majority of the non-Muslim workers are required to take up the slack.

Unlike religion in Western civilization, Islam permeates every function of human endeavour. There does not exist a separation of church, state, and judiciary. Indeed, in purist circles, the question does not arise. The hybrid systems existing in certain Arab countries are considered aberrations created by Western colonial influences. Accordingly, to function successfully, the expatriate must understand and learn to accept a very different structuring of a society.

Women in Bahrain

Bahrain tended to be more progressive than many Middle Eastern countries in its attitude towards women. Although traditions were strong, Bahraini women had some freedom. For example, all women could work outside the home, although the hours they could work were restricted both by convention and by the labor laws. They could only work if their husbands, fathers, or brothers permitted them, and could not take potential employment away from men. Work outside the home was to be conducted in addition to, not instead of, duties performed inside the home, such as child-rearing and cooking. Most women who worked held secretarial or clerical positions; very few worked in management.

Bahraini women were permitted to wear a variety of outfits, from the conservative full length black robe with head scarf which covers the head and hair, to below-the-knee skirts and dresses without head covering.

> Arabic women who sincerely want change and more decision-making power over their own lives face an almost impossible task, as the male influence is perpetuated not only by men, but also by women who are afraid to alter views they understand and with which they have been brought up all their lives. I once asked a female co-worker the reason why one of the women in the office, who had previously been "uncovered," was now sporting a scarf over her head. The response was that this woman had just been married, and although her husband did not request that she become "covered," she personally did not feel as though she was a married woman without the

head scarf. So she simply asked her husband to demand that she wear a scarf on her head. It was a really interesting situation: some of the more liberal Bahraini women were very upset that she had asked her husband to make this demand. They saw it as negating many of the progressive steps the women's movement had made in recent years.

Although Bahrainis had been exposed to Western cultures for the two decades of industrial expansion, they were still uncomfortable with Western notions of gender equality and less traditional roles for women.

One day a taxi driver leaned back against his seat and, while keeping one eye on the road ahead, turned to ask me, "How many sons do you have?" I replied that I didn't have any children. His heartfelt response of "I'm so sorry" and the way he shook his head in sympathy were something my North American upbringing didn't prepare me for. My taxi driver's response typifies the attitude projected towards women, whether they are expatriates from Europe or North America, or are Bahrainis. Women are meant to have children, preferably sons. Although Bahrain is progressive in many ways, attitudes on the role of women in society run long and deep, and it is quite unlikely these sentiments will alter in the near, or even distant, future.

Another time I was greeted with gales of laughter when I revealed to the women in the office that my husband performed most of the culinary chores in our household. They assumed I was telling a joke, and when I insisted that he really did most of the cooking, they sat in silent disbelief. Finally, one woman spoke up and informed the group that she didn't think her husband even knew where the kitchen was in their house, let alone would ever be caught touching a cooking utensil. The group nodded in agreement. Although these women have successful business careers—as clerks, but in the workforce nonetheless—they believe women should perform all household tasks without the assistance of their husbands. The discovery that this belief holds true in Bahrain is not remarkable as I know many North American and European businesswomen who believe the same to be true. What is pertinent is these women allow themselves to be completely dominated by the men in their lives.

The one concept I faced daily but never accepted was that my husband was regarded as the sole decision maker in our household. He and I view our marriage as a partnership in which we participate equally in all decisions. But when the maintenance manager for our housing compound came by, repairs were completed efficiently only if I preceded my request with "my husband wants the following to be completed." It's a phrase I hated to use as it went against every rational thought I possess, but I frequently had to resort to it.

These attitudes also affected how Ellen was treated as a manager by Bahraini managers:

One manager, I'll call him Fahad, believed that women were only capable of fulfilling secretarial and coffee serving functions. One day I was sitting at my desk, concentrating on some documents. I didn't notice Fahad having a discussion with another male manager nearby. When I looked up from my papers, Fahad noticed me and immediately began talking in French to the other manager. Although my French was a bit rusty, my comprehension was still quite serviceable. I waited for a few moments and then broke into their discussion in French. Fahad was completely dismayed. Over the new few years, Fahad and I worked together on several projects. At first, he was pompous and wouldn't listen to anything I presented. It was a difficult situation, but I was determined to remain above his negative comments. I ignored his obvious prejudice towards me, remained outwardly calm when he disregarded my ideas, and proceeded to prove myself with my work. It took a lot of effort and patience but, in time, Fahad and I not only worked out our differences, but worked as a successful team on a number of major projects. Although this situation had a happy ending, I really would have preferred to have directed all that energy and effort towards more productive issues.

Bahraini nationals were not the only ones who perpetuated the traditional roles of women in society. Many of the expatriates, particularly those from Commonwealth countries, tended to view their roles as "the colonial charged with the responsibility to look after the developing country." This was reflected in an official publication for new expatriates that stated: "Wives of overseas employees are normally sponsored by their husbands' employers, and their Residence Permits are processed at the same time. . . ." However, wives were not permitted to work unless they could obtain a work permit for themselves.

The first question I was often asked at business receptions was "What company is your husband with?" When I replied that I worked as well, I received the glazed over look as they assumed I occupied myself with coffee mornings, beach, tennis and other leisure activities as did the majority of expatriate wives.

Social gatherings were always risky. At typical business and social receptions the men served themselves first, after which the women selected their food. Then women and men positioned themselves on opposite sides of the room. The women discussed "feminine" topics, such as babies and recipes, white the men discussed the fall (or rise) of the dollar and the big deal of the day. At one Bahraini business gathering, I hesitated in choosing sides: should I conform and remain with the women? But most of these women did network outside their homes, and, consequently, they spoke and understood very little English. I joined the men. Contrary to what I expected, I was given a gracious welcome.

However, on another occasion I was bored with the female conversation, so I ventured over to the forbidden male side to join a group of bankers discussing correspondent banking courses. When I entered the discussion, a British bank general manager turned his nose up at me. He motioned towards the other side of the room, and told me I should join the women. He implied that their discussion was obviously over my head. I quickly informed him that although I personally had found the banking courses difficult to complete while holding a full time banking position, I not only managed to complete the program and obtain my Fellowship, but at the time was the youngest employee of my bank ever to be awarded the diploma. The man did a quick turnabout, was thoroughly embarrassed, and apologized profusely. Although it was nice to turn the tables on the man, I was more than a little frustrated with the feeling that I almost had

to wear my resume on my sleeve to get any form of respect from the men, whether European, North American, or Arab.

A small percentage of Bahraini women had completed university degrees in North America and Europe. While residing in these Western cultures, they were permitted to function as did their Western counterparts. For example, they could visit or phone friends when they wished without first obtaining permission. After completing their education, many of these women were qualified for management positions; however, upon returning to Bahrain they were required to resume their traditional female roles.

The notion of pink MBA diplomas for women and blue for men is very real. Although any MBA graduate in North America, male or female, is generally considered to have attained a certain level of business sense, I had to constantly "prove" myself to some individuals who appeared to believe that women attended a special segregated section of the university with appropriately tailored courses.

Ellen discovered that, despite being a woman, she was accepted by Bahrainis as a manager as a result of her Western nationality, her education, and her management position in the company.

Many of my male Arabic peers accepted me as they would any expatriate manager. For example, when a male employee returned from a holiday, he would typically visit each department, calling upon the other male employees with a greeting and a handshake. Although he might greet a female co-worker, he would never shake her hand. However, because of my management position in the company and my status as a Western expatriate, male staff members gave me the same enthusiastic greeting and handshake normally reserved for their male counterparts.

Ellen also found herself facilitating Bahraini women's positions in the workplace.

As I was the only female in a senior management position in our office, I was often asked by the female employees to speak to their male superiors about problems and issues they experienced in their departments. I also had to provide a role model for the women because there were no female Bahraini managers. Some of them came to me not just to discuss career issues but to discuss life issues. There was just no one else in a similar position for them to talk to. On the other hand, male managers would ask me to discuss sensitive issues, such as hygiene, with their female staff members.

The government of Bahrain introduced legislation that restricted the amount of overtime hours women could work. Although the move was being praised by the (female) Director of Social Development as recognition of the contribution women were making to Bahraini industry, Ellen saw it as further discriminatory treatment restricting the choices of women in Bahrain. Her published letter to the editor of the *Gulf Daily News* read:

> . . . How the discriminatory treatment of women in this regulation can be seen as recognition of the immense contribution women make to the Bahrain workforce is beyond comprehension. Discrimination of any portion of the population in the labor legislation does not recognize anything but the obvious prejudice. If the working women in Bahrain want to receive acknowledgement of their indispensable impact on the Bahrain economy, it should be through an increase in the number of management positions available to qualified women, not through regulations limiting the hours they work. All this regulation means is that women are still regarded as second class citizens who need the strong arm tactics of the government to help them settle disputes over working hours. Government officials could really show appreciation to the working women in Bahrain by making sure that companies hire and promote based on skill rather than gender. But there is little likelihood of that occurring.

The letter was signed with a pseudonym, but the day it was published one of Ellen's female employees showed her the letter and claimed "if I didn't know better, Ellen, I'd think you wrote this letter."

CAREER DECISIONS

When Ellen first arrived in Bahrain, she had great expectations that she would work somewhere where she could make a difference. She received several offers for positions and turned down, among others, a university and a high profile brokerage house. She decided to take a position as a Special Projects Coordinator at a large American financial institution.

> In fact the records will show I was actually hired as a "Financial Analyst," but this title was given solely because at that time, the government had decided that expatriate women shouldn't be allowed to take potential positions away from Bahrain nationals. The expertise required as a Financial Analyst enabled the company to obtain a work permit for me as I had the required experience and academic credentials, although I performed few duties as an analyst.

In her special projects role, Ellen learned a great deal about international finance. She conducted efficiency studies on various operating departments. She used her systems expertise to investigate and improve the company's micro computer usage, and developed a payroll program which was subsequently integrated into the company's international systems. She was a member of the Strategic Review Committee, and produced a report outlining the long term goals for the Middle East market, which she then presented to the Senior Vice President of Europe, Middle East, and Africa.

After one year, Ellen was rewarded for her achievements by a promotion to Manager of Business Planning and Development, a position which reported directly to the Vice President and General Manager. She designed the role herself, and was able to be creative and quite influential in the company. During her year in this role, she was involved in a diverse range of activities. She managed the Quality Assurance department, coordinated a product launch, developed and managed a senior management information system, was an active participant in all senior management meetings, and launched an employee newsletter.

At the end of her second year in Bahrain, Ellen was informed that two positions in Operations would soon be available, and the General Manager, a European expatriate, asked if she would be interested in joining the area. She had previously only worked in staff positions, and quickly decided to accept the challenge and learning experience of a line post. Both positions were in senior management, and both had responsibility for approximately thirty employees.

The first position was for Manager of Accounts Control, which covered the Credit, Collection and Authorization departments. The manager's role was to ensure that appropriate information was used to authorize spending by clients, to compile results of client payment, and to inform management of nonpayment issues. The manager also supervised in-house staff and representatives in other Gulf countries for the collection of withheld payments.

The second post was Manager of Customer Services, New Accounts, and Establishment Services. The manager's role was to ensure that new clients were worthy and that international quality standards were met in all Customer Service activity. The manager also worked with two other departments: with Marketing to ensure that budgets were met, and with Sales to manage relationships with the many affiliate outlets of the service.

After speaking with the two current managers and considering the options carefully, Ellen decided that she would prefer working in the Accounts Control area. The job was more oriented to financial information, the manager had more influence on operations at the company, and she would have the opportunity to travel to other countries to supervise staff. Although she was not familiar with the systems and procedures, she knew she could learn them quickly. Ellen went into her meeting with the General Manager excited about the new challenges.

Ellen Meets with the General Manager

Ellen told the General Manager she had decided to take the Accounts Control position, and outlined her reasons. Then she waited for his affirmation and for the details of when she would begin.

"I'm afraid I've reconsidered the offer," the General Manager announced. "Although I know you would probably do a terrific job in the Accounts Control position, I can't offer it to you. It involves periodic travel into Saudi Arabia, and women are not allowed to travel there alone." He went on to tell Ellen how she would be subject to discriminatory practices, would not be able to gain the respect of the company's Saudi Arabian clients, and would experience difficulty travelling there.

Ellen was astonished. She quickly pointed out to him that many businesswomen were representatives of American firms in Saudi Arabia. She described one woman she knew of who was the sole representative of a large American bank in the Eastern Province of Saudi Arabia who frequently travelled there alone. She explained that other women's experiences in Saudi Arabia showed professional men there treated professional women as neither male nor female, but as business people. Besides, she continued, there were no other candidates in the company for either position. She reminded the General Manager of the pride the company took in its quality standards and how senior management salaries were in part determined by assuring quality in their departments. Although the company was an equal opportunity employer in its home country, the United States, she believed the spirit of the policy should extend to all international offices.

The General Manager informed her that his decision reflected his desire to address the interests of both herself and the company. He was worried, he said, that Ellen would have trouble obtaining entry visas to allow her to conduct business in Saudi Arabia, and that the customers would not accept her. Also, if there were ever any hostile outbreaks, he believed she would be in danger, and he could not have lived with that possibility.

Ellen stated that as a woman, she believed she was at lower risk of danger than her Western male counterparts since in the event of hostility, the Saudi Arabians would most likely secure her safety. There was much greater probability that a male representative of the firm would be held as a hostage.

The General Manager was adamant. Regardless of her wishes, the company needed Ellen in the Customer Service position. New Accounts had only recently be firm been added to the department, and the bottom line responsibility was thus doubled from what it had been in the past. The General Manager said he wanted someone he could trust and depend upon to handle the pressure of New Accounts, which had a high international profile.

Ellen was offered the Customer Service position, then dismissed from the meeting. In frustration, she began to consider her options.

Take the Customer Services Position. The General Manager obviously expected her to take the position. It would mean increased responsibility and challenge. Except for a position in high school where she managed a force of sixty student police, Ellen had not yet supervised more than four employees at any time in her professional career. On the other hand, it went against her values to accept the post

since it had been offered as a result of gender roles when all consideration should have been placed on competence. She knew she had the abilities and qualifications for the position. She viewed the entire situation as yet another example of how the business community in Bahrain had difficulty accepting and acknowledging the contributions of women to international management, and didn't want to abandon her values by accepting the position.

Fight Back. There were two approaches which would permit Ellen to take the matter further. She could go to the General Manager's superior, the Senior Vice President of Europe, Middle East, and Africa. She had had several dealings with him, and had once presented a report to him with which he was very impressed. But she wasn't sure she could count on his sympathy regarding her travelling to Saudi Arabia as his knowledge of the region was limited, and he generally relied on local management's decisions on such issues. She could consider filing a grievance against the company. There were provisions in Bahraini Labor Law that would have permitted this option in her case. However, she understood that the Labor Tribunals, unlike those held in Western countries, did not try cases based on precedents or rules of evidence. In other words, the judge would apply a hodgepodge of his own subjective criteria to reach a decision.

Stay in the Business Planning and Development Job. Although the General Manager had not mentioned it as an option, Ellen could request that she remain in her current position. It would mean not giving in to the General Manager's prejudices. Since she had been considering the two Operations positions, though, she had been looking forward to moving on to something new.

Leave the Company. Ellen knew she was qualified for many positions in the financial center of Bahrain and could likely obtain work with another company. She was not sure, though, whether leaving her present company under these circumstances would jeopardize her chances of finding work elsewhere. Furthermore, to obtain a post at a new company would inquire a letter of permission from her current employer, who, as her sponsor in Bahrain, had to sanction her move to a new employer who would become her new sponsor. She was not sure that she would be able to make those arrangements considering the situation.

> I always tell my employees "If you wake up one morning and discover you don't like your job, come to see me immediately. If the problem is with the tasks of the job, I'll see if I can modify your tasks. If the problem is with the department or you want a change, I'll assist you in getting another position in the company. If the problem is with the company, then I'll help you write your resume." I have stated this credo to all my employees in every post I've held. Generally, they don't believe that their manager would actually assist with resume writing, but when the opportunity arises, and it has, and I do come through as promised, the impact on the remaining employees is priceless. Employees will provide much more effort towards a cause that is supported by someone looking out for their personal welfare.

Ellen's superior did not have the same attitude towards his employees. As she considered her options, Ellen realized that no move could be made without a compromise either in her career or her values. Which choice was she most willing to make?

ELLEN MOORE (B)

What decision did you make and why?

I accepted the Customer Services position because I was looking for a win-win situation. The Customer Services post was, despite

everything, a promotion. Fighting back was not really an option. I would never have received the Accounts Control position, no matter how hard I fought. There was no doubt of this at all. The General Manager had already made up his mind. Any effort I might have made to fight for the Accounts Control post would have compromised my effectiveness in the company, as I would be perceived as someone unwilling to accept senior management decisions.

I could have left the company, but that action would have placed me in a difficult situation, as my husband still had one year remaining on his contract and I wanted to continue working in Bahrain. I could have looked for a post with another company in Bahrain, but the economic situation had changed, and a number of companies were closing, so there was a limited number of available jobs.

When I was making the decision regarding the position I would prefer, the discussion involved three people: the General Manager, the Director of Operations, and me. No one else was aware of this discussion. If the issue had been in the public forum, and if everyone knew I had unsuccessfully requested the Accounts Control position, I would have been perceived to have lost face. It would have been difficult, if not impossible, to work there afterwards and to maintain the level of respect I had in the company. If everyone had known about the situation, I probably would have had to fight the General Manager's decision. One reason which allowed me to work so effectively was that people had a high degree of respect for me. They felt that I had approval, tremendous approval, from senior management. If they saw that I wanted this particular position and that senior management disagreed, for whatever reason, they would assume that senior management no longer held me in the same regard.

I actually did receive a portion of the Accounts Control area because one segment, New Accounts, had been moved from Accounts Control to the area which was under my responsibility. Management had been reviewing the move during this decision process. I also received a high degree of international exposure from my Customer Service post. My reports and documents, and the statistics from my group, went to all international centers, so it was a high profile post. Interestingly, the majority of my clients were from Saudi Arabia, and I dealt with them personally when they occasionally visited our center, and when they called by phone. I didn't experience any problems when I personally handled their accounts. In fact, as I was the Senior Manager, these clients actually were pleased when I would take the time to deal with them directly. They understood that they were receiving professional attention.

I left the job and the company after three months in the Customer Service post. I was working seven days a week, seventeen hours a day when I woke up one morning and realized that I didn't want to go to work. I recognized the signal I had always asked my employees to be aware of. I tried to salvage the situation. I phoned the Senior Vice President in Europe to see if there might be an available post in the United Kingdom. I knew him because I had made a successful presentation to him. He was keen, very enthusiastic. He found a post in London which was exactly what I was looking for at the time, but the company couldn't get the required work permit. He was very embarrassed. By this time, the people in the Bahrain unit found out I was looking and I could no longer remain with the company. I did some private consulting for about six months, assisting a company to obtain research on the Bahrain market, as well as designing the office layout and systems.

How did you decide which job to take?

I really did not have a choice. I had to accept the Customer Service post or leave the company. I could not stay where I was, as this option had not been offered. Basically, I sat down and thought about what was important to me. I said okay, it is a line position, and I want a line position; tick one in the "pro" column. Is there an appropriate number of staff reporting to me? Tick another in the "pro" column, and so on. I didn't actually make a list, but I reviewed the pro's and con's of accepting the Customer Service post, and made what I felt was a slight compromise to my values at the time. That was how I came to accept the decision.

Did you compromise your values?

I don't really think so, because I was looking for a senior management position, and this post provided that opportunity. There were times, however, when I would sit back and think, perhaps I did compromise. But, it's all relative. If that situation had occurred in North America, then, yes, it would definitely be a compromise. But given that same situation and in Bahrain, I don't believe I compromised my values. I was just incredibly fortunate to get the positions I did receive.

I have been asked if I have any regrets regarding my move to Bahrain or with my decision to take the Customer Service post. In both cases, I believe the experiences have been generally positive influences on my career. I am not looking for easy ways out or quick jumps up the corporate ladder. I expect to work hard and hope that my efforts will be recognized. When situations arise where I must compromise slightly, I evaluate my decision carefully, and once satisfied that I am not compromising more than is appropriate, I accept the situation and move on from there.

What was your experience when you returned to North America?

My husband remained in Bahrain when I returned to North America to look for a new post, rent a house, and get us settled. We were moving to Toronto, a city where I had not lived before. Everyone seemed so cold and unfriendly. I really was not prepared for this atmosphere, and it took a while for me to get used to it. And although I am a Canadian, when I returned I didn't really feel the same attachment towards Canada. I felt more like a citizen of the world. That is how both my husband and I feel right now. We're not really attached to Bahrain, although our hearts are still there with our friends. Our hearts are also here in Canada with our parents, families and friends, but we don't feel the same nationalistic ties that we felt before.

Also, someone recently commented to me about how much easier it would be to be accepted in a similar professional role in North America. My response was "Don't be so sure. Think again!" I've been a guinea pig in most places where I have worked. I'm the youngest to do, or the first to be, or the only female ever. I'm always breaking new ground, and it's very, very difficult. In fact, I believe I was accepted more readily as a professional in Bahrain by the Arab men because I had education and experience, and I was in a senior position. Here, having an MBA isn't necessarily a ticket towards acceptance. Also, I am now working in the railroad industry and in Information Systems, both fields typically dominated by men. I have had to prove myself here once again.

How do women get international experience?

In my opinion, there are two ways that you can get a position in international business. The first is that you can enter a country on a visitor's visa, which is usually valid for several weeks for most countries. During your stay, you should go to recruitment agencies and companies. This method allows you to see what the country is like in terms of both lifestyle and working environment. You may find out that, although the country appears to be exactly what you want and looks great in a movie, it may not meet your expectations. The other route is to seek work in your own country from a company which has a large international operation. Over time, you may obtain a post within its international system. This option is much more difficult these days, particularly as firms tighten their expenses, and, therefore, limit the number of available international posts.

Do you think that if you had worked for this company in the United States, it would have transferred you to Bahrain?

Probably not. We had a small percentage of people who were placed on international assignment. The company doesn't normally hire through its international posting system for the level of position at which I was hired. It is very expensive to transfer employees internationally, they generally attempt to hire locally. I was, therefore, a local hire for that company.

What tips would you have for women about being effective in management positions?

I believe that it is very important not to become complacent once you attain the next level on the way up the ladder. Never assume that you will be automatically given the respect normally accorded to your position. For example, when I am introduced to someone in business as "Here is Ellen," I immediately stick my hand out and say, "Hello my name is Ellen

Moore, I'm the Manager of X Group for Company Y." If I am introduced as "here's Ellen" by one of my employees, I'll add "and X (the staff member) is a member of my team working on your project." You have to eliminate any ambiguity in such situations.

I strongly believe that women can obtain recognition for their efforts by understanding that they are employees first, and women second. While I was in Bahrain, I was generally regarded by Arab males as a professional, not as a female. I work very hard to ensure that I am professional at all times. I believe that treating people, at any level, from any background, with respect will usually create a positive atmosphere.

Although I am normally very professional, I will play the stereotypical feminine role when required. If I must state to the housing compound manager that "my husband would like this repair," I'll do that. I am very pragmatic, and recognize that sometimes I must resort to play-acting to get something accomplished, without being totally ridiculous about it. However, I'm not about to "sell my soul to the devil."

Do you have any ideas about how men can help women in international business? Or have you worked with any men who have been particularly helpful?

Yes, but I think it's not just in international business, I think it's anywhere. Men often talk about the mentors they have had in their careers who have assisted them in their progress up the ladder. Women very rarely have that source of assistance. There are few women in senior positions at this time; therefore, there are few role models. In my current position, I am often regarded as a role model by female employees at lower levels. I am very cognizant of this fact and strive to maintain a positive image. For example, although I may be frustrated by some aspects of my work, I will portray a positive outlook to my employees. I believe that employees can become disconcerted by negative views expressed by management. That is not to say that I hide reality, but there's a difference between communicating a realistic and pessimistic view. I take my responsibility as a role model very seriously.

It is very difficult for most men in senior positions to become a mentor for a woman. Constant justifications of the relationship are necessary because many people perceive it as being something entirely different. As a result the majority of men don't enter into these situations. But, while I was in Bahrain, a director of another area reporting to the General Manager often discussed business tactics with me. He and I talked about our views on management styles, as well as the future direction of the company. He was there for me when I needed assistance, and when I wanted to bounce an idea off someone. I think that a coach is what most women don't have, a person with whom they can discuss their ideas, someone who has been there before and who is willing to share his knowledge and expertise.

What is your feeling about imposing your value system or your beliefs regarding women's roles in a culture like that in Bahrain? For example, why did you write the letter to the editor of the local newspaper?

I wrote that letter because I felt very strongly about the interpretation made by the Director of Social Development. She believed that the inclusion of women in this labour legislation indicated that their contributions to the workforce were being recognized. I didn't write the letter in an effort to influence anyone's views regarding the legislation itself; that would have been a completely unrealistic purpose. I wrote the letter in order to provide an alternative viewpoint. I had often seen in Bahrain that individuals would accept the views of others without thoroughly understanding or examining all the issues, and I wanted to do my part to prevent that from occurring with this situation.

I am generally a very enthusiastic person, and people tend to follow my lead. I have to be very careful with that side of myself. I would like to believe that I have made some positive changes within my small group of colleagues. But one has to recognize that, at the same time, there is a limited amount of change possible, particularly changes for Bahraini women.

As a North American woman I was generally accorded a high degree of professional respect by Arab males in Bahrain. I have been asked if I believe the same respect would be shown to women with an Arab background who were born in North America. My response is that I don't believe they would be treated equally. Their Arab background would be considered primarily, and as Arab women, their role in society would be set forth by long standing traditional values. There are numerous changes I would like to see for Arab women, but I am realistic at the same time.

As well, individuals from Western countries often incorrectly perceive that a country such as Bahrain is similar to any Western country because of the presence of office buildings and Western firms. They don't understand that as a guest in someone's country, you must respect the cultural values of the host country. I recently read of a North American woman working in Bahrain who said that, although she knew the custom was to wear more conservative clothing, she insisted on wearing shorts in public and didn't care that people stared at her. One Bahraini woman confided in me that when a woman wears such clothing in public, it is the same as if she were walking up to all the people she meets and slapping

them across the face. I wonder if that woman would feel as comfortable wearing her shorts if she took the time to understand the impact of her attire on the people she met on the street. This blatant disrespect for cultural values, while indicating a lack of acceptance for local customs, also demonstrates why many individuals from the West fail to succeed in foreign countries.

You said you were generally respected as a professional by the Arab men. Yet we hear of situations where, for example, a female bank manager working in North America is not invited by Arab male clients to attend a meeting. What are your views on this issue?

Although there could be other factors involved here, my understanding of this type of situation is that the Arab clients are not concerned with the fact that she is a woman. Instead, they most likely believe that her position in the bank is a low level post with limited decision making power. In Bahrain, for example, the leaders of the country are fairly accessible to the people. Given that one can meet with the leader of a country, within a business environment one should be permitted to meet with the president of a given firm. In business I have found most Arab men would like to ensure that they are accorded respect by North American firms, which generally means they wish to meet with senior management who have the authority to make decisions. Individuals from Western countries may interpret these requests incorrectly.

You said that there were no Americans in this American company, you were the token North American?

Yes. Well, I'm Canadian. Most of the executives were European or from other countries in the Middle East, a situation which is not unusual for large multinational firms. The remaining staff were locally hired in Bahrain.

How about your personal relationship?

When we first met over fifteen years ago, my husband and I decided that our relationship was a partnership, and as partners that we would make decisions jointly. And, we recognized early on that we would both have very demanding careers. We sat down and tried to determine, believe it or not it actually took months to accomplish this, what criteria we would use to choose a city, if that situation occurred during our careers. How would we decide if we were offered posts in different cities?

We first thought we should base our decision on salary, with the highest paying job determining the city. But we quickly eliminated that factor as a determinant as I might have a job that pays more today, but if the post is a dead end with no promise of a future, it isn't worth a high investment. We finally decided the position which offered the most long term growth opportunity would be our primary decision criterion. And, that is how we have handled these situations. We actually sit down and say: Well, this is what I've been presented with by this recruitment agency or by this company, and your job is currently at this level. We evaluate the pro's and con's of each posting, and the long term benefits. As well, another key determinant is that good posts would have to be available for both my husband and me in whatever city we select. We seem to go through this decision process fairly often. In fact, we're going through it again. My husband just left for England to be Vice President for an American bank. He is going on a short term contract, but we will be evaluating our alternatives shortly when we have more information on the scope of his post.

My husband and I have a partnership in which each of us respects and assists the other person at all times. For example, he does all the cleaning, dusting, washing the dishes, buying the groceries and the cooking. At one point, a few years ago, I was cooking our dinners about three or four times a week, but I recently haven't had the time as my job has become much more demanding. We know that sometimes my job is more demanding, and sometimes his job requires more of his time. And we share the work in the house based on demands made on our time by our current work situation. We joke about who is the better cook; for example, there are some recipes which I usually prepared and he had his specialty dishes. It happened a few times that he prepared one of my dishes and would say "I think I make it better than you," and I would say, "Really? I guess that one should be your dish from now on." So, little by little I started giving him a few more recipes, but he loves it. He is not cooking our dinners and hating it, he really likes contributing to our relationship in this way.

I think that both people in a relationship have to be flexible, and be willing to make compromises. They have to recognize the needs of each other and understand that these needs will change as time goes on. We often go out for dinner, just so we have special time together, to talk about everything, with no interruptions or television to take us away from each other. We don't fight like most couples I know. We talk about issues, and generally attempt to make decisions based on the "us" rather than the "you" or "I." For example, this Christmas I would like to go to a beach for a holiday. I have not had a holiday for so long, and just need a holiday where I can completely relax. He, on the other hand, would like me to go to London to be with him. We have decided to compromise. I am going to London, and will relax and do nothing much while he is at work during the days.

Then, we are planning to take a beach holiday sometime in February or March.

We have also made a conscious decision not to have children. I guess I have had a lot of time to think about this decision. I remember when I was in elementary school some of my friends had mothers who worked, and these friends would come home from school and no one would be there. I would come home, and my mother was there to hear about my day at school, and her presence was very special. This comparison was always at the back of my mind.

On the other hand, I recognized that in order to be truly successful at anything, you have to devote a fair amount of time to that effort For example, someone training to be the best at a certain sport will have to give up something else, like being a great pianist. Both goals would require more time than is ever available. Alternatively, someone could choose to be adequate at the sport and to have average skills playing the piano, and that would be perfectly all right as long as the person recognized, and accepted, the fact that he or she would not be the best at either the sport or the piano. I view having children in a similar fashion. Although I agree that you can have children and also work, you have to recognize that you simply can't be the best at both. For example, an out-of-town business trip may come up on the day that the child has a school recital. Time is required to be the best at anything, and, I determined I couldn't be the best in work and the best with children. Together, my husband and I decided to choose each other and our career accomplishments.

However, you could decide to compromise, to go half way for both career and children. You could say I don't necessarily want to be the best in my career, half way is fine. But then you still have to say it's half way for the children as well. So you have to realize that you certainly can't be the best at both, but you could choose to have both. If you choose to accept that you won't be the best at both that's fine. I personally don't know how anyone who is raising children could consciously choose this route.

Case Study

Nike's Suppliers in Vietnam

Sasha Lyutse

Following allegations of worker abuse, an investigation was launched in 1998 of Nike practices in subcontracted factories in Vietnam. This investigation created a public relations problem for the American manufacturer of athletic apparel. The report found that by not directly running the factories where its products were being made, Nike had little direct control over how employees were treated.

The report focused on Nike subcontracted factories in and around Ho Chi Minh City. It found local supervisors using abusive and

---

This case was written by Sasha Lyutse. Basic sources were: "*The Living Wage Project to Brief Members of Congress on Nike Labor Abuses.*" PR Newswire Association, Inc., Copyright 2001, April 3, 2001; "*Labor-rights Group: Nike, Knight Not Living up to 1998 Promises.*" The Associated Press State & Local Wire, May 16, 2001; and "*Nike Battles Labour Charges U.S. Firm Makes Changes after Alleged Worker Abuses in Vietnam,*" Toronto Star Newspapers, Ltd., Copyright 1998, April 2, 1998. Reprinted with permission.

humiliating practices to punish Vietnamese workers. Nike insisted that it did not tolerate abuse and required its manufacturers to take "immediate and effective measures to deal with it." A Nike training manager, the company said, works with subcontractors on sexual harassment, physical and verbal abuse, as well as on listening skills. The report found mat Nike had "a fine code of conduct," but that its local contractors often violated it.

In 1998 Nike employees at the Sam Yang factory, just outside Ho Chi Minh City, were paid $1.84 a day. Their average monthly salary was $48—slightly better than Vietnam's $45 minimum wage for this region. With this salary, Nike workers could meet needs for food and shelter, but little else. In a 1998 survey, however, Nike suppliers were found to be paying competitive wages—no worse and no better than those paid by other foreign shoemakers.

Phillip Knight, founder of Nike's $9 billion sports-apparel empire, signs sports superstars to multimillion dollar contracts to advertise Nike sneakers that sometimes sell for $100 or more on the American market. A pair of Nike sneakers is unattainable for a worker at the Sam Yang factory, who works six days a week and makes roughly $600 a year, half the average income in Ho Chi Minh City, but about four times the annual earnings in more remote rural regions of Vietnam.

In 1999 Nike responded to mounting pressures by creating a labor monitoring department and translated its code of conduct into 11 languages so that more workers could read it. At the Sam Yang factory the local owners issued a 10-point "action plan" based on many of the 1998 report's recommendations. They held a union election, signed a labor contract with workers and improved working conditions. The factory also got a new manager, increased trainees' wages and cut overtime. Most workers got a 5 percent raise, which came to about 8 cents more a day.

However, a 2001 report by the Global Alliance, an initiative sponsored by Nike in response to persistent criticism, documented proof of continued abusive labor practices in Southeast Asia, including physical, verbal and sexual abuse. According to the report, 96 percent of workers stated that they did not make enough money to meet their basic needs.

In its early days, before costs escalated and orders shifted to lower cost suppliers in Taiwan and South Korea, Nike imported all of its shoes from Japan. Soon, even Taiwan and South Korea became expensive, and suppliers moved their factories to China and Indonesia. In its global search for low-cost labor, Nike found Vietnam. By 1998, one out of every 10 pairs of Nike shoes came from subcontractors in Vietnam.

Vietnam is one of Southeast Asia's poorest countries. It has an official rural unemployment of about 27 percent in some regions. It aggressively seeks foreign investment to create jobs and bring manufacturing expertise. However, unlike those countries that turn a blind eye to worker abuses by overseas employers, Vietnam pays close attention to foreign investors' behavior and has some of the region's toughest laws aimed at protecting workers; it ensures a minimum wage, sets overtime limits, permits strikes, etc.

At the same time, Vietnamese government officials sometimes appear to have divided priorities. They feel that they are duty-bound to defend workers (which union leaders say is their primary responsibility), but they also feel that they must accommodate investment planners who want trade unions to back off and not scare away desperately needed foreign investments.

In 1998 Nike employed more workers than any other foreign business in Vietnam (through its five Nike-aligned shoe factories). At the time, shipments of Nike shoes accounted for 5 percent of Vietnam's total exports. If Nike were to pull out of Vietnam, 35,000 Vietnamese would be out of work.

Case Study

Chrysler and Gao Feng: Corporate Responsibility for Religious and Political Freedom in China

Michael A. Santoro

INTRODUCTION

For multinational corporations, doing business in China presents may complex ethical issues. The Gao Feng incident exemplified the challenging decisions that confront corporate executives trying to run a business in a country run by a totalitarian government that violates the human rights of its own citizens.

THE GAO FENG INCIDENT

In May 1994, Gao Feng, a devout Christian, was arrested in Beijing for planning a private worship service and candlelight vigil to commemorate the fifth anniversary of the Tiananmen Square massacre. Gao was a 26-year employee of Beijing Jeep, Chrysler's joint venture with the Chinese government. Gao was accused of violating Chinese laws against the practice of religion outside of a state-authorized venue.

Technically, Gao appears to have violated Chinese law. Article 36 of the Chinese Constitution nominally provides for freedom of religious belief. However, the government restricts religious practice to government sanctioned organizations in order to control the growth and scope of activity of religious groups. State Council Regulation 145, signed into law by then Premier Li Peng in January 1994, requires all places of worship to register with government religious affairs bureaus and come under the supervision of official "patriotic"

religious organizations. There are almost 85,000 approved venues for religious activities in China. Many religious groups, however, have been reluctant to comply with the regulation either out of principled opposition to state control of religion or due to fear of adverse consequences if they reveal, as the regulations require, the names and addresses of church leaders.

The Universal Declaration of Human Rights, endorsed by a resolution of the United Nations General Assembly in 1948, contains the following relevant provisions:

> **Article 18.** Everyone has the right to freedom of thought, conscience and religion; this right includes freedom to change his religion or belief, and freedom, either alone or in community with others and in public or private, to manifest his religion or belief in teaching, practice, worship and observance.

> **Article 19.** Everyone has the right to freedom of opinion and expression; this right includes freedom to hold opinions without interference and to seek, receive and impart information and ideas through any media and regardless of frontiers.

> **Article 20.** (1) Everyone has the right to freedom of peaceful assembly and association. (2) No one may be compelled to belong to an association.

According to press reports, Gao remained under administrative detention for five weeks.

He was never formally charged. In early July, Gao returned to work at Beijing Jeep and told his supervisor that the Chinese Public Safety Bureau had imprisoned him for over a month. Chrysler asked Gao to produce proof of his detention. The Chinese police gave Gao a note that said that he had been detained for three days and then released without trial.

Beijing Jeep's general manager was faced with a tough decision. The Chinese joint venture partner was pressuring Chrysler to fire Gao Feng. If he does not fire him, millions of dollars of Chrysler's invested capital in China would be put at risk. If, however, Chrysler fires Gao Feng, the company would become complicit in the violation of his right to religious freedom and political expression.

The commercial interests at stake for Chrysler cannot be ignored. One of the keys to success in the Chinese markets is good relations with the Communist Party which keeps rigid control over the economy. Multinational corporations spend years cultivating good *guanxi* or connections in China. They are thus extremely vulnerable to retaliation. Even powerful corporations such as Motorola, Hewlett-Packard and General Motors are well aware that they could jeopardize billions of dollars of investments if they take a position on human rights that angers the Chinese government. At the time of the Gao Feng incident, for example, Chrysler was very aware that failure to accede to the government's request could result in losing a valuable minivan contract to its German competitor Daimler-Benz. (United States–based Chrysler subsequently merged its worldwide businesses with the Germany-based Daimler-Benz.) As a consequence, the basic instinct of most foreign businesspeople in China is to stay as far away from the subject of human rights as possible. However, when a situation like the Gao Feng incident arises, corporate executives must make a decision and take action. Avoidance is simply not an option.

THE DECISION

Put yourself in the position of Chrysler's general manager. How would you handle the situation? Would you fire Gao Feng? Would you refuse to fire him? Is there some other course of action you would consider?

Would it be a sign of "cultural imperialism" if Chrysler refused to fire Gao Feng? After all, didn't Gao Feng violate Chinese law on the practice of religion? Does it matter that the enforcement of the law would appear to be in violation of the Universal Declaration of Human Rights?

How much should you factor in the financial consequences of your decision? What if your refusal to fire Gao Feng cost Chrysler millions of dollars in potential profits? Is there some way of handling the situation that would minimize the potential financial consequences?

When asked how he would handle the Gao Feng scenario, one executive with many years of business experience in China replied as follows: "The first thing I would do is to tell my secretary to hold my calls and then I would close my door to think. Because this would be a very serious situation, which, if not handled properly could have serious repercussions for my company. I would take this very seriously."

OUTCOME

Chrysler, presumably reasoning that Gao Feng had no documented reason for failing to report to work for the bulk of the time he was missing, fired him for poor attendance. Gao Feng's case became widely publicized when the advocacy group Human Rights Watch took up his cause. Due to the personal intervention of Chrysler's chairman, Robert J. Eaton, Gao was eventually reinstated, but his case dramatically illustrates the moral and financial pitfalls of operating in a country where there are serious and pervasive human rights abuses.

Gao's freedom was, however, short-lived once the publicity surrounding his case subsided. A few months after his reinstatement at Chrysler, Gao was rearrested and without benefit of a legal proceeding sent to a reeducation through labor camp. Gao Feng was again released in 1998 following the highly publicized visit of a interdenominational group of clergy appointed by President Clinton to investigate religious freedom in China.

Case Study

H. B. Fuller in Honduras

John Boatright

In 1985, journalists began writing about a new social problem in Honduras that created an acute dilemma for H. B. Fuller Company, based in St. Paul, Minnesota. The news stories described the ravaging effects of glue sniffing among the street children of Tegucigalpa, the capital of Honduras, and other Central American cities. The drug of choice for these addicts was Resistol, a glue produced by a Honduran subsidiary of H. B. Fuller, and the victims of this debilitating habit were known, in Spanish, as *resistoleros*. The negative publicity was sullying the company's stellar reputation for corporate social responsibility, and company executives came under great pressure to address the problem quickly.

Poverty in Honduras had forced many families to send their children into the streets to beg or do odd jobs. The earnings of these children were critical to the support of many families, especially those headed by a single mother. Some children lived in the streets in order to avoid abusive homes; others were abandoned or orphaned. Many children, some as young as five or six, sought relief from their misery by sniffing glue containing volatile solvents which produces a temporary elation and sense of power. These chemicals are addictive and lead to irreversible damage to the brain and liver. The victims of solvent abuse generally stagger as they walk and exhibit tense, aggressive behavior.

Resistol is a brand name for a line of adhesives manufactured by a wholly owned subsidiary of H. B. Fuller and marketed throughout Latin America. The solvent-based adhesives favored by glue sniffers were widely used in shoemaking and shoe repair and were readily available on the street. H. B. Fuller had urged the press not to use the term *resistoleros* because other brands of adhesives were used as well and the problem was with the abuse of Resistol, not the product itself. Nevertheless, the name was commonly used in Honduras to describe the street children addicted to solvents. One of H. B. Fuller's most successful brands had thus become synonymous with a major social problem.

Criticism of H. B. Fuller for the company's involvement in this problem came not only from activists and public health officials in Honduras but also from customers and shareholders in the United States. One shareholder asked, "How can a company like H. B. Fuller claim to have a social conscience and continue to sell Resistol, which is

---

'literally burning out the brains' of children in Latin America?" The company's mission statement placed its commitment to customers first, followed by its responsibilities to employees and shareholders. And the statement affirms: "H. B. Fuller will conduct business legally and ethically . . . and be a responsible corporate citizen." When the company acquired its subsidiary in Honduras, the CEO at the time said:

> We were convinced that we had something to offer Latin America that the region did not have locally. In our own small way, we also wanted to be of help to that part of the world. We believed that by producing adhesives in Latin America and by employing only local people, we would create new jobs and help elevate the standard of living. We were convinced that the way to aid world peace was to help Latin America become more prosperous.

Company executives faced the dilemma of whether these expressions of H. B. Fuller's aspirations could be reconciled with the continued production of Resistol in Honduras.

Community activists in Honduras proposed the addition of oil of mustard to all solvent-based adhesives. This chemical, allyl isothiocyanate, produces a reaction that has been compared to getting an overdose of horseradish. Adding it to Resistol would effectively deter anyone attempting to inhale the fumes. However, research revealed that oil of mustard has many side effects, including severe irritation of the eyes, nose, throat, and lungs, and it can even be fatal if inhaled, swallowed, or absorbed through the skin. In addition, adhesives with oil of mustard have a shelf life of only six months. H. B. Fuller executives were convinced that the addition of oil of mustard was not an acceptable solution. However, in 1989, the Honduran legislature passed a law

requiring oil of mustard, despite the lobbying efforts of H. B. Fuller.

Another alternative was a community relations effort to alert people about the dangers of glue sniffing and to address the underlying social causes. By working with community groups and the government, the company could spread the responsibility and expand its resources. On the other hand, the community groups in Honduras and elsewhere in the region were not well organized, and the government was unstable and unreliable. In 1982, the Gillette Company had faced a similar problem with its solvent-based typewriter correction fluid, Liquid Paper, which was being abused by youngsters in the United States. Gillette also rejected the possibility of adding oil of mustard, but the company's community relations effort was facilitated by the existing network of private and government-sponsored drug education programs. In Honduras, H. B. Fuller did not have the same base of community and government support. A community relations effort would be much more difficult in a less developed country.

H. B. Fuller executives also considered withdrawing all solvent-based adhesives from the market and perhaps substituting water-based products, but these alternatives were not very attractive from a business point of view. Furthermore, they would have no impact on the critical social problem of glue sniffing by street children. The waste of young lives would continue unless conditions were changed. But what could a modest-sized company located in St. Paul, Minnesota, do to address a problem caused by deep cultural, social, political, and economic forces? A failure to act, however, would seriously damage H. B. Fuller's carefully built reputation for corporate social responsibility.

Women in the Workplace

Leave It to Beaver, the popular television show of the late 1950s and early 1960s, was a situation comedy not a documentary. And yet a lot of people then (and perhaps even now) thought it represented an ideal portrait of the American family—Dad at work, Mom home with the kids. Sociologist Stephanie Coontz maintains that the model of Dad earning a living and Mom in the kitchen resonates with a deep-seated bias regarding what we then thought to be natural and proper: Men were providers, women were nurturers. In her book, *The Way We Never Were: American Families and the Nostalgia Trap*, she argued that this model existed for only a brief moment in the cultural history of this country.

Perhaps the single most important event in the American labor market in the second half of the twentieth century was the unprecedented entry of large numbers of women into the workforce seeking full-time employment and careers, with more than 66 million women working full time in the United States, representing (depending on statistical method) 49 to 51 percent of the workforce. Working couples—whether dual income, no kids (DINKs) or dual income, some kids (DISKs)—now make up 39 percent of the workforce.

Feeding the rising tide of working women were the feminist movement, changes in social custom, the evolving needs of business, enhanced educational opportunities, the need to seek individual identity, and the rising cost of the middle-class lifestyle. In contrast to the 1950s and 1960s, when 43 percent of all families were supported on a single income, today only 14 percent do. Traditional *Leave It to Beaver*–like families are now a minority of two-parent households with children—in the 1980s, 15 percent; some studies place the current figure at 25 percent.

Because today's families have two breadwinners, are more mobile, are less stable, and are much more dependent on child-care centers, schools, restaurants, and elder-care services to perform what were once strictly family functions, the essays and cases in this section address some of the issues that attend women in the workplace and the problem of achieving an elusive work/life balance for both men and women. "Women in the Workplace" offers an overview of the entire phenomenon and its impact on our lives. "Management Women and the New Facts of Life" is the article that sparked the ongoing debate creating a "mommy track" for women who want both careers and kids. "Homeward Bound" advances the argument that affluent women choosing to leave careers for motherhood is harmful to society and future generations of women. "Where Are the Women?" seeks to explain why women, so well represented in business schools and middle management, remain conspicuous by their absence from C-level jobs. The title of "How Women Are Changing Corporate America" is self-explanatory. "How Corporate America Is Betraying Women" tells a different story. "Gender Issues at Your House" and "Worth the Effort?" provide realistic workplace scenarios of what can happen when a sexual harassment charge is made.

Essay

Women in the Workplace

Al Gini

Perhaps the single most important event in the American labor market in the twentieth century has been the unprecedented entry of large numbers of women into the workforce.

> When the history of the last quarter of the 20th century is written scholars may well conclude that the nation's most important social development has been the rise to positions of power and influence of its most vigorous majority: American women. So many women have flocked to the labor force . . . that more Americans are now employed than ever before. This is no less than a revolutionary change, one that has created profound shifts not only in the family and the workplace but also in basic U.S. economic policy making.[1]

When Freud cited work and love as the foundations of human behavior, he might as well have used the words work and family. These are the two major institutions on which any society is based. Work and family are the two primary pillars of human existence, and every society in every age must grapple with the delicate mechanisms and relationships that influence and support these two fundamental phenomena.[2] As we step onto Bill Clinton's proverbial "bridge to the twenty-first century," the sheer numbers of women who have entered the workforce threaten to irreparably alter both the quality and quantity of our work and family lives. And, like it or not, we must be prepared to adapt or modify some of our most sacred social ideals and stereotypes about work and the family.

Cultural critic Barbara Ehrenreich once commented that in the 1960s the stereotypical liberated women was a braless radical, hoarse from denouncing the twin evils of capitalism and patriarchy.[3] Today's stereotype is more often a blue-suited executive carrying an attaché case and engaging in leveraged buyouts—before transmogrifying into a perfect mother, gourmet cook, and seductive lover in the evenings. Neither stereotype is or ever was perfectly true, but they can tell us a great deal about what many women and men would like to believe. What is true, according to newspaper columnist Carol Kleiman, is that the official organizational policy of most workplaces continues to operate as if white men constituted the majority of the workforce and most women are still at home managing the multiple roles of homemaking and child-rearing. As a result, both male and female employees must cope with the mounting stress of balancing work and family demands.[4] Workplaces need to accept and accommodate the inescapable demographic fact that since

---

the mid-1980s, women and minority males make up the majority of the workforce.[5]

Women have always been part of the workforce and working mothers are not simply a "new demographic phenomenon of the later-half of the 20th century."[6] Stephanie Coontz has documented that women's active participation in the workforce has always been dependent on need, circumstance, and, to a very large extent, "cultural permission," which has varied over the years. A classic example is "Rosie the Riveter" the icon of American women during World War II. When the GI Joe husbands, brothers, and sons of "Rosie" marched off to war, "Rosie" marched into factories across America and took on complicated new jobs, gained new skills, and produced both the necessary domestic goods and the military hardware needed to win the war, doing her bit to once again "make the world safe for democracy." When the war was won and our GIs came home, many of the women were happy to leave the workplace to the men. Others were reluctant to give up their newly won responsibilities, independence, and income, and expressed a desire to continue working. Management, however, went to extraordinary lengths to purge women from high-paying and nontraditional jobs. The women who wanted or needed to work were not expelled from the labor force, but were downgraded to lower-paid, "female" jobs. Nevertheless, according to Coontz:

> Even at the end of the purge, there were more women working than before the war, and by 1952 there were two million more wives at work than at the peak of wartime production. The jobs available to these women, however, lacked the pay and the challenges that had made war time work so satisfying, encouraging women to define themselves in terms of home and family even when they were working.[7]

During the war, working as "Rosie the Riveter" was a badge of honor, a mark of distinction, a woman's patriotic duty. After the war, however, "cultural permission" once again shifted. *Esquire* magazine called working wives a "menace," and *Life* termed married women's employment a "disease." Being a full-time wife and mother was lauded as a woman's true vocation, the only job that could provide a woman with a "sense of fulfillment, of happiness, of complete pervading contentment."[8]

Sixty years ago, the notion of an unfulfilled homemaker was for most—but certainly not all—women unheard of. Prior to World War II, the maintenance of a house and, often, a large family was a full-time occupation and acknowledged as such. Those women who did venture outside the home in search of full- or part-time employment did so either out of dire financial need or in an attempt to earn a little "pin money" to subsidize a few household extras. Only in recent years have the everyday tasks of meal-making and home maintenance become less than full-time jobs. When combined with the decrease in family size, large numbers of women became, in the view of many, underemployed and underestimated.

It wasn't until the late 1950s and early 1960s, however, that women once again received "cultural permission" to enter the workforce in search of jobs or careers and a new sense of identity. Contributing to this cultural shift were the feminist movement and its impact on social consciousness, technological advances in the information and communications industries, the conversion from a manufacturing to a service economy, increased access to education, fair employment and affirmative action legislation, and the ever-increasing costs of a higher standard of living. Women now find full-time work outside the home not only possible and desirable, but, in many cases, financially necessary.

At the beginning of the twentieth century, only 5 million of the 28 million working Americans were women. One-quarter of these were teenagers and only a very few were married. As recently as 1947, women accounted for fewer than 17 million of the 59 million employed. Since that time, however, six of every ten additions to the workforce have been women. Between 1969 and 1979 women took on two-thirds of the 20 million newly created jobs;[9] between 1980 and 1992 women accounted for 60 percent of the increase in the American workforce.[10]

In 1984 the Census Bureau reported that for the first time in our history the prototype of American worker—the adult white male—no longer made up the majority of the labor force.[11] Women and minority men now hold approximately 57 percent of all jobs. In 1995, 57.5 million women were in the labor force of 125 million. In 1960, 35.5 percent of all women and 78.8 percent of all men worked full-time; by 1995, those numbers had risen to 55.6 percent of all women and 70.8 percent of all men.[12]

Depending on how you crunch the numbers, women now make up 46 to 49 percent of the entire workforce. Between 1947 and 1995 women's participation in the workforce increased 17 percent. Some demographers predict that women may represent a simple majority of the workforce early in the twenty-first century.[13] The Bureau of Labor Statistics more conservatively estimates that women will maintain but not necessarily exceed their present percentage in the workforce. They project that in 2005 the total labor force will be 150.5 million workers, and that 71.8 million of them will be women.[14]

While single and divorced women have long had relatively high labor force participation rates, fewer than 25 percent of married women were working full-time in 1960. That number today is 33.3 million, or 61 percent of married women. Of these working married women 70.2 percent have children under seventeen years of age.[15] It is estimated that two-thirds of all mothers are now in the labor force. Two-job families now make up 58 percent of married couples with children.[16] One set of statistics indicates that 20 percent of women in double-income families earn more than their husbands.[17] More recent research conducted by the Women's Voice Project, an ongoing study by the Center for Policy Alternatives in Washington, suggests that as many as 55 percent of all married women earn at least half of their family's income.[18]

According to social commentator John W. Wright, an unmistakable sign of the social change going on in the workplace is the significant increase in the number of women who return to work after having a baby. In 1976, about 31 percent of the women who gave birth returned to or entered the labor force, by 1985 it had climbed to 48 percent.[19] In a series of interviews I conducted with human resources specialists, most estimated that at their places of employment 75 percent of new mothers returned to work within twelve weeks of giving birth.

Fueling these rising statistics are the ever-widening professions now open to women. While traditional "women's" jobs such as nurses, teachers, librarians, and clerical workers are still predominantly women, the proportion of female engineers, architects, and public officials—while still small—has more than doubled since 1960.[20] Classes in law and medical schools are now typically composed of 40 to 50 percent women.

According to the Department of Labor special report "Working Women Count," 30 percent of working women are engaged in service and sales jobs, 13.1 percent have factory, craft, construction, or technical jobs or jobs in the transportation industry, 27.6 percent of working women have professional or executive jobs, and 40 percent of all corporate middle-management positions are held by women.[21] In general, although women are grossly overrepresented at the entry and low levels of all kinds of work, it is clear that the historical distinctions between "women's" work and "men's" work have begun to blur.

Obviously, the entrance of women into the labor market has changed the composition of the workforce, the workplace, and the structure of family life. According to "Working Women Count," it is now expected that 99 percent of all American women will work for pay sometime during their lives.[22] The 1950s traditional family—dad at work and mom at home with the kids—is no longer the predominant pattern; nontraditional families are now the majority.[23] Again, depending on whose figures you are willing to accept, it is estimated that fewer than 15 percent of all households fit the traditional family model.[24] As recently as 1960, 43 percent of all families conformed to the single-earner model,[25] but in less than thirty-six years we have become a nation of DINKS (Double-Income-No-Kids) and DISKS (Double-Income-Some-Kids) families. According to sociologist Uma Sekaran, "The number of two-career families, single-parent families, and unmarried working couples living together is steadily increasing. This population constitutes more than 90 percent of today's labor force. Organizations are . . . beginning to feel the impact of this new breed of employee."[26]

In addition, women are now demanding the right to define themselves in the way that men always have—through their jobs. Being a wife, a mother, a homemaker has over the course of the past two or three generations simply changed until it no longer meets the definition of work to which most people now subscribe. It has been suggested that when the first wave of female baby boomers arrived at college in the early 1960s, many expected to marry shortly thereafter and raise children.[27] Not anymore! According to a survey cited by Arlie Russell Hochschild, less than 1 percent of 200,000 female college freshmen

wanted to be a "full-time homemaker." In a 1986 survey of female college seniors, 80 percent thought it was "very important" to have a career.[28] Nine years later, 86 percent of recent female college graduates defined themselves as "careerist."[29]

Women now want to be known by their accomplishments and occupations and not merely as "Mrs. John Smith" or "Johnny's mommy." When First Lady Barbara Bush gave the commencement speech at Wellesley College in 1991, many members of the all-female student body protested her appearance because her most significant accomplishment was being somebody's wife.[30] Gloria Emerson has pointed out that every twelve-year-old boy in America knows what must be done to achieve identity and "make it" as a man: Money must be made. Nothing else is as defining or as masculine as this.[31] Women now want to forge their own identity by means of paid employment—the principal definition of work. In the words of demographer Daniel Yankelovich, women now view a paid job as "a badge of membership in the larger society and an almost indispensable symbol of self-worth."[32]

In a very real sense women's desire to define themselves through work was spurred by Betty Friedan, Gloria Steinem, and the feminist movement. The "new breed" of women sought to be autonomous agents, able to guide and direct themselves, determining their purpose and role in life by their own choices and actions. They no longer wanted to be viewed as "second-class citizens," relegated to hearth and home, and totally dependent on men. In addition to the ideological motivations, however, practical reasons played an important role. Many women sought jobs or careers to keep up with the ever-increasing costs of middle-class existence: suburban homes, safe cars, good schools, kids' music lessons, and prestigious colleges.

As recently as 1980, only 19 percent of working women said that their incomes were necessary to support their family, while 43 percent said they worked to bring in extra money.[33] In 1995, however, 44 percent of employed women said that they worked out of necessity, and only 23 percent to earn extra cash. The survey concluded that most married working women now view their incomes as essential to their family's well-being.[34] The new piece of cynical conventional wisdom currently circulating around college campuses today reads something like this: "Guys, look around. Don't just marry the pretty one. Marry the smart one. The one who's got the best chance of landing a good job. Why? Because you're going to need each other to acquire the things and lifestyle that your parents managed to achieve on one salary!" For example, in 1989, 79 percent of homes bought were purchased by two-income households.[35] Some realtors estimate that in the mid-1990s, that number rose to 85 percent.[36]

The bottom line is that women may once have entered the workforce out of desire, but, today, they stay because of need. Not only have they been granted "cultural permission" to seek work, they have now acquired a financial imperative to do so. In the most recent past, most women had three choices about employment: Don't work at all, work part-time, or work full-time. Now, like men, their options have been reduced to one.

As a final note on the many ways in which women's increased presence in the workforce has changed family life, one must mention divorce. Ninety percent of men and women marry, but 50 percent of all first marriages end in divorce, and an alarming 60 percent of second marriages also end in divorce.[37] The traumatic effect of divorce is felt by all members of a family, especially the children. Because of America's rising divorce rates in the last fifty years, 60 percent of all children will live in a single-parent household for a significant period of time before they are eighteen.[38] Although 70 percent of divorced adults will remarry, 25 percent of all children grow up primarily in a one-parent household.[39]

Whatever the causes of a divorce, the practical and financial fallout of the separation is much harder on the woman. According to psychologist Lenore Weitzman, in the first year after divorce women experience a 73 percent loss in their standard of living, whereas men experience a 42 percent gain.[40] Even when divorced fathers dutifully comply with child-support payments and remain emotionally involved with their children, the primary responsibility for children's day-to-day and long-term well-being falls to the mother.

Divorce is now an accepted part of our social tapestry. Another trend gaining acceptance is single motherhood, from unmarried teenage mothers to adult women who choose to have children out of wedlock (à la TV's *Murphy Brown*). One of the major lessons now learned by women and girls alike is self-sufficiency. According to Karen Nussbaum, former head of the U.S. Department of Labor's Women's Bureau, "There should be no girl out there [anymore] who thinks someone else is going to take care of [her]." Life has changed and the expectations of women must also change. For women work is now less of an option and more of a necessity. "If girls [today] aren't working when they get out of high school," Nussbaum has stated, "they will be at some point."[41] While, for many women, work can be a badge of honor and a symbol of self-worth, it has also become a fundamental element of survival.

JUSTICE ON THE JOB

Women are now being recruited more than men for entry positions in various industries. In this way, corporations can claim, at least prima facie, that they are complying with the rules of affirmative action and open employment. The issue for most women is not getting a job, but, what happens to them once they have it. Although not all women encounter prejudicial behavior, too many are forced to endure personal and institutional resistance to their careers and professional advancement.

According to management scholar Judy Rosener, few women encounter a level playing field on the job. Most are forced to cope with a problem she calls "sexual static." Rosener argues that most male managers and workers—especially those over the age of forty—see females in the workplace, first and foremost, as females, not as colleagues. Too many men are unable to see female coworkers outside their traditional sex roles—as mothers, sisters, daughters, and potential mates. Sexual static interferes with communication and hampers normal business conduct between men and women, resulting in mixed signals, misunderstanding, embarrassment, anger, confusion, and fear.[42] Sexual static, suggests business ethicist Patricia Werhane, may make a work environment hostile or just uncomfortable. It may be "sexually charged" or create an atmosphere in which "men and women feel uneasy about their professional interrelationships and how these might be misinterpreted as sexual ones."[43]

Sexual static is not the same thing as sexual harassment. Sexual static is more insidious. Sexual harassment is about inappropriate sexual comments, unwelcome sexual advances, or requests for sexual favors as a condition of an individual's employment, advancement, or success. Sexual static is an attempt to avoid and defuse even the suggestion of sexual harassment. It is the tension that occurs when men and women are not sure how to comport themselves in a business or social environment. The personal sexual insecurity of male managers often leads to dysfunctional corporate decision-making. A senior male attorney at a major firm admitted, "We have a real bright woman who has what it takes to be a partner, but I can't bring myself to vote to promote her because she turns me on, and it gets in my way." Fear of gossip motivates other men. "Every time I promote a woman," reported a fifty-year-old male advertising executive, "I worry about people suspecting I have a romantic interest in her."[44]

Rosener and Werhane agree that although everyone involved loses both personally and professionally in an atmosphere of sexual static, women are the primary victims. Sexual static perpetuates stereotypical female roles, denies women the opportunity to acquire new skills and experiences, too often denies women the support of a senior male mentor who can act as a role model, and, finally, precludes professional objectivity.[45] Professional objectivity maintains that management practices should be unbiased and impersonal. It requires that the most skilled and effective persons be hired and promoted to leadership positions. Unfortunately, concludes Werhane, "we live in a society in which business is conducted in an atmosphere where merit or worthiness is the ideal but not the practice."[46] Not only do we not live in a sex-gender-color-ethnic-age–neutral environment, sexual static reinforces the divisive notion that men and women are two separate and competitive species loosely connected by sex, children, and financial arrangements.

The major organizational problem facing working women is the proverbial glass ceiling—an invisible barrier that keeps women from ascending to the highest levels of management. The glass ceiling does not just apply to elite workers aspiring to corporate management; it also refers to the institutional and personal prejudices that women encounter in every kind of job at every level in the workplace. A majority of American women in the workplace, regardless of race, class, type of job, or job location, feel that the glass ceiling is keeping them in their place. According to the nationally based report "Working Women Count," more than 60 percent of women believe that they have little or no opportunity for advancement.[47]

Even though women now represent 46 to 49 percent of the workforce, more than 97 percent of all senior management is still male. Where women are starting to achieve representation equal with their numbers is in the lower and middle ranks of management. Even those women who manage to pass through this transparent barrier often find themselves in jobs that have a "glass floor," that is, where their every move can be seen and scrutinized, and where their first big mistake has them figuratively crashing down.

Business Week has reported that half the lowest management levels are staffed with female workers and that soon the middle ranks will be, too. Overall, women now occupy an unprecedented 41 to 43 percent of lower- and middle-management positions.[48] However, a report by Catalyst, Inc., released in October 1996 found that only 10 percent of the top jobs at the nation's 500 largest companies are held by women. Alarmingly, 105 of these 500 companies have no female corporate officers at all, and only 2.4 percent of all the women employed in these 500 companies have achieved the rank of chairperson, president, CEO, or executive vice president. Only four of the twenty-four "Best Companies for Women to Work For," featured in a *Business Week* cover story, had women in more than 25 percent of their corporate officer posts in 1996.[49]

In a related report, Catalyst announced that women's representation on boards of directors of Fortune 500 companies had finally exceeded 10 percent. Of the 6,123 Fortune 500 board seats, women now hold 626, or 10.2 percent. Altogether, 83 percent of Fortune 500 companies have at least one woman on their boards. According to Sheila

Wellington, president of Catalyst, while these numbers are important, they're "absolutely minuscule. What this shows is that people who say the gains have been made, so let's move on, are dead wrong. It shows that the numbers of women who have made it to the apex are still so few. . . . Clearly, there's a lot more work to be done."[50]

The absence of women from positions of power in business is also reflected in our political system. In 1995, the seventy-fifth anniversary of women's suffrage in America, the Center for Policy Alternatives reported that across the nation, women represented only 20 percent of state legislators, 25 percent of statewide elective executive officers, 10 percent of U.S. representatives, 8 percent of U.S. senators, and 2 percent of governors.[51] As Katherine Spillar, national coordinator for the Fund for the Feminist Majority, so wryly put it, "At the current rates of increase it will be four hundred and seventy-five years before women reach equality in executive suites."[52]

Some critics suggest that those few women who have broken through the glass ceiling have done so not by embracing feminism but by outperforming men on their own terms. These are classic careerists, who happen to be women. Like any dedicated careerist, they did their jobs, made their numbers, and, when necessary, did battle. In fact, according to Chicago-based consultants Megan Buffington and Jane Neff, some of these successful women are more combative and ruthless than their male counterparts because they feel they have to prove they can be rough, tough, and resilient. Buffington and Neff call this the "only bra in the room syndrome" and cite Chicago's first female mayor, Jane Byrne, as its icon.

By all accounts Byrne may have been a "lady" when the situation required but in her heart she was one of the boys. A longtime operative in Richard J. Daley's political machine, Byrne earned her spurs because she did her job, could keep a secret, and over the years built up alliances. After Daley died, she rose to his post. In a tough campaign that "reeked of testosterone," as one pundit put it, she convinced the electorate that she had more of the "right stuff" than her rival. After she was out of office, she said in an interview that she really hated losing the mayor's job because she had worked so hard at it; she had wanted to be an effective mayor, and she feared that people attributed her mistakes not just to miscalculation or shortcomings of character, but to being "just a woman."

According to Buffington and Neff, a characteristic of these types of achievers is their lack of empathy for and support of other working women, especially their subordinates. Having achieved success by playing hardball and working hard, they expect the same from others. Having made it despite being a woman, their focus is on success and not sensitivity. They tend to be intolerant of office schmoozing or signs of friendship in the office, such as birthday celebrations. They leave their private lives at home, and they expect others to do so as well. But, worst of all, out of either a twisted sense of elitism or simple selfishness, too many of these successful women do not reach back to mentor other women. Some of them seem to think "I made it without any help, and if you're any good so will you" or "since I'm already here, there's no more room at the table." Buffington and Neff suggest that consequently, many women do not like to work for female bosses. In a recent Gallop poll conducted in twenty-two countries, women overwhelmingly preferred male to female bosses in all but three countries surveyed (India, where they preferred to work for women, and El Salvador and Honduras, where they were evenly split in their preferences). In the United States 45 percent of men and women surveyed prefer a man as a boss while only 20 percent prefer a woman (the rest did not indicate a preference).[53]

Although the term *glass ceiling* is metaphorical, the effect it describes is very real. Not only does it prohibit some women from advancing to senior corporate management, it also denies women on the shop floor and in the lower offices equal opportunities for training, advancement, and promotion. Worse still, it has a limiting effect on salaries. According to the Department of Labor, the second most common complaint voiced by the 250,000 women surveyed as part of its study "Working Women Count," was "unequal and unfair pay."[54] Even though the Equal Pay Act passed Congress in 1963 and the discrepancy between men's and women's pay has narrowed, the gap remains significant. In 1993 in annual earnings of full-time, full-year workers, women earned 71 cents for every dollar earned by a man in the same job, and in 1996 the International Labor Organization reported that a majority of women in America earn 75 cents for every dollar earned by men doing the same job.[55]

Nationwide it is estimated that, on average, women with college degrees earn slightly more than men with high-school degrees and $10,000 a year less than men with comparable educations. Of the women who took part in the "Working Women Count" survey, 23 percent had part-time jobs (less than 35 hours per week) and 77 percent had full-time jobs (40 hours or more per week). Their income reporting was as follows: 16.3 percent earned less than $10,000 per year; 39 percent earned $10,000 to $25,000; 15.8 percent earned $25,000 to $35,000; 10.4 percent earned $35,000 to $50,000; and 4.8 percent earned $50,000 to $75,000. It is worth noting that 71.1 percent of these women earned less than $35,000 per year, and 58 percent earned less than $25,000. At the same time, 35 percent of the sample reported being the sole support of themselves and their families.[56] While women may nearly constitute the simple majority of the workforce, it was clear that they are a long way from matching men in pay.

Another factor that impedes women's advancement at work is babies. According to the Women's Bureau of the Department of Labor the greatest concern of working women is finding a way to balance work, family, and child care. Never has the number of women with young children in the workplace been higher. Sixty-seven percent of women with children under eighteen are working or actively seeking employment. This includes 54 percent of mothers with children under three, 58 percent of mothers with children under six, and 75 percent of mothers with school-age children. These mothers report that juggling kids and work results in a constant state of anxiety, fatigue, frustration, and guilt, both on and off the job. As one working woman told me, "I don't even know what I should feel bad about first! The job? Because I always feel I should be working harder? The kids? Because I miss them so much, and I know I'm missing so much. The house? Because it doesn't feel like a home anymore, it's just a place where we live. Or, my husband? Good old—what the hell is his name?!"

In the "Working Women Count" survey, 56 percent of mothers complained about not being able to find adequate, affordable child-care services, 49 percent wanted paid leaves "to care for a newborn and sick relatives," and 35 percent wanted more "flexible working schedules" in an attempt to balance the day-to-day necessities of work and private life.[57] In some sense, these demands and desires reflect a piece of "occupational wisdom" that all working women have been forced to absorb: "You can take time to baby a client, but you can't take time to baby your own baby."[58]

In 1989, in an attempt to address the needs of babies, women, and men, Felice Schwartz published an article in which she proposed that corporations establish two parallel working tracks for female employees: the "career primary" track and the "career and family" track. Those who chose the career primary track would be considered for any and all tasks, and the career and family track women would be given more limited responsibilities than their career primary colleagues. Schwartz also proposed that at different points in a woman's career she could change career tracks. In this way, corporations would be able to retain experienced employees, and women could pursue their careers without being forced to totally abdicate their responsibilities as mothers.[59] Critics immediately attacked Schwartz's ideas and relabeled her categories the "breeders" versus the "achievers." Although Schwartz offered her track system as a means of balancing the needs of women, children, and families, many commentators saw her proposal as a passport to permanent second class status and a one-way ticket to a mediocre career. The "mommy track," as her proposal was commonly called, was seen as singling out women for complete parental responsibility or sacrifice. The mommy track became not a new alternative, but a dead end.

In a 1997 article in *Fortune* magazine Betsy Morris argued that the issues raised by Schwartz—balancing careers, babies, and long-term family responsibilities—have neither been resolved nor gone away. In fact, Morris claims things have gotten much worse. For all their politically correct talk, most companies don't much care about or like kids.

> Today, in the corridors of business as elsewhere, families are getting more lip service than ever. Being on the right side of work and family issues—having the proper programs, letting Mom and Dad slip out to watch a T-ball game—is very PC. But corporate America harbors a dirty secret. People in human resources know it. So do a lot of CEOs, although they don't dare discuss it. Families are no longer a big plus for a corporation; they are a big problem. An albatross. More and more, the business world seems to regard children not as the future generation of workers but as luxuries you're entitled to after you've won your stripes. Its fine to have kid's pictures on your desk—just don't let them cut into your billable hours.[60]

[handwritten margin notes: "PROBLEM"; "Baby is not income generator"]

Companies want all their employees to clock as much time as possible. They are interested in results, productivity, and success, not child-care commitments and kindergarten recitals. In the spirit of full disclosure, Morris suggested, all corporate manuals should carry a warning: "Ambitious workers beware. If you want to have children, proceed at your own risk. You must be very talented, or on very solid ground, to overcome the damage a family can do to your career."[61]

JUSTICE AT HOME

The problems, prejudices, and injustices that women face in the workplace are, unfortunately, mirrored and often intensified on the home front. As Arlie Hochschild put it, "Women can have fame and fortune, office affairs, silicon injections, and dazzling designer clothes. But the one thing they can't have, apparently, is a man who shares the work at home."[62] There is a price to pay for having "made it," and, by all accounts, women are picking up most of the tab. In her important book *The Second Shift,* Hochschild claims that even though women have won certain rights in the workplace, they have not won many rights at home—in fact, many women are losing ground. According to Hochschild, women in dual-income families not only carry the burdens and responsibilities of their profession, but 80 percent of working women also carry the burden of a second job—caring for the home, the kids, and the husband.

On average, Hochschild claims, in the 1960s and 1970s American women worked around the house 15 hours more per week than men did. Over a year, this adds up to women putting in "an extra month of twenty-four-hour days" on household chores. One study showed that "women averaged three hours a day on housework while men averaged 17 minutes; women spent fifty minutes a day of time exclusively with their children; men spent 12 minutes." According to Hochschild's computations, 61 percent of men do little or no housework, 21 percent attempt, on an irregular basis, to do their share of household chores, and only 18 percent of men share housework equally.[63] In effect, the second shift means that women put in a double day: They're on duty at work, they're on duty at home. As one angry woman put it, "I do my half. I do half of his half. And the rest doesn't get done!"[64]

Some of Hochschild's findings are unexpected (for example, working-class husbands did more around the house than ostensibly more liberal, middle-class professional husbands), but the cultural causes of the second shift phenomenon are painfully predictable. Most men feel that their work is more important than their wives' jobs. Although their wives' salaries may be necessary, most men, because they earn more and because they have been traditionally seen as the head of the family, view their work as the primary ingredient defining household status. Although domestic chores may be aesthetically and hygienically necessary, they are neither creative nor important and therefore are not the concern of the progenitor and main provider of the family. Most men believe that women are natural nurturers and are better suited for child care.

Hochschild argues that the sudden surge of women into the workplace has not been accompanied by a new cultural understanding of both marriage and work that would have made this transition smoother. Families have changed, women have changed, work has changed, but most workplaces have remained inflexible in the face of their workers' family demands. At home, most men have yet to fundamentally adapt their lifestyles to accommodate the changes in women's lives. Because of this absence of change, said Hochschild, and because of the burdens of the second shift, the movement of women into the workforce in search of identity, independence, and financial security remains at best a "stalled revolution."[65]

In her most recent book, *The Time Bind*, Hochschild suggests that the revolution not only is still "stalled" but that the burdens and fallout of the second shift have gotten more complex. Even with men actively contributing to child care and household chores, men and women still find themselves desperately trying to juggle their commitments to family and work. The demands of a workaholic corporate system and the needs of families and children have us rushing from one responsibility to another and have us trapped in a "time bind" of guilt. Unfortunately, Hochschild says, "many working families are both prisoners and architects of the time bind in which they find themselves."[66] They want it all: great jobs, great families, and all the goodies that go along with it. But the increased energy and time they pump into work is taken from the home, and their lives become more emotionally stressful. Surprisingly, Hochschild discovered, in her three-year study of a "family friendly" Fortune 500 firm, that for a growing number of two-career couples, when work and family compete, work wins. Many workers choose to escape into work because life at home has become a "frantic exercise in beat-the-clock, while work, by comparison, seems a haven of grown-up sociability, competence and relative freedom."[67]

According to Hochschild, the roles of home and work have begun to reverse. Work has become a form of "home" (a village of associates, peers, coworkers) and home has become "hardwork" (a locus of duty, chores, and demanding personalities). Work is the new "neighborhood," where we spend most of our time, where we talk to friends and develop relationships and expertise. Meanwhile, home is now where we are least secure and most harried. "At home the divorce rate has risen, and the emotional demands have become more baffling and complex. In addition to teething, tantrums and the normal development of growing children, the needs of elderly parents are creating more tasks for the modern family—as are the blending, unblending, reblending of new step parents, step children, exes, and former in-laws."[68] By comparison work is less chaotic, cleaner, more enriching, and much less personal. As one female worker admitted to Hochschild, "I put in for [overtime]. . . . I get home, and the minute I turn the key, my daughter is right there . . . the baby is still up . . . the dishes are still in the sink. . . . My husband is in the other room hollering at my daughter, 'I don't ever get any time to talk to your mother. You're always monopolizing her time!' They all come at me at once."[69]

Is it any wonder that work becomes home and home becomes work? Work is less demanding, a surrogate, a refuge from our troubled private lives. It is also a place where conflicts that originate in the home can be discussed, debated, and subjected to sympathetic scrutiny. In the sanctuary of work, says Hochschild, increasing numbers of women are discovering the "great male secret"—work can be an escape from the pressures of home. In the words of a James Thurber character as he leaves for work after a long weekend of kit and kin, "Ah, thank God it's Monday!" Somewhat reluctantly, Hochschild concludes that for more and more women "the world of 'male' work seems more honorable and valuable than the 'female' world of home and children."[70] The paradoxical result of such a shift, suggests Hochschild, is altogether clear: That for which we work—families—is that which is most hurt by our work!

Hochschild implies that every dual-career family needs a full-time wife. In my review of *The Time Bind* I argued that given Hochschild's findings and insights, perhaps the only way to save the family is to change it.

In the future, individuals who want to "have it all"—children and a career—without short-changing one or the other, or both, will be required to enter into a communal marriage involving six precertified adults. Two of them will work full-time in order to support the family; two will be in charge of the house and kids; and two of them will be held in ready reserve, to fill in wherever they are needed. Divorce will be forbidden; all property will be owned in joint tenancy; sleeping arrangements are negotiable; and sex will be strictly optional. Hey, why not give it a try? Nothing else seems to be working.[71]

Women have changed. The economy has changed. The workplace has changed. Families have changed. Unfortunately, most men have not changed, either privately or professionally. The rules of work also have not changed sufficiently to accommodate the new reality. Are women in the workplace to stay? Absolutely! Women report that they both need and want to work. Current research also suggests that no matter how taxing and hectic their lives, women who do paid work feel less depressed, have a higher sense of personal worth, and are happier and more satisfied than women who do not have jobs. Do men need women in the workplace? Yes! Demographic trends regarding birthrates, urban population patterns, and college graduation rates necessitate women's active participation in the workplace. Do men want women in the workplace? Yes and no. For a lot of men, women simply represent another group of individuals to compete with for jobs, salaries, promotions; and for some men there yet remains a sense of social awkwardness about women's roles and men's appropriate response.

For too many men, women's commitment to work and their general dependability remains suspect because of "the one immutable, enduring difference between men and women . . . maternity."[72] On the job, families and babies are seen as a vulnerability, an impediment rather than a normal and necessary part of life that should be accommodated. According to

Betsy Morris, in an interesting shift in values, the new ultimate male status symbol "is not a fancy car or a fancy second home, or a wife with a fancy career. You've really made it, buddy, if you can afford a wife that doesn't work. She may be a drag on earnings, but she provides a rare modern luxury: peace on the home front."[73]

Finally, will women rise in the ranks and assume power proportional to their numbers in the workplace? I fear not. But the reasons are much more straightforward and much less gender-specific and sexually biased than some social commentators would have us think. To begin with, the rules of work are, by and large, still being written by men, and these rules communicate an indifference to any concerns beyond the job at hand. As both Robert Bly and Gloria Emerson have argued, the primary masculine imperative is to fulfill their role as worker-provider. Consequently, most workplace rules reflect primarily professional, and not personal, issues. Second, although it is true that the predominantly male corporate structure has been unwilling to share the power base, this reluctance is not necessarily misogynistic in its origins. The term *power* comes from the Latin *posse*: to do, to be able, to change, to influence, to affect. Power is about control or the ability to produce intended results. To have power is to possess the capacity to control or direct change. The first maxim of power is self-perpetuation; nobody gladly gives up power. This principle is not testosterone-based or predominantly masculine in its origins. It is purely Machiavellian, that is, those who have power (in this case, men) will give it up only reluctantly. The goal of power, said Machiavelli, is not to allow change, because change always leads to the alienation of power and of the status quo, and an alteration of the status quo is never in the best interest of those who possess power. Although the issue at hand is the power of the "good-old-boy network,"

254   Women in the Workplace

we are not talking about a cabal of evil men conspiring to keep women in their place. In effect, the motivating principle involved in this and every power struggle is much more visceral than simple machismo.

Things are not going to radically change anytime soon, but gradual change is occurring. As singer-actress-director Barbra Streisand said upon her 1992 induction into the Women in Film Hall of Fame, "Not so long ago we were referred to as dolls, tomatoes, chicks, babes, broads. We've graduated to being called tough cookies, foxes, bitches and witches. I guess that's progress."[74]

NOTES

1. "Changing Profile of the U.S. Labor Force." *U.S. News & World Report*, September 2, 1985, 46–47.

2. Bradley K. Googins, *Work/Family Conflicts* (New York: Auburn House, 1991), 1, 286.

3. Barbara Ehrenreich, "Strategies of Corporate Women," *New Republic,* January 27, 1987, 28.

4. Carol Kleiman, "On the Job," *Chicago Tribune,* November 1, 1998, Jobs section, 1.

5. Kathryn M. Borman, "Fathers, Mothers, and Child Care in the 1980s," in K. M. Borman et al., eds., *Women in the Workplace: Effects on Families* (Trenton, N.J.: Ablex Publishing, 1984), 73.

6. Stephanie Coontz, *The Way We Never Were: American Families and the Nostalgia Trap* (New York: Basic Books, 1992), 31–41.

7. Ibid., 31.

8. Ibid., 32.

9. Ralph E. Smith, ed., *The Subtle Revolution: Women at Work* (Washington, D.C.: Urban Institute, 1979), 1.

10. "Are Men Becoming the Second Sex?" *Chicago Tribune,* February 9, 1997, Women's News section, 6.

11. "Sixth Annual Salary Survey," *Working Woman,* January 5, 1985, 65.

12. *Statistical Abstract of the United States,* 116th ed., no. 626, "Employment Status of Women" (Latham, Md.: Bernan Press, 1996), 400.

13. Borman, "Fathers, Mothers, and Child Care in the 1980s," 73.

14. John Schmeltzer, "Daughters Will Face Many of Mom's Barriers at Work," *Chicago Tribune,* April 28, 1994, Business section, 1.

15. *Statistical Abstract of the United States,* 116th ed., no. 626.

16. Arlie Russell Hochschild, *The Second Shift* (New York: Viking, 1989), 2.

17. Ibid., 93–94; Daniel Evan Weiss, *The Great Divide: How Females and Males Really Differ* (Crofton, Md.: Poseidon Press, 1991), 32.

18. Carol Kleiman, "Women's Voices Poll Speaks of Solutions as Well as Questions," *Chicago Tribune,* November 12, 1996, Business section, 3.

19. John W. Wright, *The American Almanac of Jobs and Salaries* (New York: Avon, 1997), 650–51.

20. *Working Woman,* January 1985, 65.

21. *Working Women Count! A Report to the Nation,* U.S. Department of Labor Women's Bureau, 1994, 13; Lisa Anderson, "Women Escape Affirmative Action Feud," *Chicago Tribune,* May 16, 1995, 1.

22. *Working Women Count,* 10.

23. Coontz, *The Way We Never Were,* 23.

24. Googins, *Work/Family Conflicts,* 95.

25. Ibid., 4.

26. Ibid., 5.

27. Sara Ann Friedman, *Work Matters* (New York: Viking, 1996), xii.

28. Hochschild, *The Second Shift,* 263.

29. Maureen Brendan, Director, Career Center and Placement, Loyola University, Chicago, 1996.

30. Friedman, *Work Matters,* xii.

31. Gloria Emerson, *Some American Men* (New York: Simon and Schuster, 1985), 32.

32. Daniel Yankelovich, "The New Psychological Contracts at Work," *Psychology Today,* May 1978.

33. Roper Starch Worldwide survey, quoted in *Working Woman,* October 1995, 22.

34. Ibid.

35. Coontz, *The Way We Never Were,* 266.

36. David R. Koller, president, Cornerstone Realty Advisors, Inc., Chicago, 1996.

37. Coontz, *The Way We Never Were,* 22.

38. Googins, *Work/Family Conflict,* 22.

39. Coontz, *The Way We Never Were,* 3, 15.

40. Hochschild, *The Second Shift,* 249.

41. Schmeltzer, "Daughters Will Face Many of Mom's Barriers at Work," 2.

42. Judith Rosener, "Coping with Sexual Static," *New York Times Magazine,* December 7, 1986, 89 ff.

43. Patricia H. Werhane, "Sexual Static and the Ideal of Professional Objectivity," in A. R. Gini and T. J. Sullivan, eds., *It Comes with the Territory* (New York: Random House, 1989), 170.

44. Rosener, "Coping with Sexual Static."

45. Werhane, "Sexual Static and the Ideal of Professional Objectivity," 173.

46. Ibid., 171.

47. *Working Women Count,* 36.

48. Amanda T. Segal and Wendy Zeller, "Corporate Women," *Business Week*, June 8, 1992, 76.

49. "Breaking Through," *Business Week*, February 17, 1997, 64. Survey by Catalyst, Inc., a New York research firm that focuses on women in business.

50. Barbara Sullivan, "Women Cross 10% Barrier in Presence on Boards," *Chicago Tribune*, December 12, 1996, Business section, 1–2.

51. "The State of the States for Women and Politics" (Washington, D.C.: Center for Policy Alternatives, n.d.), 2–3.

52. Segal and Zeller, "Corporate Women," 74.

53. Mike Dorning, "Poll Details Global Role of Gender Bias," *Chicago Tribune*, March 27, 1996, 1.

54. *Working Women Count*, 20.

55. Carol Kleiman, "Equal Pay for Work of Equal Value: A Gender-Free Gain," *Chicago Tribune*, September 17, 1996, Business section, 3.

56. *Working Women Count*, 13.

57. Ibid., 31–32.

58. Hochschild, *The Second Shift*, 96.

59. Felice N. Schwartz, "Management Women and the New Facts of Life," *Harvard Business Review*, January–February 1989, 65–76.

60. Betsy Morris, "Is Your Family Wrecking Your Career?" *Fortune*, March 17, 1998, 71–72.

61. Ibid., 72.

62. Ibid., 26.

63. Ibid., 3–4, 260.

64. Ibid., 259.

65. Ibid., 12.

66. Arlie Russell Hochschild, *The Time Bind* (New York: Metropolitan Books, 1997), 249.

67. Laura Shapiro, "The Myth of Quality Time," *Newsweek*, May 12, 1997, 64.

68. Arlie Russell Hochschild, "There's No Place Like Work," *New York Times Magazine*, April 20, 1997, 53.

69. Ibid., 53.

70. Ibid., 84.

71. Al Gini, "Work, Time, and Hochschild," *Metropolis*, WBEZ, Chicago, May 21, 1997.

72. Schwartz, "Management Women and the New Facts of Life," 66.

73. Morris, "Is Your Family Wrecking Your Career?" 72.

74. Friedman, *Work Matters*, 231.

Essay

Management Women and the New Facts of Life

Felice N. Schwartz

The cost of employing women in management is greater than the cost of employing men. This is a jarring statement, partly because it is true, but mostly because it is something people are reluctant to talk about. A new study by one multinational corporation shows that the rate of turnover in management positions is 2½ times higher among top-performing women than it is among men. A large producer of consumer goods reports that one half of the women who take maternity leave return to their jobs late or not at all. And we know that women also have a greater tendency to plateau or to interrupt their careers in ways that limit their growth and development. But we have become so sensitive to charges of sexism and so afraid of confrontation, even litigation, that we rarely say what we know to be true. Unfortunately, our bottled-up awareness leaks out in misleading metaphors ("glass ceiling" is one notable example), veiled hostility, lowered expectations, distrust, and reluctant adherence to Equal Employment Opportunity requirements.

Career interruptions, plateauing, and turn-over are expensive. The money corporations invest in recruitment, training, and development is less likely to produce top executives among women than among men, and the invaluable company experience that developing executives acquire at every level as they move up through management ranks is more often lost.

The studies just mentioned are only the first of many, I'm quite sure. Demographic realities are going to force corporations all across the country to analyze the cost of employing women in managerial positions, and what they will discover is that women cost more.

But here is another startling truth: The greater cost of employing women is not a function of inescapable gender differences. Women *are* different from men, but what increases their cost to the corporation is principally the clash of their perceptions, attitudes, and behavior with those of men, which is to say, with the policies and practices of male-led corporations.

It is terribly important that employers draw the right conclusions from the studies now being done. The studies will be useless—or worse, harmful—if all they teach us is that women are expensive to employ. What we need to learn is how to reduce that expense, how to stop throwing away the investments we make in talented women, how to become more responsive to the needs of the women that corporations *must* employ if they are to have the best and the brightest of all those now entering the work force.

The gender differences relevant to business fall into two categories: those related to maternity and those related to the differing traditions and expectations of the sexes. Maternity is biological rather than cultural. We can't alter it, but we can dramatically reduce its impact on the workplace and in many cases eliminate its negative effect on employee development. We can accomplish this by addressing the second set of differences, those between male and female socialization. Today, these differences exaggerate the real costs of maternity and can turn a relatively slight disruption in work schedule into a serious business problem and a career derailment for individual women. If we are to overcome the cost differential between male and female employees, we need to address the issues that arise when female socialization meets the male corporate culture and masculine rules of career development—issues of behavior and style, of expectation, of stereotypes and preconceptions, of sexual tension and harassment, of female mentoring, lateral mobility, relocation, compensation, and early identification of top performers.

The one immutable, enduring difference between men and women is maternity. Maternity is not simply childbirth but a continuum that begins with an awareness of the ticking of the biological clock, proceeds to the anticipation of motherhood, includes pregnancy, childbirth, physical recuperation, psychological adjustment, and continues on to nursing, bonding, and child rearing. Not all women choose to become mothers, of course, and among those who do, the process varies from case to case depending on the health of the mother and baby, the values of the parents, and the availability, cost, and quality of child care.

In past centuries, the biological fact of maternity shaped the traditional roles of the sexes. Women performed the home-centered functions that related to the bearing and nurturing of children. Men did the work that required great physical strength. Over time, however, family size contracted, the community assumed greater responsibility for the care and education of children, packaged foods and household technology reduced the work load in the home, and technology eliminated much of the need for muscle power at the workplace. Today, in the developed world, the only role still uniquely gender related is childbearing. Yet men and women are still socialized to perform their traditional roles.

Men and women may or may not have some innate psychological disposition toward these traditional roles—men to be aggressive, competitive, self-reliant, risk taking; women to be supportive, nurturing, intuitive, sensitive, communicative—but certainly both men and women are capable of the full range of behavior. Indeed, the male and female roles have already begun to expand and merge. In the decades ahead, as the socialization of boys and girls and the experience and expectations of young men and women grow steadily more androgynous, the differences in workplace behavior will continue to fade. At the moment, however, we are still plagued by disparities in perception and behavior that make the integration of men and women in the workplace unnecessarily difficult and expensive.

Let me illustrate with a few broadbrush generalizations. Of course, these are only stereotypes, but I think they help to exemplify the kinds of preconceptions that can muddy the corporate waters.

Men continue to perceive women as the rearers of their children, so they find it understandable, indeed appropriate, that women should renounce their careers to raise families. Edmund Pratt, CEO of Pfizer, once asked me in all sincerity, "Why would any woman choose to be a chief financial officer rather than a full-time mother?" By condoning and taking pleasure in women's traditional behavior, men reinforce it. Not only do they see parenting as fundamentally female, they see a career as fundamentally male—either an unbroken series of promotions and advancements toward CEOdom or stagnation and disappointment. This attitude serves to legitimize a woman's choice to extend maternity leave and even, for those who can afford it, to leave employment altogether for several years. By the same token, men who might want to take a leave after the birth of a child know that management will see such behavior as a lack of career commitment, even when company policy permits parental leave for men.

Women also bring counterproductive expectations and perceptions to the workplace. Ironically, although the feminist movement was an expression of women's quest for freedom from their home-based lives, most women were remarkably free already. They had many responsibilities, but they were autonomous and could be entrepreneurial in how and when they carried them out. And once their children grew up and left home, they were essentially free to do what they wanted with their lives. Women's traditional role also included freedom from responsibility for the financial support of their families. Many of us were socialized from girlhood to expect our husbands to take care of us, while our brothers were socialized from an equally early age to complete their educations, pursue careers, climb the ladder of success, and provide dependable financial support for their families. To the extent that this tradition of freedom lingers subliminally, women tend to bring to their employment a sense that they can choose to change jobs or careers at will, take time off, or reduce their hours.

Finally, women's traditional role encouraged particular attention to the quality and substance of what they did, specifically to the physical, psychological, and intellectual development of their children. This traditional focus may explain women's continuing tendency to search for more than monetary reward—intrinsic significance, social importance, meaning—in what they do. This too makes them more likely than men to leave the corporation in search of other values.

The misleading metaphor of the glass ceiling suggests an invisible barrier constructed by corporate leaders to impede the upward mobility of women beyond the middle levels.

A more appropriate metaphor, I believe, is the kind of cross-sectional diagram used in geology. The barriers to women's leadership occur when potentially counterproductive layers of influence on women—maternity, tradition, socialization—meet management strata pervaded by the largely unconscious preconceptions, stereotypes, and expectations of men. Such interfaces do not exist for men and tend to be impermeable for women.

One result of these gender differences has been to convince some executives that women are simply not suited to top management. Other executives feel helpless. If they see even a few of their valued female employees fail to return to work from maternity leave on schedule or see one of their most promising women plateau in her career after the birth of a child, they begin to fear there is nothing they can do to infuse women with new energy and enthusiasm and persuade them to stay. At the same time, they know there is nothing they can do to stem the tide of women into management ranks.

Another result is to place every working woman on a continuum that runs from total dedication to career at one end to a balance between career and family at the other. What women discover is that the male corporate culture sees both extremes as unacceptable. Women who want the flexibility to balance their families and their careers are not adequately committed to the organization. Women who perform as aggressively and competitively as men are abrasive and unfeminine. But the fact is, business needs all the talented women it can get. Moreover, as I will explain, the women I call career-primary and those I call career-and-family each have particular value to the corporation.

Women in the corporation are about to move from a buyer's to a seller's market. The sudden, startling recognition that 80% of new entrants in the work force over the next decade will be women, minorities, and immigrants has stimulated a mushrooming incentive to "value diversity."

Women are no longer simply an enticing pool of occasional creative talent, a thorn in the side of the EEO officer, or a source of frustration to corporate leaders truly puzzled by the slowness of their upward trickle into executive positions. A real demographic change is taking place. The era of sudden population growth of the 1950s and 1960s is over. The birth rate has dropped about 40%, from a high of 25.3 live births per 1,000 population in 1957, at the peak of the baby boom, to a stable low of a little more than 15 per 1,000 over the last 16 years, and there is no indication of a return to a higher rate. The tidal wave of baby boomers that swelled the recruitment pool to overflowing seems to have been a one-time phenomenon. For 20 years, employers had the pick of a very large crop and were able to choose males almost exclusively for the executive track. But if future population remains fairly stable while the economy continues to expand, and if the new information society simultaneously creates a greater need for creative, educated managers, then the gap between supply and demand will grow dramatically and, with it, the competition for managerial talent.

The decrease in numbers has even greater implications if we look at the traditional source of corporate recruitment for leadership positions—white males from the top 10% of the country's best universities. Over the past decade, the increase in the number of women graduating from leading universities has been much greater than the increase in the total number of graduates, and these women are well represented in the top 10% of their classes.

The trend extends into business and professional programs as well. In the old days, virtually all MBAs were male. I remember addressing a meeting at the Harvard Business School as recently as the mid-1970s and looking out at a sea of exclusively male faces.

Today, about 25% of that audience would be women. The pool of male MBAs from which corporations have traditionally drawn their leaders has shrunk significantly.

Of course, this reduction does not have to mean a shortage of talent. The top 10% is at least as smart as it always was—smarter, probably, since it's now drawn from a broader segment of the population. But it now consists increasingly of women. Companies that are determined to recruit the same number of men as before will have to dig much deeper into the male pool, while their competitors will have the opportunity to pick the best people from both the male and female graduates.

Under these circumstances, there is no question that the management ranks of business will include increasing numbers of women. There remains, however, the question of how these women will succeed—how long they will stay, how high they will climb, how completely they will fulfill their promise and potential, and what kind of return the corporation will realize on its investment in their training and development.

There is ample business reason for finding ways to make sure that as many of these women as possible will succeed. The first step in this process is to recognize that women are not all alike. Like men, they are individuals with differing talents, priorities, and motivations. For the sake of simplicity, let me focus on the two women I referred to earlier, on what I call the career-primary woman and the career-and-family woman.

Like many men, some women put their careers first. They are ready to make the same trade-offs traditionally made by the men who seek leadership positions. They make a career decision to put in extra hours, to make sacrifices in their personal lives, to make the most of every opportunity for professional development. For women, of course, this decision also requires that they remain single or at least childless or, if they do have children, that

they be satisfied to have others raise them. Some 90% of executive men but only 35% of executive women have children by the age of 40. The *automatic* association of all women with babies is clearly unjustified.

The secret to dealing with such women is to recognize them early, accept them, and clear artificial barriers from their path to the top. After all, the best of these women are among the best managerial talent you will ever see. And career-primary women have another important value to the company that men and other women lack. They can act as role models and mentors to younger women who put their careers first. Since upwardly mobile career-primary women still have few role models to motivate and inspire them, a company with women in its top echelon has a significant advantage in the competition for executive talent.

Men at the top of the organization—most of them over 55, with wives who tend to be traditional—often find career women "masculine" and difficult to accept as colleagues. Such men miss the point, which is not that these women are just like men but that they are just like the *best* men in the organization. And there is such a shortage of the best people that gender cannot be allowed to matter. It is clearly counterproductive to disparage in a woman with executive talent the very qualities that are most critical to the business and that might carry a man to the CEO's office.

Clearing a path to the top for career-primary women has four requirements:

1. Identify them early.
2. Give them the same opportunity you give to talented men to grow and develop and contribute to company profitability. Give them client and customer responsibility. Expect them to travel and relocate, to make the same commitment to the company as men aspiring to leadership positions.
3. Accept them as valued members of your management team. Include them in every kind of communication. Listen to them.

4. Recognize that the business environment is more difficult and stressful for them than for their male peers. They are always a minority, often the only woman. The male perception of talented, ambitious women is at best ambivalent, a mixture of admiration, resentment, confusion, competitiveness, attraction, skepticism, anxiety, pride, and animosity. Women can never feel secure about how they should dress and act, whether they should speak out or grin and bear it when they encounter discrimination, stereotyping, sexual harassment, and paternalism. Social interaction and travel with male colleagues and with male clients can be charged. As they move up, the normal increase in pressure and responsibility is compounded for women because they are women.

Stereotypical language and sexist day-to-day behavior do take their toll on women's career development. Few male executives realize how common it is to call women by their first names while men in the same group are greeted with surnames, how frequently female executives are assumed by men to be secretaries, how often women are excluded from all-male social events where business is being transacted. With notable exceptions, men are still generally more comfortable with other men, and as a result women miss many of the career and business opportunities that arise over lunch, on the golf course, or in the locker room.

The majority of women, however, are what I call career-and-family women, women who want to pursue serious careers while participating actively in the rearing of children. These women are a precious resource that has yet to be mined. Many of them are talented and creative. Most of them are willing to trade some career growth and compensation for freedom from the constant pressure to work long hours and weekends.

Most companies today are ambivalent at best about the career-and-family women in their management ranks. They would prefer that all employees were willing to give their all

to the company. They believe it is in their best interests for all managers to compete for the top positions so the company will have the largest possible pool from which to draw its leaders.

"If you have both talent and motivation," many employers seem to say, "we want to move you up. If you haven't got that motivation, if you want less pressure and greater flexibility, then you can leave and make room for a new generation." These companies lose on two counts. First, they fail to amortize the investment they made in the early training and experience of management women who find themselves committed to family as well as to career. Second, they fail to recognize what these women could do for their middle management.

The ranks of middle managers are filled with people on their way up and people who have stalled. Many of them have simply reached their limits, achieved career growth commensurate with or exceeding their capabilities, and they cause problems because their performance is mediocre but they still want to move ahead. The career-and-family woman is willing to trade off the pressures and demands that go with promotion for the freedom to spend more time with her children. She's very smart, she's talented, she's committed to her career, and she's satisfied to stay at the middle level, at least during the early child-rearing years. Compare her with some of the people you have there now.

Consider a typical example, a woman who decides in college on a business career and enters management at age 22. For nine years, the company invests in her career as she gains experience and skills and steadily improves her performance. But at 31, just as the investment begins to pay off in earnest, she decides to have a baby. Can the company afford to let her go home, take another job, or go into business for herself? The common perception now is yes, the corporation can afford to lose her unless, after six or eight weeks or even three months of disability and maternity leave, she returns to work on a full-time schedule with the same vigor, commitment, and ambition that she showed before.

But what if she doesn't? What if she wants or needs to go on leave for six months or a year or, heaven forbid, five years? In this worst-case scenario, she works full-time from age 22 to 31 and from 36 to 65—a total of 38 years as opposed to the typical male's 43 years. That's not a huge difference. Moreover, my typical example is willing to work part-time while her children are young, if only her employer will give her the opportunity. There are two rewards for companies responsive to this need: higher retention of their best people and greatly improved performance and satisfaction in their middle management.

The high-performing career-and-family woman can be a major player in your company. She can give you a significant business advantage as the competition for able people escalates. Sometimes too, if you can hold on to her, she will switch gears in mid-life and reenter the competition for the top. The price you must pay to retain these women is threefold: you must plan for and manage maternity, you must provide the flexibility that will allow them to be maximally productive, and you must take an active role in helping to make family supports and high-quality, affordable child care available to all women.

The key to managing maternity is to recognize the value of high-performing women and the urgent need to retain them and keep them productive. The first step must be a genuine partnership between the woman and her boss. I know this partnership can seem difficult to forge. One of my own senior executives came to me recently to discuss plans for her maternity leave and subsequent return to work. She knew she wanted to come back. I wanted to make certain that

she would. Still, we had a somewhat awkward conversation, because I knew that no woman can predict with certainty when she will be able to return to work or under what conditions. Physical problems can lengthen her leave. So can a demanding infant, a difficult family or personal adjustment, or problems with child care.

I still don't know when this valuable executive will be back on the job full-time, and her absence creates some genuine problems for our organization. But I do know that I can't simply replace her years of experience with a new recruit. Since our conversation, I also know that she wants to come back, and that she *will* come back—part-time at first—unless I make it impossible for her by, for example, setting an arbitrary date for her full-time return or resignation. In turn, she knows that the organization wants and needs her and, more to the point, that it will be responsive to her needs of working hours and child-care arrangements.

In having this kind of conversation it's important to ask concrete questions that will help to move the discussion from uncertainty and anxiety to some level of predictability. Questions can touch on everything from family income and energy level to child care arrangements and career commitment. Of course you want your star manager to return to work as soon as possible, but you want her to return permanently and productively. Her downtime on the job is a drain on her energies and a waste of your money.

For all the women who want to combine career and family—the women who want to participate actively in the rearing of their children and who also want to pursue their careers seriously—the key to retention is to provide the flexibility and family supports they need in order to function effectively.

Time spent in the office increases productivity if it is time well spent, but the fact that most women continue to take the primary responsibility for child care is a cause of distraction, diversion, anxiety, and absenteeism—to say nothing of the persistent guilt experienced by all working mothers. A great many women, perhaps most of all women who have always performed at the highest levels, are also frustrated by a sense that while their children are babies they cannot function at their best either at home or at work.

In its simplest form, flexibility is the freedom to take time off—a couple of hours, a day, a week—or to do some work at home and some at the office, an arrangement that communication technology makes increasingly feasible. At the complex end of the spectrum are alternative work schedules that permit the woman to work less than full-time and her employer to reap the benefits of her experience and, with careful planning, the top level of her abilities.

Part-time employment is the single greatest inducement to getting women back on the job expeditiously and the provision women themselves most desire. A part-time return to work enables them to maintain responsibility for critical aspects of their jobs, keeps them in touch with the changes constantly occurring at the workplace and in the job itself, reduces stress and fatigue, often eliminates the need for paid maternity leave by permitting a return to the office as soon as disability leave is over, and, not least, can greatly enhance company loyalty. The part-time solution works particularly well when a work load can be reduced for one individual in a department or when a full-time job can be broken down by skill levels and apportioned to two individuals at different levels of skill and pay.

I believe, however, that shared employment is the most promising and will be the most widespread form of flexible scheduling in the future. It is feasible at every level of the corporation except at the pinnacle, for both the short and the long term. It involves two people taking responsibility for one job.

Two red lights flash on as soon as most executives hear the words "job sharing": continuity and client-customer contact. The answer to the continuity question is to place responsibility entirely on the two individuals sharing the job to discuss everything that transpires—thoroughly, daily, and on their own time. The answer to the problem of client-customer contact is yes, job sharing requires reeducation and a period of adjustment. But as both client and supervisor will quickly come to appreciate, two contacts means that the customer has continuous access to the company's representative, without interruption for vacation, travel, or sick leave. The two people holding the job can simply cover for each other, and the uninterrupted, full-time coverage they provide together can be a stipulation of their arrangement.

Flexibility is costly in numerous ways. It requires more supervisory time to coordinate and manage, more office space, and somewhat greater benefits costs (though these can be contained with flexible benefits plans, prorated benefits, and, in two-paycheck families, elimination of duplicate benefits). But the advantages of reduced turnover and the greater productivity that results from higher energy levels and greater focus can outweigh the costs.

A few hints:

Provide flexibility selectively. I'm not suggesting private arrangements subject to the suspicion of favoritism but rather a policy that makes flexible work schedules available only to high performers.

Make it clear that in most instances (but not all) the rates of advancement and pay will be appropriately lower for those who take time off or who work part-time than for those who work full-time. Most career-and-family women are entirely willing to make that trade-off.

Discuss costs as well as benefits. Be willing to risk accusations of bias. Insist, for example, that half time is half of whatever time it takes to do the job, not merely half of 35 or 40 hours.

The woman who is eager to get home to her child has a powerful incentive to use her time effectively at the office and to carry with her reading and other work that can be done at home. The talented professional who wants to have it all can be a high performer by carefully ordering her priorities and by focusing on objectives rather than on the legendary 15-hour day. By the time professional women have their first babies—at an average age of 31—they have already had nine years to work long hours at a desk, to travel, and to relocate. In the case of high performers, the need for flexibility coincides with what has gradually become the goal-oriented nature of responsibility.

Family supports—in addition to maternity leave and flexibility—include the provision of parental leave for men, support for two-career and single-parent families during relocation, and flexible benefits. But the primary ingredient is child care. The capacity of working mothers to function effectively and without interruption depends on the availability of good, affordable child care. Now that women make up almost half the work force and the growing percentage of managers, the decision to become involved in the personal lives of employees is no longer a philosophical question but a practical one. To make matters worse, the quality of child care has almost no relation to technology, inventiveness, or profitability but is more or less a pure function of the quality of child care personnel and the ratio of adults to children. These costs are irreducible. Only by joining hands with government and the public sector can corporations hope to create the vast quantity and variety of child care that their employees need.

Until quite recently, the response of corporations to women has been largely symbolic and cosmetic, motivated in large part by the will to avoid litigation and legal penalties. In some cases, companies were also moved by a genuine sense of fairness and a vague discomfort and frustration at the absence of women above the middle of the corporate pyramid. The actions they took were mostly quick, easy, and highly visible—child care information services, a three-month parental leave available to men as well as women, a woman appointed to the board of directors.

When I first began to discuss these issues 26 years ago, I was sometimes able to get an appointment with the assistant to the assistant in personnel, but it was only a courtesy. Over the past decade, I have met with the CEOs of many large corporations, and I've watched them become involved with ideas they had never previously thought much about. Until recently, however, the shelf life of that enhanced awareness was always short. Given pressing, short-term concerns, women were not a front-burner issue. In the past few months, I have seen yet another change. Some CEOs and top management groups now take the initiative. They call and ask us to show them how to shift gears from a responsive to a proactive approach to recruiting, developing, and retaining women.

I think this change is more probably a response to business needs—to concern for the quality of future profits and managerial talent—than to uneasiness about legal requirements, sympathy with the demands of women and minorities, or the desire to do what is right and fair. The nature of such business motivation varies. Some companies want to move women to higher positions as role models for those below them and as beacons for talented young recruits. Some want to achieve a favorable image with employees, customers, clients, and stockholders. These are all legitimate motives. But I think the companies that stand to gain most are motivated as well by a desire to capture competitive advantage in an era when talent and competence will be in increasingly short supply. These companies are now ready to stop being defensive about their experience with women and to ask incisive questions without preconceptions.

Even so, incredibly, I don't know of more than one or two companies that have looked into their own records to study the absolutely critical issue of maternity leave—how many women took it, when and whether they returned, and how this behavior correlated with their rank, tenure, age, and performance. The unique drawback to the employment of women is the physical reality of maternity and the particular socializing influence maternity has had. Yet to make women equal to men in the workplace we have chosen on the whole not to discuss this single most significant difference between them. Unless we do, we cannot evaluate the cost of recruiting, developing, and moving women up.

Now that interest is replacing indifference, there are four steps every company can take to examine its own experience with women:

1. Gather quantitative data on the company's experience with management-level women regarding turnover rates, occurrence of and return from maternity leave, and organizational level attained in relation to tenure and performance.
2. Correlate this data with factors such as age, marital status, and presence and age of children, and attempt to identify and analyze why women respond the way they do.
3. Gather qualitative data on the experience of women in your company and on how women are perceived by both sexes.
4. Conduct a cost-benefit analysis of the return on your investment in high-performing women. Factor in the cost to the company of women's negative reactions to negative experience, as well as the probable cost of corrective measures and policies. If women's value to your company is greater than the cost to recruit, train, and develop them—and of course I believe it will be—then you will want to do everything you can to retain them.

We have come a tremendous distance since the days when the prevailing male wisdom saw women as lacking the kind of intelligence that would allow them to succeed in business.

For decades, even women themselves have harbored an unspoken belief that they couldn't make it because they couldn't be just like men, and nothing else would do. But now that women have shown themselves the equal of men in every area of organizational activity, now that they have demonstrated that they can be stars in every field of endeavor, now we can all venture to examine the fact that women and men are different.

On balance, employing women is more costly than employing men. Women can acknowledge this fact today because they know that their value to employers exceeds the additional cost and because they know that changing attitudes can reduce the additional cost dramatically. Women in management are no longer an idiosyncrasy of the arts and education. They have always matched men in natural ability. Within a very few years, they will equal men in numbers as well in every area of economic activity.

The demographic motivation to recruit and develop women is compelling. But an older question remains: Is society better for the change? Women's exit from the home and entry into the work force has certainly created problem—an urgent need for good, affordable child care; troubling questions about the kind of parenting children need; the costs and difficulties of diversity in the workplace; the stress and fatigue of combining work and family responsibilities. Wouldn't we all be happier if we could turn back the clock to an age when men were in the workplace and women in the home, when male and female roles were clearly differentiated and complementary?

Nostalgia, anxiety, and discouragement will urge many to say yes, but my answer is emphatically no. Two fundamental benefits that were unattainable in the past are now within our reach. For the individual, freedom of choice—in this case the freedom to choose career, family, or a combination of the two. For the corporation, access to the most gifted individuals in the country. These benefits are neither self-indulgent nor insubstantial. Freedom of choice and self-realization are too deeply American to be cast aside for some wistful vision of the past. And access to our most talented human resources is not a luxury in this age of explosive international competition but rather the barest minimum that prudence and national self-preservation require.

Essay

Homeward Bound

Linda Hirshman

"Choice feminism" claims that staying home with the kids is just one more feminist option. Funny that most men rarely make the same "choice." Exactly what kind of choice is that?

I. THE TRUTH ABOUT ELITE WOMEN

Half the wealthiest, most-privileged, best-educated females in the country stay home with their babies rather than work in the market economy. When in September *The New York Times* featured an article exploring a piece of this story, "*Many Women at Elite Colleges Set Career Path to Motherhood*," the blogosphere went ballistic, countering with anecdotes and sarcasm. *Slate*'s Jack Shafer accused the *Times* of "*weasel-words*" and of *publishing the same story*—essentially, "*The Opt-Out Revolution*"—every few years, and, recently, every few weeks. (A month after the flap, the *Times'* only female columnist, Maureen Dowd, invoked the elite-college article in her contribution to the *Times'* running soap, "*What's a Modern Girl to Do?*" about how women must forgo feminism even to get laid.) The colleges article provoked such fury that the *Times* had to post an *explanation* of the then–student journalist's methodology on its Web site.

There's only one problem: There is important truth in the dropout story. Even *though* it appeared in *The New York Times.*

I stumbled across the news three years ago when researching a book on marriage after feminism. I found that among the educated elite, who are the logical heirs of the agenda of empowering women, feminism has largely failed in its goals. There are few women in the corridors of power, and marriage is essentially unchanged. The number of women at universities exceeds the number of men. But, more than a generation after feminism, the number of women in elite jobs doesn't come close.

Why did this happen? The answer I discovered—an answer neither feminist leaders nor women themselves want to face—is that while the public world has changed, albeit imperfectly, to accommodate women among the elite, private lives have hardly budged. The real glass ceiling is at home.

Looking back, it seems obvious that the unreconstructed family was destined to re-emerge after the passage of feminism's storm of social change. Following the original impulse to address everything in the lives of women, feminism turned its focus to cracking open the doors of the public power structure. This was no small task. At the beginning, there were

---

From *The American Prospect*, Dec. 20, 2005, vol. 16, no. 12. Reprinted with permission.

male juries and male Ivy League schools, sex-segregated want ads, discriminatory employers, harassing colleagues. As a result of feminist efforts—and larger economic trends—the percentage of women, even of mothers in full- or part-time employment, rose robustly through the 1980s and early '90s.

But then the pace slowed. The census numbers for all working mothers leveled off around 1990 and have fallen modestly since 1998. In interviews, women with enough money to quit work say they are "choosing" to opt out. Their words conceal a crucial reality: the belief that women are responsible for child-rearing and homemaking was largely untouched by decades of workplace feminism. Add to this the good evidence that the upper-class workplace has become more demanding and then mix in the successful conservative cultural campaign to reinforce traditional gender roles and you've got a perfect recipe for feminism's stall.

People who don't like the message attack the data. True, the *Times* based its college story on a survey of questionable reliability and a bunch of interviews. It is not necessary to give credence to Dowd's book, from which her *Times Magazine* piece was taken and which seems to be mostly based on her lifetime of bad dates and some e-mails from fellow *Times* reporters, to wonder if all this noise doesn't mean something important is going on in the politics of the sexes.

What evidence *is* good enough? Let's start with you. Educated and affluent reader, if you are a 30- or 40-something woman with children, what are you doing? Husbands, what are your wives doing? Older readers, what are your married daughters with children doing? I have asked this question of scores of women and men. Among the affluent-educated-married population, women are letting their careers slide to tend the home fires. If my interviewees are working, they work largely part time, and their part-time careers are not putting them in the executive suite.

Here's some more evidence: During the '90s, I taught a course in sexual bargaining at a very good college. Each year, after the class reviewed the low rewards for child-care work, I asked how the students anticipated combining work with child-rearing. At least half the female students described lives of part-time or home-based work. Guys expected their female partners to care for the children. When I asked the young men how they reconciled that prospect with the manifest low regard the market has for child care, they were mystified. Turning to the women who had spoken before, they said, uniformly, "But she chose it."

Even Ronald Coase, Nobel Prize–winner in economics in 1991, quotes the aphorism that "the plural of anecdote is data." So how many anecdotes does it take to make data? I—a 1970s member of the National Organization for Women (NOW), a donor to EMILY's List, and a professor of women's studies—did not set out to find this. I stumbled across the story when, while planning a book, I happened to watch *Sex and the City*'s Charlotte agonize about getting her wedding announcement in the "Sunday Styles" section of *The New York Times*. What better sample, I thought, than the brilliantly educated and accomplished brides of the "Sunday Styles," circa 1996? At marriage, they included a vice president of client communication, a gastroenterologist, a lawyer, an editor, and a marketing executive. In 2003 and 2004, I tracked them down and called them. I interviewed about 80 percent of the 41 women who announced their weddings over three Sundays in 1996. Around 40 years old, college graduates with careers: Who was more likely than they to be reaping feminism's promise of opportunity? Imagine my shock when I found almost all the brides from the first Sunday at home with their children. Statistical anomaly? Nope. Same result for the next Sunday. And the one after that.

Ninety percent of the brides I found had had babies. Of the 30 with babies, five were still working full time. Twenty-five, or 85 percent, were not working full time. Of those not working full time, 10 were working part time but often a long way from their prior career paths. And half the married women with children were not working at all.

And there is more. In 2000, Harvard Business School professor Myra Hart surveyed the women of the classes of 1981, 1986, and 1991 and found that only 38 percent of female Harvard MBAs were working full time. A 2004 survey by the Center for Work-Life Policy of 2,443 women with a graduate degree or very prestigious bachelor's degree revealed that 43 percent of those women with children had taken a time out, primarily for family reasons. Richard Posner, federal appeals-court judge and occasional University of Chicago adjunct professor, reports that "the [*Times*] article confirms—what everyone associated with such institutions [elite law schools] has long known: that a vastly higher percentage of female than of male students will drop out of the workforce to take care of their children."

How many anecdotes to become data? The 2000 census showed a decline in the percentage of mothers of infants working full time, part time, or seeking employment. Starting at 31 percent in 1976, the percentage had gone up almost every year to 1992, hit a high of 58.7 percent in 1998, and then began to drop—to 55.2 percent in 2000, to 54.6 percent in 2002, to 53.7 percent in 2003. Statistics just released showed further decline to 52.9 percent in 2004. Even the percentage of working mothers with children who were not infants declined between 2000 and 2003, from 62.8 percent to 59.8 percent.

Although college-educated women work more than others, the 2002 census shows that graduate or professional degrees do not increase work-force participation much more than even one year of college. When their children are infants (under a year), 54 percent of females with graduate or professional degrees are not working full time (18 percent are working part time and 36 percent are not working at all). Even among those who have children who are not infants, 41 percent are not working full time (18 percent are working part time and 23 percent are not working at all).

Economists argue about the meaning of the data, even going so far as to contend that more mothers are working. They explain that the bureau changed the definition of "work" slightly in 2000, the economy went into recession, and the falloff in women without children was similar. However, even if there wasn't a falloff but just a leveling off, this represents not a loss of present value but a loss of hope for the future—a loss of hope that the role of women in society will continue to increase.

The arguments still do not explain the absence of women in elite workplaces. If these women were sticking it out in the business, law, and academic worlds, now, 30 years after feminism started filling the selective schools with women, the elite workplaces should be proportionately female. They are not. Law schools have been graduating classes around 40-percent female for decades— decades during which both schools and firms experienced enormous growth. And, although the legal population will not be 40-percent female until 2010, in 2003, the major law firms had only 16-percent female partners, according to the American Bar Association. It's important to note that elite workplaces like law firms grew in size during the very years that the percentage of female graduates was growing, leading you to expect a higher female employment than the pure graduation rate would indicate. The Harvard Business School has produced classes around 30-percent female. Yet only 10.6 percent of Wall Street's corporate officers are women, and a mere nine are Fortune 500 CEOs. Harvard Business School's dean, who extolled the virtues of interrupted careers on *60 Minutes*, has a 20-percent female academic faculty.

It is possible that the workplace is discriminatory and hostile to family life. If firms had hired every childless women lawyer available, that alone would have been enough to raise the percentage of female law partners above 16 percent in 30 years. It is also possible that women are voluntarily taking themselves out of the elite job competition for lower status and lower-paying jobs. Women must take responsibility for the consequences of their decisions. It defies reason to claim that the falloff from 40 percent of the class at law school to 16 percent of the partners at all the big law firms is unrelated to half the mothers with graduate and professional degrees leaving full-time work at childbirth and staying away for several years after that, or possibly bidding down.

This isn't only about day care. Half my *Times* brides quit *before* the first baby came. In interviews, at least half of them expressed a hope never to work again. None had realistic plans to work. More importantly, when they quit, they were already alienated from their work or at least not committed to a life of work. One, a female MBA, said she could never figure out why the men at her workplace, which fired her, were so excited about making deals. "It's only money," she mused. Not surprisingly, even where employers offered them part-time work, they were not interested in taking it.

II. THE FAILURE OF CHOICE FEMINISM

What is going on? Most women hope to marry and have babies. If they resist the traditional female responsibilities of child-rearing and householding, what Arlie Hochschild called "The Second Shift," they are fixing for a fight.

But elite women aren't resisting tradition. None of the stay-at-home brides I interviewed saw the second shift as unjust; they agree that the household is women's work. As one lawyer-bride put it in explaining her decision to quit practicing law after four years, "I had a wedding to plan." Another, an Ivy Leaguer with a master's degree, described it in management terms: "He's the CEO and I'm the CFO. He sees to it that the money rolls in and I decide how to spend it." It's their work, and they must do it perfectly. "We're all in here making fresh apple pie," said one, explaining her reluctance to leave her daughters in order to be interviewed. The family CFO described her activities at home: "I take my [3-year-old] daughter to all the major museums. We go to little movement classes."

Conservatives contend that the dropouts prove that feminism "failed" because it was too radical, because women didn't want what feminism had to offer. In fact, if half or more of feminism's heirs (85 percent of the women in my *Times* sample), are not working seriously, it's because feminism wasn't radical enough: It changed the workplace but it didn't change men, and, more importantly, it didn't fundamentally change how women related to men.

The movement did start out radical. Betty Friedan's original call to arms compared housework to animal life. In *The Feminine Mystique* she wrote, "[V]acuuming the living room floor—with or without makeup—is not work that takes enough thought or energy to challenge any woman's full capacity. . . . Down through the ages man has known that he was set apart from other animals by his mind's power to have an idea, a vision, and shape the future to it . . . when he discovers and creates and shapes a future different from his past, he is a man, a human being."

Thereafter, however, liberal feminists abandoned the judgmental starting point of the movement in favor of offering women "choices." The choice talk spilled over from people trying to avoid saying "abortion," and it provided an irresistible solution to feminists trying to duck the mommy wars. A woman could work, stay home, have 10 children or one, marry or stay single. It all counted as "feminist" as long as she *chose* it. (So dominant has the concept of choice become that when Charlotte, with a push from her insufferable first husband, quits her job, the writers at *Sex and the City* have her screaming, "I choose my choice! I choose my choice!")

Only the most radical fringes of feminism took on the issue of gender relations at home, and they put forth fruitless solutions like socialism and separatism. We know the story about socialism. Separatism ran right into heterosexuality and reproduction, to say nothing of the need to earn a living other than at a feminist bookstore. As feminist historian Alice Echols put it, "Rather than challenging their subordination in domestic life, the feminists of NOW committed themselves to fighting for women's integration into public life."

Great as liberal feminism was, once it retreated to choice the movement had no language to use on the generated ideology of the family. Feminists could not say, "Housekeeping and child-rearing in the nuclear family is not interesting and not socially validated. Justice requires that it not be assigned to women on the basis of their gender and at the sacrifice of their access to money, power, and honor."

The 50 percent of census answerers and the 62 percent of Harvard MBAs and the 85 percent of my brides of the *Times* all think they are "choosing" their gendered lives. They don't know that feminism, in collusion with traditional society, just passed the gendered family on to them to choose. Even with all the day care in the world, the personal is still political. Much of the rest is the opt-out revolution.

III. WHAT IS TO BE DONE?

Here's the feminist moral analysis that choice avoided: The family—with its repetitious, socially invisible, physical tasks—is a necessary part of life, but it allows fewer opportunities for full human flourishing than public spheres like the market or the government. This less-flourishing sphere is not the natural or moral responsibility only of women. Therefore, assigning it to women is unjust. Women assigning it to themselves is equally unjust. To paraphrase, as Mark Twain said, "A man who chooses not to read is just as ignorant as a man who cannot read."

The critics are right about one thing: Dopey *New York Times* stories do nothing to change the situation. Dowd, who is many things but not a political philosopher, concludes by wondering if the situation will change by 2030. Lefties keep hoping the Republicans will enact child-care legislation, which probably puts us well beyond 2030. In either case, we can't wait that long. If women's flourishing does matter, feminists must acknowledge that the family is to 2005 what the workplace was to 1964 and the vote to 1920. Like the right to work and the right to vote, the right to have a flourishing life that includes but is not limited to family cannot be addressed with language of choice.

Women who want to have sex and children with men as well as good work in interesting jobs where they may occasionally wield real social power need guidance, and they need it early. Step one is simply to begin talking about flourishing. In so doing, feminism will be returning to its early, judgmental roots. This may anger some, but it should sound the alarm before the next generation winds up in the same situation. Next, feminists will have to start offering young women not choices and not utopian dreams but *solutions* they can enact on their own. Prying women out of their traditional roles is not going to be easy. It will require rules—rules like those in the widely derided book *The Rules*, which was never about dating but about behavior modification.

There are three rules: Prepare yourself to qualify for good work, treat work seriously, and don't put yourself in a position of unequal resources when you marry.

The preparation stage begins with college. It is shocking to think that girls cut off their options for a public life of work as early as college. But they do. The first pitfall is the liberal-arts curriculum, which women are good at, graduating in higher numbers than men. Although many really successful people start out studying liberal arts, the purpose of a liberal education is not, with the exception of a miniscule number of academic positions, job preparation.

So the first rule is to use your college education with an eye to career goals. Feminist organizations should produce each year a survey of the most common job opportunities for people with college degrees, along with the average lifetime earnings from each job category and the characteristics such jobs require. The point here is to help women see that yes, you can study art history, but only with the realistic understanding that one day soon you will need to use your arts education to support yourself and your family. The survey would ask young women to select what they are best suited for and give guidance on the appropriate course of study. Like the rule about accepting no dates for Saturday after Wednesday night, the survey would set realistic courses for women, helping would-be curators who are not artistic geniuses avoid career frustration and avoid solving their job problems with marriage.

After college comes on-the-job training or further education. Many of my *Times* brides—and grooms—did work when they finished their educations. Here's an anecdote about the difference: One couple, both lawyers, met at a

firm. After a few years, the man moved from international business law into international business. The woman quit working altogether. "They told me law school could train you for anything," she told me. "But it doesn't prepare you to go into business. I should have gone to business school." Or rolled over and watched her husband the lawyer using his first few years of work to prepare to go into a related business. Every *Times* groom assumed he had to succeed in business, and was really trying. By contrast, a common thread among the women I interviewed was a self-important idealism about the kinds of intellectual, prestigious, socially meaningful, politics-free jobs worth their incalculably valuable presence. So the second rule is that women must treat the first few years after college as an opportunity to lose their capitalism virginity and prepare for good work, which they will then treat seriously.

The best way to treat work seriously is to find the money. Money is the marker of success in a market economy, it usually accompanies power, and it enables the bearer to wield power, including within the family. Almost without exception, the brides who opted out graduated with roughly the same degrees as their husbands. Yet somewhere along the way the women made decisions in the direction of less money. Part of the problem was idealism; idealism on the career trail usually leads to volunteer work, or indentured servitude in social-service jobs, which is nice but doesn't get you to money. Another big mistake involved changing jobs excessively. Without exception, the brides who eventually went home had much more job turnover than the grooms did. There's no such thing as a perfect job. Condoleezza Rice actually wanted to be a pianist, and Gary Graffman didn't want to give concerts.

If you are good at work you are in a position to address the third undertaking: the reproductive household. The rule here is to avoid taking on more than a fair share of the second shift. If this seems coldhearted, consider the survey by the Center for Work-Life Policy. Fully 40 percent of highly qualified women with spouses felt that their husbands create more work around the house than they perform. According to Phyllis Moen and Patricia Roehling's *Career Mystique*, "When couples marry, the amount of time that a woman spends doing housework increases by approximately 17 percent, while a man's decreases by 33 percent." Not a single *Times* groom was a stay-at-home dad. Several of them could hardly wait for Monday morning to come. None of my *Times* grooms took even brief paternity leave when his children were born.

How to avoid this kind of rut? You can either find a spouse with less social power than you or find one with an ideological commitment to gender equality. Taking the easier path first, marry down. Don't think of this as brutally strategic. If you are devoted to your career goals and would like a man who will support that, you're just doing what men throughout the ages have done: placing a safe bet.

In her 1995 book, *Kidding Ourselves: Babies, Breadwinning and Bargaining Power*, Rhona Mahoney recommended finding a sharing spouse by marrying younger or poorer, or someone in a dependent status, like a starving artist. Because money is such a marker of status and power, it's hard to persuade women to marry poorer. So here's an easier rule: Marry young or marry much older. Younger men are potential high-status companions. Much older men are sufficiently established so that they don't have to work so hard, and they often have enough money to provide unlimited household help. By contrast, slightly older men with bigger incomes are the most dangerous, but even a pure counterpart is risky. If you both are going through the elite-job hazing rituals simultaneously while having children, someone is going to have to give. Even the most devoted lawyers with the hardest-working nannies are going to have weeks

when no one can get home other than to sleep. The odds are that when this happens, the woman is going to give up her ambitions and professional potential.

It is possible that marrying a liberal might be the better course. After all, conservatives justified the unequal family in two modes: "God ordained it" and "biology is destiny." Most men (and most women), including the liberals, think women are responsible for the home. But at least the liberal men should feel squeamish about it.

If you have carefully positioned yourself either by marrying down or finding someone untainted by gender ideology, you will be in a position to resist bearing an unfair share of the family. Even then you must be vigilant. Bad deals come in two forms: economics and home economics. The economic temptation is to assign the cost of child care to the woman's income. If a woman making $50,000 per year whose husband makes $100,000 decides to have a baby, and the cost of a full-time nanny is $30,000, the couple reason that, after paying 40 percent in taxes, she makes $30,000, just enough to pay the nanny. So she might as well stay home. This totally ignores that both adults are in the enterprise together and the demonstrable future loss of income, power, and security for the woman who quits. Instead, calculate that all parents make a total of $150,000 and take home $90,000. After paying a full-time nanny, they have $60,000 left to live on.

The home-economics trap involves superior female knowledge and superior female sanitation. The solutions are ignorance and dust. Never figure out where the butter is. "Where's the butter?" Nora Ephron's legendary riff on marriage begins. In it, a man asks the question when looking directly at the butter container in the refrigerator. "Where's the butter?" actually means butter my toast, buy the butter, remember when we're out of butter. Next thing you know you're quitting your job at the law firm because you're so busy managing the butter. If women never start playing the household-manager role, the house will be dirty, but the realities of the physical world will trump the pull of gender ideology. Either the other adult in the family will take a hand or the children will grow up with robust immune systems.

If these prescriptions sound less than family-friendly, here's the last rule: Have a baby Just don't have two. Mothers' Movement Online's Judith Statdman Tucker reports that women who opt out for child-care reasons act only after the second child arrives. A second kid pressures the mother's organizational skills, doubles the demands for appointments, wildly raises the cost of education and housing, and drives the family to the suburbs. But cities, with their Chinese carryouts and all, are better for working mothers It is true that if you follow this rule, your society will not reproduce itself. But if things get bad enough, who knows what social consequences will ensue? After all, the vaunted French child-care regime was actually only a response to the superior German birth rate.

IV. WHY DO WE CARE?

The privileged brides of the *Times*—and their husbands—seem happy. Why do we care what they do? After all, most people aren't rich and white and heterosexual, and they couldn't quit working if they wanted to.

We care because what they do is bad for them, is certainly bad for society, and is widely imitated, even by people who never get their weddings in the *Times*. This last is called the "regime effect," and it means that even if women don't quit their jobs for their families, they think they should and feel guilty about not doing it. That regime effect created the mystique around *The Feminine Mystique*, too.

As for society, elites supply the labor for the decision-making classes—the senators, the newspaper editors, the research scientists, the entrepreneurs, the policy-makers, and the policy wonks. If the ruling class is overwhelmingly male, the rulers will make mistakes that benefit males, whether from ignorance or from indifference. Media surveys reveal that if only one member of a television show's creative staff is female, the percentage of women on-screen goes up from 36 percent to 42 percent. A world of 84-percent male lawyers and 84-percent female assistants is a different place than one with women in positions of social authority. Think of a big American city with an 86-percent white police force. If role models don't matter, why care about Sandra Day O'Connor? Even if the falloff from peak numbers is small, the leveling off of women in power is a loss of hope for more change. Will there never again be more than one woman on the Supreme Court?

Worse, the behavior tarnishes every female with the knowledge that she is almost never going to be a ruler. Princeton President Shirley Tilghman described the elite colleges' self-image perfectly when she told her freshmen last year that they would be the nation's leaders, and she clearly did not have trophy wives in mind. Why should society spend resources educating women with only a 50-percent return rate on their stated goals? The American Conservative Union carried a column in 2004 recommending that employers stay away from such women or risk going out of business. Good psychological data show that the more women are treated with respect, the more ambition they have. And vice versa. The opt-out revolution is really a downward spiral.

Finally, these choices are bad for women individually. A good life for humans includes the classical standard of using one's capacities for speech and reason in a prudent way, the liberal requirement of having enough autonomy to direct one's own life, and the utilitarian test of doing more good than harm in the world. Measured against these time-tested standards, the expensively educated upper-class moms will be leading lesser lives. At feminism's dawning, two theorists compared gender ideology to a caste system. To borrow their insight, these daughters of the upper classes will be bearing most of the burden of the work always associated with the lowest caste: sweeping and cleaning bodily waste. Not two weeks after the Yalie flap, the *Times* ran a story of moms who were toilet training in infancy by vigilantly watching their babies for signs of excretion 24–7. They have voluntarily become untouchables.

When she sounded the blast that revived the feminist movement 40 years after women received the vote, Betty Friedan spoke of lives of purpose and meaning, better lives and worse lives, and feminism went a long way toward shattering the glass ceilings that limited their prospects outside the home. Now the glass ceiling begins at home. Although it is harder to shatter a ceiling that is also the roof over your head, there is no other choice.

Essay

Where Are the Women?

Linda Tischler

Brenda Barnes knows what it takes to hold a top job in a highly competitive company. As president and chief executive of the North American arm of PepsiCo, a place famous for its driven culture, she set a fast pace. Rising at 3:30 A.M., she would blitz through a few hours of work before waking her three children at 7 A.M., then dash off to the office, where she'd grind through an 11- or 12-hour day crammed with meetings, conference calls, and strategy sessions. Then it was home for dinner and bedtime stories before finishing up with phone calls or email before falling into bed. Three rights a week, she was on the road. Seven times, she relocated when the company wanted her in another office. For eight years, she and her husband lived in separate cities, trying valiantly to juggle both job demands and those of marriage and family. And all the effort was paying off: Barnes was widely considered a real contender for the top job at PepsiCo when CEO Roger Enrico retired. But in September 1997, at 43, she suddenly stepped down when the toll of the job began, in her mind, to outstrip its rewards.

Unlike some women executives who have famously dropped out, Barnes did not go home to write her memoirs or devote herself to charity and her children's soccer schedules. She just chose what is for her, a less demanding path: She serves on the board of six major companies, among them Seas, Avon, and The New York Times; she's taught at the Kellogg School of Management, and stepped in as interim president of Starwood Hotels and Resorts in early 2000. Although she's had many offers for other enticing jobs, she's unwilling to consider another gig at the top. "When you talk about

---

those big jobs, those CEO jobs, you just have to give them your life," she says. "You can't alter them to make them accommodate women any better than men. It's just the way it is."

Six years after the fact, Barnes is still happy with her decision. But she admits that despite her considerable post-PepsiCo accomplishments, she's been forever branded as The Woman Who Walked Away. Small wonder. In a workplace where woman CEOs of major companies are so scarce that they can be identified, like rock stars, by first name only—Carly and Martha and Andrea and Oprah and Meg—it's shocking each time a contender to join their august ranks steps down.

It wasn't supposed to turn out this way. By 2004, after three decades of the women's movement, when business schools annually graduate thousands of qualified young women, when the managerial pipeline is stuffed with capable, talented female candidates for senior positions why are they still so few women at the top?

In part, the answer probably still lies in lingering bias in the system. Most women interviewed for this story say that overt discrimination is rare; still, the executive suites of most major corporations remain largely boys' clubs. Catalyst, the women's business group, blames the gap on the fact that women often choose staff jobs, such as marketing and human resources, while senior executives are disproportionately plucked from the ranks of those with line jobs, where a manager can have critical profit-and loss responsibility. Others fault the workplace itself, saying corporations don't do enough to accommodate women's often more-significant family responsibilities.

All those things are true. But there may be a simpler—and in many ways more disturbing—reason that women remain so underrepresented in the corner office: For the most part, men just compete harder than women. They put in more hours. They're more willing to

relocate. They're more comfortable putting work ahead of personal commitments. And they just want the top job more.

Let's be clear: Many, many individual women work at least as hard as men. Many even harder. But in the aggregate, statistics show, they work less, and as long as that remains true, it means women's chances of reaching parity in the corner office will remain remote. Those top jobs have become all-consuming: In today's markets, being CEO is a global, 24-hour-a-day job. You have to, as Barnes says, give it your life. Since women tend to experience work-life conflicts more viscerally than their male peers they're less likely to be willing to do that. And at the upper reaches of corporate hierarchy, where the pyramid narrows sharply and the game becomes winner-take-all, a moment's hesitation—one important stint in the Beijing office that a woman doesn't take because of a sick child or an unhappy husband—means the odds get a little worse for her and a little better for the guy down the hall.

And let's be clear, too, that we're not talking about women who simply opt out. They've been getting a lot of press and sparking a lot of controversy lately—those young women investment bankers and lawyers who are quitting to become stay-at-home moms (and, really, they're still using those MBA skills on the board of the PTA). That's still a fringe phenomenon affecting relatively few privileged women with high-earning husbands.

No, the women we're talking about here work, want to work, want to continue to work. But not the way you have to work in order to reach the top these days. That's the conclusion that Marta Cabrera finally came to four years ago. By 1999, Cabrera was a vice president at JP Morgan Chase, one of only two women on the emerging-markets trading desk. True, the demands were steep—12-hour days were the norm. But the rewards, at the peak of the boom, were pretty delicious, too: an apartment in Manhattan, a country home, and the chance for an artist husband to pursue his vocation.

Not only was Cabrera at the top of her game, but she had, by all measures, managed to pull off the career woman's trifecta—a great job, a happy marriage, and two beautiful, healthy little daughters—all by age 43. But in October of that year, as she watched her second-grader blow out the candles on her birthday cake, Cabrera had an unsettling realization: She didn't know her own child as well as most of the friends and family who had gathered to celebrate the big event. "I realized seven years had gone by, and I had only seen her and my five-year-old on weekends," she says. No first words. No school plays. No class trips. "I asked myself, 'What the hell am I doing?'" Then she thought about her job. To walk away would mean upheaval. Plus, there was a principle at stake: "I had the sense I was letting down my sex by leaving."

It took another seven months, and much soul-searching, to reach her decision, but in May of 2000, Cabrera quit. Like Barnes, she did not opt out. No 180-degree turn to a life of play dates or book groups. No reconnecting with her inner tennis-lady. Instead, she became executive director of EMPower, a microlender in developing countries. Facing a precipitous drop in income, she and her husband rented out their Manhattan place and moved to the country. Now she works from home three days a week, and is in the city the other two, an arrangement that lets her do rewarding work and still spend time with her kids.

And what did her experience at JP Morgan Chase teach her? "There's a different quality of what men give up versus what women give up" when they attempt to reconcile the demands of a senior job with those of family responsibilities. "The sacrifices for women are deeper, and you must weigh them very

consciously if you want to continue," she says. "I didn't want to be the biggest, best, greatest. I didn't feel compelled to be number one."

She was doing what women often do: scaling back on work for the sake of family, with a clear-eyed realization that she was, simultaneously, torpedoing her chances for a climb up the ladder. What's more, she didn't care. It's a choice women often make, with no particular social sanctions. For some, it's even an easy and convenient way to escape an increasingly hostile and unfriendly work world, an out that men simply don't have. But it's also the reason women may continue to be stalled at the lower rungs in organizations and men may continue to rule.

Charles A. O'Reilly III, professor of organizational behavior at Stanford Graduate School of Business, has been particularly interested in women's career attainment and the problem of why, despite notable gains in education and experience, women are still so woefully underrepresented in the top ranks of American corporations. In 1986, he began following a group of University of California, Berkeley MBAs to see if he could isolate those qualities that led to a corner office. His conclusion is starkly simple: Success in a corporation is less a function of gender discrimination than of how hard a person chooses to compete. And the folks who tend to compete the hardest are generally the stereotypical manly men.

Think of careers as a tournament, he says. In the final rounds, players are usually matched pretty equally for ability. At that point, what differentiates winners from losers is effort—how many backhands a tennis player hits in practice, how many calls a sales rep is willing to make. "From an organization's perspective," he says, "those most likely to be promoted are those who both have the skills and are willing to put in the effort. Individuals who are more loyal, work longer hours, and are willing to sacrifice for the organization are the ones who will be rewarded."

Today's women, he says, are equal to their male counterparts in education, experience, and skill. But when it's a painful choice between the client crisis and the birthday party, the long road trip and the middle schooler who needs attention, the employee most likely to put company over family is the traditional, work-oriented male. Interestingly, the women in O'Reilly's study reported levels of career satisfaction equal to those of their more-drive male peers, even if they were not as outwardly successful. In other words, women may be happier not gunning for power positions if it means they can work less and have a life.

After seven years with the big computer leasing company Comdisco, Diane Brandt, for example, left to form a small investment banking firm with two male colleagues. She decided to leave that job, too, when the growing business's hours increased and the moment approached when her only son would leave for college. Recently, she launched a small company, Captio Corp., that offers budgeting and scheduling tools for college students. "I've made choices all through my career," she says from her home in Menlo Park, California, days before heading to Germany to visit her son, who's studying abroad. "I've not pursued promotions in the same way I might have had I not been trying to balance other things in my life. It's been important to me to be home and have dinner with my family. You can't do that and move up the ladder."

Beth Johnson, a banker in Chicago, describes herself as "very ambitious," and says she has always loved business: the deal making, the challenge, the money. But she still remembers when her son was a baby, calculating the percentage of his waking hours that she could, if all went well, actually be present. "I doubt that his father was doing the same," she says dryly.

Recently, when the fund she was managing fell victim to the stock market, she decided to take some time off to help her son negotiate his final precollege year. Her brief attempt to be a "golf lady" didn't pan out. "I just couldn't do it," she confesses. She's now mulling various job offers. While she will go back to work, she knows there are sacrifices she and most other women are less willing to make than men. "People may get mad if I describe women as a group," she says, "but we are relational family beings. We do not have a world that's structured to understand that, to know how to account for it, and I don't know that we ever will."

There's a scene near the end of the 1956 movie *The Man in the Gray Flannel Suit* in which Fredric March, who plays a work-obsessed network president, turns on Gregory Peck, who plays his conflicted speechwriter. "Big, successful companies just aren't built by men like you, nine-to-five and home and family," March says. "They're built by men like me, who give everything they've got to it, who live it body and soul." March, of course, has sacrificed his own happiness to the company, a choice that Peck is unwilling to make.

Not much has changed in 48 years, says David Nadler, chairman of Mercer Delta Consulting. Nadler, who advises senior managers, says that because top jobs are typically crushing in their demands, they require a certain psychological type. "I've worked closely with 20 CEOs over the past two decades—both men and women," he says. "All of them are characterized by being driven. Something in them says, 'This is important enough for me to make the sacrifices that are inherent with the job.' "

Certainly, there are women willing and able to compete by those draconian rules. A 2003 Catalyst study found that more than half of the women not yet in senior leadership positions within their companies aspired to be there (although 26% also said they weren't interested). And some women want nothing less than a hill-throttle engagement with work. "I don't seek balance. I want to work,

Average Hours Worked per Week

	Men	Women
Lawyers*	47.5	43.0
Management, business, and financial operations occupations*	46.1	40.4
Doctors (primary care physicians)**	50.0	45.0

Sources: *Bureau of Labor Statistics, Current Population Surrey 1989 (lawyers), 2002 (business); **Medical Economics, 2003

work, work," Ann Livermore, executive vice president of Hewlett-Packard, told Karin Kauffmann and Peggy Baskin for their book, *Beyond Superwoman* (Carmel, 2003). Or as Kim Perdikou, CIO of Juniper Networks, told the author, "I'm wired 24 hours a day."

But such decisions continue to have consequences that thoughtful women are all too aware of. Asked what advice she would give to a daughter, M.R.C. Greenwood, chancellor of the University of California at Santa Cruz. warns, "Remember that the assumption that one's marriage will remain intact as she moves up is a false assumption. You really have to know yourself and know it will take a toll."

Conversely, there are plenty of men who would like the option to lead saner lives. A recent study of 101 senior human-resource managers found that men are also starting to leave big companies to try to improve the balance between their home lives and their worklives. Still, many more men than women seem to get an adrenaline rush from work that allows them to log long hours, zoom through time zones, and multitask savagely.

As a nation, we now clock more time on the job than any other worker on earth, some 500 hours a year more than the Germans, and 250 hours per year more than the British. But

the true heavy lifters in the productivity parade are American men. According to the Bureau of Labor Statistics, men work longer hours in every industry, including those traditionally identified with women. In financial fields, for example, men worked an average of 43.8 hours per week compared with women's 38.7; in management, it was men 47.2, women 39.4; in educational services, men 39.2, women 36.0; in health services, men 43.1, women 36.4.

The same pattern holds true in professions whose elaborate hazing rituals are designed to separate potential chiefs from the rest of the tribe. Young associates at prestigious law firms, for example, often put in 60- to 70-hour weeks for long periods of time. "It's almost an intentional hurdle placed by the firms to weed out those who simply don't have the drive and ambition to do it," says Stanford University economist Edward Lazear. "It may be excessive, but you select out a very elite few, and those are the ones who make it to partner and make very high salaries."

Women are as scarce in the upper reaches of the legal profession as they are in top-tier corporate offices. According to the National Directory of Legal Employers and Catalyst, women represented only 15.6% of law partners nationwide and 13.7% of the general counsels of Fortune 500 companies in 2000 (even though they have accounted for at least 40% of enrollments at top law schools since 1985 and nearly 50% since 2000). Women in these firms say personal or family responsibilities are the top barrier to advancement, with 71% of women in law firms reporting difficulty juggling work and family, and 66% of women in corporate legal departments citing the same struggle.

Depending on the specialty, medical practices can be similarly pitiless. Among doctors, women work 45 hours per week compared with men's 50. Male physicians also see 117 patients per week, compared with 97 for women. And, as with the law, the top rungs of the medical ladder are populated by men who are willing to put work ahead of family, with women doctors concentrated in lower-paying positions in hospitals, HMOs, and group practices.

Meanwhile, back in the executive suite, researchers at Catalyst say some progress has been made. Women made up 15.7% of corporate officers in the *Fortune* 500 in 2002, up from 8.7% in 1995. In 2003, they held 13.6% of board seats in the same companies, up from 12.4% in 2001. But their actual numbers, compared to the percentage of women in the workforce, are still minuscule. This has occasioned much hand-wringing among business organizations and women's advocacy groups. But maybe all that angst is misplaced.

"When a woman gets near the top, she starts asking herself the most intelligent questions," says Warren Farrell, the San Diego-based author of *The Myth of Male Power* (Simon & Schuster, 1993). The fact that few women make it to the very top is a measure of women's power, not powerlessness, he maintains. "Women haven't learned to get their love by being president of a company," he says. "They've learned they can get respect and love in a variety of different ways—from being a good parent, from being a top executive, or a combination of both." Free of the ego needs driving male colleagues, they're likelier to weigh the trade-offs and opt for saner lives.

Mary Lou Quinlan has seen the view from the top and decided it's not worth the price. In 1998, she stepped down as CEO of the big advertising agency N.W. Ayer when she realized she was no longer enjoying a life that had no room for weekends, vacations, or, often, sleep. She went on to found Just Ask a Woman, a New York-based consulting firm

that helps big companies build business with women. The decision wasn't driven by guilt over giving family responsibilities short shrift (Quinlan has no children); it was about calibrating the value of work in one's life. Quinlan thinks that calculation is different for women. "The reason a lot of women aren't shooting for the corner office is that they've seen it up close, and it's not a pretty scene," she says. "It's not about talent, dedication, experience, or the ability to take the heat. Women simply say, 'I just don't like that kitchen.'"

Catalyst and other groups have suggested that the heat can be turned down in that kitchen—that senior jobs can be changed to allow for more flexibility and balance, which will in turn help more women to the top of the heap. Catherine Hakim thinks that is bunk. Hakim, a sociologist at the London School of Economics, has been investigating the attitudes toward work among European men and women, and says reengineering jobs won't solve two fundamental problems: First, many women have decidedly mixed feelings about working, and second, top jobs by their very nature will remain relentlessly demanding. In surveys of 4,700 workers in Britain and Spain, she found that only 20% of women considered themselves "work-centered"—they made their careers a primary focus of their lives, and said they would work even if they didn't have to. By contrast, 55% of men said they focused primarily on work. Given those numbers, most top jobs will continue to go to men, she says, despite the equal-opportunity movement and the contraceptive revolution.

That's because work-centered employees are most likely to leap to the tasks that are most disruptive to life. "That's the bottom line, and it's not a sexist bottom line," Hakim says. "Of course, you could say jobs shouldn't be so greedy, but in practice, the higher up you go, by and large, jobs get greedier and greedier. The idea that some people have, that if only employers would reshape jobs they would be perfectly easy for women to do, is just nonsense."

Not surprisingly, the suggestion that the fault lies with women and not with the system drives many women nuts. Margaret Heffernan, the outspoken former CEO of the CMGI company iCast, for example, goes apoplectic at what she calls the perennial "little black dress stories"—tales of how various women have stepped down from their big jobs to spend more time with their families. Their implicit message, she says, is that women can't cut it and would prefer to be back in the kitchen. Indeed, she says, the conclusion we should be drawing is, "Another company just f***d up big time. Another company just trained somebody and made them incredibly skilled and still couldn't keep them."

Heffernan says the hordes of women refusing to play the career-advancement game aren't doing so because they can't hack it, but because they've lost faith in the institutions they've worked for and are tired of cultures driven by hairy-chested notions of how companies must function. Instead, they are founding businesses where they can use the experience in an environment they can better

Percentage of Workers in Top Jobs

	Men	Women
Lawyers (partner)*	84.4%	15.6%
Corporate officers in the Fortune 500**	84.3%	15.7%
Top-earning doctors***	93.4%	6.6%

Sources: *National Directory of Legal Employers, NALP 2000, and 2000 Catalyst Census of Women Corporate Officers and Top Earners; **2002 Catalyst; ***Medical Economics: cardiology, gastroenterology, and orthopedic surgery are top-earning specialities. Percentages of women m those fields calculated from data on doctors (by gender and speciality), from American Medical Association.

control. "They leave to create companies where they don't have to be the change agents, where they can start from scratch without the fights, without the baggage, and without the brawls," she says.

Stanford's Lazear so envisions a different scenario for women, one in which they wouldn't have to leave corporate America to get the jobs they want. Given the coming labor shortage, which the U.S. Department of Labor predicts will hit by 2010, companies maybe forced to redesign jobs to attract talented workers. And that, combined with technology that will let people work from a variety of locations, he says, will make it possible for more women to reach the top. He predicts that 20% of CEOs in top organizations will be women in 15 to 20 years. But total parity? "I don't expect it ever to be equal—ever," he says.

Brenda Barnes thinks as today's business-school students gain power in companies, they will force changes that benefit men and women. When she taught at Kellogg, she asked her students to write a paper describing how they saw their careers playing out. "They were far more focused on having a life than my generation was," she says. "And it wasn't just a female thing. They grew up seeing their parents killing themselves and then being downsized despite their loyalty. How much this generation is willing to give to any enterprise is a totally different ballgame."

We can hope so. Unfortunately, her students' desire for more balance could be one more form of youthful idealism. As a 24-hour global economy makes it ever more difficult to turn off the office, it's hard to imagine a day when the promotions won't go to the worker who makes just a little more effort, who logs on just a little longer. Or to envision a day when there won't be plenty of contenders—maybe most of them men—who will be willing to do just that.

Essay

How Women Are Changing Corporate America

Yoji Cole

The American work force has changed dramatically in the past several decades. Where women once were the "girls in the office" even if they were in their 60s, they now are CEOs and presidents as well as just about everything else. Yet they aren't just female clones of male executives. Women approach management and leadership differently, emphasizing relationship-building and attentiveness to employee needs, both of which focus a team on common goals.

What most women do not do now is wear those dreaded man ties.

"It's not like we make up half of the country's CEOs, but now we're doing it our own way," says Peluso, 33.

As more women rise in the ranks of corporate America, smart companies are noticing their distinctive leadership qualities and rewarding them. Among DiversityInc's Top 10 Companies for Executive Women, the advancement of female employees is taken so seriously that nine out of 10 link managers' pay to diversity initiatives for women. At these companies, women are visible, powerful and supported with programs that balance their lives in the office and at home.

The numbers tell the story. The Top 10 Companies for Executive Women hire more females than males and employ a quarter more women in management than the typical American employer. Almost a third of their top 10 percent of highest-paid employees are women, 14 percent more than at the Top 50 Companies for Diversity. Additionally, the Top 10 Companies for Executive Women outperform the Fortune 500's percentage of female board directors by a third.

Why do some companies surpass others when it comes to advancing women? Many claim that their inclusiveness is a deeply ingrained part of their culture dating back many years. But even the top companies had to start somewhere, and change usually begins with leadership.

Peluso and the other executives in this story are a snapshot of corporate America's women leaders. They are GenXers, they are baby boomers, and they are CEOs, CFOs and senior vice presidents. Some of them entered corporate America when male CEOs thought married men were the best employees, when women could not become vice presidents and when survival meant assimilating dress and management tactics to male mores.

The personal leadership styles of the four women here represent the promise of greater inclusiveness as corporate America evolves.

In addition to Peluso. *DiversityInc* spoke with Diane Parks, 53, senior vice president and general manager, specialty biotherapeutics and managed care for Genentech; Sallie Krawcheck, 39, CFO and head of strategy at Citigroup; and Amy S. Butte, 37, CFO of the New York Stock Exchange (NYSE). They all have brought value to their respective organizations through their business acumen and effort to build morale through inclusive management tactics.

"It's important to reach out to people who make us intellectually uncomfortable," says Krawcheck. "You have to lead people who are independent self-starters."

Krawcheck, after joining Citigroup in 2002 as the chairman and CEO of "Smith Barney—Citigroup's private wealth-management and equity-research unit—guided the restructuring of Smith Barney's equity-research business and strengthened the quality and transparency of its research.

Krawcheck attributes her success to a practice of purposely seeking out assignments that forced her to stretch her abilities. Women, she says, should be "unflinching and open-eyed about [their] strengths and weaknesses and not just accepting of critiques but asking for them and acting upon them."

Parks, as the senior member of the group interviewed, recalls the days when women executives were passed over for promotion simply because they were women. At the outset of her career in the mid-1970s, Parks worked at a Kansas City-based pharmaceutical company called Marion Laboratories, now Aventis. Women at that time mostly were relegated to sales-support functions. That's where Parks found herself, even though she had wanted to be a product manager. She believes that married men were preferred because the management believed they were motivated to provide for their families.

So Parks, not wanting to leave her hometown of Kansas City, dealt with the limiting corporate culture by trying her hand at as many jobs as possible. She made lateral moves working in therapeutics, wound care, cardiovascular medicine and other areas.

In the 1980s, Marion's management decided it was time to include more women in its sales department and launched a rotational training program that placed candidates in different areas of the business for six months at a time. Parks joined.

"[These lateral moves] enabled me to show I could do other things, learn other things and have a broad line of experience," says Parks.

Training programs such as these are the first step in transforming a company into a diversity leader. Nine of the Top 10 Companies for Executive Women have employee-resource groups and seven of the 10 offer official mentoring and training programs.

The experience Parks gained helped her to move up the corporate ladder. In 1998, she beat three male candidates out of a vice-presidential position at the pharmaceutical company. She contends that lateral moves do not always spell doom.

"I see some women not being flexible and [not] taking lateral moves because they're so focused on 'upward' they don't see the benefit in broadening their experience," says Parks.

Parks left the company for Genentech in 1999, where her presence sends a signal to aspiring female recruits that their gender won't impede their upward mobility. Before a company can become a top company for women, it must open its upper ranks to them.

Butte, by noticing the unnoticed, created a more inclusive corporate culture at the NYSE. "People in the [NYSE] finance department would point to the fact that my presence has made a difference in terms of how we operate and changing the expectations," says Butte.

She joined the NYSE as an executive vice president in February 2004 and the following April was named its CFO. Throughout her career, she's been a producer, she says, "whether it was a client relationship, sale[s], [or as] an analyst building coverage and attracting clients to the firm. And today I'm viewed as someone who produces by setting our mission and meeting objectives."

One of her objectives has been to recognize talented employees in the NYSE's financial department.

Since becoming CFO of the NYSE, Butte has used her position to promote financial services as a career choice for women. She's also proud of the role she played in promoting Rae Amen, a 29-year NYSE veteran who was moved up from manager to assistant controller of operations, and 26-year NYSE veteran Doreen Bloise, who was promoted to manager of collection from collection coordinator.

"They are an example of women I've seen come alive and are making a difference," says Butte.

Women executives, like men, want to be valued members of their organizations. Like men, women report that they are frustrated with a lack of mentor programs and having to navigate through office politics.

One of the traits that set top companies apart is the degree to which they create formal development opportunities for women. Marriott, which ranks No. 9 on the Top 10 Companies for Women, for example, hosts regional women's leadership councils so that women can gain visibility in the organization. SBC Communications, which ranks No. 8, offers a three-year leadership-development program that prepares women for greater responsibility.

While none of the executives in this story benefited from formal mentoring programs, they all endorsed mentoring and are themselves mentors. For example, Krawcheck partners with Citigroup's employee network groups to organize a leadership-training program for women executives. Citigroup ranks No. 7 on the Top 10 Companies for Executive Women list and No. 2 on the Top 50 Companies for Diversity.

Another result of the influx of women into corporate America is choices.

"I see women who are 25 and are saying by the time they're 40, they want to be a CEO somewhere, and I see women who love what they're doing and move on when they've accomplished their goals," says Parks, before adding with a laugh: "And I have a 21-year-old daughter who says she doesn't want to work, period."

Such choices are the result of progressive companies, such as those on the Top 50 Companies for Diversity list, which have created diversity programs and/or women's initiatives to augment male-dominated corporate cultures to ensure women are included in succession planning and other high-profile activities.

As a result, progressive companies have reaped financial rewards. In studying companies that appeared on the Fortune 500 between 1996 and 2000, the women's research organization Catalyst found that companies with the highest percentage of women on their top management teams had better financial performance than those companies with the lowest representation—total return to shareholders was 34 percent higher and return on equity was 35.1 percent higher.

Despite stereotypes that women aren't aggressive enough to run major companies, the reality is that entrepreneurialism runs strong in executive women.

Since becoming Travelocity's CEO in December 2003, Peluso has overseen the company's effort to diversify its revenue streams in an attempt to reclaim its position as the No. 1 online travel Website, a position currently held by Expedia. Under Peluso's direction, Travelocity developed technology that provides a direct connection to hotels and allows consumers to build their own vacation packages. This diverted the company's focus away from bookings.

"It was risky," says Peluso, who during her tenure as Travelocity's vice president of hotels and COO increased annual gross bookings by 11.6 percent in 2003 to $3.9 billion. "But that's how you differentiate who you are," she says.

Peluso is also trying to differentiate Travelocity in the minds of diverse consumers. She expects to dedicate more effort to attracting diverse travelers in the upcoming year.

Top 10 Companies for Executive Women

Top 10 Rank	Company
1	AstraZeneca
2	Merck & Company
3	PricewaterhouseCoopers
4	Abbot Laboratories
5	Prudential Financial
6	Thompson Hospitality
7	Citigroup
8	SBC Communications
9	Marriott International
10	KPMG

In April, the company launched a section on its site for gay and lesbian travelers.

Peluso attributes her success at Travelocity to her staff more than she does herself and in doing so does not do her management techniques justice. She, like the other women in this story, seeks to build team unity by paying attention to her employees' personal and professional needs.

"Women understand what it's like to get pregnant and still want your job. Women understand what it's like to be in a meeting where you're the only one. I think we think about those issues a little harder or differently [than male leaders] because we have the experience base," says Peluso.

Krawcheck agrees: "Women tend to be good at interpersonal relationships."

To further build a collegial, interpersonal atmosphere at Travelocity, Peluso has organized parties using the company's theme of making over its product. One party called "extreme makeover day" had employees come to work as their alter egos. Peluso took the lead in this as well, showing up to work dressed in an army-fatigue skirt and T-shirt with an anarchy symbol. She has also been known to dance on stage at company parties, is a practical joker and will e-mail phrases to employees who win a prize if they can guess who said the phrase.

"Work should feel like a mission and not a job," says Peluso.

Thinking of work as a mission might come easier for women since each time a woman sits in a meeting or boardroom, moves upstairs to a corner office or has her name etched on the company's front door, it is not only a personal success but a success shared by other women. It is a success won by trudging through corporate and gender politics, and while it is getting easier, as exemplified by the experiences of Peluso, Butte, Krawcheck and Parks, it still is difficult.

Essay

How Corporate America Is Betraying Women

Betsy Morris

The deluge began last May. That's when Boeing agreed to cough up as much as $72.5 million to settle a class-action lawsuit brought by female employees; they had asserted that the company paid them less than men and did not promote them as quickly. The next

FEEDBACK *bmorris@fortunemail.com*
Reprinted from the January 10, 2005, pp. 64, 66–74 issue of *Fortune*, by Betsy Morris. Copyright © 2005 by Time Inc. All rights reserved.

month, in June, a court ruled that a lawsuit charging Wal-Mart with discriminatory pay and promotion practices proceed as a class action. In July, Morgan Stanley stunned a courtroom jam-packed with Wall Street women by announcing an 11th-hour $54 million settlement to a class-action suit that made similar allegations. Then, in August, an assistant store manager for Costco sued the retailer for denying her a promotion. Her lawyers have asked the court to allow that case, too, to proceed as a class action.

Just because a company is sued doesn't mean it's guilty, but the flood of sex-discrimination headlines is sobering. After all, didn't we get through this long ago? Don't men and women have a pretty level playing field? Aren't women paid basically the same amount as men for doing the same job? And don't women have an equal shot at getting promoted?

Not exactly. For most management jobs it's still not even close. And if men don't know it, women certainly do. They are bringing these cases, and winning big settlements, because it appears that the evidence is overwhelmingly on their side. Forty years after the Civil Rights Act made discrimination on the basis of sex illegal, studies show that women—virtually across all job categories—are still paid less for doing the very same job. And through women now hold about half of all managerial and professional positions, they account for only about 8% of executive vice presidents and above at FORTUNE 500 companies. "Everybody expected a lot more progress by now," says Ilene Lang, president of Catalyst, the research firm that gathered the data. "There are so many women in the workplace. You just assumed this was a 20th-century battle, and by the 21st century it would be over."

Why the explosion in litigation now? Well, just as the economy went south, the market tanked, and stock options dried up, a critical mass of career women began reaching their 40s and 50s and 60s. And they are shouldering way more financial responsibility than ever before: About 62% of all working women are contributing half or more of their household income, according to an AFL-CIO survey of 800 working women earlier this year. A difference of several thousand dollars between a woman's entry-level salary and a man's may not have mattered much at the start of their careers, but over a lifetime, the gap widens— adding up to a world of difference in, say, which worker's kids will be burdened with a boatload of college debt.

Changes in civil rights legislation enacted in 1991 made it easier for women to do something about the problem. The changes allowed for jury trials and substantial compensatory and punitive damages against companies that discriminate by gender. Suddenly those cases became "incredibly lucrative," says one defense lawyer. "Companies settle them because they don't want to go to trial and look like a bigot in front of a jury." What's more, recent technological advances make it easy for plaintiffs' lawyers to gather and analyze mountains of data across vast geographies and gather prospective class members. Women can join such cases with the click of a mouse.

The threat of a sex-discrimination case has become one of corporate America's worst nightmares. When the Houston-based law firm Fulbright & Jaworski surveyed 300 company general counsels last summer, 62% said their biggest area of litigation exposure— and greatest fear—was employment lawsuits, which include suits claiming sex discrimination. The American Bar Association is currently advertising a seminar entitled *Wal-Mart Class Certification: How an Individual Can Take On a Whole Company—And How to Prevent It.* Many legal and human resources experts expect the number of suits to increase dramatically. Nobody knows exactly how costly they'll be to business. But a brief filed recently by the U.S. Chamber of Commerce litigation center in support of Wal-Mart's appeal of the class-action certification of its lawsuit estimates the damage somewhere in the "billions and billions of dollars." One analyst says the potential damages to Wal-Mart alone, if it is found liable, could amount to $2 billion to $4 billion—and that doesn't include what the company would probably have to pay to equalize skewed salaries.

The cases cast a cold, harsh glare on practices corporate America would prefer to keep out of the spotlight: the way it rewards its workers, determines entry-level salaries, makes promotion decisions, and divvies up merit raises. Traditionally those matters have been largely secret and, except in unionized shops, left to the discretion of management. Now, some say, a byproduct of the lawsuits will be to push companies, for defensive reasons if nothing else, to raise some salaries and put pressure on others at a time when extra money is especially hard to come by, and to adopt quotas (though nobody is using that word), making sure they have enough women in all ranks of management to keep them out of trouble. "I have heard corporate executives say, 'We are going to be forced to do this,'" says Robin Conrad, senior VP of the Chamber of Commerce litigation center, who is apoplectic about the implications of the Wal-Mart class action. "Then we're regimented, right? Like the federal government. It sort of flies in the face of a system of meritocracy in this country—that we work hard and should be rewarded for it."

It's no surprise that the lawsuits have stoked workplace distrust. "Employers are pissed. They say, 'How dare you bite the hand that feeds you!'" says Johnny Taylor Jr., an employment lawyer and chair of the Society of Human Resource Management. "Employees already mistrust employers. So each time a case reveals the secret that was never told, employees think, 'Aha! They really are paying men more than women.'" That breeds more cases, more inquiries, more management defensiveness. "The mindset of employers is: 'Which one of

my employees is going to sue me tomorrow?'" says John Harper, a partner at Fulbright, which conducted the general counsel survey.

Forty years ago women's biggest battle was simply to get access to the workplace at all. That changed with the Civil Rights Act of 1964, which made it illegal for employers to discriminate on the basis of race, creed, and—as an afterthought—sex. (Congressman Howard Smith of Virginia slipped the gender provision into the bill in a last-ditch effort to kill it.) The law provided for the creation of the Equal Employment Opportunity Commission and required that any company with 100 employees or more file annual accounts of how many women and minorities it had at all levels of the organization.

In the 1970s the EEOC took on the automakers, oil companies, and AT&T—where, in 1971, only 1% of all but the lowliest supervisory jobs were held by women, according to the *New York Times*, even though the company ran on an army of female telephone operators. The big blue chip replied that the commission "failed to recognize that the primary reason the Bell System exists is to provide communications service to the American public, not merely to provide employment to all comers, regardless of ability." But two years and $70 million-plus in settlement costs later, the chastened company agreed to promote more women. It's no coincidence that two of the eight women running FORTUNE 500 companies today—Carly Fiorina at Hewlett-Packard and Pat Russo at Lucent—are both products of the enlightened post-lawsuit AT&T.

In the '80s the EEOC (headed by Clarence Thomas from 1982 to 1990) became less feisty; conservative Reagan-era courts all but eliminated the class-action suit and made it much tougher to prove sex discrimination. But under mounting pressure from civil-rights and women's groups, in 1991 Congress passed the law that made it easier for women to file sex discrimination charges. While the economy was booming, not much happened. But in the latter part of the decade, cases against big companies started trickling in: Mitsubishi settled for $34 million in 1996; Home Depot for $104.5 million in 1997; Merrill Lynch for an undisclosed sum in 1998; American Express for $42 million in 2002. And on to Boeing and Morgan Stanley in 2004.

When the courts pondered whether to give the green light to those class-action suits, they turned to statistical analysis. The courts have said that if data on pay or job levels indicate a pattern that is "two deviations from the norm," then there is a "legal inference" that discrimination is present—and a suit can proceed. The norm is generally defined as what might be expected, say, given the number of women in your workforce.

Calculating a standard deviation can be devilishly complex. But at Wal-Mart and Costco, allege the plaintiffs' lawyers, it wasn't hard to tell that the numbers were out of whack. At Wal-Mart women make up more than 72% of hourly workers and hold only about a third of the store manager jobs, according to charges in *Betty Dukes v. Wal-Mart.* A Wal-Mart spokesperson disputes that figure, saying that 60% of the company's associates are women and more than 40% of its managers and professionals are women—and adding that "Wal-Mart does not tolerate discrimination of any kind." At Costco women make up half the workforce but hold only one in six of the richly paying top management jobs, according to charges in *Ellis v. Costco.* (Costco denies the allegations; a spokesperson didn't return calls asking for comment.) Says the Chamber of Commerce's Conrad of the allegations: "You know how you can play around with statistics. You can make them say anything you want to say. There is an element of junk science in all of this."

To be sure, there are several reasons a pay gap between men and women exists. Biology is one: Working women who have children often take time off, delaying promotions. Preference is another: Some women choose professions

that pay less or quit high-powered jobs when they don't seem worth it (see "Power: Do Women Really Want It?" on fortune.com). The oft-quoted Census Bureau statistic—women working full-time earn just 75½ cents for every dollar a man earns—doesn't correct for those things.

So Hilary Lips, a Radford University psychology professor who has studied the pay gap, recently decided to conduct a study that *did* control for those factors. The study caused quite a stir. She found that only in jobs that pay $25,000 to $30,000 a year do men and women earn roughly the same. The further up the pay scale and the higher the education, the wider the earnings gap. Women psychologists earn 83 cents to the male dollar; women college professors earn 75 cents; women lawyers and judges earn 69 cents (see chart for more examples). Even in "women's industries," women consistently earn less than men: women elementary-school teachers earn 95 cents to the dollar; women bookkeepers earn 94 cents; women secretaries earn 84 cents. Says Lips; "It cannot be explained in any way except that people think that what men do is more important and more valuable than what women do."

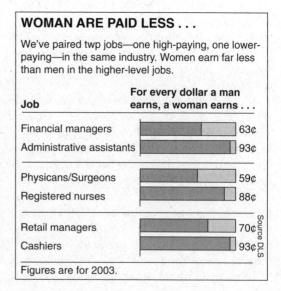

WOMAN ARE PAID LESS . . .

We've paired twp jobs—one high-paying, one lower-paying—in the same industry. Women earn far less than men in the higher-level jobs.

Job	For every dollar a man earns, a woman earns . . .
Financial managers	63¢
Administrative assistants	93¢
Physicans/Surgeons	59¢
Registered nurses	88¢
Retail managers	70¢
Cashiers	93¢

Source DLS

Figures are for 2003.

A top financial services executive who has appeared on FORTUNE'S list of the 50 Most Powerful Women in American Business will never forget the weekend she spent several years ago analyzing the pay scales of her direct reports. She was taken aback to find that time and again the men outearned the women. Her father was visiting her at the time, and she was sitting on the floor of her porch, surrounded by paper, on a Sunday. "Dad, look at this. How can this be?" she asked. "Well," her father replied to his daughter, "maybe women just don't work as hard."

But research shows that women—including women with children—are every bit as hardworking and ambitious as men. Earlier this year Catalyst conducted a survey of 950 top executives, both men and women. Fifty-five percent of the women said they wanted to be CEOs, almost exactly the same as the men. About as many mothers aspired to be CEOs as fathers. Women, like men, believed they needed to outperform expectations, take on big assignments, and work long hours and weekends to get ahead.

So what was the difference? Lack of operational experience accounted for some of it—36% of women in the Catalyst study said it was a problem for them, compared with 25% of men. But the far bigger reasons cited by the women were exclusion from informal networks—the boys' after-dinner drinks, the golf games, the men's clubs—and persistent stereotypes and assumptions their bosses made about their ambitions, their aspirations, and their abilities. Men, for example, may assume a woman wants to cut back or quit when she has a baby. But in a story two years ago on the growing number of women with stay-at-home husbands (see "Trophy Husbands" on fortune.com), FORTUNE found that when the playing field is level for women, they keep working. The decision about which spouse stays home with the kids has little to do with gender. The biggest determinants are serendipity, timing, and, most of all, which parent has the greatest earning potential.

Over a lifetime that earning potential can be significantly affected by seemingly small disparities in pay—Marc Bendick Jr., an economist and expert witness for the Wal-Mart plaintiffs, calls them "micro-inequities." Consider the stories from Boeing. Charles Phillips, a former training manager there, notes that when it was time to dole out annual raises, there was no way to rectify the fact that in the same job category men usually made the most, and women and minorities, the least. Even if you subtracted two percentage points from the 7% raise for the man making $100,000 and added two percentage points to the 7% raise for the deserving woman making $50,000, the man would get $5,000 to the woman's $4,500—widening the gap still further. "There was never enough money to fix the problem," Phillips says. "It was heart-wrenching to figure out how to bring the women up and at the same time not penalize the men. Eventually we just gave up."

If you start out too low, it's almost impossible to catch up. Consider Phillips' wife, Terri, 50. She wanted so badly to have a career at Boeing that she accepted a $13,000 job as a clerk there in 1989, figuring she'd work her way up. Soon after, she was making $27,000; by the time she was laid off in 2003, she was making about $70,000 as a senior manager in HR. At least that's what the org chart reflected, and that's what her boss called her. In payroll, though, she was a Level 1 employee (one step lower than a senior manager) and paid accordingly. When she tried to fix the discrepancy, higher-ups told her she didn't have enough direct reports to be called senior manager; another time she was told Boeing was afraid that if it corrected the problem, she might sue. When she left the company, she was still making $15,000 to $20,000 less than the other senior managers. She says she figures her gender cost her about $200,000 during her management years. A Boeing spokesperson says that the company "is firmly committed to an environment in which employees are treated fairly," adding that Boeing never admitted wrongdoing.

One explanation for women's lower pay and status is that women don't negotiate as deftly as men, according to economist Linda Babcock, co-author of the 2003 book *Women Don't Ask.* Studies show that women are much more likely to accept a salary offer without quibbling. A study of Carnegie Mellon graduate students reports that men were eight times more likely than women to negotiate an initial salary, resulting in starting pay an average of 7.4%, or $4,000, more than their female classmates.

Many companies argue, in effect, that failing to negotiate is the job candidate's problem; not theirs. "If [a woman] will work for $8 and a guy will hold out for $9," asks one defense lawyer, "is that discrimination, or is it market reality?" Retorts employment lawyer Taylor: "That's like saying, 'If I could hire children to work for $1 an hour in a coal mine, why wouldn't I?' There are a lot of decisions and practices we could justify on the basis of pure market analysis."

Wal-Mart has gotten religion. The retailer has made big changes to its employee practices that one analyst warns could drive up its operational costs. The far greater consequence, though, may be the standard it sets for the rest of corporate America. Recently Wal-Mart began to tie 15% of a manager's bonus (which can amount to 85% of salary for top executives) to meeting diversity goals. What that includes, explains the company's new chief diversity officer, Charlyn Jerrells Porter, is that the sex and race of those promoted closely reflect the percentages of those who apply. This is not a quota system, she says. Only the most qualified are to be promoted. But if the company is recruiting effectively, "at some point, the stats take over" and the percentages naturally match up. Wal-Mart is also taking another bold, possibly precedent-setting step: It has begun to require that new hires with the same experience receive the same starting pay—no matter what their pay was in the past. (This applies to hourly hires; the company is reviewing changes for salaried types.) Says Porter: "We don't bring a female in at $6 and a male in at $7, where both have similar prior work experience, because if you do, then you have an immediate issue."

Of course, gender disparities in pay and promotions aren't always glaring. In companies where the problem is subtler, many people in power tend to think there is no problem. Remember the financial executive whose father thinks women don't work hard enough? Last year she was on a diversity committee made up of herself and white men. She says the men were convinced that women were getting promoted faster than men—until she got them the stats that showed otherwise. Laura Liswood, a senior adviser and former managing partner at Goldman Sachs and head of the Council of Women World Leaders at Harvard's Kennedy School, says that the groups that dominate (usually white men) "tend to think the system is meritocratic, that it works correctly, and that if changes are needed, they're minor." In the exact same organization, she says, women—and minorities—believe the opposite.

That disconnect between what working men and women think underlines the need for transparency about pay and promotions, according to a growing consensus among legal and HR experts and defense lawyers. So far, of course, transparency has been in very short supply. For example, Boeing spent four years and enough legal challenges to fill 31 feet of shelf space, according to the plaintiffs' lawyers, just to keep from having to reveal that it had conducted its own internal studies and found that it was indeed underpaying its women. Boeing settled one day before the start of the trial, which would have forced the company to share those details. Boeing agreed to settle "because it was in the best interests of the company, its employees, and shareholders, and enables the company to move forward and avoid the continued exposure and distraction of protracted litigation," says a spokesman.

One simple solution would be for the EEOC to make public the reams of employment data that companies are required to file every year. But it won't—because, according to the 1964 Civil Rights Act, it can't except in some cases. The EEOC can supply data to be used in certain lawsuits. It also sometimes shares information with academics for research on the condition that no companies be identified. Isn't the EEOC supposed to sniff out discrimination whenever it occurs? Yes, says EEOC chair Can Dominguez, but it has limited resources. When it comes to litigation, it must pick its shots, such as the Morgan Stanley case settled last summer. "We can't boil the ocean," says Dominguez.

For companies that may be vulnerable to sex-discrimination lawsuits, here's the prescription from one defense lawyer handling a high-profile case. Be much more formal in setting up systems for selection and promotion. Define the required competencies. Always post jobs. Be able to justify your sections either for hire or for promotion: Have a good explanation when pay and promotion don't look even-steven. Establish guidelines for how you set pay—both entry-level and raises—so that you are consistent. "Some companies do a good job and some do a terrible job in outlining expectations and being candid about performance," says the defense lawyer. "Make sure that women are getting the explanations and feedback they need to honestly understand the skills they need to advance." Finally, when you deny a woman a promotion, explain why. The companies in which all this is a closed and secret process are the ones that get into trouble.

Taking that kind of action may not eliminate the pay gap or suddenly catapult more women to the top. But at least it might lead to happier and more productive employees. And it would certainly reduce the risk of lawsuits from people like Terri Phillips, the former Boeing manager. "There wasn't anything in my nature to sue," she says. "That's not the way I was taught to deal with things." In the end, though, her reasoning for joining the class-action suit went according to an imprecise formula used by many of the other plaintiffs in sex-discrimination suits: "I don't want to hurt the company. But if companies continue to be run like this, it will end up hurting my granddaughters."

Case Study

Gender Issues at Your House

John Hasnas

DOMINIQUE FRANCON

You are Dominique Francon, a senior account representative in the advertising department of the successful architecture magazine, *Your House*. In this position, you supervise the junior account reps who directly contact potential advertisers to sell advertising space. You and Peter Keating, the other senior account representative, are each responsible for

---

half the staff, although your half consistently out-performs Keating's. Both of you report directly to Henry Cameron, the manager of the advertising department. Recently, you were excited to learn that Cameron will soon be promoted to the magazine's editorial board. Since by any performance standard your results are greatly superior to Keating's, you feel sure that you are slated to replace Cameron.

You think of yourself as a self-assured and assertive woman and have a strong desire to succeed in what you view as the male-dominated publishing industry. Accordingly, you behave in what you consider a professional manner at all times. Although somewhat demanding, you are never unfair to your subordinates; a combination that you believe helps account for your staff's superior bottom-line performance. You feel some regret that this posture prevents you from developing the kind of work-place friendships that others do, but you see this as part of the price you have to pay to make it as a woman manager. You keep a strict separation between your social and professional lives and would never consider pursuing a personal relationship with any of your co-workers. In addition, you are a hard worker, typically putting in many hours beyond the 40 per week required by your position.

You get along fairly well with everyone at the magazine except Ellsworth Toohey, one of the senior editors. Even before the run-in you had with him last year, you considered Toohey to be a typical "male chauvinist pig." Toohey, a man in his mid-fifties from Lubbock, Texas, habitually engages in behavior that you find offensive and demeaning to the women who work at the magazine. Regardless of their position, he typically addresses the women on the staff as "Honey" or "Dear" and refers to them collectively as the magazine's "fillies." In addition, he will invariably greet them with some comment on their appearance such as "Looking good today, Dear" or "Nice dress. I don't know how I'll keep my mind on my work while you're around, Honey."

Last year, after a private meeting in his office concerning the advertising budget, Toohey asked you to go out with him. You told him that since he was a superior of yours whose judgment could have an effect on your future career, you thought it would be inappropriate and that you had a personal policy of never dating co-workers. Rather than accept your refusal, Toohey responded to this by saying, "Oh, loosen up. People go out with co-workers all the time. Let your hair down. I guarantee you won't be disappointed." Although you found this to be both condescending and offensive, you retained your calm and said, "Mr. Toohey, you are putting me in a very awkward situation. I don't think it would be a good idea and I'd appreciate it if you would drop the subject."

A few days following this, you overheard two of the female secretaries discussing Toohey at lunch. Upon inquiring, you learned that he had propositioned many of the single women at the magazine, something that upset several of them. The final straw, however, came the following week when you were leaning over to take a drink from the water fountain. Toohey, who was passing by at the time, said, "Whoa, nice view!" and when you stood up, "Have you reconsidered my proposal of last week? You should get to know me better. I can really be of help to you in this business."

Following this incident, you went immediately to the manager of personnel, Howard Roark, to complain. Roark listened to your description of both incidents and your claim that other female employees had had similar experiences and told you he would look into it. Less than a week later, he came by your office to say that the problem had been taken care of and if you had any further trouble with Toohey to inform him immediately. Although you have no idea what action Roark took, it was clear something had been done. From that point on, Toohey never said a word to you that was not strictly business related. His manner toward you had become completely cold and formal, and he seemed to try to avoid you whenever possible.

This state of affairs suited you fine until today. Yesterday afternoon, you were shocked to learn that the editorial board had voted to promote Peter Keating to manager of the advertising department. The editorial board is made up of the senior managers and editors and is empowered to fill any opening at the managerial level by majority vote. The board presently has nine members, none of whom are women.

Upset, you had gone to Roark's office to ask why you had been passed over. He informed you that although the vote was as close as it possibly could be, the board elected to go with Keating because it was impressed with his "people skills." However, when you came in this morning, one of your account reps asked you what you had ever done to Toohey. When you asked her what she meant, she said that she had been talking to the secretary who had kept the minutes of yesterday's Board meeting, and she had said that Toohey really had it in for you. Before you could stop yourself, you heard yourself saying. "Why, that son of a bitch. I'll sue him for sexual harassment and the entire board for sex discrimination."

When you calmed down, you found yourself wondering whether this was, in fact, a case of sexual harassment or sex discrimination. You also found yourself wondering what would be the best steps for you to take in this situation. What should you do? (You may ask to meet with either Roark or Toohey or both

in addition to any other action you deem appropriate.)

ELLSWORTH TOOHEY

You are Ellsworth Toohey, a senior editor of the successful architecture magazine, *Your House*. This position has both editorial and managerial responsibilities. As an editor, you both decide which articles will be printed in the magazine and make editorial recommendations regarding them. However, as a senior editor, you are also a member of the editorial board, which makes the important managerial decisions for the magazine. The board is comprised of the nine men who are senior managers or editors. It has responsibility for planning the magazine's budget, establishing editorial policy, and selecting those who are to be hired or promoted to managerial positions.

You were born in 1937 in Lubbock, Texas. Your family was extremely poor and you always had to work as a boy, but you managed to put yourself through college, getting a B.A. in English. Following graduation, you married your college sweetheart, got a position as a reporter for the *Dallas Morning News*, and began your career. By 1982, you had worked your way up to editor of the *Morning News*. At that time, you left Dallas to join the staff of *Your House*, then a new magazine just starting out. You were quite happy with your new position and things were going very well for you until your wife died 18 months ago. After a very rough 6 or 7 months, you began to put your life back together and have rededicated yourself to your work, perhaps in order to compensate for some of the emptiness in your personal life.

You think of yourself as a skilled professional, but one who has never forgotten the importance of a friendly demeanor that your Southern upbringing impressed upon you. Accordingly, you try to maintain an informal and friendly manner with your co-workers and subordinates. You will often chat with the male employees about sports or politics. You also try to make small talk with the female employees, although you find this more difficult since your upbringing and life experience seems to have left you ignorant of what subjects are of interest to women. You have a personal policy of attempting to greet all co-workers with a complimentary comment in an effort to overcome the intimidating effect your high-level position can have on lower-level employees. Even when you don't know their names, you might greet an employee with a comment such as, "Nice suit, Son," or "Looking good today, Dear."

You believe you get along fairly well with everyone at the magazine except Dominique Francon, one of the two senior account representatives in the advertising department. A senior account representative supervises the junior account reps who directly contact potential advertisers to sell advertising space. Even before the run-in you had with her last year, you considered Francon to be an example of an "uptight, feminist bitch"; cold, aloof, and demanding. She had the reputation for driving the accounts reps under her unmercifully hard while hardly ever dispensing a "Nice job" or "Well done." Although her section usually sold the most advertising, in your opinion these results came at the expense of a happy workforce.

Last year, about six months after your wife's death, you made what you now consider some terrible errors in judgment. Seeking escape from your loneliness, you asked several of the single women at the magazine to go out with you. Since you had not asked a woman out in over 35 years, you were not particularly good at it and felt foolish and inept trying to do so.

One day last year, you were having a private meeting with Francon in your office concerning the advertising budget. It was one of those days when you were feeling particularly lonely and couldn't stand the thought of going home to an empty house again. As a result, you asked Francon to go out with you despite the negative impression you had of her personality. To your surprise, she did not turn you down directly, but simply stated that she had a policy against dating people from the office. At the time, you interpreted this to mean that she would like to go out with you, but was concerned with the appearance of impropriety. Rather than let the matter drop, you said something to the effect that she should not be so concerned with appearances and that people on the magazine's staff go out with each other all the time. However, Francon responded by saying that she thought it would create an awkward situation and that she would rather not.

A week later, Francon was getting a drink at the water fountain when you passed by. After saying hello, you said "Have you reconsidered my proposal of last week? I would really like to get to know you better. I know you're trying to make a career in publishing. I have a lot of experience in the field. Maybe I can be of some help to you." To your surprise, she just stormed off.

The next thing you knew, Howard Roark, the manager of personnel, was in your office telling you that Francon had complained to him that you were sexually harassing her as well as other women on the magazine's staff. Angry and extremely embarrassed, you admitted to Roark that you had been lonely since your wife's death and had asked several women out. You assured him that since these actions had apparently been misinterpreted, you would not do so again. Since then, although you still have endeavored to remain on friendly terms with most of the women at the magazine, you have never been familiar with Francon again. You have kept all your dealings with her on a formal and professional level.

Yesterday, the editorial board met to vote on who should be named manager of the advertising department now that the former manager, Henry Cameron, had been promoted to senior manager and member of the editorial board. Although four members of the board wanted to promote Francon because of her sections superior sales performance, Cameron, now a board member, recommended Peter Keating, the other senior account representative. Cameron stated that he thought Keating had more "people skills" than did Francon and would make a better manager. You certainly

agreed with this and said so. In the end, the board voted 5–4 to promote Keating.

Today, you learned that upon hearing that Keating had been promoted rather than her, Francon had told one of her account reps that she was going to sue you and the magazine for sexual harassment and sex discrimination. Your initial reaction to this was to exclaim, "Isn't that just like the bitch." However, after you calmed down, you realized that this could present a damaging situation both for you and the magazine. What should you do? (You may ask to meet with either Roark or Francon or both in addition to any other action you deem appropriate.)

Case Study

Worth the Effort?

Raymond S. Pfeiffer and Ralph P. Forsberg

HANDLING SEXUAL HARASSMENT

Violet Spear had done her homework. But then, she felt she had to in order to know whether or not she should file a grievance against her colleague, Theo Lucasey. Violet did not want to jeopardize her job as a junior marketing executive by appearing to be a "bad sport," "overly sensitive woman," or any "hysterical female." Theo had called her all of these in the last few months when she complained to him about his conduct toward her.

Violet was trying to find out whether the way Theo had been treating her constituted sexual harassment. What she found out was interesting. First, she looked for the legal guidelines for sexual harassment. Under Title

VII of the 1964 Civil Rights Act, sexual harassment is defined as

> Unwelcome sexual advances, requests for sexual favors, and other verbal or physical conduct of a sexual nature constitute sexual harassment when (1) submission to such conduct is made either explicitly or implicitly a term or condition of an individual's employment, (2) submission to or rejection of such conduct by an individual is used as the basis for employment decisions affecting such individual, or (3) such conduct has the purpose or effect of unreasonably interfering with an individual's work performance or creating an intimidating, hostile, or offensive working environment.[1]

This seemed pretty clear to Violet and seemed to definitely apply to the way Theo had been treating her.

Violet is very successful in her marketing position. She attributes part of her success to the fact that her clients trust her professionalism as well as her knowledge of her job. Part of what Violet sees as important to her professional image is her wardrobe: she dresses in very conservative business suits that are feminine yet reassuring to her conservative male clients. Before Theo's remarks, no one had ever referred to her wardrobe as anything but tasteful or stylish.

Theo was transferred from a regional branch about six months earlier and almost immediately began to make comments to Violet whenever they worked together. At first it had just been things like "Very nice suit," but soon he began to add a growl or a low barking noise to his comments. She had called him on this right away, but he accused her of being overly sensitive. The comments continued and gradually became more suggestive. Again Violet told him to keep his comments to himself. He responded by accusing her of being a bad sport.

The situation reached its peak about a week ago when once again Theo made a comment about her clothes: "That suit is so sexy I can't stand it. Why don't we go into my office where you can take it off so I can get some work done? You know what kind of work I mean, right?"

Violet replied angrily, "Why don't you just knock it off. Act like a grown man instead of a 14-year-old with a hormone problem. I simply will not tolerate these remarks any more. One more and I'm going to have to file a complaint."

"Don't be a hysterical female, dear. Those business suits of yours really turn me on. I've always had a thing for women who dress in those 'power suits.' I like power. Why not just stop wearing those clothes? Maybe then I'll be able to control myself," was Theo's response.

Violet had walked away in disgust. In the next week she looked up the harassment guidelines and talked to a number of women at her office about what had happened. When she asked what to do, the replies were not encouraging. One woman said it couldn't be harassment, because Theo wasn't her boss and had no power over her employment. Another said that she had no confidence that any of the male executives would take her complaints seriously. A third said that unless one of the male executives actually witnessed the harassment, nothing would be done. In all, five different women expressed the sentiment that no male executive would take her seriously, and probably they'd believe Theo's comment about her being overly sensitive or hysterical.

"It's the way men are. Must be genetic. No government guidelines are going to reverse 41,000 years of habit," one had said.

Violet was confused. The terms of the guidelines seemed to cover Theo's action—work was becoming oppressive. Yet she had gotten no encouragement from other women at the company. She had also come across some statistics that stated that 67 percent of the women who complained of harassment lost their jobs within one year, either by being fired or by voluntarily leaving. The same source stated that only 9 percent of the complaints ever resulted in the harassment ceasing. There was a procedure for sexual harassment claims at Violet's firm, but each step of the process involved some male executive who might react just as the other women predicted.

Violet is afraid of being labeled a complainer or a troublemaker. She began to think Theo's comments might be correct, maybe if she just stopped wearing those suits he'd leave her alone. She didn't want to compromise her career; she had worked too hard and been too professional to give it up for a jerk like Theo. But her clients responded well to her professional style of dressing and had never insulted her like Theo. Would they be bothered by a switch in her wardrobe? Yet if she didn't complain, work would continue to be oppressive, and there was no telling how many other women Theo would insult. Violet has to make a decision about how she's going to get this problem RESOLVED.

Put yourself in her position to complete the analysis and reach a decision.

NOTE

1. "Guidelines on Discrimination on the Basis of Sex" (Washington, DC: Equal Employment Opportunity Commission, November 10, 1980).

Diversity in the Workplace

Former New Jersey senator and presidential candidate Bill Bradley has argued that "slavery was America's original sin, and race remains our unresolved dilemma." Internationally recognized African American legal scholar Derrick Bell couldn't agree more. The U.S. Constitution, the Bill of Rights, and the Declaration of Independence, says Bell, suggest, specify, and argue that all human beings have a right to life, liberty, and the pursuit of happiness, equal protection under the law, and an equal opportunity for, if not an absolute guarantee of, an equal outcome. These documents claim that all human beings are equal, and therefore everyone must be treated equally unless there are compelling reasons to treat them differently. In 1964, Title VII of the Civil Rights Act attempted to update, encapsulate, and bring into the workplace the spirit of the founding documents:

> It shall be unlawful employment practice for an employer to fail or refuse to hire or discharge any individual or otherwise discriminate against any individual with respect to his compensation, terms, conditions, or privileges of employment because of such individual's race, color, religion, sex, or national origin.

This is our creed, our faith commitment, our mantra, says Bell, but it is not our lived reality. We remain a society that discriminates by disposition, habit, and institutional tradition. Bell believes that only continued education and legislation can eradicate racism, and one of the best and most common places for this to occur is the workplace. He agrees with former President Clinton that affirmative action needs to be augmented and mended but certainly not ended!

Whether in the workplace, in government contracting, or in university admissions, affirmative action policies remain controversial—albeit not for the reasons they were initially so. Today's opponents see in affirmative action policies, their application, and their extension a betrayal of the principles of fundamental fairness that motivated their adoption. Where once the goal of affirmative action policies was to level playing fields that were historically tilted against women and ethnic minorities, opponents claim, legal and regulatory interpretations of affirmative action seek to tilt those same playing fields in the other direction. This is often expressed as the idea that affirmative action policies promote "reverse discrimination"—countering one form of odious discrimination with another, equally odious form; a textbook case of two wrongs not making a right. Affirmative action policies were predicated initially on impeccable principles of compensatory justice: Those who were unfairly held down ought to get a leg up, as compensation. That argument is compelling when principles of affirmative action are applied to identifiable victims of past discrimination. But opponents complain that the focus of today's affirmative action policies has shifted from compensation of individual, identifiable victims of past discrimination to spoils for *groups*. Discrimination against *any* member of an affirmative action–protected group demands preferential treatment for *all* members of the group. Opponents complain that this makes affirmative action less a vehicle for achieving a commonsense conception of compensatory justice and more a vehicle for achieving a debatable and divisive conception of distributive justice—the idea that jobs, government contracts, and university admissions ought to be distributed to persons based on group membership and each group's representation in society. That idea repudiates, rather than realizes, the day of which the Reverend Dr. Martin Luther King spoke movingly in his famous speech:

> I have a dream that my four little children will one day live in a nation where they will not be judged by the color of their skin but by the content of their character.

Under today's affirmative action policies, opponents argue, we are more than ever judged by color of our skin.

"Racism in the Workplace" is an article that concludes that no matter what the legal prohibitions in place, workplace prejudice and the harassment of minorities have not entirely ceased. The "Texaco" and "Denny's" cases show how prejudice and the harassment keep occurring in both complicated and secretive, as well as blatant and obvious, ways in the business world. "Management Dilemma" reaches beyond race, addressing ageism, sexism, and stereotypes regarding being single or married, or being affluent or poor. "Keeping It Real" focuses on racial discrimination and its effects at Coca-Cola. "Sexual Discrimination at Eastern Airlines?" moves the debate to the next frontier—protection against employment discrimination for the transgendered.

Essay

Racism in the Workplace

Aaron Bernstein

When Wayne A. Elliott was transferred in 1996 from a factory job to a warehouse at Lockheed Martin Corp.'s sprawling military-aircraft production facilities in Marietta, Ga., he says he found himself face to face with naked racism. Anti-black graffiti was scrawled on the restroom walls. His new white colleagues harassed him, Elliott recalls, as did his

---

manager, who would yell at him, call him "boy," and tell him to "kiss my butt." He complained, but Elliot says the supervisor was no help. Instead, he assigned Elliott, now 46, to collecting parts to be boxed, which involves walking about 10 miles a day. Meanwhile, the eight whites in his job category sat at computer terminals and told him to get a move on—even though Elliott outranked them on the union seniority list.

The atmosphere got even uglier when Elliott and a few other blacks formed a small group in 1997 called Workers Against Discrimination, which led to the filing of two class actions. One day, he and the other two black men among the 30 warehouse workers found "back-to-Africa tickets" on their desks, he says, which said things like "Just sprinkle this dingy black dust on any sidewalk and piss on it, and, presto! hundreds of n—s spring up!" They reported this, but the Lockheed security officials who responded took the three victims away in their security cars as if they were the wrongdoers, he says, and interrogated them separately.

Then, one day in 1999, according to Elliott, a hangman's noose appeared near his desk. "You're going to end up with your head in here," Elliott recalls a white co-worker threatening. Another noose appeared last November, he says. He and the other whites "hassle me all the time now, unplugging my computer so I lose work, hiding my bike or chair; it's constant," says Elliott, who gets counseling from a psychologist for the stress and says he has trouble being attentive to his two children, ages 7 and 8, when he's at home.

Lockheed spokesman Sam Grizzle says the company won't comment on any specific employee. But regarding the suits, which Lockheed is fighting, he says, "we do not tolerate, nor have we ever tolerated, harassment or discrimination of any form. We take such complaints very seriously, and we always have investigated them and taken appropriate action when needed."

The alleged incidents at Lockheed are part of an extensive pattern of charges of racial hatred in U.S. workplaces that *Business Week* investigated over a two-month period. Nearly four decades after the Civil Rights Act of 1964 gave legal equality to minorities, charges of harassment at work based on race or national origin have more than doubled, to nearly 9,000 a year, since 1990, according to the Equal Employment Opportunity Commission.

The problem is not confined to small Southern cities such as Marietta. In addition to high-profile suits at Lockheed, Boeing, and Texaco, dozens of other household names face complaints of racism in their workforce. Noose cases have been prosecuted in cosmopolitan San Francisco and in Detroit, with a black population among the largest in the nation.

It's true that minorities' share of the workforce grew over the decade, which could have led to a corresponding rise in clashes. Yet racial harassment charges have jumped by 100% since 1990, while minority employment grew by 36%. What's more, most charges involve multiple victims, so each year the cases add up to tens of thousands of workers—mostly blacks, but also Hispanics and Asians.

It's hard to reconcile such ugly episodes with an American culture that is more accepting of its increasing diversity than ever before. Today, immigrants from every ethnic and racial background flock to the U.S. There is a solid black middle class, and minorities are active in most walks of life, from academia to the nightly news. When we do think about race, it's usually to grapple with more subtle and complex issues, such as whether affirmative action is still necessary to help minorities overcome past discrimination, or whether it sometimes constitutes reverse discrimination against whites.

To some extent, the rise in harassment cases may actually reflect America's improved race relations. Because more minorities believe that society won't tolerate blatant bigotry anymore, they file EEOC charges rather than keep quiet out of despair that their complaints won't be heard, says Susan Sturm, a Columbia University law professor who studies workplace discrimination. Many cases involve allegations of harassment that endured for years.

Multimillion-dollar settlements of racial discrimination or harassment claims at such companies as Coca-Cola Co. and Boeing Co. also give victims greater hope that a remedy is available. Such suits became easier in 1991, after Congress passed a law that allowed jury trials and compensatory and punitive damages in race cases. "It's like rape, which everyone kept silent about before," says Boeing human resources chief James B. Dagnon. "Now, prominent individuals are willing to talk publicly about what happened, so there's a safer environment to speak up in."

But many experts say they are seeing a disturbing increase in incidents of harassment. Minority workers endure the oldest racial slurs in the book. They're asked if they eat "monkey meat," denigrated as inferior to whites, or find "KKK" and other intimidating graffiti on the walls at work.

Even office workers are not exempt. In May, 10 current and former black employees at Xerox Corp. offices in Houston filed harassment charges with the EEOC. One, Linda Johnson, says she has suffered racial slurs from a co-worker since 1999, when glaucoma forced her to quit the sales department and become a receptionist. Last year, a white colleague doctored a computer photo of her to make her look like a prostitute, she says. After she complained, her boss printed out the picture and hung it in his office, her charge says. "I tried to do what company procedures suggested and complain to my supervisor, then on up to human resources at headquarters," says Johnson, 47. "But they just sweep it under the rug." Xerox declined to comment on her case.

Worse yet are hangman's nooses, a potent symbol of mob lynchings in America's racial history. The EEOC has handled 25 noose cases in the past 18 months, "something that only came along every two or three years before," says Ida L. Castro, outgoing EEOC chairwoman. Management lawyers concur that racial harassment has jumped sharply. "I've seen more of these cases in the last few years than in the previous 10, and it's bad stuff," says Steve Poor, a partner at Seyfarth, Shaw, Fairweather & Geraldson, a law firm that helps companies defend harassment and discrimination suits.

Some lay the blame on blue-collar white men who think affirmative action has given minorities an unfair advantage. Their feelings may be fueled by the long-term slide in the wages of less-skilled men, which have lagged inflation since 1973. Since many whites see little evidence of discrimination anymore, the small number who harbor racist views feel more justified in lashing out at minorities, whom they perceive as getting ahead solely due to their race, says Carol M. Swain, a Vanderbilt University law professor who is writing a book about white nationalism.

SILENCE

Incidents of open racism at work occur below the national radar because all the parties have powerful incentives to keep it quiet. Plaintiffs' lawyers don't want employees to go public before a trial for fear of prejudicing their case in court *Business Week* spoke for more than a month with some lawyers before they agreed to let their clients talk. Even then, most workers refused to give their names, fearful of retaliation. Management and plaintiffs' lawyers alike say it takes tremendous nerve to file a suit or EEOC charges, given the likelihood that co-workers or bosses will strike back. Since 1990, the number of minorities filing charges of retaliation with the EEOC after they complained about racial mistreatment has doubled, to 20,000 a year.

Companies have an even greater desire to avoid bad publicity. Many suits end when employers settle. They routinely buy employees' silence with extra damage award money.

Because racial harassment allegations can be so embarrassing, they pose a difficult challenge for companies. Some quickly go on the offensive and take steps to change. Other employers hunker down for a fight, arguing that allegations are inaccurate or exaggerated. Northwest Airlines Corp., for example, is fighting charges made by black construction workers who found a noose last July at the airline's new terminal under construction at Detroit Metro Airport. Northwest also recently settled two noose-related suits, although it denied liability. Northwest spokeswoman Kathleen M. Peach says none of the noose incidents "rise to the level of harassment. You have to ask was it a joke at a construction site? Or was it in a cargo area where a lot of ropes are used? It's not as cut-and-dried as it seems."

Some employers dismiss nooses and slurs as harmless joking. This seems to be the view taken by Lakeside Imports Inc., New Orleans' largest Toyota Motor Corp. dealer. Last August, it signed a consent decree with the EEOC to settle charges brought by six black salesmen in its 50-person used car department. The men said that their manager, Chris Mohrman, hit and poked them with two 3½-foot-long sticks with derogatory words on them that he called his "n—sticks."

Lakeside brushed aside the incident; according to case depositions. Mohrman's manager at the time, a white man named David Oseng, had hired the black salesmen. When he heard what was going on, Oseng said in his deposition, he told the dealership's top brass. Oseng said the top two managers "told me they were tired of all the problems with the n—s. And if we hired another n—, [I] would be terminated."

Lakeside lawyer Ralph Zatzkis says the dealer didn't admit any guilt and denies that anything serious happened. He says the sticks, which the EEOC obtained by subpoena, did have writing on them, but "those weren't racial remarks." Zatzkis dismissed the episode as "horseplay." Mohrman and the black salesmen left Lakeside and couldn't be reached. Zatzkis says Lakeside's top managers declined to comment.

Frivolous harassment charges do occur, say experts, but they're rare. "It takes a lot of energy to raise a complaint, and you can make major mistakes assuming what the employees' motives are," warns Haven E. Cockerham, head of human resources at R. R. Donnelley & Sons Co., which is fighting a class action for alleged racial discrimination and harassment that included claims of whites donning KKK robes.

Consider Adelphia Communications Corp., a $2.9 billion cable-TV company based in Coudersport, Pa. In February, the EEOC filed suit on behalf of Glenford S. James, a 12-year veteran, and other black employees in the company's Miami office. A manager there racially harassed minorities "on a daily basis" after he took over in August, 1999, the suit says. The manager twice put a noose over James's door, it says. Once, says the complaint, the manager told an employee to "order monkey meat or whatever they eat" for James.

In a suit filed in June, James says that Adelphia didn't stop the problem until he complained to the EEOC in May, 2000. Then, the manager was terminated or resigned. Adelphia declined to comment. However, its brief in the EEOC suit admits that the manager displayed a noose and "made inappropriate statements of a racial nature." The brief says Adelphia "promptly and severely disciplined" the manager "as a result of his actions." The manager couldn't be reached.

REVENGE

Whites who stand up for co-workers also can run into trouble. Ted W. Gignilliat, a worker at the Marietta facility of Lockheed since 1965, says he was harassed so badly for speaking up about two nooses that he had to take a leave of absence. He says he was threatened, his truck was broken into, and he got anonymous phone calls at work and at home—one telling him he would "wind up on a slab, dead." In March, 2000, a psychologist told Gignilliat to stop work: he went on disability leave until May of this year. He now works as an alarm-room operator in the plant's fire station. It's in the middle of the security office, with guards, but I feel they will retaliate against me again for stepping forward," says Gignilliat.

Usually, of course, minorities bear the brunt of revenge. Roosevelt Lewis, who delivers Wonder bread for an Interstate Bakeries Corp. bakery in San Francisco, says his white superiors have been making his life miserable ever since he and other blacks filed a race suit in 1998. A jury awarded them $132 million last year (late reduced by a judge to $32 million). Lewis says this only exacerbated the

behavior. "They're trying to make you insubordinate, to create an excuse to fire you," charges Lewis. He says he has complained to higher-ups, but the hassling continues.

Jack N. Wiltrakis, Interstate's head of human resources, says the company has a hotline to headquarters in Kansas City but has received no complaints. "If they have a problem, it's incumbent on them to tell us," he says. Interstate, which has 34,000 workers in 64 bakeries around the U.S., has been sued for race problems in New York, Orlando, Indianapolis, and Richmond, Va. It has settled the two cases, denying liability, and is still fighting the others, including Lewis.' Wiltrakis says the suits haven't prompted Interstate to launch new policies.

In the end, racist behavior by employees lands at the door of corporate executives. They face a dilemma: If they admit there's a problem, the company is exposed to lawsuits and negative publicity. But denial only makes matters worse. Until more employers confront the rise of ugly racism head on, Americans will continue to see behavior they thought belonged to a more ignominious age.

Case Study

Texaco: The Jelly Bean Diversity Fiasco

Marianne M. Jennings

In November, 1996, Texaco, Inc., was rocked by the disclosure of tape-recorded conversations among three executives about a racial discrimination suit pending against the company. The suit, seeking $71 million, had

been brought by 6 employees, on behalf of 1500 other employees, who alleged the following forms of discrimination:

> I have had KKK printed on my car. I have had my tires slashed and racial slurs written about

---

me on bathroom walls. One co-worker blatantly me a racial epithet to my face.

Throughout my employment, three supervisors in my department openly discussed their view that African-Americans are ignorant and incompetent, and, specifically, that Thurgood Marshall was the most incompetent person they had ever seen.

Sheryl Joseph, formerly a Texaco secretary in Harvey, Louisiana was given a cake for her birthday which occurred shortly after she announced that she was pregnant. The cake depicted a black pregnant woman and read, "Happy Birthday, Sheryl. It must have been those watermelon seeds."

The suit also included data on Texaco's workforce:

1989	Minorities as a percentage of Texaco's workforce	15.2%
1994	Minorities as a percentage of Texaco's workforce	19.4%

of Years to Promotion by Job Classification

Minority Employers	Job	Other Employees
6.1	Accountant	4.6
6.4	Senior Accountant	5.4
12.5	Analyst	6.3
14.2	Financial Analyst	13.9
15.0	Assistant Accounting Supervisor	9.8

Senior Managers

	White	Black
1991	1,887	19
1992	2,001	21
1993	2,000	23
1994	2,029	23

Racial Composition (% of Blacks) by Pay Range

Salary	Texaco	Other Oil Companies
$51,000	5.9%	7.2%
$56,900	4.7%	6.5%
$63,000	4.1%	4.7%
$69,900	2.3%	5.1%
$77,600	1.8%	3.2%
$88,100	1.9%	2.3%
$95,600	1.4%	2.6%
$106,100	1.2%	2.3%
$117,600	0.8%	2.3%
$128,800	0.4%	1.8%

(African-Americans make up 12% of the U.S. population)

The acting head of the EEOC wrote in 1995, "Deficiencies in the affirmative-action programs suggest that Texaco is not committed to insuring comprehensive, facility by facility, compliance with the company's affirmative-action responsibilities."

Faced with the lawsuit, Texaco's former treasurer, Robert Ulrich, senior assistant treasurer, J. David Keough, and senior coordinator for personnel services, Richard A. Lundwall, met and discussed the suit. A tape transcript follows:

They look through evidence, deciding what to turn over to the plaintiffs.

LUNDWALL: Here, look at this chart. You know, I'm not really quite sure what it means. This chart is not mentioned in the agency, so it's not important that we even have it in there. . . . They would never know it was here.

KEOUGH: They'll find it when they look through it.

LUNDWALL: Not if I take it out they won't.

The executives decide to leave out certain pages of a document; they worry that another version will turn up.

ULRICH: We're gonna purge the [expletive deleted] out of these books, though. We're not going to have any damn thing that we don't need to be in them—

LUNDWALL: As a matter of fact, I just want to be reminded of what we discussed. You take your data and . . .

KEOUGH: You look and make sure it's consistent to what we've given them already for minutes. Two versions with the restricted and that's marked clearly on top—

ULRICH: But I don't want to be caught up in a cover-up. I don't want to be my own Watergate.

LUNDWALL: We've been doing pretty much two versions, too. This one here, this is strictly my book, your book . . .

ULRICH: Boy, I'll tell you, that one, you would put that and you would have the only copy. Nobody else ought to have copies of that.

LUNDWALL: O.K.?

ULRICH: You have that someplace and it doesn't exist.

LUNDWALL: Yeah, O.K.

ULRICH: I just don't want anybody to have a copy of that.

LUNDWALL: Good, No problem.

ULRICH: You know, there is no point in even keeping the restricted version anymore. All it could do is get us in trouble. That's the way I feel. I would not keep anything.

LUNDWALL: Let me shred this thing and any other restricted version like it.

ULRICH: Why do we have to keep the minutes of the meeting anymore?

LUNDWALL: You don't, you don't.

ULRICH: We don't?

LUNDWALL: Because we don't, no, we don't because it comes back to haunt us like right now—

ULRICH: I mean, the pendulum is swinging the other way, guys.

The executives discuss the minority employees who brought the suit.

LUNDWALL: They are perpetuating an us/them atmosphere. Last week or last Friday I told . . .

ULRICH: [Inaudible.]

LUNDWALL: Yeah, that's what I said to you, you want to frag grenade? You know, duck, I'm going to throw one. Well, that's what I was alluding to. But the point is not, that's not bad in itself but it does perpetuate us/them. And if you're trying to get away and get to the we . . . you can't do that kind of stuff.

ULRICH: [Inaudible.] I agree. This diversity thing. You know how black jelly beans agree. . . .

LUNDWALL: That's funny. All the black jelly beans seem to be glued to the bottom of the bag.

ULRICH: You can't have just we and them. You can't just have black jelly beans and other jelly beans. It doesn't work.

LUNDWALL: Yeah. But they're perpetuating the black jelly beans.

ULRICH: I'm still having trouble with Hanukkah. Now, we have Kwanza (laughter).

The release of the tape prompted the Reverend Jesse Jackson to call for a nationwide boycott of Texaco. Sales fell 8%, Texaco's stock fell 2%, and several institutional investors were preparing to sell their stock.

Texaco did have a minority recruiting effort in place and the "jelly bean" remark was tied to a diversity trainer the company had hired. The following are excerpts from Texaco's statement of vision and values:

Respect for the Individual

Our employees are our most important resource. Each person deserves to be treated with respect and dignity in appropriate work environments, without regard to race, religion, sex, age, national origin, disability or position in the company. Each employee has the responsibility to demonstrate respect for others.

The company believes that a work environment that reflects a diverse workforce, values diversity, and is free of all forms of discrimination, intimidation, and harassment is essential for a productive and efficient workforce. Accordingly, conduct directed toward any employee that is unwelcome, hostile, offensive, degrading, or abusive is unacceptable and will not be tolerated.

A federal grand jury began an investigation at Texaco to determine whether there had been obstruction of justice in the withholding of documents.

Within days of the release of the tape, Texaco settled its bias suit for $176.1 million, the largest sum ever allowed in a discrimination case. The money will allow an 11% pay raise for blacks and other minorities who joined in the law suit.

Texaco's chairman and CEO, Peter I. Bijur, issued the following statement after agreeing to a settlement:

Texaco is facing a difficult but vital challenge. It's broader than any specific words and larger than any lawsuit. It is one we must and are attacking head-on.

We are a company of 27,000 people worldwide. In any organization of that size, unfortunately, there are bound to be people with unacceptable, biased attitudes toward race, gender and religion.

Our goal, and our responsibility, is to eradicate this kind of thinking wherever and however it is found in our company. And our challenge is to make Texaco a company of limitless opportunity for all men and women.

We are committed to begin meeting this challenge immediately through programs with concrete goals and measurable timetables.

I've already announced certain specific steps, including a redoubling of efforts within Texaco to focus on the paramount value of respect for the individual and a comprehensive review of our diversity programs at every level of our company.

We also want to broaden economic access to Texaco for minority firms and increase the positive impact our investments can have in the minority community. This includes areas such as hiring and promotion; professional services such as advertising, banking, investment management and legal services; and wholesale and retail station ownership.

To assist us, we are reaching out to leaders of minority and religious organizations and others for ideas and perspectives that will help Texaco succeed in our mission of becoming a model of diversity and workplace equality.

It is essential to this urgent mission that Texaco and African-Americans and other minority community leaders work together to help solve the programs we face as a company—which, after all, echo the problems faced in society as a whole.

Discrimination will be extinguished only if we tackle it together, only if we join in a unified, common effort.

Working together, I believe we can take Texaco into the 21st century as a model of diversity. We can make Texaco a company of limitless opportunity. We can make Texaco a leader in according respect to every man and woman.

Even after the announcement, Texaco stock was down $3 per share, a loss of $800 million total, and the boycott was continued. Texaco's proposed merger with Shell Oil began to unravel as Shell's CEO expressed concern about Texaco's integrity. However, after the settlement, additional information about the case began to emerge.

Holman W. Jenkins, Jr. wrote the following piece for the *Wall Street Journal:*

Quietly, corporate America is debating whether Texaco's Peter Bijur did the right thing.

Mr. Bijur gets paid to make the hard calls, and with the airwaves aflame over "nigger" and "black jelly beans," Texaco took a battering in the stock and political markets. He had every reason for wanting to put a stop-loss on the media frenzy. "Once the taped conversations were revealed," he says, settling was "reasonable and honorable." So now Texaco is betting $176 million that paying off minority employees and their lawyers is the quickest way out of the news.

But as the company's own investigation showed, the truly inflammatory comments reported in the media never took place. They were purely a fabrication by opposing lawyers, and trumpeted by a credulous *New York Times.* And some digging would have shown this problem cropping up before in the career of Mike Hausfeld, lead attorney for the plaintiffs.

In an antitrust case years ago, he presented a secret recording that he claimed showed oil executives conspiring to threaten gasoline dealers. But a check by the same expert who handled the Nixon Watergate tapes showed no such thing. Says Larry Sharp, the Washington antitrust lawyer who opposed Mr. Hausfeld: "To put it generously, he gave himself the benefit of the doubt in making the transcript."

But this time the lie has been rewarded, and the broader public, unschooled in legal cynicism, heads home believing Texaco an admitted racist.

The catechism of corporate crisis management says you can't fight the media. Mr. Bijur had to consider that Jesse Jackson was threatening a boycott if Texaco failed to "regret, repent and seek renewal." Mr. Jackson pointedly added that "any attempt to shift to denial would add insult to injury"—a warning against trying to spread some egg to the faces of those who were fooled by the fake transcript.

There may have been wisdom, if not valor, in Mr. Bijur's decision to run up the white flag. But he also evinced symptoms of Stockholm Syndrome, telling CNN that Texaco was just the "tip of the iceberg" of corporate racism. Ducking this fight so ignominiously may yet prove a penny-wise, pound-foolish strategy. The City of Philadelphia has decided to dump its Texaco holdings anyway, partly out of fear of more litigation.

What else could Texaco have done? It could have apologized for any offense, but stuck up for its former treasurer Bob Ulrich, who was wronged by the phony transcript and stripped of his medical benefits by Texaco. And the company could have vowed to fight the lawsuit like the dickens, arguing that Texaco is not the cause of society's racial troubles but has tried to be part of the solution.

Start with the tapes: A fair listening does not necessarily reveal a "racist" conversation by executives at Texaco, but certainly a candid conversation about the problems of race at Texaco. They spoke of "jelly beans" dividing into camps of "us" and "them," an honest representation of life at many companies, not just in the oil patch.

Mr. Bijur could have made this point, starting with the *New York Times*, which has been embroiled in its own discrimination lawsuit with Angela Dodson, once its top-ranking black female. In a complaint filed with New York City's Human Rights Commission, she claims the paper was "engaged in gender-based harassment and disability-based discrimination . . . because *The Times* no longer wanted me, as a black person, to occupy a position as Senior editor."

Her deepest ire is reserved for *Times* veteran Carolyn Lee, who is white and more accustomed to being lauded as a champion of women and minorities. Ms. Dodson told the *Village Voice*: "It got to the point that whenever I was in her presence or earshot she made remarks [about other black people] that could only be taken as negative."

This sounds remarkably like the anecdotes filed in the Texaco complaint. All an outsider can safely conclude is that race makes everything more complicated, as sensitivity begets sensitivity. Mr. Bijur would have done more for racial understanding had he used his platform to open up this subject.

Yes, the cartoonist racists are out there, he might have said, but the *Times* coverage of Texaco only found cartoonist racists. The paper could have looked to its own experience for another story—a story about how garden-variety interpersonal conflict can land even decent people in the snares of racial mistrust.

This is what affirmative action, by throwing people together, was supposed to get us past. And it may be no accident that our most quota-ridden newspaper, *USA Today*, jumped off the bandwagon on the Texaco tapes, noting the ambiguity of whether the "jelly bean" remarks were meant to be hostile or friendly to blacks.

And McPaper kept on asking intelligent questions, like whether the *New York Times* had been "used by plaintiffs in the case to promote a faulty but more inflammatory transcript?" ("Not unless the court was used," answered *Times* Business Editor John Geddes, sounding like a lawyer himself.)

So Mr. Bijur was not facing a uniformly hopeless media torrent. The truth, even a complicated truth, catches up with the headlines eventually.

In time, he might have found surprising allies drifting to his side. The *New Republic* and the *New Yorker* have run thoughtful articles arguing that businesses should be allowed to use quotas but shouldn't be subject to harassment litigation if they don't. Right now, we do the opposite: Forbid companies to promote by quota, then sue them under federal "adverse impact" rules when they don't.

In effect, liberal voices are arguing that business could do more for minorities with less conflict if freedom of contract were restored. The world is changing, and companies have their own reasons nowadays for wanting minorities around. They need input from different kinds of people on how to deal with different kinds of people. No doubt this is why McPaper feels free to thumb its nose at the conformity crowd on stories like Texaco and church-burnings. (See September's *Harvard Business Review* for what business is thinking about diversity now.)

If companies were set free to assemble the work forces most useful to them, they could sweep away a heap of excuses for recrimination. Whites couldn't feel cheated out of jobs. Blacks wouldn't end up at companies that want them only for window-dressing. And the world could go back to feeling OK about being an interesting place. We might even allow that cultural patterns other than racism may explain why so many rednecks, and so few blacks, become petroleum engineers.

Mr. Bijur may have made the best of a bad deal for his shareholders. Whether it was best for America is a different judgment.[1]

Richard Lundwall, the executive who taped the sessions with the other executives, was charged with one count of obstruction of justice. Lundwall had turned over the tapes of the conversations to lawyers for the plaintiffs in the discrimination suit on October 25, 1996. Lundwall had been terminated.

Texaco hired attorney Michael Armstrong to investigate the underlying allegations. Mr. Armstrong found the tapes had not been transcribed correctly.

As part of its settlement, Texaco agreed to, at a cost of $55 million, assign a task force to police hiring and promotion as well as requiring mentors for black employees and sensitivity training for white employees.

The following interview with CEO Bijur appeared in *Business Week:*

Q: How did your legal strategy change once the news of the tapes was printed?

A: When I saw [the story], I knew that this lawsuit was pending and moving forward. I made the judgment that we needed to accelerate the settlement process. And those discussions on settlement commenced almost immediately.

Q: It has been reported that you didn't get the board of directors involved with the settlement talks and other issues. Why not?

A: You're drawing conclusions that are erroneous. The board was fully involved throughout the entire process. I talked to numerous directors personally. We had several board and executive committee meetings. The board was fully supportive of our actions.

Q: Have you met with shareholders?

A: Yes, of course. I went down to [New York] and met with the Interfaith Center on Corporate Responsibility, which is a group of religious shareholders. I expressed our position on this and listened carefully to their position and got some good counsel and guidance. But I wanted to provide our side of the issue as well. I have met with [New York State Comptroller] Carl McCall and [New York City Comptroller] Alan Hevesi about concerns that they had, and I will continue to meet with other shareholders as I normally do.

Q: Why do you think the oil industry has such a poor reputation on issues of racial diversity and gender equality? How does Texaco stack up against the others?

A: The percentage of minorities within Texaco is just about average for the petroleum industry. We have made really significant progress in the last several years in improving the percentage. But there are some very interesting points that need to be examined to place in context what may be going on in this industry. I just read a study that showed that in 1995, there were only nine petroleum engineering minority graduates that came out of all engineering schools in the United States—only nine. That's not an excuse. But it is indicative of why it is difficult for this industry to have a lot of people in the pipeline. Now, of course, that does not apply to accountants, finance people, and anybody else. But we are a very technically oriented industry.

Q: Have you personally witnessed discrimination at Texaco?

A: In the nearly 31 years I have been with Texaco, I have never witnessed an incident of racial bias or prejudice. And had I seen it, I would have taken disciplinary action. I've never seen it.

Q: Is there a widespread culture of insensitivity at Texaco?

A: I do not think there is a culture of institutional bias within Texaco. I think we've got a great many very good and decent human beings, but that unfortunately we mirror society. There is bigotry in society. There is prejudice and injustice in society. I am sorry to say that, and I am sorry to say that probably does exist within Texaco. I can't do much about society, but I certainly can do something about Texaco.

Q: What are your views on affirmative action?

A: Texaco's views on affirmative action have not changed a bit. We have supported affirmative action, and we will continue to support affirmative action.

Q: This is your first big trial since taking over. What have you learned?

A: I've learned that as good as our programs are in the company—and they really are quite good, even in this area—there's always more we can do. We've got to really drill down into the programs. We've got to make certain that they're meeting the objectives and goals we've set for them.

Q: Are there other lessons in terms of your style of management?

A: I don't think I would do anything different the next time than what I did this time.

Q: How will you make sure the spirit as well as the letter of the policy is followed at Texaco?

A: We're going to put more and more and more emphasis on it until we get it through everybody's head: Bigotry is not going to be tolerated here.[2]

Robert W. Ulrich was indicted in 1997. Mr. Lundwall entered a "not guilty" plea on July 8, 1997, and J. David Keough has sued Texaco for libel. Texaco named Mary Bush, a financial consultant, as its first black female board member.

As Lundwall's prosecution has proceeded, new discoveries have been made. For example, "purposeful erasures" have been found on the tapes.

In an interim report on its progress toward the settlement goals, Texaco revealed the following:

Polishing the Star

As part of its settlement of a discrimination lawsuit brought by black employees, Texaco has moved on a half-dozen fronts to alter its business practices.

Hiring Asked search firms to identify wider arrays of candidates. Expanded recruiting at historically minority colleges. Gave 50 scholarships and paid internships to minority students seeking engineering or technical degree.

Career Advancement Wrote objective standards for promotions. Developing training program for new managers. Developing a mentoring program.

Diversity Initiatives Conducted two-day diversity training for more than 8,000 of 20,000 U.S. employees. Tied management bonuses to diversity goals. Developing alternative dispute resolution and ombudsman programs.

Purchasing Nearly doubled purchases from minority- or women-owned businesses. Asking suppliers to report their purchases from such companies.

Financial Services Substantially increased banking, investment management and insurance business with minority- and women-owned firms. A group of such firms underwrote a $150 million public financing.

Retailing Added three black independent retailers, 18 black managers of company-owned service stations, 12 minority or female wholesalers, 13 minority- or women-owned Xpress Lube outlets and 6 minority- or women-owned lubricant distributors.

In May 1998, the Texaco executives were acquitted of all criminal charges.

NOTES

1. Reprinted with permission of *The Wall Street Journal* © 1996 Dow Jones & Company, Inc. All rights reserved.
2. Smart, Tim. "Texaco: Lessons From A Crisis-in-Progress." Reprinted from December 2, 1996, issue of *Business Week* by special permission, © 1997 by McGraw-Hill, Inc.

Case Study

Denny's

Ronald M. Green

On the morning of April 1, 1993, 21 agents of the Secret Service Uniformed Division entered the West Street, Annapolis, Denny's restaurant for breakfast. The agents were part of a detail assigned to protect President Clinton while he addressed the American Society of Newspaper

---

Editors at the U.S. Naval Academy in Annapolis. The unit hoped to grab a quick bite before returning to the Naval Academy to set up metal-detecting equipment.

Six black Secret Service Agents, including Alfonso Dyson, Leroy Snyder, and Robin Thomson, sat together. Their white colleagues sat at neighboring tables. The entire detail was dressed in full uniform—badges, black shoes, black pants with wide gold stripes, white shirts, black ties, and guns strapped on. All 21 agents, who had less than an hour to eat, ordered quickly, one after another, but the six black agents, who sat together, waited 50 minutes after ordering without being served. Watching as their white colleagues finished second and third helpings, agent Robin Thompson complained to their waitress. She replied that their meals were on the way. Thompson then asked to see the manager, but the waitress said he was on the phone. White agents report that the waitress rolled her eyes after turning to leave the black agents' table. The agents saw several dishes sitting for several minutes under heat lamps next to the kitchen. Meanwhile, a small group of white customers, who had entered the uncrowded restaurant after the black agents, were promptly served.

When the other agents had finished their meals, and after numerous complaints, the black agents stood to leave. Only then was food offered to them. The agents refused it because there was no time to eat. The food arrived so late and after so many complaints that the agents believed they were effectively denied service. "We had to go to Roy Rogers and eat in the van," said agent Dyson.

Ironically, the incident occurred the same day that Flagstar, Denny's parent corporation, settled a federal lawsuit in California by a consent decree in which Denny's agreed to stop allegedly discriminatory treatment of black customers. Now Denny's faced another suit, soon filed by the six Secret Service agents, who claimed that the chain violated their civil rights during the April 1 incident. Agent Thompson said he "felt humiliated" by the events of that April morning. "I was somewhat invisible that day. I felt we (black and white agents) were coequals. But after I left the restaurant, I felt belittled, less than a person. This should not happen to anyone." Agent Alfonso Dyson said that he concluded that poor service was not the reason for the delay. "You would never think it would happen to you, especially not in full uniform. I was definitely unprepared. I had let my guard down."

This incident was part of a larger pattern of discrimination of which the Denny's chain was being accused. (See Exhibit 1.) The lawsuit filed by the Secret Service agents brought Denny's under renewed fire. At a press conference, the agents said that the Secret Service had been supportive of their effort, adding that the decision to break from the agency's traditional stoicism and file the lawsuit had been difficult.

As the agents' suit grabbed headlines, the NAACP demanded negotiations with Flagstar Corporation to amend their alleged discriminatory hiring and serving practices. Rupert Richardson, an NAACP member, pointing to the California consent decree and the Annapolis incident, said, There has got tobe something radically wrong with Denny's, because the moment you take care of a problem here, it pops up somewhere else." Around the country, editorial writers blasted the chain and held it up as an example of how far the United States was from eliminating racism.

Denny's top management was caught unprepared by the intensity and extent of the criticisms. The company thought of itself as a family-oriented business, serving reasonably priced food 24 hours a day in a sit-down, friendly atmosphere. Over the years, Denny's had tried to distinguish itself from many other fast food chains by its emphasis on sit-down service and by the creation of a welcoming atmosphere with practices like complimentary meals on customers' birthdays. Flagstar Corporation, the parent company, owns some of the nation's largest restaurant chains. In addition to Denny's, its franchises include Hardee's, Quincy's Family Steakhouse, and El Polio Loco. Flagstar also owns Canteen Company, a food services and concessions business. With 3.7 billion dollars in sales in 1992, and nearly 2,000 restaurants nationwide, Flagstar is one of the nation's largest corporations, employing 120,000 people. There are 1,460 Denny's Restaurants nationwide alone, employing 46,000 people. Seventy percent of these restaurants are owned by Flagstar, while the others are owned and operated by individual franchisers. After the Annapolis incident, sales were down in restaurants across the nation, and Flagstar's stock was trading near the lowest price since the company went public in 1989.

Flagstar executives, realizing that their company was in trouble and insisting that these incidents were not examples of company policy, struggled to understand and explain the cause of the widespread allegations. Thirty-six percent of Flagstar's employees are minorities, twenty percent of whom are black (twice the proportion of the U.S. population). But Flagstar has no senior black managers, and no minority officers or directors. Only one of its franchises is minority owned. Although Flagstar obviously had a lack of minority leadership, Marilyn Loven, a San Francisco management and diversity consultant, offered a sympathetic view of the company's problems. In most cases, she claimed, discrimination results from employees acting individually without the approval of management. A company can have enlightened, well-intentioned leaders, only to be undercut by low-level front line employees. She argued that no company can eliminate racism, "but any company that doesn't spend a lot of time

---

EXHIBIT 1

1990: Marcus Daniels accuses Denny's manager of harassing him for his skin color. Tyrone Jackson, a Denny's employee, alleges that he was ordered not to allow blacks to receive separate checks.

October, 1992: U.S. Justice Department informs Denny's that it plans to file lawsuit alleging discriminatory practices against black customers in Northern California. Government offers Denny's opportunity to settle complaint.

March 24, 1993: Black customers file class-action lawsuit in San Francisco, accusing Denny's of discrimination. Complaint is also filed with the Equal Opportunity Commission alleging job discrimination and asking the company to hire a civil rights monitor.

March 25: Denny's reaches settlement with Justice Department, promising to train employees against racial discrimination and to hire a civil rights monitor.

April 1: A waitress at a Denny's restaurant in Annapolis, Maryland, allegedly refuses to serve breakfast to six black Secret Service agents. The Justice Department demands an explanation. Federal judge approves consent decree between Denny's and U.S. Justice Department. Denny's agrees to reinforce policies of equitable treatment and to communicate guidelines to all employees.

Other: Individual charges of discrimination on April 1, April 18, April 24, May 7, May 8, May 9, May 10, May 20, and May 26, 1993.

educating employees is going to run into problems."

Jerome Richardson, head of Flagstar, readily accepted some of the blame. The company has recently come through a long period of financial turbulence. Richardson sold Flagstar in 1979, bought it out again in 1989, and took it public. In 1992, Kohlberg Kravis Roberts invested $300 million to acquire 47% of the company. Richardson acknowledges that constantly dealing with finances blinded him to other aspects of running a corporation.

"I should have invested the time earlier, and I regret it."

Whatever the causes, Denny's, with numerous charges of discrimination facing it and a tarnished reputation, had run into serious problems. Flagstar executives now confronted an urgent responsibility—convincing the public and their employees that they truly believed that discrimination is bad business. Richardson, with a company $2 billion in debt, summed up the challenge. "We need all the customers we can get."

Case Study

Management Dilemma

Fred E. Schuster

Stan Fritzhill, Manager of the Data Analysis Department of Aerostar, Inc., a small research firm; pondered how he should utilize a salary increase budget of $32,900 (10% of total payroll) to reward the five semi-professional employees in his unit. He knew that he did not have to spend the full budget, but under no circumstances could he exceed it. In his opinion, all of these individuals were properly paid in relation to their relative performance and seniority one year (12 months) ago, when he last adjusted their compensation. The rate of inflation last year was 7%.

Fritzhill had assembled a summary of his performance appraisals (see Appendix A) and other pertinent data to assist in determining his recommendations, which he knew were needed immediately.

Questions for Discussion

1. Is the information provided in the column titled "personal circumstances" relevant to Mr. Fritzhill's decision? Why or why not?
2. Is the information provided in the column titled "years in department" relevant to Mr. Fritzhill's decision? Why or why not?
3. If it appears that an employee has been unfairly denied raises in the past, should special "makeup" raises be given? Are there any employees in this case who appear to have been unfairly treated?
4. How should Fritzhill distribute the money? What role, if any, should inflation play in his deliberations?

APPENDIX A

Name	Present Salary	Title	Salary Grade	Years in Dept.	Performance	Personal Circumstances
John Mason	$87,000	Analyst	6	5	Acceptable quality, several important deadlines have been missed but may not be his fault.	Married. Large family dependent on him as sole support.
G. W. Jones	$76,000	Analyst	6	2	Outstanding. Sometimes a bit "pushy" in making requests and suggestions about the department.	Single. No dependents. Has no pressing need for money. Reported to lead a rather "wild" life outside the office.
Jane Boston	$66,000	Junior Analyst	5	8	Consistently an excellent performer, though not assigned to the full range of duties of an analyst. Dependable. Often initiates improvements in work methods.	Married. Husband is a successful architect. Children in high school.
Ralph Schmidt	$88,000	Senior Analyst	7	15	Acceptable, but not outstanding. Few original contributions recently. Seems to be a "plodder." Content to get by with minimum performance and participation.	Married. Financially pressed because he has 2 children in college (one plans to go on to Med. School).
Hillary Johnson	$68,000	Junior Analyst	5	6	Acceptable volume of performance, but continues to make costly mistakes. Has repeatedly been warned about this over last years.	Single. Has a dependent mother who is chronically ill.

Case Study

Keeping it Real

Patricia S. Parker

This case explores norms and practices of racial discrimination at Coca-Cola, which limited the contributions and the pay of African American employees. According to the case, the hostile work environment also created unusually high rates of stress-related illnesses, such as depression, among the employees. The case raises important issues regarding the rights of minority employees, as well as the utility of creating organization-wide differences in compensation, promotion and career advancement that, in effect, exclude the contributions of some employees.

The Coca-Cola Company, based in Atlanta, Georgia, is a Fortune 500 multinational corporation operating in nearly 200 countries. It is arguably one of the world's most recognizable brands. In November 2000, Coca-Cola agreed to pay $192.5 million to settle a racial discrimination lawsuit filed a year earlier by Linda Ingram and three other former and current African American employees. The settlement was the largest ever among an increasing number of racial discrimination lawsuits, surpassing the $176.1 million awarded in the highly publicized case against Texaco, in which an audio tape revealed high-ranking Texaco executives referring to African American employees as "black jelly beans . . . glued to the bottom of the bag" ("Excerpts from tapes in discrimination lawsuit," 1996).

The suit against Coca-Cola accused the company of constructing a corporate hierarchy in which African American workers were clustered at the bottom of the pay scale, averaging $26,000 a year less than white employees. Furthermore, workers depicted an environment so hostile that African American employees at Coca-Cola suffered from unusually high rates of stress-related illnesses, such as depression. Many African American workers reported that upon complaining about these conditions, they were denounced, spied on by management, or fired.

The terms of the Coca-Cola settlement agreement and the events leading up to it illustrate the continued significance of race in the workplace and the complex ethical dilemmas associated with race and difference in organizations. The settlement agreement mandated that the Coca-Cola Company grant unprecedented monitoring powers to an outside task force that would oversee Coca-Cola's progress toward (a) promoting equal opportunity in compensation, promotion, and career advancement for all employees regardless of race, color, gender, religion, age, national origin, or disability; and (b) promoting an environment of inclusion, respect, and freedom from retaliation. However, this mandate raises several ethical questions: What are the limits and opportunities for corporate decision makers to create and promote an environment of inclusion, respect, and fairness for all employees? Who should lead the effort? Whose voices should be heard on important related issues? To what extent and under what circumstances are differences in compensation, promotion, and career advancement justified? What criteria should be used? How are personal biases influenced by corporate values about race and difference and vice versa? How should corporate discourse about race and difference be structured? In what ways can corporate culture influence dialogues about race, difference, and organizational outcomes?

Ethical questions such as these are central to the ongoing debates in the scholarly literature and popular culture about race, difference, and workplace democracy. These questions, and the ethical issues they bring to the forefront, can be fruitfully explored in the case of *Ingram et al. v. The Coca-Cola Company.*

RACE (STILL) MATTERS IN ORGANIZATIONS

The Coca-Cola case and the increasing number of racial discrimination complaints filed with the Equal Employment Opportunity Commission (EEOC)—the government agency that monitors and enforces compliance with federal nondiscrimination statutes—illustrate the continued significance of race in the workplace. Historically, issues of race and work in the United States were primarily centered on racial justice in hiring and access to jobs for African Americans as they moved from forced labor during 200 years of slavery into legally sanctioned segregation and exclusion from certain jobs during the latter part of the 19th century and into the 1950s. The passage of Title VII of the Civil Rights Act of 1964 brought new opportunities for jobs and access to management positions for African American workers. Title VII prohibited employment discrimination on the basis of race, color, religion, national origin, and sex in the private, public, and federal sectors. It also established the EEOC, which developed affirmative action policies to redress the impact of socio-historical patterns of discrimination against disenfranchised groups, especially African Americans and women, and to end discrimination in hiring, college admissions, and awarding contracts.

However, the central struggle over racial justice has shifted from corporate hiring practices to corporate culture, bringing into focus the complex issues of differences related to race, ethnicity, migration, and immigration. According to EEOC figures reported in the *New York Times,* the number of complaints about discrimination in *hiring* has fallen 20 percent in the last decade. Yet charges of *racial harassment* in the workplace rose nearly 100% between 1990 and 2000 (Winter, 2000). The increase in claims of racial conflict in the workplace directs attention to organizations' internal practices that promote or inhibit workplace fairness.

Ironically, the apparent rise in racial conflict in the workplace occurred as organizations were placing increasing resources into managing diversity (Cox, 1991, 1993). Johnston and Packer's (1987) influential report, *Workforce 2000,* alerted organizations to the prospect of dramatic demographic changes—along dimensions such as gender, race, ethnicity, migration, and immigration—that would transform the U.S. workforce. However, despite the proliferation of managerial philosophies espousing the value of diversity and multiculturalism in organizations, there is growing consensus that past strategies and theoretical approaches have had limited effectiveness in addressing the more complex issue of *difference* in organizations (Allen, 2004; Prasad, Mills, Elmes, & Prasad, 1997). *Difference* is associated with issues of social identity that create race tensions, gender conflicts, and cultural frictions that impede the development of organizational diversity (Prasad et al., 1997). Past strategies equated diversity management with "learning to get along," which in effect tended to obscure, conceal, and deny the real human differences among people at work (Prasad & Elmes, 1997, p. 373). Increasingly, however, organizational practitioners and researchers are searching for new approaches to facilitate the negotiation of differences and understand how organizational discourses and power relations promote or hinder the development of equal opportunity for a diverse workforce.

CORPORATE CULTURE, DIFFERENCE, AND FAIRNESS

An organization's culture is a primary means for creating an environment of inclusion, respect, and fairness, and fostering ethical practices by organizational members (Arnold & Lampe, 1999). Broadly, "culture is a system of meaning that guides the construction of reality in a social community" (Cheney, Christensen, Zorn, & Ganesh, 2004, p. 76). For formal organizations, culture can foster an environment where ethical practice regarding race and difference is the norm or, conversely, promote an environment in which unethical practices signaling racial bias are accepted behaviors. Thomas and Gabarro (1999), present a framework for analyzing corporate cultures, such as the Coca-Cola Company, that promote or inhibit workplace fairness for diverse employees. They studied the cultures of three Fortune 500 organizations that had successfully implemented diversity programs, focusing on the careers of 54 African American, Asian American, and Hispanic American executives and managers who had reached the top ranks of their respective companies. Although the companies differed widely in the types of cultures they created and in their approaches to fostering discourses about race and difference, they each achieved diversity as an integral part of the organization's image and philosophy.

Conversely, based on their extensive review of the literature on diversity, Thomas and Gabarro (1999) report that firms that tend to limit the advancement of racial and ethnic cultural groups fall into two categories. First are those corporations where there is a widely shared set of unchallenged biases that have the effect of setting low targets for minority advancement. As a result, the best of their minority employees leave (Thomas & Gabarro, 1999). The second type of organization is one in which there is some genuine intent to diversify the workforce; however, there is a lack of alignment between the organization's diversity strategy and its culture and values. These organizations are often pursuing diversity as a goal, but are using a strategy that consists of a patchwork of disconnected programs and compliance efforts. Minorities often make it to threshold positions in middle or upper-middle management, but are not able to advance further (Thomas & Gabarro, 1999).

The above framework can be used to analyze organizations' efforts toward creating and sustaining cultures that promote fairness and opportunity. Where does the Coca-Cola Company fit into this framework? As with any framework, actual practices do not always fit neatly into fixed categories. And it is clear from Coke's history and recent handling of a race discrimination lawsuit that sustaining and promoting a commitment to valuing diversity is a complex and ongoing process.

COCA-COLA AS "THE REAL THING": THE MAKING OF A MEGA BRAND

The Coca-Cola Company was founded in Atlanta, Georgia, just after the Civil War. From the very beginning, even during that tumultuous time of racial conflict and reconstruction, Coke emerged as a company marketing a feel-good product intended for every race, creed, and color. Coke's creator, John Pemberton, arrived in Atlanta four years after President Lincoln's assassination, having served as a cavalryman in the Confederate Army. He embarked on a highly successful postwar career selling medicines and other products that promised relief, as one writer put it, "for anxious southern Whites and newly liberated Blacks, and people who had been in Atlanta for generations, as well as the carpetbaggers come to afflict them" (Hays, 2004). In 1886, searching for something unique to be patented, Pemberton created a syrup he called French Wine Coca and, after some

TABLE 8.1 Three Cultural Approaches to Organization Diversity*

Assimilationist Cultures: Melting Pot	*Pluralist Cultures:* Valuing Differences	*Hybrid Cultures:* Leveling the Playing Field/Intergroup Negotiations
Premise Racial differences are irrelevant. Individual attitudes are the problem. The goal is to be color-blind.	*Premise* Differences matter. Race is central to identity. Being valued for who you are is critical to empowerment and contributes to performance.	*Premise* Biases are built into the system. The system(s) can be changed. Mobilization of minorities is good if focused on performance and advocacy.
Principal Targets Individual attitudes and behavior	*Principal Targets* Individual attitudes Relationships	*Principal Targets* Total system Power relations Practices that unfairly advantage or disadvantage any group
Motivating Rhetoric "All people are people" and deserve "fair and equal treatment." "It's not the color of your skin that matters, it's how green [the company's logo] your blood is that counts."	*Motivating Rhetoric* "Do the right thing." "People are effective when valued for who they are." "People [and organizations] are more effective if they can engage their differences." "Our diversity effort is about empowering people."	*Motivating Rhetoric* "We need to change the system so that it works for all employees." "The most important thing for minorities to focus on is performance, even in the face of bias." "Minorities' efforts at self-help benefit the company because they are better able to contribute." "Working with minorities to improve the system [level the playing field] is a form of employee involvement."
Core Tactics Active sponsoring of minorities Strong mandate from the top Leadership models behavior Anti-bias training Benchmarking and monitoring	*Core Tactics* Dialogue groups (vehicles for understanding differences/ confronting stereotypes) Development of networks	*Core Tactics* Self-help/advocacy groups Joint problem solving and negotiating Altering/changing unfair systems or practices Benchmarking and monitoring Top-down support of bottom-up initiative

refinements, mixed it with carbonated water and began selling it from a soda fountain as Coca-Cola, a "tonic," good for brain and body.

Two years later, Asa Candler, also from Atlanta, purchased the secret formula from Pemberton and began an intensive campaign to sell Coca-Cola syrup to every soda fountain he could, first in Atlanta, then across the South, and by 1895 in every state and territory in the United States. Even as some pharmacists found it easier to make their own concoctions, Candler's aggressive marketing strategies convinced drugstore owners to sell only "the real thing." In 1902, Candler reluctantly expanded the business to include bottled Coca-Cola, in addition to the soda fountain product. In doing so, he issued contracts to independent bottlers who quickly transformed the company into a national phenomenon. By 1915, no longer restricted by the Main Street hours and Sunday-best formality required of the soda fountain dispensers, Coke was widely available in bottles to anyone in America with a nickel to spend.

Coca-Cola bottling factories sprang up across America's heartland, making its independent owners rich and propelling the Coca-Cola Company into a multinational colossus by the time of its 100th anniversary in 1986. The Coke brand was everywhere, imprinting itself upon cultures around the world, appearing in movies, paintings, sculptures, and song lyrics. Under the leadership of past presidents and CEOs, such as Don Keough and Cuban-born Roberto Goizueta, the company was labeled by Wall Street as a growth stock, beckoning a multitude of investors.

By the late 1990s, under the aggressive leadership of president and then CEO Doug Ivester, the Coca-Cola Company had wrestled control of the lucrative independent bottling enterprise and was a sprawling empire employing 29,000 people worldwide. About 6,000 of them worked in the company's headquarters in Atlanta, where the executives at the top maintained tight control over decision making. As Constance

L. Hays writes in her book, *The Real Thing: Truth and Power at the Coca-Cola Company,* "As global as the Coca-Cola Company was, it was still, in its heart of hearts, a southern place. It craved formality as much as it craved profits . . . it remained in many ways hierarchical and in the grip of certain old fashioned customs" (p. 198). For many of the African American employees, the old-fashioned customs translated into limited opportunity for upward mobility at the Coca-Cola Company.

RACE AND CORPORATE CULTURE AT THE COCA-COLA COMPANY

In the 1990s, during a time of aggressive growth at the Coca-Cola Company, there was growing discontent among African American employees who believed that they did not have the same kinds of successes as whites in the company. There were very few senior executives who were black, even though by the 1980s, many African Americans were being hired by the company. Talented and ambitious, they came to Coca-Cola, lasted a couple of years, and left. Some of those who stayed formed support groups and met secretly to exchange stories about their perceptions of unfair practices and racially charged incidents at Coke. As would be revealed later, some African American employees noticed that they were paid less than people they supervised, all of them white. One African American employee working in the benefits office noticed that when he organized seminars for people receiving stock options, there were almost no blacks in the standing-room-only crowds. Others shared that they were viewed inappropriately as lacking the skills and intelligence to succeed in certain areas. The general feeling among African American employees was that Coke had created an atmosphere, consciously or unconsciously, that came across as hostile to blacks and offered little opportunity for advancement.

Conversely, many white employees at Coca-Cola did not think there was racial discrimination at their company. For people who did not receive stock options, one employee observed, "everyone is treated equally bad." In a similar vein, some Coke officials would say later that employees suffered from "benign neglect" because the company had been so intent on increasing its share price. Moreover, by the 1990s, whites in Atlanta often proclaimed that there was no "race problem" in that city, and certainly not at the Coca-Cola Company. Nevertheless, African American employees at Coke believed Coke had had a problem for a long time.

One African American executive who did ascend the ranks at Coke was Carl Ware, a former Atlanta city council member. Recruited in 1974 as a corporate affairs executive, Ware became a senior vice president in the mid 1990s, with responsibility for all of Coke's business in Africa. However, aware that he was the only black senior vice president in the company's 109-year history, and privy to the growing discontent among African Americans in the company, Ware approached then-Coke president, Doug Ivester, requesting permission to convene a committee to examine the issue of race at Coca-Cola. Was Coke doing a good job hiring, promoting, and keeping African Americans like him? Although Ivester gave Ware the go-ahead to convene the committee, the company president apparently missed the opportunity to learn from its findings.

A Missed Opportunity to Listen to African American Employees

With Ivester's approval, Ware convened a committee consisting of African American employees in some of the higher-ranking management positions at Coke to discuss what it meant to be a black executive at the Coca-Cola Company. Assisted by a consultant who facilitated their conversations, the committee produced a report that Ware delivered to Ivester in December 1995. The report concluded, "There is no evidence that the company, in the absence of laws requiring affirmative action, has a commitment to achieve further diversification of its workforce. . . . The company has no clearly articulated vision of how diversification of the workforce is linked to business success." The report contained instances recounting senior black employees' experiences of feeling "humiliated, ignored, overlooked, or unacknowledged," to which employees felt compelled to use "diplomacy, resourcefulness, and the ability to depersonalize prejudicial behavior" to minimize the psychological and material effects of these experiences (Excerpts from report cited in Hays, 2004).

The report also contained several areas where courses of action could be implemented. One of the main issues was the concern that there were so few African Americans in certain levels of the business. However, there were broader concerns cited, including "the lack of tolerance by the organization toward those who are different," the suggestion that Ivester, as president and CEO, define the company's philosophy or approach to diversity and then champion the activation of this approach in the company's business plan, policies, and programs. As a follow-up to the report, Ivester scheduled a lunch meeting with Ware to discuss the committee's findings. However, subsequent to the meeting, no apparent further action was taken.

By 1997, race issues at the Coca-Cola Company had gained the attention of the U.S. Labor Department, which requires companies with sizable federal contracts to address inequities and push forward with an affirmative action plan. In its review, the Labor Department found that Coke had violated federal anti-discrimination laws and directed the company to address the problems. At issue was the highly subjective process by which employees were reviewed and promoted. The company reached an agreement with the Labor Department in 1998 to address the problems, but it did little to revamp the highly subjective review and promotion process.

FORMAL CHARGES OF RACIAL DISCRIMINATION

Linda Ingram, who is African American, had been an information analyst at Coke since 1988, but she had not been a member of Ware's committee on race relations, nor was she aware of the report delivered to Ivester recommending changes in Coke's culture. However, in 1996, a year after Ware's report, Ingram experienced a series of encounters that led her to file a suit in 1999, charging racial discrimination against the Coca-Cola Company.

By most accounts, Ingram was a loyal Coke employee who enjoyed her work and liked her colleagues. However, things changed suddenly one day when she was engaged in an intense discussion with her supervisor, Elaine Arnold. Arnold, who is white, abruptly leaned close into Ingram's face and scolded her, saying, "This is why you people don't get anywhere." The only African American in her department Ingram said she felt shock and shame, stunned by the tenor and tone of what she heard, taken aback by having "someone . . . standing in your face and you can feel their breath on your face . . . and you start to ask yourself, 'Where am I? Am I in the fifties?'"

Committed to following corporate protocol, Ingram reported the incident to human resources executives and the company's director of equal employment opportunity. After an investigation, Arnold was fired. However, this sparked tension in Ingram's department that seemed to spiral out of control. People in her department, who had liked Arnold,

blamed Ingram for their boss's dismissal. She was ignored by some of her coworkers, while others openly refused to talk to her. Feeling isolated and depressed, Ingram repeatedly asked to be moved to another part of the company, but to no avail. Ingram felt unable to escape the fallout from the incident as people continued blaming her for an incident she believed had been precipitated by nothing more than the color of her skin. As time went on, she felt helpless to change her situation. She began taking more and more sick days, and by 1998, she had stopped working and obtained a long-term disability leave.

Ingram felt that worse than the incident itself was the way Coca-Cola executives handled its aftermath. The company seemed to have no mechanisms for dealing professionally with racially charged confrontations. However, rather than an act of omission, to Ingram the company's handling of the conflict in her department, where she was the only African American, seemed to be an intentional way of avoiding race issues. Ingram found that people in the company talked about doing something about her situation, but no one seemed willing to take any action. Eventually, Ingram solicited the help of a lawyer, Cyrus Mehri, the attorney in the 1994 racial discrimination lawsuit against Texaco that had ended in a $176 million settlement. After hearing her story and that of other African American Coke employees, Mehri decided to take the case. On April 22, 1999, Ingram and three other Coke employees filed a lawsuit charging that a pattern of racial discrimination existed in the company.

Coca-Cola's Response to the Racial Discrimination Lawsuit

The summer before the lawsuit was filed, Coca-Cola stock was topping $79 a share and reaching new highs on a daily basis. However, serious problems were brewing at Coke, including sluggish growth in the United States, antitrust investigations into its business practices by regulators abroad, and an incident involving Coca-Cola being suspected of making Belgian schoolchildren sick. The charges of a racial discrimination lawsuit came as these problems and more began making news headlines.

Company officials immediately advised Ivester, who had become Coke's chief executive in 1997, to resolve the lawsuit. However, Ivester refused and vowed to fight. He denied the allegations in an e-mail sent to employees and in public statements to the media. He also announced that he had formed a special Diversity Council that would report to him on matters such as those that had spawned the lawsuit, positioning himself as the channel through which needed changes would come.

However, as Ivester and other company representatives publicly denied the allegations, and as more details of the lawsuit were made public, civil rights groups, public relations experts, and consumers from around the world hounded Coke about the allegations, some accusing the firm of acting defensively and being slow to respond to the charges. The reputation of one of the world's most recognizable brands was being tarnished, not only by the allegations of racial intolerance, but also by its response to them.

An important turning point came with the announcement of the resignation of Carl Ware, the Coca-Cola Company's one and only African American senior vice president. In what seemed to be one of many desperate attempts to stem the tide of problems Coke faced on multiple continents, Ivester had made the decision to change the top management structure. Ware would no longer report to Ivester regarding his progress in the Africa division, but to his peer, a fellow senior vice president, Douglas Daft, who controlled the Asia division. Within a week, Ware decided to

quit, but agreed to announce his departure as an early retirement to spend time with his family. Six months earlier, Ware had been one of the Coke representatives saying publicly that the charges of race discrimination had no merit, despite his confidential 1995 report to Ivester describing the plight of black executives at Coke.

As news of Ware's intended retirement spread, buoying the position of the plaintiffs in the racial discrimination lawsuit, Coke officials announced that Ware had graciously agreed to remain at Coke until the end of the following year as head of the Africa division. However, a negative public image was emerging of a Coca-Cola Company so intolerant that even its top Hack executive was leaving. More than the slow growth and the antitrust allegations, and on the heels of the Belgian schoolchildren incident, the word of the racial discrimination lawsuit was resounding around the world.

Coke Agrees to Largest Settlement Ever in Racial Discrimination Case

In December 1999, Ivester was fired as Coke's chief executive. The new CEO, Doug Daft, set about addressing some of the most obvious problems afflicting Coke. In January 2000, he persuaded Carl Ware to reconsider his retirement, announcing that Ware would become Coke's executive vice president for corporate affairs, an operations position that involved working with governments as well as Wall Street. He also made it clear that he wanted the racial discrimination lawsuit behind him, which had become even more complicated by the announcement of thousands of job cuts in which black employees were offered a better severance package if they agreed not to pursue the lawsuit.

Meanwhile, there was more public pressure for Coke to settle the racial discrimination lawsuit. In March, the trustee of the New York

State Common Retirement Fund, which owns $370 million in Coke stock, encouraged the company to take steps to halt the suit's damage to Coca-Cola's reputation and stock price. In April, a caravan of current and former employees, led by the Reverend Jesse Jackson, organized a "Ride for Corporate Justice," traveling from Atlanta to Washington, D.C., and ending at Coke's shareholders meeting in Wilmington, Delaware.

By the middle of June, Coke had reached a tentative settlement of the lawsuit, with the final agreement made in November 2000. At $192 million, it was the largest sum ever awarded in a racial discrimination case. The settlement provided as many as 2,000 current and former African American salaried employees an average of $40,000 in cash, while the four plaintiffs whose names were on the lawsuit would receive 5300,000 each.

A NEW OPPORTUNITY TO LISTEN

In addition to the monetary award, the settlement agreement mandated that the Coca-Cola Company make sweeping changes, costing an additional $36 million, and grant unprecedented monitoring powers to an outside task force, headed by former labor secretary Alexis Herman. In the agreement, the Coca-Cola Company committed to evaluate, and where appropriate, implement specific changes to human resource programs for its non-hourly U.S.-based employees. The Statement of Principle made the objectives of the agreement clear:

> The Coca-Cola Company commits to excel among Fortune 500 Companies in *promoting and fostering equal opportunity in compensation, promotion, and career advancement for all employees in all levels and areas of business,* regardless of race, color, gender, religion, age, national origin, or disability, *and to promote and foster an environment of inclusion, respect, and freedom from retaliation.*

The company recognizes that diversity is a fundamental and indispensable value and that the Company, its shareholders, and all of its employees will benefit by striving to be a premier "gold standard" company on diversity. The Company will set measurable and lawful business goals to achieve these objectives during the next four years. (Excerpt from the Settlement Agreement in *Ingram et al. v. The Coca-Cola Company,* cited in Herman et al., 2003; emphasis added.)

As of this writing, the task force has made two of four reports on the Coca-Cola Company's progress toward changing its culture and improving the lot for all employees at Coca-Cola. In its second report, the committee noted that the company has done well implementing, for example, diversity training for its employees and implementing an ombudsman office. However, the report suggests that the company has been slow to implement significant changes in the areas of promotion and development of diverse employees and creating a diversity strategy that is a critical element of its overall business strategy. When it comes to diversity and difference at the Coca-Cola Company, what constitutes "the real thing"?

Discussion Questions

1. What do the terms *inclusion, respect,* and *fairness* mean to you?
2. Do corporations such as the Coca-Cola Company have an ethical obligation to create and promote an environment of inclusion, respect, and fairness for all employees? Why or why not? If so, what are the limits of that obligation? If not, what should employees do if they feel they are being treated unfairly?
3. To what extent and under what circumstances are differences in compensation, promotion, and career advancement justified? What criteria should be used?
4. Of all the challenges faced by the Coca-Cola Company, why do you think the racial discrimination lawsuit received such strong public reaction?
5. What role should the public play in monitoring the activities of corporations such as Coca-Cola? Explain.

6. How should corporate discourse about race and difference be structured? How are personal biases influenced by corporate values about race and difference and vice versa? Explain.
7. In what ways can corporate culture influence dialogues about race, difference, and organizational outcomes? Explain.
8. In which category does the Coca-Cola Company fit in Thomas and Gabarro's (1999) framework? Explain.
9. In what ways do other organizational communication theories, such as organizational learning, leadership, and change, apply in this case?

REFERENCES

Allen, B.A. (2004). *Difference matters: Communicating social identity.* Long Grove, IL: Waveland.

Arnold, V., & Lampe, J. C. (1999, Summer). Understanding the factors underlying ethical organizations: Enabling continuous ethical improvement. *Journal of Applied Business Research, 15,* 1–20.

Cheney, G., Christensen, L., Zorn, T., & Ganesh, S. (2004). *Organizational communication in an age of globalization: Issues, reflections, practices.* Prospect Heights, IL: Waveland Press.

Cox, T. (1991). The multicultural organization. *Academy of Management Executive, 5,* 34–37.

Cox, T. (1993). *Cultural diversity in organizations.* San Francisco: Berrett-Koehler.

Excerpts from tapes in discrimination lawsuit. (1996, November 4). *New York Times,* p. D4.

Hays, C. L. (2004). *The real thing: Truth and power at The Coca-Cola Company.* New York: Random House.

Herman, A., Burns, M., Casellas, G., Cooke, Jr., E., Knowles, M., Lee, B., et al. (2003, December 1). *United States District Court Northern District of Georgia, Ingram et al., Plaintiffs, v. The Coca-Cola Company, Defendant, Case No. 1–98-CV-679 (RWS): Second annual report of the task force,* p. 17. Retrieved October 16, 2004, from http://www2.coca-cola.com/ourcompany/taskforce_report. html

Ingram et al. v. The Coca-Cola Company, Case No. 1–98-CV-3679 (RWS). June 7, 2001.

Johnston, W. B., & Packer, A. H. (1987). *Workforce 2000: Work and workers for the 21st century.* Hudson Institute, Indianapolis, IN.

Prasad, P., & Elmes, M., (1997). From showcase to shadow: Understanding the dilemmas of managing workplace diversity. In P. Prasad, A. J. Elmes, & A. Prasad (Eds.), *Managing the organizational melting pot: Dilemmas of workplace diversity* (pp. 3–30). Thousand Oaks, CA: Sage.

Prasad, P., Mills, A. J, Elmes, M., & Prasad, A. (Eds.). (1997). *Managing the organizational melting pot: Dilemmas of workplace diversity.* Thousand Oaks, CA: Sage.

Thomas, D., & Gabarro, J. J. (1999). *Breaking through: The making of minority executives in corporate America.* Boston: Harvard Business School Press.

Thomas, R. R. (1992). Managing diversity: A conceptual framework. In S. E. Jackson (Ed.), *Diversity in the workplace: Human resource initiatives* (pp. 306–318). New York: Guilford.

Quinn, M. (2000, July 29). Ga. Power learns from Coca-Cola; bias suit cases similar: Utility's response shows lessons gleaned from soft drink giant's actions. *Atlanta Journal-Constitution,* p. F1.

Unger, H. (1999, April 24). Discrimination lawsuit: Coca-Cola accused of company wide patterns. *Atlanta Journal-Constitution,* p. H1.

Winter, G. (2000, November 17). Coca-Cola settles racial bias case. *New York Times.* Retrieved October 16, 2004, from www. nytimes. com

Case Study

Sexual Discrimination at Eastern Airlines?

Al Gini

On December 28, 1983, a federal judge ordered Eastern Airlines to reinstate a pilot who had been fired following a sex-change operation in 1980. The pilot, who flew for the airline for 12 years as Kenneth Ulane, is now known as Karen Ulane. Before joining Eastern in 1968, Ulane had previously been an Army pilot and was decorated for valor in connection with missions flown in Vietnam.[1]

In 1979, following years of psychiatric consultation, Ulane took a leave of absence and underwent a sex-change operation in April 1980. When she returned to work, the airline would not reinstate her as a pilot. After refusing to accept other administrative positions, Eastern fired her on April 24, 1981. Ulane charged that her dismissal was a direct result of her sex-change operation and filed a sex-discrimination suit. "In terms of sexual discrimination," said one of her lawyers, "Karen Ulane was kind of a perfect control group. As a male pilot, Eastern's own witnesses acknowledge that she was one of their better pilots. When she changed her sex, she was all of a sudden not acceptable. Eastern was willing to retain one sex in their employ, but not willing to retain the other."[2] At the time, only two of Eastern's 4,200 pilots were women.

In an emotionally charged two-hour oral opinion, Judge John Grady found in favor of Ulane and berated Eastern for their "ostrich-like and contemptuous attitude toward transsexuals."[3] Grady based his decision on Title VII of the Civil Rights Act of 1964. This statute provides that

> It shall be an unlawful employment practice for an employer to fail or refuse to hire or to discharge any individual or otherwise to discriminate against any individual with respect to his compensation, terms, conditions or privileges of employment because of such individual's race, color, religion, sex, or national origin.

The specific question before the court, Judge Grady suggested, is whether the phrase "because of the individual's sex" encompasses a person such as the plaintiff who alleges that she is a transsexual or, alternatively, that having gone through sex-reassignment surgery, she is now no longer a man but a woman. In other words, is a person's sexual identity a protected category under the Civil Rights Act?[4]

Judge Grady pointed out that this section of the Civil Rights Act had originally prohibited discrimination on the basis of race but not sex. An amendment introducing sex into the statute was offered by a southern senator who hoped that by this gambit he would prevent the bill's passage. His ploy obviously did not work, but neither was there much discussion at that time concerning the scope of the term *sex*. Grady therefore set himself the task of defining *sex* in the context of Title VII. He first distinguished between our understanding of the terms *homosexual* and *transvestite* on the one hand, and *transsexual* on the other. The later group, he argued, have problems relative to their sexual identities as men or women, while the former do not. He indicated that, while the statute in question cannot reasonably be extended to matters of sexual preference it is an altogether different matter as to whether the matter of sexual identity is included in our general understanding of the term *sex*.[5]

In his ruling, Grady interpreted the word *sex* to reasonably include the question of sexual identity. He said that, prior to his participation in this case, he would have had nodoubt that the question of gender was straightforward. But after hearing the testimony, he realized that there is no settled definition in the medical community as to what we mean by *sex*. He argued that sex is defined by something more than the biological. It is also defined by society, because the way an individual is perceived by society plays a crucial role in a person's sense of sexual identity.[6]

Having concluded that the term *sex* in Title VII reasonably includes the question of sexual identity, Grady then considered whether Ulane was indeed a transsexual. The defendants argued that Ulane is really a transvestite and hence is not protected by the statute. Grady contended that both the Gender Identity Board of the University of Chicago Medical School and her own doctor had found Ulane to be a transsexual. The defense countered that the plaintiff had only managed to persuade these medical practitioners—through some retrospective distortion—that she is transsexual. Grady dismissed this claim, saying that Ulane knew as much as most psychiatrists about her condition and the possible risks of her operation, and that she could hardly have any ulterior motive in undergoing such a radical procedure. He contended that the fact of Ulane's operation argues for her being a true transsexual, since she must have been aware that transvestites have very poor prognosis after sex-reassignment surgery.[7]

Grady then considered the question of whether Ulane had been discharged because of her sex. The evidence presented at the trial indicated that Eastern began to develop their brief leading to Ulane's discharge just after her surgery. Prior to that time, Eastern had no complaints about her performance as a pilot.[8] Eastern's legal department drafted two separate discharge letters which contained seven essential arguments, each of which they felt represented independent "nondiscriminatory" reasons for dismissal.[9]

1. Eastern alleged that because of Ulane's "underlying psychological problem" her presence in the cockpit represented an unjustifiable safety hazard to passengers and crew. Grady argued that Eastern was prejudiced from the start and had invented all sorts of dangers that inhered in the so-called "underlying psychological problem." Furthermore, Eastern never gave Ulane a fair hearing on this issue or the opportunity to show that they were wrong or at least had no reason for concern in her particular situation.[10]

2. Eastern charged that Ulane's medical certification was not unconditional after her surgery. Here, Grady compared her case to that of alcoholic pilots, whose certificates are also conditional. The FAA had, in fact, indicated that Ulane was fit to fly, and had ordered her to undergo periodic counseling only in order to help her deal with any problems created by unfriendly co-workers.[11]

3. Eastern complained that sex-reassignment surgery does not solve the underlying psychological problem. Grady indicated that there was no evidence of change in the plaintiff's psychological adjustment profile. Ulane, therefore, would be no more dangerous in the cockpit than before her surgery. Moreover, the judge cited evidence that such surgery actually decreases the patient's anxieties and makes them more stable in regard to their own sense of self-esteem. Grady concluded that the fact of transsexuality does not in itself constitute a safety problem, any more than does, say, left-handedness.[12]

4. Eastern claimed that Ulane's presence in the cockpit would counteract its efforts to assure the public that airline travel is safe. Grady drew a parallel here between Eastern and those who at one time believed that black salesclerks or waiters would drive customers away. The American public, said Grady, is a lot smarter than Eastern gives them credit for, and rejected their contention as prejudicial.[13]

5. Eastern alleged that, by virtue of her operation, Ulane was no longer the same person they had hired, and that, knowing what they do now, they would not have hired her in the first place. According to Grady, Eastern reacted to the situation as a public-relations problem: "A transsexual in the cockpit? The public wouldn't accept it! We will be the laughing stock of the airline industry! We have got to do something about it!" Grady ruled that this line of argumentation was a virtual admission of discrimination based on sex.[14]

6. Eastern alleged that Ulane had failed to disclose to the company the medication and medical and psychiatric treatments she had received over the years for her condition. Grady pointed out that the drugs Ulane had taken were approved by the FAA as not being dangerous. Therefore, he concluded that her flying ability was not impaired by the medication she was taking. He again drew a parallel between Ulane and male pilots who were alcoholics. Alcoholic pilots rarely, if ever, disclose their problems to the company, but they are not fired for that, even though the dangers of alcohol are well known. Female hormones, on the other hand, have no known effects on flying ability. Grady contended that Eastern had not followed its normal procedure in this case as a result of its initial prejudice against Ulane. If one employee is fired for failure to disclose, all should be treated alike.[15]

7. Eastern alleged that Ulane had instigated publicity damaging to Eastern Airlines. Grady countered that the company must have known that this case would inevitably draw publicity even as it drew up its letters of discharge. Besides, Eastern had raised no similar fuss when some of its female employees were featured nude in *Playboy* magazine.[16]

Grady dismissed all of Eastern's justifications for firing Ulane as mere pretexts. He concluded that, but for her being a transsexual, Ulane would not have been discharged.

I am satisfied from this evidence that while some transsexuals, just as some tall people and some left-handers, some fat people, and some Irishmen would not be safe airline pilots, it is true that some transsexuals would not be safe airline pilots. But it cannot be said with any rationality that all transsexuals are unsafe airline pilots. Neither can it be said with any rationality that it is impossible to make this determination of whether or not a safety hazard is really involved on an individualized basis.[17]

Grady ordered Ulane reinstated with back pay and seniority. The amount of the award was not set during the hearing, but was estimated at about $142,000. Ulane had been receiving an annual salary of $50,000 at the time of her dismissal in 1981.[18]

Eastern said it would appeal what it calls Judge Grady's "novel view of the law" and stated that "Eastern remains confident that its position in this case is correct under the law."[19] Grady indicated that if the U.S. Courts of Appeals rules that transsexuals are not protected under Title VII, he will reconsider the question of whether Ulane could claim discrimination because she is a woman. Ulane had originally contended that she was fired because she' is a transsexual and a woman. Grady said he was unsure if he could rule that Ulane is a woman. "I don't think I can find the plaintiff is both a transsexual and a woman," he said. "She's either one or the other. . . ."[20]

In the end, Judge Grady saw Eastern's dismissal of Ulane as an attempt by the company to maintain its image at the expense of a good employee's career. But, according to labor-relations attorney Gerald Skoning, the basic premise behind Grady's decision—that sexual identity is defined by something more than the number of X and Y chromosomes present at birth—could have far more extensive implications.[21] Until now the courts have generally refused to grant employment protection for homosexuals under Title VII, saying that although it prohibits discrimination based on sex, it was not intended to prohibit discrimination based on "sexual preference." Many legal scholars believe, however, that if Grady's ruling is upheld on appeal, the decision may be used to try to win protection for homosexuals. Although other scholars are not sure Grady's decision can be extended that far, the ruling, if upheld, not only protects reassigned transsexuals, but all men who feel like a woman but have not undergone surgery.[22]

UPDATE

"Transsexual Pilot Loses Job Appeal"
Adrienne Drell
Chicago Sun Times
August 3, 1984

A federal appeals court ruled yesterday that Karen Ulane, a former Eastern Airlines pilot fired after undergoing a sex-change operation, is not entitled to regain her job.

The 7th Circuit Court of Appeals reversed a Dec. 28 decision by U.S. District Judge John F. Grady that Eastern had violated federal sex discrimination laws.

The 12-page opinion by a three-judge panel, written by Harlington Woods Jr., said *the law does not cover transsexuals or anyone with a "sexual identity disorder. . . ."*

The appellate court said federal law "implies that it is unlawful to discriminate against women because they are women and against men because they are men. . . . A prohibition against discrimination based on an individual's sex is not synonymous with a prohibition against discrimination based on an individual's sexual identity disorder or discontent with the sex into which they were born."

Ulane is entitled to any "personal belief about her sexual identity she desires," the opinion notes. "But even if one believes that a woman can be so easily created from what remains of a man, that does not decide this case."

NOTES

1. *New York Times,* December 29, 1983, p. 18.
2. Ibid.
3. *Chicago Tribune,* January 1, 1984.
4. *Karen Frances Ulane v. Eastern Airlines, Inc., et al.,* No. 81 C 4411, U.S. District Court, Northeastern Illinois.
5. Ibid., p. 5.
6. Ibid., p. 6.
7. Ibid., pp. 15, 16, 17.
8. Ibid., p. 19.
9. Ibid., p. 33.
10. Ibid., p. 22.
11. Ibid., p. 27.
12. Ibid., p. 30.
13. Ibid., p. 32.
14. Ibid., p. 14.
15. Ibid., p. 15.
16. Ibid., p. 16.
17. *Chicago Tribune,* January 11, 1984, sect. 2, p. 8.
18. *Ulane v. Eastern Airlines,* p. 47.
19. *New York Times,* December 29, 1983, p. 18.
20. *Chicago Tribune,* January 11, 1984, sect. 2, p. 8.
21. *Chicago Tribune,* January 8, 1984, p. 1.
22. Ibid., p. 10.

Business and the Environment

The Eskimo and some subcultures of India regard pollution as a philosophical concept: To pollute is to injure the harmony that exists between person and nature. Hence one should avoid polluting not only the physical environment but also one's social environment. In Western Europe and the United States, we have tended to view pollution more narrowly. We have defined it in a largely physical manner, referring primarily to air, water, radiation, waste disposal, and noise pollution. For our present purposes, we define pollution as "the presence in the environment of a substance produced by human beings that renders the environment less fit for life."

Concern about pollution mushroomed during the 1960s with the appearance of books like Rachel Carson's *Silent Spring*, a chilling forecast of the destruction that pesticides such as DDT could bring to bird and animal populations. During the 1960s, not only were DDT and other pesticides restricted by legislation, but broad regulatory mechanisms were also established under the Clean Air Act and Clean Water Act. Strong enforcement of the acts awaited passage of the Clean Air Amendments Act and Clean Water Amendments Act in the early 1970s.

An economic concept crucial to understanding pollution issues is that of a *negative externality*. Economists define negative externalities as "costs of production borne by someone other than the producer." Under this definition, the production of steel would involve both external costs (negative externalities) and internal costs. Producing steel requires the acquisition of iron ore, coal, and skilled labor. These are all internal costs because they are borne directly by the producer. But steel production typically involves also the discharge of pollutants such as sulfur dioxide and sulfur trioxide into the atmosphere. These pollutants are notorious for defacing and weakening steel and marble structures. To the extent that the structures damaged are not owned by the steel producer (and typically they are not), the costs that flow from the defacing and weakening of the structures (e.g., restoration of marble facades) are negative externalities. From an ethical and efficiency point of view, then, there is good reason to devise regulatory and market institutions that as much as possible internalize what would otherwise be external costs. For example, legal liability rules might require steel producers to compensate those who are harmed by their pollution or, owing to the difficulty of attributing harm to an individual producer, regulatory regimes might demand the installation of pollution-control devices as a condition of the right to produce.

Thinking clearly about pollution issues also requires a healthy dose of realism. *Zero discharge*—that is, no pollution at all—is neither a realizable nor desirable goal. Pollution experts note that the cost of eliminating pollutants from a given production process is inversely and exponentially related to the percentage of pollutants remaining. That is, the first 50 percent of pollution is relatively inexpensive to eliminate, but each remaining percentage point of pollution is dramatically more expensive than the last to eliminate. Eliminating the next 2 percent of automobile emissions, for example, has cost orders of magnitude more in research and development than did the elimination of the first 97 percent. A zero emissions automobile may soon be technically feasible, but it is an open question whether it will be so expensive as to be commercially nonviable.

Although as a nation and a world we are more aware of the issues and dangers of pollution than we were when the first edition of this text was published (1984), some believe the dire effects and consequences of pollution are escalating rather than receding. Others, pointing to a veritable renaissance in environmental cleanup, environmentally friendly design, and urban green space, aren't so sure. Whatever the case, controversies surrounding endangered species, natural resources, the accumulation of garbage and toxic waste, deforestation, the loss of plant life, and global warming (whether real or imagined) promise to be with us for some time.

"Save the Turtles" is a case about the disappearance and possible extinction of six species of sea turtle that have existed since the time of the dinosaurs. It raises questions like these: *Do these turtles and, by extension, most if not all animals have a right to exist for their own sake?* and *Should we create and enforce laws that protect and provide specific animals with a haven from extinction?* "Edible Carpets, Anyone!?" examines the short- and long-term consequences of chemically polluting our environment and our bodies in the pursuit of products that supposedly constitute "the good life." "Texaco in the Ecuadorean Amazon" deals with the tradeoff between pollution and economic survival. "The Fight over the Redwoods" tells the story of how a hostile takeover can have an environmental issue at its core. "The New Market Opportunity" asks whether China's drive to modernize, industrialize, and especially automotivize should be opposed in the name of the environment.

Case Study

Save the Turtles

Rogene A. Buchholz

The Endangered Species Act was originally passed in 1973 to protect animal species threatened with extinction. It marked the first time a law had been passed in the United States that recognized that animals have a right to exist for their own sake, and that

---

animals must be protected both from human beings and from projects that threaten their existence. The law was based in part on the notion that animals have an intrinsic value apart from their value for human welfare. As such, a law was needed to protect this value as well as give animals a haven from extinction. Since the law's passage, various animals have been placed on the endangered list when their species have become threatened for one reason or another.[1]

Since 1978 all six species of sea turtles found in U.S. waters have been labeled threatened and have been placed on the endangered list to protect them from further decimation. Sea turtles are powerful and imposing creatures that evolved about the time of the dinosaurs. They are fascinating in their own right, and some people are loath to see them disappear. Turtle populations in North America have declined in recent years due to the development of beaches where they breed; butchery of nesting females and theft of eggs from their nests; oil slicks; eating plastic garbage; and nets used to catch fish and shellfish.[2]

The Kemp Ridley sea turtle nests only on one beach—near Rancho Nuevo, Mexico—and is one of the world's most threatened species of sea turtles. The Kemp Ridley's population has declined from 40,000 nesting females a day in the late 1940s to 10,000 in 1960 to little more than 500 in the 1980s. The decline continues at an annual rate of about 3 percent. Their nesting beach is now protected by a detachment of Mexican marines who guard the site against poachers. Shrimp nets are the major suspect in their continuing decline. According to some estimates, approximately 48,000 sea turtles are caught each year on shrimp trawlers in the southeast, and about 11,000 of these turtles die because of drowning, since they must come to the surface every hour or so to breathe. About 10,000 of the turtles that

die are Loggerheads, and 750 are Kemp Ridleys.[3]

The Kemp Ridley has a diameter of about 32 inches and may weigh as much as 85 pounds. The breeding season starts in early April and lasts through the first week of September. During this period biologists from the United States and Mexico, together with a contingent of volunteers from both countries, work at the Rancho Nuevo site to improve the turtles' reproduction rate. After a female turtle digs her nest in the sand and lays her 100 or so eggs, she leaves the scene and heads out to sea the moment her clutch has been buried. When left unguarded, the nest may be victimized by predators. To protect the eggs, volunteers transfer them to nests in a nearby corral guarded by the marines.[4]

The shrimping industry disputes government figures showing a close correlation between the number of dead turtles found on beaches and the number of trawlers working in the vicinity. While any one boat may not catch many turtles, the cumulative impact of approximately 7,000 offshore commercial vessels towing 4 to 5 million hours per year can be serious. Shrimpers claim dead turtles are mostly victims of pollution or disease rather than shrimpers' nets. There is evidence supporting both points of view, but there is no doubt that shrimpers are killing a number of turtles along with other nonshrimp organisms. For every pound of shrimp caught, 9 pounds of fish, such as juvenile trout, redfish, whiting, and flounder, are dumped dead over the side of the boat in what is called the by-catch.[5] The by-catch has become more of a problem as shrimping has increased.

Americans eat an average of 2.4 pounds of shrimp a year, making it the most popular seafood in the country. In 1988, 331 million pounds of shrimp, worth $506 million, were caught. The shrimping industry provides jobs for many people in the southeastern part of the United States. More than 30,000 commercial fishermen and their families rely on shrimp for their livelihood, and many more work in shoreside processing plants.[6] Many shrimpers are second and third generation, following in the paths of their fathers and grandfathers. As such, the industry has great social as well as economic value, and any threat to the industry is likely to be met with great resistance.[7]

THE SOLUTION

Such a threat appeared in the form of turtle excluder devices (TEDs), which act as trapdoors in the nets of the shrimpers. The TED is a panel of large-mesh webbing or a metal grid inserted into the funnel-shaped nets of the shrimpers. When these nets are dragged along the bottom of the ocean, shrimp and other small animals pass through the TED and into the narrow bag at the end of the funnel where the catch is collected. Sea turtles, sharks, and other marine species too large to get through the panel are deflected out the trapdoor. The problem is that some of the shrimp escape as well, as much as 20 percent or more of the catch, according to some estimates.[8]

Some fishermen call the TEDs a trawler elimination device. They claim the TEDs, which are about 3 feet in diameter, are dangerous, wasteful, expensive, and unnecessary, often leading to wholesale losses of catch. "Would you all like to go to work with a big hole in the back of your pants?" asked the wife of a Louisiana fisherman. "That's what they're asking us to do. We can't pull a TED." Many shrimpers simply refuse to use TEDs in spite of laws requiring their installation.[9]

Ironically, TEDs were developed to save the shrimp industry. Since the law requires that endangered species in the public domain be protected regardless of the cost, the industry was in danger of being totally shut down if environmental groups were to sue the industry or the federal government. To prevent a total shutdown, the National Marine Fisheries Service (NMFS) sought a technological solution. Between 1978 and 1981 the NMFS spent $3.4 million developing and testing the TED device. By 1981, the agency was promoting voluntary usage of the device and in 1983 began distributing free TEDs to further encourage shrimpers to use them. However, shrimpers rejected the TEDs, claiming they were difficult to use and lost a significant percentage of the shrimp catch.[10]

As more dead turtles washed ashore, environmental groups like Greenpeace and the Center for Marine Conservation demanded an end to the killing. Since the voluntary approach to TEDs had failed, the U.S. Fish and Wildlife Service mandated the use of TEDs, and the Center for Marine Conservation threatened to sue the NMFS and close down the industry completely. Industry representatives agreed to phase in use of TEDs, but rank-and-file fishermen rose up in rebellion. They vowed civil disobedience against what they saw as a threat to their survival, and filed lawsuit after lawsuit, which were all eventually lost in court.[11]

The fight then moved to Congress where the Endangered Species Act was up for renewal. It was hoped that Congress would not require the devices until a study was done to determine (1) whether the turtles to be protected were really endangered; (2) if so, whether the TEDs would protect them; and (3) whether there were better ways, such as increased use of hatcheries, to protect the sea turtle population.[12] After prolonged debate, amendments were passed in early fall 1988 that made the use of TEDs mandatory by May 1, 1989, but only in offshore waters, with the exception that regulations already in effect in the Canaveral, Florida, area remain in effect. Regulations for inshore areas were to go into effect by

May 1, 1990, unless the secretary of commerce determined that other conservation measures were proving equally effective in reducing sea turtle mortality by shrimp trawling. Further testing was to be done on TEDs under inshore conditions, but until 1990, inshore turtles had virtually no protection.[13]

FURTHER CONTROVERSY

Disaster struck almost immediately after the amendments were passed. Record numbers of dead turtles began washing up on beaches from Georgia to New Smyrna Beach, Florida. From October to December 1980–1986, 32 Kemp Ridleys had washed ashore, but during these same months in 1988, 70 dead Kemp Ridleys washed ashore along with several other species of sea turtles. Altogether, 201 dead turtles were counted, and since there were 150 to 200 boats working in the area, shrimpers were again blamed.[14] In December 1988 environmentalists pressured the state of Florida into requiring emergency use of TEDs in state waters off Florida's northeast coasts. Florida's mandated use of TEDs was now set for an earlier date than required by the federal government.[15]

As the May 1 federal deadline for implementing TEDs drew closer, fishermen in Louisiana rallied to oppose installation of the device. Officials from across the South pledged to help stop TED legislation from being implemented. Governor Roemer of Louisiana said that state wildlife agents should boycott TED laws until studies showed conclusively that the device worked. Roemer said he would take his concerns to Washington, D.C., and tell George Bush to "read my lips."[16]

Louisiana congressional representatives persuaded the secretary of commerce, who was responsible for implementing TED regulations, to further delay their implementation. This would allow shrimpers additional time to buy and install the devices. Only warnings would be issued through the end of June while a National Academy of Sciences committee studied the issue.[17] However, shrimpers who were caught many times not pulling a TED would be branded flagrant abusers of the new law and could be held liable for civil penalties of up to $12,000 per violation.[18] When the warning period ended, penalties as high as $10,000 would go into effect and the catch confiscated. Criminal violators—those who repeatedly thumbed their noses at the law—could be convicted of a felony and fined $20,000 in addition to losing their catch. Emotions ran high in some Louisiana communities, and many shrimpers vowed to break the law by not pulling TEDs, and dared officials to haul them off to jail. Some vowed to shoot the man who tried to take away their living.[19]

In order to comply with the regulations, many shrimpers installed and tried to use the device. Then nature struck with the largest bloom of seaweed in several years, which clogged the excluder panels and prevented much of a shrimp catch from being taken. Shrimpers who had installed TEDs cut them out of their nets, and the Coast Guard temporarily suspended the regulations for Louisiana coastal waters. Representatives from the state hoped that the secretary of commerce would make the suspension permanent.[20]

Then the secretary of commerce, after initially telling the Coast Guard not to enforce the law, reversed himself. When the shrimpers heard this, they streamed into port to protest, blocking shipping channels in Galveston and Corpus Christi, Texas, as well as several Louisiana locations. The blockade in Galveston halted all ship and ferry traffic, although by midafternoon the shrimpers agreed to let ferries pass through the blockade. The blockade threatened to shut down Houston's oil refineries. There was some violence. An Alabama man was arrested after firing a semi-automatic rifle from his boat in Galveston, and two men were arrested in Corpus Christi for throwing an object through a window of a 41-foot Coast Guard patrol boat. Angry fishermen set fire to a huge pile of TEDs on shore.[21]

The secretary of commerce then announced that he was suspending the use of TEDs until the National Academy of Sciences completed its study. Environmental groups filed suit, claiming that the secretary had caved in to terrorism and had put the Bush administration on a collision course with the Endangered Species Act. Robert E. McManus, president of the Center for Marine Conservation, said the secretary of commerce's decision "is a capitulation to organized violence, assaults against government and private property and individuals, and legitimizes organized efforts by a minority of shrimpers to promote illegal activity."[22]

Meanwhile, researchers for the National Marine Fisheries Service released the results of their research, which showed that nets equipped with TEDs resulted in only a 2 to 5 percent reduction in the shrimp catch. These results were at considerable variance with the 20 to 50 percent loss claimed by shrimpers. The results were based on 1,555 hours of trawling off the coast of Louisiana, which produced 12,185 pounds of shrimp in nets equipped with TEDs and 12,391 pounds of shrimp in nonequipped nets. Shrimpers accused the researchers of fudging their data to keep sea turtle research money flowing into their organization.[23]

Experts on the use of TEDs defended their results and accused the shrimpers of refusing to learn how to use the devices correctly. They argued that if TEDs were installed properly the shrimp catch could even be increased. But shrimpers, as victims of a depressed economy that resulted in an increase in the number of competing boats thus contributing to stagnant prices, believed they were fighting for their lives. TEDs were seen as the deathblow to a dying industry, and research data regarding the use of TEDs were rejected. With such a hardened position, nothing short of a court-ordered settlement seemed likely to resolve the issue.[24]

With respect to the lawsuit filed by environmental groups, a federal judge refused to immediately force offshore shrimpers to use TEDs, but directed the secretary of commerce to enforce some immediate turtle protection until he ruled on the TEDs issue. The judge stated that the secretary of commerce's decision to suspend the use of TEDs left sea turtles totally unprotected, but it was not the court's responsibility to determine what protection was appropriate. The secretary then published regulations that required shrimpers to limit their tows to 105 minutes so that any sea turtles caught would not drown. Environmental groups were unhappy with these results, and said they would appeal the judge's decision, arguing that restricting tow times is not nearly as effective in protecting the turtles as TEDs. They claimed that turtles could not survive even 90 minutes underwater.[25]

In order to enforce the trawl limits, the secretary of commerce planned to embargo shrimping altogether for 30 minutes after each 105-minute period. The normal trawl times for shrimpers ranged between 2 and 6 hours. Shrimping would be banned for 11 half-hour periods during a 24-hour day. This fixed routine would allow Coast Guard officials to spot violators. Fishermen who pulled TEDs, however, would not have to adhere to this schedule.[26]

After the Coast Guard reported that 88 percent of the shrimp fleet was not complying with the shorter tow times, the secretary withdrew the limited tow times and required TEDs to be installed once again.[27] The new regulations were to go into effect Friday,

September 8, 1989, but until September 22 violators would not be fined if they immediately installed a TED upon being caught. Violators caught between September 22 and October 15 would be eligible for reduced fines if they purchased and installed TEDs; otherwise, the fines ranged between $8,000 and $20,000 depending on the circumstances. Agents of the federal government could also confiscate both the boats and their catch.[28]

When President Bush visited New Orleans in September 1989 to address the U.S. Hispanic Chamber of Commerce and the National Baptist Convention, shrimpers and their families lined his motorcade route protesting the use of TEDs, and more than 50 shrimpers blocked nearby waterways. Instead of confronting the shrimpers, the Coast Guard issued citations that could have amounted to $55,000 per vessel. Shrimpers, who scaled off Belle Pass in Lafourche Parish and the Intracoastal Waterway near Intercoastal City, were cited under two little-used maritime laws. Many shrimpers were cited for one count of anchoring in and blocking a narrow channel and two counts of violating a safety zone as designated by a port captain.[29]

Shrimpers then protested an editorial that appeared in the *Times-Picayune* under the headline "Shrimpers as Scofflaws." The protest took place outside the newspaper's main offices in downtown New Orleans. The shrimpers resented being compared to outlaws and wanted the newspaper to listen to their side.[30] The president of Concerned Shrimpers of America then said his group might sue the federal government for cash compensation for losses caused by being forced to use TEDs. Comparisons were made with ranchers who are subsidized by the federal government if endangered animals feed on their cattle. These payments are designed to stop ranchers from killing the endangered species.[31]

To protect shrimpers from an unfair competitive advantage given to countries that did not require the use of TEDs or other actions to protect endangered sea turtles, Congress considered a law barring these cheaper imports. Even though imports constitute 80 percent of shrimp consumption in this country, the law was not expected to have much of an impact. Most of the shrimp imported into the United States are produced by an aquaculture industry that relies on shrimp farming. China and Ecuador, for example, each of which accounts for about 104 million pounds of shrimp imports, run aquaculture industries. The import provision was inserted into a spending bill by U.S. Senators J. Bennett Johnston and John Breaux, both from Louisiana. The measure ordered the state department to negotiate agreements with countries that do not protect sea turtles to institute similar turtle protection measures to those found in the United States.[32]

In February 1990 shrimpers sued the federal government again, saying TED laws placed an unconstitutional burden on their businesses. The suit was filed in federal court in Corpus Christi, Texas, and sought immediate suspension of the regulations requiring the use of TEDs for offshore shrimpers. Attorney Robert Ketchand, who filed the suit on behalf of the Concerned Shrimpers of America, called the TED laws "regulatory taking" of shrimpers' profits.[33]

The controversy had now come full circle, with the shrimpers pursuing the cause through the courts as they did before the amendments to the Endangered Species Act were passed. Nothing yet has been resolved, and a solution to the problem seems nowhere in sight.

1. Is there a technological solution to this problem, or is the nature of the controversy so political at this point that the parties to the controversy have ceased to believe a technological solution exists? If so, what kind of a

political solution will work to resolve the controversy?

2. Should the fishermen be paid compensation for the losses they claim because of using TEDs? How should these losses be determined? Who should pay for the protection of endangered species? What is a fair resolution of this issue?

3. Is the on-again nature of the regulations a serious problem? Was the secretary of commerce right in suspending TED regulations when shrimpers blockaded ports along the Gulf Coast? What else could have been done at this point?

4. What should be done now? Is our system structured in such a way that it can resolve conflicts of this nature? What makes this conflict different from others that seem to get resolved without resort to violence or stonewalling tactics that drag on forever?

NOTES

1. Roderick Frazier Nash, *The Rights of Nature: A History of Environmental Ethics* (Madison: University of Wisconsin Press, 1989), pp. 175–179.

2. Jack and Anne Rudlow, "Shrimpers and Lawmakers Collide over a Move to Save the Sea Turtles," *Smithsonian*, December 1989, p. 47.

3. Ibid.

4. "TEDs Couldn't Keep Gilbert from Attacking Turtle's Beach," *Times-Picayune* (New Orleans), September 20, 1988, p. A-4.

5. Rudlow, "Shrimpers and Lawmakers Collide," p. 49.

6. Ibid., p. 47.

7. Ibid., p. 49.

8. Ibid., p.45.

9. Christopher Cooper, "La. Shrimpers Get Break on TEDs," *Times-Picayune* (New Orleans), July 11, 1989, p. B-1.

10. Rudlow, "Shrimpers and Lawmakers Collide," p. 50.

11. Ibid.

12. Susan Finch, "Congress May Delay TEDs Date," *Times-Picayune* (New Orleans), July 16, 1988, p. A-13.

13. Endangered Species Art Amendments of 1988. Conference Report 100–928 to Accompany H.R. 1467. House of Representatives, 100th Congress, 2d Session, p. 5.

14. Rudlow, "Shrimpers and Lawmakers Collide," pp. 26, 50–51.

15. Ibid., pp. 52–53.

16. Christopher Cooper, "Shrimpers Vow to Defy Law on TEDs," *Times-Picayune* (New Orleans), April 9, 1989, p. B-1.

17. Rudlow, "Shrimpers and Lawmakers Collide," pp. 52–53.

18. Christopher Cooper, "TED Honeymoon May Be a Short One," *Times-Picayune* (New Orleans), May 6, 1989, p. B-2.

19. Christopher Cooper, "Furious Shrimpers Flouting TEDs Law," *Times-Picayune* (New Orleans), July 9, 1989, p. B-1.

20. Cooper, "La. Shrimpers Get Break on TEDs." p. B-1.

21. Christopher Cooper, "Shrimpers' TEDs Protest Turns Violent," *Times-Picayune* (New Orleans), July 23, 1989, p. A-1.

22. Christopher Cooper, "Environmentalists Plan Legal Challenge of TEDs Suspension," *Times-Picayune* (New Orleans), July 26, 1989, p. B-1.

23. James O'Byrne, "Research Disputes Shrimpers' Claims," *Times-Picayune* (New Orleans), July 27, 1989, p. A-1.

24. Ibid.

25. Rick Raber and Christopher Cooper, "Judge Refuses to Force Shrimpers to Use TEDs," *Times-Picayune* (New Orleans), August 4, 1989, p. A-1.

26. Christopher Cooper, "Trawling Schedules Start for Shrimpers," *Times-Picayune* (New Orleans), August 8, 1989, p. A-1.

27. Rudlow, "Shrimpers and Lawmakers Collide," p. 55.

28. Christopher Cooper, "Commerce Department Reinstates TED Regulation," *Times-Picayune* (New Orleans), September 6, 1989, p. A-1.

29. Christopher Cooper, "555,000 Fines Are Urged for TEDs Blockage." *Times-Picayune* (New Orleans), September 13, 1989, p. B-1.

30. Christopher Cooper, "Shrimpers Picket Newspaper to Protest Blockade Editorial," *Times-Picayune* (New Orleans), September 22, 1989, p. B-5.

31. "Shrimpers May Sue U.S. for Losses," *Times-Picayune* (New Orleans), October 4, 1989, p. B-5.

32. Rick Raber, "TED Provision OK'd for Shrimp Imports," *Times-Picayune* (New Orleans), October 21, 1989, p. A-4.

33. Christopher Cooper, "Shrimpers File Federal Suit against TEDs." *Times-Picayune* (New Orleans), February 22, 1990, p. B-1.

Case Study

Edible Carpets, Anyone!? Interface Corporation, a Sustainable Business

Joe DesJardins and Janalle Aaron

The old cliché suggests that business ethics is, like jumbo shrimp and working vacations, an oxymoron. To that list, one might wish to add "industrial ecology." Yet if Interface Corporation, a Georgia-based carpeting manufacturer, has its way, industrial ecology will become the standard for twenty-first century manufacturing and the model for sustainable business.

The concept of industrial ecology requires manufacturing processes be designed to mimic biological processes. Since 1994, Interface has worked to transform its business operations to become a leader in industrial ecology. In the words of their Mission Statement:

> Interface will become the first name in commercial and institutional interiors worldwide through its commitment to people, process, product, place and profits. We will strive to create an organization wherein all people are accorded unconditional respect and dignity: one that allows each person to continuously learn and develop. We will focus on product (which includes service) through constant emphasis on process quality and engineering, which we will combine with careful attention to our customers' needs so as always to deliver superior value to our customers, thereby maximizing all stakeholders' satisfaction. We will honor the places where we do business by endeavoring to become the first name in industrial ecology, a corporation that cherishes nature and restores the environment. Interface will lead by example and validate by results, including profits, leaving the world a better place than when we began, and we will be restorative through the power of our influence in the world.

But it was not always this way.

Interface was founded in 1973 when Ray Anderson, current chairman of the board, recognized a growing market for flexible floor coverings for office environments. Interface soon began manufacturing and distributing modular carpet tiles, essentially carpeting that can easily be installed and replaced in modular sections. Over the years the company has grown to its current status as the world's leading producer of soft-surfaced modular floor coverings. Through the years Interface hasgrown by over 50 acquisitions. Today, Interface is a global company with sales offices in over 100 countries, 26 factories, more than 7,000 employees, and annual sales in excess of $1.3 billion.

For more than two decades, Interface could rightly he described as a typical and responsible business. They were a good corporate citizen, treated their employees, customers, and suppliers well, and produced a quality product. Like most business, Interface believed that it was fulfilling its social responsibility simply by responding to consumer demand as reflected in the market and by obeying the law. It was, in short, doing all that society asked of it.

Carpet manufacturing, however, is not normally thought of as an environmentally commendable industry. Most carpeting is derived from petroleum, a non-renewable resource. Petroleum-based products are synthesized with fiberglass and PVC, two known carcinogens, to create the fibers used to man-ufacture carpeting. The carpeting is dyed, and the waste produced from this process can con-tain various toxins and heavy metals. Carpet manufacturing factories are heavy industrial producers of CO_2 emissions. Used carpeting, especially nylon-based products, is not recy-cled and therefore usually ends up in landfills. One estimate holds that carpeting products add nearly 10 million pounds to American landfills each day.[1] Interface estimates that over 5 billion pounds of its own carpeting now exists in landfills. This carpet waste is toxic and nonbiodegradable. Thus, for twenty-five years Interface was living up to normal stan-dards of corporate social responsibility in a way that was environmentally dreadful.

The company's transformation from one that merely sold floor coverings while comply-ing with social expectations to a leader in environmental responsibility was dramatic. Anderson states that

> For the first twenty-one years of Interface's exis-tence, I never gave one thought to what we took from or did to the Earth, except to be sure we obeyed all laws and regulations. Frankly, I didn't have a vision, except "comply, comply, comply." I had heard statesmen advocate "sustainable development," but I had no idea what it meant.

The traditional standard of corporate social responsibility, a standard which asks business only to respond to consumer demand and obey the law, no longer seemed sufficient. Reflecting on this friction between ecological responsi-bility and compliance with the demands of the law and the marketplace, Anderson now believes that "In the future, people like me will go to jail.[2]

By all accounts Interface's dramatic trans-formation has been spearheaded by the personal commitment of Ray Anderson. As Anderson recounts the story, his own conver-sion began with a book on sustainable busi-ness. In 1994 he was invited to deliver a

keynote address at a conference of Interface managers. The conference was called to review Interface's environmental activities and Anderson realized that he had little to offer on this topic. In preparation for the address. Anderson read Paul Hawken's *Ecology of Commerce*, a book that provided a vision and rationale for sustainable business practices.[3] The resulting speech challenged Interface's employees to turn the company into a model of sustainable business.

FRAMEWORKS FOR SUSTAINABLE BUSINESS

"Sustainability" and "sustainable develop-ment" have perhaps become overused phrases in recent years. To some, sustainability is little more than environmental window-dressing to rationalize the status quo. From this perspec-tive, a sustainable business simply is one that can continue business as usual for the long-term. But this superficial understanding is not what Hawken, or Anderson, had in mind. Their concept of sustainable business can be traced to a U.N. report authored by then-Prime Minister Gro Bruntland of Norway in which sustainability was defined as the ability "to meet the needs of the present without compromising the ability of future genera-tions to meet their own needs."

True sustainability requires radical changes in the status quo and a recognition that com-pliance is not enough. To meet the needs (and not simply the desires) of the present without jeopardizing the morally equal needs of future generations requires action along three dimensions: economic, ecological, and social. These "three pillars of sustainability" require that business activities be economi-cally, ecologically, and socially sustainable. As reflected in the Mission Statement quoted previously, Interface has committed itself to becoming sustainable on all three grounds.

The three pillars of sustainability suggest that no business can be truly sustainable unless it satisfies three related and mutually dependent criteria. A sustainable business must be *economically* sustainable, which means not just that it be profitable but that it be capable of maintaining profitability over the long-term. A business that maintains revenues by liquidating its capital is not sustainable in this sense, nor is one that does not reinvest in capital, that takes on expenses greater than revenues, or that relies exclusively on nonrenewable resources. A sustainable business must also be *ecologically* sustainable, which means that it must recognize the biophysical limits to its activities. The worldwide fishing industry is an example of an unsustainable industry because it has harvested fish at a rate that the ocean's ecosystems cannot sustain. The automotive industry is learning that the internal combustion engine, with its reliance on nonrenewable fossil fuels and resultant CO_2 pollution, is not ecologically sustainable, but fuel-cell-driven cars may well be. Finally, a business must be *socially* or *ethically* sustainable. A company, such as Enron, that relies on a strategy of "pushing the envelope" on fraud, or a global business that ignores or disrespects local culture, is unsustainable. So, too, is a company that exploits child labor, mistreats its employees, or makes profits by defrauding its investors, deceiving its customers, or squeezing its suppliers.

More generally, three global facts show why these criteria of sustainable business are ultimately connected. First, worldwide poverty and inequality, judged according to any reasonable measure of quality of life, show that tremendous economic growth in the near term would be required to meet even the basic needs of hundreds of millions of people. Quite literally, billions of people lack basic minimal levels of clean water, adequate nutrition, health care, or education. The amount of economic growth required to men

the very real present needs of billions of people is staggering. Second, even conservative estimates hold that worldwide population will increase significantly in the coming decades, with most of the increase coming in the already poor urban areas in the undeveloped world. The problems of poverty and inequality will increase exponentially in the face of this population growth. Third, the only source for the resources needed to address these problems is the productive capacity of the earth and there are already clear signs that the biosphere is under stress from present economic activity.

In light of these factors, it seem unduly optimistic to assume that economic growth and business as usual can meet the basic needs of the billions of people already lacking, plus the hundreds of millions of children who will join them in the very near future, without causing the already fragile biosphere to collapse. It is also morally repugnant to think that business as usual can continue without attention to these real and fundamental needs of the world's poor. Yet, attempting to meet these needs by continuously growing the economy threatens the earth's capacity to sustain the very lives we seek to protect.

The three general sustainability criteria can be applied more specifically to business. Some refer to similar criteria as the "triple bottom line" of sustainable business.[4] This "triple bottom line" holds that business must be judged by its performance on three bottom lines: financial, ecological, and ethical. In fact, this was the type of strategy being pursued by Paul Hawken in the book that so inspired Anderson. To be sustainable, business ought to be arranged in such a way that it adequately meets the economic expectations of society (i.e., jobs, income, goods and services) in an efficient and sustainable manner. But in meeting these responsibilities, business must also be arranged in a way that supports, rather than degrades, the ability of the biosphere to sustain life, especially but not exclusively human life, over the long-term. Business also ought to be arranged in ways that address minimum demands of social justice.

Some models exist for what such sustainable economic and business institutions might look like. *Natural Capitalism*, a more recent book co-authored by Hawken, provides both a framework for and numerous examples of sustainable business practice.[5] Interface is prominently featured in this book as a model for sustainable business. *Natural Capitalism* offers four strategies for creating sustainable business: radical resource productivity (or eco-efficiency); biomimicry; service and flow economy; and investment in natural capital. These strategies can be thought of as reasonable means for attaining the three pillars/triple-bottom-line sustainability goals. *Natural Capitalism* argues that business can and must be made more efficient in use of natural resources and energy, suggesting that even a ten-fold increase in resource and energy efficiency is already attainable with present technologies. Biomimicry involves redesigning industrial systems to mimic biological processes, essentially enabling the constant reuse of materials and the elimination of waste. The service and flow economy would have business create value by providing services rather than by selling products. Instead of purchasing light bulbs, carpeting, copying machines, and air conditioners, the service economy has business renting or leasing illumination, floor-covering, copying, or climate control services. By investing in natural capital business comes to recognize and value the significant benefits provided by living systems and natural resources. The ultimate capital on which all business relies is natural capital, not financial capital. Just as it would be a mistake to spend one's financial capital without reinvestment, so it is a mistake to spend one's natural capital without reinvesting.

SUSTAINABLE PRACTICE AT INTERFACE

This sustainability model permeates all aspects of Interface's business. Their corporate vision statement commits itself

> To be the first company that, by its deeds, shows the entire industrial world what sustainability is in all its dimensions: People, process, product, place and profits—by 2020—and in doing so we will become restorative through the power of influence.

In its annual reports and on the company's website Interface explains why this goal is so important:

> Here's the problem in a nutshell. Industrialism developed in a different world from the one we live in today: fewer people, less material well-being, plentiful natural resources. What emerged was a highly productive, take-make-waste system that assumed infinite resources and infinite sinks for industrial wastes. Industry moves, mines, extracts, shovels, burns, wastes, pumps and disposes of four million pounds of material in order to provide one average, middle-class American family their needs for a year. Today, the rate of material throughput is endangering our prosperity, not enhancing it. At Interface, we recognize that we are part of the problem. We are analyzing all of our material flows to begin to address the task at hand.

> What's the solution? We're not sure, but we have some ideas. We believe that there's a cure for resource waste that is profitable, creative and practical. We must create a company that addresses the needs of society and the environment by developing a system of industrial production that decreases our costs and dramatically reduces the burdens placed upon living systems. This also makes precious resources available for the billions of people who need more. What we call the next industrial revolution is a momentous shift in how we see the world, how we operate within it, what systems will prevail and which will not. At Interface, we are completely reimagining and redesigning everything we do, including the way we define our business. Our vision is to lead the way to the next industrial revolution by becoming the

first sustainable corporation, and eventually a restorative enterprise. It's an extraordinarily ambitious endeavor; a mountain to climb that is higher than Everest.

To attain this goal, Interface has articulated seven steps along the way. Again from the company's own literature, these steps are:

1. **Eliminate Waste**—The first step to sustainability, QUEST is Interface's campaign to eliminate the concept of waste, not just incrementally reduce it.
2. **Benign Emissions**—We're focusing on the elimination of molecular waste emitted with negative or toxic impact into our natural systems.
3. **Renewable Energy**—We're reducing the energy used by our processes while replacing nonrenewable sources with sustainable ones.
4. **Closing the Loop**—Our aim is to redesign our processes and products to create cyclical material flows.
5. **Resource Efficient Transportation**—We're exploring methods to reduce the transportation of molecules (products and people) in favor of moving information. This includes plant location, logistics, information technology, videoconferencing, e-mail, and telecommuting.
6. **Sensitivity Hookup**—The goal here is to create a community within and around Interface that understands the functioning of natural systems and our impact on them.
7. **Redesign Commerce**—We're redefining commerce to focus on the delivery of service and value instead of the delivery of material. We're also engaging external organizations to create policies and market incentives that encourage sustainable practices.

The relationships among these steps and the synergies created by them can be seen in what is perhaps the most significant transformation at Interface. Interface is making a transition from a company that manufactures and sells carpeting to become a company that provides floor-covering services. This is very much the shift to the service and flow economy described in *Natural Capitalism*.

On a traditional business model, carpet is sold to consumers who, once they become dissatisfied with the color or style or once the carpeting becomes worn, are responsible for disposal of the carpet, typically sending the old carpeting to landfills. There is little incentive here for the manufacturer to produce long-lasting or easily recyclable carpeting. The old-time manufacturing strategy of planned obsolescence seems the rational corporate strategy in this situation. But once Interface shifted to leasing floor-covering services, incentives are created to produce long-lasting, easily replaceable and recyclable carpets. By selling carpeting services rather than the carpeting itself, Interface thereby accepts responsibility for the entire life-cycle of the product it markets. Because they retain ownership and are responsible for maintenance, Interface strives to produce carpeting that can be easily replaced in sections rather than in its entirety, that is more durable, and that can eventually be remanufactured. Redesigning their carpets and shifting to a service lease have also improved production efficiencies and reduced material and energy costs significantly. Consumers benefit by getting what they truly desire at lower costs and fewer burdens.

Thus, the shift to becoming a service provider addresses several of the seven goals outlined above. By providing carpeting in modules and by being responsible to replace worn sections, Interface has made great strides to eliminate waste. Strong incentives exist to create a fully closed loop process; carpeting that will be taken back is designed to be recycled and remanufactured. What was formerly waste now becomes resource, and any material that is destined for the landfill represents lost potential revenues. Because Interface's own employees will be recycling and remanufacturing its waste products, there is also a strong incentive to produce non-toxic and benign products. This shift truly does pioneer a new business model of delivering service and value rather than simply delivering the material of a planned obsolescence product model. Finally, a service lease creates an on-going and stable relationship with customers, something that should benefit both the business and its customer.

A second area in which Interface has made great strides towards sustainability is in the design of their manufacturing plants. In the late 1990s, Interface was building a new manufacturing plant in Shanghai, China. Consciously looking for design changes that would radically increase energy efficiency, its engineers redesigned the piping and pumping process throughout the plant. The original and standard design included 14 large pumps with 95 horsepower and an intricate system of small pipes arranged throughout the factory. With normal plant design, the factory is set up first and the pipes are then arranged to flow throughout the pre-existing design. Such an approach results in many secondary pipes coming off of the major trunk, and many bends and turns throughout the system. In this case, Interface's engineers laid out the pipes first, emphasizing a more efficient and straighter design. The new design and larger pipes reduced friction and allowed smaller and fewer pumps. Ultimately the redesign required pumping capacity of only 7 horsepower, a 92 percent savings on energy efficiency, and resulted in a simplified and therefore more reliable production process, and an overall reduction in capital expenditures.[6]

In the decade that Interface has been moving towards a sustainable model its economic outlook has been mixed. In the first four years, Interface's revenues doubled, its employment almost doubled, and its profits increased almost three-fold. The recession of the early 2000s resulted in a noticeable downturn in Interface's business. Nevertheless, the company is committed to a sustainable future. Ray Anderson's vision continues to inspire the company:

> We look forward to the day when our factories have no smokestacks and no effluents. If successful, we'll spend the rest of our days harvesting yesteryear's carpets, recycling old petrochemicals into new materials, and converting sunlight into energy. There will be zero scrap going into landfills and zero emissions into the ecosystem. Literally, it is a company that will grow by cleaning up the world, not by polluting or degrading it.[7]

NOTES

1. See P. Warshall, "The Tensile and the Tantric," *Whole Earth* 90: 4–7, summer 1997, as quoted in *Natural Capitalism* by Paul Hawken, Amory Lovins, and Hunter Lovins (Boston: Little Brown, 1999), p. 77.

2. *"In the Future, People Like Me Will Go to Jail,"* in *Fortune*, May 24, 1999, pp. 190–200. Other quotes from the Interface Mission Statement are from the company website: www.interface.com. Further information for this case was taken from *Mid-Course Correction: Toward a Sustainable Enterprise: The Interface Model* by Ray Anderson (White River Junction, VT: Chelsea Green Publishers, 1999), a public lecture and interview with Anderson at St. John's University, and *Natural Capitalism.*

3. *Ecology of Commerce*, by Paul Hawken (New York: Harper Business Books, 1994).

4. The "triple bottom line" was most notably introduced in John Elkington, *Cannibals with Forks: The Triple Bottom Line of 21st Century Business* (Gabriola Island, British Columbia: New Society Publishers, 1998).

5. *Natural Capitalism.*

6. As described in *Natural Capitalism*, pp. 116–117.

7. *Interface Sustainability Report*, 1997, as quoted in *Natural Capitalism*, pp. 168–169.

Case Study

Texaco in the Ecuadorean Amazon

Denis G. Arnold

Ecuador is a small nation on the northwest coast of South America. During its 173-year history, Ecuador has been one of the least politically stable South American nations. In 1830 Ecuador achieved its independence from Spain. Ecuadorean history since that time has been characterized by cycles of republican government and military intervention and rule. The period from 1960–1972 was marked by instability and military dominance of political institutions. From 1972–1979 Ecuador was governed by military regimes. In 1979 a popularly elected president took office, but the military demanded and was granted important governing powers. The democratic institutional framework of Ecuador remains weak. Decreases in public sector spending, increasing unemployment, and rising inflation have hit the Ecuadorean poor especially hard. World Bank estimates indicate that in 1994 thirty-five percent of the Ecuadorean population lived in poverty, and an additional seventeen percent were vulnerable to poverty.

The Ecuadorean Amazon is one of the most biologically diverse forests in the world and is home to an estimated five percent of the Earth's species. It is home to cicadas, scarlet macaws, squirrel monkeys, freshwater pink dolphins, and thousands of other species. Many of these species have small populations, making them extremely sensitive to disturbance. Indigenous Indian populations have lived in harmony with these species for centuries. They have fished and hunted in and around the rivers and lakes. And they have raised crops of cacao, coffee, fruits, nuts, and tropical woods in *chakras*, models of sustainable agroforestry.

Ten thousand feet beneath the Amazon floor lies one of Ecuador's most important resources: rich deposits of crude oil. Historically, the Ecuadorean government regarded the oil as the best way to keep up with the country's payments on its $12 billion foreign debt obligations. For twenty years American oil companies, led by Texaco, extracted oil from beneath the Ecuadorean Amazon in partnership with the government of Ecuador. (The U.S. is the primary importer of Ecuadorean oil.) They constructed four hundred drill sites and hundreds of miles of roads and pipelines, including a primary pipeline that extends for 280 miles across the Andes. Large tracts of forest were clear-cut to make way for these facilities. Indian lands, including *chakras*, were taken and bulldozed, often without compensation. In the village of Pacayacu the central square is occupied by a drilling platform.

Officials estimate that the primary pipeline alone has spilled more than 16.8 million gallons of oil into the Amazon over an eighteen-year period. Spills from secondary pipelines have never been estimated or recorded; however, smaller tertiary pipelines dump ten thousand gallons of petroleum per week into the Amazon, and production pits dump approximately 4.3 million gallons of toxic production wastes and treatment chemicals into the forest's rivers, streams, and groundwater each day. (By comparison, the *Exxon Valdez* spilled 10.8 million gallons of oil into Alaska's Prince William Sound.) Significant portions of these spills have been carried downriver into neighboring Peru.

Critics charge that Texaco ignored prevailing oil industry standards that call for the reinjection of waste deep into the ground. Rivers and lakes were contaminated by oil and petroleum; heavy metals such as arsenic, cadmium, cyanide, lead, and mercury; poisonous industrial solvents: and lethal concentrations of chloride salt, and other highly toxic chemicals. The only treatment these chemicals received occurred when the oil company burned waste pits to reduce petroleum content. Villagers report that the chemicals return as black rain, polluting what little fresh water remains. What is not burned off seeps through the unlined walls of the pits into the groundwater. Cattle are found with their stomachs rotted out, crops are destroyed, animals are gone from the forest, and fish disappear from the lakes and rivers. Health officials and community leaders report adults and children with deformities, skin rashes, abscesses, headaches, dysentery, infections, respiratory ailments, and disproportionately high rates of cancer. In 1972 Texaco signed a contract requiring it to turn over all of its operations to Ecuador's national oil company, Petroecuador, by 1992. Petroecuador inherited antiquated equipment, rusting pipelines, and uncounted toxic waste sites. Independent estimates place the cost of cleaning up the production pits alone at 600 million dollars. From 1995–1998 Texaco spent 40 million dollars on cleanup operations in Ecuador. In exchange for these efforts the government of Ecuador relinquished future claims against the company.

Numerous international accords—including the 1972 Stockholm Declaration on the Human Environment signed by over one hundred countries, including the United States and Ecuador—identify the right to a clean and healthy environment as a fundamental human right and prohibit both state and private actors from endangering the needs of present and future generations. Ecuadorean and Peruvian plaintiffs, including several indigenous tribes, have filed billion-dollar class-action lawsuits against Texaco in U.S. courts under the Alien Tort Claims Act (ATCA). Enacted in 1789, the law was designed to provide noncitizens access to U.S. courts in cases involving a breach of international law, including accords. Texaco maintains that the case should be tried in Ecuador. However, Ecuador's judicial system does not recognize the concept of a class action suit and has no history of environmental litigation. Furthermore, Ecuador's judicial system is notoriously corrupt (a poll by George Washington University found that only sixteen percent of Ecuadoreans have confidence in their judicial system) and lacks the infrastructure necessary to handle the case (e.g., the city in which the case would be tried lacks a courthouse). Texaco defended its actions by arguing that it is in full compliance with Ecuadorean law and that it had full approval of the Ecuadorean government.

In May 2001 U.S. District Judge Jed Rakoff rejected the applicability of the ATCA and dismissed the case on grounds of forum non conveniens. Judge Rakoff argued that since "no act taken by Texaco in the United States bore materially on the pollution-creating activities," the case should be tried in Ecuador and Peru. In October 2001 Texaco completed a merger with Chevron Corporation. Chevron and Texaco are now known as Chevron Texaco Corporation. In August 2002 the U.S. Court of Appeals for the Second Circuit upheld Judge Rakoff's decision.

NOTE

This case was prepared by Denis G. Arnold and is based on James Brooke, "New Effort Would Test Possible Coexistence of Oil and Rain Forest," *The New York Times*, February 26, 1991; Dennis M. Hanratty, ed., *Ecuador: A Country Study*, 3rd ed. (Washington D.C.: Library of Congress, 1991); Anita Isaacs, *Military Rule and Transition in Ecuador, 1972–92* (Pittsburgh:

University of Pittsburgh Press, 1993); *Ecuador Poverty Report* (Washington D.C.: The World Bank, 1996); Joe Kane, *Savages* (New York: Vintage Books, 1996); Eyal Press, "Texaco on Trial," *The Nation*, May 31, 1999; "Texaco and Ecuador," *Texaco: Health, Safety and the Environment*, 27 September 1999. <www.texaco.com/she/index. html> (16 December 1999); and *Aguinda v. Texaco, Inc.*, 142 F. Supp. 2d 534 (S.D.N.Y 2001).

Case Study

The Fight over the Redwoods

William H. Shaw

Dense forests of coastal redwood trees once covered 2.2 million acres of southern Oregon and northern California. Today, only about 86,000 acres of virgin redwood forest remain. Most of this is in public parks and preserves, but about 6,000 acres of old-growth forest are privately owned—nearly all of it by the Pacific Lumber Company, headquartered in San Francisco.

Founded in 1869, Pacific Lumber owns 220,000 acres of the world's most productive timberland, including the old-growth redwoods. For years the family-run company was a model of social responsibility and environmental awareness. Pacific Lumber paid its employees well, supported them in bad times, funded their pensions, and provided college scholarships for their children. It sold or donated nearly 20,000 acres of forest to the public, and instead of indiscriminate clearcutting, the company logged its forests carefully and selectively. Throughout its history, the company harvested only about 2 percent of its trees annually, roughly equivalent to their growth rate. After other timber firms had logged all their old-growth stands, Pacific Lumber had a virtual monopoly on the highly

durable lumber that comes from the heart of centuries-old redwood trees.

Because Pacific Lumber was debt free and resource rich, its potential value drew attention on Wall Street, where the firm of Drexel Burnham Lambert suspected that the company was undervalued—and thus ripe for raiding. In 1985 Drexel hired a timber consultant to fly over Pacific Lumber's timberland to estimate its worth. With junk-bond financing arranged by its in-house expert, Michael Milken, Drexel assisted Charles Hurwitz, a Texas tycoon, and his firm, Maxxam, Inc., to take over Pacific Lumber for $900 million. After initially resisting the leveraged buyout, the timber company's directors eventually acquiesced, and by the end of the year Hurwitz and Maxxam had control of Pacific Lumber. At the time, Hurwitz was primary owner of United Financial Group, the parent company of United Savings Association of Texas. In exchange for Milken's raising the money for the takeover of Pacific Lumber, Hurwitz had United Savings purchase huge amounts of risky junk bonds from Drexel. Three years later, the savings and loan failed, and taxpayers were stuck with a bill for $1.6 billion.

The takeover of Pacific Lumber left Maxxam with nearly $900 million in high-interest debt. To meet the interest payments, Maxxam terminated Pacific Lumber's pension plan and replaced it with annuities purchased from an insurance company owned by Hurwitz. Worse still, Maxxam tripled the rate of logging on Pacific Lumber's lands, and it was soon clear that Hurwitz intended to log the now-famous Headwaters forest, a 3,000-acre grove of virgin redwoods—the largest single stand of redwoods still in private hands. The value of the grove is astronomical: Milled into lumber, some of the trees are worth $100,000 each.

The potential lumber may be worth a fortune to Hurwitz, but environmentalists consider the Headwaters grove to be priceless as it is, and they have stepped in to do battle with Hurwitz. They see the Headwaters forest with its 500- to 2,000-year-old trees as an intricate ecosystem that took millions of years to evolve, a web of animals and plants that depend not just on living trees but also on dead, fallen redwoods that provide wildlife habitat and reduce soil erosion. Some of these activists—including Darryl Cherney, a member of the environmental group Earth First!—have devoted their lives to stopping Hurwitz.

Earth First! is not a mainstream conservation organization; it has a reputation for destroying billboards, sabotaging bulldozers and lumber trucks, and spiking trees with nails that chew up the blades of saws. "Hurwitz is a latter-day robber baron," says Cherney. "The only thing that's negotiable . . . is the length of his jail sentence."

Other environmental organizations have opposed Hurwitz in court. The Sierra Club Legal Defense Fund and the Environmental Protection Information Center have filed sixteen lawsuits against Pacific Lumber, giving the company's legal experts a run for their money. One of these suits bore fruit in 1995,

when a judge blocked the company's plan to harvest timber in a smaller old-growth forest known as Owl Creek Grove. The legal reason was protection of the marbled murrelet, a bird about the size of a thrush, which breeds in the forest and is close to extinction. The judge also noted that "after the logging of an old-growth forest, the original cathedral-like columns of trees do not regenerate for a period of 200 years."

Pacific Lumber appealed the Owl Creek decision, but the ruling was upheld a year later. However, at the same time, the company won the right to appeal to another court to be allowed to harvest timber in the larger Headwaters forest. Meanwhile, both conservationists and a number of public officials are making strenuous efforts to acquire Headwaters and nine other surrounding redwood groves of about 200 acres each from Hurwitz. Although Hurwitz continues to fight both environmentalists and the government in court, he has quietly taken some steps to facilitate a sale, both through an indirect public relations campaign and by refinancing his takeover debt so that if the grove is sold, the proceeds would flow to Maxxam free and clear. Hurwitz has never named a price, but his deputies claim that the U.S. Forest Service has appraised the Headwaters forest at $500 million.

Some environmentalists balk at paying Hurwitz what amounts to ransom. They point to the fact that several government agencies, including the Federal Deposit Insurance Corporation, have filed suit against Hurwitz; they want $250 million from Hurwitz and $500 million from United Financial Group for their role in the $1.6 billion crash of United Savings. The environmentalists argue that Hurwitz should be forced to swap the forest in exchange for being forgiven the federal government's claims against him: The public gets Headwaters; Hurwitz gets off. Hurwitz, however, says that the lawsuits are without merit and denies any wrongdoing in the failure of the savings and loan.

Other environmentalists worry that too much attention is being directed toward saving the 3,000-acre Headwaters grove while leaving Pacific Lumber free to log the rest of its land with abandon. They are less concerned about the murrelets in particular or even the redwoods themselves; rather, what disturbs them is the dismantling of an ancient and intricate ecosystem—an irreplaceable temperate rain forest, home to some 160 species of plants and animals. Their aim is to build a new style of forestry based on values other than board feet of lumber and dollars of profit. They seek sustainable forest management and a new resource ethic devoted to rebuilding and maintaining habitats for coho salmon, the murrelet, the weasel-like fisher, and the northern spotted owl. As a first step, these conservationists call for protection, not just of the 3,000 Headwaters acres, but for an area nearly twenty times that amount, called the Headwaters Forest Complex. This tract includes all the ancient redwoods that Hurwitz owns and large areas of previously logged forest. "We have a vision that's bigger than Headwaters," says Cecelia Lanman of the Environmental Protection Information Center.

Her vision is definitely more sweeping than that of the Pacific Lumber workers in Scotia, California, a village containing 272 company-owned homes. Because Hurwitz has instituted stepped-up logging, which has meant more jobs, his employees tend to side with him, not the environmentalists. Workers say that Hurwitz has reinvested more than $100 million in modernizing his mills and has kept up the tradition of paying college scholarships for their children. The environmentalists are the real threat, says one employee. "You've got a group of people who hate Mr. Hurwitz, and they're using the Endangered Species Act and anything they can to hurt him. And we're caught in the middle."

Update

In March 1999, Hurwitz signed a deal that a federal team led by Senator Dianne Feinstein and Deputy Interior Secretary John Garamendi had begun negotiating with him several years earlier. In exchange for a 7,500-acre tract that includes the Headwaters grove and 2,500 additional acres of old-growth forest, the U.S. government and the state of California agreed to pay Pacific Lumber $480 million. The agreement also bans logging for fifty years on 8,000 other acres of company land in order to safeguard the murrelet, and it sets up buffer zones to protect the river habitats of endangered coho salmon and steelhead trout. A Habitat Protection Plan regulates how and where Pacific Lumber harvests timber on the rest of its land. However, because Hurwitz transferred the $868 million debt that still remains from his original hostile takeover of Pacific Lumber from Maxxam to Pacific Lumber itself, the company will need to log as much as it can to make its interest payments.

Feinstein and Garamendi defended the deal as the best that they could get, and President Clinton and California Governor Gray Davis called the pact that saved Headwaters "historic." But Darryl Cherney and other activists have criticized the agreement as a sellout. They would like to see Pacific Lumber more closely regulated, claiming that the company still engages in overharvesting, clear-cutting instead of thinning, and various other poor logging practices. They also note that for 10,000 acres the government is paying Hurwitz half of what he originally spent for the entire company with its 220,000 acres of timberland.

Pacific Lumber, for its part, contends that state and federal agencies are so rigidly enforcing the habitat conservation plan that it can't cut enough lumber to keeps its mills running, and in late 2001 it closed down

Scotia's 104-year-old mill. "We are being strangled by the operating restraints," said Robert Manne, current president of Pacific Lumber, which are "not working to meet the company and its employees' economic needs." To this complaint, conservationists and governmental officials respond that Pacific Lumber, which will continue to operate two smaller and much newer mills in neighboring towns, is scapegoating them for problems stemming from falling timber prices and the company's depletion of its old-growth redwood groves by clear-cutting. According to Paul Mason, president of a local environmental organization, "The lumber market is right in the tank, and that takes a bite out of your profit margin. The company has been operating at an unsustainable level for a number of years."

Case Study

The New Market Opportunity

Manuel G. Velasquez

In 1994, anxious to show off the benefits of a communist regime, the government of China invited leading auto manufacturers from around the world to submit plans for a car designed to meet the needs of its massive population.[1] A wave of rising affluence had suddenly created a large middle class of Chinese families with enough money to buy and maintain a private automobile. China was now eager to enter joint ventures with foreign companies to construct and operate automobile manufacturing plants inside China. The plants would not only manufacture cars to supply China's new internal market, but could also make cars that could be exported for sale abroad and would be sure to generate thousands of new jobs. The Chinese government specified that the new car had to be priced at less than $5000, be small enough to suit families with a single child (couples in China are prohibited from having more than one child), rugged enough to endure the poorly maintained roads that criss-crossed the nation, generate a minimum of pollution, be composed of parts that were predominantly made within China, and be manufactured through joint-venture agreements between Chinese and foreign companies. Experts anticipated that the plants manufacturing the new cars would use a minimum of automation and would instead rely on labor-intensive technologies that could capitalize on China's cheap labor. China saw the development of a new auto industry as a key step in its drive to industrialize its economy.

The Chinese market was an irresistible opportunity for General Motors, Ford, and Chrysler, as well as for the leading Japanese, European, and Korean automobile companies. With a population of 1.2 billion people and almost double-digit annual economic growth rates, China estimated that in the next 40 years between 200 and 300 million of the new vehicles would be purchased by Chinese citizens. Already cars had become a symbol of affluence for China's new rising

---

middle class, and a craze for cars had led more than 30 million Chinese to take driving lessons despite that the nation had only 10 million vehicles, most of them government-owned trucks.

Environmentalists, however, were opposed to the auto manufacturers' eager rush to respond to the call of the Chinese government. The world market for energy, particularly oil, they pointed out, was based in part on the fact that China, with its large population, was using relatively low levels of energy. In 1994, the per-person consumption of oil in China was only one sixth of Japan's and only a quarter of Taiwan's. If China were to reach even the modest per person consumption level of South Korea, China would be consuming twice the amount of oil the United States currently uses. At the present time, the United States consumes one fourth of the world's total annual oil supplies, about half of which it must import from foreign countries.

Critics pointed out that if China were to eventually have as many cars on the road per person as Germany does, the world would contain twice as many cars as it currently does. No matter how "pollution-free" the new car design was, the cumulative environmental effects of that many more automobiles in the world would be formidable. Even clean cars would have to generate large amounts of carbon dioxide as they burned fuel, thus significantly worsening the greenhouse effect. Engineers pointed out that it would be difficult, if not impossible, to build a clean car for under $5000. Catalytic converters, which diminished pollution, alone cost over $200 per car to manufacture. In addition, China's oil refineries were designed to produce only gasoline with high levels of lead. Upgrading all its refineries so they could make low-lead gasoline would require an investment China seemed unwilling to make.

Some of the car companies were considering submitting plans for an electric car because China had immense coal reserves which it could burn to produce electricity. This would diminish the need for China to rely on oil, which it would have to import. However, China did not have sufficient coal burning electric plants nor an electrical power distribution system that could provide adequate electrical power to a large number of vehicles. Building such an electrical power-system also would require a huge investment that the Chinese government did not seem particularly interested in making. Moreover, because coal is a fossil fuel, switching from an oil-based auto to a coal-based electric auto would still result in adding substantial quantities of carbon dioxide to the atmosphere.

Many government officials were also worried by the political implications of having China become a major consumer of oil. If China were to increase its oil consumption, it would have to import all its oil from me same countries that other nations relied on, which would create large political, economic, and military risks. Although the United States imported some of its oil from Venezuela and Mexico, most of its imports came from the Middle East—an oil source that China would have to turn to also. Rising demand for Middle East oil would push oil prices sharply upward, which would send major shocks reverberating through the economies of me United States and those of other nations that relied heavily on oil. State Department officials worried that China would begin to trade weapons for oil with Iran or Iraq, heightening the risks of major military confrontations in the region. If China were to become a major trading partner with Iran or Iraq, this would also create closer ties between these two major power centers of the non-Western world—a possibility that was also laden with risk. Of course, China might also turn to tapping the large reserves of oil that were thought to be lying under Taiwan and other areas neighboring its coast However, this would bring it into competition with Japan, South Korea, Thailand, Singapore, Taiwan, the Philippines, and other nations that were already drawing on these sources to supply their own booming economies. Many of these nations, anticipating heightened tensions, were already pouring money into their military forces, particularly their navies. In short, because world supplies of oil were limited, increasing demand seemed likely to increase me potential for conflict.

Questions

1. In your judgment, is it wrong, from an ethical point of view, for the auto companies to submit plans for an automobile to China? Explain your answer.
2. Of the various approaches to environmental ethics outlined in this section, which approach sheds most light on the ethical issues raised by this case? Explain your answer.
3. Should the U.S. government intervene in any way in the negotiations between U.S. auto companies and the Chinese government? Explain.

NOTE

1. All information for this case is drawn from the following sources: "Is China's 'People's Car' Good or Bad?" *San Jose Mercury News*, 1 December 1996, pp. IE, 5E; John W. Wright, ed., *The Universal Almanac* (Kansas City: Andrews and McMeel, 1996).

Internet Ethics and Electronic Commerce

Information technology has had a profound effect on business and business ethics, bringing new moral problems as well as accelerating the impact of existing ethical issues on all participants in the economy. Information technology allows us to do things we couldn't do before as well as things we could do before—only now more quickly, efficiently, and accurately. However, it's not enough simply to discuss whether we *can* do a particular thing; we must also consider whether we *ought* to do that thing or not.

Information flow is at the forefront of this technological transformation of business, enabling business firms to create, store, merge, analyze, and recombine data in ways never before possible. This can be seen most clearly in the humble cash register: What was once merely a cash box is now a sophisticated interactive communications device that, simultaneously, processes credit card transactions, generates receipts for purchase, deletes purchased goods from inventory, prints coupons targeted to buyers based on their purchases, flags items for reorder, credits a salesperson his or her commissions, and generates sophisticated summary data that allows management to determine what is being sold, to whom, by whom, using what medium (cash, check, or charge), and at what hour of the day—all to make pricing, vendor, scheduling, inventory, and other decisions.

Firms with which you've done business now often know what *you've* bought—information other business firms are willing to pay for. Although this sharing is obviously beneficial to business, it brings to consumers both benefits (in the form of products, pricing, and promotion well tailored to the individual consumer) and concerns about their privacy. Sometimes it seems that George Orwell's famous dictum from *1984* has been made manifest: "Big Brother is watching."

Electronic information is plentiful, fast moving, and free flowing. It is no longer so easily sequestered from prying eyes. With the invention of planes, trains, and automobiles came the observation that the world was becoming a smaller place. Information technology and high-speed telecommunications have made the world even smaller. News travels at the speed of light, and not always the news we want to travel, nor to whom. Whereas the protection of privileged information is a technological and a business problem, the invasion of privacy is a moral problem. Who owns information? Who should have access to that information?

Electronic commerce has changed not just the communications mediums through which consumers purchase their products or the speed of their transactions, it has transformed consumers themselves. As few as fifteen years ago, it would have seemed impossible that large numbers of consumers would enter *auctions* to make purchases—as people do today routinely on websites such as eBay. Where once auctions were common only for brokering the sale of rare art works, farm equipment, and liquidating businesses, now just about anything that can be had in bricks-and-mortar retail stores can be purchased and *priced* via online auction. Sites like PriceLine invite consumers to name their own prices for airline tickets, rental cars, and hotels—and have the providers of those services bid for the right to provide them to a consumer at his or her price. The low cost of conducting an online auction, or of setting up an online business through the e-commerce tools available through websites like Yahoo!, has democratized business—making us all potential entrepreneurs. Where once the many were consumers of products and sellers *only* of their own labor, innovations in electronic commerce leave almost anyone a few mouse clicks away from starting a new business.

The cases and essays in this section seek to begin the process of sorting out some of the ethical issues this bold, new commercial landscape brings. Excerpts from "Cyberethics" give us short but specific cases regarding employee e-mail, spam, and cookies. "E-Mail Policy at Johnson & Dresser" addresses corporate confidentiality and communication. "Reckonings: What Price Fairness?" and "Much Ado About Price Discrimination" address the phenomenon of *dynamic pricing*—offering different prices to different consumers for the same product, based on buying habits or other data a firm may have about its customers. "Snipers Draw Ire of Auction Site Fans" and "Snipers, Stalkers, and Nibblers" address a controversy that would have been inconceivable before the advent of online auctions.

Case Study

Cyberethics: Seven Short Cases

Richard A. Spinello and Herman T. Tavani

CASE STUDY I

The Librarian's Dilemma (Hypothetical)

Assume that you have just taken over as the head librarian of a library system in a medium-size city in the United States. You discover that the main library building in the heavily populated downtown area has six Macintosh computers, but they are used only sporadically by this library's many patrons. The computers lack any interesting software and do not have Internet connectivity. As one of your first orders of business, you decide to

---

purchase some popular software packages and to provide Internet access through Netscape's Navigator browser. The computer room soon becomes a big success. The computers are in constant use, and the most popular activity is Web surfing. You are pleased with this decision because this is an excellent way for those in the community who cannot afford computer systems to gain access to the Internet.

Soon, however, some problems begin to emerge. On one occasion, some young teenagers (probably about twelve or thirteen years old) are seen downloading graphic sexual material. A shocked staff member tells you that these young boys were looking at sadistic obscene images when they were asked to leave the library. About ten days later, an older man was noticed looking at child pornography for several hours. Every few weeks, there are similar incidents.

Your associate librarian and several other staff members recommend that you purchase and immediately install some type of filtering software. Other librarians remind you that this violates the ALA's code of responsibility. You re-read that code and are struck by the following sentence: "The selection and development of library resources should not be diluted because of minors having the same access to library resources as adult users." They urge you to resist the temptation to filter, an activity they equate with censorship. One staff member argues that filtering is equivalent to purchasing an encyclopedia and cutting out articles that do not meet certain standards. Another librarian points out that the library does not put pornographic material in its collection, so why should it allow access to such material on the Internet?

As word spreads about this problem, there is also incipient public pressure from community leaders to do something about these computers. Even the mayor has weighed in—she too is uncomfortable with unfettered access. What should you do?

Questions

1. Is filtering of pornographic Web sites an acquisition decision or does it represent an attempt to censor the library's collection?
2. Do libraries have any legal and/or moral duty to protect children from indecent and obscene material?
3. What course of action would you take? Defend your position.

CASE STUDY II

Spam or Free Speech at Intel?

Mr. Kenneth Hamidi is a disgruntled, former employee of Intel who has problems with the way Intel treats its workers. Hamidi is the founder and spokesperson of an organization known as FACE, a group of current and former Intel employees, many of whom claim that they have been mistreated by Intel. Hamidi was dismissed from Intel for reasons that have not been made public, but he claims to be a victim of discrimination.

Shortly after his dismissal in the fall of 1996, Hamidi began e-mailing Intel employees, informing them of Intel's unfair labor practices. He alleges that the company is guilty of widespread age and disability discrimination, but Intel firmly denies this allegation. According to Intel, Hamidi sent about 30,000 e-mail messages complaining about Intel's employment policies between 1996 and 1998. One message, for example, accused Intel of grossly underestimating the size of an impending layoff.

Intel's position was that Hamidi's bulk e-mail was the equivalent of spam, congesting its e-mail network and distracting its employees. Intel's lawyers have contended that these unsolicited mailings were intrusive and costly for the corporation. Moreover, the unwanted messages are analogous to trespass on Intel's property: just as a trespasser forces his or her way onto someone's else's property so these messages were being forced upon Intel and its employees.

In summary, their basic argument is that Hamidi does not have a right to express his personal views on Intel's proprietary e-mail system. They also point out that Hamidi has many other forums to express his opinions, such as the FACE Web site.

In November 1998, a California Superior Court judge agreed with these arguments and issued an injunction prohibiting Hamidi from sending any more bulk e-mail to Intel's employees.

Defenders of Hamidi's actions argue that the injunction is an unfair overreaction and that his free speech rights are being violated. They claim that this bulk e-mail should not be categorized as spam because it took the form of noncommercial speech, which deserves full First Amendment protection. Hamidi's speech involves ideas; it is not an attempt to sell goods or services over the Internet. Hamidi, therefore, has a First Amendment right to disseminate his e-mail messages to Intel's employees, even if the company is inconvenienced in the process.

Questions

1. Does Hamidi's speech deserve First Amendment protection? Should he be allowed to send these messages without court interference?
2. What do you make of Intel's argument that its censoring of Hamidi's bulk e-mail amounts to protecting its private property?
3. Should there be new laws to clarify this issue? How might those laws be crafted?

CASE STUDY III

The www.nga Domain Name Dispute (Hypothetical)

The National Gun Association (NGA) of America is a powerful lobbying organization established more than fifty years ago to protect the public's constitutional right to own firearms. The organization has millions of members concentrated in the western and southern regions of the country. It has a strong presence in Washington, D.C., where it advocates against efforts to restrict the right to own a gun. The NGA's vocal support of that right has spawned opposition groups, which believe that the NGA helps contribute to a climate of violence through its encouragement of gun ownership.

The NGA has a Web site, www.nga.org, where it disseminates information about the right to bear arms and other issues related to gun ownership and gun control. The site also informs members about impending legislation and advises them how to register their opinions with elected officials. The Web site is popular with members and averages more than 25,000 hits a day.

One of the more radical groups opposing the NGA, called Pacifists for Gun Control (PGC), has set up a nonprofit organization that distributes literature and organizes its own lobbying efforts. It has created a Web site for which it was able to secure the domain name www.nga-assassins.org. The PGC has admitted that one purpose in using this accusatory domain name is to intercept users looking for www.nga.org through its meta tags. Its home page has the following message.

Don't be fooled by the NGA. Look here to see the damage that guns can really do!

The PGC's Web site is filled with material on the perils of gun ownership and the virtues of gun controls, particularly for automatic weapons and handguns. There are also links to other sites that discuss the excesses and the tendentious views of the NGA. Through the contents of this Web page, the PGC seeks to convert gun owners and others sympathetic to the NGA's objectives to its ideological views regarding violence and firearms.

The NGA has filed a lawsuit to block this Web site on the grounds that the domain name is deceptive and misleading. It also alleges that its trademark, "NGA," has been violated and diluted. The PGC contends that it is merely exercising its free speech rights. It is using this derivative domain name to help propagate its political ideas about gun ownership. It also points out that NGA members who are temporarily diverted to this site can easily move on to the real NGA Web site, so no harm is done. A court in the NGA's home state of Texas has taken up the matter and will soon issue a preliminary ruling.

Questions

1. Is this a free speech issue? Does the PGC have any right to use the domain name www.nga. assassins.org?
2. If you were litigating this case on behalf of the National Gun Association, which arguments would you use to support their position?
3. Can the PGC's unorthodox actions be morally justified in any way?

CASE STUDY IV

Framing as Property Theft?

In May 1998, a significant property dispute arose between *The Journal Gazette*, a major daily newspaper published in Fort Wayne, Indiana, and a Web site called www.Ft-Wayne. com. This Web site was created as a public service to provide announcements about community activities and local social events in Fort Wayne and its environs.

The newspaper alleged that when the Web site linked to its newspaper articles, the article would appear within a "frame," that is, surrounded by Ft-Wayne.com's own ads and banners along with its site address. *The Journal Gazette* filed suit against the Web site, claiming that its property was being systematically "looted" by this practice. The lawsuit cited

federal trademark and copyright infringement as the basis for its claim. *The Journal Gazette* also alleged that Ft.Wayne.com was acting as a free rider by exhibiting the *Journal's* articles surrounded by its own advertisements.

The Ft-Wayne.com Web site did stop framing the newspaper's articles after the lawsuit was filed but insisted that it did not violate any laws or do anything wrong. Defenders of the Web site observed that they were guilty only of providing more readers for *The Journal Gazette*. One of the Web site's creators also defended the practice "as a means to keep viewers from roaming away form the Ft-Wayne com site.[1]

Questions

1. Comment on the merits of this lawsuit. Should there be unambiguous laws that prohibit framing? Does it make any difference that this was a community service site?
2. Defenders of framing use the analogy that this practice is similar to a newsstand running advertising banners over the area where it sells its newspapers. Does this analogy make any sense to you?

CASE STUDY V

Using Cookies at greatcarcers.com (Hypothetical)

You have just opened a new Web site called *www.greatcareers.com*. The purpose of this Web site is to be a clearing house of information for people looking for jobs, especially in the Boston and New York areas. Users can sign up for this site free of charge to look through the extensive job listings, which are displayed weekly. The major sections of the Web page are divided according to different fields of work and different professions.

Your projected source of revenues is primarily from the ads that display on each page. One advertising agency that supplies you with some of your advertisers requests to be provided with some "cookie" information of your subscribers. They intend to use the "cookie" information, which includes the user's search criteria, to generate a more personalized stream of ads for each user. Thus, individuals searching for teaching jobs would see different ads than someone looking for a nursing job. Such customized ads have the potential to generate more revenue.

This seems like a reasonable proposition, but you wonder whether it is legitimate to use cookie technology in this way. If so, should your users be informed about this practice? Should they be given an opportunity to "opt-out"?

Questions

1. Discuss the pros and cons of this proposal. What would you choose to do?
2. Is the principle of informed consent applicable here?

CASE STUDY VI

AOL and On-Line Privacy

Steve Case and other executives at America Online (AOL) were not prepared for the firestorm of controversy that greeted their latest press release. In that release, AOL verified that it was planning to sell the home phone numbers of their 8.5 million customers to selected telemarketers. Many AOL customers and even some government leaders called or e-mailed the company to register their dissatisfaction. In the wake of this strident protest, AOL needed to make some quick decisions.

Before their acknowledgment of this plan, AOL had signed deals with two marketing organizations: CUC International, a vendor of discount shopping services, and TelSave Holdings, Inc., a discount phone service. Apparently, AOL planned to give these two companies the phone numbers of their

customers so that they could follow up with targeted telemarketing calls.

This was the second time in less than six months that AOL, America's largest on-line service provider, found itself besieged with customer complaints. In January of 1997, AOL began offering a flat monthly fee of $19.95 in exchange for unlimited Internet access. However, the company failed to upgrade its network capacity to accommodate peak traffic. As a result, AOL could not handle the added volume generated by this promotion and it was forced to provide rebates to many irate subscribers. The company was just recovering from the ill-effects of this public relations debacle, and in the view of many outsiders, it could ill-afford another publicity setback.

As AOL executives read over some the more vehement complaints of their subscribes, they reflected upon their options. They could forge ahead with their plans or perhaps use their own employees to make the marketing phone calls on behalf of CUC International and TelSave. AOL had assembled a proficient telemarketing group within its organization to peddle goods such as the AOL Visa card to its customer base. Under this plan, their role would simply be expanded.

As the controversy intensified, AOL managers faced some difficult questions. Should it stick with its plans to disseminate the phone numbers of its on-line subscribes and hope that the negative attention would soon dissipate? Also, how should it deal with those subscribers who did not want to receive these calls?

Questions

1. Recommend a specific course of action for AOL. Which philosophical or ethical principle underlies your position?
2. Should these phone numbers be off limits for AOL under any circumstances? Is the company violating their subscribers' privacy by making these calls?

CASE STUDY VII

The Case of the Pretty Good Privacy Encryption Program

In June 1991, Philip Zimmerman completed a complex and elaborate encryption program, which he called *Pretty Good Privacy*, or PGP. The program is based on public key cryptography (RSA) and allows ordinary users to encrypt their messages so that they cannot be deciphered by unauthorized individuals, including law enforcement authorities. To the dismay of government officials, the program was made available free of charge to the general public. Zimmerman handed PGP over to an unidentified "friend" in the summer of 1991. That individual subsequently placed the program on a bulletin board system on the Internet for anyone to access, with no fees to pay, registration forms to fill out, or questions to answer.

Since Zimmerman has distributed this user-friendly program, it has become the most widely used encryption program in cyberspace. Zimmerman himself never shipped the product to other countries (in violation of U.S. export laws), but there is no doubt that others have taken this free program and made it available to users all over the globe. According to Zimmerman, PGP was dispersed through cyberspace "like thousands of dandelion seeds blowing in the wind."

Although Zimmerman is admired by many civil libertarians and those who oppose U.S. export controls on encryption products, he does not enjoy the same status with law enforcement officials. They have contended for years that PGP interferes with their efforts to apprehend criminals and stop crime. The problem is that PGP makes it possible for terrorists or criminals to encrypt their communications, thereby making them off limits for surveillance.

According to the government's perspective, PGP has undermined U.S. export controls of encryption software and efforts to prevent uncrackable encryption programs from falling into the wrong hands. Several years ago, California police reported that PGP encryption prevented them from reading the electronic diary of a pedophile, which would have helped them crack an expanding ring of child pornographers.

Zimmerman has been investigated by the FBI and by a federal grand jury, but he has never been convicted of any wrongdoing. He has explained and justified his actions in many forums. In an essay written when PGP was just completed, he cites the need for privacy protection for all citizens as his primary motivation for writing this program:

> If privacy is outlawed, only outlaws will have privacy. Intelligence agencies have access to good cryptographic technology. So do the big arms and drug traffickers. So do defense contractors, oil companies, and other corporate giants. But ordinary people and grassroots political organizations mostly have not had access to affordable "military grade" public-key cryptographic technology. Until now.
>
> PGP empowers people to take their privacy into their own hands. There's a growing social need for it. That's why I wrote it.[2]

Questions

1. From a moral standpoint, do you agree with Zimmerman's decision to release PGP so freely on the Internet?
2. Are U.S. legal restrictions on programs such as PGP sound and warranted?

NOTES

1. Kaplan, C. Lawsuit may determine whether framing is thieving. *Cyber Law Journal.* Available at http://www.nytimes.com/library/tech/98/05/cyberlaw.
2. Zimmerman, P. 1996. How PGP works/why do you need PGP? In Ludlow, P. (Ed.), *High noon on the electronic frontier.* Cambridge, MA: MIT Press, p. 184.

Case Study

E-Mail Policy at Johnson & Dresser

Richard A. Spinello

Jason Perry left the executive office suite of Johnson & Dresser shortly after 3:30 P.M. and returned to his own office on the floor below. He had made a rare visit to the company's Chief Operating Officer (COO) in order to discuss the company's questionable e-mail policies. The meeting had gone reasonably well and Perry was wondering about his next steps. As he checked over his notes and waited for his next appointment he reviewed the events leading up to this meeting.

Perry had joined Johnson & Dresser, a moderate sized retail brokerage firm, about seven years ago. He was hired as a senior systems analyst but within two years he was promoted to the position of Information Systems (IS) Director. He was relatively well known in the industry and aspired to work for one of the major brokerage houses on Wall Street.

A year or two after Perry's promotion he oversaw the purchase and installation of an advanced electronic mail system that would be used throughout the company. Although many were slow to make the transition to an on-line communication system, within a short time almost the entire organization became dependent on e-mail.

The new product had been introduced at several training sessions where electronic mail was frequently compared to regular postal mail and where the confidentiality of one's communications was certainly intimated. Users were not told that all of the company's e-mail messages were archived and available for future inspection at any time. Moreover, users were strongly encouraged to use e-mail for communicating with their fellow employees. The firm clearly saw this form of electronic communication as preferable to the use of phone calls or quick office visits.

Perry did not expect that Johnson & Dresser would make much use of the archived messages, but when an insider trading scandal broke at the firm it was decided to check the e-mail of several brokers who had been implicated. All of the brokers involved resigned quietly and nothing further came of the matter. The brokerage house had a strong reputation on Wall Street for integrity, and always acted quickly when there were problems of this nature. The company was keenly aware of the importance of an unimpeachable reputation in order to maintain its current clients and attract new business.

In the aftermath of this potential scandal senior managers at the firm decided to routinely inspect employee e-mail. This was to make sure that no one else was involved in the insider trading scandal and to ferret out any other compliance problems or suspicious behavior. As a result some managers regularly asked for a compilation of e-mail messages before an employee's annual review. In the vast majority of cases they found nothing incriminating or damaging in these messages and the individuals never knew that anyone had been checking their electronic mail messages.

But there were some exceptions to this. One incident that bothered Perry a great deal involved a young analyst named Lisa Curry. She was a 10-year veteran at the company responsible for following the utility industry. She worked closely with brokers, providing reports and advice on various utility stocks. Like others at Johnson & Dresser, she was a little wary at first of using the e-mail system. Soon, however, she came to heavily rely on electronic mail for a large portion of her communications with her fellow employees. Indeed over time she felt much less inhibited when she composed e-mail messages. Thus, although she was usually pretty diffident around the company, she found herself engaging in some intense e-mail discussions with one of the few women brokers at the firm, Margaret Leonard. She often sent Leonard messages that complained about sexist corporate policies or messages that conveyed the latest company gossip. None of these messages were especially incendiary or provocative but they were fairly critical of Johnson & Dresser. Also, on occasion she criticized her boss for his lack of sensitivity on certain issues; she was perturbed, for example, at his condescending attitude toward some of the other women analysts.

Curry never dreamed that anyone would ever see these messages. Leonard assured her that she promptly erased the messages right after she read them. Curry let her know that she did the same with Leonard's messages. Both of them assumed that when they hit the delete key the messages would be permanently erased from the system. When Curry was due for her annual review her manager decided to check her e-mail communications and found the messages which she sent to Leonard. He was furious that she was so critical of Johnson & Dresser and also chastised her for wasting so much time sending "trivial, gossipy" e-mail messages. He told her that she did not seem to be a real team player and that

maybe she should look around for a company that had a philosophy closer to her own. The end result was that despite her excellent track record as an analyst Curry received a small salary increment and a mixed performance review.

Curry was completely shocked by this. She could not believe that her messages were not considered completely confidential. She expected such confidentiality especially since she was not told anything to the contrary indeed, in her view she had been led to believe by the IS department that her privacy would be protected.

Among those she called in the company to complain about her treatment was Perry. She told him that his department's training sessions had duped people into believing that their e-mail messages would be confidential. She also pointed out that users should be told that messages would be archived and might be available for future scrutiny. Finally she stressed that she would be loath to continue using e-mail if everything she wrote would one day be scrutinized by her manager and "God knows who else at this paranoid company!"

Perry was sympathetic. He had received a few other complaints, and was beginning to question the company's fairness. He told Curry that he would look into the matter and try to craft a more open and responsible policy. He could make no promises since he knew that others in the company would need to be involved in any such policy emendations. Perry felt sorry for what happened to Curry, and he did not want to see other employees get blindsided in the same way that she did.

Consequently, Perry decided to ask for a meeting with the Chief Operating Officer in order to broach the issue of a revised e-mail policy that would better protect the privacy of Johnson & Dresser employees. During this session Perry argued that the company should probably at least take steps to inform employees that their messages were being stored and might be intercepted. However, while the COO did not disagree, he was worried about the ramifications of announcing to everyone that e-mail was being monitored. For one thing users might be less inclined to use e-mail, and the productivity gains realized by adopting this technology would be lost.

When asked about the legal implications of all this, Perry noted that according to current law the company was well within its rights to read an employee's e-mail. He wondered, however, if the company was living up to its high moral ideals by inspecting these messages. Isn't it a violation of confidentiality to read someone's postal letters? Why should electronic mail be any different? Should the company be proactive and declare electronic mail off limits except under unusual circumstances? Should it even continue to collect and store the large volume of e-mail messages generated by its many employees?

The COO was ambivalent about these suggestions, and he pointed out to Perry how the policy of archiving and inspecting e-mail helped the firm to uncover the insider trading scandal and take swift action. Maybe it needed to compromise employee privacy sometimes in order to protect the company against such abuses in the future. The more sources it could tap, the better it could discover problems and ensure that everyone at Johnson & Dresser was complying with the regulations of the Securities and Exchange Commission (SEC).

As the meeting came to a conclusion Perry was told to propose and defend a tenable and responsible e-mail policy that could be presented to the Executive Committee. He now began to think about what that policy should be. Clearly, there were many complex issues to untangle and key decisions to make.

Essay

Reckonings: What Price Fairness?

Paul Krugman

Why do I buy books from Amazon.com? Location, location, location. Not Amazon's—mine. The bookstores of central New Jersey are actually better than you might expect, but London it's not.

Browsing in a physical bookstore is still the best way to find books you weren't looking for. But if there's a specific book I want, I go online. Convenience, not price, is the selling point: I would buy those books from Amazon even if I were charged a couple of dollars extra. And maybe Amazon will charge me a few dollars extra.

Recently it came to light that Amazon has been charging different customers different prices (for movies, not books). The company insists that the price differentials were random, a way of testing the market.

But many buyers accused the online retailer of tailoring its price to the consumer's characteristics. And even if Amazon's prices really were random, the outrage of those who had paid a few dollars extra suggests that "dynamic pricing" is about to become a major consumer issue, maybe even a political issue.

You see, despite that outrage, dynamic pricing won't go away. Both the nature of e-commerce—the ease with which sellers can figure out who you are and what you want—and the nature of "new economy" business in general make it almost irresistible. The only thing that is likely to stop it is government action.

Dynamic pricing is a new version of an old practice: price discrimination. It uses a potential buyer's electronic fingerprint—his record of previous purchases, his address, maybe the other sites he has visited—to size up how likely he is to balk if the price is high. If the customer looks price-sensitive, he gets a bargain; if he doesn't he pays a premium.

To see why this is not just attractive to sellers but arguably good for the economy, look at how the publishing business works now. Books must be sold at a price well above the actual cost of producing one more copy. Otherwise the publisher couldn't cover costs that don't depend on how many books are sold—editing, typesetting and, yes, writing. But by charging, say, $25 for a book that costs only $3 to produce the publisher loses some potential profitable sales.

So publishers try to sort customers indirectly. Most books are offered first in hardcover, then some time later in paperback. The paperback is cheaper to produce; but mainly its lower price is a way of pulling in price-sensitive customers after the juice has been squeezed out of the well heeled and impatient.

But in the world of e-commerce, such crude market segmentation isn't necessary. When I log on to Amazon, the site offers me quite accurate recommendations—not just for books but for music, which is spooky considering that I've never bought music online. In other words, Amazon's computers have got my tastes pretty well pegged. So I'm sure similar algorithms would have no trouble figuring out which customers are likely to be repelled by a high price and which are likely to ignore it—and tailoring the prices customers are actually offered accordingly.

This would obviously be good for Amazon. But it would also be good for the overall book business. Publishers would be willing to publish more titles, book buyers who would otherwise have delayed their purchase until the thing came out in paper would be spared the wait And it would be good for any other business with high fixed costs (it's expensive to offer the thing at all) but low marginal costs (it's cheap to satisfy one more customer)— a combination that has become ever more common as we have moved from an economy that mainly made physical things to one that increasingly deals in digital embodiments of ideas.

But dynamic pricing is also undeniably unfair: some people pay more just because of who they are.

In fact, dynamic pricing might already be illegal. I'm no lawyer, but it looks to me as if the Robinson-Patman Act, which outlaws price discrimination across state lines (though strictly speaking only if it hurts competition), could be invoked to prevent dynamic pricing. But it's a judgment call—one that depends on how much you value fairness versus how much you want to promote e-commerce.

One thing is clear: The next battle in the eternal conflict between equity and efficiency may well be in cyberspace.

Essay

Much Ado About Price Discrimination

Alexei M. Marcoux

Online selling technology raises the specter of widespread dynamic pricing, or *price discrimination* (PD). Articulating a widely held view, Paul Krugman writes, "[D]ynamic pricing is undeniably unfair: some people pay more just because of who they are." Implicit in this view are two claims: (C1) PD is unfair because it violates the *equal treatment* norm; and (C2) equal treatment of buyers by sellers requires *unitary pricing*—the same price for one and all. These claims may be thought to underwrite a third: (C3) PD ought to be met with public policy initiatives deterring it. I argue that this view is mistaken: (1) On any reasonable concept of equal treatment, buyers are treated *more* equally under PD. (2) Although some public policy initiatives aim to deter PD; it is not because PD treats *some* buyers unfairly with respect to *other* buyers. (3) Despite emerging online selling technology, PD promises to be *ephemeral.*

INTRODUCTION

The advancing technology of electronic commerce (e-commerce) raises the specter of widespread and more sophisticated price discrimination or, as it is often called in e-commerce, *dynamic pricing*. Discovery of their experiments in dynamic pricing and the ensuing public outcry led Amazon.com (Amazon) both to apologize publicly for and to abandon the practice:

> In September 2000, Amazon.com got headlines when customers found that the same DVDs were being offered to different buyers at discounts of 30, 35, or 40 percent. Amazon insisted the discounts were part of a random "price test," but critics suggested they were based on customer profiling.
>
> After weeks of bad press, the firm offered to refund the difference to buyers who had paid the higher prices. The company vowed it wouldn't happen again.[1]

In a recent and widely remarked upon paper, Andrew Odlyzko predicts that online price discrimination will become both more common and more cleverly concealed.[2] It will become more common because advances in technology will permit firms to more accurately estimate a buyer's reservation price. It will be more cleverly concealed through marketing strategies such as personal bundling (i.e., offering consumers a basket of goods at a single price that is unlike other baskets offered to other consumers and hence not directly price comparable) because of the negative public reaction price discrimination elicits when it is practiced transparently.

Price discrimination strikes most people as being *unfair*. In a *New York Times* column written in the aftermath of the Amazon controversy, Paul Krugman articulates this widely held view: "[D]ynamic pricing is undeniably unfair, some people pay more just because of who they are."[3] Because of the outrage that dynamic pricing generates, Krugman predicts that it may become a major consumer and perhaps even political issue.[4]

In the present article, I argue that the widely held view about the unfairness of price discrimination is untenable; fairness considerations incline either no more against or else strongly in favor of price discrimination, as against other pricing regimes. Although there exist public policy initiatives intended to combat price discrimination (e.g., the Robinson-Patman Act), these are motivated by concerns far different from those informing Krugman and most others who claim that price discrimination is unfair. Whatever the concern, it is generally believed that the specter of widespread price discrimination calls for new public policy initiatives designed to deter it. To the contrary, I argue that price discrimination promises to be ephemeral and, where it does not, if there is legitimate locus of concern, it is not price discrimination but *monopoly power*— for the deterrence of which a well-developed public policy apparatus exists already. Consequently, the prudent public policy response is a dispositionally conservative one: Launch no new initiatives.

GROUND RULES

In this exploration of price discrimination, I will say nothing about the current state of online selling technology. No argument will turn on its limitations. Every argument will be compatible with the assumption that sellers possess the means to predict potential customers' reservation prices[5] exactly.

Similarly, no argument that I advance will turn on the efficiency-enhancing characteristics of price discrimination; for example, marketable products with high fixed costs but low variable costs.[6] The principal complaint against price discrimination is that it is unfair. It is a widely held intuition that fairness considerations, in most cases, most of the time, have normative priority over efficiency considerations. Whatever the merits of that intuition, no argument of mine will depend upon overthrowing it or claiming that price discrimination presents

a case in which efficiency considerations should trump fairness.

By the same token, no argument I advance will turn on the fact that there exists widespread opposition to price discrimination or that sellers known to be practicing price discrimination tend to lose business for that reason. All of my arguments are equally compatible with public ignorance of or indifference to price discrimination.

Finally, I will say nothing about privacy. I take it as uncontroversial that if online sellers gather information about their prospective customers in ways that violate customers' privacy rights, that conduct is wrongful. It is wrongful *irrespective* of the uses to which the information acquired is subsequently put because *the manner of its gathering* is violative of those rights. We gain a clear picture of price discrimination's moral contours by considering the case where price discrimination is practiced on its own, rather than where it is practiced in conjunction with other, obvious wrongs.[7]

PRICE DISCRIMINATION AND FAIRNESS

Two claims inform the view that price discrimination is unfair to some buyers as against others:

C1. Price discrimination is unfair because it violates the *equal treatment norm.*

C2. Equal treatment of buyers by sellers requires a *unitary price*—the same price for one and all.[8]

Taken in conjunction with the observation that online selling technology promises to make price discrimination both more prevalent and more sophisticated, these two claims may be thought to underwrite a third:

C3. Online sellers practicing price discrimination ought to be met with public policy initiatives intended to deter price discrimination.

Presumably, the equal treatment norm is apt because buyers differ in no relevant respect that could underwrite disparate treatment. If price discrimination is an example of disparate treatment, and there exists no relevant distinction among buyers that could justify disparate treatment, then price discrimination is for that reason unfair.

If price discrimination is unfair because it violates the equal treatment norm, there remains the question of what treatment the equal treatment norm demands of sellers. The view C2 articulates that equal treatment of buyers by sellers demands a unitary price—the same price for one and all. The appeal of unitary pricing is presumably that it affords all buyers *equal welfare* or perhaps equal welfare *diminution*. Under a unitary pricing regime, all buyers are out-of-pocket to the same degree; each surrenders the same to get the same. The visceral appeal of this view is obvious, but it raises an important question: Is out-of-pocket expense a welfare measure?

Consider the market demand curve, familiar from introductory economics (see Figure 1). The market demand curve represents the quantities of a good or service that the market demands at different prices. For each price represented on the vertical axis, there is a quantity of the good or service demanded at

that price represented on the horizontal axis. In Figure 1, at price P, Q units are demanded. The market demand curve is thus a kind of graphical input-output matrix, in which prices are inputs and quantities demanded are outputs, or *vice versa*. It is also something less obvious: Because quantities demanded vary inversely with price, the market demand curve is a *schedule of reservation prices*—that is, a schedule of prices above which different buyers will not buy.

The familiar downward sloping demand curve represents the differing reservation prices of buyers. Quantity demanded at lower prices is greater than quantity demanded at higher prices because some buyers have lower reservation prices than others. With each successive reduction in price, some buyers are priced into (and with each augmentation of price, some buyers are priced out of) the market because their reservation prices, exceeded at higher prices, are met at lower ones. Each point on the market demand curve is thus a tipping point, representing the price above which some buyers refrain from purchasing the good or service on offer.[9]

Consumer surplus is the utility derived by the buyer from a purchase. It is the utility enjoyed from the monetary sum that is the difference between the buyer's reservation price and the price at which the buyer transacts. Put differently, consumer surplus *is* a welfare measure. It is a measure of the *utility* derived by the buyer from the transaction.

If buyers are subject to a unitary price and some buyers have higher reservation prices than others, it follows that those with higher reservation prices derive greater utility from their purchases than those with lower reservation prices. If I sell my widget for twenty dollars and your reservation price is fifty dollars, you derive greater consumer surplus than does another buyer whose reservation price for the same widget is twenty-five dollars. Consequently, a unitary price affords *unequal*

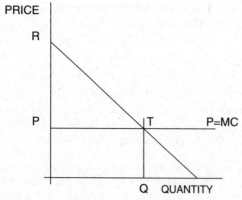

Figure 1:   Competitive Market Equilibrium

degrees of utility enhancement to buyers—some derive more utility, and others less, when paying the same price. The more steeply sloped the demand curve (i.e., the more price inelastic the demand), the greater this inequality across buyers.[10] To borrow Krugman's terms, under unitary pricing *some people derive more consumer surplus just because of who they are.*

Compare a regime of price discrimination under which the seller charges each buyer his reservation price. The seller thereby *equalizes* the consumer surplus each buyer derives from his transaction. Each receives only that smidgen of consumer surplus necessary to induce him to buy rather than refrain, but it is the same smidgen, equal across all buyers. The lesson is clear: If fairness demands that each buyer enjoy the same welfare from purchasing the same product, then some form of price discrimination (whether one that charges each his reservation price or another price that affords each the same degree of consumer surplus) is *necessary* to achieve fairness. For *only* a regime of price discrimination could equalize consumer welfare. Any principle of equal treatment that appeals to equal welfare considerations must for that fact favor *any* consumer-surplus-equalizing scheme of price discrimination (such as, *charge each his reservation price*) over unitary pricing.[11]

One could take the alternative course, seeking to establish the superiority of unitary pricing by appeal to a concept of equal treatment that does not refer to welfare considerations. For instance, one might argue that unitary pricing is *procedurally* fair to buyers and procedural fairness ought not be abandoned when adopting pricing policies. The problem with this approach is that there exist many pricing rules one could apply, all of which could be applied in a procedurally fair manner to all buyers and so satisfy the procedurally focused equal treatment norm. *Charge each his reservation price* is exactly such a pricing rule. Thus, whereas equal welfare

considerations conclusively disfavor unitary pricing, appeal to procedural equality inclines no more heavily in favor of unitary pricing than it does price discrimination.

PRICE DISCRIMINATION AND PUBLIC POLICY: EXISTING INITIATIVES

Here, the proponent of unitary pricing may appeal to public policy. The Robinson-Patman Act,[12] for example, is intended explicitly to deter some forms of price discrimination. If law is a reliable guide to our moral intuitions,[13] and we have legal norms aimed at deterring price discrimination, then there are likely some considerations in terms of which price discrimination is believed to be harmful or wrongful. The questions on the table, then, are two:

1. What are the considerations informing the Robinson-Patman Act?
2. Do those considerations, when applied to the practice of price discrimination, show that it is unfair?

The Robinson-Patman Act is a New Deal era amendment to the Clayton Antitrust Act[14] that makes it illegal to engage in price discrimination practices that have the effect of diminishing competition. For example, if wholesaler W offers better prices to retailer R_1, than to retailers $R_2, \ldots, R_n$, and this affords an advantage to R_1 that diminishes competition in the market in which retailers $R_1, \ldots, R_n$ compete, then the Robinson-Patman Act provides that those injured by diminished competition may recover from W (or from R_1).

At root, the Robinson-Patman Act seeks to protect consumer-welfare-enhancing competition by keeping upstream (wholesale) pricing policies from fostering downstream (retail) monopolies. In the example above, R_1, the beneficiary of more favorable wholesale pricing, may drive out competition through predatory pricing. Having monopolized the market by limiting output, R_1 may transform what in a competitive market would have been consumer surplus into producer surplus (monopoly rents) and deadweight losses.[15]

In Figure 2, P is the competitive market price and P* is the price extracted by the monopolist. By reducing output to Q*, the monopolist enforces P*. Consumer surplus is diminished by the area bounded by P*UTP. The area bounded by P*UVP is captured by the monopolist as producer surplus, and the area bounded by VUT is deadweight loss—lost to consumers but not gained by the monopolist.

Two things are worth noting about the Robinson-Patman Act in connection with the present exploration of price discrimination's fairness. First, the Act is addressed to pricing policies that have the effect of diminishing competition among sellers in another market. A seller who charges different prices to consumers does *not* thereby diminish competition among sellers in another market because consumers can hardly be said to be in competition with one another, much less as sellers.

Second, although the concern that informs the Robinson-Patman Act appeals to consumer welfare, it is not a concern about how *some* consumers are treated as against *others*. If it can be considered a fairness concern at all, it is a concern that consumers *in the aggregate* be treated fairly with respect to producers *in the aggregate*. Price discrimination is objectionable, on this account, because it facilitates monopoly. Monopoly upsets the fair division of the aggregate transactional surplus between aggregate consumer surplus and aggregate producer surplus that prevails in competitive markets. Price theory tells us that one of the distinguishing characteristics of a competitive market is that aggregate consumer surplus is large and aggregate producer surplus is small. In a monopolized market, some consumer surplus is transformed into producer surplus (in the form of monopoly rents) and that upsets the fair (read: competitive market) division of the transactional surplus.

Whatever the merits of regarding the Robinson-Palman Act as a public policy initiative concerned with fairness, the *treatment of some consumers as against others* plays no role in its indictment of price discrimination. The Act is indifferent to price discrimination except insofar as its practice promises to diminish competition among sellers. Retail price discrimination affords no seller an opportunity to monopolize his market. Thus, the Robinson-Patman Act implies nothing about the fairness of charging some consumers prices that are different from those charged to others.

PRICE DISCRIMINATION AND PUBLIC POLICY: NEW INITIATIVES

By stopping here, one may be tempted to conclude that the whole of my argument consists in chastising opponents of price discrimination for misidentifying the *justification* for opposing the practice. If price discrimination is objectionable on other grounds (e.g., upsetting fair division of the transactional surplus) and advances in online selling technology threaten (per Odlyzko) its expansion,

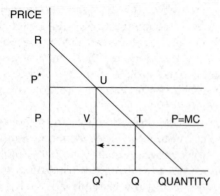

Figure 2: Monopoly Pricing

then new public policy initiatives would seem to be underwritten for these reasons, if not for the reasons with which we began. Indeed, were I stopping here, that would be the entire upshot of my argument. However, the question now on the table is whether circumstances merit new public policy initiatives.

Entertain the following as a commonsense normative principle of public policy initiatives. Call it the *public policy prudence principle* (4P):

4P. Durable public policy initiatives ought to be adopted to address what promise to be durable phenomena. They ought not be adopted to address phenomena promising to be ephemeral.

A number of compelling reasons support 4P. Bureaucracies implement public policy initiatives, and new public policy initiatives tend to be implemented by new bureaucracies. Bureaucracies tend to be self-perpetuating for reasons that economic historians and public choice economists have explicated skillfully.[16] Legislatures are significantly more inclined to enact legislation designed to combat a perceived problem than they are to repeal legislation the animating problems of which have since dissipated. Government and mainstream media are imbued by a culture of legislative achievement—authoring and passing new legislation is the *sine qua non* of a legislator's worthiness.

In combination, these factors imply that the costs of hastily adopted or poorly chosen public policy initiatives have an inbuilt tendency to outlive and, in the long run, outweigh their benefits. Thus, 4P is a rough political analogue to Ockham's Razor. It says that one ought not to multiply public policy initiatives beyond necessity. If 4P is correct, then public policy initiatives designed to combat online price discrimination are warranted only if the practice and the harm that flows from it promise to be durable without such initiatives.[17]

Online price discrimination, even if technologically perfected, promises to be ephemeral. To see this, suppose that Amazon develops technology that affords crystalline insight into a potential customer's reservation price. Suppose further than Amazon uses this insight to quote prices exactly equal to that customer's reservation price and will quote such prices to customers so long as their reservation prices are at or above marginal cost.[18] In short, suppose that Amazon becomes a *perfect price discriminator*.

Noting that Amazon is not a monopolist, consider: What is a competitor's best response? Barnes & Noble (for example) may secure profits and take market share from Amazon by applying the same technology, undercutting Amazon's (discriminatory) prices by a fixed percentage. Barnes & Noble can quote all such prices that are at or above marginal cost and win customers away from Amazon. Note that other competitors can do the same to Barnes & Noble, and Amazon to the other competitors, and so forth. The logical limit of this price competition is the point where price equals marginal cost. In other words, even where technology facilitates fine-grained price discrimination, *competition* pushes optimal pricing back toward a unitary price—the price equivalent to marginal cost.

What of the case where not all competitors possess the technology? Suppose that patents or prohibitive cost preclude some or all of Amazon's competitors from developing the technology. If a competitor lacks the requisite technology to be a perfect price discriminator, that competitor's best response to Amazon is to charge a unitary price. Amazon and other competitors do best to follow suit. Again, competitive pressure pushes toward a unitary price.

Of course, a successful cartel arrangement among competitors could forestall the competitive pressures that eventuate in a unitary price. However, if successful online price discrimination depends upon effective cartellization of the market, then we find ourselves in well-trod territory. Existing antitrust law and enforcement mechanisms are designed to combat durable cartel arrangements.[19]

In sum, there are scant reasons to suppose that online price discrimination will be any more durable than the less technologically sophisticated kind.[20] Because durable price discrimination is the *fruit of*, not the *means to*, monopoly power, price discrimination without monopoly power promises to be ephemeral, whatever the technological sophistication with which it is effected. New antiprice discrimination public policy initiatives therefore fail the 4P test. Forces that could afford price discrimination durability (e.g., cartel arrangements) are those for which a public policy apparatus exists already.

Because durable price discrimination is the consequence rather than the cause of monopoly power, wise public policy will seek, paradoxically, to *encourage* it. By *observing* attempts at price discrimination and seeing which are durable, we may discover *which* are the firms possessing monopoly power and, hence, which should be pursued under existing antitrust law.

CONCLUSION

The conclusions of this discussion are three:

First, price discrimination is no less fair to buyers vis-à-vis other buyers than unitary pricing; if the concern is to achieve fairness through equal welfare, it is more so.

Second, to the extent that public policy should be concerned about price discrimination, it is not for its own sake but because the durable form evidences monopoly power. To the extent that we should be concerned about monopoly power, a well-developed public policy apparatus for addressing it already exists.

Third, the advance of online selling technology does not alter either of the first two conclusions. Technology affords sellers the means to do more accurately and in a more fine-grained way what they have heretofore done in broad brushstrokes.[21] However, this added precision does not add durability to price discrimination—only monopoly power can do that.

Consequently, the case for public policy initiatives to combat emerging online price discrimination is a poor one.[22]

NOTES

1. Joseph Turow, "Have they got a deal for you," *Washington Post* , June 19, 2005, B01. [Available online at: http://www.washingtonpost.com/wp-dyn/content/article/2005/06/18/AR2005061800070.html]

2. Andrew Odlyzko, "Privacy, Economics, and Price Discrimination on the Internet." *Proceedings of the Fifth International Conference on Electronic Commerce*, ed. N. Sadeh (New York: ACM Press, 2003), 355–66. [Available online at http://www.dtc.umn.edu/~odlyzko/doc/eworld.html]

3. Paul Krugman, "What price fairness?" *New York Times*, October 4, 2000, A31. [Available online at http://www.pkarchive.org/column/100400.html]

4. Ibid.

5. A buyer's reservation price is the highest price the buyer is willing to pay—the price above which the buyer declines to purchase. A seller's reservation price is the lowest price the seller is willing to accept—the price below which the seller declines to sell.

6. Krugman, "What price fairness?"

7. In an otherwise thoughtful piece on how online price discrimination threatens to promote a "culture of suspicion" in e-commerce, Turow, "Have they got a deal for you," tars price discrimination with the privacy brush. That is, he argues in effect that price discrimination is harmful or wrongful because invasions of privacy are.

8. Strictly speaking, C2 is most plausibly the view that equal treatment of buyers by sellers requires the same price for one and all *at any one time and place* , for surely it does not violate the equal treatment norm to raise or lower prices in response to changing market conditions. However, nothing I say subsequently will turn on this elaboration of C2.

9. Or, alternatively, the price above which some will reduce their consumption of the good or service on offer.

10. Of course, it may be the case that the inequality is diminished by variations in the declining marginal utility of money across persons. If those with higher

reservation prices derive lesser utility from an additional monetary unit than do those with lower reservation prices, then the inequality in consumer surpluses derived will be proportionally less than the differences in their reservation prices.

11. In some circumstances, this strikes people as being intuitively obvious. Journal subscriptions and memberships in scholarly organizations are frequently priced on rough ability-to-pay terms to the general approbation of their subscribers and members. Thus, graduate students and retirees pay less than tenured and tenure-track professors without anyone complaining about price discrimination.

12. 15 U.S.C. §13.

13. Robert Goodin, *Protecting the Vulnerable* (Chicago: University of Chicago Press, 1985), argues that the law is a reliable, though not infallible, guide to widely held moral intuitions.

14. 15 U.S.C. §§2–27.

15. This is not to say that the Robinson-Patman Act is grounded in sound economics. As Richard Posner (*The Robinson-Patman Act: Federal Regulation of Price Differences* [Washington, D.C.: American Enterprise Institute, 1976], 1) observes, "The Robinson-Patman Act . . . is almost uniformly condemned by professional and academic opinion, both legal and economic."

16. In his *Crisis and Leviathan* (New York: Oxford University Press, 1989), Robert Higgs emphasizes the role that crises—for example, wars, depressions—play in the growth of government and bureaucratic authority. Public choice theorists have emphasized the role that bureaucratic and legislative inertia play in the perpetuation of bureaucracies. See, for example, William A. Niskanen, *Bureaucracy: Servant or Master?* (London: Institute of Economic Affairs, 1973).

17. Note that this is a necessary, but not a sufficient, condition for prudent adoption of public policy initiatives. A further necessary condition is that the public policy initiative passes the *comparative institutions test*. In some cases, some of the time, the problem we hope to address through public policy may itself be the best we can accomplish. The comparative institutions test demands evidence that the proposed cure will be better in practice than the disease it seeks to eliminate. A regulatory initiative to address a market failure is justified only if it can be shown that life under the regulatory initiative will be better in practice than life under the market failure. On the comparative institutions test, see N. Scott Arnold, "Economists and Philosophers as Critics of the Free Enterprise System," *The Monist* 73 (October 1990): 621–41.

18. If the buyer's reservation price is below marginal cost, the seller is better off quoting a price equal to marginal cost and not selling to the buyer because the seller loses money on each transaction consummated at a price below marginal cost.

19. In adverting to existing antitrust law, I do not endorse it uncritically. Some critics of antitrust focus on doctrinal detail, arguing that particular features of antitrust law and its development undermine what is, in concept, a worthwhile public policy initiative. Other critics argue that antitrust is objectionable in concept. For problems in doctrinal detail see, for example, Robert Bork, *The Antitrust Paradox* (New York: Basic Books, 1978). For problems with antitrust in concept see, for example, Dominick T. Armentano, *Antitrust and Monopoly* (New York: John Wiley & Sons, 1982). I mention antitrust law only to consider the case most favorable to the proponent of public policy initiatives.

20. Odlyzko, "Privacy," argues that online sellers will seek to conceal price discrimination, and hence make it more durable, through personal bundling, membership schemes, and the like. It is easy to see how this could make price discrimination harder for consumers to detect. It is more difficult, however, to see how these practices would insulate a seller from price competition. A competitor who sells identical but lower-priced bundles, or who unbundles products and sells them at more attractive prices promises to win customers away from the assiduous, price-discriminating bundler.

21. Anyone who has been quoted round trip airfares differing markedly depending upon whether a Saturday night stay over is included, or who has purchased earlier and in hardback a book that may be had later and in softcover at a significantly lesser price, has encountered price discrimination in its less sophisticated and heuristic form.

22. An early draft of this article was presented as a paper at Santa Clara University. I wish to thank Dennis Moberg for the invitation and for his incisive comments. The article is much improved by discussions with Nicholas Capaldi, Jim Child, and Spencer Weber Waller. I thank them, as well. The Social Philosophy and Policy Center at Bowling Green State University hosted me as a visiting scholar in the fall of 2004, during which visit I completed the article's penultimate draft. I thank the directors of the Social Philosophy and Policy Center for their support.

Essay

"Snipers" Draw Ire of Auction Site Fans

Doug Bedell

Dallas photographer Jay Brousseau can still feel the indignation—the horror—of his first encounter with an online auction sniper.

"In the last 17 seconds, this guy came out of nowhere and took the auction," says Mr. Brousseau.

"I had the bid with eight minutes to go. Then he just jumped in and grabbed it away."

Losing that $22 Kensington track ball was a bitter lesson, Mr. Brousseau says. "It made me realize that that's the way the game is played, but it makes the whole thing a pain in the butt. I e-mailed the guy that he was a schmuck, but he never responded. And I've been much less active ever since."

Sniping is one of several cutthroat tactics that have soured some users of popular Internet auction sites on *eBay, Ubid, Yahoo* and *Amazon.com.*

Complaints about sniping—the practice of entering a bid just before the close of an auction—are escalating as millions of bargain-hunters take their first forays into these new worldwide bazaars.

CALL TO ACTION

Spurred by customer complaints, some online auction houses have instituted anti-sniping measures.

At the same time, software companies have developed programs that help snipers become even more efficient.

The pioneering auction site eBay says that only a minuscule fraction of its 12 million customers are griping about sniping.

There are also more serious schemes that bear watching. They include bid-shielding, in which two bidders collude. One bids low, the other bids very high to frighten off other shoppers. Seconds before the auction ends, the high bid is retracted, and the low bidder wins by default.

Shilling—putting an item up for auction, then assuming a different identity to bid up the price—is also a growing tactic, according to auction bulletin boards.

Nearly everybody agrees that shilling and bid-shielding are morally out of bounds.

Most services will investigate persistent complaints, then expel perpetrators they can catch.

But when it comes to sniping, there is no consensus about what's right and wrong.

SNIPING'S EFFECTS

Sniping "essentially preys on the ignorance of other bidders and contributes to a general sense of unfairness and unpleasantness at eBay," Barry Goldberg of Somerville, Mass., wrote to *Auctionwatch.com,* which monitors online auctioning.

"I hate the feeling that somebody is lurking in the bushes, just waiting to jump out at the last moment in an effort to catch me by surprise."

But for every complaint by the Mr. Goldbergs and Mr. Brousseaus of the world, there are equally ardent defenders.

Many are quick to point out that terms such as *shill* and *snipe* stem from common practices in live auctions conducted for centuries.

Says Barry Scott Will of Richmond, Va.: "Sniping is frustrating, but so is getting cut off while driving. There's not much you can do about either, so you can either learn to put up with a little frustration or get off the highway."

Officials at eBay also say sniping is hard to control.

"The only way to protect yourself from being outbid at the last second (also called being 'sniped') is to bid the highest maximum you are willing to pay," the service advises.

"Remember, it's not the last bid that wins, it's the highest. There is a common misconception that snipers always win. This isn't so. To win, they must outbid you. If someone places a last-second bid that isn't high enough, they almost never have enough time to try again and place a winning bid before the listing ends."

Sniping is one reason that eBay and its cousins provide automated proxy bid mechanisms.

If you find something you really want, you can sit at your computer all day and incrementally outbid each new offer until you've reached your self-imposed ceiling.

Proxy mechanisms simplify that process by confidentially bidding up to your maximum amount, freeing you from constant checking and rechecking.

Deft use of proxy bidding would solve most people's sniping worries, says North Carolina student Arthur Crenshaw.

"As long as people underbid and don't use the proxy bidding properly, the snipers will continue to thrive," Mr. Crenshaw says. "If everyone bid what they were willing to pay from the start, there wouldn't be any benefit to sniping, would there?"

David Coursey, an electronics industry consultant, online ZDNet columnist and recent sniping victim, drew hundreds of responses to a recent anti-sniping diatribe.

"The experience left a bad taste in my mouth since I felt like I'd played by the rules and the sniper hadn't," says Mr. Coursey.

"Of course, he who owns the playground makes the rules. And if eBay wants to run things like this, they can run them without me."

As auction observers point out, in-person auctions link all the participants together by putting them in the same physical spot. The person with the greatest will wins.

"On eBay, this equation is broken because the bidders don't all show up at once—except to snipe at the end, of course," says Mr. Coursey. "And proxy bidding doesn't quite deal with the issue of the greatest will wins."

Amazon.com has attempted to deter sniping by automatically extending any auction when a bid comes in during the last 10 minutes. Some regular users are pushing eBay to do the same.

"If you are bidding at Sotheby's . . . there is no ending time for this kind of auction," says Chris Rampson of Dearborn, Mich. "It's the going once, going twice call by the auctioneer. This is the element that is missing from eBay and creates snipers."

Scott Neuman of Recordweb Communications, who is both a seller and sniper, says the open nature of auctions presents multiple problems for all participants.

"Sniping on eBay—I do it all the time. I wait till the last 10 seconds and bang! Since eBay set up this . . . way of doing business by not adding five minutes to the auction for the last bid, then what they're really saying is they don't care if you get the highest price for an item."

There are also calls to hide auction data in an electronic sealed bid.

Others insist that snipers should be forced to pay, say, 20 percent over the last bid to participate at all. Still others argue that sniped high bidders should be allowed one last chance to win by submitting a supplemental offer by e-mail.

Mr. Coursey's brief, unfulfilling venture into eBay left him with one conclusion on the process.

"I am convinced that sniping is the only way to win in the environment eBay has created," he writes.

That's exactly how a sadder but wiser Mr. Brousseau handles his eBay pursuits today.

"I put it in my daily planner to check the spots I've researched, then get a clock and sit it by the computer," he says.

"If the bidding hasn't gone over my established price parameter, I move in."

"Bidding on eBay is not a game; it is a legal financial transaction," Bonnie Barrett of New York recently warned sniper sufferers.

"If you get sniped, chances are there is another seller with the exact same item and you can bid again. You might even get a better deal than you had before."

Essay

Snipers, Stalkers, and Nibblers: Online Auction Business Ethics

Alexei M. Marcoux

Few disputes inflame the passions of online auction participants more than that over *sniping*. A common feature of contested online auctions, sniping is the practice of delaying one's bid; placing it only in the closing seconds of an auction.

Practitioners of sniping (*snipers*) observe that it is both an effective strategy for winning auctions and a tactic well within the rules of time-limited auctions like those on eBay, the most prominent online auction site and the object of much of the debate over sniping. Detractors (*anti-snipers*) maintain that sniping is unfair, a form of cheating that circumvents the requirements of fair play. Journalistic commentators have taken up the detractors' complaint, counting sniping among the tactics discussed in articles about fraudulent or abusive online auction practices like shill bidding (See, e.g., Bedell, 2000).

Some prominent online auction sites (e.g., Amazon), in response to complaints about sniping, have adopted auction formats that eliminate or discourage sniping. Among auction sites adopting sniper-unfriendly formats, at least one (IronPlanet) claims to have done so explicitly as a matter of ethics. Given both the popularity of online auctions and the fact that they constitute one of the few pure-play success stories in e-commerce, it is a matter of some moment if these auctions are, as detractors claim, plagued by systematic unfairness in the bidding process—an unfairness due to sniping.

In the present paper, I argue that moral criticism of sniping is misplaced. To the extent that the anti-snipers' complaint is conceived as one about the ethics of online auction *participation*, it is wholly misguided; but conceived as a complaint about the ethics of online auction *hosting*, it gains coherence and recasts the question in terms of business ethics. Even recast, however, the argument fails on the merits, for on no plausible conception of fairness is sniping, or adopting auction formats that facilitate sniping, revealed to be unfair. I conclude by observing that the most interesting question about sniping is not whether it is fair but why *bidders* are the ones complaining about it.

AUCTIONS: ONLINE AND BRICKS-AND-MORTAR COMPARED

Typically, online auctions are conducted under rules that differ significantly from those of more familiar, bricks-and-mortar auctions. As the attractions of sniping depend critically upon the rules of online auctions, an understanding of the debate and the ethical issues (both real and imagined) surrounding sniping depends upon an understanding of those rules.

Throughout this discussion, I shall focus on the rules of eBay auctions for two important reasons. First, eBay is by far the largest and most familiar online auction site. Second, eBay's rules make the sniping tactic both attractive and effective.

Rules which give rise to sniping are of two kinds, *pricing* rules and *closing* rules. I discuss each in turn.

Pricing Rules

In eBay auctions the final, or *hammer*,[1] price of items on auction is the lesser of (a) the *maximum* bid offered by the top bidder, and (b) one *bid increment*[2] above the maximum bid offered by the second-highest bidder. That is, regardless of how high the top bidder bids, she is obligated to pay no more than one bid increment above the second-highest bidder's maximum bid. Auctions with these pricing rules are *second-price* (2P) auctions (Ockenfels and Roth, 2002).

Compare the *English* auction, the standard auction format employed in bricks-and-mortar auction houses like Christie's and Sotheby's and the one with which most people are familiar, through television and film if not by direct participation. In an English auction, the

hammer price is the highest bidder's highest bid. Auctions with these pricing rules are *first-price* (1P) auctions.

Closing Rules

Closing rules determine the circumstances under which an auction is concluded. eBay auctions are *hard-close* (HC) auctions, meaning that they end at a specified time (e.g., 11:21:46 AM PST) regardless of the willingness of bidders to continue bidding and raising the price.

Compare the English auction, which ends when all bids are exhausted or when no further bids are registered within a few seconds of a warning, e.g., "Going once, going twice . . ." Auctions closing on these terms are "going, going, gone" (3G) auctions.

Armed with distinctions based upon pricing and closing rules, one may characterize eBay auctions as second-price, hard-close (2PHC) auctions and familiar, bricks-and-mortar English auctions as first-price, going-going-gone (1P3G) auctions.

Other Important Differences: Bidding Agents (Proxy Bidding)

In addition to their pricing and closing rules, eBay auctions are characterized by bidding agents, or what eBay calls *proxy bidding*. Proxy bidding is a consequence of the 2P rule. Rather than bidding frequently throughout the auction period and raising her bid in response to the bids of others, as she would do in 1P3G bricks-and-mortar auctions, a bidder may specify a maximum price she is willing to pay and eBay's proxy bidding software will raise her bid one increment above the next-highest bidder's bid until her maximum is exceeded, at which point she is no longer the highest bidder. Her maximum price is secret, withheld from other bidders and the seller of the item up for auction.

For example, imagine an auction for a vintage metal Josie and the Pussycats lunchbox that opens at $1 with a $0.25 bid increment.[3] If Alice opens bidding and specifies a maximum of $3, the current price will be $1 (the opening bid), but will rise as others bid. The second bidder to enter the auction must enter a bid of at least $1.25 (one bid increment above the current price), but Alice will remain the top bidder until either (a) another bidder bids more than $3, or (b) the auction closes.[4] If no one but Alice bids, Alice wins the auction at a hammer price of $1 (the opening price). If other bidders enter the auction and the highest bid among them is $2.50, then Alice wins the auction at a hammer price of $2.75 (one bid increment above $2.50). If only one bidder (call him Brent) exceeds Alice's bid, then Brent wins at a hammer price of the lesser of (a) Brent's maximum price, and (b) $3.25 (one bid increment above Alice's maximum).

SNIPING: A PRIMER

Sniping is accomplished by delaying one's bid until the closing seconds of the auction. Rather than specify a maximum bid early in the auction period and let eBay's proxy bidding software raise it, as necessary, to maintain his spot as top bidder, the sniper strikes without warning, his identity and interest in the item concealed until the closing seconds of the auction. The practice is called *sniping* (and the persons who engage in it *snipers*) because it bears a rough resemblance to the work of military snipers—sharpshooters who lie in wait, taking out targets who, if the sniper does his job well, "never saw it coming."

Why Snipe?

Why not just specify one's maximum bid early in the proceedings, as eBay recommends (http://pages.ebay.com/aw/notabuse.html,

1999, quoted in Roth and Ockenfels, 2002), and ignore the auction until it is over? The answer is that by bidding early, one risks attracting the attention of other bidders. These other bidders are called *stalkers* and *nibblers.*

Stalkers. Stalking is the tactic of bidding in the auctions that others bid in, because others bid in them. Stalkers bypass auctions with no bids but participate in otherwise identical auctions where others have already bid. Thus, a stalker interested in purchasing vintage metal Josie and the Pussycats lunchboxes may bid only in lunchbox auctions that have already attracted other bidders.

In essence, stalkers engage in a form of research. Uncertain about whether a lunchbox is worth bidding on or what to bid for it, they use the presence of others in the auction and *those others'* maximum bids as a guide to what they themselves should bid on the item. Stalkers reason that if someone else is willing to bid $10 on the lunchbox, then they can in good conscience bid $11; if others are willing to bid $12, then they can bid $13; and so on. Call these stalkers, who use the willingness of anyone to bid as a reason to bid, *naive* stalkers.

Another, more discriminating form of stalking is that of bidding in auctions that *particular* others bid in, because those particular others bid in them. Imagine that the community of vintage metal lunchbox collectors is relatively small and that some among them are known to be expert in identifying more desirable (e.g., initial-issue) lunchboxes and distinguishing them from similar, but less desirable examples. An expert bidding in a lunchbox auction stands as a good indication that the lunchbox is worth bidding on.[5] Because the identities of bidders are discoverable through consulting an auction's bid history (available as a link from the auction's main page), one is often able to determine whether a known expert has bid on the item or not. Call stalkers who use the willingness of experts to bid as a reason for themselves to bid *sophisticated* stalkers.

Whether naïve or sophisticated, stalkers pose a strategic problem for early bidders. That stalkers use one's willingness to bid as a reason to bid means that bidding one's maximum price and bidding it early in an auction, as eBay recommends, raises the likelihood that one will draw responsive bids from stalkers. These bids threaten either to increase the hammer price that one pays for the item or to win the item outright for others. That is, but for the early placement of one's bid, one would either win the item at a lower price or, in the extreme case, win instead of lose.

Nibblers. Whether in conjunction with stalking or not, some bidders bid in small increments above the item's current price, usually the minimum bid (one bid increment above the current price), and continue to do so until they exceed the maximum of the top bidder, just as one does in an English (1P3G) auction. Those who bid in this manner are *nibblers*.

Nibblers typically bid multiple times in an auction. They bid until they achieve top bidder status, usually with a maximum bid that is one bid increment above the next highest bidder's maximum bid, and re-enter the auction subsequently if they are outbid, repeating the process of gaining top bidder status with a bid that barely exceeds the maximum of the previous top bidder. Thus, the nibbler's bidding strategy approximates participation in a 1P3G auction, outbidding the current top bidder by one increment only (Roth and Ockenfels, 2002).

Nibblers too pose a strategic problem for early bidders. Because nibblers, having once secured the top bidder position, bid only in response to other bidders, the early bidder who displaces a nibbler invites a responsive bid.

Sniping

Bidding early, as eBay recommends in its tips for bidders, exposes the bidder to stalking and nibbling.[6] The early bidder either loses the item to the stalker or nibbler or pays a hammer price that is a higher proportion of her maximum bid than she would have paid if the stalker or nibbler had not been attracted to the auction.

If the bidder instead delays her bid until the closing seconds of the auction, stalkers and nibblers are thwarted. The stalker lacks the time necessary to discover the bidder's presence and register a responsive bid. The nibbler lacks the time necessary to discover the bidder's presence and bid the multiple times necessary to nibble away at the high bid. Specifying the same maximum, this late bidder (the sniper) is more likely both to win and to pay a lower hammer price (Varian, 2000; Roth and Ockenfels, 2002).

This is not to say that sniping is risk-free. For by delaying her bid until the closing seconds of the auction, the sniper herself lacks the ability to reassess and rebid (which is to say, to nibble). Suppose that Charles, whose secret maximum is $10, is the top bidder at $4.25 (meaning that there is another bidder in the auction whose maximum is $4). Darcy, a sniper, delays her bid until the closing seconds. Darcy bids $8. Darcy's bid pushes the hammer price to $8.50 (one bid increment above $8) and Charles is the winner. Even if Darcy would be willing, having seen the price go to $8.50, to bid $11, by sniping she loses the ability to reassess and bid again.

So understood, sniping, like other bidding strategies, has both strengths and weaknesses. The principal strength is that the snipe bid is invulnerable to a responsive bid placed by a stalker or a nibbler. The principal weakness is that the tactic similarly denies the sniper the opportunity to place a revised bid if, e.g., her snipe bid fails to secure the top spot. This risk is similar to that assumed by the basketball team that "plays for the last shot" in the closing seconds of a tight game.

The sniper runs the additional risk that her bid will not be registered. The imperfect reliability of internet connections and of auction servers presents the risk that a bid attempted in the closing seconds of an online auction will not be registered before time expires. In their interviews with online auction participants, Ockenfels and Roth (2002) found that among those who employ the sniping tactic, a significant proportion had on at least one occasion failed to register an attempted bid before time expired:

> In a survey of 73 bidders who successfully bid at least once in the last minute of an eBay auction, 86 percent replied that it had happened at least once to them that they started to make a bid, but the auction was closed before the bid was received (Ockenfels and Roth, 2002).

Bidding Strategies

The foregoing discussion reveals that there are, in essence, three basic bidding strategies: (1) proxy bidding (bidding one's maximum price as soon as one determines one's willingness to bid), which eBay recommends; (2) nibbling (entering the minimum bid in an auction, continuing to do so until one is the top bidder, and repeating the process if one is displaced as top bidder); and (3) sniping (placing one's bid, usually a maximum, in the closing seconds of the auction).[7] The important strengths and weaknesses of each strategy are summarized in Table 10.1.

Sniping Ethics

Some eBay auction participants and their sympathizers complain loudly and bitterly about sniping. eBay's discussion forums are awash in messages decrying the practice and offering proposals for reform. In a message to auction-watch.com, disgruntled auction participant Barry Goldberg complained that sniping "essentially preys on the ignorance of other bidders and contributes to a general sense of unfairness and unpleasantness at eBay" (Quoted in Bedell, 2000). In an open memorandum to eBay, computer columnist David Coursey complained about being sniped and requested that eBay adopt measures to punish snipers and benefit bidders who had placed earlier bids or held the top-bidder position for longer (http://kewlstuff.editthispage.com/stories/storyReader$195, 2002). IronPlanet, a B2B online auction site devoted to the sale of used heavy construction

TABLE 10.1   Strengths and Weaknesses of Bidding Strategies

	Proxy bidding	*Nibbling*	*Sniping*
Strengths	Bidder either wins at or below price she is happy to pay or loses at a price she is happier not to pay.	Bidder always knows exactly what she will pay if she wins.	Invulnerable to stalking and nibbling. If high bid, then winning bid.
Weaknesses	Vulnerable to stalking and nibbling.	Time-consuming. Requires constant attention to auction. If others recognize top bidder as nibbler, easy to determine the bid needed to outbid the nibbler.	If not high bid, no opportunity to reassess and re-enter auction. Risk of failing to enter bid before time expires.

machinery, makes a commitment to stop snip-ing an explicit part of its code of ethics and adopts closing rules that preclude sniping:

> IronPlanet's Code of Ethics: In order to build a reliable, secure and trusted marketplace, we maintain the following guidelines: [. . .] 2. No sniping. IronPlanet prevents "sniping" by only ending auctions after a five-minute period of inactivity. Any bid placed within that period extends the auction another five minutes. Auctions can be extended multiple times until there is a total period of five minutes without bidding activity (http://www.ironplanet.com/help/faqs_selling.shtml, 2002).

Amazon, while not referring specifically to the ethics of sniping, tailors its closing rules and its advice for bidders to those who are bothered by sniping:

> We know that bidding can get hot and heavy near the end of many auctions. Our Going, Going, Gone feature ensures that you always have an opportunity to challenge last-second bids. Here's how it works: Whenever a bid is cast in the last 10 minutes of an auction, the auction is automatically extended for an additional 10 minutes from the time of the latest bid. This ensures that an auction can't close until 10 minutes have passed with no further bids. The bottom line? If you're attentive at the end of an auction, you'll always have the opportunity to challenge a new bidder (http://www.amazon.com/exec/obidos/tg/browse/-/537850/qid=1014783710/sr=1-1/104-2469150-4326361, 2002).

Proposals for discouraging sniping range from the feasible to the absurd.[8] The most basic of these is the *automatically-extended* (AE) auction format—the format adopted by IronPlanet, Amazon, and many others. In the AE auction, any bid registered in the last m minutes of the auction extends the auction by n minutes, any bid in the extension period triggers a further extension, and so on until an extension period passes with no bids.

In an AE auction, bidding in the closing seconds extends the auction and affords other bidders an opportunity to place responsive bids

TABLE 10.2   Auction Formats Offered by the Major Online Auction Sites

	2PHC	2PAE
Amazon		*
eBay	*	
Yahoo![a]	*	*

[a] Auction format is determined by the seller of the item.

(which bids themselves extend the auction still further). As such, an AE auction approximates a 3G auction insofar as both are likely to end when all bids have been exhausted. It is not surprising, therefore, that Amazon refers to its AE format as its "Going, Going, Gone feature" in the quoted passage above. The auction formats offered by the three major, consumer-oriented online auction sites (Amazon, eBay, Yahoo!) are represented in Table 10.2.

AE and other auction mechanisms may, with varying degrees of success, discourage sniping, but offering proposals for reform presupposes that there exists a reason for the reform. The case against sniping, as it exists in internet discussion forums and journalistic accounts, is a jumble of emotional appeals, name-calling, *ad hominem* attacks, claims about what is in the best interests of eBay as a business, claims about the character of those who engage in sniping, and the like. Generally, it is just assumed or, what is much the same, claimed to be obvious or self-evident that sniping is harmful or wrong.

Although anti-snipers fail to articulate coherently the harm that flows from sniping, it does not follow that sniping is innocuous. Therefore, the present task is that of constructing a plausible account of sniping's harm. The usual and probably the most plausible claim is that sniping is *unfair* in some way to those who are sniped. One must be certain, however, to unpack this notion carefully and to specify what is the source of the unfairness claimed and what about sniping is unfair. I consider these in turn.

The Ethics of Auction Participation and the Ethics of Auction Hosting

One avenue of approach is to focus on snipers themselves. The claim that sniping is unfair can be advanced as part of the *ethics of auction participation*. Most online discussions of sniping have this claim as a backdrop, whether explicit or implicit. Thus, critics of sniping claim that it is unsporting, that snipers deviate from an unwritten but widely adhered-to code of practice that informs the great bulk of online auction participants.[9]

This understanding of the ethics of online auction participation, however, would seem to wreck itself on the rocks of eBay rules. As a matter of online auction participation, sniping is straightforwardly fair: A snipe bid is a bid placed during the auction period, the same as any other. eBay rules permit and count any bid placed during the auction period. Therefore, a snipe bid is fair.

The more sophisticated anti-sniper does not deny the force of this argument, but rather claims that it misses the point of the claim that sniping is unfair: It is not that *sniping is unfair* under eBay rules, but that *eBay rules are unfair* to the extent that they permit, encourage, or reward sniping. Here, the claim that sniping is unfair is advanced as part of the *ethics of auction hosting*. Rather than a claim about the ethics of auction participation, and so not a part of business ethics, this claim is one about the ethics of transaction hosting (of which auction hosting is a part), a form of business practice.

The distinction is an important one, explicated in detail by Rawls (1955). To observe that sniping is fair under the rules of eBay is to claim merely that sniping is fair *under a practice*—the practice constituted by the rules of eBay auctions. It is not to claim that *the practice itself* is fair. Our sophisticated anti-sniper seeks a change in eBay rules that afford an advantage to sniping as a bidding strategy because the rules themselves are unfair.

What about Sniping Is Unfair?

Usually, when one claims that an action, a rule, or a practice is unfair one means either of two things:

1. *The action, rule, or practice affords someone an advantage unavailable to others because those others are formally barred or otherwise precluded from availing themselves of it.*

Thus, e.g., it would be unfair to permit motorists whose cars bear Policemen's Benevolent Association (PBA) bumper stickers to exceed the speed limit while enforcing the speed limit against others. Exceeding the speed limit with impunity affords the advantage of more speedy arrival at one's destination and that advantage is denied to those who lack PBA bumper stickers.

2. *Although the advantages of the action, rule, or practice can be made available to all, making them available to all would be harmful or wrongful such that all are better served if the advantages are available to none than if they are available to all.*

Thus, e.g., it would be intolerable to permit all motorists to exceed the speed limit (whether or not their cars bear PBA bumper stickers) because that would undermine road safety.

The first sense of unfairness is informed by a widely-held intuition about *distributive justice:* Advantages made available to some ought not to be denied to others absent a compelling reason or justification (e.g., need, merit). The second sense of unfairness is informed by an intuition about the proper *content* of morality that finds expression in a number of ethical theories. This second sense is expressed, e.g., in Kantian ethics through the Categorical Imperative, which demands that one "act only on the maxim through which you can at the same time will that it be universal law" (O'Neill, 1990, quoting Kant, 1953). Whether an advantage ought to be denied to all or denied to none depends in part upon the character of the advantage under consideration.

Distributive justice. Sniping is not unfair by reference to distributive justice. Although sniping does afford the sniper certain advantages over non-snipers (in particular, nibblers), those advantages are available to all, if only they will snipe. No bidder is precluded from sniping, so the claim that the opportunity to snipe constitutes an unfair advantage afforded to some (snipers) and denied to others (non-snipers) is false.

Some anti-snipers claim that sniping is nonetheless unfair in this way because it *precludes other bidders from bidding in response to the sniper's bid.* This is in one, trivial sense true and in another, more important sense false.

Trivially, it is true that a bid placed in the closing seconds of an online auction precludes the placing of a bid specifically in response to it. That is, one cannot recognize a snipe bid and bid subsequently.

More importantly, however, the proxy bidding system permits bidders to *anticipate* snipe bids (and other bids) and to enter a bid at the price at which one would wish to counter it. Unlike an English auction, bids registered "against oneself" (i.e., bids Ernesto places when Ernesto is the top bidder) do not raise the current price and so do not work to one's disadvantage. Therefore, because of the 2P pricing rule and the availability of proxy bidding, anyone willing to bid q in response to a sniper ought to be willing to enter a proxy bid of q at any time during the auction, regardless of whether or when anyone else has bid.[10]

The Content of Morality

Kant's Categorical Imperative demands that one act only in a manner that one would will that all others act, i.e., as a universal law. One ought not to choose courses of action that one would not willingly make available equally to others. An important intuition informing the Categorical Imperative is that of *moral equality.* One may not regard one's own as a special case merely because it is one's own.

Another intuition, more relevant for present purposes, is that one ought not to will intolerable courses of action and that *one test of* intolerability is the character of the state of affairs that would obtain if a particular course of action were adopted universally. The Categorical Imperative calls upon moral agents deliberating about alternative courses of action to assess each by reference to a thought experiment motivated by a familiar question: *What if everyone did that?* In the instant case, that familiar question takes this form: *What if all bidders sniped?*

If all bidders snipe, the auction process is identical to that which would obtain in a *second-price, sealed-bid* (2PSB) auction. All bid in ignorance of the existence and identity of other bidders. As (i) a 2PHC auction in which all bidders snipe is in all relevant particulars identical to a 2PSB auction, (ii) a 2PSB auction is but one version of a sealed-bid auction, and (iii) neither the sealed-bid auction format nor the second-price mechanism is morally intolerable, it follows by parity of reasoning and by operation of the Categorical Imperative that sniping (iv) is something that a rational moral agent could will as a maxim, and therefore, (v) is not unfair in the second sense.[11]

Auction Structure

The parallels between 2PHC auctions and sealed-bid auctions are interesting to pursue. Widespread sniping transforms the bulk of the auction period into an inspection period. This is interesting because, far from showing that widespread sniping circumvents the intentions of eBay, it seems to illustrate why eBay auctions are structured as multi-day events (three-, five-, seven-, or ten-day auctions, at the option of the seller).

It is not that items will necessarily incite a multi-day bidding war (although, if they do, this works to the advantage of the seller and, by extension, of eBay), but that over time potential bidders will *discover* the auction, *research* the item, *question* the seller, and then, armed with the necessary information to make an informed bid, *enter* the auction. That eBay places "ask seller a question" links on each auction page suggests that the bulk of an auction's duration is regarded as an inspection period. Indeed, eBay explicitly encourages potential bidders to ask questions of the seller, research the seller's feedback profile (which indicates whether the seller's past transactions have gone well or poorly), and to be as informed as possible about the item up for bids before placing a bid.[12]

Whereas a bricks-and-mortar auction devotes discrete time periods to publicity, to inspection, and to bidding, in an eBay auction these run concurrently. Auction periods are sufficiently long to permit discovery of the auction (the publicity phase), information gathering about the item on auction (the inspection phase), and bidding on the item (the auction phase). Moreover, structuring the auction as a multi-day event permits each potential bidder to determine how much time she devotes to information gathering.

The benefits flowing from this auction structure render implausible the claim of some anti-snipers, e.g., Coursey, that early bidders ought to have some sort of priority in determining who wins. Presumably, those who enter (and lead) an auction earliest have researched the item the least. Structuring auctions so that they assign priority to those who have led the bidding the longest would have the perverse effect of *discouraging* information gathering and thereby of increasing the incidence of post-auction disputes between sellers and buyers over issues of quality, defects, wear, etc.[13]

Given that sniping is (i) available to all, (ii) morally innocuous, and (iii) countered in an agreeable way by proxy bidding, the important remaining question is this: *Why are some people resistant to employing the proxy-bidding system or, in the alternative, to engaging in sniping?*

Another Complaint, a Genuine Problem

An answer to the foregoing question is perhaps not difficult to find. Common among the complaints registered by anti-snipers is that sniping is not the way people bid in "real" auctions. "Real" auctions are those with 3G closing rules, like the familiar English auction. Whereas nibblers play by the rules of "real" auctions, snipers do not. Nibblers are resistant to sniping (and, indeed, to proxy-bidding) because that would mean participating in online auctions in a manner that is further removed from, rather than closer to, "real" auctions.

The important observation to make about the claim that snipers are failing to play by the rules of "real" auctions is this: If the anti-sniper recognizes that eBay auctions are not, by his standards, "real" auctions and it is important to him to participate in a "real" auction, then the obvious remedy would be to avoid participating in eBay auctions. There are many other venues at which one may participate in auctions with rules that more closely approximate what the anti-sniper calls a "real" auction, some of which (e.g., Amazon) are online.[14]

Of course, this response depends critically upon the anti-sniper *recognizing that eBay auctions are not conducted by the auction rules with which he is most familiar*. To see the importance of this point, consider an analogous case:

Suppose that Luckless Larry's Casino has a poker room in which is played an atypical but not implausible version of five-card stud. In each hand, each player has the option of having her hand dealt with one concealed (*hole*) card (i.e., she receives one card down and four cards up), or two hole cards (i.e., she receives one card down, three cards up, and one card down). Some players, recognizing the strategic advantages afforded by an additional hole card, choose to take two. Others, convinced that it is not "real" five-card stud unless one has only one hole card, choose to take only one. Predictably, over time two hole card players win more hands and more pots than do one hole card players. One hole card players, rather than adopting the available two hole-card strategy, deride two hole card players as cheats and scoundrels. They insist that Luckless Larry's is morally obligated to convert its five-card stud tables to one-hole-card-only rules.

There are many things one may wish to say about this case, but among them is not that Luckless Larry's is obligated to convert its five-card stud tables to one-hole-card-only rules. Presumably, the careful observer would wish to say two things. First, to the extent that one hole card players recognize the rules, the availability of a second hole card under those rules, and the advantages that it affords, then those players ought to adopt the two hole card strategy or not play. Second, to the extent that one hole card players *do not* recognize the rules, the availability of a second hole card under those rules, or the advantages that it affords, then perhaps Luckless Larry's is duty-bound to take some steps to *inform* or to *educate* players about the rules and their implications.[15]

As it is for Luckless Larry's, so too for eBay. Although there is no justification for holding that eBay is duty-bound to abandon the 2PHC auction format in favor of another (e.g., 2PAE) that discourages sniping, the existence of the controversy and of not insignificant numbers of bidders who bid in 2PHC auctions *as if* they were 1P3G auctions suggests the possibility that some bidders may be unaware of the auction format. Auction data gathered and analyzed by Ockenfels and Roth (2002) reveal that the propensity to snipe is positively correlated with bidder experience and, more importantly, that the propensity to bid multiple times in the same auction is correlated with a *lack* of experience. This may suggest that some bid in 2PHC auctions as if they were 1P3G auctions because they do not recognize that they are participating in 2PHC auctions. To the extent that this is true, eBay may be duty-bound to inform or to educate players about the rules and their implications.

Whether duty-bound or not, there can be little doubt that eBay has made considerable efforts to inform and to educate both bidders and sellers about the rules of eBay auctions and their implications. eBay's site is laden with tips for bidders, answers to frequently asked questions, online help, and discussion forums in which bidding strategies and other aspects of the auction process are addressed in considerable detail. Thus, if there is anything that ought morally to be done about the sniping controversy, the most reasonable conclusion is that eBay is already doing it.

Although it may be correct to observe that sniping "essentially preys on the ignorance of other bidders [...]" (Goldberg, quoted in Bedell, 2000), to make that observation is merely to raise the question of what, if anything, ought to be done about it. In the present case, as in Luckless Larry's Casino, seeking to eliminate the ignorance is far more reasonable than seeking to eliminate the tactics that profit from it.

CONCLUSION

The applied ethicist is generally called upon to lend his knowledge, experience, and analytical rigor to matters of genuine moral controversy; to moral dilemmas that afford no easy solution. An at least equally important service the applied ethicist can provide, however, is that of employing the same knowledge, experience, and analytical rigor to show that cases or controversies *thought* to include important moral dimensions really do not. In the sniping controversy anti-snipers have a *position*, but they don't have a *point*.

The interesting question raised by the debate over sniping is not "Is sniping ethical?" but "What does the existence of anti-snipers tell us about online auctions with second-price, hard-close rules?" The answer is that, at least for those auctions that attract both snipers and bidders who would have bid in response to them had the clock not run out, money is being left on the table—money that would otherwise go to sellers and, by extension, to eBay. Therefore, one wonders why *sellers* register no complaints with eBay and why there is no exodus of sellers from eBay (2PHC) auctions to Amazon (2PAE) or Yahoo! (2PHC or 2PAE, at the option of the seller) auctions.

ACKNOWLEDGEMENT

This paper was presented at the 2002 Society for Business Ethics Annual Meeting in Denver and at the Markkula Center for Applied Ethics, Santa Clara University. My thanks to John Boatright, Dennis Moberg, Michael Scripps, Manuel Velasquez, and Spencer Waller for challenging and helpful comments on an earlier draft.

NOTES

1. So-called because the end of an English auction is typically marked by a gaveling, or "hammering down" of the auction.
2. Bid increments are determined by the current price of the auction. For instance, if the current price of an eBay auction is between $1 and $5, the bid increment is $0.25—meaning that the minimum bid one must enter to participate in the auction is $0.25 over the current price. Current prices and their associated bid increments are (http://webhelp.ebay.com/cgi-bin/eHNC/showdoc-ebay.tcl?docid=445&queryid=bid_increment, 2002):

Current Price	Bid Increment
$0–$1	$0.05
1–5	0.25
5–25	0.50
25–100	1.00
100–250	2.50
250–500	5.00
500–1000	10.00
1000–2500	25.00
2500–5000	50.00
5000+	100.00

3. The opening bid is discretionary, determined by the seller.
4. If a subsequent bidder bids exactly $3 (which is possible because Alice's maximum is secret and bidders are required only to place a bid that exceeds the current price by one bid increment), Alice remains the high bidder, at $3, because eBay rules provide that for equivalent bids those placed earlier defeat those placed later.
5. Bajari and Hortaçsu (2003) argue that this phenomenon is an important factor in explaining late bidding (sniping).
6. Which may be why eBay recommends it. Facilitating bid-stalking raises the hammer price, making more money for the seller and for eBay, which collects from sellers both a listing fee (based on the opening bid) and a commission (based on the hammer price).
7. Stalking is not a basic bidding strategy, but instead one that is practiced in conjunction with one of the basic ones. Thus, there may be stalker-proxy bidders, stalker-nibblers, and stalker-snipers.
8. For an exhaustive (and biting) discussion of the often hilarious proposals and the vicissitudes of the sniping debate, see http://members.cox.net/cruenti/ebay/solutions.html (2003).
9. Ockenfels and Roth (2002) found that, in fact, sniping is widely practiced and, in some auction categories, upwards of 40 percent of the bids placed in auction are placed in the last 5 minutes of the auction period.
10. That among anti-snipers posting in eBay forums this is the most common claim advanced for why sniping is unfair tells one something important about the bidding strategies employed by the anti-snipers: they are nibblers.

11. Interestingly, in eBay forums some anti-snipers propose sealed-bid auctions as the appropriate anti-sniping reform. They seem not to have recognized that if everyone snipes, 2PHC auctions essentially become 2PSB auctions. Indeed, bidding early in a 2PHC auction is virtually the equivalent of placing a bid in a sealed-bid auction and publicizing the fact to other potential bidders.

12. Each eBay auction page contains a text box bearing the following advice:

    "How to Bid

    1. Register to bid—if you haven't already. It's free!

    2. Learn about this seller—read feedback comments left by others.

    3. Know the details—read the item description and payment & shipping terms closely.

    4. If you have questions—contact the seller [eBay ID of seller] *before* you bid.

    5. Place your bid!"

13. Presumably, fairness demands that those who bid late *earnestly* (i.e., those who discover an auction only in its closing minutes) and place the highest bid ought to win the auction. Therefore, proponents of rules giving priority to early bidders encounter two challenges, one practical and one theoretical. The practical challenge is that of distinguishing earnest from strategic late bidders (i.e., snipers). The theoretical challenge, of course, is that of providing an account of why strategic late bidders warrant different treatment.

14. Moreover, even if there were not other venues with 3G or 3G-like rules, absent an account of why auctions structured in other (e.g., HC) ways are morally deficient there seem no legitimate grounds for complaint.

15. Many casinos, recognizing the likelihood that some newcomers may not recognize that some games

(e.g., blackjack, craps) are played by rules different from those depicted in television or film, offer classes to familiarize newcomers with the rules (and the etiquette) of gaming. Whether they do this out of sense of moral obligation or as a marketing tool is less important for present purposes than the fact that they have recognized a need (of whatever origin) to educate participants.

REFERENCES

Bajari, P. and A. Hortaçsu: 2003, 'Winner' Curse, Reserve Prices, and Endogenous Entry: Empirical Insights from Ebay Auctions,' *Rand Journal of Economics* 34(2), in press.

Bedell, D.: 2000, '"Snipers" draw ire of auction site fans,' *Dallas Morning News*, December 5. [Accessed: http://www.dougbedell.com/sniping.html, February 26, 2002.]

Kant, I.: 1953, *Groundwork of the Metaphysic of Morals*, H. Paton, trans. (Hutchinson, London).

Ockenfels, A. and A. Roth: 2002, 'The Timing of Bids in Internet Auctions: Market Design, Bidder Behavior, and Artificial Agents,' *Artificial Intelligence Magazine* (Fall), 79–87.

O'Neill, O: 1990, 'Kantian Ethics,' in P. Singer (ed.), *A Companion to Ethics* (Blackwell, Oxford).

Rawls, J.: 1955, 'Two Concepts of Rules, ' *The Philosophical Review* 64, 3–13.

Roth, A. and A. Ockenfels: 2002, 'Last-Minute Bidding and the Rules for Ending Second-Price Auctions: Evidence From Ebay and Amazon Auctions on the Internet,' *American Economic Review* 92(4), 1093–1103.

Varian, H.: 2000, 'Economic Scene: Online Users as Laboratory Rats,' *New York Times*, November 16.

Leadership

In the final section, we return to the primary questions of this text: Why is it so hard for businesses to do the right thing? Why is it so hard to be ethical? We are convinced that without committed ethical leadership, ethical standards will not be established, maintained, and retained in the life of any organization. Ethical standards and values can originate anywhere within an organization, but without the backing, encouragement, and support of leadership, the best intentions and ideas more often than not wither on the vine.

The ethics of all forms of leadership—good or bad, positive or negative—affect the ethos of the workplace and thereby help form the ethical choices and decisions of the workers themselves. Leaders set the tone, develop the vision, and shape the behavior in the organization. The critical point to understand here is—like it or not—business and politics serve as the metronome for our society. The meter and behavior established by leaders set the pattern and provide the model for the behavior of others. Although the terms *business ethics* and *moral leadership* are technically separate, they're practically connected.

An age-old principle underlies this thesis regarding leadership and ethical conduct. In his *Nicomachean Ethics,* Aristotle suggested that one cannot learn morality simply by reading a treatise on virtue. The spirit of morality, said Aristotle, is awakened in the individual only through the behavior and conduct of a virtuous person. In claiming that workers and followers derive their models for ethical conduct from the action of leaders, we in no way deny that workers and followers are responsible for the overall conduct and culture of an organization. The aim is not to exonerate followers but to explain the process involved. The actions of leaders both communicate the ethics of our institutions and establish the standards and expectations of the leaders. Although it would be naive to assert that employees simply and unreflectively absorb the manners and mores of the workplace, it would be equally naive to suggest that they are unaffected by those same manners and mores. Work is how we spend our lives, and the lessons learned in the workplace play a part in the development of our moral perspective and how we formulate ethical choices. Many business ethicists believe that without the intervention of effective moral leadership, we are doomed forever to wage a rearguard action. Students of organizational development are never really surprised when poorly managed, badly led businesses end up doing unethical things.

This final section offers cases and essays that both positively and negatively support the thesis that, for good or ill, leadership directly influences the conduct and character of organizational life. The first two essays, "Leadership: An Overview" and "The Call of Leaders," offer a working definition of and theoretical perspective on the roles, rights, and responsibilities of leaders and the function of leadership. "Ethics: Take It from the Top" and "Moral Mazes" wind up arguing for the same thesis: Leaders influence and sometimes dictate the standards, values, and behavior of organizations—but with radically different outcomes. "Ways Women Lead" offers some interesting and provocative insights into the differences between men and women in leadership roles. "Not a Fool, Not a Saint" and "Malden Mills: When Being a Good Company Isn't Good Enough" tell the story of Aaron Feuerstein and Maiden Mills, celebrating the difficulties, discipline, integrity, and commitment it takes to do the right thing. "Merck and Roy Vagelos" tells of Merck's remarkable history of developing and giving away lifesaving but unprofitable drugs.

Essay

Leadership: An Overview

Al Gini

INTRODUCTION

In 1948, Chester Barnard, noted management scholar, wrote that research in "leadership has been the subject of an extraordinary amount of dogmatically stated nonsense."[1] In 1978, the dean of modern leadership studies, James MacGregor Burns, put it slightly more charitably when he wrote: "Leadership is one of the . . . least understood phenomena on earth."[2]

The sting and the irony of this criticism is even more painful when you consider that no other topic in the behavioral sciences has been more studied and more written about than leadership.[3] Ralph Stogdill and Bernard Bass, in their separate and combined works, itemized and analyzed some 4,725 studies of leadership prior to 1981; and a recent study claims that, not counting magazine and newspaper articles, there were 132 books published on leadership during the 1980s alone.[4]

The problem then is not a lack of research, but rather a lack of agreement on fundamentals. As one wag has put it: "Next to economic theory never has so much been written on the same topic—resulting in so little agreement on the most elemental propositions in the field."

Joseph C. Rost, in his important book *Leadership for the Twenty-First Century*, claims that the problem is rock-bottom basic. The field of leadership studies lacks definitional clarity and consensus regarding its two most primary terms: "leadership" and "leader(s)."

Rost claims that most leadership scholarship has been a mishmash of mythology, mistakes, and misunderstanding.[5] Of the 587 books, chapters and articles (written between 1900 and 1989) Rost researched in preparation for his text, only 221 of them gave a definition of leadership. The other 366 offered no definition, either, he claims, because they assumed knowledge on everyone's part or because they feared that an explicit definition would be proven wrong. Moreover, said Rost, of the 190 definitions offered, most did not distinguish leadership from the numerous other social processes which human beings use to coordinate, direct, control, and govern others. And worse still, all of them, after analysis, can be reduced to the equation: "Good Leadership is equal to Good Management." (What Rost refers to as the fallacy of the "Industrial Paradigm of Leadership.") Rost contends that, for any discipline to be on solid ground and to pursue its topic in a focused manner, it must at least be able to define itself clearly.[6]

Unfortunately, even with this admonition, the problem which remains is that leadership is still conventionally defined, by scholars and laymen alike, either by the social role of leadership or by what leaders do.

According to John Gardner, leadership should never be confused with status, power, position, rank, or title.

> Even in large corporations and government agencies, the top-ranking person may simply be bureaucrat number one. We have all occasionally encountered top persons who couldn't lead a squad of seven-year-olds to the ice cream counter.[7]

Jill Graham has correctly pointed out: "Appropriate labels for the person giving orders, monitoring compliance, and administering performance-contingency rewards and punishment include 'supervisor' and 'manager,' but *not* 'leader.' "[8]

Just as leadership is not equivalent to office-holding, prestige, authority, or decision making,[9] a true and complete definition of leadership cannot be drawn simply from the personality traits and behaviors of particular leaders. Such an attempt may produce an informative biographical account of the leader in question, but may not result in any real insights into the art of leadership.

So the question remains, what is leadership and how can it be defined? I believe that leadership is a delicate combination of *the process*, the techniques of leadership, the *person*, the specific talents and traits of a/the leader, and the general requirements of the *job* itself. I am convinced that although the concept of leadership can and must be distinguishable and definable separately from our understanding of what and who leaders are, the phenomenon of leadership can only be known and measured in the particular instantiation of a leader doing a job. In other words, while the terms "leadership" and "leader" are not synonymous, the reality of leadership cannot be separated from the person as leader and the job of leadership. . . .

THE PROCESS

Leadership is a power and value laden relationship between leaders and followers/constituents who intend real change(s) that reflect their mutual, purpose(s) and goal(s).[10]

Given this definition there are a number of essential elements that must be present if leadership exists or is occurring.

Power

All forms of leadership must make use of power. However, power need not be coercive, dictatorial or punitive to be effective. Power can also be used in a non-coercive manner to orchestrate, mobilize, direct, and guide members of an institution or organization in the pursuit of a goal or series of objective.

The term "power" comes from the Latin *posse:* to do, to be able, to change, to effect. In general power is about control, the ability to produce intended effects or results. To have power is to possess the capacity to control or direct change. . . .[11]

The central issue of power in leadership is not will it used; but, rather, will it be used wisely and well? In the best of all possible worlds scenario, those who seek power should seek it out of a sense of stewardship and not for the purposes of personal aggrandizement and career advancement. The ideal model of this can be found in *The Republic* where Socrates' guardians see their office as a social responsibility, a trust, a duty and not as a symbol of their personal identity, prestige and lofty status.

Of course, the juggling act of wielding power ultimately lies in the ability to balance and integrate the natural conflict which exists between standard definitions, utopian ideals, historic necessity and the peculiar quirks and needs of the individual personalities who aspire to power.

Value Laden

I believe that Tom Peters and Bob Waterman were correct when they stated: "The real role of leadership is to manage the values of an organization."[12] All leadership is value laden. All leadership, whether good or bad, is moral leadership.

To put it more accurately, all leadership is ideologically driven or motivated by a certain philosophical perspective which may or may not prove to be moral in a more colloquial or normative sense. The point is, all leadership claims a particular point of view or philosophical package of ideas it wishes to advocate and advance. All forms of leadership try to establish the guidelines, set the tone, and control the manners and morals of the constituency of which they are a part.

Although we regularly hold up for praise the moral leadership of Lincoln, Churchill, Gandhi, and Mother Teresa; like it or not Hitler, Stalin, Hussein, and David Koresh must also be considered moral leaders of a sort!

Leaders and Followers/Constituents

One of the most common errors in leadership literature is the equation of leadership with the ability of a leader to lead.[13] Leadership, however, does not exclusively reside in the leader. Rather it is a dynamic relationship between leaders and followers alike. Leadership is always plural; it always occurs within the context of others.

E. P. Hollander has argued that while the leader is the central and often the most vital part of the leadership phenomenon, followers are important and necessary factors in the equation.

> Without responsive followers there is no leadership . . . (Leadership) involves someone who exerts influence, and those who are influenced . . . The real "power" of a leader lies in his or her ability to influence followers . . . Leadership is a process of influence which involves an ongoing transaction between a leader and followers.[14]

In fact, I believe the argument can be advanced—in partial response to the "bewhiskered question"[15] are leaders born or made?—that leaders, good or bad, great or small arise out of the needs and opportunities of a specific time and place. I believe that great leaders require great causes, great issues, and most importantly, a hungry and willing constituency. If this were not true, at least in part, would any of us have ever heard of Lech Walesa, Martin Luther King, Jr., or Nelson Mandela? "Leaders and followers," Burns wrote, "are engaged in a common enterprise; they are dependent on each other, their fortunes rise and fall together."[16]

Leaders and Followers Intend Real Change(s)

All forms of leadership are essentially about transformation.[17] Leadership is not about maintaining the status quo; it is about initiating change in an organization. Simply sustaining the status quo is equivalent to institutional stigmatism. "The leadership process," said Burns, "must be defined . . . as carrying through from decision-making stages to the point of concrete changes in people's lives, attitudes, behaviors (and) institutions . . ."[18] While the process of leadership always involves a certain number of transactional exchanges—that is, short-term changes and the trading of benefits to meet immediate and appropriate wants and needs—transformational change means the pursuit of new concrete, substantive, and not incidental changes.

Of course, while the ultimate test of practical leadership is the realization of actual change that meets people's enduring the long term needs, the real issue in the process is the Kantian one of intent.[19] Transformation is about leaders and followers *intending* real changes to happen and pursuing them actively. As John Gardner has pointed out, consequences are never a reliable assessment of leadership.[20] The quality and worth of leadership cannot be measured solely in terms of achievements. Ultimately and ethically, commitment and concerted effort are as important as outcome.

Mutual Purposes and Goals

If leadership is an active and ongoing relationship between leaders and followers, then the central requirement of the leadership process is for leaders to evoke consensus in their constituencies, and conversely, for followers to inform and influence their leadership.

"Leadership mobilizes, naked power coerces," said Burns.[21] Leadership must "engage" its followers, not merely direct them. Leaders must serve as models and mentors, not martinets. Leaders must be effective teachers and through education and the policy of empowerment make their followers "collaborators"[22] and reciprocally co-responsible in the pursuit of a common enterprise. In the end, says Abraham Zaleznik, "Leadership is based on a compact that binds those who lead with those who follow into the same moral, intellectual and emotional commitment."[23]

However, as both Bums and Rost warn us, the nature of this "compact" is inherently unequal because the influence patterns existing between leaders and followers are unequal. Responsive and responsible leadership requires, as a minimum, that democratic mechanisms be put in place which recognize the right of followers to have adequate knowledge of alternative leadership styles, goals and programs, as well as the capacity to choose between them. In leadership, writ large, mutually agreed upon purposes help people achieve consensus, assume responsibility, work for the common good and build community.[24]

THE PERSON

Given my definition of leadership and the thesis that the process of leadership cannot be separated from the person as leader, I now want to examine those traits and talents that are required of an individual if he or she is going to adequately fulfill the role of leader.

Character

In *Character: America's Search for Leadership,* Gail Sheehy argues, as did Aristotle, that character is the most crucial and most illusive element of leadership. The root of the word "character" comes from the Greek word for engraving. As applied to human beings, it refers the enduring marks, engravings, or etched-in factors in our personality which include our inborn talents as well as the learned and acquired traits imposed upon us by life and experience. These engravings define us, set us apart, and motivate our behavior.

In regard to leadership, says Sheehy, character is both fundamental and prophetic. The "issues (of leadership) are today and will change in time. Character is what was yesterday and will be tomorrow."[25] For Sheehy, character establishes both our day-to-day demeanor and our destiny. Therefore it is not only useful but essential to examine the character of those who desire to lead us. As a journalist and long time observer of the political scene, Sheehy contends that the Watergate affair of the early 1970s serves as a perfect example of the links between character and leadership. As Richard Nixon demonstrated so well: "The Presidency is not the place to work out one's personal pathology . . ."[26]

Leaders rule us, run things, wield power. Therefore, says Sheehy, we must be careful about who we chose to lead. Because who we chose, is what we shall be. If character is destiny, the destiny our leaders reap will be our own.

Charisma

While the exact role, definition, and function of a charismatic leader is the center of much controversy in the literature of leadership, I want to make a much more modest claim for the necessity of charisma in the person of the leader.

I am convinced that leadership is as much an emotional relationship between leaders and followers as it is a jural or legalistic one.[27] Whether through personality, performance, presentation, image, mind, or message, effective leaders must win-over, at a very basic human level, those they lead.

By charisma I do not mean spiritual aura, celebrity status, hypnotic powers, or even rhetorical eloquence. I mean, as a minimum, that leaders must possess enough self esteem to be seen, heard, and understood in order to engender confidence and cooperation from

their constituency. Warren Bennis in his book, *On Becoming a Leader*, offered a definition of a leader which he did not specifically refer to as charismatic, but one, I think, that nicely sums up the definition I am suggesting

> [Leaders are] People who are able to express themselves fully. They know who they are, what their strengths and weaknesses are, and how to fully deploy their strengths and compensate for their weaknesses. They also know what they want, why they want it, and how to communicate what they want to others in order to gain their cooperation andsupport.[28]

Political Ambition

Although I have argued against those that covet power for purposes of personal aggrandizement or career advancement, there must be those who seek and want power. Without ambition we are caught in the Socratic conundrum of having to force leadership on otherwise reluctant individuals by dint of mythology, prescribed duty, and the force of law.

Ambition is not necessarily bad or pathological, and political ambition need not simply be the quest for power to the exclusion of other motives. Citing the works of Abraham Maslow, Burns contends that ambition, fueled by a strong sense of self-esteem, is the most potent and beneficial motivator for those who seek power. According to Maslow, people who possess self-esteem (self-actualization) have a clearer sense of self and others, egoism and objectivity, individual and communal rights, basic and growth needs and are not threatened by ambiguity, conflict, and consensus. Self actualizes, Maslow believes, are not motivated by unfulfilled ego needs. They do not need "recognition" or to "make a mark." Rather they seek to "make a difference," by contributing to the collective whole."[29] They seek to contribute in the way that John Adams sought to contribute.

I must study politics and war, that my sons may have liberty to study mathematics and philosophy. My sons ought to study mathematics and philosophy, geography, natural history and naval architecture, in order to give their children the right to study painting, poetry, music, architecture, statuary, tapestry and porcelain.[30]

Know-How

Perhaps the most important contribution of Joseph Rost's *Leadership for the Twenty-First Century* is his thesis that leadership should not be studied solely from the perspective of a single discipline such as business leadership, educational leadership, or political leadership. Leadership studies, he claims, requires a multidisciplinary and interdisciplinary approach to fully understand and practice leadership.[31]

While I want to agree with this overall thesis, I also want to uphold the principle that leadership as practiced in a particular profession is different from leadership as practiced in other professions. In other words, while the general techniques of leadership and the qualities of the leader remain the same, the specific task requirements of leadership vary with the "business" at hand.

Leadership in different areas requires different technical expertise. To use Warren Bennis' term, leaders must possess "business literacy." That is, leaders must have knowledge of and be experts at what they are doing. They must have horizontal and vertical knowledge of how the "business" works and a full understanding of what is required to do the task well.[32]

THE JOBS OF LEADERSHIP

Lifting a page from John Gardner, I want to turn to a short list of the jobs of leadership and the leader. While individuals differ strikingly in how well they perform these various jobs, how they perform them will determine, to a large extent, how their leadership skills will be evaluated.[33]

Vision

The first and central job of leadership is that effective leaders must create and communicate a clear vision of what they stand for, what they want to achieve and what they expect from their followers. . . .

However, even though vision is central to leadership, the visions offered need not always be Nobel Prize winning accomplishments or involve Herculean efforts. For success to be possible, visions must be doable, attainable. Any task or vision—no matter how vital or important—when too large, will, more often than not, prove too overwhelming to accomplish or even attempt. At the very least, the visions of leadership must offer direction as well as hope.

Managing

Leadership and management are not the same thing. One can be a leader without being a manager. Conversely, one can manage without leading. Nevertheless, logistically these two jobs often overlap.

Abraham Zaleznick offers a reasonably neutral definition and distinction between the two terms.

> The crucial difference between managers and leaders is in their respective commitments. A manager is concerned with *how* decisions get made and *how* communications flow; a leader concerned with *what* decisions get made and *what* he or she communicates.[34]

This definition implies that leaders are involved in strategy, and that managers are more concerned with the operational side of a given enterprise. But what this definition does not imply is the all-too-common fallacy of associating the people practicing leadership with the "good guys in white hats"; and the people practicing management as the "bad guys in black hats" who are mediocre, bungling, bureaucrats, unqualified, and unsuited to lead.[35] Nor does this definition imply that management is an important but insufficient process in the operation of organizations; whereas leadership is necessary and needed at all times.

Management and leadership are two distinct and necessary ingredients in the life of every organization. Leadership is not just good management, but good management is pan of the overall job description of every leader. To turn around a quote from H. Ross Perot: "In successful organizations, both its people and its inventories are well led and well managed."[36] Moreover, given our definition of leadership as a dynamic relationship between leaders and followers, at times—leaders must manage managers, and managers must manage by leading.

Stakeholdership

Through their conduct and policy, leaders, within the context of any job, must try to make their fellow constituents aware that they are all stakeholders in a conjoint activity that cannot succeed without their involvement and commitment. Successful leadership believes in and communicates some version of the now famous Hewlett Packard motto: "The achievements of an organization arc the results of the combined efforts of each individual."

At the operational or "shop-floor" level, at least three overlapping policies must be operative in order to translate the concept of stakeholdership from theory to fact. *Participation*: Leaders must actively participate in the life of an organization. But it is not enough to just walk through the shop, say hello, and be seen. Participation means asking questions, getting

involved, spending time, and trouble shooting.[37] *Trust:* Trusting one's constituents means living out the belief that people will respond well when treated like adults. Certainly, some individuals will abuse that trust, but the hope is that most will thrive, grow, and prove more productive because of it. *Risk taking*: Successful leaders must clearly communicate that creativity and innovation are prized commodities. Therefore, autonomy and experimentation are encouraged, and, conversely, failure is tolerated and not viewed negatively. The message here should be a clear one: "Only those with confidence and ability sometimes fail. The mediocre and those who are insecure in what they are doing never dare to risk either success or failure."

Responsibility

"Leadership," said Burns, "is grounded in conscious choice among real alternates. Hence, leadership assumes competition and conflict, and brute power denies it."[38] Leaders, of whatever particular profession, do not shun conflict; they confront it, exploit it and ultimately take responsibility for the choices and decisions they are able to hammer out of it.[39]

Leaders must assume full responsibility for their choices and commitments, successes and failures. If and when they promise certain kinds of change and cannot bring about that change, they must be willing to stand down.

The final job of leadership is knowing when to go.

CONCLUSION

Leadership is never tidy. "Any attempt to describe a social process as complex as leadership inevitably makes it seem more orderly than it is."[40] Few examples neatly fit into the definitional molds we have fashioned. Nevertheless, I want to conclude my remarks with an example which, perhaps, brings together the three issues of this paper "the *Process*, the *Person*, and the *Job*."

In a recent book, *The Mask of Command*, the British war historian John Keegan argues that Alexander the Great was one of the most, if not the most, effective generals in history. Keegan's contention is based on the fact that Alexander both made the plans for battle and then literally led his troops into battle.

Keegan maintains that Alexander's men followed him, had confidence in him as well as in themselves, because Alexander shared their life and all of their risks. In many ways, said Keegan, Alexander's army was a collection of individuals who shared the same ideals and goals. They knew that their literal survival—not just financial success and career advancement—was totally dependent on the commitment and energy of their fellow worker-warriors.

For Keegan, Alexander was an heroic leader because he inspired achievement and took the risks. Alexander did not simply command or demand obedience from his men. Rather, he convinced them of his vision and lived it out with them.

Not so surprisingly, said Keegan, when, because of his many wounds. Alexander was no longer able to participate in battle and lead by example, he lost control of his army and they voted to stop their conquests, turn back, and go home.[41]

To reiterate the words of Abraham Zaleznick: "Leadership is based on a compact that binds those that lead with those who follow into the same moral, intellectual and emotional commitment."[42]

NOTES

1. C. I. Bernard: 1948, *Organizations and Management* (Harvard University Press, Cambridge), p. 80.
2. James MacGregor Burns: 1979, *Leadership* (Harper Torchbooks, New York), p. 2.
3. W. B. Bennis: 1959, "Leadership Theory and Administrative Behavior: The Problem With Authority." *Administrative Science Quarterly* 4, 259–301.
4. J. C. Rost: 1993, *Leadership for the Twenty First Century* (Praeger, Westport, CT), p. 69.
5. Rost, p. 149.
6. Rost, pp. 94, 136, 179.
7. J. W. Gardner: 1990, *On Leadership* (The Free Press, New York), p. 2.
8. J. W. Graham: 1988, "Transformational leadership: Fostering Follower Autonomy, Not Automatic Followership." In J. G. Hunt, B. R. Baliga, H. P. Crachler and C. A. Schriescheim (eds.), *Emerging Leadership Vistas* (Lexington Books, Lexington, MA), p. 74.
9. P. Selznick: 1957. *Leadership in Administration* (Row, Peterson, Evanston, IL), p. 24.
10. Rost, p. 102.
11. A. A. Berle: 1969, *Power* (Harcourt, Brace and World, Inc., New York), p. 37.
12. T. Peters. B. Waterman; 1982, *In Search of Excellence* (Harper and Row, New York), p. 245.
13. Rost, p. 43.
14. E. P. Hollander 1978, *Leadership Dynamics* (The Free Press, New York), pp. 4, 5, 6, 12.
15. Gardner, p. 6.
16. Burns, p. 426.
17. Rost, p. 123.
18. Burns, p. 414.
19. Burns, p. 461.
20. Gardner, p. 8.
21. Burns, p. 439.
22. B. Nanus: 1989, *The Leader's Edge* (Contemporary Books, Chicago), pp. 51, 52.
23. A. Zaleznik: 1990, "The Leadership Gap," *Academy of Management Executive* 4(1), 12.
24. Rost, p. 124.
25. G. Sheehy: 1990, *Character: America's Search for Leadership* (Bantam Books, New York), p. 311.
26. Sheehy, p. 66.
27. W. H. Kracke: 1978, *Force and Persuasion: Leadership in an Amazonian Society* (University of Chicago Press, Chicago), p. 34.
28. W. G. Bennis: 1989, *On Becoming a Leader* (Addison-Wesley, Reading, MA), p. 89.
29. Burns, pp. 116, 117.
30. Burns, p. 31.
31. Rost, pp. 1, 2.
32. W. G. Bennis: Sept. 7, 1992, *NPR—Marketplace* (USC Radio).
33. Gardner, p. 11.
34. Zaleznick, p. 14.
35. Rost, pp. 140, 141.

36. Rost, p. 141 (H. Ross Perot, "People cannot be man-
     aged, Inventories can be managed, but people must
     be led").
37. John McDonald: 1989, *Global Quality* (Mercury
     Books, John Piggott Lowdon).
38. Burns, p. 36.

39. Burns, p. 39.
40. Gardner, p. 22.
41. J. Keegan: 1987, *The Mask of Command* (Viking Press,
     New York).
42. Zaleznick, p. 12.

Essay

The Call of Leaders

Gary Wills

I had just turned seventeen, did not know Los Angeles, had never even driven in a big city. I had certainly never backed a swivel trailer up to a loading dock. But my father gave me a map, marked a warehouse's location, and told me to deliver a refrigerator there. I would have to get someone to help me unload it when I arrived. It was very clever of him. I knew what he was doing. But I complied anyway.

I had a chip on my shoulder, since my father had left my mother to marry a (much younger) Hollywood model. While I was in California for a high school contest, he asked me to work at his nascent business for the rest of the summer. But for that offer, I would not have stayed—I needed a job in any event. He knew that the way to recruit a resisting son-employee was to give me independence—not only in things like deliveries, but in sales and purchasing of household equipment. If I failed, that might break down my resistance. If I didn't, pride in the work might renew a bond that had been broken. Paradoxically, by giving me independence he got me to do his will. That is the way leadership works, reciprocally engaging two wills, one leading (often in disguised ways), the other following (often while resisting). Leadership is always a struggle, often a feud.

Why, after all, should one person do another person's will? The answer that used to be given is simple: the leader is a superior person, to whom inferiors should submit. But modern democracies are as little sympathetic to this scheme as I was to the authority of my father. Patriarchal society, it is true, was rooted in a radical inequality between leaders and followers. Even ancient Athens, the first western democracy, submitted to "the best man," according to Thucydides:

> [Pericles], a man clearly above corruption, was enabled, by the respect others had for him and his own wise policy, to hold the multitude in a voluntary restraint. He led them, not they him; since he did not win his power on compromising terms, he could say not only what pleased others but what displeased them, relying on their respect.[1]

Some still subscribe to that notion of leadership. How often have we heard that we lack great leaders now, the clearly virtuous kind, men like George Washington and Abraham Lincoln? The implication is that we could become great again with a great man to guide us. We would not mind submitting to anyone *that* good. (Of others we continue to be wary.)

I shall be arguing in this book that the Periclean type of leadership occurs rarely in

---

history, if at all. Scholars have questioned Thucydides' description of Pericles' position— Athenians seemed quicker than most to *ostracize* leaders who thought themselves above the people.[2] Why *should* people immolate their own needs and desires to the vision of some superior being? That has happened in some theocratic societies—but then people were obeying *God* in his representative; and it was their own belief in God's will that constrained them.

In a democracy, supposedly, the leader does not pronounce God's will to the people but carries out what is decided *by* the people. Some might object that the leader is, in this case, mainly a follower—he or she does what the community says when it "speaks" through elections, through polls, through constituent pressure. Such leaders are not, like the Pericles of Thucydides, able to displease their followers. They compromise their principles. They are bribed, if not with money, then with acceptance, or office, or ego satisfaction.

We seem stuck, then, between two unacceptable alternatives—the leader who dictates to others, or the one who truckles to them. If leaders *dictate*, by what authority do they take away people's right to direct their own lives? If, on the contrary, they truckle, who needs or respects such weathervanes?

Most of the how-to manuals on leadership assume one or other of these models—or, inconsistently, both. The superior-person model says the leader must become *worthy* of being followed—more disciplined than others, more committed, better organized. This sends aspiring leaders to the mirror, to strike firm-jawed poses, to cultivate self-confidence and a refusal to hedge.

Or the leader is taught to be ingratiating. This is the salesmanship or Dale Carnegie approach—how to win friends and influence people. It treats followers as customers who "buy" the leader's views after these have been consumer-tested and tailored to maximum acceptance.

The *followers* are, in this literature, a hazy and not very estimable lot—people to be dominated or served, mesmerized or flattered. We have thousands of books on leadership, none on followership. I have heard college presidents tell their students that schools are meant to train leaders. I have never heard anyone profess to train followers. The ideal seems to be a world in which everyone is a leader—but who would be left for them to be leading?

Talk about the nobility of leaders, the need for them, our reliance on them, raises the clear suspicion that followers are *not* so noble, not needed—that there is something demeaning about being a follower. In that view, leaders only rise by sinking others to subordinate roles. Leaders have a vision. Followers respond to it. Leaders organize a plan. Followers get sorted out to fit the plan. Leaders have willpower. Followers let that will replace their own.

We have long lists of the leader's requisites— he or she needs determination, focus, a clear goal, a sense of priorities, and so on. We easily forget the first and all-encompassing need. The leader most needs followers. When those are lacking, the best ideas, the strongest will, the most wonderful smile have no effect. When Shakespeare's Welsh seer, Owen Glendower, boasts that "I can call spirits from the vasty deep," Hotspur deflates him with the common-sense answer: "Why, so can I, or so can anyone. But will they come when you do call them?"[3] It is not the noblest call that gets answered, but the *answerable* call.

Abraham Lincoln did not have the highest vision of human equality in his day. Many abolitionists went farther than he did in recognizing the moral claims of slaves to instant freedom and something approaching a recognition of their human dignity. Lincoln had limited political goals, and he was willing to compromise even those. He knew that no one could be elected in or from Illinois if he espoused full equality for blacks—so he unequivocally renounced that position:

> I am not, nor ever have been, in favor of bringing about, in any way, the social and political equality of the white and black races . . . I am not, nor ever have been, in favor of making voters or jurors of negroes, nor of qualifying them to hold office, nor of intermarrying with white people; and I will say, in addition to this, that there is a physical difference between the white and black races which I believe will forever forbid the two races living together on terms of political and social equality. And inasmuch as they cannot so live, while they do remain together, there must be the position of superior and inferior; and I, as much as any other man, am in favor of having the superior position assigned to the white race.[4]

But for that pledge, Lincoln had no hope of winning office. The followers were setting the terms of acceptance for their leader. He could not issue calls they were unprepared to hear. (He *could* do it, of course—as Owen Glendower can shout summonses down into the deep. But it would be a waste of time.)

This Lincoln has disappointed people who think followers should submit to a leader's superior vision, those who want the leader to be active, the followers passive. Lincoln's career shows response from both sides of the process. His leadership was a matter of *mutually* determinative activity, on the part of the leader *and* the followers. Followers "have a say" in what they are being led to. A leader who neglects that fact soon finds himself without followers. To sound a certain trumpet does not mean just trumpeting one's own certitudes. It means sounding a specific call to specific people capable of response.

Docs this remove or reduce the heroic note from Lincoln's leadership—as if he were only *allowed* to lead, by followers who could withhold their response? Well, what is the alternative— people who cannot refuse to follow? If that were the case, the leader would be marshaling automatons, not voluntary respondents.

It is odd that resentment should be felt toward the demands of followers when the limiting power of *circumstance* is so readily accepted. Even the most ardent hero worshipers of Winston Churchill admit that he needed an occasion for the exercise of his skills. But for World War II, we would never have known what he could do in the way of rallying English spirit. Yet the followers are even more intimate in their cooperation with the leader than are external circumstances. The leader can have the skill for his or her role, the occasion for its use, and still lack followers who will respond to the person or the moment.

So much for the idea that a leader's skills can be applied to all occasions, that they can be taught outside a historical context, learned as a "secret" of control in every situation. A leader whose qualities do not match those of potential followers is simply irrelevant. The world is not playing his or her game. My favorite example of this is the leadership of Syrian holy men in the fifth century of the Common Era.[5] Those men, who made policy for whole communities, were revered for their self-ravaging austerity. The man who had starved himself most spectacularly was thought the best equipped to advise pious consultants. So delegations went to consult Simeon the "Stylite" (Pillar Man), perched in his midair hermitage. Leadership was entirely conditioned by the attitudes of contemporary followership. Who would now write a manual called *The Leadership Secrets of Simeon Stylites*, telling people to starve and whip and torture themselves into command positions?

Closer to our time, Thomas Jefferson thought the French Revolution had been less successful than the American one, not because the French lacked leaders but because they lacked discerning followers. A corrupt people is not responsive to virtuous leadership. The French spirit had been sapped, he claimed, by superstition (Catholicism) and despotism (monarchy). Napoleon, to retain the people's allegiance, had to revert to both, calling on the pope to crown him emperor.[6]

It may seem that the Lincoln example has moved us too far from the Periclean "best man" toward the Dale Carnegie accommodator. If the leader is just an expediter of what other people want, a "resource" for their use, the people are not being led but serviced.

But Lincoln had no clear expression of popular will to implement. He had to *elicit* the program he wanted to serve, and that always involves *affecting* the views one is consulting. Even pollsters, seeking to understand what is on the minds of people, affect the outcome by their mode of questioning. In Lincoln's constituency were some abolitionists, many defenders of slavery, many more who wanted to avoid facing the issue of slavery. Unlike the abolitionists, who were leaders of a small elite putting pressure on the government from outside, Lincoln had to forge a combination of voters who would join him in at least minimal disapproval of slavery. He had to convince some people that it was in their own interest not to let the problem fester—he told them they could not *afford* to take Stephen Douglas's "hands-off" attitude.

Many voters resisted Lincoln—as I did my father in the summer of 1951. Lincoln deferred to some of their prejudices—left them independent in that sense—in order to win agreement on a policy of (at least) some hope for ultimate manumission. He argued in terms of his listeners' own commitment. They celebrated the Declaration of Independence, with its claim that all men are created equal. How could they stay true to their political identity, based on the Declaration, if they did not at some level oppose slavery? By keeping this option open for gradual approximation, Lincoln was able to move at a later period for more direct action on the problem. In that sense, he temporized not to evade the problem but to *prevent* its evasion. G. K. Chesterton perfectly captured the delicacy of his operation:

> He loved to repeat that slavery was intolerable while he tolerated it, and to prove that something ought to be done while it was impossible to do it. . . . But, for all that, this inconsistency beat the politicians at their own game, and this abstracted logic proved most practical after all. For, when the chance did come to do something, there was no doubt about the thing to be done. The thunderbolt fell from the clear heights of heaven.[7]

In order to know just how far he could go at any moment, Lincoln had to understand the mix of motives in his fellow citizens, the counterbalancing intensities with which the different positions were held, and in what directions they were changing, moment by moment. This is the time-consuming aspect of leadership. It explains why great thinkers and artists are rarely the leaders of others (as opposed to influences on them). The scientist absorbed in the solution of his problems does not have the energy or patience to understand the needs of a number of other people who might be marshaled to deal with the problem. That is something the popularizer of the great man's thought usually does. More important, the pure scientist does not *tailor* his view of, say, the atom to whatever audience he hopes to influence, as Lincoln trimmed and hedged on slavery in order to make people take small steps in the direction of facing the problem.

My father was a natural leader who acted in small arenas. Even as a child, I thought it childish of him to want to get his way all the time. I did not notice then that he got his way by entering into the minds of others and finding something there that would respond to his attentions—as, on a vastly different scale, Lincoln found a grudging acceptance of the Declaration's pledge on which to build his strategy of emancipation. My father's tactics were different with me, with my sister, with the golfing friends I observed him with while caddying. There is something selfless in the very selfishness of leaders—they must see things as the followers see them in order to recruit those followers.

If the followers get marshaled toward action by a leader, the leader need not be loved or admired (though that can help). I had no great admiration for my father when I found myself responding to his initiatives. Conversely, one can admire or love people who are not, by virtue of that love, leaders.

Imagine a meeting called to consider a course of action—let us say, to mount a protest against an employer whose hiring and promotion practices discriminate against women. A speaker rises who is stunningly eloquent. Listener A knows and admires the speaker, would go anywhere to hear her speak, hopes to emulate her eloquence in his own way; but he does not care about the issue, and the speech does not bring him any closer to caring. Listener B, on the contrary, has never met the speaker, does not particularly like her, is disposed to resent the employer but had no hope of finding allies to resist him, and is now heartened to act in conjunction with others responding to the speaker. Who is the follower here? If, as seems certain, it is Listener B, then admiration, imitation, and affection are not necessary to followership. Agreement on a *goal* is necessary.

So far I have been discussing just two things—leaders and followers. That is better at least, than treatments dealing with only one thing—leaders. But the discussion cannot get far without a third thing—the goal. This is not something *added on* to the other two. It is the reason for the other two's existence. It is also the equalizer between leader and followers. The followers do not submit to the person of the leader. They *join* him or her in pursuit of the goal. My father and I were working together for the success of his new business. Of course, he had separate motives

for wanting me there, and I had motives for not wanting to be there. We could not share *those* motives, unique to our own situation. It was the thing we *could* share that created the possibility of leadership.

It is time for a definition: the leader is one who mobilizes others toward a goal shared by leader and followers. In that brief definition, all three elements are present, and indispensable. Most literature on leadership is unitarian. But life is trinitarian. One-legged and two-legged chairs do not, of themselves, stand. A third leg is needed. Leaders, followers, and goals make up the three equally necessary supports for leadership.

The goal must be *shared*, no matter how many other motives are present that are not shared. Go back to the meeting that called for a protest at employer discrimination. The speaker may have had many ancillary motives for speaking—to show off her rhetorical style, to impress a sexual partner in the audience, to launch a larger political career. Her listeners surely would have many motives—some to improve their prospects with the employer, or their regard among fellow workers. But the followers *become* followers only insofar as they agree with the speaker on a plan of action against the employer.

This plan is cast in terms of justice, though it is easy to think this is only a rationale for the mix of various motives, some shared, some not. Each is in this to get something different. David Hume, the eighteenth-century philosopher, said people obey others for their *own* advantage, and this writhing of various wormlike urges for advantage is far from the picture of idealistic leaders and docile followers.

Yet Hume, perceptive as he was, knew that people follow most reliably when they are convinced that what they are doing is right. He knew the *utility* of that belief.[8] If, at the meeting to discuss discrimination, only those who would benefit directly by the protest were to join the speaker, that would limit the followership from the outset. And that small number would always be fraying away. The boss could buy off dissent by special favors to a few of the activists, or threats to the weak-hearted. Once one person got what *she* wanted, there would be no future motive for supporting her sisters. Private advantage shifts constantly, and is a poor basis for public action. That is why Lincoln based his policy on the *moral* claim of the Declaration of Independence. Some thought he did not go far enough, others that he went too far; but the moral ground of the Declaration was both broad and narrow enough to accommodate many positions while remaining fixed itself.

Lincoln had to persuade voters. He could not force them. Where coercion exists, to the extent of its existence, leadership becomes unnecessary or impossible. Loose uses of the word "lead" can mislead. We talk of a policeman leading his prisoner to jail. But the captor is not a leader in our sense—he is a captor. Though he is mobilizing another toward a goal, it is not a goal they share in their intentions. The prisoner's goal is to get as far away from the prison as possible.

A slave master buying labor can "lead" slaves to his plantation, but that does not make him their leader. He is their owner. If I had worked for my father only because I needed the money and could get it nowhere else, I would not have been a follower, just an employee. Coercion is not leadership, any more than is mesmerism. Followers cannot be automatons. The totalitarian jailer who drugs a prisoner into confession of a crime has not *led* him to some shared view of reality.[9]

James MacGregor Burns's well-known definition of leadership, though it tries to cover all bases, is inadequate precisely because it leaves out this note of a goal *shared* by leader and followers:

Leadership over other human beings is exercised when persons with certain motives and purposes mobilize, in competition or conflict with others, institutional, political, psychological, and other resources so as to arouse, engage, and satisfy the motives of followers.[10]

Any person who *affects* others is a leader, by this definition. Hitler's enormities, let us say, arouse hatred in me, mobilize me, and that hatred is satisfying to me—am I, then, a follower of Hitler? Not when the goals of our action are so different. My aim is to destroy Hitler. That is not his aim. Hitler's followers shared, at some level, his goals—vindication of German complaints about the Versailles treaty, the restoration of discipline in society, the glorification of the German nation (and, to varying degrees, the German race) at the expense of others.

Burns's definition would cover all kinds of influence on others—a musician's arousing of pleasure in the audience, a celebrity's gratification of curiosity. A person does not become a "follower" of Bach by being aroused and satisfied. A reader of the *National Enquirer* "follows" reports on Cher or Michael Jackson, but is not a follower of them toward some shared goal. A thinker may be influenced by the philosophy of Ludwig Wittgenstein, but their wills were never consciously engaged in cooperative movement toward a goal. A fan of Madonna is not like a soldier in Joan of Arc's army. Influence is not, of itself, leadership. The weather influences us. So do earthquakes, or background music in public places.

The leader does not just vaguely affect others. He or she takes others toward the object of their joint quest. That object defines the *kind* of leadership at issue. Different types of leaders should be distinguished more by their goals than by the personality of the leader (the most common practice). The crisis of mere subsistence on a life raft calls for one type of leader. Democratic stability for another. Revolutionary activity for still a third. The compromise and flexibility of Lincoln were appropriate for his kind of leadership. But in his own time other leaders had to be quite different in their methods. General Grant could not sound out his military "constituents." William Lloyd Garrison could not temporize on principle when leading the abolitionists. Harriet Tubman, organizing raids to rescue slaves in the South, could not lead by discussion-group methods.

It is one of the major disservices of the "superman" school of leadership that it suggests a leader can command *all* situations with the same basic gifts. Businessmen study the leadership style of General Patton. People assume that Napoleon would make a good CEO—which is like assuming that he would make a good Simeon Stylites. General Grant proved that a great military commander is not necessarily, by reason of his marital success, a good political leader in an electoral democracy—as Lyndon Johnson proved that a superb Senate leader can make a poor president.

Since leadership must differ from situation to situation, it will not be treated in the book as a single thing. I have considered sixteen different *kinds* of leadership—and, of course, there are subdivisions within those. Those chosen are not the "greatest" leaders, but the ones who seemed to exemplify the distinctive type. Skills overlap from type to type, without obscuring the fact that the military leader's goal is quite different from the social reformer's. A Napoleon's leadership resembles only very distantly an Eleanor Roosevelt's. It is the goal that, in the first place, sets the type. The tactics will be affected, also, by the followers available.

It is easier to see the type when the exemplar is large in scale. Yet not every military leader can be (or should be) a Napoleon, not every politician an FDR, not every intellectual leader a Socrates. What is said about the outsize figure can be applied, *mutatis mutandis*, to

leaders in a smaller sphere. The military adjutant has something to ponder in the career of Napoleon, or the precinct worker in Roosevelt's techniques. Templates from the past can be laid over living leaders around us.

I try further to define each person I study by considering an *antitype* to him or her, one who exemplifies the same characteristics by contrast. Roger Smith shows how Perot succeeded by the way he (Smith) failed. The marketing leadership Perot had is made clearer by considering its lack in Smith. For both types and the antitypes I do not offer brief biographies. Only the aspects of their careers that exemplify the stated kind of leadership (or its lack) will be emphasized. Thus Napoleon's military career is considered apart from his legislative and imperial politics.

Most important, I hope that readers will keep in mind the different types of *followers* appropriate to historically conditioned goals. Not many of us will be leaders; and even those who are leaders must also be followers much of the time. This is the crucial role. Followers judge leaders. Only if the leaders pass that test do they have any impact. The potential followers, if their judgment is poor, have judged themselves. If the leader takes his or her followers to the goal, to great achievements, it is because the followers were capable of that kind of response. Jefferson said the American people responded to revolution in a way that led to a free republic, while the French responded to their revolution in a way that led to an imperial dictatorship. The followers were as much to blame for the latter development as was Napoleon. In the same way, the German people were jointly responsible for Hitler's atrocities. He was powerless to act without followers.

Show me your leader, and you have bared your soul. You respond only to one who has set certain goals. You are responsible for that activity, for motion toward those goals. If leadership is mysterious and often scary, so is followership. That is why some would prefer not to follow at all. At the dawn of the ancient Greek achievement, Hesiod had already identified the problem with people who will neither lead nor follow:

> The best is he who calls men to the best.
> And those who heed the call are likewise blessed.
> But worthless who call not, heed not, but rest.[11]

Some people lament a current lack of leaders, implying that they would become wonderful followers if only some leader worthy of them came along. But perhaps they have not been looking very hard. Others think that if the president is not a leader to their liking, the whole national scene is empty. But, throughout our history, the great leaders have not been only or mainly in the White House. Except in time of war or other crisis, a democratic leader is usually a reconciler of voting blocs rather than a leader of embattled causes. Resisted change has been accomplished by abolitionists, suffragists, labor organizers, civil rights defenders, antiwar activists.

In our own day, vast changes have been taking place, with strong leaders on both sides of each issue. Dr. King led the integration struggle, and George Wallace opposed it, with great skill. No social change has been more vast than that of women's place in society. Leaders on one side, like Gloria Steinem and Faye Wattleton, have been met and resisted by a Phyllis Schlafly or a Beverly LaHaye. The environmental movement, the consumer movement, the gay rights movement have had devoted leaders, and devoted opposition. Randall Terry and his followers have been inventive and determined in their opposition to abortion. A Ralph Nader on the left faces a leader on the right like William F. Buckley. We do not lack leaders. Various trumpets are always being sounded. Take your pick. We lack sufficient followers. That is always the real problem with leadership. Calls are always going down into the vasty deep; but what spirits will respond?

Essay

Ethics: Take It from the Top

Maynard M. Dolecheck and Carolyn C. Dolecheck

"History teaches us that no free society or free economy can long survive without an ethical base. It is only through a shared moral foundation—a set of binding rules for fair conduct—that free associations, be they social, diplomatic, or commercial, can flourish and endure. Far from being a luxury, a sound business ethic is essential to preservation of free enterprise."[1]

Few in the business community would disagree with the foregoing statement by William Simon, businessman and former U.S. Secretary of the Treasury. However, the problem of unethical business practices needs to be periodically reviewed, interpreted, and

---

analyzed. Therefore, this article discusses unethical business practices and suggests steps business executives might take to reduce or alleviate such practices.

SCALE OF ETHICAL/UNETHICAL PRACTICES

Ethical/unethical business practices can be viewed on a scale from Highly Ethical to Highly Unethical as shown in Exhibit 1. Practices to the left of Point A on the scale represent unethical actions, while practices to the left of Point B represent not only unethical but illegal actions. A gray area exists as to whether a practice is ethical or unethical, since different individuals may locate Point A differently on the scale. Most individuals, however, agree that Point A is to the right of Point B. In other words, business practices occur which are unethical but not illegal. Such agreement was confirmed by the authors' 1986 study of business persons employed in the southern United States; 89% of those responding thought that business ethics is more than operating a business organization in such a way as to stay within the law.[2]

This example of a business practice that would fall into the gray area of ethical/unethical was reported in the 6 January 1988 *Wall Street Journal*: The Best Western Hotel in Winter Park, Florida, charges guests daytime long-distance rates 24 hours a day without informing the guests; the hotel then pockets the difference between what the telephone company charges and what the guest pays. When the general manager was asked about the practice, his reply was, "There's nothing in the Florida law that requires us to (inform the guests), so we don't."[3]

In this case the manager apparently believes that Points A and B coincide on the ethical/unethical scale and therefore the practice is ethical. One could even argue that use of the telephone is no different from the hotel's buying soft drinks for $0.25 and selling them to its guests for $2.00. Therefore, the practice in question is ethical. However, most people would argue that the practice is unethical because the hotel does not inform the guests that it is charging daytime rates at all times; guests probably assume they are paying night rates for nighttime calls and thus they are being misled.

SERIOUS PROBLEM OF UNETHICAL PRACTICES

Conceding that some business practices fall into a gray area of ethical/unethical, the apparent frequency of unethical practices indicates a serious and continuing problem facing American business organizations. Reporters and commentators have publicly exposed business wrongdoing with seemingly ever-greater frequency. During the 1970s, the media focused on illegal activities involving

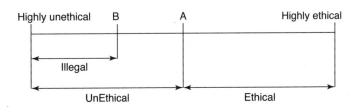

Exhibit 1:   Scale of ethical/unethical practices

political contributions; discrimination due to age, sex, and race; lack of concern for workers' and the public's health and safety; mishandling of pension funds; and bribing of foreign officials. During the 1980s, the media has concentrated on flagrant abuses of financial information, overcharging the government for military supplies, and mislabeling of products. *Time* magazine recently stated, "While common street crime costs the United States an estimated $4 billion/year in losses, white-collar lawbreaking drains at least $40 billion—and probably much more—from corporations and government."[4] A study by Amitai Etzioni, professor of sociology at George Washington University, concluded that during the past ten years about two-thirds of America's 500 largest corporations have been involved in some form of illegal behavior.[5]

Managers themselves acknowledge the problem exists. A *Wall Street Journal* article on 8 September 1987 noted that one-fourth of 671 managers surveyed by a research firm believed ethics can impede a successful career and that better than one-half of all executives they know would bend the rules to get ahead.[6]

Furthermore, the general public believes that fraud, lying, and shoddy practices are typical of American business. A New York Times/CBS News Poll conducted in June 1985 revealed that 55% of the American public believe that most corporate executives are dishonest; 59% think that white-collar crime occurs very often.[7]

Most of the wrongdoing just noted is not only unethical but illegal. Illegal behavior compared to unethical, but legal, behavior is easier to document (measure) because it stems from litigation and is usually more sensational. If illegal behavior occurs as frequently as reports indicate, unethical practices that may not be illegal also occur frequently.

CHANGING ENVIRONMENT CONTRIBUTES

The frequency of unethical business practices appears to have several basic causes, but many seem to stem from changing environmental conditions. Examples are changing regulations, widespread mergers and acquisitions, rapid computerization, and increased international trade. Changing environmental conditions can result in the breaking down of established corporate cultures, widening the previously noted gray area of ethical/unethical practices, creating areas where appropriate controls are nonexistent and fostering extreme pressures to achieve organizational goals—all of which can lead to unethical behavior.

An example of changing regulations is the lessening of government intervention in business. The United States has a long history of establishing laws, regulations, and agencies for the protection of consumers, investors, employees, and the public. The current U.S. government administration and, to a lesser extent the previous two administrations, have curtailed and even dismantled many regulatory agencies. Examples are the trucking, airline, and banking industries. Deregulation may have resulted in managers feeling compelled or pressured to cut corners to compete with rivals, as the airline industry appears to have done. If media reports are true, some airlines have acted unethically, if not illegally, in an effort to compete with other airlines particularly in areas of flight delays, and the maze of ticket prices and restrictions that tend to confuse and mislead the public.

The decline in American businesses ability to compete internationally with foreign firms has added impetus to the pressures that managers perceive in order to regain lost markets. Such pressures can result in unethical actions, such as paying bribes to foreign governments.

Large business organizations, particularly those formed by mergers and acquisitions, typically decentralize by establishing profit centers as a means of control. Such profit centers can easily lead to pressures for managers to act unethically to achieve organizational goals (primarily profits). Research has shown that managers at the lower levels in an organization feel greater pressure to do this than do managers higher up.[8]

The ethical problems that business organizations are facing are analogous to ethical problems the U.S. government is currently encountering. Examples are government officials abusing Civil Service rules, misspending government money, conspiring to end enforcement actions against a client represented by a relative, participating in conflicts of interest, and using government personnel for private business. The House Subcommittee on Civil Service has compiled an index that lists 225 top administration personnel or nominees who have been the subject of allegations of ethical infractions. Whitney North Seymour who prosecuted and convicted former White House aide Michael Deaver recently stated, "Unless the attitudes of government leaders change, there is little that prosecutors can do except put a thumb in the dike."[9]

ALLEVIATING THE ETHICS PROBLEM

Realistically, unethical practices in business can never be totally eliminated—it is an imperfect world. As in government, the legal system—even with more laws and regulations—is not the answer nor is an attempt to slow environmental change. However, with appropriate management attitudes and actions, businesses can alleviate or control the problem.

Business organizations should strive to employ only individuals with integrity. Too often companies are careless about checking prospective employees' statements concerning education, military service, and accomplishments in previous jobs. Regardless of a business organization's efforts to employ only individuals with impeccable integrity, it is not always possible to perform thorough background checks.

All is not lost, however. While clichés such as "ethics is learned at home" or "once a thief—always a thief" may be partially true, attitudes of unethical individuals can be changed or at the very least held in check by an ethical business organization.

Attitudes toward ethics involve a complex set of values derived from experiences and emotions that are learned at home, church, and school as well as the many varied influences of other formal and informal groups to which one belongs. Business organizations also have a great influence on the attitudes and values systems of individuals; this is particularly true since employees spend a minimum of eight hours a day at work. In fact, those in some quarters propose that a business organization can have a conscience.[10]

To achieve a corporate conscience requires that management focus on three areas: (1) commit to the goal of ethical conduct and serve as a role model; (2) strive toward openness; and (3) establish and implement rules, policies, and procedures to achieve the goal.

Commit to Ethical Goals and Serve as a Role Model

It is mandatory that an organization as a whole—from top to bottom—make a commitment to ethical behavior; however, the commitment has to originate from the top. One study of business executives of manufacturing firms located in the Southeast found that in a listing of eight factors that could influence ethical standards, the factor selected most frequently (32.6%) was "Top management emphasis on ethical action."[11] Traditionally, mission statements of a business refer to market niches in terms of goods and services. To incorporate the relative importance of values within the organization, the mission statement should also embrace ethical behavior. Top management must then continually stress that ethical behavior is demanded and that company loyalty will not be accepted as an excuse for unethical acts. Such a philosophy must be reiterated at every level and each manager held responsible for seeing that ethical behavior occurs at all lower levels.

What management says is important, but management action is even more important. Management serves as an ethical role model; through its capacity to set highly visible personal examples of sound ethical behavior, it establishes the tone for the entire organization. Serving as an ethical role model also requires sound employee relations, such as dealing with employees in a fair and just manner, never attempting to use subordinates in such a way as to profit from their efforts without considering their welfare, and representing subordinates' points of view at higher management levels. Sound employee relations result in a climate of trust and confidence within the organization. Without such a climate, total commitment to ethical behavior cannot be attained.

The daily contact between supervisor and subordinate provides the best opportunity for integrating the top management commitment to ethical activity into everyday conduct and decision making throughout all levels of an organization. Research has shown that an individual's immediate supervisor plays a very important role in ethical/unethical behavior. In the authors' 1986 study, U.S. business personnel in the South were asked to rank by relative importance six factors contributing to unethical behavior. Behavior of superiors was ranked first, with behavior of one's peers and personal financial need ranked a distant

second and third.[12] Other studies have consistently indicated that behavior of superiors ranks first as a contributor to unethical behavior.[13] Also, in the authors' 1986 study, when asked who of eight possible individuals they consulted when faced with an ethical dilemma on the job, 42% of those responding indicated that they consulted their boss.[14] The percentage would probably have been even higher if more employees believed their bosses were ethical.

A personal example may illustrate the importance of supervisors' leading by example: Early in his career one of us worked as a management trainee for a large alcoholic beverage distillery. Shortly after he began work, it was learned that an error had been made in the selection of barrels of aged whiskey. Only whiskey aged in oak barrels for at least six years was to be bottled, since the label on the bottles indicated that it had been aged six years. But in this particular batch, about 4% of the whiskey had been aged less than six years by only one to four months. The whiskey had already been bottled but not shipped to the wholesaler when the error was detected. Retrieving all the cases and emptying each bottle by hand (the whiskey itself could have been reused in a blend) would have been very time-consuming and costly. It was the author's judgment as well as that of three other management trainees that nothing should be done since (1) only 4% of the whiskey was aged less than six years, (2) the average age of the whiskey was considerably in excess of six years, (3) research had shown that individuals cannot detect any taste difference after five years of aging in a barrel, and (4) no one except a few people within the department knew that the error had occurred.

The production foreman, however, without a second thought, ordered all bottles from the batch dumped. The gist of the foreman's comment was, "When the company states "aged six years in an oak barrel,' that's what it means."

The point was well made, and it had a profound effect on all four management trainees. Furthermore, over time it became apparent that ethical behavior consistently permeated all levels of the organization.

The performance review between supervisor and subordinate is an opportune time to emphasize the importance of discussing an ethical situation with someone—preferably the superior. Counseling with others about ethical situations in the workplace can provide perspective, understanding, and comfort. Sanford McDonnell, chairman of McDonnell Douglas Corporation, recently stated, "When you talk things out, you get a better feel for the company's value system."[15] Recently, a partner in an accounting firm knowingly approved another firm's false financial statements and is now facing a prison sentence. He stated in retrospect, "If I had sought counsel from someone that I had respect for, if I had even talked to my wife . . ."[16]

During a performance review, goals to be met by a subordinate are usually agreed on. Realistic goals must be set. If goals are too high, the temptation is to cut corners to achieve them. Certainly, setting a goal that requires effort to achieve is sound management practice, but the effort should be reasonable or the subordinate may feel the goal can be attained only through unethical practices. Supervisors must demand that ethical practices be maintained even at the expense of not achieving profit goals. During such contacts it is also important to attempt to identify situations (sometimes referred to as forward control) that may arise in pursuit of goals where ethical or legal problems are likely to occur.

Strive for Openness

Openness is essential to the establishment of mutual confidence and trust within an organization; therefore, openness must be an integral part of management's commitment to ethical conduct. Business organizations tend to be very secretive both internally and externally. Secretiveness too often enables managers to avoid responsibility for their decisions. Any decision not open for scrutiny is too often unethical. Even ethical actions and decisions that arc not open for all to see or are only partially known by others in an organization (often through the grapevine) are often perceived as unethical because not all facts and circumstances are known. False perceptions may be as detrimental to an organization as reality. Furthermore, openness allows employees to feel comfortable when speaking out and discussing ethical questions and problems. Openness encourages employees to talk freely about an organization's policies and procedures, thus reducing the gray area on the ethical/unethical scale. Optimum decisions in terms of ethics are made only after discussion and debate within an organization.

An argument can be made against openness in certain situations. For instance, performance evaluations should be strictly between a supervisor and the subordinate. However, most arguments against openness are specious and usually benefit only those who wish to maintain secrecy at the expense of the organization.

Openness is also the best way to reduce outsiders' suspicions of an organization's motives and actions. Sir Adrian Cadbury, chairman of Cadbury Schweppes, recently stated, "Disclosure is not a panacea for improving the relations between business and society, but the willingness to operate an open system is the foundation of those relations."[17] The recent disclosure that Chrysler cars with disconnected speedometer cables were driven by company employees and then sold as new (a practice which most would describe as unethical) was diffused by openness concerning the incident. Chrysler President Lee Iaccoca publicly admitted the practice, offered compensation to buyers of such cars, and promised such a practice would not occur again.

Openness also involves top management's acknowledgment that it is accountable for unethical behavior occurring at lower levels. Too often, one hears a manager saying, "But I didn't know such an activity was going on"; or, "It's impossible for me to know everything going on below me." Such statements may be partially true, but too often they are only an excuse. Marshall Clinard, professor emeritus at the University of Wisconsin, found in his survey of retired middle managers that 72% believed that upper management knew about improper conduct either while it was going on or soon after.[18] Furthermore, a truly open organization with appropriate controls reduces the likelihood that managers really do not know what is going on at lower levels.

Establish Rules, Policies, and Procedures

Appropriate rules, policies, and procedures must be established to reinforce and augment management's commitment toward achievement of the ethical goal—

1. A code of ethics should be established. In recent years, most large business organizations have devised codes. The Center for Business Ethics at Bentley College found that of 279 large companies surveyed, 208 had written codes.[19] While most large firms have an ethics code, many, if not most, smaller firms have not taken the time or effort to establish one. Even firms with ethics codes have too often devised them for the wrong reason—an erroneous belief that having a code absolves top managers from responsibility if wrongdoing occurs at lower levels.

A meaningful ethics code should be both general and specific. The code should contain general statements outlining management's total commitment to ethical behavior; these statements serve as a guide to behavior and decision making within the total organization. A code should also contain specific "do" and "don't" statements that are enforceable. An example of a specific statement would be "All facts necessary for an informed purchase of a product or service must be provided to a potential customer." Such a statement would have been clearly violated in the earlier example of the hotel that did not inform guests they were being charged daytime telephone rates for night calls. Even supposedly specific statements can be open to interpretation, and codes should indicate that when a question of interpretation is involved, it must be referred to a higher level in the organization. Ethics codes must be continually updated. As environmental changes occur, revisions and additions to the code may be needed. For instance, rapid computerization or a merger may require updating an organization's ethics code.

2. Policies and procedures for reporting ethical problems must be established. The traditional upward communication channel flowing from subordinate through superior is not always appropriate. As previously noted, an individual's supervisor may be part of the problem. An organization must designate individuals to whom information can be communicated. The Bentley College study of 279 top U.S. companies found that only 17 had an ombudsman or a telephone hot line for employees to use when they wished to bypass normal channels.[20]

The establishment of a hot line is an effective upward communication channel. A hot line also serves notice that the organization encourages individuals to report what they believe is unethical behavior within the organization, sometimes referred to as whistle-blowing. The fate of whistle-blowers in some organizations—demotion or even termination—has been frequently publicized in the media. Thus, it is management's responsibility to convince employees of the following:

• Whistle-blowing is encouraged.
• Confidentiality will be maintained.
• Appropriate action will be taken when wrongdoing is reported.

Management's total commitment to ethical behavior can overcome most employees' fears concerning use of an ombudsman. However, establishing an ombudsman who is an outsider (for example a retired executive) can aid in overcoming fears of confidentiality and reprisals. At the very least, the ombudsman should be a manager near the top of the organization.

3. Policies and procedures must be devised to communicate downward to employees. Methods for communicating downward are many and include bulletin boards, policy manuals, company

newsletters, and meetings. Too often a company sends out a memo to all employees citing the organization's commitment to ethical behavior, and the subject is never mentioned again. As previously noted, each supervisor is the key to downward communication and is responsible for the following:

- Reemphasizing the ethical commitment of the organization.
- Explaining policies and procedures such as the hot line.
- Reiterating that performance will be measured first in terms of ethical standards and second in terms of profitability.

Training sessions are often useful in communicating downward and to some extent upward. Training sessions should include employees from all levels in order to promote common understanding of management's commitment to ethical behavior as well as to discuss the policies and procedures for implementing the commitment. It is doubtful that such sessions can teach ethics per se, but they should accomplish the following:

- Sensitize employees as to the importance of ethical conduct.
- Alert employees to possible ethical situations.
- Help individuals think more clearly about relevant issues and discuss concerns and doubts.
- Reduce the gray area on the ethical/unethical scale.

4. A formal enforcement system is necessary to put teeth into rules. Regardless of an organization's positive commitment to ethical behavior, it is imprudent to rely solely on good intentions. Human behavior still necessitates deterrents. People must be afraid to break the rules because they know they are likely to be punished. A formal auditing system should be devised to detect unethical behavior and a judicial board (ethics committee) empowered to judge internal violations and to guarantee due process to those accused of wrongdoing. Membership on a judicial board depends on many factors, such as size of the organization, number of levels within the organization, and so forth, but the members must be individuals whose impeccable integrity is generally recognized throughout the organization.

When unethical behavior is found, prompt action (commensurate with the misdeed) must be taken. Management should publicize the misconduct and the punishment should be administered for all to see—the element of openness. Too often, a manager's first reaction is to avoid an embarrassing situation which to some extent derives from the feeling that "I'm at least partially responsible." However, little or no action sends a clear message to other employees about what top management really thinks is or is not important. If an infraction is deemed very serious, frequently the action is to allow the guilty individual to resign, and the whole affair is handled as quietly as possible. Companies have even been known to give a good recommendation for the individual who was asked to resign. Such actions do not serve as a deterrent to unethical behavior.

One must remember, however, that while an enforcement system is necessary, an organization has to be careful to address issues of ethics in a positive manner. Instituting a police-state atmosphere only intimidates and alienates employees and results in a loss of confidence in and loyalty to the organization.

In the final analysis, top management must set the ethical tone and send a clear and pragmatic message to all employees that ethical conduct is demanded regardless of other organizational goals. To ensure compliance, such a mandate must be supplemented by appropriate rules, policies, and procedures. The key, however, is for an organization to never let up on its vigilance to achieve ethical practices. Only then can an organization have a conscience.

NOTES

1. William E. Simon, "A Challenge to Free Enterprise," in *The Ethical Basis of Economic freedom*, Ivan Hill, ed. (Chapel Hill, North Carolina: American Viewpoint, 1976), 405–06.
2. Maynard M. Dolecheck, James Caldwell, and Carolyn C. Dolecheck, "Ethical Perceptions and Attitudes of Business Personnel," *American Business Review* (January 1988): 47–54.

3. Jonathan Dahl, Tracking Travel," *Wall Street Journal*, 6 January 1988, 17.

4. Stephen Koepp, "Having It All, Then Throwing It All Away,' *Time*, 25 May 1987, 23.

5. Saul W. Gellerman, "Why Good Managers Make Bad Ethical Choices," *Harvard Business Review* (July/August 1986): 85.

6. "Ethics Art Nice, But They Can Be a Handicap Some Executives Declare," *Wall Street Journal*, 8 September 1987, 1.

7. *Hong Kong Business Today* reporting the New York Times/CBS News poll, September 1985. 42.

8. Barry Z. Posner and Warren H. Schmidt, "Values and the American Manager: An Update," *California Management Review* (Spring 1984): 210–11.

9. "Ethical Problems Plague Reagan's Administration," *News-Star-World*, 20 December 1987, 11A.

10. Kenneth Goodpaster and John Mathews, "Can a Corporation Have a Conscience?" *Harvard Business Review* (January/February 1982): 132–41.

11. S. J. Vitell and T. A. Festervand, "Business Ethics Conflict, Practices and Beliefs of Industrial Executives," *Journal of Business Ethics* (May 1987): 16.

12. Dolecheck, Caldwell, and Dolecheck, "Ethical Perceptions."

13. Ibid.

14. Ibid.

15. Alan J. Otten, "Ethics on the Job: Companies Alert Employees to Potential Dilemmas," *Wall Street Journal*, 1 July 1986, 17.

16. Martha Brannigan, "Auditor's Downfall Shows a Man Caught in Trap of His Own Making," *Wall Street Journal*, 4 March 1987, 31.

17. Sir Adam Cadbury, "Ethical Managers Make Their Own Rules," *Harvard Business Review*, (September/October 1987): 69.

18. Stan Crock, "How to Take a Bite Out of Corporate Crime," *Business Week*, 15 July 1985, 122.

19. Otten, "Ethics on the Job."

20. Ibid.

Essay

Ways Women Lead

Judy B. Rosener

The command-and-control leadership associated with men is not the only way to succeed.

Women managers who have broken the glass ceiling in medium-sized, nontraditional organizations have proven that effective leaders don't come from one mold. They have demonstrated that using the command-and-control style of managing others, a style generally associated with men in large traditional organizations, is not the only way to succeed.

The first female executives, because they were breaking new ground, adhered to many of the "rules of conduct" that spelled success for men. Now a second wave of women is making its way into top management, not by adopting the style and habits that have proved successful for men but by drawing on the skills and attitudes they developed from their shared experience as women. These second-generation managerial women are drawing on what is unique to their socialization as women and creating a different path to the top. They are seeking and finding opportunities in fast-changing and growing organizations to show that they can achieve results—in a different way. They are succeeding because of—not in spite of—certain characteristics generally considered to be "feminine" and inappropriate in leaders.

The women's success shows that a nontraditional leadership style is well suited to the conditions of some work environments and can increase an organization's chances of surviving in an uncertain world. It supports the belief that there is strength in a diversity of leadership styles.

In a recent survey sponsored by the International Women's Forum, I found a number of unexpected similarities between men and women leaders along with some important differences. Among these similarities are characteristics related to money and children. I found that the men and women respondents earned the same amount of money (and the household income of the women is twice that of the men). This finding is contrary to most studies, which find a considerable wage gap between men and women even at the executive level. I also found that just as many men as women experience work-family conflict (although when there are children at home, the women experience slightly more conflict than men).

But the similarities end when men and women describe their leadership performance and how they usually influence those with whom they work. The men are more likely than the women to describe themselves in ways that characterize what some management experts call "transactional" leadership. That is, they view job performance as a series of transactions with subordinates, which includes exchanging rewards for services rendered or punishment for inadequate performance. The men are also more likely to use power that comes from their organizational position and formal authority.

The women respondents, on the other hand, described themselves in ways that characterize "transformational" leaderships—getting subordinates to transform their own self-interest into the interest of the group through concern for a broader goal. Moreover, they ascribe their power to personal characteristics like charisma, interpersonal skills, hard work, or personal contacts rather than to organizational stature.

Intrigued by these differences, I interviewed some of the women respondents who described themselves as transformational. These discussions gave me a better picture of how these women saw themselves as leaders and a greater understanding of the important ways in which their leadership style differs from the traditional command-and-control style. I call their leadership style "interactive leadership" because these women actively work to make their interactions with subordinates positive for everyone involved. More specifically, the women encourage participation, share power and information, enhance other people's self-worth, and get others excited about their work. All these things reflect their belief that allowing employees to contribute and to feel powerful and important is a win-win situation—good for the employees and the organization.

INTERACTIVE LEADERSHIP

From my discussions with the women interviewees, several patterns emerged. The women leaders made frequent reference to their efforts to encourage participation and share power and information—two things that are often associated with participative management. But their self-description went beyond the usual definitions of participation. Much of what they described were attempts to enhance other people's sense of self-worth and to energize followers. In general, these leaders believe that people perform best when they feel good about themselves and their work, and they try to create situations that contribute to that feeling.

Encourage Participation

Inclusion is at the core of interactive leadership. In describing nearly every aspect of management, the women interviewees made reference to trying to make people feel part of the organization. They try to instill this group identity in a variety of ways, including encouraging others to have a say in almost every aspect of work, from setting performance goals to determining strategy. To facilitate inclusion, they create mechanisms that get people to participate and they use a conversational style that sends signals inviting people to get involved.

One example of the kinds of mechanisms that encourage participation is the "bridge club" that one interviewee, a group executive in charge of mergers and acquisitions at a large East Coast financial firm, created. The club is an informal gathering of people who have information she needs but over whom she has no direct control. The word bridge describes the effort to bring together these "members" from different functions. The word club captures the relaxed atmosphere.

Despite the fact that attendance at club meetings is voluntary and over and above the usual work demands, the interviewee said that those whose help she needs make the time to come. "They know their contributions are valued, and they appreciate the chance to exchange information across functional boundaries in an informal setting that's fun." She finds participation in the club more effective than memos.

Whether or not the women create special forums for people to interact, they try to make people feel included as a matter of course, often by trying to draw them into the conversation or soliciting their opinions. Frieda Caplan, founder and CEO of Frieda's Finest, a California-based marketer and distributor of unusual fruits and vegetables, described an approach she uses that is typical of the other women interviewed: "When I face a tough decision, I always ask my employees, 'What would you do if you were me?' This approach generates good feedback and introduces my employees to the complexity of management decisions."

Of course, saying that you include others doesn't mean others necessarily feel included.

The women acknowledge the possibility that their efforts to draw people in may be seen as symbolic, so they try to avoid that perception by acting on the input they receive. They ask for suggestions before they reach their own conclusions, and they test—and sometimes change—particular decisions before they implement them. These women use participation to clarify their own views by thinking things through out loud and to ensure that they haven't overlooked an important consideration.

The fact that many of the interviewees described their participatory style as coming "naturally" suggests that these leaders do not consciously adopt it for its business value. Yet they realize that encouraging participation has benefits. For one thing, making it easy for people to express their ideas helps ensure that decisions reflect as much information as possible. To some of the women, this point is just common sense. Susan S. Elliott, president and founder of Systems Service Enterprises, a St. Louis computer consulting company, expressed this view: "I can't come up with a plan and then ask those who manage the accounts to give me their reactions. They're the ones who really know the accounts. They have information I don't have. Without their input I'd be operating in an ivory tower."

Participation also increases support for decisions ultimately reached and reduces the risk that ideas will be undermined by unexpected opposition. Claire Rothman, general manager of the Great Western Forum, a large sports and entertainment arena in Los Angeles, spoke about the value of open disagreement: "When I know ahead of time that someone disagrees with a decision, I can work especially closely with that person to try to get his or her support."

Getting people involved also reduces the risk associated with having only one person handle a client, project, or investment. For Patricia M. Cloherty, senior vice president and general partner of Alan Patric of Associates, a New York venture capital firm, including people in decision making and planning gives investments longevity. If something happens to one person, others will be familiar enough with the situation to "adopt" the investment. That way, there are no orphans in the portfolio, and a knowledgeable second opinion is always available.

Like most who are familiar with participatory management, these women are aware that being inclusive also has its disadvantages. Soliciting ideas and information from others takes time, often requires giving up some control, opens the door to criticism, and exposes personal and turf conflicts. In addition, asking for ideas and information can be interpreted as not having answers.

Further, it cannot be assumed that everyone wants to participate. Some people prefer being told what to do. When Mary Jane Rynd was a partner in a Big Eight accounting firm in Arizona (she recently left to start her own company—Rynd, Carneal & Associates), she encountered such a person: "We hired this person from an out-of-state CPA firm because he was experienced and smart—and because it's always fun to hire someone away from another firm. But he was just too cynical to participate. He was suspicious of everybody. I tried everything to get him involved—including him in discussions and giving him pep talks about how we all work together. Nothing worked. He just didn't want to participate."

Like all those who responded to the survey, these women are comfortable using a variety of styles. So when participation doesn't work, they act unilaterally. "I prefer participation," said Elliott, "but there are situations where time is short and I have to take the bull by the horns."

Share Power and Information

Soliciting input from other people suggests a flow of information from employees to the "boss." But part of making people feel included is knowing that open communication flows in two directions. These women say they willingly share power and information rather than guard it and they make apparent their reasoning behind decisions. While many leaders see information as power and power as a limited commodity to be coveted, the interviewees seem to be comfortable letting power and information change hands. As Adrienne Hall, vice chairman of Eisaman, Johns & Laws, a large West Coast advertising firm, said: "I know territories shift, so I'm not preoccupied with turf."

One example of power and information sharing is the open strategy sessions held by Debi Coleman, vice president of information systems and technology at Apple Computer. Rather than closeting a small group of key executives in her office to develop a strategy based on her own agenda, she holds a series of meetings over several days and allows a larger group to develop and help choose alternatives.

The interviewees believe that sharing power and information accomplishes several things. It creates loyalty by signaling to coworkers and subordinates that they are trusted and their ideas respected. It also sets an example for other people and therefore can enhance the general communication flow. And it increases the odds that leaders will hear about problems before they explode. Sharing power and information also gives employees and coworkers the wherewithal to reach conclusions, solve problems, and see the justification for decisions.

On a more pragmatic level, many employees have come to expect their bosses to be open and frank. They no longer accept being dictated to but want to be treated as individuals with minds of their own. As Elliott said, "I work with lots of people who are bright and intelligent, so I have to deal with them at an intellectual level. They're very logical, and they want to know the reasons for things. They'll buy in only if it makes sense."

In some cases, sharing information means simply being candid about work-related issues. In early 1990, when Elliott hired as employees many of the people she had been using as independent contractors, she knew the transition would be difficult for everyone. The number of employees nearly doubled overnight, and the nature of working relationships changed. "I warned everyone that we were in for some rough times and reminded them that we would be experiencing them together. I admitted that it would also be hard for me, and I made it clear that I wanted them to feel free to talk to me. I was completely candid and encouraged them to be honest with me. I lost some employees who didn't like the new relationships, but I'm convinced that being open helped me understand my employees better, and it gave them a feeling of support."

Like encouraging participation, sharing power and information has its risks. It allows for the possibility that people will reject, criticize, or otherwise challenge what the leader has to say or, more broadly, her authority. Also, employees get frustrated when leaders listen to—but ultimately reject—their ideas. Because information is a source of power, leaders who share it can be seen as naive or needing to be liked. The interviewees have experienced some of these downsides but find the positives overwhelming.

Enhance the Self-Worth of Others

One of the byproducts of sharing information and encouraging participation is that employees feel important. During the interviews, the women leaders discussed other ways they build a feeling of self-worth in coworkers and subordinates. They talked about giving others credit and praise and sending small signals of recognition. Most important, they expressed how they refrain from asserting their own superiority, which asserts the inferiority of others. All those I interviewed expressed clear aversion to behavior that sets them apart from others in the company-reserved parking places, separate dining facilities, pulling rank.

Examples of sharing and giving credit to others abound. Caplan, who has been the subject of scores of media reports hailing her innovation of labeling vegetables so consumers know what they are and how to cook them, originally got the idea from a farmer. She said that whenever someone raises the subject, she credits the farmer and downplays her role. Rothman is among the many note-writers; when someone does something out of the ordinary, she writes them a personal note to tell them she noticed. Like many of the women I interviewed, she said she also makes a point of acknowledging good work by talking about it in front of others.

Bolstering coworkers and subordinates is especially important in businesses and jobs that tend to be hard on a person's ego. Investment banking is one example because of the long hours, high pressures, intense competition, and inevitability that some deals will fail. One interviewee in investment banking hosts dinners for her division, gives out gag gifts as party favors, passes out M&Ms at meetings, and throws parties "to celebrate ourselves." These things, she said, balance the anxiety that permeates the environment.

Rynd compensates for the negativity inherent in preparing tax returns: "In my business we have something called a query sheet where the person who reviews the tax return writes down everything that needs to be corrected. Criticism is built into the system. But at the end of every review, I always include a positive comment—your work paper technique looked good, I appreciate the fact that you got this done on time, or something like that. It seems trivial, but it's one way to remind people that I recognize their good work and not just their shortcomings."

Energize Others

The women leaders spoke of their enthusiasm for work and how they spread their enthusiasm around to make work a challenge that is exhilarating and fun. The women leaders talked about it in those terms and claimed to use their enthusiasm to get others excited. As Rothman said, "There is rarely a person I can't motivate."

Enthusiasm was a dominant theme throughout the interviews. In computer consulting: "Because this business is on the forefront of technology, I'm sort of evangelistic about it, and I want other people to be as excited as I am." In venture capital: "You have to have a head of steam." In executive search: "Getting people excited is an important way to influence those you have no control over." Or in managing sports arenas: "My enthusiasm gets others excited. I infuse them with energy and make them see that even boring jobs contribute to the fun of working in a celebrity business."

Enthusiasm can sometimes be misunderstood. In conservative professions like investment banking, such an upbeat leadership style can be interpreted as cheerleading and can undermine credibility. In many cases, the women said they won and preserved their credibility by achieving results that could be measured easily. One of the women acknowledged that her colleagues don't understand or like her leadership style and have called it cheerleading. "But," she added, "in this business you get credibility from what you produce, and they love the profits I generate." While energy and enthusiasm can inspire some, it doesn't work for everyone. Even Rothman conceded, "Not everyone has a flame that can be lit."

PATHS OF LEAST RESISTANCE

Many of the women I interviewed said the behaviors and beliefs that underlie their leadership style come naturally to them. I attribute this to two things: their socialization and the career paths they have chosen. Although socialization patterns and career paths are changing, the average age of the men and women who responded to the survey is 51—old enough to have had experiences that differed because of gender.

Until the 1960s, men and women received different signals about what was expected of them. To summarize a subject that many experts have explored in depth, women have been expected to be wives, mothers, community volunteers, teachers, and nurses. In all these roles, they are supposed to be cooperative, supportive, understanding, gentle, and to provide service to others. They are to derive satisfaction and a sense of self-esteem from helping others, including their spouses. While men have had to appear to be competitive, strong, tough, decisive, and in control, women have been allowed to be cooperative, emotional, supportive, and vulnerable. This may explain why women today are more likely than men to be interactive leaders.

Men and women have also had different career opportunities. Women were not expected to have careers, or at least not the same kinds of careers as men, so they either pursued different jobs or were simply denied opportunities men had. Women's career tracks have usually not included long series of organizational positions with formal authority and control of resources. Many women had their first work experiences outside the home as volunteers. While some of the challenges they faced as managers in volunteer organizations are the same as those in any business, in many ways, leading volunteers is different because of the absence of concrete rewards like pay and promotion.

As women entered the business world, they tended to find themselves in positions consistent with the roles they played at home: in staff positions rather than in line positions, supporting the work of others, and in functions like communications or human resources where they had relatively small budgets and few people reporting directly to them.

The fact that most women have lacked formal authority over others and control over resources means that by default they have had to find other ways to accomplish their work. As it turns out, the behaviors that were natural and/or socially acceptable for them have been highly successful in at least some managerial settings.

What came easily to women turned out to be a survival tactic. Although leaders often begin their careers doing what comes naturally and what fits within the constraints of the job, they also develop their skills and styles over time. The women's use of interactive leadership has its roots in socialization, and the women interviewees firmly believe that it benefits their organizations. Through the course of their careers, they have gained conviction that their style is effective. In fact, for some, it was their own success that caused them to formulate their philosophies about what motivates people, how to make good decisions, and what it takes to maximize business performance.

They now have formal authority and control over vast resources, but still they see sharing power and information as an asset rather than a liability. They believe that although pay and promotion are necessary tools of management, what people really want is to feel that they are contributing to a higher purpose and that they have the opportunity as individuals to learn and grow. The women believe that employees and peers perform better when they feel they are part of an organization and can share in its success. Allowing them to get involved and to work to their potential is a way of maximizing their contributions and using human resources most efficiently.

ANOTHER KIND OF DIVERSITY

The IWF survey shows that a nontraditional leadership style can be effective in organizations that accept it. This lesson comes especially hard to those who think of the corporate world as a game of survival of the fittest, where the fittest is always the strongest, toughest, most decisive, and powerful. Such a workplace seems to favor leaders who control people by controlling resources, and by controlling people, gain control of more resources. Asking for information and sharing decision-making power can be seen as serious disadvantages, but what is a disadvantage under one set of circumstances is an advantage under another. The "best" leadership style depends on the organizational context.

Only one of the women interviewees is in a traditional, large-scale company. More typically, the women's organizations are medium-sized and tend to have experienced fast growth and fast change. They demand performance and/or have a high proportion of professional workers. These organizations seem to create opportunities for women and are hospitable to those who use a nontraditional management style.

The degree of growth or change in an organization is an important factor in creating opportunities for women. When change is rampant, everything is up for grabs, and crises are frequent. Crises are generally not desirable, but they do create opportunities for people to prove themselves. Many of the women interviewees said they got their first break because their organizations were in turmoil.

Fast-changing environments also play havoc with tradition. Coming up through the ranks and being part of an established network is no longer important. What is important is how you perform. Also, managers in such environments are open to new solutions, new structures, and new ways of leading.

The fact that many of the women respondents are in organizations that have clear performance standards suggests that they have gained credibility and legitimacy by achieving results. In investment banking, venture capital, accounting, and executive placement, for instance, individual performance is easy to measure.

A high proportion of young professional workers—increasingly typical of organizations—is also a factor in some women's success. Young, educated professionals impose special requirements on their organization. They demand to participate and contribute. In some cases, they have knowledge or talents their bosses don't have. If they are good performers, they have many employment options. It is easy to imagine that these professionals will respond to leaders who are inclusive and open, who enhance the self-worth of others, and who create a fun work environment. Interactive leaders are likely to win the cooperation needed to achieve their goals.

Interactive leadership has proved to be effective, perhaps even advantageous, in organizations in which the women I interviewed have succeeded. As the work force increasingly demands participation and the economic environment increasingly requires rapid change, interactive leadership may emerge as the management style of choice for many organizations. For interactive leadership to take root more broadly, however, organizations must be willing to question the notion that the traditional command-and-control leadership style that has brought success in

earlier decades is the only way to get results. This may be hard in some organizations, especially those with long histories of male-oriented, command-and-control leadership. Changing these organizations will not be easy. The fact that women are more likely than men to be interactive leaders raises the risk that these companies will perceive interactive leadership as "feminine" and automatically resist it.

Linking interactive leadership directly to being female is a mistake. We know that women are capable of making their way through corporations by adhering to the traditional corporate model and that they can wield power in ways similar to men. Indeed, some women may prefer that style. We also know from the survey findings that some men use the transformational leadership style.

Large, establishing organizations should expand their definition of effective leadership. If they were to do that, several things might happen, including the disappearance of the glass ceiling and the creation of a wider path for all sorts of executives—men and women—to attain positions of leadership. Widening the path will free potential leaders to lead in ways that play to their individual strengths. Then the newly recognized interactive leadership style can be valued and rewarded as highly as the command-and-control style has been for decades. By valuing a diversity of leadership styles, organizations will find the strength and flexibility to survive in a highly competitive, increasingly diverse economic environment.

Essay

Moral Mazes: Bureaucracy and Managerial Work

Robert Jackall

Corporate leaders often tell their charges that hard work will lead to success. Indeed, this theory of reward being commensurate with effort has been an enduring belief in our society, one central to our self-image as a people where the "main chance" is available to anyone of ability who has the gumption and the persistence to seize it. Hard work, it is also frequently asserted, builds character. This notion carries also conviction because businessmen, and our society as a whole, have little patience with those who make a habit of finishing out of the money. In the end, it is success that matters, that legitimates striving, and that makes work worthwhile.

What if, however, men and women in the big corporation no longer see success as necessarily connected to hard work? What becomes of the social morality of the corporation—I mean the everyday rules in use that people play by—when there is thought to be no "objective" standard of excellence to explain how and why winners are separated from also-rans, how and why some people succeed and others fail?

This is the puzzle that confronted me while doing a great many extensive interviews with managers and executives in several large corporations, particularly in a large chemical company and a large textile firm. I went into these corporations to study how bureaucracy—the prevailing organizational form of our society and economy—shapes moral consciousness. I came to see that managers' rules for success are at the heart of what may be called the bureaucratic ethic.

This article suggests no changes and offers no programs for reform. It is, rather, simply an interpretive sociological analysis of the moral dimensions of managers' work. Some readers may find the essay sharp-edged, others familiar. For both groups, it is important to note at the outset that my materials are managers' own descriptions of their experiences.[1] In listening to managers, I have had the decided advantages of being unencumbered with business responsibilities and also of being free from the taken-for-granted views and vocabularies of the business world. As it happens, my own research in a variety of other settings suggests that managers' experiences are by no means unique; indeed they have a deep resonance with those of other occupational groups.

WHAT HAPPENED TO THE PROTESTANT ETHIC?

To grasp managers' experiences and the more general implications they contain, one must see them against the background of the great historical transformations, both social and cultural, that produced managers as an occupational group. Since the concern here is with the moral significance of work in business, it is important to begin with an understanding of the original Protestant Ethic, the world view of the rising bourgeois class that spear-headed the emergence of capitalism.

The Protestant Ethic was a set of beliefs that counseled "secular asceticism"—the methodical, rational subjection of human impulse and desire to God's will through "restless, continuous, systematic work in a worldly calling."[2] This ethic of ceaseless work and ceaseless renunciation of the fruits of one's toil provided both the economic and the moral foundations for modern capitalism.

On one hand, secular asceticism was a ready-made prescription for building economic capital; on the other, it became for the upward-moving bourgeois class—self-made industrialists, farmers, and enterprising artisans—the ideology that justified their attention to this world, their accumulation of wealth, and indeed the social inequities that inevitably followed such accumulation. This bourgeois ethic, with its imperatives for self-reliance, hard work, frugality, and rational planning, and its clear definition of success and failure, came to dominate a whole historical epoch in the West.

But the ethic came under assault from two directions. First, the very accumulation of wealth that the old Protestant Ethic made possible gradually stripped away the religious basis of the ethic, especially among the rising middle class that benefited from it. There were, of course, periodic reassertions of the religious context of the ethic, as in the case of John D. Rockefeller and his turn toward Baptism. But on the whole, by the late 1800s the religious roots of the ethic survived principally among the independent farmers and proprietors of small businesses in rural areas and towns across America.

In the mainstream of an emerging urban America, the ethic had become secularized into the "work ethic," "rugged individualism," and especially the "success ethic." By the beginning of this century, among most of the economically successful, frugality had become an aberration, conspicuous consumption the norm. And with the shaping of the mass consumer society later in this century, the sanctification of consumption became widespread, indeed crucial to the maintenance of the economic order.

Affluence and the emergence of the consumer society were responsible, however, for the demise of only aspects of the old ethic—namely, the imperatives for saving and investment. The core of the ethic, even in its later, secularized form—self-reliance, unremitting devotion to work, and a morality that postulated just rewards for work well done—was undermined by the complete transformation of the organizational form of work itself. The hallmarks of the emerging modern production and distribution systems were administrative hierarchies, standardized work procedures, regularized time-tables, uniform policies, and centralized control—in a word, the bureaucratization of the economy.

This bureaucratization was heralded at first by a very small class of salaried managers, who were later joined by legions of clerks and still later by technicians and professionals of every stripe. In this century, the process spilled over from the private to the public sector and government bureaucracies came to rival those of industry. This great transformation produced the decline of the old middle class of entrepreneurs, free professionals, independent farmers, and small independent businessmen—the traditional carriers of the old Protestant Ethic—and the ascendance of a new middle class of salaried employees whose chief common characteristic was and is their dependence on the big organization.

Any understanding of what happened to the original Protestant Ethic and to the old morality and social character it embodied—and therefore any understanding of the moral significance of work today—is inextricably tied to an analysis of bureaucracy. More specifically, it is, in my view, tied to an analysis of the work and occupational cultures of managerial groups within bureaucracies. Managers are the quintessential bureaucratic work group; they not only fashion bureaucratic rules, but they are also bound by them. Typically, they are not just *in* the organization; they are *of* the organization. As such, managers represent the prototype of the white-collar salaried employee. By analyzing the kind of ethic bureaucracy produces in managers, one can begin to understand how bureaucracy shapes morality in our society as a whole.

PYRAMIDAL POLITICS

American businesses typically both centralize and decentralize authority. Power is concentrated at the top in the person of the chief executive officer and is simultaneously decentralized; that is, responsibility for decisions and profits is pushed as far down the organizational line as possible. For example, the chemical company that I studied—and its structure is typical of other organizations I examined—is one of several operating companies of a large and growing conglomerate. Like the other operating companies, the chemical concern has its own president, executive vice presidents, vice presidents, other executive officers, business area managers, entire staff divisions, and operating plants. Each company is, in effect, a self-sufficient organization, though they are all coordinated by the corporation, and each president reports directly to the corporate CEO.

Now, the key interlocking mechanism of this structure is its reporting system. Each manager gathers up the profit targets or other objectives of his or her subordinates, and with these formulates his commitments to his boss; this boss takes these commitments, and those of his subordinates, and in turn makes a commitment to *his* boss. (Note: henceforth only "he" or "his" will be used to allow for easier reading.) At the top of the

line, the president of each company makes his commitment to the CEO of the corporation, based on the stated objectives given to him by his vice presidents. There is always pressure from the top to set higher goals.

This management-by-objectives system, as it is usually called, creates a chain of commitments from the CEO down to the lowliest product manager. In practice, it also shapes a patrimonial authority arrangement which is crucial to defining both the immediate experiences and the long-run career chances of individual managers. In this world, a subordinate owes fealty principally to his immediate boss. A subordinate must not overcommit his boss; he must keep the boss from making mistakes, particularly public ones; he must not circumvent the boss. On a social level, even though an easy, breezy informality is the prevalent style of American business, the subordinate must extend to the boss a certain ritual deference: for instance, he must follow the boss's lead in conversation, must not speak out of turn at meetings, and must laugh at the boss's jokes while not making jokes of his own.

In short, the subordinate must not exhibit any behavior which symbolizes parity. In return, he can hope to be elevated when and if the boss is elevated, although other important criteria also intervene here. He can also expect protection for mistakes made up to a point. However, that point is never exactly defined and always depends on the complicated politics of each situation.

Who Gets Credit?

It is characteristic of this authority system that details are pushed down and credit is pushed up. Superiors do not like to give detailed instructions to subordinates. The official reason for this is to maximize subordinates' autonomy; the underlying reason seems to be to get rid of tedious details and to protect the privilege of authority to declare that a mistake has been made.

It is not at all uncommon for very bald and extremely general edicts to emerge from on high. For example, "Sell the plant in St. Louis. Let me know when you've struck a deal." This pushing down of details has important consequences:

1. Because they are unfamiliar with entangling details, corporate higher echelons tend to expect highly successful results without complications. This is central to top executives' well-known aversion to bad news and to the resulting tendency to "kill the messenger" who bears that news.

2. The pushing down of detail creates great pressure on middle managers not only to transmit good news but to protect their corporations, their bosses, and themselves in the process. They become the "point men" of a given strategy and the potential "fall guys" when things go wrong.

Credit flows up in this structure and usually is appropriated by the highest ranking officer involved in a decision. This person redistributes credit as he chooses, bound essentially by a sensitivity to public perceptions of his fairness. At the middle level, credit for a particular success is always a type of refracted social honor; one cannot claim credit even if it is earned. Credit has to be given, and acceptance of the gift implicitly involves a reaffirmation and strengthening of fealty. A superior may share some credit with subordinates in order to deepen fealty relationships and induce greater future efforts on his behalf. Of course, a different system is involved in the allocation of blame, a point I shall discuss later.

Fealty to the "King"

Because of the interlocking character of the commitment system, a CEO carries enormous influence in his corporation. If, for a moment, one thinks of the presidents of individual operating companies as barons, then the CEO of the parent company is the king. His word is law; even the CEO's wishes and whims are taken as commands by close subordinates on the corporate staff, who zealously turn them into policies and directives.

A typical example occurred in the textile company last year when the CEO, new at the time, expressed mild concern about the rising operating costs of the company's fleet of rented cars. The following day, a stringent system for monitoring mileage replaced the previous casual practice.

Great efforts are made to please the CEO. For example, when the CEO of the large conglomerate that includes the chemical company visits a plant, the most important order of business for local management is a fresh paint job, even when, as in several cases last year the cost of paint alone exceeds $100,000. I am told that similar anecdotes from other organizations have been in circulation since 1910; this suggests a certain historical continuity of behavior toward top bosses.

The second order of business for the plant management is to produce a complete book describing the plant and its operations, replete with photographs and illustrations, for presentation to the CEO; such a book costs about $10,000 for the single copy. By any standards of budgetary stringency, such expenditures are irrational. But by the social standards of the corporation, they make perfect sense. It is far more important to please the king today than to worry about the future economic state of one's fief, since if one does not please the king, there may not be a fief to worry about or indeed any vassals to do the worrying.

By the same token, all of this leads to an intense interest in everything the CEO does and says. In both the chemical and the textile companies, the most common topic of conversation among managers up and down the line is speculation about their respective

CEOs' plans, intentions, strategies, actions, styles, and public images.

Such speculation is more than idle gossip, Because he stands at the apex of the corporation's bureaucratic and patrimonial structures and locks the intricate system of commitments between bosses and subordinates into place, it is the CEO who ultimately decides whether those commitments have been satisfactorily met. Moreover, the CEO and his trusted associates determine the fate of whole business areas of a corporation.

Shake-Ups & Contingency

One must appreciate the simultaneously monocratic and patrimonial character of business bureaucracies in order to grasp what we might call their contingency. One has only to read the *Wall Street Journal* or the *New York Times* to realize that, despite their carefully constructed "eternal" public image, corporations are quite unstable organizations. Mergers, buy-outs, divestitures, and especially "organizational restructuring" are commonplace aspects of business life. I shall discuss only organizational shake-ups here.

> Usually, shake-ups occur because of the appointment of a new CEO and/or division president, or because of some failure that is adjudged to demand retribution; sometimes these occurrences work together. The first action of most new CEOs is some form of organizational change. On the one hand, this prevents the inheritance of blame for past mistakes; on the other, it projects an image of bareknuckled aggressiveness much appreciated on Wall Street. Perhaps most important, a shake-up rearranges the fealty structure of the corporation, placing in power those barons whose style and public image mesh closely with that of the new CEO.

A shake-up has reverberations throughout an organization. Shortly after the new CEO of the conglomerate was named, he reorganized the whole business and selected new presidents

to head each of the five newly formed companies of the corporation. He mandated that the presidents carry out a thorough reorganization of their separate companies complete with extensive "census reduction"—that is, firing as many people as possible.

The new president of the chemical company, one of these five, had risen from a small but important specialty chemicals division in the former company. Upon promotion to president, he reached back into his former division, indeed back to his own past work in a particular product line, and systematically elevated many of his former colleagues, friends, and allies. Powerful managers in other divisions, particularly in a rival process chemicals division, were: (1) forced to take big demotions in the new power structure; (2) put on "special assignment"—the corporate euphemism for Siberia (the saying is: "No one ever comes back from special assignment"); (3) fired; or (4) given "early retirement," a graceful way of doing the same thing.

Up and down the chemical company, former associates of the president now hold virtually every important position. Managers in the company view all of this as an inevitable fact of life. In their view, the whole reorganization could easily have gone in a completely different direction had another CEO been named or had the one selected picked a different president for the chemical company, or had the president come from a different work group in the old organization. Similarly, there is the abiding feeling that another significant change in top management could trigger yet another sweeping reorganization.

Fealty is the mortar of the corporate hierarchy, but the removal of one well-placed stone loosens the mortar throughout the pyramid and can cause things to fall apart. And no one is ever quite sure, until after the fact, just how the pyramid will be put back together.

SUCCESS & FAILURE

It is within this complicated and ambiguous authority structure, always subject to upheaval, that success and failure are meted out to those in the middle and upper middle managerial ranks. Managers rarely spoke to me of objective criteria for achieving success because once certain crucial points in one's career are passed, success and failure seem to have little to do with one's accomplishments. Rather, success is socially defined and distributed. Corporations do demand, of course, a basic competence and sometimes specified training and experience; hiring patterns usually ensure these. A weeding-out process takes place, however, among the lower ranks of managers during the first several years of their experience. By the time a manager reaches a certain numbered grade in the ordered hierarchy—in the chemical company this is Grade 13 out of 25, defining the top 8 1/2% of management in the company—managerial competence as such is taken for granted and assumed not to differ greatly from one manager to the next. The focus then switches to social factors, which are determined by authority and political alignments—the fealty structure—and by the ethos and style of the corporation.

Moving to the Top

In the chemical and textile companies as well as the other concerns I studied, five criteria seem to control a person's ability to rise in middle and upper middle management. In ascending order they are:

1. *Appearance and dress.* This criterion is so familiar that I shall mention it only briefly. Managers have to look the part, and it is sufficient to say that corporations are filled with attractive, well-groomed, and conventionally well-dressed men and women.

2. *Self-control.* Managers stress the need to exercise iron self-control and to have the ability to mask all emotion and intention behind bland, smiling, and agreeable public faces. They believe it is a fatal weakness to lose control of oneself, in any way, in a public forum. Similarly, to betray valuable secret knowledge (for instance, a confidential reorganization plan) or intentions through some relaxation of self-control—for example, an indiscreet comment or a lack of adroitness in turning aside a query—can not only jeopardize a manager's immediate position but can undermine others' trust in him.

3. *Perception as a team player.* While being a team player has many meanings, one of the most important is to appear to be interchangeable with other managers near one's level. Corporations discourage narrow specialization more strongly as one goes higher. They also discourage the expression of moral or political qualms. One might object, for example, to working with chemicals used in nuclear power, and most corporations today would honor that objection. The public statement of such objections, however, would end any realistic aspirations for higher posts because one's usefulness to the organization depends on versatility. As one manager in the chemical company commented: "Well, we'd go along with his request but we'd always wonder about the guy. And in the back of our minds, we'd be thinking that he'll soon object to working in the soda ash division because he doesn't like glass."

Another important meaning of team play is putting in long hours at the office. This requires a certain amount of sheer physical energy, even though a great deal of this time is spent not in actual work but in social rituals—like reading and discussing newspaper articles, taking coffee breaks, or having informal conversations. These rituals, readily observable in every corporation that I studied, forge the social bonds that make real managerial work—that is, group work of various sorts—possible. One must participate in the rituals to be considered effective in the work.

4. *Style.* Managers emphasize the importance of "being fast on your feet"; always being well organized; giving slick presentations complete with color slides; giving the appearance of knowledge even in its absence; and possessing a subtle, almost indefinable sophistication, marked especially by an urbane, witty, graceful, engaging, and friendly demeanor.

I want to pause for a moment to note that some observers have interpreted such conformity, team playing, affability, and urbanity as evidence of the decline of the individualism of the old Protestant Ethic.[3] To the extent that commentators take the public images that managers project at face value, I think they miss the main point. Managers up and down the corporate ladder adopt the public faces that they wear quite consciously; they are, in fact, the masks behind which the real struggles and moral issues of the corporation can be found.

Karl Mannheim's conception of self-rationalization or self-streamlining is useful in understanding what is one of the central social psychological processes of organizational life.[4] In a world where appearances—in the broadest sense—mean everything, the wise and ambitious person learns to cultivate assiduously the proper, prescribed modes of appearing. He dispassionately takes stock of himself, treating himself as an object. He analyzes his strengths and weaknesses, and decides what he needs to change in order to survive and flourish in his organization. And then he systematically undertakes a program to reconstruct his image. Self-rationalization curiously parallels the methodical subjection of self to God's will that the old Protestant Ethic counseled; the difference, of course, is that one acquires not moral virtues but a masterful ability to manipulate personae.

5. *Patron power.* To advance, a manager must have a patron, also called a mentor, a sponsor, a rabbi, or a godfather. Without a powerful patron in the higher echelons of management, one's prospects are poor in most corporations. The patron might be the manager's immediate boss or someone several levels higher in the chain of command. In either case the manager is still bound by the immediate, formal authority and fealty patterns of his position; the new—although more ambiguous—fealty relationships with the patron are added.

A patron provides his "client" with opportunities to get visibility, to showcase his abilities, to make connections with those of high status. A patron cues his client to crucial political developments in the corporation, helps arrange lateral moves if the client's upward progress is thwarted by a particular job or a particular boss, applauds his presentations or suggestions at meetings, and promotes the client during an organizational shake-up. One must, of course, be lucky in one's patron. If the patron gets caught in a political crossfire, the arrows are likely to find his clients as well.

Social Definitions of Performance

Surely, one might argue, there must be more to success in the corporation than style, personality, team play, chameleonic adaptability, and fortunate connections. What about the bottom line—profits, performance?

Unquestionably, "hitting your numbers"— that is, meeting the profit commitments already discussed—is important, but only within the social context I have described. There are several rules here. First, no one in a line position—that is, with responsibility for profit and loss—who regularly "misses his numbers" will survive, let alone rise. Second, a person who always hits his numbers but who lacks some or all of the required social skills will not rise. Third, a person who sometimes misses his numbers but who has all the desirable social traits will rise.

Performance is thus always subject to a myriad of interpretations. Profits matter, but it is much more important in the long run to be perceived as "promotable" by belonging to central political networks. Patrons protect those already selected as rising stars from the negative judgments of others; and only the foolhardy point out even egregious errors of those in power or those destined for it.

Failure is also socially defined. The most damaging failure is, as one middle manager in the chemical company puts it, "when your boss or someone who has the power to determine your fate says: 'You failed.'" Such a godlike pronouncement means, of course, out-and-out personal ruin; one must, at any cost, arrange matters to prevent such an occurrence.

As it happens, things rarely come to such a dramatic point even in the midst of an organizational crisis. The same judgment may be made but it is usually called "nonpromotability." The difference is that those who are publicly labeled as failures normally have no choice but to leave the organization; those adjudged nonpromotable can remain, provided they are willing to accept being shelved or, more colorfully, "mushroomed"—that is, kept in a dark place, fed manure, and left to do nothing but grow fat. Usually, seniors do not tell juniors they are nonpromotable (through the verdict may be common knowledge among senior peer groups). Rather, subordinates are expected to get the message after they have been repeatedly overlooked for promotions. In fact, middle managers interpret staying in the same job for more than two or three years as evidence of a negative judgment. This leads to a mobility panic at the middle levels which, in turn, has crucial consequences for pinpointing responsibility in the organization.

Capriciousness of Success

Finally, managers think that there is a tremendous amount of plain luck involved in advancement. It is striking how often managers who pride themselves on being hardheaded rationalists explain their own career patterns and those of others in terms of luck. Various uncertainties shape this perception. One is the sense of organizational contingency. One change at the top can create profound upheaval throughout the entire corporate structure, producing startling reversals of fortune, good or bad, depending on one's connections. Another is the uncertainty of the markets that often makes managerial planning simply elaborate guesswork, causing real economic outcome to depend on factors totally beyond organizational and personal control.

It is interesting to note in this context that a line manager's credibility suffers just as much from missing his numbers on the upside (that is, achieving profits higher than predicted) as from missing them on the down side. Both outcomes undercut the ideology of managerial planning and control, perhaps the only bulwark managers have against market irrationality.

Even managers in staff positions, often quite removed from the market, face uncertainty. Occupational safety specialists, for instance, know that the bad publicity from one serious accident in the workplace can jeopardize years of work and scores of safety awards. As one high-ranking executive in the chemical company says, "In the corporate world, 1,000 'Attaboys!' are wiped away by one 'Oh, shit!' "

Because of such uncertainties, managers in all the companies I studied speak continually of the great importance of being in the right place at the right time and of the catastrophe of being in the wrong place at the wrong time. My interview materials are filled with stories of people who were transferred immediately before a big shake-up and, as a result, found themselves riding the crest of a wave to power; of people in a promising business area who were terminated because top management suddenly decided that the area no longer fit the corporate image desired; of others caught in an unpredictable and fatal political battle among their patrons; of a product manager whose plant accidentally produced an odd color batch of chemicals, who sold them as a premium version of the old product, and who is now thought to be a marketing genius.

The point is that managers have a sharply defined sense of the *capriciousness* of organizational life. Luck seems as good an explanation as any of why, after a certain point, some people succeed and others fail. The upshot is that many managers decide that they can do little to influence external events in their favor. One can, however, shamelessly streamline oneself, learn to wear all the right masks, and get to know all the right people. And then sit tight and wait for things to happen.

"GUT DECISIONS"

Authority and advancement patterns come together in the decision-making process. The core of the managerial mystique is decision-making prowess, and the real test of such prowess is what managers call "gut decisions," that is, important decisions involving big money, public exposure, or significant effect on the organization. At all but the highest levels of the chemical and textile companies, the rules for making gut decisions are, in the words of one upper middle manager; "(1) Avoid making any decisions if at all possible; and (2) if a decision has to be made, involve as many people as you can so that, if things go south, you're able to point in as many directions as possible."

Consider the case of a large coking plant of the chemical company. Coke making requires a gigantic battery to cook the coke slowly and evenly for long periods; the battery is the most important piece of capital equipment in a coking plant. In 1975, the plant's battery showed signs of weakening and certain managers at corporate headquarters had to decide whether to invest $6 million to restore the battery to top form. Clearly, because of the amount of money involved, this was a gut decision.

No decision was made. The CEO had sent the word out to defer all unnecessary capital expenditures to give the corporation cash reserves for other investments. So the managers allocated small amounts of money to patch the battery up until 1979, when it collapsed entirely. This brought the company into a breach of contract with a steel producer and into violation of various Environmental Protection Agency pollution regulations. The total bill, including lawsuits and now federally mandated repairs to the battery, exceeded $10 million. I have heard figures as high as $150 million, but because of "creative accounting," no one is sure of the exact amount.

This simple but very typical example gets to the heart of how decision making is intertwined with a company's authority structure and advancement patterns. As the chemical company managers see it, the decisions facing them in 1975 and 1979 were crucially different. Had they acted decisively in 1975—in hindsight, the only rational course—they would have salvaged the battery and saved their corporation millions of dollars in the long run.

In the short run, however, since even seemingly rational decisions are subject to widely varying interpretations, particularly decisions which run counter to a CEO's stated objectives, they would have been taking a serious risk in restoring the battery. What is more, their political networks might have unraveled, leaving them vulnerable to attack. They chose short-term safety over long-term gain because they felt they were judged, both by higher authority and by their peers, on their short-term performances. Managers feel that if they do not survive the short run, the long run hardly matters. Even correct decisions can shorten promising careers.

By contrast, in 1979 the decision was simple and posed little risk. The corporation had to meet its legal obligations; also it had to either repair the battery the way the EPA demanded or shut down the plant and lose several hundred million dollars. Since there were no real choices, everyone could agree on a course of action because everyone could appeal to inevitability. Diffusion of responsibility, in this case by procrastinating until total crisis, is intrinsic to organizational life because the real issue in most gut decisions is: Who is going to get blamed if things go wrong?

"Blame Time"

There is no more feared hour in the corporate world than "blame time." Blame is quite different from responsibility. There is a cartoon of

Richard Nixon declaring: "I accept all of the responsibility, but none of the blame." To blame someone is to injure him verbally in public; in large organizations, where one's image is crucial, this poses the most serious sort of threat. For managers, blame—like failure—has nothing to do with the merits of a case; it is a matter of social definition. As a general rule, it is those who are or who become politically vulnerable or expendable who get "set up" and become blamable. The most feared situation of all is to end up inadvertently in the wrong place at the wrong time and get blamed.

Yet this is exactly what often happens in a structure that systematically diffuses responsibility. It is because managers fear blame time that they diffuse responsibility; however, such diffusion inevitably means that someone, somewhere is going to become a scapegoat when things go wrong. Big corporations encourage this process by their complete lack of any tracking system. Whoever is currently in charge of an area is responsible—that is, potentially blamable—for whatever goes wrong in the area, even if he has inherited others' mistakes. An example from the chemical company illustrates this process.

When the CEO of the large conglomerate took office, he wanted to rid his capital accounts of all serious financial drags. The corporation had been operating a storage depot for natural gas which it bought, stored, and then resold. Some years before the energy crisis, the company had entered into a long-term contract to supply gas to a buyer—call him Jones. At the time, this was a sound deal because it provided a steady market for a stably priced commodity.

When gas prices soared, the corporation was still bound to deliver gas to Jones at 20¢ per unit instead of the going market price of $2. The CEO ordered one of his subordinates to get rid of this albatross as expeditiously as possible. This was done by selling the operation to another party—call him Brown—with the agreement that Brown would continue to meet the contractual obligations to Jones. In return for Brown's assumption of these costly contracts, the corporation agreed to buy gas from Brown at grossly inflated prices to meet some of its own energy needs.

In effect, the CEO transferred the drag on his capital accounts to the company's operating expenses. This enabled him to project an aggressive, asset-reducing image to Wall Street. Several levels down the ladder, however, a new vice president for a particular business found himself saddled with exorbitant operating costs when, during a reorganization, those plants purchasing gas from Brown at inflated prices came under his purview. The high costs helped to undercut the vice president's division earnings and thus to erode his position in the hierarchy. The origin of the situation did not matter. All that counted was that the vice president's division was steadily losing big money. In the end, he resigned to "pursue new opportunities."

One might ask why top management does not institute codes or systems for tracking responsibility. This example provides the clue. An explicit system of accountability for subordinates would probably have to apply to top executives as well and would restrict their freedom. Bureaucracy expands the freedom of those on top by giving them the power to restrict the freedom of those beneath.

On the Fast Track

Managers see what happened to the vice president as completely capricious, but completely understandable. They take for granted the absence of any tracking of responsibility. If anything, they blame the vice president for not recognizing soon enough the dangers of the situation into which he was being drawn and for not preparing a defense—even perhaps finding a substitute scapegoat. At the same time, they realize that this sort of thing could easily happen to them. They see few defenses against being caught in the wrong place at the wrong time except constant wariness, the diffusion of responsibility, and perhaps being shrewd enough to declare the ineptitude of one's predecessor on first taking a job.

What about avoiding the consequences of their own errors? Here they enjoy more control. They can "outrun" their mistakes so that when blame time arrives, the burden will fall on someone else. The ideal situation, of course, is to be in a position to fire one's successors for one's own previous mistakes.

Some managers, in fact, argue that outrunning mistakes is the real key to managerial success. One way to do this is by manipulating the numbers. Both the chemical and the textile companies place a great premium on a division's or a subsidiary's return on assets. A good way for business managers to increase their ROA is to reduce their assets while maintaining sales. Usually they will do everything they can to hold down expenditures in order to decrease the asset base, particularly at the end of the fiscal year. The most common way of doing this is by deferring capital expenditures, from maintenance to innovative investments, as long as possible. Done for a short time, this is called "starving" a plant; done over a longer period, it is called "milking" a plant.

Some managers become very adept at milking businesses and showing a consistent record of high returns. They move from one job to another in a company, always upward, rarely staying more than two years in any post. They may leave behind them deteriorating plants and unsafe working conditions, but they know that if they move quickly enough, the blame will fall on others. In this sense, bureaucracies may be thought of as vast systems of organized irresponsibility.

FLEXIBILITY & DEXTERITY WITH SYMBOLS

The intense competition among managers takes place not only behind the agreeable public faces I have described but within an extraordinarily indirect and ambiguous linguistic framework. Except at blame time, managers do not publicly criticize or disagree with one another or with company policy. The sanction against such criticism or disagreement is so strong that it constitutes, in managers' view, a suppression of professional debate. The sanction seems to be rooted principally in their acute sense of organizational contingency; the person one criticizes or argues with today could be one's boss tomorrow.

This leads to the use of an elaborate linguistic code marked by emotional neutrality, especially in group settings. The code communicates the meaning one might wish to convey to other managers, but since it is devoid of any significant emotional sentiment, it can be reinterpreted should social relationships or attitudes change. Here, for example, are some typical phrases describing performance appraisals followed by their probable intended meanings:

Stock Phrase	Probable Intended Meaning
Exceptionally well qualified	Has committed no major blunders to date
Tactful in dealing with superiors	Knows when to keep his mouth shut
Quick thinking	Offers plausible excuses for errors
Meticulous attention to detail	A nitpicker
Slightly below average	Stupid
Unusually loyal	Wanted by no one else

For the most part, such neutered language is not used with the intent to deceive; rather, its purpose is to communicate certain meanings within specific contexts with the implicit understanding that, should the context change, a new, more appropriate meaning can be attached to the language already used. In effect, the corporation is a setting where people are not held to their word because it is generally understood that their word is always provisional.

The higher one gets in the corporate world, the more this seems to be the case; in fact, advancement beyond the upper middle level depends greatly on one's ability to manipulate a variety of symbols without becoming tied to or identified with any of them. For example, an amazing variety of organizational improvement programs marks practically every corporation. I am referring here to the myriad ideas generated by corporate staff, business consultants, academics, and a host of others to improve corporate structure; sharpen decision making; raise morale; create a more humanistic workplace; adopt Theory X, Theory Y, or, more recently, Theory Z of management; and so on. These programs become important when they are pushed from the top.

The watchword in the large conglomerate at the moment is productivity and, since this is a pet project of the CEO himself, it is said that no one goes into his presence without wearing a blue *Productivity!* button and talking about "quality circles" and "feedback sessions." The president of another company pushes a series of managerial seminars that endlessly repeats the basic functions of management: (1) planning, (2) organizing, (3) motivating, and (4) controlling. Aspiring young managers attend these sessions and with a seemingly dutiful eagerness learn to repeat the formulas under the watchful eyes of senior officials.

Privately, managers characterize such programs as the "CEO's incantations over the assembled multitude," as "elaborate rituals with no practical effect," or as "waving a magic wand to make things wonderful again." Publicly, of course, managers on the way up adopt the programs with great enthusiasm, participate in or run them very effectively, and then quietly drop them when the time is right.

Playing the Game

Such flexibility, as it is called, can be confusing even to those in the inner circles. I was told the following by a highly placed staff member whose work requires him to interact daily with the top figures of his company:

"I get faked out all the time and I'm part of the system. I come from a very different culture. Where I come from, if you give someone your *word*, no one ever questions it. It's the old hard-work-will-lead-to-success ideology. Small community, Protestant, agrarian, small business, merchant-type values. I'm disadvantaged in a system like this."

He goes on to characterize the system more fully and what it takes to succeed within it:

"It's the ability to play this system that determines whether you will rise. . . . And part of the adeptness [required] is determined by how much it bothers people. One thing you have to be able to do is to play the game, but you can't be disturbed by the game. What's the game? It's bringing troops home from Vietnam and declaring peace with honor. It's saying one thing and meaning another.

"It's characterizing the reality of a situation with *any* description that is necessary to make that situation more palatable to some group that matters. It means that you have to come up with a culturally accepted verbalization to explain why you are *not* doing what you are doing. . . . [Or] you say that we had to do what we did because it was inevitable; or because the guys at the [regulatory] agencies were dumb; [you] say we won when we really lost; [you] say we saved money when we squandered it; [you] say something's safe when it's potentially or actually dangerous. . . . Everyone knows that it's bullshit, but it's *accepted*. This is the game."

In addition, then, to the other characteristics that I have described, it seems that a prerequisite for big success in the corporation is a certain adeptness at inconsistency. This premium on inconsistency is particularly evident in the many areas of public controversy that face top-ranking managers. Two things come together to produce this situation. The first is managers' sense of beleaguerment from a wide array of adversaries who, it is thought, want to disrupt or impede management's attempts to further the economic interests of their companies. In every company that I studied, managers see themselves and their traditional prerogatives as being under siege, and they respond with a set of caricatures of their perceived principal adversaries.

For example, government regulators are brash, young, unkempt hippies in blue jeans who know nothing about the business for which they make rules; environmental activists—the bird and bunny people—are softheaded idealists who want everybody to live in tents, bum candles, ride horses, and eat berries; workers' compensation lawyers are out-and-out crooks who prey on corporations to appropriate exorbitant fees from unwary clients; labor activists are radical troublemakers who want to disrupt harmonious industrial communities; and the news media consist of rabble-rousers who propagate sensational antibusiness stories to sell papers or advertising time on shows like *60 Minutes*.

Second, within this context of perceived harassment, managers must address a multiplicity of audiences, some of whom are considered adversaries. These audiences are the internal corporate hierarchy with its intricate and shifting power and status cliques, key regulators, key local and federal legislators, special publics that vary according to the issues, and the public at large, whose goodwill and favorable opinion are considered essential for a company's free operation.

Managerial adeptness at inconsistency becomes evident in the widely discrepant perspectives, reasons for action, and presentations of fact that explain, excuse, or justify corporate behavior to these diverse audiences.

Adeptness at Inconsistency

The cotton dust issue in the textile industry provides a fine illustration of what I mean. Prolonged exposure to cotton dust produces in many textile workers a chronic and eventually disabling pulmonary disease called byssinosis or, colloquially, brown lung. In the early 1970s, the Occupational Safety and Health Administration proposed a ruling to cut workers' exposure to cotton dust sharply by requiring textile companies to invest large amounts of money in cleaning up their plants. The industry fought the regulation fiercely but a final OSHA ruling was made in 1978 requiring full compliance by 1984.

The industry took the case to court. Despite an attempt by Reagan appointees in OSHA to have the case removed from judicial consideration and remanded to the agency they controlled for further cost/benefit analysis, the Supreme Court ruled in 1981 that the 1978 OSHA ruling was fully within the agency's mandate, namely, to protect workers' health and safety as the primary benefit exceeding all cost considerations.

During these proceedings, the textile company was engaged on a variety of fronts and was pursuing a number of actions. For instance, it intensively lobbied regulators and legislators and it prepared court materials for the industry's defense, arguing that the proposed standard would crush the industry and that the problem, if it existed, should be met by increasing workers' use of respirators.

The company also aimed a public relations barrage at special-interest groups as well as at the general public. It argued that there is probably no such thing as byssinosis; workers suffering from pulmonary problems are all heavy smokers and the real culprit is the government-subsidized tobacco industry. How can cotton cause brown lung when cotton is white? Further, if there is a problem, only some workers are afflicted, and therefore the solution is more careful screening of the work force to detect susceptible people and prevent them from ever reaching the workplace. Finally, the company claimed that if the regulation were imposed, most of the textile industry would move overseas where regulations are less harsh.[5]

In the meantime, the company was actually addressing the problem but in a characteristically indirect way. It invested $20 million in a few plants where it knew such an investment would make money; this investment automated the early stages of handling cotton, traditionally a very slow procedure, and greatly increased productivity. The investment had the side benefit of reducing cotton dust levels to the new standard in precisely those areas of the work process where the dust problem is greatest. Publicly, of course, the company claims that the money was spent entirely to eliminate dust, evidence of its corporate good citizenship. (Privately, executives admit that, without the productive return, they would not have spent the money and they have not done so in several other plants.)

Indeed, the productive return is the only rationale that carries weight within the corporate hierarchy. Executives also admit, somewhat ruefully and only when their office doors are closed, that OSHA's regulation on cotton dust has been the main factor in forcing technological innovation in a centuries-old and somewhat stagnant industry.

Such adeptness at inconsistency, without moral uneasiness, is essential for executive success. It means being able to say, as a very high-ranking official of the textile company said to me without batting an eye, that the industry has never caused the slightest problem in any worker's breathing capacity. It means, in the chemical company, propagating an elaborate hazard/benefit calculus for appraisal of dangerous chemicals while internally conceptualizing "hazards" as business risks. It means publicly extolling the carefulness of testing procedures on toxic chemicals while privately ridiculing animal tests as inapplicable to humans.

It means lobbying intensively in the present to shape government regulations to one's immediate advantage and, ten years later, in the event of a catastrophe, arguing that the company acted strictly in accordance with the standards of the time. It means claiming that the real problem of our society is its unwillingness to take risks, while in the thickets of one's bureaucracy avoiding risks at every turn; it means as well making every effort to socialize the risks of industrial activity while privatizing the benefits.

THE BUREAUCRATIC ETHIC

The bureaucratic ethic contrasts sharply with the original Protestant Ethic. The Protestant Ethic was the ideology of a self-confident and independent propertied social class. It was an ideology that extolled the virtues of accumulating wealth in a society organized around property and that accepted the stewardship responsibilities entailed by property. It was an ideology where a person's word was his bond and where the integrity of the handshake was seen as crucial to the maintenance of good business relationships. Perhaps most important, it was connected to a predictable economy of salvation—that is, hard work will lead to success, which is a sign of one's election by God—a notion also containing its own theodicy to explain the misery of those who do not make it in this world.

Bureaucracy, however, breaks apart substance from appearances, action from responsibility, and language from meaning. Most important, it breaks apart the older connection between the meaning of work and salvation. In the bureaucratic world, one's success, one's sign of election, no longer depends on one's own efforts and on an inscrutable God but on the capriciousness of one's superiors and the market; and one achieves economic salvation to the extent that one pleases and submits to one's employer and meets the exigencies of an impersonal market.

In this way, because moral choices are inextricably tied to personal fates, bureaucracy erodes internal and even external standards of morality, not only in matters of individual success and failure but also in all the issues that managers face in their daily work. Bureaucracy makes its own internal rules and social context the principal moral gauges for action. Men and women in bureaucracies turn to each other for moral cues for behavior and come to fashion specific situational moralities for specific significant people in their worlds.

As it happens, the guidance they receive from each other is profoundly ambiguous because what matters in the bureaucratic world is not what a person is but how closely his many personae mesh with the organizational ideal; not his willingness to stand by his actions but his agility in avoiding blame; not what he believes or says but how well he has mastered the ideologies that serve his corporation; not what he stands for but whom he stands with in the labyrinths of his organization.

In short, bureaucracy structures for managers an intricate series of moral mazes. Even the inviting paths out of the puzzle often turn out to be invitations to jeopardy.

NOTES

I presented an earlier version of this paper in the Faculty Lecture Series at Williams College on March 18, 1982. The intensive field work done during 1980 and 1981 was made possible by a Fellowship for Independent Research from the National Endowment for the Humanities and by a Junior Faculty Leave and small research grant from Williams College.

1. There is a long sociological tradition of work on managers and I am, of course, indebted to that literature. I am particularly indebted to the work, both joint and separate, of Joseph Bensman and Arthur J. Vidich, two of the keenest observers of the new middle class. See especially their *The New American Society: The Revolution of the Middle Class* (Chicago: Quadrangle Books, 1971).

2. See Max Weher, *The Protestant Ethic and the Spirit of Capitalism,* translated by Talcott Parsons (New York: Charles Scribner's Sons, 1958), p. 172.

3. See William H. Whyte, *The Organization Man* (New York: Simon & Schuster, 1956), and David Riesman, in collaboration with Reuel Denney and Nathan Glazer, *The Lonely Crowd: A Study of the Changing American Character* (New Haven: Yale University Press, 1950).

4. Karl Mannheim, *Man and Society in an Age of Reconstruction* [London: Paul (Kegan), Trench, Trubner Ltd., 1940], p. 55.

5. On February 9, 1982, the Occupational Safety and Health Administration issued a notice that it was once again reviewing its 1978 standard on cotton dust for "cost-effectiveness." See *Federal Register,* vol. 47, p. 5906. As of this writing (May 1983), this review has still not been officially completed.

Essay

Not a Fool, Not a Saint

Thomas Teal

Malden Mills owner Aaron Feuerstein was both ridiculed and canonized when he kept his 1,000 employees on the payroll after a fire burned down his factory last Christmas. But now he's proving that treating workers well is just plain good business.

At a European trade show in Brussels during the first week of September, Malden Mills of Lawrence, Massachusetts, introduced a broad new line of high-end upholstery fabrics. Buyers snapped up the sleek material, derived from the company's hugely successful line of Polartec and Polarfleece apparel knits. A victory, certainly. And one more step in an uphill comeback by a factory that suffered one of the biggest industrial fires in New England history less than a year ago, a factory whose owner achieved heroic stature by keeping more than 1,000 jobless employees at full pay for several months after the blaze.

Yet Aaron Feuerstein, owner, president, and CEO of Malden Mills, has good reason to feel unappreciated. It's true that his work force adores him, that almost every newspaper, TV station, and business magazine in the U.S. has sung his praises, that Bill Clinton invited him to Washington for the State of the Union address, and that columnists, unions, and religious leaders all across the country have declared him a saint. But much of this celebrity is based on the misleading premise that this 70-year-old acted selflessly, against his own best interests, which is another way of saying that he acted the way a saint might act: irrationally.

In fact, it seems pretty clear that some people call Feuerstein a saint because they don't quite have the courage to call him a fool. They don't think he should be rebuilding his mill, at least not in Lawrence. They think he should have pocketed the insurance proceeds, closed the business, and walked away. Or else they think he should have grabbed the chance to move the company to some state or country with lower labor costs.

Some commentators have even accused him of risking the very survival of his business with a lot of grandstanding magnanimity that served no purpose but self-advertisement. There's a suggestion that real businessmen are tougher than Feuerstein, that responsible owners never pay any employee a dime more than they have to, and that no factory owner could possibly have done what Feuerstein has done unless he'd been touched by God or is just touched, period. These people, for instance, argue that Feuerstein certainly could have skipped the grand gesture of paying out some $15 million in wages and benefits to already overpaid workers when they no longer had a place to work. One business school professor has suggested pointedly that not everyone should look to him as a model.

Most of this carping is nonsense. But in a way, so is much of the praise. Why in the world should it be a sign of divinely inspired nuttiness to treat a work force as if it was an asset, to cultivate the loyalty of employees who hold the key to recovery and success, to take risks for the sake of a large future income stream, even to seek positive publicity? These are the things Aaron Feuerstein has done, and most people stand in amazement as if they were witnessing a miracle or a traffic accident.

I was one of them until I discovered that Feuerstein is at heart a hard-nosed businessman. He has some minor eccentricities—a weakness for little bursts of Shakespeare, a tendency to wander off into far corners of the room as he thinks and talks—and his Old Testament intensity and biblical pronouncements can be slightly intimidating, despite his warmth. The two hours I spent with him, however, convinced me that he is as tough-minded as he is righteous, a man entirely up to the job of running a factory for profit.

Take downsizing. Would anyone have guessed that Feuerstein was a devotee? At one point, as he was warming to an attack on the unconscionable Al Dunlap (the man who dismantled Scott Paper and fired a third of its work force), I interrupted to suggest that maybe Scott Paper was overstaffed and Feuerstein surprised me: "If one-third of the people in that company were wastefully employed, then Dunlap did the right thing." And then the new patron saint of working Americans surprised me some more. "Legitimate down-sizing as the result of technological advances or as a result of good industrial engineering? Absolutely. I'm in favor of it. And we do it here all day long. . . . We try to do it in such a way as to minimize human suffering, but the downsizing must be done." Under the benevolent, angular exterior lurks a businessman—a businessman who understands labor. The trick, he told me, is to keep growing fast enough to give new jobs to the people technology displaces, to weed out unnecessary jobs "without crushing the spirit of the work force." If all you're after is cutting costs, if you "just have a scheme to cut people—that sort of thing is resented by labor, and you're never forgiven." Feuerstein has a union shop, has long invested heavily in technology that eliminates jobs, and has never had a strike—not exactly the hallmarks of a fool.

Or take the insurance question. Feuerstein could certainly have closed the factory, sold the business, pocketed the proceeds, and spent the rest of his days in a hammock. But men in their 70s who still come to work every day for the sheer exhilaration of the job don't turn to hammocks in a crisis. His decision to rebuild seems to have been spontaneous and immediate, made more or less by the light of the flames and without much thought to the insurance proceeds. And still it was a rational decision. Factories are insured for their replacement cost, and if you don't replace them, you have to settle for the depreciated value of the lost building and machinery, in this case a lot of modern machinery and several antediluvian buildings. You can solve this equation without the higher math. An insurance payoff is likely to be much larger when it's taken as a contribution toward a state-of-the-art manufacturing facility, partly because it has the potential to produce income for your family for two or three generations to come. Last year's pre-fire, pre-tax profits was $20 million on sales of $400 million. Twenty million times two or three generations comes to an awful lot of money.

Or take self-advertisement. Feuerstein has not been shy with the media. Malden Mills has been featured everywhere from *People* to *Dateline* to the Lands' End catalogue, and it's all been free. What's more, if the insurance settlement should wind up in court—not wildly improbable—will it hurt Feuerstein's chances of winning that half the people in the country worship the ground he walks on? Do insurance companies care about their reputations? You bet.

As for the idea that he might relocate the company somewhere with lower wages, Feuerstein moved the company to Lawrence (from Malden, just outside Boston) in 1956, at a time when New England textile mills thought local labor too expensive and were streaming south like carpetbaggers. A great many of those companies failed anyway, despite the lower wages they spent so much money to find, and Feuerstein is sure he knows why: They gave too much attention to costs and not enough to quality. He responds with contempt to suggestions that Malden Mills should move offshore. (Labor in the South is no longer such a bargain.)

"Why would I go to Thailand to bring the cost lower when I might run the risk of losing the advantage I've got, which is superior quality?" In any case, he goes on, lower wages are a temporary advantage. Quality lasts. At least it can last if you focus hard on expertise and the freedom to innovate. But to do that, you have to focus hard on employees. When Feuerstein came to Lawrence, he wasn't looking for cheap labor but for skilled labor—capable, experienced textile designers, engineers, and workers who could give him the edge he needed to compete more effectively.

It's here he has shown his real genius. Any idiot with a strong enough stomach can make quick money, sometimes a lot of it, by slashing costs and milking customers, employees, or a company's reputation. But clearly that's not the way to make a lot of money for a long time. The way to do that is to create so much value that your customers wouldn't dream of looking for another supplier. Indeed, the idea is to build a value creation system of superior products, service, teamwork, productivity, and cooperation with the buyer. Reduced to its essence, that means superior technology and superior employees. Reduced still further, as Aaron Feuerstein can tell you, it means superior employees. The correlation between loyal customers and loyal employees is no coincidence.

For Malden Mills, the first test and the breakthrough came in the early 1980s with the total collapse of the market for what was then a company mainstay—artificial furs. It was the R&D and production employees who saved the company over the next few years, using their superior expertise in synthetic fibers, napping, and finishing to create a series of lightweight, thermal, resilient, woollike fabrics under the brand names Polarfleece and Polartec. They look good, feel good, wick well, don't pill, and hold up to repeated washing. Moreover, they're all engineered to order. The retailer wants, say, a fabric for cyclists that's windproof and light but also soft, absorbent, and quick-drying. Malden's ability to satisfy such orders has made Polartec a favorite of upscale retailers like Lands' End, L. L. Bean, Patagonia, the North Face, Eddie Bauer, and a dozen more.

Best of all, these customers are loyal. Customer retention at Malden Mills runs roughly 95%, which is world class. Employee retention runs above 95%, which is prodigious but can hardly come as a surprise to anyone familiar with Feuerstein's approach to personnel. As for productivity, from 1982 to 1995, revenues in constant dollars more than tripled while the work force barely doubled. Compare that with an overall productivity increase for the U.S. of a little better than 1% per year. Thanks to its employees, Malden Mills has risen from at least one five-alarm crisis in the past. No wonder Aaron Feuerstein loves those employees enough to risk $15 million to keep them available and motivated and to help him rise from the literal ashes of last year's catastrophe. This isn't the work of a saint or a fool, it's the considered and historically successful policy of a genial manufacturing genius who might serve as a model for every man and woman in business.

<h2 style="text-align:center">. Essay</h2>

Malden Mills: When Being a Good Company Isn't Good Enough

Al Gini and Alexei M. Marcoux

I

In American business literature, the concept of "corporate social responsibility" (CSR) was enunciated, if not completely defined, during the height of our Industrial Revolution by no less major a player than United States Steel founder Andrew Carnegie. Believing that "to whom much had been given, much is expected," Carnegie was convinced that successful businesses were duty bound to be charitable to those in need, and to be diligent stewards and guardians of the wealth and property entrusted to them. Since this initial parochial and paternalistic description, the exact nature of CSR continues to be debated and redefined as the issues in business become increasingly complex and sophisticated.[1]

There is, of course, a core of theorists and practitioners who claim that while business ought to try to behave ethically, the primary business of business is to maximize owner value. As one pundit put it:

> The modern firm solves one (but only one) of the major problems of humankind—the creation of wealth. That wealth then allows individuals in their various roles the opportunity to protect values they care about.[2]

However, as Rotman School of Management Dean Roger Martin has suggested, a "tipping-point" in our social conscience has occurred regarding the role and responsibilities of business: Corporations aren't just in the business of making money; they don't operate in a universe composed solely of shareholders. They exist within smaller and larger political and social entities, and are subject to pressures from members of those networks. Moreover, in the wake of recent corporate scandals, corporate leaders are now painfully aware that they need to think more rigorously about responsible corporate conduct—whether they want to or not. Failure to do so, warns Martin, may mean that the option to act will be taken out of their hands.[3]

According to Richard DeGeorge, since the 1950s the growing size, impact, import, and power of corporations have not gone unnoticed.[4] In 2000, the Institute for Policy Studies reported that of the largest 100 economies in the world, 51 are companies/corporations, not countries.[5] Today the approximately 4.8 million U.S corporations generate collectively annual revenues of 17.3 trillion dollars. On the other side of the ledger, there are approximately 23.5 million small and family businesses nationwide that provide 63% of all employment in the United States.[6] Because of these numbers, an increasing segment of the general public both expects and demands that corporations and businesses in general recognize and accept the fact the "power and size begets *self-monitored* obligations." In a 2005 poll conducted by Mark Clements Research Inc., 89% of the respondents believed that businesses and corporations have a social responsibility to behave fairly and honestly with their employees and the community at large.[7]

Although the original formulation of CSR was based on the notion of noblesse oblige, the main focus of the contemporary version of CSR revolves around the allied principles of "stakeholder responsibility" and "corporate citizenship." All accounts of contemporary CSR are predicated on the fundamental proposition that all businesses/corporations are players in the context of a larger social drama. Businesses/corporations are part of the web-work and geography of life, and, as such, share obligations and rights with other players in the scenario. At a minimum, according to the *Wall Street Journal*, responsible corporate citizenship includes:

1. Strong, sustainable economic performance.
2. Rigorous compliance with financial and legal rules.
3. Ethical actions beyond formal requirements which reflect a corporation's sense of integrity and appropriate concern for issues beyond self and the needs of self.[8]

II

Issues of social, political, and economic justice have long been part of the magisterium of the church. In the late nineteenth century and early twentieth century "Catholic social thought" (CST) joined the ongoing debate among Marxism, Socialism and Capitalism by focusing on an important question: *What are the rights and obligations of property (capital) versus labor, and which of them has priority over the other?* Or, more contemporaneously: *What expectations and rights do workers carry with them into the workplace, and beyond the rights and needs of the place of business to earn a profit, what other obligations does the business/employer have to the worker?*

In 1891, Pope Leo XII published the encyclical *Rerum novarum* (On the Condition of Labor) which, according to commentator Thomas A. Shannon, set the agenda and established a baseline for future CST analysis and commentary. *Rerum novarum* addressed four critical socioeconomic issues of the day:

1. A defense of the right of private property.
2. The right/obligation to earn a profit.
3. The right to earn a living wage.

4. The right of labor to organize and when necessary, strike.[9]

Subsequent social writings and encyclicals of Leo XIII's successors went on to develop and expand CST on how "good work," "good business," and a "good company" can and should be defined.

In a very real sense, Leo XIII's initial message on the "nature of work" and the "rights of the worker" waited ninety years to find its completion in Pope John Paul II's publication of *Laborem exercens* (On Human Work) in 1981. Mirroring the words of Pius XI, "[We] are born to labor, as a bird to fly,"[10] John Paul II argues that while toil may be a part of our collective "curse," work is also a part of our destiny and character. Work is not just a burden to be tolerated and endured. Work is the mechanism by which we fulfill and establish ourselves in the world.[11] Work, said John Paul II, is the agency by which we complete ourselves and transform the world. It is in work that we come to know and define ourselves. It is in work that we come to recognize our rights and obligations in regard to others.

> Work is a good thing for man—a good thing for humanity because through work man not only transforms nature, adopting to its own needs, but he also achieves fulfillment as a human being and indeed, in a sense becomes more a human being.[12]

In his 1991 encyclical *Centesimus annus* (On the One Hundredth Anniversary of *Rerum novarum*), John Paul II argues that if work is a necessary condition for human existence, then it can also be argued that people have a "right to work."

> The obligation to earn one's bread by the sweat of one's brow also presumes the right to do so. A society in which the right is systematically denied, in which economic policies do not allow workers to reach satisfactory levels of employment, cannot be justified from an ethical point of view, nor can the society attain social peace.[13]

For John Paul II the "right to work" is a fundamental human right, because it is a necessary condition for personhood at the most primary physical, moral, and psychological levels.[14] In *Economic Justice for All* American Catholic Bishops took John Paul II's position one step further. If "people have a right to work/employment," then "the community has an obligation to fulfill these basic needs unless an absolute scarcity of resources makes this strictly impossible."[15] Thus, "businesses in particular and societies in general are to be judged morally based on their ability to generate jobs."[16] The bishops call full employment "the foundation of a just economy."

The bottom line here is, we think, obvious. Within the CST tradition the "right to work" is a fundamental human right necessary for personal and social well-being; and the "priority of labor" must be seen as the first postulate in the establishment of a just and secure "social morality." Hence, the primary ethical duty of the state, the Church, and all employers is "to promote the dignity of work" and to subordinate all work to man, "the proper subject of work," and not simply to "economic advantage(s)."

In tandem, the traditions of CSR and CST constitute a collective model or template for responsible and responsive moral business conduct. In ethical terms, these positions both advocate the continuous attempt to work out the rights and obligations we have and share with others in our public lives, on the job, and in our businesses.

III

Until recently under the leadership of Aaron Feuerstein, Malden Mills is taken by many CSR proponents to be the archetype of the socially responsible firm. Viewed from the joint perspective of CSR and CST, it is hard to find a more exemplary firm than Malden Mills.

On December 11, 1995, three of eight factory buildings in Lawrence, Massachusetts, burned to the ground, displacing thousands of workers and seriously endangering the future of the family business founded in 1906. Feuerstein, the then-majority shareholder, president, and CEO of closely held Malden Mills, had a number of options available to him. He could have pocketed the insurance money, closed the business, and walked away. He could have used the insurance proceeds to move operations to some other state or country with lower labor costs. Or, he could use the money to hang on to his workforce, rebuild the factories, and keep Malden Mills where it was.

For Feuerstein, the decision was a clear one. An observant Jew motivated by his religious convictions, a strong sense of personal and family responsibility, and confidence in his own ability to handle adversity, Feuerstein couldn't and wouldn't walk away from this problem. Corporate responsibility, he said, *does mean* you have to take care of your stockholders. But, he went on, it *also means* you have responsibility to your workers and to your community. Closing down—giving up—was unthinkable. It meant putting 3000 people out of work and delivering a deathblow to the city of Lawrence.[17]

In choosing to do "the right thing for the right reason," Aaron Feuerstein passed the CSR/CST test with flying colors.

> Feuerstein was pronounced a corporate hero when he promised his workers that he would continue to pay their salaries out of his own pocket while he rebuilt the factories, even though his workers wouldn't be producing.
>
> As a result, Feuerstein was invited to speak at colleges and universities all across the U.S. He was given honorary degrees, and was the subject of a flattering profile on the television program *60 Minutes.*[18]

But, unfortunately, as things turned out, Feuerstein's actions failed the test of the marketplace. The very virtues for which Malden Mills is lauded among CSR proponents are recognized also to be significant causes of Malden Mills' recent bankruptcy (which found former creditor GE Capital its largest shareholder) and of Feuerstein's fall from leadership (in favor of new President and CEO Michael Spillane).

> Feuerstein's pledge to continue paying his workers eventually cost them their jobs, and cost Feuerstein his company. Feuerstein ran out of money, and Malden Mills was forced to declare bankruptcy. . . . After its bankruptcy, Malden Mills was dangerously close to going out of business completely. Only the last minute heroics of a group of corporate lenders saved the company from going under.[19]

In short, *passing* the CSR lest meant, for Malden Mills, *failing* the test of the marketplace.

IV

Ought implies can means that if one *ought* to perform an action *A*, then it must be the case that one *can* perform *A*. Its negative corollary is that if one *cannot* perform *A*, then it is *not* the case that one ought to perform *A*.[20]

Capitalism won the debate amongst Marxism, Socialism, and Capitalism *theoretically* because it won *practically*. Only Capitalism satisfies the *can* in *ought implies can* because only Capitalism is capable of supporting a sustainable, flourishing economic community. Capitalism provides for a sustainable, flourishing economic community because (i) only those firms whose operations cover their costs survive market competition, and (ii) the bankruptcy system facilitates the efficient redeployment to other uses of assets held by firms whose operations don't cover their costs. If only Capitalism satisfies the *can* in *ought implies*

can, and if it does this through the discipline imposed by market competition and the bankruptcy system, then it follows that compatibility with *passing the market test* must be implicit in any candidate principle of CSR capable of being action-guiding for capitalist firms.

Ought implies can is relevant to the evaluation of Feuerstein-led Malden Mills' insolvency because, to the extent that Feuerstein's actions on behalf of Malden Mills in the wake of the 1995 fire are responsible for the firm's subsequent insolvency, it suggests that one *cannot* sustainably manage Malden Mills (or other firms similarly-situated to Malden Mills) in the manner that Feuerstein and, by extension, Feuerstein-impressed CSR advocates claim one ought. If ought implies can and one cannot, then it is not the case that one ought. Those claiming that one ought to do so anyway advance a claim in contravention of *ought implies can.*

Consequently, Feuerstein-led Malden Mills' insolvency calls for a re-examination of CSR in light of capitalist reality. Trivially, CSR is either relevant to capitalist firms doing business in a competitive market economy or it is not. If it is, then CSR advocates seem forced to acknowledge that their enthusiasm for Feuerstein's leadership of Malden Mills in the wake of the 1995 fire is misplaced. However admirable Feuerstein's *intentions*, his *actions* were ultimately destructive of Malden Mills as an engine of sustainable and flourishing economic community. Those who today work at Malden Mills owe their good fortune not to the leadership of Aaron Feuerstein, but to the financial might of GE Capital. GE Capital's existence and financial might issue from the leadership of Jack Welch. Welch is rarely (if ever) identified among the CSR-impressed as an exemplary corporate leader. To the contrary, his leadership style and his notorious, fire-the-bottom-ten-percent method of personnel evaluation are more often identified among the CSR-impressed as products of the *absence* of a social conscience. His book *Winning*[21] is characterized as a how-to manual for the most distasteful form of corporate psychopathy. A CSR relevant to capitalist firms seems forced to place greater value on Welch's leadership than on Feuerstein's.

There remains, of course, the opposite tack. Perhaps CSR is *not* relevant to capitalist firms doing business in a competitive market economy. For some, Feuerstein's actions just feel so *right*—and if those actions are incompatible with Feuerstein-led Malden Mills' survival in a competitive market economy, then so much the worse for the competitive market economy. The clear implication is that we ought to *change our economic institutions* to make them more hospitable to firms like the Feuerstein-led Malden Mills (and perhaps less hospitable to firms like the flourishing Welch-led GE entities).

This opposite tack is, of course, available—and many pursue it: antiglobalization protesters being the most prominent, recent example. But if that is what CSR is to become, it thereby abandons its historic mission. It becomes instead—as Kenneth Goodpaster once said of stakeholder theory—a more radical critique of capitalism and of the corporate form than its proponents intend.[22] In other words, it abandons the *C* in CSR, embracing instead the economic nonsense (and often, nihilism) that informs the more vocal critics of capitalism.[23]

V

Economic activity is as much the proper subject of moral reflection as any other form of human action—and perhaps more so, given its intimate connection to sustaining human life. Capitalist economic institutions and capitalist firms are not without moral fault. We do well, morally and prudently, as children of God, to seek their improvement.

Those who would do the difficult work of offering moral guidance for economic activity are duty-bound first to *understand* economic activity, and to understand particularly its most successful and fecund form—capitalist economic activity. Admiration for Aaron Feuerstein's leadership of Malden Mills, regardless of its actual effects, is symptomatic of a partial blindness that afflicts so many of the CSR-impressed. It is a blindness to economic theory, to economic practice, and to the relationship between the two.

If the measure of an economic system's moral worth is in the economic opportunity it provides and in the jobs it creates,[24] then there really is no moral contest: supposedly ruthless Anglo-American capitalist economic institutions and their equally ruthless firms win, going away. A CSR worth paying attention to ought to acknowledge as much—looking a bit more kindly on the likes of Jack Welch, and a bit more critically at the likes of Aaron Feuerstein.

NOTES

1. R. Edward Freeman and Patricia H. Werhane, "Corporate Responsibility," in *A Companion to Applied Ethics*, ed. by R. G. Frey, C. H. Wellman (New York: Blackwell Publishing, 2003) 552, 553.
2. "Corporate Social Responsibility: Good Citizenship or Investor Rip-off?," *The Wall Street Journal*, January 9, 2006, R6.
3. Roger Martin, "The Virtue Matrix," *Rotman Management*, Spring/Summer 2003, 7, 8.
4. R. T. DeGeorge, "The Status of Business Ethics," Research Workshop, Stanford University, August 1985, 14–17.
5. Sandra Waddock, "Corporate Citizenship" in *The Blackwell Encyclopedia of Management: Business Ethics*, Second Edition, ed. by P. H. Werhane, R. E. Freeman (New York: Blackwell Publishing, 2005), 114.
6. Matt Bai, "New World Economy," *New York Times Magazine*, December 18, 2005, 15, 16.
7. David Wallechinsky, "Is the American Dream Still Possible?," *Parade Magazine*, April 23, 2006, 5.
8. "Corporate Social Responsibility: Good Citizenship or Investor Rip-off?," *The Wall Street Journal*, January 9, 2006, R6.

9. Thomas A. Shannon, "Commentary on *Rerum novarum*" in *Modern Catholic Social Teaching* ed. by Kenneth R. Hines, O.F.M. (Washington, D.C.: Georgetown University Press, 2004), 127–129.

10. Pope Pius XI, *Quadragesimo anno* (*On Reconstructing the Social Order*), May 15, 1931 in *Justice in the Workplace* ed. by David M. Byers (Washington, D.C.: United States Catholic Conference, 1985), 63.

11. John Paul II, *Laborem exercens* (*On Human Work*), 18.

12. John Paul II, *Laborem exercens* (*On Human Work*), 9.

13. John Paul II, *Centesimus annus* (On the One Hundredth Anniversary of *Rerum Novarum*) (Boston: St. Paul Books, n.d.), 62.

14. R. T. DeGeorge, "The Right to Work: Law and Ideology," *Valparaiso University Law Review* 19 (Fall 1984), 15, 16.

15. National Conference of Catholic Bishops, *Economic Justice for All*, 136.

16. "Jobless Recoveries, Displaced Workers, and the Responsibility to Create Jobs," an unpublished article submitted to *Business Ethics Quarterly*, Spring 2006.

17. "Competing Vision at Malden Mills," in John R. Boatright, *Ethics and the Conduct of Business*, 5th Edition (Upper Saddle River, New Jersey: Prentice Hall, 2007), 364–366.

18. Radley Balko, "Altruism? Bah, Humbug," *Apple Daily*, December 24, 2004. [Accessed via World Wide Web at http://www.cato.org/dailys/12-24-04.html on September 15, 2006]

19. Balko, "Altruism? Bah, Humbug," *op. cit.*

20. This negative corollary is just an application of modus tollens. Let Oa = ought to perform *a* and let Ca = can perform *a*. Adopt as conventional logical operators '←' for 'implies' and '~' for 'not.' 'Ought to perform *a* implies can perform *a*' is expressed as: Oa←Ca. 'Cannot perform *a*' is expressed as: ~Ca. From Oa←Ca and ~Ca, it follows by modus tollens that ~Oa.

21. Jack Welch with Suzy Welch, *Winning* (New York: HarperCollins, 2005).

22. Kenneth E. Goodpaster, "Business Ethics and Stakeholder Analysis," *Business Ethics Quarterly* 1(1) (1991): 53–73.

23. See, e.g., Franklin Foer, "Meet the New New Left: Bold, Fun and Stupid," *The New Republic*, May 1, 2000 (arguing that "anarchy is socialism without the state" is the closest thing to an idea informing antiglobalization protesters' activities—and it's not very close). [Accessed via World Wide Web at http://web.nps.navy.mil/~relooney/3040_1432. htm on September 15, 2006]

24. See note 16, above.

Case Study

Merck and Roy Vagelos: The Values of Leaders

Joanne B. Ciulla

Prior to becoming CEO, Vagelos was director of Merck Sharp & Dohme's research laboratories.[1] In 1979 a researcher named William Campbell had a hunch that an antiparasite drug he was working on called Ivermectin might work on the parasite that caused river blindness, a disease that threatens the eyesight and lives of 85 million people in 35 developing countries. He asked Vagelos if he could have the resources to pursue his research. Despite the fact that the market for this drug was essentially the poorest people in the world, Vagelos gave Campbell the go ahead. While the decision was Vagelos's, it was also reinforced by Merck's axiom "health precedes wealth."

Campbell's hunch about Ivermectin proved to be right, and he developed a drug called Mectizan, which was approved for use by the government in 1987. By this time Vagelos had become the CEO of Merck. Now that the drug was approved, he sought public underwriting to produce Mectizan. Vagelos hired Henry Kissenger to help open doors for Merck. They approached several sources, including the U.S. Agency for International Development and the World Health Organization, but couldn't raise money for the drug. Merck was left with a drug that was useful only to people who couldn't buy it. Vagelos recalled, "We faced the possibility that we had a miraculous drug that would sit on a shelf."[2] After reviewing the company's options, Vagelos and his directors announced that they would give Mectizan away for free, forever, on October 21, 1987. A decade later, the drug give-away cost Merck over $200 million. By 1996 Mectizan had reached 19 million people. In Nigeria alone it saved 6 million people from blindness.

Few business leaders ever have the opportunity to do what Vagelos did. When asked how he could commit his company to produce a product that cost rather than generated money, he said he had "no choice. My whole life has been dedicated" to helping people, and "this was *it* for me."[3] His values guided his decisions in this case, but so did the values of the founder. George C. Merck, son of the company's American founder, said that from the very beginning. Merck's founders asserted that medicine was for people, not profits. However, he quickly added that they also believed that if medicine is for people profits will follow.[4]

Like many corporate mission statements, Merck's says its mission "is to provide society with superior products and services." The statement goes on to assert, "We are in the business of preserving and improving human life. . . . All of our actions must be measured by our success at achieving this goal." It concludes that "We expect profits from work that satisfies customer needs and that benefits humanity.[5] Merck's corporate leaders acted on and hence instilled and reinforced these values long before Vagelos donated Mectizan.

After World War II, tuberculosis thrived in Japan. Most Japanese couldn't afford to buy Merck's powerful drug, Streptomycin, to fight it. Merck gave away a large supply of the drug to the Japanese public. The Japanese did not forget. In 1983 the Japanese government allowed Merck to purchase 50.02 percent of Banyu Pharmaceutical. At the time, this was the largest foreign investment in a Japanese company. Merck is currently the largest American pharmaceutical company in Japan. The story makes Merck's mission statement come alive. It is the kind of story that employees learn and internalize when they come to work there.

Vagelos' moral leadership in this case extended beyond his organization into the industry. As Michael Useem pointed out, Merck has become the benchmark by which the moral behavior of other pharmaceutical companies is judged. Sometimes the moral actions of one CEO or company set the bar higher for others. Useem observed that the message hit home at Glaxo. In comparing Glaxo to Merck, a business writer once called Glaxo "a hollow enterprise lacking purpose and lacking soul."[6] Merck's values seemed to inspire Glaxo's new CEO Richard Sykes. In 1993 Glaxo invested in developing a drug to combat a form of tuberculosis that is connected to AIDS and found mostly among the poor. In 1996 Glaxo donated a potent new product for malaria. Similarly, Dupont is now giving away nylon to filter guinea worms out of drinking water in poor countries, and American Cyanamid is donating a larvacide to control them.

A cynic might regard Merck's donation of Streptomycin and Mectizan as nothing more than public relations stunts. But what is most interesting about the actions of Merck's leaders is that while they believed that "by doing good they would do well," at the time that they acted, it was unclear exactly when and how the company would benefit. Neither the

Japanese after the war nor the poor people of the world who are threatened by river blindness seemed likely to return the favor in the near future. While this wasn't an altruistic act, it was not a purely self-interested one either. Since it was unclear if, when, and how Merck would benefit, it is reasonable to assume that Merck's leaders and the values upon which they acted were authentic. They intentionally acted on their values. Any future benefits required a leap of faith on their part.

Business leaders' values matter to the organization only if they act on them. In business ethics and in life, we always hope that doing the right thing, while costly and sometimes painful in the short run, will pay off in the long run.

NOTES

1. The information about this case is from Michael Useem, *The Leadership Moment* (New York: Times Business Books, 1998), chap. 1.
2. Ibid., p. 23.
3. Ibid., p. 42.
4. Ibid., p. 29.
5. Ibid., p. 29.
6. Ibid., p. 31.